Introduction to
Artificial
Neural Systems

JACEK M. ZURADA

Professor of Electrical Engineering and of
Computer Science and Engineering

PWS Publishing Company

I(T)P **An International Thomson Publishing Company**

Boston • Albany • Bonn • Cincinnati • Detroit • London • Madrid • Melbourne • Mexico City
New York • Paris • San Francisco • Singapore • Tokyo • Toronto • Washington

PWS PUBLISHING COMPANY
20 Park Plaza, Boston, MA 02116-4324

Reprinted in 1995 by PWS Publishing Company

ISBN 0-534-95460-X

Text Design:	Geri Davis, Quadrata
Composition and Art:	Technique Typesetting
Copyediting:	Loretta Palagi
Indexing:	Barbara Farabaugh

WEST'S COMMITMENT TO THE ENVIRONMENT

In 1906, West Publishing Company began recycling materials left over from
the production of books. This began a tradition of efficient and responsible
use of resources. Today, up to 95 percent of our legal books and 70 percent
of our college texts are printed on recycled, acid-free stock. West also recycles
nearly 22 million pounds of scrap paper annually—the equivalent of 181,717
trees. Since the 1960s, West has devised ways to capture and recycle waste
inks, solvents, oils, and vapors created in the printing process. We also recycle
plastics of all kinds, wood, glass, corrugated cardboard, and batteries, and
have eliminated the use of styrofoam book packaging. We at West are proud
of the longevity and the scope of our commitment to our environment.

Production, Prepress, Printing and Binding by West Publishing Company.

Library of Congress Cataloging-in-Publication Data

Zurada, Jacek M.
    Introduction to artificial neural systems / Jacek M. Zurada
       p. cm.
    Includes index.
    ISBN 0-314-93391-3 (alk. paper)
    1. Neural networks (Computer science)   I. Title
QA76.87.Z87 1992
006.3–dc20

                            92-712
 CIP

To Anna, Joanna, and Mark

Contents

2 **Fundamental Concepts and Models of Artificial Neural Systems** 25

3 **Single-Layer Perceptron Classifiers** 93

9 Neural Networks Implementation   565

Appendix

Index

Preface

MOTIVATION FOR THE BOOK

The recent resurgence of interest in neural networks has its roots in the recognition that the brain performs computations in a different manner than do conventional digital computers. Computers are extremely fast and precise at executing sequences of instructions that have been formulated for them. A human information processing system is composed of neurons switching at speeds about a million times slower than computer gates. Yet, humans are more efficient than computers at computationally complex tasks such as speech understanding. Moreover, not only humans, but even animals, can process visual information better than the fastest computers.

The question of whether technology can benefit from emulating the computational capabilities of organisms is a natural one. Unfortunately, the understanding of biological neural systems is not developed enough to address the issues of functional similarity that may exist between the biological and man-made neural systems. As a result, any major potential gains derived from such functional similarity, if they exist, have yet to be exploited.

This book introduces the foundations of artificial neural systems. Much of the inspiration for such systems comes from neuroscience. However, we are not directly concerned with networks of biological neurons in this text. Although the newly developed paradigms of artificial neural networks have strongly contributed to the discovery, understanding, and utilization of potential functional similarities between human and artificial information processing systems, many questions remain open. Intense research interest persists and the area continues to develop. The ultimate research objective is the theory and implementation of massively parallel interconnected systems which could process the information with an efficiency comparable to that of the brain.

To achieve this research objective, we need to define the focus of the study of artificial neural systems. *Artificial neural systems, or neural networks, are physical cellular systems which can acquire, store, and utilize experiential knowledge.* The knowledge is in the form of stable states or mappings embedded in networks that can be recalled in response to the presentation of cues. This book focuses on the foundations of such networks. The fundamentals of artificial neural systems theory, algorithms for information acquisition and retrieval, examples of applications, and implementation issues are included in our discussion. We explore a rather new and fundamentally different approach to computing and information processing.

Programmed computing, which has dominated information processing for more than four decades, is based on decision rules and algorithms encoded into the form of computer programs. The algorithms and program-controlled computing necessary to operate conventional computers have their counterparts in the learning rules and information recall procedures of a neural network. These are not exact counterparts, however, because neural networks go beyond digital computers since they can progressively alter their processing structure in response to the information they receive.

The purpose of this book is to help the reader understand the acquisition and retrieval of experiential knowledge in densely interconnected networks containing cells of processing elements and interconnecting links. Some of the discussed networks can be considered adaptive; others acquire knowledge *a priori*. Retrieval of knowledge is termed by some authors as neural computation. However, "neural computation" is only a segment of the artificial neural systems focus. This book also addresses the concepts of parallel machines that are able to acquire knowledge, and the corresponding issues of implementation.

I believe that the field of artificial neural systems has evolved to a point where a course on the subject is justified. Unfortunately, while the technical literature is full of reports on artificial neural systems theories and applications, it is hard to find a complete and unified description of techniques. The beginning student is likely to be bewildered by different levels of presentations, and a widespread spectrum of metaphors and approaches presented by authors of diverse backgrounds.

This book was conceived to satisfy the need for a comprehensive and unified text in this new discipline of artificial neural systems. It brings students a fresh and fascinating perspective on computation. The presentation of the material focuses on basic system concepts and involves learning algorithms, architectures, applications, and implementations. The text grew out of the teaching effort in artificial neural systems offered for electrical engineering and computer science and engineering senior and graduate students at the University of Louisville. In addition, the opportunity to work at Princeton University has considerably influenced the project.

This book is designed for a one semester course. It is written at a comprehensible level for students who have had calculus, linear algebra, analytical geometry, differential equations, and some exposure to optimization theory. As such, the book is suitable for senior-level undergraduate or beginning graduate students. Due to the emphasis on systems, the book should be appropriate for electrical, computer, industrial, mechanical, and manufacturing engineering students as well as for computer and information science, physics, and mathematics students. Those whose major is not electrical or computer engineering may find Sections 9.2 to 9.5 superfluous for their study. They can also skip Sections 5.4 to 5.6 without any loss of continuity.

With the mathematical and programming references in the Appendix, the book is self-contained. It should also serve already-practicing engineers and scientists who intend to study the neural networks area. In particular, it is assumed that the reader has no experience in neural networks, learning machines, or pattern recognition.

PHILOSOPHY

The fundamentals of artificial neural systems are the main concern of this book. Concepts are introduced gradually. The basic neural network paradigms are conveyed using a system perspective and mathematics exposition suitable for thorough understanding. Although only some of the algorithms are provided with proofs, the book uses mathematical exposition at the depth essential for artificial neural systems implementation and simulation, and later, initiation of research in the area. The reader is not only shown how to get a result, but also how to think about and possibly extend it.

Neural network processing typically involves dealing with large-scale problems in terms of dimensionality, amount of data handled, and the volume of simulation or neural hardware processing. This large-scale approach is both essential and typical for real-life applications. Although the study of such applications show dramatically *what* has been done, a student needs to find out *how* and *why* it has happened. Peeling off the complexity of large-scale approaches, diversity of applications, and overlapping aspects can facilitate the study.

When serious readers look behind the easy articles on neural networks in popular books or magazines, they may notice an involved mosaic of theories taken from mathematics, physics, neurobiology, and engineering. Fortunately, there are unified and pedagogical approaches to studying such complex subjects as neural networks. In order to understand digital computer organization and architecture, for example, one needs to study basic axioms of Boolean algebra, binary arithmetic, sequential circuits, control organization, microprogramming, etc. A similar decomposition of the neural network knowledge domain into basic but coherent parts should simplify the study. Such an approach is employed in this text.

An additional difficulty in studying the field arises from the large number of publications appearing in the neural network field. They make use of a variety of mathematical approaches, notations, and terminologies. Authors with diverse backgrounds bring a myriad of perspectives from numerous disciplines, ranging from neurobiology and physics to engineering and computer science. While the field has benefitted from having experts with a variety of backgrounds and perspectives, the resulting differences in approach have made it difficult to see the underlying similarities of substance. To blend interdisciplinary aspects of the discipline, I present a unified perspective, and also link the approaches and terminologies among them.

As the reader will hopefully notice, the fundamental concepts of neural processing are often rather lucid. Because they combine simplicity and power, they are also appealing. The approach often taken in this text is to reduce both high dimensionality and data volume whenever possible without loss of generality, and to demonstrate algorithms in two- or three-dimensional space and with a small amount of data. An algorithm is often introduced along with an explanatory example showing how and why it works. Later on, the algorithm is formally outlined and formulated for any size of the problem. Some proofs of algorithms are included; others are omitted for simplicity. Some proofs of neural algorithms, however, have yet to be constructed.

Examples within chapters usually follow this philosophy of material presentation. I feel strongly that illustrative examples need to be made available to readers to develop intuitive understanding and to facilitate study. The end-of-chapter problems typically also have a reduced size and complexity. They focus on enhancing the understanding of principles; some of them are short proofs. I also believe that solving problems should enhance the understanding of algorithm principles and related concepts. Since the use of existing algorithms does not contribute much to the understanding of the subject, only a limited number of end of chapter problems is devoted to the "simulate and see" approach.

At the same time, I realize that the practical significance of neural computation becomes apparent for large or very large-scale tasks. To illustrate neural networks practical applications, computationally intensive problems are also included at the ends of most chapters. Such problems are highlighted with asterisks and can be considered mini-projects. Their size is usually between the "pencil and paper" problem size and the large-scale application. Because some of these problems are rather computationally intensive, the coding of algorithms or the use of the ANS program (available with this text) or other software is recommended for their solution. Unless software is available, the mini-project problems usually take much more time to solve than other problems.

Problems marked with asterisks also tend to overlap somewhat throughout the chapters with regard to input data, training sets, and similar aspects, but the algorithms used differ among problems in various chapters. As the course has been developed, students should have created an integrated program package for selected neural algorithms by the end of a semester. The input of the package includes user-specified problem size, choice of an algorithm, entering training data, training the network, and commands for running the program for test data in the recall mode. Obviously, neither the package code nor the applications of the algorithms are optimized, but they are not meant to be, since they address a spectrum of neurocomputing paradigms for project work.

Rather than focusing on a number of algorithms, another alternative for project content of the course is proposed. Students can be assigned one large-scale project, which can be the outgrowth, or fusion, of the computationally intensive end-of-chapter problems. In this mode, instead of using the spectrum of several algorithms, one neural processing algorithm is covered in depth. Alternatively, one practical application problem can be studied and approached using more than one paradigm. Study of the literature referenced at the end of each chapter, or extension of applications covered in Chapter 8, can provide the reader with more guidelines for further work.

SUMMARY BY CHAPTERS

Chapter 1 presents a number of neural network examples and applications. It provides an overview of what neural networks can accomplish. Brief historical remarks of artificial neural network development are presented, followed by a future outlook of the discipline.

Chapter 2 introduces the terminology and discusses the most important neural processing paradigms, network properties, and learning concepts. Basic assumptions, definitions, and models of neurons and neural architectures are introduced in this chapter. The chapter concludes with the analysis of networks and their learning rules.

The foundations of supervised learning machines are presented in Chapter 3. Feedforward single-layer architectures are studied. The concept of the nonparametric training of a linear machine composed of discrete perceptrons is introduced. The training is discussed in geometric terms, and the steepest descent minimization of the classification error function is accomplished for a network with continuous perceptrons.

The concept of error function minimization is extended in Chapter 4 to multilayer feedforward neural networks. Emphasis is placed on the pattern-to-image space mapping provided through the first network layer. The generalized delta learning rule is derived based on the steepest descent minimization rule. The error back-propagation algorithm is discussed and illustrated with examples. Application examples of multilayer feedforward networks are also covered. The chapter ends with presentation of functional link networks.

Chapter 5 covers the foundations of recurrent networks. Discrete-time and continuous-time gradient-type networks are introduced. The time-domain behavior of single-layer feedback networks is emphasized. Particular attention is paid to the energy minimization property during the evolution of the system in time, and to the use and interpretation of trajectories in the output space. A comprehensive example involving analog-to-digital converters and an optimization problem solving using gradient-type networks are presented to illustrate the theory.

Associative memories are introduced in Chapter 6. The exposition proceeds from the linear associator to single-layer recurrent networks. Two-layer recurrent networks, known as bidirectional associative memories, are introduced. They are then generalized to perform as multidirectional and spatio-temporal memories. Performance evaluation of single- and double-layer memory is covered and illustrated with examples. Memory capacity and retrieval performance versus distances between stored patterns are discussed.

Chapter 7 covers networks that for the most part learn in an unsupervised environment. These networks typically perform input vector matching, clustering or feature extraction. Diverse architectures covered in this chapter include the Hamming networks, MAXNET, clustering and counterpropagation networks, self-organizing feature mapping networks, and adaptive resonance networks.

Chapter 8 provides examples of neural network applications for computation, control, and information processing. An optimization network for a linear programming task is discussed. Character recognition architectures using hidden-neuron layers are described, and applications in robotics and control systems are reviewed. Other application examples treat the implementation of connectionist expert systems for medical diagnosis. Such systems first acquire and then use the knowledge base to diagnose a patient's disease when provided with a list of symptoms. The application of a self-organizing feature mapping network for semantic map processing is covered.

The final chapter, Chapter 9, is devoted to hardware implementation issues. A brief review of digital neurocomputing and simulation issues is followed by an extensive discussion of microelectronic implementation techniques. The emphasis of this chapter is on adaptive analog and learning circuit configurations which can be implemented in MOS technology.

The Appendix contains essential mathematical references needed for the understanding of neural network paradigms covered in the book. It also contains the listing of the main procedures of the program ANS in Pascal, which is capable of running on IBM-PC compatible microcomputers. The program implements most computational algorithms discussed in the book, and can provide numerical solutions to a number of examples and problems contained in the text.

ACKNOWLEDGMENTS

First and foremost, I would like to thank my wife, Anna, for her encouragement and cooperation during the time I spent writing the book. I was introduced to the subject in the outstanding lectures of Professor J. Seidler at the Technical University of Gdansk, Poland, who had an early influence on this project. Also, I am indebted to a number of individuals who, directly or indirectly, assisted in the preparation of the text. In particular, I wish to extend my appreciation to Professors M. Bialko of the Technical University of Gdansk, Poland, D. Mlynski of the Technical University of Karlsruhe, Germany, M. H. Hassoun of Wayne State University, S. K. Park of Tennessee Technical University, B. Dickinson of Princeton University; J. Starzyk of Ohio University; R. W. Newcomb of the University of Maryland; and P. B. Aronhime and J. H. Lilly of the University of Louisville whose criticism, comments, and suggestions have been very helpful. The list of individuals who have contributed to the development of this text include graduate students whose effort I gratefully acknowledge. I also wish to thank Diane S. Eiland for her commitment to and skillful effort of processing the manuscript in many iterations.

I would like to thank Peter Gordon, Engineering Editor at West Publishing, for sharing his enthusiasm and supporting the evolving project.

I also thank Sharon Adams, Developmental Editor, Mélina Brown, Production Editor, and Jo Anne Bechard at West Publishing.

The following colleagues were extremely helpful in offering comments and suggestions:

James Anderson
Brown University

Donald Glaser
University of California-Berkeley

Leonard Myers
California Polytechnic University-San Luis Obispo

Bahram Nabet
Drexel University

Edgar Sanchez-Sinencio
Texas A&M University

Gene A. Tagliarini
Clemson University

John Uhran
University of Notre Dame.

Jacek M. Zurada

Notation and Abbreviations

ANS	— artificial neural systems simulation program from appendix page A9
ART	— adaptive resonance theory
BAM	— bidirectional associative memory
C	— capacitance matrix of Hopfield network (diagonal)
CPS	— connections per second
d	— desired output vector of a trained network
D	— digital control word
det **A**	— determinant of matrix **A**
e	— error
E	— error function to be minimized during learning (for feedforward networks)
E	— energy function to be minimized during recall (for feedback networks)
	— (E can be termed as a loss, or an objective function)
EBPTA	— error back-propagation training algorithm
$f(\cdot)$	— neuron's activation operator
$f(net)$	— activation function
$\mathbf{f}^{(i)}$	— memory forced response vector
$f_{\mathrm{sat}+}, f_{\mathrm{sat}-}$	— operational amplifier saturation voltages
F	— memory forced response matrix
$g(\mathbf{x})$	— discriminant function
G	— conductance matrix of Hopfield network (diagonal)
$h(\mathbf{x})$	— multivariable function to be approximated
H	— Hessian matrix (also ∇^2)
HD	— Hamming Distance
$H(\mathbf{w}, \mathbf{x})$	— neural network-produced approximation of function $h(\mathbf{x})$
$i_o(\mathbf{x})$	— decision function
i	— network input current vector (bias vector)
I	— number of input nodes of multilayer feedforward network
I	— identity matrix
I_+	— excitatory current
I_-	— inhibitory current
I_{ds}	— drain-to-source current
J	— number of hidden nodes of multilayer feedforward network
J	— Jacobian matrix
k	— device transconductance of MOS transistor
k'	— process transconductance of MOS transistor
K	— number of output nodes of multilayer feedforward network
KCL	— Kirchhoff's current law
L	— channel length of MOS transistor

MDAC	— multiplying digital-to-analog converter
n	— normal vector to hyperplane
net	— activation vector for neuron layer (general notation)
net	— activation value of a neuron
o	— output vector of a neuron layer
P	— number of patterns in the training set
r	— learning signal
r	— unit normal vector to hyperplane
RAMSRA	— recurrent associative memory storage and retrieval algorithm
RDPTA	— R-category discrete perceptron training algorithm
R_{ds}	— tunable weight resistance produced by MOS transistor
$r(t)$	— reference signal (Chapter 8)
sgn(x)	— signum function
$\mathbf{s}^{(i)}$	— vector stored in memory (or classifier)
S	— vectors stored in memory, arranged in matrix
SCPTA	— single continuous perceptron training algorithm
SDPTA	— single discrete perceptron training algorithm
T	— neuron (or perceptron) threshold
TLU	— threshold logic unit
u	— activation vector (only for Hopfield layer)
v	— output vector of continuous-time feedback or memory network
V	— weight matrix (v_{ij} is the weight from node j toward node i)
V_{ds}, V_{gs}	— drain-to-source and gate-to-source voltage of MOS transistor, respectively
v_o	— output voltage
V_{th}, V_{dep}	— threshold, depletion voltages of MOS transistor, respectively
VTC	— voltage transfer characteristics
w	— weight vector (or augmented weight vector)
W	— channel width of MOS transistor
W	— weight matrix (w_{ij} is the weight from node j toward node i)
w′	— updated weight vector (or augmented weight vector)
$\hat{\mathbf{w}}$	— normalized weight vector
x	— input pattern vector
y	— input vector, or augmented input vector, also output of hidden layer neuron
$\mathbf{y}^k$	— matching score at input of MAXNET
z	— input vector for multilayer network

Greek

| α | — learning constant |
| β | — learning constant |

$\Gamma[\cdot]$ — nonlinear diagonal matrix operator with operators $f(\cdot)$ on the diagonal

$\boldsymbol{\delta}$ — error signal vector

$\boldsymbol{\delta}_y$ — error signal vector of hidden layer

$\boldsymbol{\delta}_o$ — error signal vector of output layer

δ_{ij} — Kronecker delta function

η — learning constant

$\boldsymbol{\eta}$ — memory output noise vector

$\theta_1,\ \theta_2$ — joint angles of planar robot manipulator

λ — gain (steepness) factor of the continuous activation function, also used in Chapter 9 to denote the channel length modulation factor

ρ — vigilance test level (Chapter 7) (also used as measure of distance in Chapter 2, and as radius of attraction Chapter 6)

$\nabla_x E(\mathbf{x})$ — gradient of a multivariable function $E(\mathbf{x})$ with respect to $\mathbf{x}$

$\nabla_x^2 E(\mathbf{x})$ — Hessian matrix of a multivariable function $E(\mathbf{x})$ with respect to $\mathbf{x}$

ARTIFICIAL NEURAL SYSTEMS: PRELIMINARIES

*Happy those who are convinced so
as to be of the general opinions.*

LORD HALIFAX

For many centuries, one of the goals of humankind has been to develop machines. We envisioned these machines as performing all cumbersome and tedious tasks so that we might enjoy a more fruitful life. The era of machine making began with the discovery of simple machines such as lever, wheel and pulley. Many equally congenial inventions followed thereafter. Nowadays engineers and scientists are trying to develop intelligent machines. Artificial neural systems are present-day examples of such machines that have great potential to further improve the quality of our life.

As mentioned in the preface, people and animals are much better and faster at recognizing images than most advanced computers. Although computers outperform both biological and artificial neural systems for tasks based on precise and fast arithmetic operations, artificial neural systems represent the promising new generation of information processing networks. Advances have been made in applying such systems for problems found intractable or difficult for traditional computation. Neural networks can supplement the enormous processing power of the von Neumann digital computer with the ability to make sensible decisions and to learn by ordinary experience, as we do.

A neural network's ability to perform computations is based on the hope that we can reproduce some of the flexibility and power of the human brain by artificial means. Network computation is performed by a dense mesh of computing nodes and connections. They operate collectively and simultaneously on most or all data and inputs. The basic processing elements of neural networks are called *artificial neurons,* or simply *neurons.* Often we simply call them *nodes.* Neurons perform as summing and nonlinear mapping junctions. In some cases they can be considered as threshold units that fire when their total input exceeds certain bias levels. Neurons usually operate in parallel and are configured in regular architectures. They are often organized in layers, and feedback connections both within the layer and toward adjacent layers are allowed. Each connection strength is expressed by a numerical value called a *weight,* which can be modified.

We have just introduced several new words describing some of the attributes of neural processing. These, and other notions introduced later in this chapter, are not yet rigorously defined. For now we will use them to discuss qualitatively several introductory examples and applications of neurocomputing. A more detailed exposition of concepts and terminology is provided in Chapter 2. Let us only mention that the artificial neural systems field alone goes under the guise of many names in the literature. The effort is not only called neural networks, but also neurocomputing, network computation, connectionism, parallel distributed processing, layered adaptive systems, self-organizing networks, or neuromorphic systems or networks. The reader may not need to assimilate all new technical jargon terms related to neurocomputing. Rather, the variety of names indicates how many different perspectives can be taken when studying a single subject of interest such as neural networks.

Artificial neural systems function as parallel distributed computing networks. Their most basic characteristic is their architecture. Only some of the networks provide instantaneous responses. Other networks need time to respond and are characterized by their time-domain behavior, which we often refer to as *dynamics.* Neural networks also differ from each other in their learning modes. There are a variety of learning rules that establish when and how the connecting weights change. Finally, networks exhibit different speeds and efficiency of learning. As a result, they also differ in their ability to accurately respond to the cues presented at the input.

In contrast to conventional computers, which are programmed to perform specific tasks, most neural networks must be taught, or trained. They learn new associations, new patterns, and new functional dependencies. *Learning corresponds to parameter changes.* As will be shown in subsequent chapters, learning rules and algorithms used for experiential training of networks replace the programming required for conventional computation. Neural network users do not specify an algorithm to be executed by each computing node as would programmers of a more traditional machine. Instead, they select what in their view is the best architecture, specify the characteristics of the neurons and initial weights, and choose the training mode for the network. Appropriate inputs are then applied to the network so that it can acquire knowledge from the environment. As a result of such exposure, the network assimilates the information that can later be recalled by the user.

Artificial neural system computation lies in the middle ground between engineering and artificial intelligence. The mathematical techniques utilized, such as mean-square error minimization, are engineering-like, but an experimental *ad hoc* approach is often necessary. Heuristic methodology and "quasi-rigorous" techniques of network learning are needed, since often no theory is available for selection of the appropriate neural system for a specific application.

Much of this book is devoted to answering questions, such as the following: How can a network be trained efficiently and why does it learn? What models of neurons need to be used for good performance? What are the best architectures for certain classes of problems? What are the best ways of extracting the knowledge stored in a network? What are the typical applications of neural computation and how accurate are they? How can a specific task be accomplished if it is modeled through a neural network? How can artificial neural systems be implemented as application-specific integrated circuits? We realize that our main objective of study is to design efficient neural systems. However, a strong understanding of the principles and behavior of networks is invaluable if a good design is to be developed.

Neural networks have attracted the attention of scientists and technologists from a number of disciplines. The discipline has attracted neuroscientists who are interested in modeling biological neural networks, and physicists who envisage analogies between neural network models and the nonlinear dynamical systems they study. Mathematicians are fascinated by the potential of mathematical modeling applied to complex large systems phenomena. Electrical and computer engineers look at artificial neural systems as computing networks for signal processing. They are also interested in building electronic integrated circuit-based intelligent machines. Psychologists look at artificial neural networks as possible prototype structures of human-like information processing. Finally, computer scientists are interested in opportunities that are opened by the massively parallel computational networks in the areas of artificial intelligence, computational theory, modeling and simulation, and others.

1.1 NEURAL COMPUTATION: SOME EXAMPLES AND APPLICATIONS

In the previous section we read about interesting and novel aspects of neural computation. We now focus on the applicability and usefulness of neural network technology in the solving of real-world problems. Below, we demonstrate sample applications and relate them to simplified neural network examples. Because mathematical exposition and more precise explanation of concepts are addressed starting in Chapter 2, this discussion is descriptive rather than quantitative.

Classifiers, Approximators, and Autonomous Drivers

This portion of our neural networks discussion introduces networks that respond instantaneously to the applied input. Let us try to inspect the performance of a simple *classifier,* and then also of similar networks that are far more complex, but can be designed as extensions of the classifier.

Assume that a set of eight points, P_0, P_1, ..., P_7, in three-dimensional space is available. The set consists of all vertices of a three-dimensional cube as follows:

$$\{P_0(-1,-1,-1), P_1(-1,-1,1), P_2(-1,1,-1), P_3(-1,1,1),$$
$$P_4(1,-1,-1), P_5(1,-1,1), P_6(1,1,-1), P_7(1,1,1)\}$$

Elements of this set need to be classified into two categories. The first category is defined as containing points with two or more positive ones; the second category contains all the remaining points that do not belong to the first category. Accordingly, points P_3, P_5, P_6, and P_7 belong to the first category, and the remaining points to the second category.

Classification of points P_3, P_5, P_6, and P_7 can be based on the summation of coordinate values for each point evaluated for category membership. Notice that for each point P_i (x_1, x_2, x_3), where $i = 0, ..., 7$, the membership in the category can be established by the following calculation:

$$\text{If } \operatorname{sgn}(x_1 + x_2 + x_3) = \begin{cases} 1, & \text{then category 1} \\ -1, & \text{then category 2} \end{cases} \tag{1.1}$$

Expression (1.1) describes the decision function of the classifier designed by inspection of the set that needs to be partitioned. No design formulas or training have been required to accomplish the design, however. The resulting neural network shown in Figure 1.1(a) is extremely simple. It implements expression (1.1) by summing the inputs x_1, x_2, and x_3 with unity weighting coefficients. The weighted sum undergoes a thresholding operation and the output of the unit is 1 for $x_1 + x_2 + x_3 > 0$, otherwise it is -1. We thus achieve the desired classification using a single *unit,* or computing node. The unit implements summation with respective weights followed by the thresholding operation.

Looking at the network just discussed and taking a different perspective, we may notice that in addition to classification, the network performs three-dimensional Cartesian space partitioning as illustrated in Figure 1.1(b). The

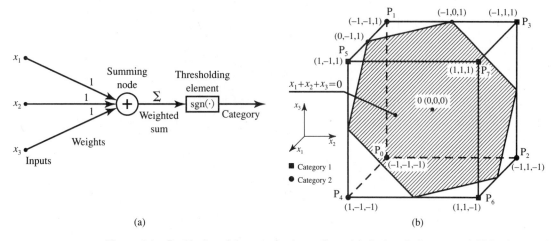

Figure 1.1 Partitioning of the set of cube vertices: (a) single-unit diagram and (b) implemented partitioning.

partitioning plane is $x_1 + x_2 + x_3 = 0$. All points above it are mapped into $+1$ and all below it are mapped into -1. Although this observation is not crucial for our understanding of classifier design, insight into the geometry of mapping will prove to be very valuable for more complex cases.

Design of neural network classifiers becomes far more involved and intriguing when requirements for membership in categories become complicated. No single-unit classifier exists, for example, that would implement assignment of P_2, P_3, and P_5 into a single category, and of the remaining five points of the set into the other category. The details of the classification discussion, however, will be postponed until Chapter 3, since they require more formal coverage.

As stated, the unit from Figure 1.1(a) maps the entire three-dimensional space into just two points, 1 and -1. A question arises as to whether a unit with a "squashed" sgn function rather than a regular sgn function could prove more advantageous. Assuming that the "squashed" sgn function has the shape as in Figure 1.2, notice that now the outputs take values in the range $(-1, 1)$ and are generally more discernible than in the previous case. Using units with continuous characteristics offers tremendous opportunities for new tasks that can be performed by neural networks. Specifically, the fine granularity of output provides more information than the binary ± 1 output of the thresholding element.

An important new feature of networks with units having continuous characteristics is that they can be trained independent of their architecture. This has not been the case for many networks with units implementing a sgn function. The principles of this training are explained beginning in Section 2.4. Meanwhile, we concentrate on what trained networks could compute for us, rather than how to

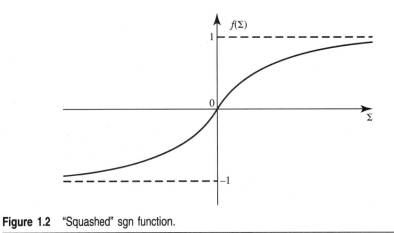

Figure 1.2 "Squashed" sgn function.

design them. As an example, let us look at a neural network classifier applied to the solution of a real-world problem of biomedical signal processing.

Neurologists often need to evaluate the electroencephalogram (EEG) signals of a patient. The EEG waveforms contain important information about the patient's abnormal brain function. The interpretation of EEG signals is used by neurologists when diagnosing the risk of seizures and deciding on corrective measures. The recordings are taken from the patient's scalp and are multichannel. Up to 64 electrodes are used to monitor fully electrical impulses generated by the patient's brain.

Evaluation of the multichannel EEG data is rather difficult and therefore done most often by qualified neurologists. In addition, large amounts of data must be handled because of the round-the-clock monitoring of each patient. To reduce the costs of monitoring and data interpretation, the EEG waves need to be processed by a computing device that provides on-line detection of signals of interest. One of the most important signal shapes that needs to be discriminated is an EEG spike which indicates an imminent epileptic seizure.

EEG spike detection using a neural network classifier was recently developed (Eberhart and Dobbins 1990). Data are monitored in four channels of interest. The EEG waves are sampled 200 or 250 times per second within a 240-ms time window. This yields 48 or 60 data samples available from each channel to be evaluated. The data samples from each channel are fed to the neural network of interconnected units with squashed characteristics as in Figure 1.2. The total of 41 units arranged in three layers does the processing of the data. Two output units are provided for the purpose of spike identification. When the first output unit responds close to unity, this identifies a spike; when the second output yields high response, the network identifies the present input as nonspike.

The network was designed by a team of signal processing engineers who developed the system and the design methodology, and by a team of four to six neurologists who provided expert identification of spikes and nonspikes. The network was extensively trained using both spike and nonspike data.

The test results for the trained network are impressive. Six series of comprehensive tests were reported. First, the network was tested with spike/nonspike waves used earlier for training. All spikes used for training were positively identified by the network. Only 2 nonspikes of the total of 260 nonspikes were classified mistakenly as spikes. Following the test of the classification with the previously used training data, the classification of entirely new spike/nonspike wave data was performed. Again, all spikes were correctly identified. However, there were also some new nonspikes incorrectly classified by the network as spikes. Despite some number of false alarms, the performance of the network has been found to be significantly better than that required for practical application in hospitals.

While classification of input data is of tremendous importance and will be revisited in more detail in subsequent chapters, let us turn our attention to other forms of mapping. An example of function approximation performed by a neural network is shown in Figure 1.3(a). The network's input is a scalar variable x, and its output is a scalar function $o(x)$. It can be seen from the figure that each of the n units operates with input that is equal to weighted input x plus individual bias that enters each of the summing nodes. Each of the n nonlinear mapping units produces the output. The outputs are then weighted and summed again. Then the nonlinear mapping is performed by the output unit and the network implements the function $o(x)$. The function $o(x)$ depends on a number of weights and biases as marked on the figure.

Notice that the network configuration shown in Figure 1.3(a) can be used to approximate a function. Figure 1.3(b) illustrates a specific example of approximation. The dashed line denotes the function that needs to be approximated and is known at P example points only. The exact function is

$$h(x) = 0.8 \sin \pi x, \qquad -1 \le x \le 1 \qquad (1.2)$$

Choosing $P = 21$, we obtain the data for function approximation as shown by the circles on the dashed curve.

Approximation of function $h(x)$ as in Equation (1.2) through function $o(x)$ can be implemented using the network from Figure 1.3(a) for $n = 10$. Parameters of the neural network have been found as a result of the training using 21 points shown as training data. The reader may notice that the number of parameters for the discussed network is 31, with 20 of them being weights and 11 being bias levels. The mapping $o(x)$ performed by the network is shown by a continuous line. Although the two functions $h(x)$ and $o(x)$ do not exactly overlap, the example shows the potential that exists for function approximation using neural networks.

While neural networks for function approximation seem useful for the purpose of mathematical modeling, we may need a more convincing argument for how networks of this class may be used in practical applications. A sample

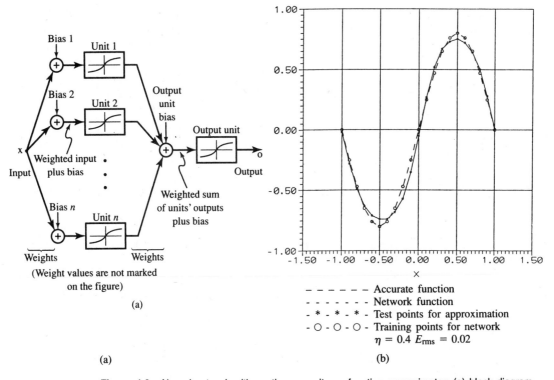

(a)

(b)

Figure 1.3 Neural network with continuous units as function approximator: (a) block diagram and (b) example approximation of Equation (1.2).

network designed for the task of road following can offer us additional insight into the applied nature and potential of artificial neural systems. Consider, for example, ALVINN (Autonomous Land Vehicle In a Neural Network) project reported by Pomerleau (1989). The ALVINN network takes road images from a camera and a laser range finder as input. It produces as output the direction the vehicle should travel in order to follow the road. Let us look at some interesting details of this system.

The architecture of ALVINN is shown in Figure 1.4. Inputs to the network consist of video and range information. The video information is provided by the 30 × 32 retina, which depicts the road scene. The resulting 960 segments of the scene are each coded into input proportional to the intensity of blue color. The blue band of the color image is used because it provides the highest contrast between the road and nonroad. The distance information is available at the input from a second retina consisting of 8 × 32 units and receiving the signal from a laser range finder. The resulting 256 inputs are each coded proportionally to the proximity of the corresponding area in the image. An additional single unit is made available in the network to indicate whether the road is lighter or darker than the nonroad in the previous image.

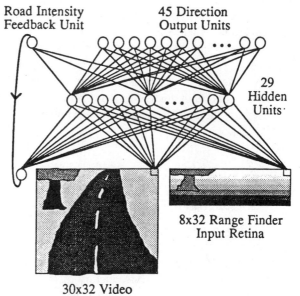

Road Intensity
Feedback Unit

45 Direction
Output Units

29
Hidden
Units

8x32 Range Finder
Input Retina

30x32 Video
Input Retina

Figure 1.4 Architecture of autonomous vehicle driver. SOURCE: (Pomerleau 1989) © Morgan-Kaufmann; reprinted with permission.

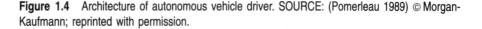

The 1217 inputs are fed to the layer consisting of 29 units with squashed sgn characteristics. Each of the 29 units is connected to each of the 46 output units. A single output unit provides feedback input information about the road intensity, and the remaining 45 units are directional. The middle unit indicating high output gives the signal to drive straight ahead. Units to the left and right represent the curvature of the necessary turn that the vehicle should perform to stay at the road center. The extreme left and right units correspond to the sharpest left and right turns, respectively.

ALVINN has been developed using computer-generated road images. The images have been used as training exemplars. The training set of different road images has involved 1200 different combinations of scenes, curvatures, lighting conditions and distortion levels. The actual neural network driver has been implemented using an on-board computer and a modified Chevy van. Performance of the network as reported by Pomerleau (1989) has been comparable to that achieved by the best traditional vision-based navigation systems evaluated under similar conditions.

It seems that the salient image features important for accurate driving have been acquired by ALVINN not from the programmer or the algorithm, but from the data environment presented to the network. As a result, the system mastered the art of driving within a half-hour training session. It would take many months of algorithm development and parameter tuning related to vision and pattern recognition work to develop a conventional autonomous driver of comparable efficiency.

Interesting observations were reported following the development of the project. The network performed much better after it had been trained to recover after making mistakes during driving. This training apparently provided the network with instructions on how to develop corrective driving measures. Presently, the project is aimed toward dealing more sensibly with road forks and intersections.

Simple Memory and Restoration of Patterns

This part of our neural network discussion introduces networks that respond, in time, to a presented pattern. Since they do so in a very characteristic way through a gradual reconstruction of a stored pattern, we call such networks simply *memories*. Only introductory discussion is presented below, with more in-depth coverage of memory analysis and design techniques to follow in Chapters 5 and 6.

Let us begin with an analysis of a very simple network as shown in Figure 1.5(a). The network consists of three units computing values of sgn($\cdot$), three summing nodes, and six weights of values +1 or −1. Signals passing through

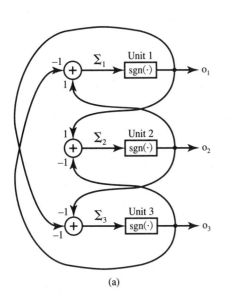

Case	Unit Number	Present Output O	Σ	sgn Σ	Next Output O
	1	1	0	x	1
1	2	1	0	x	1
	3	1	−2	−1	(−1)
	1	1	2	1	1
2	2	1	2	1	1
	3	−1	−2	−1	−1
	1	−1	2	1	(1)
3	2	1	0	x	1
	3	−1	0	x	−1
	1	1	0	x	1
4	2	−1	2	1	(1)
	3	−1	0	x	−1

x stands for sgn (0).
Encircled are updated outputs.

(a)

(b)

Figure 1.5 Simple neural network memory: (a) network diagram and (b) listing of updates.

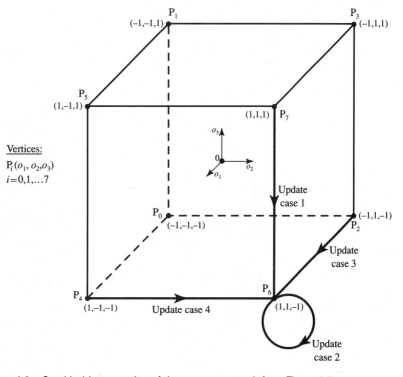

Figure 1.6 Graphical interpretation of the memory network from Figure 1.5.

weights are multiplied by the weight values. Assume that the network is initialized at its output and the initial output is $o_1 = 1$, $o_2 = 1$, $o_3 = 1$. When the network is allowed to compute, we notice that inputs to units 1 and 2 are exactly zero, while the input to unit 3 is equal to -2. As a result, o_1 and o_2 do not update their respective values since sgn(0) is an undetermined value. However, o_3 updates to -1 after it leaves the initial state of 1. Therefore, single updating activity across the network results in $o_1 = o_2 = 1$ and $o_3 = -1$.

The next computing cycle does not bring about any change since inputs to units 1, 2, and 3 are 2, 2, and -2, respectively, thus yielding $o_1 = o_2 = 1$ and $o_3 = -1$ again. The listing of discussed updates is shown in Figure 1.5(b) as cases 1 and 2. Transitions from initial output $o_1 = -1$, $o_2 = 1$, $o_3 = -1$, and $o_1 = 1$, $o_2 = -1$, $o_3 = -1$ are also displayed as cases 3 and 4, respectively. Cases 1, 3, and 4 result in a single unit update and they all terminate in the same final output of $o_1 = 1$, $o_2 = 1$, and $o_3 = -1$. In addition, analysis of case 2 indicates that this output is, in fact, a terminal one, no matter how many update cycles are allowed to take place thereafter.

Figure 1.6 provides a geometrical interpretation of updates performed by the simple memory network from Figure 1.5. It can be seen that $P_6(1, 1, -1)$ is the stable output of the discussed memory. When a single entry of the initializing

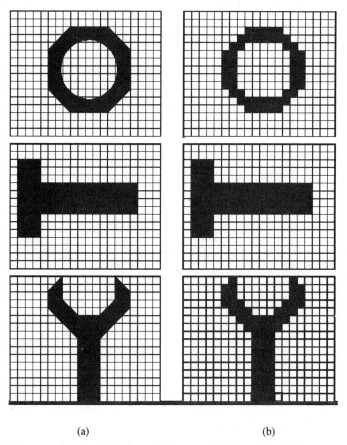

Figure 1.7 Memory network applications: (a) images of three mechanical parts and (b) images converted to bit-map forms.

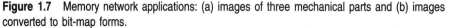

binary output vector does not agree with P_6, the network responds with the corrected entry. This output is sustained thereafter.

The memory concept demonstrated in this example can be easily extended to real-world applications. Assume that three images as shown in Figure 1.7(a) need to be stored in a memory network. They are a nut, a bolt, and a wrench as displayed on the 20×16 grid. The network, which can store any bit maps placed on the grid shown, has 320 units, each computing the sgn function. Essentially, the network is an extension of memory from Figure 1.5(a). The first preparatory step that needs to be taken is to represent the actual images through grid elements that are entirely white or black. In this way we obtain a set of three approximated

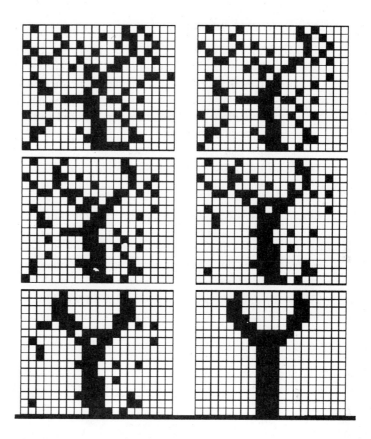

Figure 1.8 Restoration of the wrench image.

images. Examples of such images obtained from Figure 1.7(a) are illustrated in Figure 1.7(b).

A neural network memory can now be designed using the methods explained in Chapter 6. The memory holds each of the three binary patterns corresponding to bit maps from Figure 1.7(b). Once the memory is initialized at its output, it starts computing. After the evolution through intermediate states, the memory should terminate at one of its originally stored outputs. Figure 1.8 illustrates a sequence of outputs when a distorted image of the wrench is used to initialize the computation. The sequence consists of three snapshots taken during the computation performed by the memory network. It can be seen that the correct wrench shape is restored after a number of correctional transitions. This application indicates the potential of neural networks memory to restore heavily distorted images.

Optimizing Networks

Optimization is one of the most important objectives of engineering. The purpose of optimization is to minimize certain cost functions, usually defined by the user. Neural computation methods are successfully applied, among others, to the solution of some optimization problems. A more formal discussion of neural computation for optimization is covered in Chapter 5. Below we discuss only introductory concepts.

Assume that an analog value x, $0 \leq x \leq 3.5$, needs to be converted to a two-bit binary number $v_1 v_0$ such that

$$x \cong 2v_1 + v_0 \tag{1.3}$$

where v_1, $v_0 = 0, 1$. Obviously, for the conditions stated in Equation (1.3) four possible solutions to the problem exist: 00, 01, 10, 11. A simple network similar to the one depicted in Figure 1.5(a) can be designed to solve the conversion problem stated in Equation (1.3). However, the network consists of only two units described by "squashed" characteristics, each responding in the range $(0, 1)$. The block diagram of the network is shown in Figure 1.9. In addition to the two units, the network contains a number of interconnecting elements not shown on the figure.

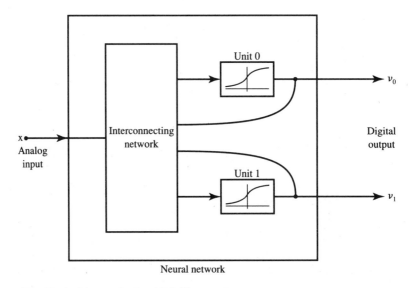

Figure 1.9 Block diagram of a two-bit A/D converter.

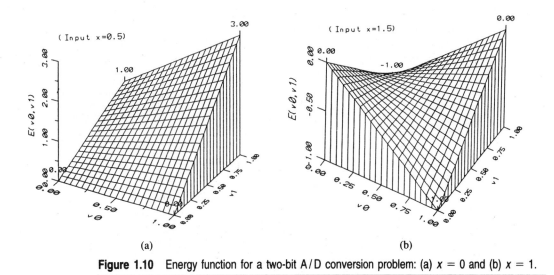

Figure 1.10 Energy function for a two-bit A/D conversion problem: (a) $x = 0$ and (b) $x = 1$.

Note that the conversion expressed by Equation (1.3) corresponds to the minimization of analog-to-digital conversion error, where

$$\text{error} = \left(x - 2v_1 - v_0\right)^2 \tag{1.4}$$

in the presence of such constraints that v_1, v_0 can take values of 0 or 1. This constrained minimization problem can be fit into a certain class of neural networks. The class has the unique property such that the so-called energy function in these networks undergoes minimization while the network is computing.

The property of energy minimization is of great importance. It states that the network seeks out, by itself, its energy minimum and then settles there. A number of optimization problems can be translated directly into the minimization of a neural network's energy function. Once the translation is accomplished and the neural network designed accordingly, the optimization task is transferred to the neural network for actual solution. Minimization of energy by the network can be considered analogous to the minimization of error expressed by Equation (1.4).

Figure 1.10 illustrates two cases of minimization of the energy function $E(v_0, v_1)$. Figure 1.10(a) shows that for input $x = 0$ the energy minimum is located at $v_0 = v_1 = 0$. Furthermore, the network output should always stabilize at that corner, since the energy function is monotonic. Similarly, convergence of the network output is guaranteed toward $v_0 = 1$ and $v_1 = 0$ for input $x = 1$. This can be seen from Figure 1.10(b). In actual networks, output approaches a corner but never reaches it since $0 < v_0 < 1$ and $0 < v_1 < 1$.

The class of neural networks exemplified here using a simple two-bit analog-to-digital (A/D) converter is very useful for the solution of a number of problems. In particular, it is useful for the solution of combinational optimization tasks. They are characterized by $N!$ or e^N possible solutions of problems that are of size N. Understandably, evaluation of the cost function at each potential solution point of such problems can be very computationally intensive. Therefore, other ways of combinational optimization are studied, and neural networks are among them.

One of the problems that can be successfully solved by this class of networks is called *job-shop scheduling*. Job-shop scheduling is a resource allocation problem, subject to allocation and sequencing constraints. The resources are typically machines and the jobs are the basic tasks that need to be accomplished using the machines. Each task may consist of several subtasks related by certain precedence restrictions. The job-shop problem is solved when the starting times of all jobs are determined and the sequencing rules are not violated. The cost function to be minimized is defined for this problem as a sum of the starting times of all jobs subject to compliance with precedence constraints (Foo and Takefuji 1988). Problems that are somewhat simpler but belong to the same group of optimization tasks include scheduling classrooms to classes, hospital patients to beds, workers to tasks they can accomplish best, etc.

Clustering and Feature Detecting Networks

A rather important group of neural networks can be used for detecting clusters of data. Such networks are tuned to certain similarity aspects that are of interest in the data being evaluated. For example, we may be interested in grouping certain measurement results together to suppress any systematic errors that may have occurred during measurements. We may also be interested in detecting regularly appearing components of inputs. These components may indicate the true signal components as opposed to the noise that is random and would not form any clusters.

Clustering and feature detecting networks exhibit remarkable properties of self-organization. These properties are closely related to the formation of knowledge representation in artificial intelligence and information theory. The networks of this class usually have a simple architecture; considerable subtleties arise mainly during the self-organization process, which is discussed in more detail in Chapter 7.

Another important function of neural networks can be feature detection. Feature detection is usually related to the dimensionality reduction of data. Some networks provide impressive planar mapping of features that are a result of multidimensional inputs of a fairly complex structure. Some of the many applications reported are discussed in Chapters 7 and 8 and one is especially intriguing. It involves mapping speech features as described below.

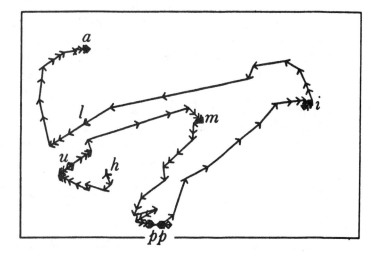

Figure 1.11 Phonotopic map of the Finnish word *humpilla* as an example of extracted features of speech. SOURCE: (Kohonen, 1988) © IEEE; reprinted with permission.

Speech processing studies indicate that speech signal consists of 15 frequency channels within the audio-frequency band. Elementary components of speech, called *phonemes,* could thus be displayed in the 15-dimensional spectral space of speech signals. The problem with such representation of phonemes is that it is of no use for us because our powers of visualization are limited to three dimensions. Through appropriate neural network mapping, however, it is possible to "flatten" the 15-dimensional spectrum of speech onto a constrained planar array. Figure 1.11 shows a so-called "phonotopic" map of a spoken word. The word *humpilla* has been used to produce the map. The rectangle is filled with units (not shown) that are selectively activated during speech. The sequence of word phonemes forms a trajectory that provides an impressive visualization of the continuous speech signal. Phonotopic maps may be invaluable for building phonetic typewriters, for speech training, and for therapy. Profoundly deaf people could have visual feedback from their speech.

1.2

HISTORY OF ARTIFICIAL NEURAL SYSTEMS DEVELOPMENT

Artificial neural systems development has an interesting history. Since it is not possible to cover this history in depth in a short introductory chapter, only major achievements are mentioned. This glimpse at the field's past milestones should provide the reader with an appreciation of how contributions to the field have led to its development over the years. The historical summary below is not exhaustive; some milestones are omitted and some are mentioned only briefly.

The year 1943 is often considered the initial year in the development of artificial neural systems. McCulloch and Pitts (1943) outlined the first formal model of an elementary computing neuron. The model included all necessary elements to perform logic operations, and thus it could function as an arithmetic-logic computing element. The implementation of its compact electronic model, however, was not technologically feasible during the era of bulky vacuum tubes. The formal neuron model was not widely adopted for the vacuum tube computing hardware description, and the model never became technically significant. However, the McCulloch and Pitts neuron model laid the groundwork for future developments.

Influential researchers of that time suggested that research in design of brain-like processing might be interesting. To quote John von Neumann's (1958) observations on the "brain language":

> We have now accumulated sufficient evidence to see that whatever language the central nervous system is using, it is characterized by less logical and arithmetical depth than what we are normally used to. The following is an obvious example of this: the retina of the human eye performs a considerable reorganization of the visual image as perceived by the eye. Now this reorganization is effected on the retina, or to be more precise, at the point of entry of the optic nerve by means of the successive synapses only, i.e. in terms of three consecutive logical steps. The statistical character of the message system used in the arithmetics of the central nervous system and its low precision, described earlier, cannot proceed very far in the message systems involved. Consequently, there exist here different logical structures from the ones we are ordinarily used to in logics and mathematics. They are characterized by less logical and arithmetical depth than we are used to under otherwise similar circumstances. Thus logic and mathematics in the central nervous system, when viewed as languages, must structurally be essentially different from those languages to which our common experience refers.

Donald Hebb (1949) first proposed a learning scheme for updating neuron's connections that we now refer to as the *Hebbian learning rule*. He stated that the information can be stored in connections, and postulated the learning technique that had a profound impact on future developments in this field. Hebb's learning rule made primary contributions to neural networks theory.

During the 1950s, the first neurocomputers were built and tested (Minsky 1954). They adapted connections automatically. During this stage, the neuron-like element called a *perceptron* was invented by Frank Rosenblatt in 1958. It was a trainable machine capable of learning to classify certain patterns by modifying connections to the threshold elements (Rosenblatt 1958). The idea caught the imagination of engineers and scientists and laid the groundwork for the basic machine learning algorithms that we still use today.

In the early 1960s a device called *ADALINE* (for ADAptive LINEar combiner) was introduced, and a new, powerful learning rule called the *Widrow-Hoff learning rule* was developed by Bernard Widrow and Marcian Hoff (1960, 1962). The rule minimized the summed square error during training involving pattern classification. Early applications of ADALINE and its extensions to MADALINE (for Many ADALINES) include pattern recognition, weather forecasting, and adaptive controls. The monograph on learning machines by Nils Nilsson (1965) clearly summarized many of the developments of that time. That book also formulates inherent limitations of learning machines with modifiable connections.

Despite the successes and enthusiasm of the early and mid-1960s, the existing machine learning theorems of that time were too weak to support more complex computational problems. Although the bottlenecks were exactly identified in Nilsson's work and the neural network architectures called *layered networks* were also known, no efficient learning schemes existed at that time that would circumvent the formidable obstacles (see Section 4.1). Neural network research entered into the stagnation phase. Another reason that contributed to this research slowdown at that time was the relatively modest computational resources available then.

The final episode of this era was the publication of a book by Marvin Minsky and Seymour Papert (1969) that gave more doubt as to the layered learning networks' potential. The stated limitations of the perceptron-class networks were made public; however, the challenge was not answered until the mid-1980s. The discovery of successful extensions of neural network knowledge had to wait until 1986. Meanwhile, the mainstream of research flowed toward other areas, and research activity in the neural network field, called at that time *cybernetics,* had sharply decreased. The artificial intelligence area emerged as a dominant and promising research field, which took over, among others, many of the tasks that neural networks of that day could not solve.

During the period from 1965 to 1984, further pioneering work was accomplished by a handful of researchers. The study of learning in networks of threshold elements and of the mathematical theory of neural networks was pursued by Sun-Ichi Amari (1972,1977). Also in Japan, Kunihiko Fukushima developed a class of neural network architectures known as *neocognitrons* (Fukushima and Miyaka 1980). The neocognitron is a model for visual pattern recognition and is concerned with biological plausibility. The network emulates the retinal images and processes them using two-dimensional layers of neurons.

Associative memory research has been pursued by, among others, Tuevo Kohonen in Finland (1977, 1982, 1984, 1988) and James A. Anderson (Anderson et al. 1977). Unsupervised learning networks were developed for feature mapping into regular arrays of neurons (Kohonen 1982). Figure 1.11 demonstrates one of the practical uses of this class of networks. Stephen Grossberg and Gail Carpenter have introduced a number of neural architectures and theories and developed the theory of adaptive resonance networks (Grossberg 1974, 1982).

During the period from 1982 until 1986, several seminal publications were published that significantly furthered the potential of neural networks. The era of renaissance started with John Hopfield (1982, 1984) introducing a recurrent neural network architecture for associative memories. His papers formulated computational properties of a fully connected network of units. Figures 1.5 through 1.10 illustrate basic concepts, examples and applications of fully connected networks originally introduced by Hopfield.

Another revitalization of the field came from the publication in 1986 of two volumes on parallel distributed processing, edited by James McClelland and David Rumelhart (1986). The new learning rules and other concepts introduced in this work have removed one of the most essential network training barriers that grounded the mainstream efforts of the mid-1960s. The publication by Mc-Clelland and Rumelhart opened a new era for the once-underestimated computing potential of layered networks. The function approximator, EEG spike detector and autonomous driver discussed in the previous section provide examples facilitated by the new learning rules.

Although the mathematical framework for the new training scheme of layered networks was discovered in 1974 by Paul Werbos, it went largely unnoticed at that time (Werbos 1974). According to the most recent statement (Dreyfus 1990), the first authors of the optimization approach for multilayer feedforward systems were Bryson (Bryson and Ho 1969) and Kelley (Kelley 1969) who obtained a gradient solution for multistage network training. In 1962, Dreyfus used a simple, new recursive derivation based on the chain-rule of differentiation to prove the Bryson-Kelley results and dealt explicitly with the optimal control problem in its discrete-stage form (Dreyfus 1962). Their work, however, has not been carried to maturity and adopted for neural network learning algorithms. Most of the developments covered in this historical overview are looked at in detail in subsequent chapters.

Beginning in 1986–87, many new neural networks research programs were initiated. The intensity of research in the neurocomputing discipline can be measured by a quickly growing number of conferences and journals devoted to the field. In addition to many edited volumes that contain collections of papers, several books have already appeared. The list of applications that can be solved by neural networks has expanded from small test-size examples to large practical tasks. Very-large-scale integrated neural network chips have been fabricated. At the time of this writing, educational offerings have been established to explore the artificial neural systems science. Although neurocomputing has had an interesting history, the field is still in its early stages of development.

1.3

FUTURE OUTLOOK

The current explosion of interest in artificial neural systems is based on a number of scientific and economic expectations. One should be aware, however, that some of the popular expectations may be exaggerated and are not realistic. The tendency for overexpectations comes to the field of artificial neural systems naturally through its name and, sometimes, through the terminology it uses. It is somewhat tempting for a human being to envisage a human-like machine with human or near-human perceptual, reasoning, and movement capabilities. Anthropomorphic terminology, inspirations, and the sensory processing applications of neural network technology may be blamed partially for linking such human-like man-made machines with what is merely a technical discipline. Such "links" should be dismissed with good humor.

We can be quite sure that neural networks will not replace conventional computers. Basic reasons preclude neurocomputers replacing conventional ones for most tasks. Conventional computers are now very inexpensive to make. They are extremely fast and accurate for executing mathematical subroutines, text processing, computer-aided design, data processing and transfer, and many other tasks. In general, conventional digital computers outperform any other computing devices in numerical calculations.

One possibility for the use of artificial neural systems is to simulate physical systems that are best expressed by massively parallel networks. Also, low-level signal processing might best be done by parallel analog or analog and digital neural networks. Perhaps the most likely applications for neural networks will be those involving classification, association, and reasoning rather than sequential arithmetic computing. Not surprisingly, the best hope for the widespread use of artificial neural systems, or neurocomputing, is in computationally intensive areas that are not successfully attacked by conventional computers. It seems that the areas requiring human-like inference and perception of speech and vision are the most likely candidates for applications. If these succeed, there will be more applications in real-time control of complex systems and other applications that we cannot yet anticipate.

Neural networks are also expected to be widely applied in expert systems and in a variety of signal processors. At present, such systems are available as aids for medical diagnosis, financial services, stock price prediction, solar flare forecasting, radar pulse identification, and other applications. As most researchers agree, future artificial neural systems are not going to replace computational and artificial intelligence simulations on conventional computers either. Rather, they will offer a complementary technology. The ultimate goal may be to exploit both technologies under the same roof, while presenting a single, flexible interface to the user.

Today's neurocomputers are often conventional programmable computers running neural simulation software. Such simulated neurocomputers provide suitable but conventional input and output interfaces. Some neurocomputers employ dedicated architectures, or neurocomputing boards, that make the neural network simulations operate faster and more accurately when compared to standard architectures. Understandably, as neurocomputers become faster, smaller, and more efficient, the limits of applications will expand beyond simulated solutions. Futhermore, it seems certain that the proliferation of application-specific very-large-scale integrated (VLSI) neural networks is of crucial importance for the long-term success of the technology.

Fortunately, artificial neural systems fabrication follows the invented computing paradigms. Optical neural network implementations are expected to become directly applicable. Since 1986, when AT&T's first neural integrated circuit memory was fabricated, we have seen the proliferation of microelectronic neural network chips. VLSI neural systems with modifiable weights have reached the market. However, general-purpose trainable neural network chips with on-chip learning are probably several years off.

In the long term, we could expect that artificial neural systems will be used in applications involving vision, speech, decision-making, and reasoning, but also as signal processors such as filters, detectors, and quality control systems. Applications are expected especially for processing large amounts of data. Also, neural networks may offer solutions for cases in which a processing algorithm or analytical solutions are hard to find, hidden, or nonexistent. Such cases include modeling complex processes, extracting properties of large sets of data, and providing identification of plants that need to be controlled. A robot system already exists that combines vision with robot arm motion control and learns hand-eye coordination. Such systems can be expected to be extended over the next few years to produce a sophisticated robotic system. Continuous, speaker-independent speech recognition systems are being developed. They are likely to be several years off, but the limited vocabulary systems may be commercially available sooner.

Artificial neural networks technology is still very new and is developing quickly. We are witnessing fast expansion of neural network-based intelligent machines. Hopefully, this expansion will enhance the quality of our lives and make many difficult tasks easier to accomplish. Further speculations may not be needed, because the technological achievements and available products will speak for themselves.

REFERENCES

Alexander, I., ed. 1989. *Neural Computing Architectures—The Design of Brain-Like Machines.* Cambridge, Mass.: MIT Press.

Amari, S. I. 1972. "Learning Patterns and Pattern Sequences by Self-Organizing Nets of Threshold Elements," *IEEE Trans. Computers* C-21: 1197–1206.

Amari, S. I. 1977. "Neural Theory of Association and Concept Formation," *Biol. Cybern.* 26: 175–185.

Anderson, J. A., J. W. Silverstein, S. A. Rite, and R. S. Jones, 1977. "Distinctive Features, Categorical Perception, and Probability Learning: Some Applications of a Neural Model," *Psych. Rev.* 84: 413-451.

Bryson, A. E., and Y. C. Ho. 1969. *Applied Optimal Control.* Waltham, Mass.: Blaisdell, 43–45.

Dayhoff, J. 1990. *Neural Network Architectures—An Introduction.* New York: Van Nostrand Reinhold.

Dreyfus, S. 1962. "The Numerical Solution of Variational Problems,"*Math. Anal. Appl.* 5(1): 30–45.

Dreyfus, S. E. 1990. "Artificial Neural Networks, Back Propagation and the Kelley-Bryson Gradient Procedure,"*J. Guidance, Control Dynamics.* 13(5): 926–928.

Eberhart, R. C., and R. W. Dobbins. 1990. "Case Study I: Detection of Electroencephalogram Spikes," in *Neural Networks PC Tools.* ed. R. C. Eberhart, R. W. Dobbins. San Diego, Calif.: Academic Press.

Foo, Y. P. S. and Y. Takefuji. 1988. "Integer Linear Programming Neural Networks for Job-Shop Scheduling," *Proc. 1988 Intern. IEEE Conf. Neural Networks,* San Diego, Calif.

Fukushima, K. and S. Miyaka. 1980. "Neocognitron: A Self-Organizing Neural Network Model for a Mechanism of Pattern Recognition Unaffected by Shift in Position," *Biol. Cybern.* 36(4): 193–202.

Grossberg, S. 1977. "Classical and Instrumental Learning by Neural Networks," in *Progress in Theoretical Biology.* vol. 3. New York: Academic Press, 51–141.

Grossberg, S. 1982. *Studies of Mind and Brain: Neural Principles of Learning Perception, Development, Cognition, and Motor Control.* Boston: Reidel Press.

Hebb, D. O. 1949. *The Organization of Behavior, A Neuropsychological Theory.* New York: John Wiley.

Hopfield, J. J. 1982. "Neural Networks and Physical Systems with Emergent Collective Computational Abilities," *Proc. Natl. Acad. Sci.* 79: 2554–58.

Hopfield, J. J. 1984. "Neurons with Graded Response Have Collective Computational Properties Like Those of Two State Neurons," *Proc. Natl. Acad. Sci.* 81: 3088–3092.

Kelley, H. J. 1960. "Gradient Theory of Optimal Flight Path," *ARS Journal,* 30(10): 947–954.

Kirrmann, H. (June) 1989. "Neural Computing: The New Gold Rush in Informatics," *IEEE Microworld.*

Kohonen, T. 1977. *Associative Memory: A System-Theoretical Approach,* Berlin: Springer-Verlag.

Kohonen, T. 1982. "A Simple Paradigm for the Self-Organized Formation of Structured Feature Maps," in *Competition and Cooperation in Neural Nets.* ed. S. Amari, M. Arbib. vol. 45. Berlin: Springer-Verlag.

Kohonen,T. 1984. *Self-Organization and Associative Memory.* Berlin: Springer Verlag.

Kohonen, T. 1988. "The 'Neural' Phonetic Typewriter," *IEEE Computer* 27(3): 11–22.

McClelland, T. L., D. E. Rumelhart 1986. *Parallel Distributed Processing.* Cambridge: MIT Press and the PDP Research Group.

McCulloch, W. S. and W. H. Pitts. 1943. "A Logical Calculus of the Ideas Imminent in Nervous Activity," *Bull. Math. Biophy.* 5:115–133.

Minsky, M. and S. Papert, 1969. *Perceptrons.* Cambridge, Mass.: MIT Press.

Minsky, M. 1954. "Neural Nets and the Brain," *Doctoral Dissertation,* Princeton University, NJ.

Nilsson, N. J. 1965. *Learning Machines: Foundations of Trainable Pattern Classifiers,* New York: McGraw Hill; also republished as *The Mathematical Foundations of Learning Machines,* Morgan-Kaufmann Publishers, San Mateo, Calif. 1990.

Pomerleau, D. A. 1989. "ALVINN: An Autonomous Land Vehicle in a Neural Network," in *Advances in Neural Information Processing.* ed. D. Touretzky. vol. 1, San Mateo, Calif.: Morgan-Kaufmann Publishers.

Rosenblatt, F. 1958. "The Perceptron: A Probabilistic Model for Information Storage and Organization in the Brain," *Psych. Rev.* 65: 386–408.

Shriver, B. D. 1988. "Artificial Neural Systems,"*IEEE Computer* (March): 8–9.

von Neumann, J. 1958. *The Computer and the Brain.* New Haven, Conn.: Yale University Press, 87.

Werbos, P. J. 1974. "Beyond Regression: New Tools for Prediction and Analysis in the Behavioral Sciences," *Doctoral Dissertation, Appl. Math.,* Harvard University, Mass.

Widrow, B. 1962. "Generalization and Information Storage in Networks of Adaline 'Neurons'," in *Self-organizing Systems.* M. C. Jovitz, G. T. Jacobi, and G. Goldstein. eds., Washington, D.C.: Spartan Books, 435–461.

Widrow, B. and M. E. Hoff, Jr. 1960. "Adaptive Switching Circuits," 1960 IRE Western Electric Show and Convention Record, part 4 (Aug. 23): 96–104.

2

FUNDAMENTAL CONCEPTS AND MODELS OF ARTIFICIAL NEURAL SYSTEMS

Nothing happens in the universe
that does not have a sense of either
certain maximum or minimum.

L. EULER

There are a number of different answers possible to the question of how to define neural networks. At one extreme, the answer could be that neural networks are simply a class of mathematical algorithms, since a network can be regarded essentially as a graphic notation for a large class of algorithms. Such algorithms produce solutions to a number of specific problems. At the other end, the reply may be that these are synthetic networks that emulate the biological neural networks found in living organisms. In light of today's limited knowledge of biological neural networks and organisms, the more plausible answer seems to be closer to the algorithmic one.

In search of better solutions for engineering and computing tasks, many avenues have been pursued. There has been a long history of interest in the biological sciences on the part of engineers, mathematicians, and physicists endeavoring to gain new ideas, inspirations, and designs. Artificial neural networks have undoubtedly been biologically inspired, but the close correspondence between them and real neural systems is still rather weak. Vast discrepancies exist between both the architectures and capabilities of artificial and natural neural networks. Knowledge about actual brain functions is so limited, however, that there is little to guide those who would try to emulate them. No models have been successful in duplicating the performance of the human brain. Therefore, the brain has been and still is only a metaphor for a wide variety of neural network configurations that have been developed (Durbin 1989).

Despite the loose analogy between artificial and natural neural systems, we will briefly review the biological neuron model. The synthetic neuron model will subsequently be defined in this chapter and examples of network classes will be discussed. The basic definitions of neuron and elementary neural networks will also be given. Since no common standards are yet used in the technical literature, this part of the chapter will introduce notation, graphic symbols, and terminology used in this text. The basic forms of neural network processing will also be discussed.

The reader may find this initially surprising, but the majority of this book's content is devoted to network learning and, specifically, to experiential training. In this chapter basic learning concepts are characterized and defined. While the exposition of artificial neural network learning is developed gradually here and throughout subsequent chapters, the reader should find it intriguing and appealing to discover how powerful and useful learning techniques can be. Since neural networks represent a rich class of learning algorithms and architectures, a taxonomy of the most important networks is presented.

2.1

BIOLOGICAL NEURONS AND THEIR ARTIFICIAL MODELS

A human brain consists of approximately 10^{11} computing elements called *neurons*. They communicate through a connection network of axons and synapses having a density of approximately 10^4 synapses per neuron. Our hypothesis regarding the modeling of the natural nervous system is that neurons communicate with each other by means of electrical impulses (Arbib 1987). The neurons operate in a chemical environment that is even more important in terms of actual brain behavior. We thus can consider the brain to be a densely connected electrical switching network conditioned largely by the biochemical processes. The vast neural network has an elaborate structure with very complex interconnections. The input to the network is provided by sensory receptors. Receptors deliver stimuli both from within the body, as well as from sense organs when the stimuli originate in the external world. The stimuli are in the form of electrical impulses that convey the information into the network of neurons. As a result of information processing in the central nervous systems, the effectors are controlled and give human responses in the form of diverse actions. We thus have a three-stage system, consisting of receptors, neural network, and effectors, in control of the organism and its actions.

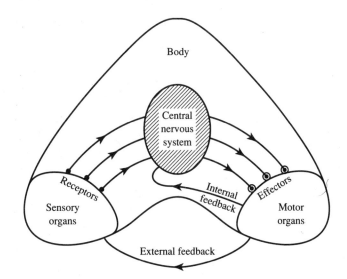

Figure 2.1 Information flow in nervous system.

A lucid, although rather approximate idea, about the information links in the nervous system is shown in Figure 2.1. As we can see from the figure, the information is processed, evaluated, and compared with the stored information in the central nervous system. When necessary, commands are generated there and transmitted to the motor organs. Notice that motor organs are monitored in the central nervous system by feedback links that verify their action. Both internal and external feedback control the implementation of commands. As can be seen, the overall nervous system structure has many of the characteristics of a closed-loop control system.

Biological Neuron

The *elementary nerve cell*, called a *neuron,* is the fundamental building block of the biological neural network. Its schematic diagram is shown in Figure 2.2. A typical cell has three major regions: the cell body, which is also called the *soma,* the *axon,* and the *dendrites.* Dendrites form a dendritic tree, which is a very fine bush of thin fibers around the neuron's body. Dendrites receive information from neurons through axons—long fibers that serve as transmission lines. An axon is a long cylindrical connection that carries impulses from the neuron. The end part of an axon splits into a fine arborization. Each branch of it terminates in a small endbulb almost touching the dendrites of neighboring neurons. The axon-dendrite contact organ is called a *synapse.* The synapse is where the neuron introduces its signal to the neighboring neuron. The signals reaching a synapse and·received

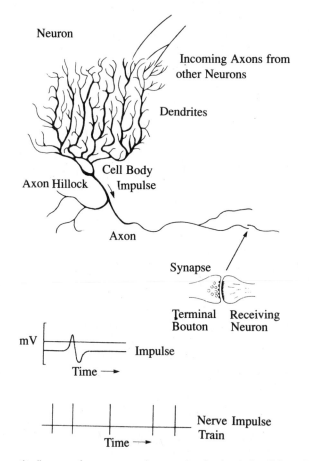

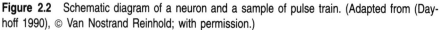

Figure 2.2 Schematic diagram of a neuron and a sample of pulse train. (Adapted from (Dayhoff 1990), © Van Nostrand Reinhold; with permission.)

by dendrites are electrical impulses. The interneuronal transmission is sometimes electrical but is usually effected by the release of chemical transmitters at the synapse. Thus, terminal boutons generate the chemical that affects the receiving neuron. The receiving neuron either generates an impulse to its axon, or produces no response.

The neuron is able to respond to the total of its inputs aggregated within a short time interval called the *period of latent summation*. The neuron's response is generated if the total potential of its membrane reaches a certain level. The membrane can be considered as a shell, which aggregates the magnitude of the incoming signals over some duration. Specifically, the neuron generates a pulse response and sends it to its axon only if the conditions necessary for firing are fulfilled.

Let us consider the conditions necessary for the firing of a neuron. Incoming impulses can be *excitatory* if they cause the firing, or *inhibitory* if they hinder the firing of the response. A more precise condition for firing is that the excitation should exceed the inhibition by the amount called the *threshold* of the neuron, typically a value of about 40 mV (Arbib 1987). Since a synaptic connection causes the excitatory or inhibitory reactions of the receiving neuron, it is practical to assign positive and negative unity weight values, respectively, to such connections. This allows us to reformulate the neuron's firing condition. The neuron fires when the total of the weights to receive impulses exceeds the threshold value during the latent summation period.

The incoming impulses to a neuron can only be generated by neighboring neurons and by the neuron itself. Usually, a certain number of incoming impulses are required to make a target cell fire. Impulses that are closely spaced in time and arrive synchronously are more likely to cause the neuron to fire. As mentioned before, observations have been made that biological networks perform temporal integration and summation of incoming signals. The resulting spatio-temporal processing performed by natural neural networks is a complex process and much less structured than digital computation. The neural impulses are not synchronized in time as opposed to the synchronous discipline of digital computation. The characteristic feature of the biological neuron is that the signals generated do not differ significantly in magnitude; the signal in the nerve fiber is either absent or has the maximum value. In other words, information is transmitted between the nerve cells by means of binary signals.

After carrying a pulse, an axon fiber is in a state of complete nonexcitability for a certain time called the *refractory period*. For this time interval the nerve does not conduct any signals, regardless of the intensity of excitation. Thus, we may divide the time scale into consecutive intervals, each equal to the length of the refractory period. This will enable a discrete-time description of the neurons' performance in terms of their states at discrete time instances. For example, we can specify which neurons will fire at the instant $k + 1$ based on the excitation conditions at the instant k. The neuron will be excited at the present instant if the number of excited excitatory synapses exceeds the number of excited inhibitory synapses at the previous instant by at least the number T, where T is the neuron's threshold value.

The time units for modeling biological neurons can be taken to be of the order of a millisecond. However, the refractory period is not uniform over the cells. Also, there are different types of neurons and different ways in which they connect. Thus, the picture of real phenomena in the biological neural network becomes even more involved. We are dealing with a dense network of interconnected neurons that release asynchronous signals. The signals are then fed forward to other neurons within the spatial neighborhood but also fed back to the generating neurons.

The above discussion is extremely simplified when seen from a neurobiological point of view, though it is valuable for gaining insight into the principles of "biological computation." Our computing networks are far simpler than their biological counterparts. Let us examine an artificial neuron model that is of special, historical significance.

McCulloch-Pitts Neuron Model

The first formal definition of a synthetic neuron model based on the highly simplified considerations of the biological model described in the preceding section was formulated by McCulloch and Pitts (1943). The McCulloch-Pitts model of the neuron is shown in Figure 2.3a. The inputs x_i, for $i = 1, 2, \ldots, n$, are 0 or 1, depending on the absence or presence of the input impulse at instant k. The neuron's output signal is denoted as o. The firing rule for this model is defined as follows

$$o^{k+1} = \begin{cases} 1 & \text{if } \sum_{i=1}^{n} w_i x_i^k \geq T \\ 0 & \text{if } \sum_{i=1}^{n} w_i x_i^k < T \end{cases}$$

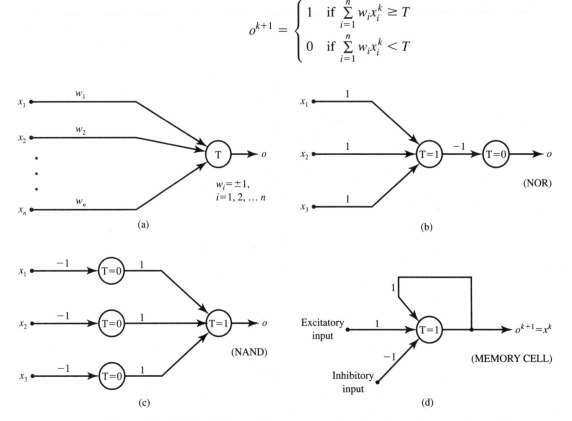

Figure 2.3 McCulloch-Pitts model neuron and elementary logic networks: (a) model diagram, (b) NOR gate, (c) NAND gate, and (d) memory cell.

where superscript $k = 0, 1, 2, \ldots$ denotes the discrete-time instant, and w_i is the multiplicative weight connecting the i'th input with the neuron's membrane. In further discussion, we will assume that a unity delay elapses between the instants k and $k + 1$. Note that $w_i = +1$ for excitatory synapses, $w_i = -1$ for inhibitory synapses for this model, and T is the neuron's threshold value, which needs to be exceeded by the weighted sum of signals for the neuron to fire.

Although this neuron model is very simplistic, it has substantial computing potential. It can perform the basic logic operations NOT, OR, and AND, provided its weights and thresholds are appropriately selected. As we know, any multivariable combinational function can be implemented using either the NOT and OR, or alternatively the NOT and AND, Boolean operations. Examples of three-input NOR and NAND gates using the McCulloch-Pitts neuron model are shown in Figure 2.3(b) and (c). The reader can easily inspect the implemented functions by compiling a truth table for each of the logic gates shown in the figure.

Both the neuron model and the example logic circuits discussed so far have been combinational and little attention has been paid to the inherent delay involved in their operation. However, the unity delay property of the McCulloch-Pitts neuron model makes it possible to build sequential digital circuitry.

First note that a single neuron with a single input x and with the weight and threshold values both of unity, computes $o^{k+1} = x^k$. Such a simple network thus behaves as a single register cell able to retain the input for one period elapsing between two instants. As a consequence, once a feedback loop is closed around the neuron as shown in Figure 2.3(d), we obtain a memory cell. An excitatory input of 1 initializes the firing in this memory cell, and an inhibitory input of 1 initializes a nonfiring state. The output value, at the absence of inputs, is then sustained indefinitely. This is because the output of 0 fed back to the input does not cause firing at the next instant, while the output of 1 does.

Thus, we see that digital computer hardware of arbitrary complexity can be constructed using an artificial neural network consisting of elementary building blocks as shown in Figure 2.3. Our purpose, however, is not to duplicate the function of already efficient digital circuitry, but rather to assess and exploit the computational power that is manifested by interconnected neurons subject to the experiential learning process.

Neuron Modeling for Artificial Neural Systems

The McCulloch-Pitts model of a neuron is characterized by its formalism and its elegant, precise mathematical definition. However, the model makes use of several drastic simplifications. It allows binary 0, 1 states only, operates under a discrete-time assumption, and assumes synchrony of operation of all neurons

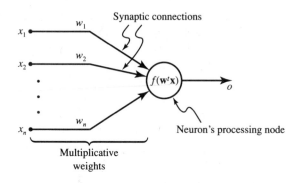

Figure 2.4 General symbol of neuron consisting of processing node and synaptic connections.

in a larger network. Weights and the neurons' thresholds are fixed in the model and no interaction among network neurons takes place except for signal flow. Thus, we will consider this model as a starting point for our neuron modeling discussion. Specifically, the artificial neural systems and computing algorithms employ a variety of neuron models that have more diversified features than the model just presented. Below, we introduce the main artificial neuron models that will be used later in this text.

Every neuron model consists of a processing element with synaptic input connections and a single output. The signal flow of neuron inputs, x_i, is considered to be unidirectional as indicated by arrows, as is a neuron's output signal flow. A general neuron symbol is shown in Figure 2.4. This symbolic representation shows a set of weights and the *neuron's processing unit,* or *node.* The neuron output signal is given by the following relationship:

$$o = f(\mathbf{w}^t\mathbf{x}), \text{ or} \tag{2.1a}$$

$$o = f\left(\sum_{i=1}^{n} w_i x_i\right) \tag{2.1b}$$

where **w** is the *weight vector* defined as

$$\mathbf{w} \overset{\Delta}{=} \begin{bmatrix} w_1 & w_2 & \cdots & w_n \end{bmatrix}^t$$

and **x** is the input vector:

$$\mathbf{x} \overset{\Delta}{=} \begin{bmatrix} x_1 & x_2 & \cdots & x_n \end{bmatrix}^t$$

(All vectors defined in this text are column vectors; superscript t denotes a transposition.) The function $f(\mathbf{w}^t\mathbf{x})$ is often referred to as an *activation function.* Its domain is the set of activation values, *net,* of the neuron model, we thus often use this function as $f(net)$. The variable *net* is defined as a scalar product of the weight and input vector

$$net \overset{\Delta}{=} \mathbf{w}^t\mathbf{x} \tag{2.2}$$

The argument of the activation function, the variable *net,* is an analog of the biological neuron's membrane potential. Note that temporarily the threshold value is not explicitly used in (2.1) and (2.2), but this is only for notational convenience. We have momentarily assumed that the modeled neuron has $n-1$ actual synaptic connections that come from actual variable inputs $x_1, x_2, \ldots, x_{n-1}$. We have also assumed that $x_n = -1$ and $w_n = T$. Since threshold plays an important role for some models, we will sometimes need to extract explicitly the threshold as a separate neuron model parameter.

The general neuron symbol, shown in Figure 2.4 and described with expressions (2.1) and (2.2), is commonly used in neural network literature. However, different artificial neural network classes make use of different definitions of $f(net)$. Also, even within the same class of networks, the neurons are sometimes considered to perform differently during different phases of network operation. Therefore, it is pedagogically sound to replace, whenever needed, the general neuron model symbol from Figure 2.4 with a specific $f(net)$ and a specific neuron model. The model validity will then usually be restricted to a particular class of network. Two main models introduced below are often used in this text.

Acknowledging the simplifications that are necessary to model a biological neuron network with artificial neural networks, we introduce in this text the following terminology: (1) *neural networks are meant to be artificial neural networks consisting of neuron models* and (2) *neurons are meant to be artificial neuron models* as defined in this chapter.

Observe from (2.1) that the neuron as a processing node performs the operation of summation of its weighted inputs, or the scalar product computation to obtain *net.* Subsequently, it performs the nonlinear operation $f(net)$ through its activation function. Typical activation functions used are

$$f(net) \overset{\Delta}{=} \frac{2}{1 + \exp(-\lambda net)} - 1 \tag{2.3a}$$

and

$$f(net) \overset{\Delta}{=} \operatorname{sgn}(net) = \begin{cases} +1, & net > 0 \\ -1, & net < 0 \end{cases} \tag{2.3b}$$

where $\lambda > 0$ in (2.3a) is proportional to the neuron gain determining the steepness of the continuous function $f(net)$ near $net = 0$. The continuous activation function is shown in Figure 2.5(a) for various λ. Notice that as $\lambda \to \infty$, the limit of the continuous function becomes the sgn (*net*) function defined in (2.3b). Activation functions (2.3a) and (2.3b) are called *bipolar continuous* and *bipolar binary functions,* respectively. The word "bipolar" is used to point out that both positive and negative responses of neurons are produced for this definition of the activation function.

By shifting and scaling the bipolar activation functions defined by (2.3), *unipolar continuous and unipolar binary activation functions* can be obtained,

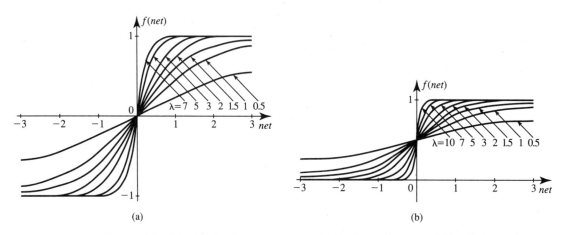

Figure 2.5 Activation functions of a neuron: (a) bipolar continuous and (b) unipolar continuous.

respectively, as

$$f(net) \triangleq \frac{1}{1 + \exp(-\lambda net)} \tag{2.4a}$$

and

$$f(net) \triangleq \begin{cases} 1, & net > 0 \\ 0, & net < 0 \end{cases} \tag{2.4b}$$

Function (2.4a) is shown in Figure 2.5(b). Again, the unipolar binary function is the limit of $f(net)$ in (2.4a) when $\lambda \to \infty$. The soft-limiting activation functions (2.3a) and (2.4a) are often called *sigmoidal characteristics,* as opposed to the *hard-limiting activation functions* given in (2.3b) and (2.4b). Hard-limiting activation functions describe the discrete neuron model.

Most neurons in this text employ bipolar activation functions. Some neural network architectures or applications do, however, specifically require the unipolar neuron responses. If this is the case, appropriate qualification for the type of activation function used is made. Essentially, any function $f(net)$ that is monotonically increasing and continuous such that $net \in R$ and $f(net) \in (-1, 1)$ can be used instead of (2.3a) in neural modeling. A few neural models that often involve some form of feedback require the use of another type of nonlinearity than that defined in (2.3) and (2.4). An example activation function that is a unipolar ramp is shown in Figure 2.6.

If the neuron's activation function has the bipolar binary form of (2.3b), the symbol of Figure 2.4 can be replaced by the diagram shown in Figure 2.7(a), which is actually a discrete neuron functional block diagram showing summation performed by the summing node and the hard-limiting thresholding performed by the *threshold logic unit* (TLU). This model consists of the synaptic weights, a summing node, and the TLU element.

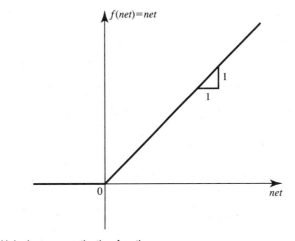

Figure 2.6 Unipolar ramp activation function.

In the case of the continuous activation function as in (2.3a), the model used is shown in Figure 2.7(b). The neuron is depicted as a summing high-gain saturating amplifier which amplifies its input signal $\mathbf{w}^t\mathbf{x}$. The models in Figure 2.7(a) and (b) can be called *discrete (binary)* and *continuous perceptrons,* respectively. The discrete perceptron, introduced by Rosenblatt (1958), was the first learning machine. It can be viewed as a precursor of many of the neural network models that we use today. Also, its study provides considerable insight into the nature of artificial neural systems.

As has been shown, neuron outputs are either discrete (binary) or continuous. Given a layer of m neurons, their output values $o_1, o_2, \ldots, o_m$ can be arranged in a layer's output vector:

$$\mathbf{o} \stackrel{\Delta}{=} \begin{bmatrix} o_1 & o_2 & \cdots & o_m \end{bmatrix}^t \tag{2.5}$$

where o_i is the output signal of the i'th neuron. The domains of vectors $\mathbf{o}$ are defined in m-dimensional space as follows for $i = 1, 2, \ldots, m$ (Hecht-Nielsen 1990):

$$(-1, 1)^m \equiv \{\mathbf{o} \in R^m, \quad o_i \in (-1, 1)\} \tag{2.6a}$$

or

$$(0, 1)^m \equiv \{\mathbf{o} \in R^m, \quad o_i \in (0, 1)\} \tag{2.6b}$$

for bipolar and unipolar continuous activation functions defined as in (2.3a) and (2.4a), respectively. It is evident that the domain of vector $\mathbf{o}$ is, in this case, the interior of either the m-dimensional cube $(-1, 1)^m$ or of the cube $(0, 1)^m$.

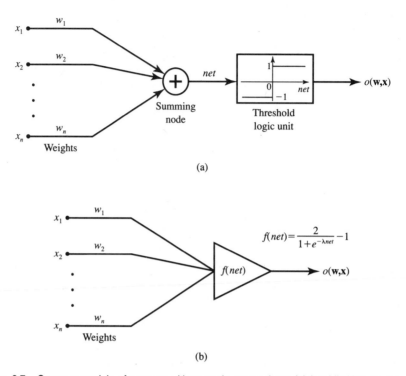

Figure 2.7 Common models of neurons with synaptic connections: (a) hard-limiting neuron (binary perceptron) and (b) soft-limiting neuron (continuous perceptron).

For binary-valued outputs o_i, the domains of $\mathbf{o}$ in m-dimensional space for $i = 1, 2, \ldots, m$, are

$$\{-1, 1\}^m \equiv \{\mathbf{o} \in R^m, \quad o_i \in \{-1, 1\}\} \tag{2.7a}$$

or

$$\{0, 1\}^m \equiv \{\mathbf{o} \in R^m, \quad o_i \in \{0, 1\}\} \tag{2.7b}$$

for bipolar and unipolar binary activation functions defined as in (2.3b) and (2.4b), respectively. The domains of vector $\mathbf{o}$ are in this case vertices of either the m-dimensional cube $[-1, 1]^m$ or of the cube $[0, 1]^m$. Each vector $\mathbf{o}$ having binary-valued entries can thus assume 2^m different values. Input vectors $\mathbf{x}$ and their domains can be described similarly.

Artificial neural systems using the models defined by (2.1) through (2.4) do not involve the biological neuron features of delay, refractory period, or discrete-time operation. In fact, the neuron models listed so far in this section represent instantaneous, memoryless networks; i.e. they generate the output response determined only by the present excitation. A delay feature can be added to the instantaneous neuron model by adding an external delay element to make the ensemble of neurons operate with memory, as shown in the next section.

2.2

MODELS OF ARTIFICIAL NEURAL NETWORKS

Our introductory definition of artificial neural networks as physical cellular networks that are able to acquire, store, and utilize experiential knowledge has been related to the network's capabilities and performance. At this point, knowing the definition of the artificial neural network neuron model, we may benefit from another definition. The neural network can also be defined as *an interconnection of neurons, as defined in (2.1) through (2.4), such that neuron outputs are connected, through weights, to all other neurons including themselves; both lag-free and delay connections are allowed.* As research efforts continue, new and extended definitions may be developed, but this definition is sufficient for the introductory study of artificial neural architectures and algorithms found in this text.

Feedforward Network

Let us consider an elementary *feedforward architecture* of m neurons receiving n inputs as shown in Figure 2.8(a). Its output and input vectors are, respectively

$$\mathbf{o} = \begin{bmatrix} o_1 & o_2 & \cdots & o_m \end{bmatrix}^t$$
$$\mathbf{x} = \begin{bmatrix} x_1 & x_2 & \cdots & x_n \end{bmatrix}^t \tag{2.8}$$

Weight w_{ij} connects the i'th neuron with the j'th input. The double subscript convention used for weights in this book is such that *the first and second subscript denote the index of the destination and source nodes, respectively.* We thus can write the activation value for the i'th neuron as

$$net_i = \sum_{j=1}^{n} w_{ij}x_j, \quad \text{for } i = 1, 2, \ldots, m \tag{2.9}$$

The following nonlinear transformation [Equation (2.10)] involving the activation function $f(net_i)$, for $i = 1, 2, \ldots, m$, completes the processing of $\mathbf{x}$. The transformation, performed by each of the m neurons in the network, is a strongly nonlinear mapping expressed as

$$o_i = f(\mathbf{w}_i^t \mathbf{x}), \quad \text{for } i = 1, 2, \ldots, m \tag{2.10}$$

where weight vector $\mathbf{w}_i$ contains weights leading toward the i'th output node and is defined as follows

$$\mathbf{w}_i \stackrel{\Delta}{=} \begin{bmatrix} w_{i1} & w_{i2} & \cdots & w_{in} \end{bmatrix}^t \tag{2.11}$$

Introducing the nonlinear matrix operator Γ, the mapping of input space x to

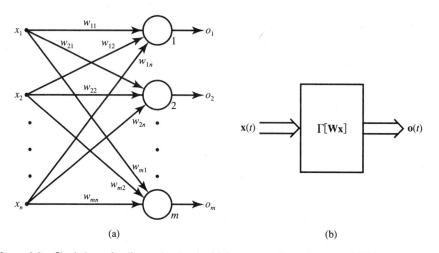

(a)　　　　　　　　　　　　　　　(b)

Figure 2.8　Single-layer feedforward network: (a) interconnection scheme and (b) block diagram.

output space o implemented by the network can be expressed as follows

$$\mathbf{o} = \Gamma[\mathbf{Wx}] \tag{2.12a}$$

where $\mathbf{W}$ is the *weight matrix*, also called the *connection matrix:*

$$\mathbf{W} \overset{\Delta}{=} \begin{bmatrix} w_{11} & w_{12} & \cdots & w_{1n} \\ w_{21} & w_{22} & \cdots & w_{2n} \\ \vdots & \vdots & \ddots & \vdots \\ w_{m1} & w_{m2} & \cdots & w_{mn} \end{bmatrix} \tag{2.12b}$$

and

$$\Gamma[\cdot] \overset{\Delta}{=} \begin{bmatrix} f(\cdot) & 0 & \cdots & 0 \\ 0 & f(\cdot) & \cdots & 0 \\ \vdots & \vdots & \cdots & \vdots \\ 0 & 0 & \cdots f(\cdot) \end{bmatrix} \tag{2.12c}$$

Note that the nonlinear activation functions $f(\cdot)$ on the diagonal of the matrix operator Γ operate componentwise on the activation values *net* of each neuron. Each activation value is, in turn, a scalar product of an input with the respective weight vector.

The input and output vectors $\mathbf{x}$ and $\mathbf{o}$ are often called *input* and *output patterns,* respectively. The mapping of an input pattern into an output pattern as shown in (2.12) is of the feedforward and instantaneous type, since it involves no time delay between the input $\mathbf{x}$, and the output $\mathbf{o}$. Thus, we can rewrite (2.12a)

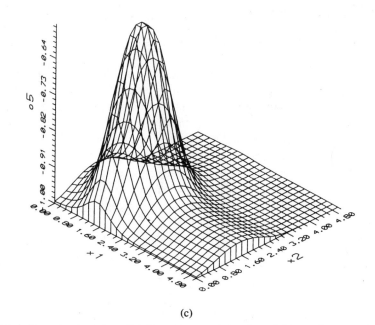

(c)

Figure 2.9c Example of two-layer feedforward network *(continued)*: (c) two-dimensional space mapping (continuous activation function, $\lambda = 2.5$).

half-plane. The response of the second layer can be easily obtained as

$$o_5 = \text{sgn}(o_1 + o_2 + o_3 + o_4 - 3.5)$$

Note that the fifth neuron responds $+1$ if and only if $o_1 = o_2 = o_3 = o_4 = 1$. It therefore selects the intersection of four half-planes produced by the first layer and designated by the arrows. Figure 2.9(b) shows that the network maps the shaded region of plane x_1, x_2 into $o_5 = 1$, and it maps its complement into $o_5 = -1$. In summary, the network of Figure2.9(a) provides mapping of the entire x_1, x_2 plane into one of the two points ± 1 on the real number axis.

Let us look at the mapping provided by the same architecture but with neurons having sigmoidal characteristics. For the continuous bipolar activation function given in (2.3a), we obtain for the first layer

$$\mathbf{o} = \begin{bmatrix} \dfrac{2}{1 + \exp(1 - x_1)\lambda} - 1 \\[2ex] \dfrac{2}{1 + \exp(x_1 - 2)\lambda} - 1 \\[2ex] \dfrac{2}{1 + \exp(-x_2)\lambda} - 1 \\[2ex] \dfrac{2}{1 + \exp(x_2 - 3)\lambda} - 1 \end{bmatrix}$$

and for the second layer

$$o_5 = \frac{2}{1 + \exp{(3.5 - o_1 - o_2 - o_3 - o_4)\lambda}} - 1$$

The network with neurons having sigmoidal activation functions performs mapping as shown in Figure 2.9(c). The figure reveals that although some similarity exists with the discrete neuron case, the mapping is much more complex. The example shows how the two-dimensional space has been mapped into the segment of one-dimensional space. In summary, the network of Figure 2.9(a) with bipolar continuous neurons provides mapping of the entire x_1, x_2 plane into the interval $(-1, 1)$ on the real number axis. Similar mapping was shown earlier in Figure 1.3. In fact, neural networks with as few as two layers are capable of universal approximation from one finite dimensional space to another. ■

Feedback Network

A feedback network can be obtained from the feedforward network shown in Figure 2.8(a) by connecting the neurons' outputs to their inputs. The result is depicted in Figure 2.10(a). The essence of closing the feedback loop is to enable

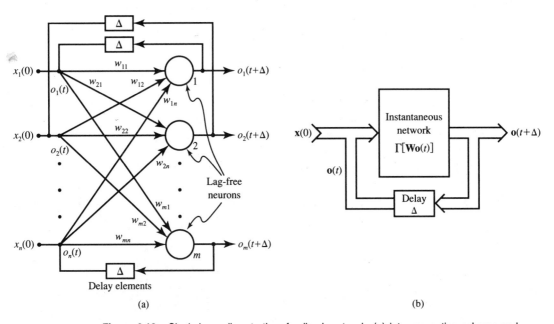

(a)   (b)

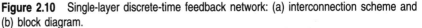

Figure 2.10 Single-layer discrete-time feedback network: (a) interconnection scheme and (b) block diagram.

control of output o_i through outputs o_j, for $j = 1, 2, \ldots, m$. Such control is especially meaningful if the present output, say $\mathbf{o}(t)$, controls the output at the following instant, $\mathbf{o}(t + \Delta)$. The time Δ elapsed between t and $t + \Delta$ is introduced by the delay elements in the feedback loop as shown in Figure 2.10(a). Here the time delay Δ has a symbolic meaning; it is an analogy to the refractory period of an elementary biological neuron model. Using the notation introduced for feedforward networks, the mapping of $\mathbf{o}(t)$ into $\mathbf{o}(t + \Delta)$ can now be written as

$$\mathbf{o}(t + \Delta) = \Gamma\,[\mathbf{Wo}(t)] \tag{2.15}$$

This formula is represented by the block diagram shown in Figure 2.10(b). Note that the input $\mathbf{x}(t)$ is only needed to initialize this network so that $\mathbf{o}(0) = \mathbf{x}(0)$. The input is then removed and the system remains autonomous for $t > 0$. We thus consider here a special case of this feedback configuration, such that $x(t) = x(0)$ and no input is provided to the network thereafter, or for $t > 0$.

There are two main categories of single-layer feedback networks. If we consider time as a discrete variable and decide to observe the network performance at discrete time instants $\Delta, 2\Delta, 3\Delta, \ldots$, the system is called *discrete-time*. For notational convenience, the time step in discrete-time networks is equated to unity, and the time instances are indexed by positive integers. Symbol Δ thus has the meaning of unity delay. The choice of indices as natural numbers is convenient since we initialize the study of the system at $t = 0$ and are interested in its response thereafter. For a discrete-time artificial neural system, we have converted (2.15) to the form

$$\mathbf{o}^{k+1} = \Gamma[\mathbf{Wo}^k], \quad \text{for } k = 1, 2, \ldots \tag{2.16a}$$

where k is the instant number. The network in Figure 2.10 is called *recurrent* since its response at the $k + 1$'th instant depends on the entire history of the network starting at $k = 0$. Indeed, we have from (2.16a) a series of nested solutions as follows

$$\mathbf{o}^1 = \Gamma[\mathbf{Wx}^0]$$
$$\mathbf{o}^2 = \Gamma\left[\mathbf{W}\Gamma[\mathbf{Wx}^0]\right]$$
$$\cdots \tag{2.16b}$$
$$\mathbf{o}^{k+1} = \Gamma\left[\mathbf{W}\Gamma\left[\ldots\Gamma[\mathbf{Wx}^0]\ldots\right]\right]$$

Recurrent networks typically operate with a discrete representation of data; they employ neurons with a hard-limiting activation function. A system with discrete-time inputs and a discrete data representation is called an *automaton*. Thus, recurrent neural networks of this class can be considered as automatons.

Equations (2.16) describe what we call the *state* $\mathbf{o}^k$ of the network at instants $k = 1, 2, \ldots$, and they yield the sequence of *state transitions*. The network begins the state transitions once it is initialized at instant 0 with $\mathbf{x}^0$, and it goes through

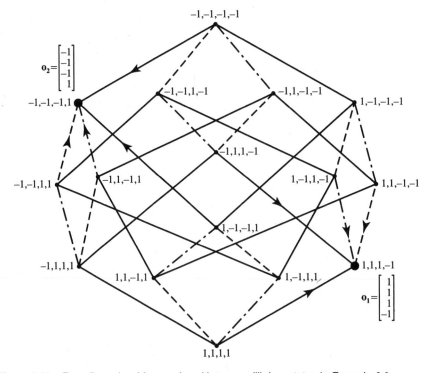

Figure 2.11　Four-dimensional hypercube with two equilibrium states in Example 2.2.

state transitions $\mathbf{o}^k$, for $k = 1, 2, \ldots$, until it possibly finds an equilibrium state. This equilibrium state is often called an *attractor*. An attractor can consist of a single state or a limited number of states. The example network of Figure 1.5(a) can be considered as having a single-state attractor of value $\mathbf{o} = \begin{bmatrix} 1 & 1 & -1 \end{bmatrix}^t$. The sequence of states of a recurrent network is generally nondeterministic. In addition, there are often many equilibrium states that can potentially be reached by the network after a number of such nondeterministic transitions. These issues will be covered in more detail in Chapters 5 and 6.

EXAMPLE 2.2 ▬▬▬▬▬▬▬

This example covers the basic concept of state transitions and the analysis of a simple recurrent discrete-time network. Figure 2.11 shows a four-dimensional hypercube, the vertices of which represent four-dimensional bipolar binary vectors, or simply, binary numbers. The cube shown visualizes state vector values and possible transitions for the four-neuron network. Four edges terminate at each vertex, since vectors that are different by a single bit component are connected with an edge. Thus, binary numbers joined by any single line can be considered to differ by only one digit. The vertices can be thought of as the output vector domain of a certain four-neuron discrete-time network with bipolar binary neurons.

Assume now that we know how to enforce the transition of states as marked by the arrows. We also can notice that each event of state transition ends at one of the two vectors as follows

$$\mathbf{o}_1 = \begin{bmatrix} 1 & 1 & 1 & -1 \end{bmatrix}^t$$
$$\mathbf{o}_2 = \begin{bmatrix} -1 & -1 & -1 & 1 \end{bmatrix}^t \tag{2.17}$$

which are apparently equilibria. Below is an example showing that a network can be devised that indeed has the equilibria as in (2.17).

Let us analyze an example of the discrete-time recurrent network shown in Figure 2.12. Its weight matrix can be set up by inspection as

$$\mathbf{W} = \begin{bmatrix} 0 & 1 & 1 & -1 \\ 1 & 0 & 1 & -1 \\ 1 & 1 & 0 & -1 \\ -1 & -1 & -1 & 0 \end{bmatrix} \tag{2.18}$$

First, it is easy to notice that none of the equilibrium states of (2.17) causes any further transitions in the network. Indeed, substituting $\mathbf{o}_1 = \mathbf{x}^0$ in (2.16b) and using (2.18) results in the first recurrence

$$\mathbf{o}^1 = \begin{bmatrix} \text{sgn}(\cdot) & 0 & 0 & 0 \\ 0 & \text{sgn}(\cdot) & 0 & 0 \\ 0 & 0 & \text{sgn}(\cdot) & 0 \\ 0 & 0 & 0 & \text{sgn}(\cdot) \end{bmatrix} \begin{bmatrix} net_1^0 \\ net_2^0 \\ net_3^0 \\ net_4^0 \end{bmatrix} \tag{2.19a}$$

or

$$\mathbf{o}^1 = \begin{bmatrix} \text{sgn}(3) & \text{sgn}(3) & \text{sgn}(3) & \text{sgn}(-3) \end{bmatrix}^t \tag{2.19b}$$

and thus no transitions take place thereafter since $\mathbf{o}^1 = \mathbf{o}^2 = \ldots = \mathbf{o}_1$. The reader may easily verify that if $\mathbf{o}_2 = \mathbf{x}^0$ then $\mathbf{o}^1 = \mathbf{o}^2 = \ldots = \mathbf{o}_2$, and no transitions take place either.

Assume now that the network is initialized at a state $\mathbf{x}^0 = \begin{bmatrix} 1 & 1 & 1 & 1 \end{bmatrix}'$, which is adjacent to $\mathbf{o}_1$. We may compute that the output $\mathbf{o}^1$ becomes

$$\mathbf{o}^1 = \begin{bmatrix} \text{sgn}(1) & \text{sgn}(1) & \text{sgn}(1) & \text{sgn}(-3) \end{bmatrix}^t \tag{2.20}$$

Therefore, the transition that takes place is

$$\begin{bmatrix} 1 & 1 & 1 & 1 \end{bmatrix} \rightarrow \begin{bmatrix} 1 & 1 & 1 & -1 \end{bmatrix}$$

and the network reaches its closest equilibrium state. The reader may easily

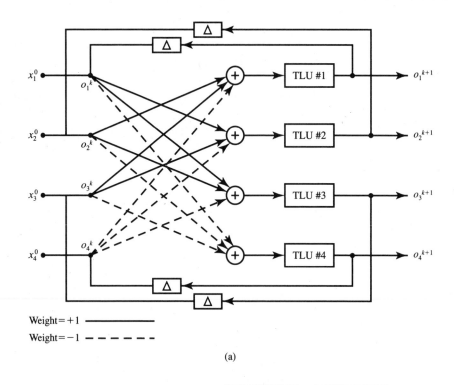

Weight $= +1$ ————————
Weight $= -1$ — — — — — —

(a)

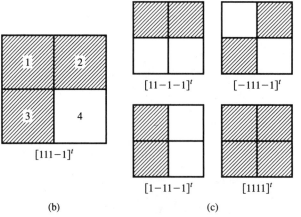

(b)   (c)

Figure 2.12 Recurrent network for two-equilibrium state diagram of Figure 2.11: (a) diagram, (b) bit map of equilibrium state vector $\mathbf{o}_1$, and (c) example bit maps that converge to the bit map of part (b).

verify that for any of the initial states as below

$$\mathbf{x}^0 = \begin{bmatrix} 1 & 1 & -1 & -1 \end{bmatrix}^t, \; \mathbf{x}^0 = \begin{bmatrix} 1 & -1 & 1 & -1 \end{bmatrix}^t, \; \text{or}$$

$$\mathbf{x}^0 = \begin{bmatrix} -1 & 1 & 1 & -1 \end{bmatrix}^t$$

there will be subsequent transitions such that $\mathbf{o}^1 = \mathbf{o}_1$ and the network will always settle at $\mathbf{o}_1$.

Bipolar binary vectors can be visualized in a bit-map form so that black and white elements of a bit map correspond to 1 and -1, respectively. The bit map in Figure 2.12(b) would thus represent $\mathbf{o}_1$. Note that the four bit maps of Figure 2.12(c), if represented as vectors, can be regarded as the initial states. Transitions from these states end at the equilibrium point $\mathbf{o}_1$. It is seen that the initial state converges in the network of Figure 2.12(a) to its closest equilibrium distant only by one bit. In cases when the initial state differs by two bits from both equilibria, the initializing input vector is equidistant to both $\mathbf{o}_1$ and $\mathbf{o}_2$. Thus, convergence to either of the equilibria would be justifiable. This assumes that the network should seek out the output which is the most similar to the initializing binary vector. Although we have not shown yet how to encode the desired equilibrium states and how to control transitions, the discussion in this example helps in understanding the concept of state transitions and the analysis of recurrent networks. ■■

In the discussion of the feedback concept, a discrete time delay Δ has been used between the input and output. The insertion of a unity delay element in the network feedback loop has made it possible to outline the formal definition of a recurrent network operating at discrete instants $k = 1, 2, \ldots$, upon its initialization at $k = 0$. To generalize the ideas just discussed, note that the feedback concept can also be implemented with any infinitesimal delay between output and input introduced in the feedback loop. The consequence of an assumption of such delay between input and output is that the output vector can be considered to be a continuous-time function. As a result, the entire network operates in continuous time. It can be seen that a *continuous-time* network can be obtained by replacing delay elements in Figure 2.10 with suitable continuous-time lag producing components.

An example of such an elementary delay network is shown in Figure 2.13(a). It is a simple electric network consisting of resistance and capacitance. In fact, electric networks are very often used to model the computation performed by neural networks. Electric networks possess the flexibility to model all linear and nonlinear phenomena encountered in our neural network studies. Because of this flexibility, they will often represent working physical models of neural networks. The differential equation relating v_2 and v_1, the output and input voltages, respectively, is

$$\frac{dv_2}{dt} + \frac{v_2}{RC} = \frac{v_1}{RC} \qquad (2.21)$$

The change of output voltage Δv_2 occurring within the small time interval Δt can be approximately expressed from (2.21) as follows:

$$\Delta v_2 \cong \frac{\Delta t}{C} \cdot \frac{v_1 - v_2}{R} \qquad (2.22)$$

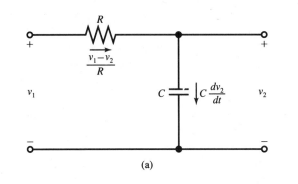

(a)

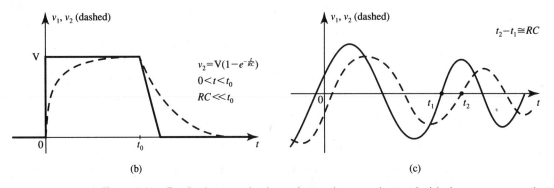

(b)   (c)

Figure 2.13 Feedback connection in continuous-time neural network: (a) elementary connecting circuit, (b) output response due to an impulse, and (c) output wave due to a damped harmonic input wave.

From (2.22) we see that for fixed C and Δt, increases of output voltage v_2 are proportional to the difference between v_1 and v_2. If v_1 is kept constant or is varied slowly with respect to the time constant RC, v_2 approximately follows v_1 in time, with a small delay. Examples of input waveforms v_1 and output responses v_2 are shown in Figures 2.13(b) and (c). Figure 2.13(b) shows $v_2(t)$ resulting from $v_1(t)$ being an impulse excitation. Figure 2.13(c) shows $v_2(t)$ due to a damped harmonic input wave excitation. Although such a wave is not very likely to be observed in artificial neural systems, it shows the explicit delay of v_2 where v_2 lags v_1 by approximately RC.

Usually, continuous-time networks employ neurons with continuous activation functions. An elementary synaptic connection using the delay network given in Figure 2.13(a) is shown in Figure 2.14. The resistance R_{ij} serves as a weight from the output of the j'th neuron to the input of the i'th neuron. Using the finite time interval Δt, Equation (2.21) can be discretized as

$$\frac{net_i^{k+1} - net_i^k}{\Delta t} \cong \frac{1}{R_{ij}C_i} \left(o_j^k - net_i^k \right) \qquad (2.23a)$$

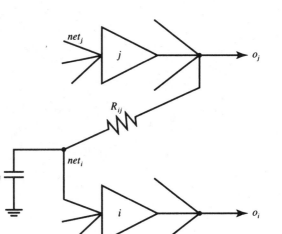

Figure 2.14 Elementary synaptic connection within continuous-time network.

The activation of the i'th neuron at the instant $k + 1$ can be expressed as

$$net_i^{k+1} \cong net_i^k + \frac{\Delta t}{R_{ij}C_i} \left(o_j^k - net_i^k \right) \tag{2.23b}$$

As can be seen, the contribution to net_i by the j'th neuron is distributed in time according to (2.23b), where Δt denotes an infinitesimal time step. When n neurons are connected to the input of the i'th neuron as shown in Figure 2.14, expression (2.23b) needs to be computed for $j = 1, 2, \ldots, n$ and summed. Numerous studies indicate that for n neurons interconnected as shown, fairly complex dynamic behavior of the network is usually obtained. The accurate description of transitions, which have been very simple for the recurrent discrete-time networks as demonstrated in Example 2.2, requires solving nonlinear differential equations for continuous-time networks. A more detailed discussion of properties of this class of networks is presented in Chapter 5. The introductory example below illustrates the main features and time-domain performance of continuous-time feedback networks.

EXAMPLE 2.3

Let us consider an electric continuous-time network of two neurons as shown in Figure2.15(a). The matrix form description, such as (2.12) for feedforward networks and (2.15) for discrete-time feedback networks, will be discussed in Chapter 5. In this example, we obtain the network equations by inspection of its diagram. We also discuss the network's main properties in terms of its dynamical behavior.

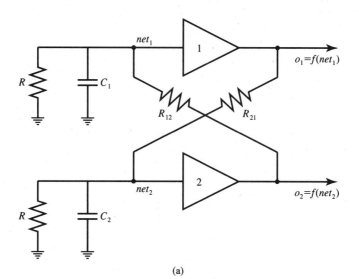

(a)

Simulation Results

Step	Run 1		Run 2		Run 3		Run 4	
	o_1	o_2	o_1	o_2	o_1	o_2	o_1	o_2
0	0.245	−0.124	0.462	−0.245	0.555	−0.555	0.704	−0.848
25	0.264	−0.146	0.493	−0.284	0.598	−0.598	0.749	−0.875
50	0.284	−0.170	0.526	−0.326	0.642	−0.642	0.790	−0.899
75	0.307	−0.195	0.560	−0.370	0.685	−0.685	0.827	−0.919
100	0.332	−0.224	0.596	−0.416	0.727	−0.727	0.860	−0.937
125	0.360	−0.254	0.633	−0.464	0.767	−0.767	0.888	−0.951
150	0.389	−0.287	0.671	−0.513	0.804	−0.804	0.912	−0.963
175	0.421	−0.323	0.708	−0.563	0.838	−0.838	0.932	−0.973
200	0.456	−0.361	0.745	−0.612	0.868	−0.868	0.948	−0.980
225	0.492	−0.402	0.781	−0.661	0.894	−0.894	0.961	−0.986
250	0.530	−0.445	0.814	−0.707	0.916	−0.916	0.971	−0.990
275	0.570	−0.489	0.845	−0.751	0.935	−0.935	0.979	−0.993
300	0.611	−0.535	0.872	−0.791	0.950	−0.950	0.985	−0.995
325	0.652	−0.582	0.897	−0.828	0.963	−0.963	0.989	−0.997
350	0.692	−0.628	0.918	−0.860	0.972	−0.972	0.993	−0.998
375	0.732	−0.674	0.936	−0.888	0.980	−0.980	0.995	−0.999
400	0.770	−0.718	0.951	−0.912	0.986	−0.986	0.997	−0.999
425	0.806	−0.760	0.963	−0.931	0.990	−0.990	0.998	−0.999
450	0.838	−0.798	0.973	−0.948	0.993	−0.993	0.999	−1.000
475	0.868	−0.833	0.980	−0.960	0.995	−0.995	0.999	−1.000
500	0.893	−0.864	0.986	−0.971	0.997	−0.997	0.999	−1.000

(b)

Figure 2.15a,b Continuous-time network from Example 2.3: (a) diagram, and (b) sample iterations for o_1, o_2

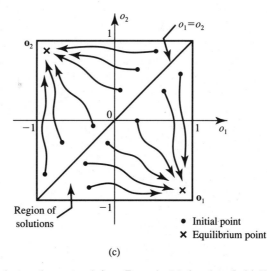

Figure 2.15c Continuous-time network from Example 2.3 *(continued)*: (c) illustration for equilibrium search.

The neuron outputs are connected to their inputs using a simple *RC* delay network, as in Figure 2.13(a). In addition, resistances *R* between each neuron input and ground are added to account for the neurons' finite input resistances. Such resistances model nonzero input currents absorbed by actual neurons. The differential equations obtained by summing currents in input nodes of the network being input neuron nodes are

$$C_1 \frac{dnet_1}{dt} = \frac{o_2 - net_1}{R_{12}} - \frac{net_1}{R}$$

$$C_2 \frac{dnet_2}{dt} = \frac{o_1 - net_2}{R_{21}} - \frac{net_2}{R}$$

(2.24)

where $o_i = f(net_i)$, $i = 1, 2$, and $f(net)$ is assumed to be given by (2.3a). We will also assume that $C_1 = C_2$ and $R_{12} = R_{21} < 0$ for this network. Although this version of the circuit involves negative resistances, we will show in Chapter 5 that they will not be needed to build actual networks. Before an analysis of this network is pursued, let us try to approach the problem intuitively.

Assume that this circuit has been initialized by storing a charge at the input capacitances, and it is allowed thereafter to seek its own equilibrium. Our initial assumption is that starting with observations of the network at $t = 0$, the value o_1 has slightly increased. This would, after a small delay Δt introduced by the *RC* network, lower the value of net_2 since R_{21} is negative. Since $f(net_2)$ is a monotonically increasing function, o_2 would also decrease within the $(0, \Delta t)$ interval. This in turn would increase net_1 and, as a final consequence, the original initial increase of o_1 would be enhanced due to the feedback interaction described. We have the cause-and-effect relationship, where the effect increases the initial cause in a closed, positive feedback, loop. If this interaction is allowed to continue for some time, the increases of o_1 will eventually slow down, since $f(net)$ flattens out far from the origin, when $o_1 \to 1^-$. Noticeably, as o_1 increases, o_2 decreases symmetrically toward -1^+ (a^+, a^- are "right" and "left" neighborhoods, respectively, of the point a while the point a is excluded). This discussion indicates that the network of Figure 2.15(a) for high-gain neurons would seek its equilibrium, or $\begin{bmatrix} o_1 & o_2 \end{bmatrix} \to \begin{bmatrix} 1^- & -1^+ \end{bmatrix}$.

The correct conclusion, however, is not unique. If the initial hypothesis on the increase of o_1 is negated, the conclusion from a similar discussion as above is just the opposite and the network seeks its equilibrium such that $\begin{bmatrix} o_1 & o_2 \end{bmatrix} \to \begin{bmatrix} -1^+ & 1^- \end{bmatrix}$. Obviously, the network cannot simultaneously be seeking two different solutions and move along opposite paths. Either the first or the second hypothesis must be true, but it is somewhat difficult to pick the right one at this point.

To gain better insight into the dynamics of the network, the equations (2.24) must be solved numerically since the closed-form solutions do not exist. Discretizing the differential equation (2.24) similar to (2.23), we obtain

$$net_1^{k+1} \cong net_1^k + \frac{\Delta t}{R_{12}C_1}\left(o_2^k - net_1^k\right) - \frac{net_1^k}{RC_1}\Delta t$$

$$net_2^{k+1} \cong net_2^k + \frac{\Delta t}{R_{21}C_2}\left(o_1^k - net_2^k\right) - \frac{net_2^k}{RC_2}\Delta t \qquad (2.25)$$

Notice that the numerical integration method chosen in (2.25) (forward Euler) is simple but usually not recommended for more sophisticated numerical computation. However, it is adequate for the purpose of this example and is also consistent with formulas (2.23). Sample results of simulations are partially listed in Figure 2.15(b) linking o_1 and o_2 as a function of k. Conditions chosen for the simulation are $\lambda = 2.5$, $dt = 0.002$, $R = 10$, and $R_{12}C_1 = R_{21}C_2 = -1$. Initial conditions are listed for $k = 0$ in the first row of the table for each of the four simulations shown. All of the partially listed runs converge to the solution $\begin{bmatrix} o_1 & o_2 \end{bmatrix} = \begin{bmatrix} 1^- & -1^+ \end{bmatrix}$.

The schematic illustration for more general cases of the equilibrium search is shown in Figure 2.15(c) for $-1 \leq o_1 \leq 1$ and $-1 \leq o_2 \leq 1$. The trajectories indicate the computed solution functions $o_2(o_1)$ with time being a parameter. The line $o_2 = o_1$ separates the two regions of attractions. For initial condition $o_1^0 > o_2^0$, $\begin{bmatrix} 1^- & -1^+ \end{bmatrix}$ is an equilibrium solution, otherwise the solution is at $\begin{bmatrix} -1^+ & 1^- \end{bmatrix}$. Note that this network maps the entire two-dimensional input space into two points, which are roughly expressed as $\mathbf{o}_1 \cong \sqrt{2} \angle -45°$ and $\mathbf{o}_2 \cong \sqrt{2} \angle 135°$. In contrast to feedforward networks, as shown in Figure 2.9(a), feedback networks require time to provide response to the mapping problem. ■

2.3

NEURAL PROCESSING

The material of the previous section has focused mainly on the computation of response **o** for a given input **x** for several important classes of neural networks. The analysis of three example networks shown in Figures 2.9(a), 2.12(a), and 2.15(a) has also been discussed. The process of computation of **o** for a given **x** performed by the network is known as *recall*. Recall is the proper processing phase for a neural network, and its objective is to retrieve the information. Recall corresponds to the decoding of the stored content which may have been encoded in a network previously. In this section we are mainly concerned with the recall mode and the tasks it can accomplish. Based on the preliminary observations made so far, we now outline the basic forms of neural information processing.

Assume that a set of patterns can be stored in the network. Later, if the network is presented with a pattern similar to a member of the stored set, it may associate the input with the closest stored pattern. The process is called *autoassociation*. Typically, a degraded input pattern serves as a cue for retrieval of its original form. This is illustrated schematically in Figure 2.16(a). The figure shows a distorted square recalling the square encoded. Another example of auto-association is provided in the Figure 1.8.

Associations of input patterns can also be stored in a *heteroassociation* variant. In heteroassociative processing, the associations between pairs of patterns are stored. This is schematically shown in Figure 2.16(b). A square input pattern presented at the input results in the rhomboid at the output. It can be inferred that the rhomboid and square constitute one pair of stored patterns. A distorted input pattern may also cause correct heteroassociation at the output as shown with dashed line.

Classification is another form of neural computation. Let us assume that a set of input patterns is divided into a number of classes, or categories. In response to an input pattern from the set, the classifier is supposed to recall the information regarding class membership of the input pattern. Typically, classes are expressed by discrete-valued output vectors, and thus output neurons of classifiers would employ binary activation functions. The schematic diagram illustrating the

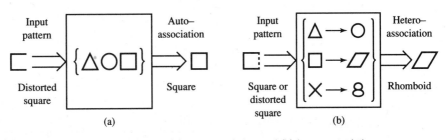

Figure 2.16 Association response: (a) autoassociation and (b) heteroassociation.

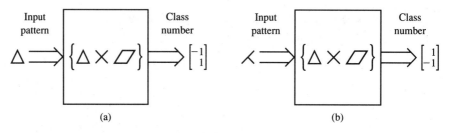

Figure 2.17 Classification response: (a) classification and (b) recognition.

classification response for patterns belonging to three classes is shown in Figure 2.17(a).

Interestingly, classification can be understood as a special case of heteroassociation. The association is now between the input pattern and the second member of the heteroassociative pair, which is supposed to indicate the input's class number. If the network's desired response is the class number but the input pattern does not exactly correspond to any of the patterns in the set, the processing is called *recognition*. When a class membership for one of the patterns in the set is recalled, recognition becomes identical to classification. Recognition within the set of three patterns is schematically shown in Figure 2.17(b). This form of processing is of particular significance when an amount of noise is superimposed on input patterns.

One of the distinct strengths of neural networks is their ability to generalize. The network is said to generalize well when it sensibly interpolates input patterns that are new to the network. Assume that a network has been trained using the data x_1 through x_5, as shown in Figure 2.18. The figure illustrates bad and good generalization examples at points that are new and are between the training points. Neural networks provide, in many cases, input-output mappings with good generalization capability.

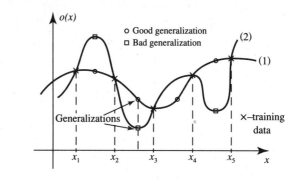

Figure 2.18 Generalization example.

When reviewing the different aspects of neural processing in this section, the assumption has been made that neural networks are able to store data. So far, we discussed the retrieval of network responses without covering any possible methods of data storage. Data are stored in a network as a result of its learning. The following section introduces basic concepts of learning.

2.4

LEARNING AND ADAPTATION

Each of us acquires and then hones our skills and abilities through the basic phenomenon of learning. Learning is a fundamental subject for psychologists, but it also underlies many of the topics in this book. In general, learning is a relatively permanent change in behavior brought about by experience. Learning in human beings and animals is an inferred process; we cannot see it happening directly and we can assume that it has occurred by observing changes in performance. Learning in neural networks is a more direct process, and we typically can capture each learning step in a distinct cause-effect relationship. To perform any of the processing tasks discussed in the previous section, neural network learning of an input-output mapping from a set of examples is needed. Designing an associator or a classifier can be based on learning a relationship that transforms inputs into outputs given a set of examples of input-output pairs. A classical framework for this problem is provided by approximation theory (Poggio and Girosi 1990).

Learning as Approximation or Equilibria Encoding

Approximation theory focuses on approximating a continuous, multivariable function $h(\mathbf{x})$ by another function $H(\mathbf{w}, \mathbf{x})$, where $\mathbf{x} = \begin{bmatrix} x_1 & x_2 & \cdots & x_n \end{bmatrix}^t$ is the input vector and $\mathbf{w} = \begin{bmatrix} w_1 & w_2 & \cdots & w_m \end{bmatrix}^t$ is a parameter (weight) vector. In the approach below, we will look at a class of neural networks as systems that can learn approximation of relationships. The learning task is to find $\mathbf{w}$ that provides the best possible approximation of $h(\mathbf{x})$ based on the set of training examples $\{\mathbf{x}\}$. An important choice that needs to be made is which approximation function $H(\mathbf{w}, \mathbf{x})$ to use. An ill-chosen, nonsmooth, approximation function example is shown in Figure 2.18 as curve (2). Even with the best choice of parameters for an ill-chosen function, the approximation is inaccurate between successive data points. The choice of function $H(\mathbf{w}, \mathbf{x})$ in order to represent $h(\mathbf{x})$ is called a *representation* problem. Once $H(\mathbf{w}, \mathbf{x})$ has been chosen, the network learning algorithm is applied for finding optimal parameters $\mathbf{w}$. A more precise formulation of the learning problem can be stated as calculation involving $\mathbf{w}^*$ such that (Poggio and Girosi 1990):

$$\rho[H(\mathbf{w}^*, \mathbf{x}), h(\mathbf{x})] \leq \rho[H(\mathbf{w}, \mathbf{x}), h(\mathbf{x})] \qquad (2.26)$$

where $\rho[H(\mathbf{w}, \mathbf{x}), h(\mathbf{x})]$, or distance function, is a measure of approximation quality between $H(\mathbf{w}, \mathbf{x})$ and $h(\mathbf{x})$. When the fit is judged according to the sum of squared differences taken for the set of training examples $\{\mathbf{x}\}$, the distance has a form of sum of squared errors. As will be shown in Chapters 3 and 4, the feed-forward networks, both single-layer and multilayer, can be taught to perform the desired mappings as described. In this chapter, only the main learning principles will be introduced.

In contrast to feedforward networks, which store mapping that can be recalled instantaneously, feedback networks are dynamical systems. The mappings in feedback networks are encoded in the equilibrium states. Similar to approximation learning, weights also determine the properties of feedback networks. Learning in feedback networks corresponds to equilibria encoding. Usually this is accomplished by a so-called "recording process," but stepwise learning approaches have also been developed for this class of networks. Equilibrium states learning will be discussed in more detail in Chapters 5 and 6.

Supervised and Unsupervised Learning

Under the notion of learning in a network, we will consider a process of forcing a network to yield a particular response to a specific input. A particular response may or may not be specified to provide external correction. Learning is necessary when the information about inputs/outputs is unknown or incomplete *a priori,* so that no design of a network can be performed in advance. The majority of the neural networks covered in this text requires training in a supervised or unsupervised learning mode. Some of the networks, however, can be designed without incremental training. They are designed by *batch learning* rather than stepwise training.

Batch learning takes place when the network weights are adjusted in a single training step. In this mode of learning, the complete set of input/output training data is needed to determine weights, and feedback information produced by the network itself is not involved in developing the network. This learning technique is also called *recording*. Learning with feedback either from the teacher or from the environment rather than a teacher, however, is more typical for neural networks. Such learning is called incremental and is usually performed in steps.

The concept of feedback plays a central role in learning. The concept is highly elusive and somewhat paradoxical. In a broad sense it can be understood as an introduction of a pattern of relationships into the cause-and-effect path. We will distinguish two different types of learning: learning *with* supervision versus

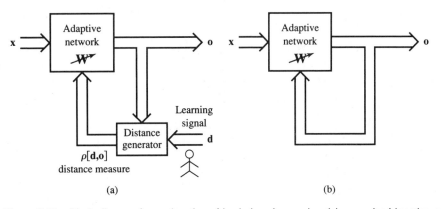

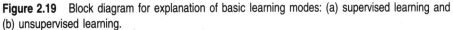

Figure 2.19 Block diagram for explanation of basic learning modes: (a) supervised learning and (b) unsupervised learning.

learning *without* supervision. The learning types block diagrams are illustrated in Figure 2.19.

In *supervised learning* we assume that at each instant of time when the input is applied, the desired response **d** of the system is provided by the teacher. This is illustrated in Figure 2.19(a). The distance $\rho[\mathbf{d}, \mathbf{o}]$ between the actual and the desired response serves as an error measure and is used to correct network parameters externally. Since we assume adjustable weights, the teacher may implement a reward-and-punishment scheme to adapt the network's weight matrix **W**. For instance, in learning classifications of input patterns or situations with known responses, the error can be used to modify weights so that the error decreases. This mode of learning is very pervasive. Also, it is used in many situations of natural learning. A set of input and output patterns called a *training set* is required for this learning mode.

Typically, supervised learning rewards accurate classifications or associations and punishes those which yield inaccurate responses. The teacher estimates the negative error gradient direction and reduces the error accordingly. In many situations, the inputs, outputs and the computed gradient are deterministic, however, the minimization of error proceeds over all its random realizations. As a result, most supervised learning algorithms reduce to stochastic minimization of error in multi-dimensional weight space.

Figure 2.19(b) shows the block diagram of unsupervised learning. In *learning without supervision,* the desired response is not known; thus, explicit error information cannot be used to improve network behavior. Since no information is available as to correctness or incorrectness of responses, learning must somehow be accomplished based on observations of responses to inputs that we have marginal or no knowledge about. For example, unsupervised learning can easily result in finding the boundary between classes of input patterns distributed as shown

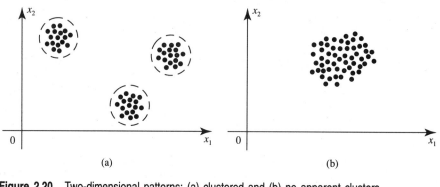

Figure 2.20   Two-dimensional patterns: (a) clustered and (b) no apparent clusters.

in Figure 2.20. In a favorable case, as in Figure 2.20(a), cluster boundaries can be found based on the large and representative sample of inputs. Suitable weight self-adaptation mechanisms have to be embedded in the trained network, because no external instructions regarding potential clusters are available. One possible network adaptation rule is: A pattern added to the cluster has to be closer to the center of the cluster than to the center of any other cluster.

Unsupervised learning algorithms use patterns that are typically redundant raw data having no labels regarding their class membership, or associations. In this mode of learning, the network must discover for itself any possibly existing patterns, regularities, separating properties, etc. While discovering these, the network undergoes change of its parameters, which is called *self-organization.*

The technique of unsupervised learning is often used to perform clustering as the unsupervised classification of objects without providing information about the actual classes. This kind of learning corresponds to minimal *a priori* information available. Some information about the number of clusters, or similarity versus dissimilarity of patterns, can be helpful for this mode of learning. Finally, learning is often not possible in an unsupervised environment, as would probably be true in the case illustrated in Figure 2.20(b) showing pattern classes not easily discernible even for a human.

Unsupervised learning is sometimes called learning without a teacher. This terminology is not the most appropriate, because learning without a teacher is not possible at all. Although, the teacher does not have to be involved in every training step, he has to set goals even in an unsupervised learning mode (Tsypkin 1973). We may think of the following analogy. Learning with supervision corresponds to classroom learning with the teacher's questions answered by students and corrected, if needed, by the teacher. Learning without supervision corresponds to learning the subject from a videotape lecture covering the material but not including any other teacher's involvement. The teacher lectures directions and methods, but is not available. Therefore, the student cannot get explanations of unclear questions, check answers and become fully informed.

2.5 ▬▬▬▬▬▬

NEURAL NETWORK LEARNING RULES

Our focus in this section will be artificial neural network learning rules. A neuron is considered to be an adaptive element. Its weights are modifiable depending on the input signal it receives, its output value, and the associated teacher response. In some cases the teacher signal is not available and no error information can be used, thus the neuron will modify its weights based only on the input and/or output. This is the case for unsupervised learning.

Let us study the learning of the weight vector $\mathbf{w}_i$, or its components w_{ij} connecting the j'th input with the i'th neuron. The trained network is shown in Figure 2.21 and uses the neuron symbol from Figure 2.4. In general, the j'th input can be an output of another neuron or it can be an external input. Our discussion in this section will cover single-neuron and single-layer network supervised learning and simple cases of unsupervised learning. Under different learning rules, the form of the neuron's activation function may be different. Note that the threshold parameter may be included in learning as one of the weights. This would require fixing one of the inputs, say x_n. We will assume here that x_n, if fixed, takes the value of -1.

The following *general learning rule* is adopted in neural network studies (Amari 1990): *The weight vector* $\mathbf{w}_i = \begin{bmatrix} w_{i1} & w_{i2} & \cdots & w_{in} \end{bmatrix}^t$ *increases in proportion to the product of input* $\mathbf{x}$ *and learning signal* r. The learning signal r is in general a function of $\mathbf{w}_i, \mathbf{x}$, and sometimes of the teacher's signal d_i. We thus have for the network shown in Figure 2.21:

$$r = r(\mathbf{w}_i, \mathbf{x}, d_i) \tag{2.27}$$

The increment of the weight vector $\mathbf{w}_i$ produced by the learning step at time t according to the general learning rule is

$$\Delta\mathbf{w}_i(t) = cr\left[\mathbf{w}_i(t), \mathbf{x}(t), d_i(t)\right]\mathbf{x}(t) \tag{2.28}$$

where c is a positive number called the *learning constant* that determines the rate of learning. The weight vector adapted at time t becomes at the next instant, or learning step,

$$\mathbf{w}_i(t+1) = \mathbf{w}_i(t) + cr\left[\mathbf{w}_i(t), \mathbf{x}(t), d_i(t)\right]\mathbf{x}(t) \tag{2.29a}$$

The superscript convention will be used in this text to index the discrete-time training steps as in Eq. (2.29a). For the k'th step we thus have from (2.29a) using this convention

$$\mathbf{w}_i^{k+1} = \mathbf{w}_i^k + cr(\mathbf{w}_i^k, \mathbf{x}^k, d_i^k)\mathbf{x}^k \tag{2.29b}$$

The learning in (2.29) assumes the form of a sequence of discrete-time weight modifications. Continuous-time learning can be expressed as

$$\frac{d\mathbf{w}_i(t)}{dt} = cr\mathbf{x}(t) \tag{2.30}$$

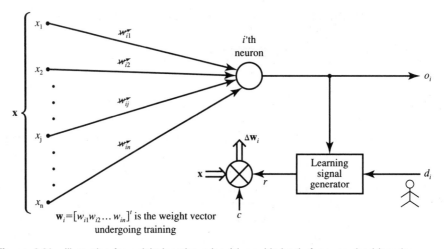

Figure 2.21 Illustration for weight learning rules (d_i provided only for supervised learning mode).

Discrete-time, or stepwise, learning is reviewed below. Weights are assumed to have been suitably initialized before each learning experiment started.

Hebbian Learning Rule

For the Hebbian learning rule the learning signal is equal simply to the neuron's output (Hebb 1949). We have

$$r \overset{\Delta}{=} f(\mathbf{w}_i^t \mathbf{x}) \tag{2.31}$$

The increment $\Delta \mathbf{w}_i$ of the weight vector becomes

$$\Delta \mathbf{w}_i = cf(\mathbf{w}_i^t \mathbf{x})\mathbf{x} \tag{2.32a}$$

The single weight w_{ij} is adapted using the following increment:

$$\Delta w_{ij} = cf(\mathbf{w}_i^t \mathbf{x})x_j \tag{2.32b}$$

This can be written briefly as

$$\Delta w_{ij} = co_i x_j, \quad \text{for } j = 1, 2, \ldots, n \tag{2.32c}$$

This learning rule requires the weight initialization at small random values around $\mathbf{w}_i = \mathbf{0}$ prior to learning. The Hebbian learning rule represents a purely feedforward, unsupervised learning. The rule implements the interpretation of the classic statement: "When an axon of cell A is near enough to excite a cell B and repeatedly or persistently takes place in firing it, some growth process or metabolic change takes place in one or both cells such that A's efficiency, as one of the cells firing B, is increased." (Hebb 1949.)

The rule states that if the crossproduct of output and input, or correlation term $o_i x_j$ is positive, this results in an increase of weight w_{ij}; otherwise the weight decreases. It can be seen that the output is strengthened in turn for each input presented. Therefore, frequent input patterns will have most influence at the neuron's weight vector and will eventually produce the largest output.

Since its inception, the Hebbian rule has evolved in a number of directions. In some cases, the Hebbian rule needs to be modified to counteract unconstrained growth of weight values, which takes place when excitations and responses consistently agree in sign. This corresponds to the Hebbian learning rule with saturation of the weights at a certain, preset level. Throughout this text note that other learning rules often reflect the Hebbian rule principle. Below, most of the learning rules are illustrated with simple numerical examples. Note that the subscript of the weight vector is not used in the examples since there is only a single weight vector being adapted there.

EXAMPLE 2.4

This example illustrates Hebbian learning with binary and continuous activation functions of a very simple network. Assume the network shown in Figure 2.22 with the initial weight vector

$$\mathbf{w}^1 = \begin{bmatrix} 1 \\ -1 \\ 0 \\ 0.5 \end{bmatrix}$$

needs to be trained using the set of three input vectors as below

$$\mathbf{x}_1 = \begin{bmatrix} 1 \\ -2 \\ 1.5 \\ 0 \end{bmatrix}, \quad \mathbf{x}_2 = \begin{bmatrix} 1 \\ -0.5 \\ -2 \\ -1.5 \end{bmatrix}, \quad \mathbf{x}_3 = \begin{bmatrix} 0 \\ 1 \\ -1 \\ 1.5 \end{bmatrix}$$

for an arbitrary choice of learning constant $c = 1$. Since the initial weights are of nonzero value, the network has apparently been trained beforehand. Assume first that bipolar binary neurons are used, and thus $f(net) = \text{sgn}(net)$.

Step 1 Input $\mathbf{x}_1$ applied to the network results in activation net^1 as below:

$$net^1 = \mathbf{w}^{1t}\mathbf{x}_1 = \begin{bmatrix} 1 & -1 & 0 & 0.5 \end{bmatrix} \begin{bmatrix} 1 \\ -2 \\ 1.5 \\ 0 \end{bmatrix} = 3$$

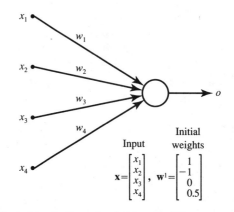

Figure 2.22 Network for training in Examples 2.4 through 2.6.

The updated weights are

$$\mathbf{w}^2 = \mathbf{w}^1 + \operatorname{sgn}(net^1)\mathbf{x}_1 = \mathbf{w}^1 + \mathbf{x}_1$$

and plugging numerical values we obtain

$$\mathbf{w}^2 = \begin{bmatrix} 1 \\ -1 \\ 0 \\ 0.5 \end{bmatrix} + \begin{bmatrix} 1 \\ -2 \\ 1.5 \\ 0 \end{bmatrix} = \begin{bmatrix} 2 \\ -3 \\ 1.5 \\ 0.5 \end{bmatrix}$$

where the superscript on the right side of the expression denotes the number of the current adjustment step.

Step 2 This learning step is with $\mathbf{x}_2$ as input:

$$net^2 = \mathbf{w}^{2t}\mathbf{x}_2 = \begin{bmatrix} 2 & -3 & 1.5 & 0.5 \end{bmatrix} \begin{bmatrix} 1 \\ -0.5 \\ -2 \\ -1.5 \end{bmatrix} = -0.25$$

The updated weights are

$$\mathbf{w}^3 = \mathbf{w}^2 + \operatorname{sgn}(net^2)\mathbf{x}_2 = \mathbf{w}^2 - \mathbf{x}_2 = \begin{bmatrix} 1 \\ -2.5 \\ 3.5 \\ 2 \end{bmatrix}$$

Step 3 For input $\mathbf{x}_3$, we obtain in this step

$$net^3 = \mathbf{w}^{3t}\mathbf{x}_3 = \begin{bmatrix} 1 & -2.5 & 3.5 & 2 \end{bmatrix} \begin{bmatrix} 0 \\ 1 \\ -1 \\ 1.5 \end{bmatrix} = -3$$

The updated weights are

$$\mathbf{w}^4 = \mathbf{w}^3 + \text{sgn}\,(net^3)\mathbf{x}_3 = \mathbf{w}^3 - \mathbf{x}_3 = \begin{bmatrix} 1 \\ -3.5 \\ 4.5 \\ 0.5 \end{bmatrix}$$

It can be seen that learning with discrete $f(net)$ and $c = 1$ results in adding or subtracting the entire input pattern vectors to and from the weight vector, respectively. In the case of a continuous $f(net)$, the weight incrementing/decrementing vector is scaled down to a fractional value of the input pattern.

Revisiting the Hebbian learning example, with continuous bipolar activation function $f(net)$, using input $\mathbf{x}_1$ and initial weights $\mathbf{w}^1$, we obtain neuron output values and the updated weights for $\lambda = 1$ as summarized in Step 1. The only difference compared with the previous case is that instead of $f(net) = \text{sgn}\,(net)$, now the neuron's response is computed from (2.3a).

Step 1

$$f(net^1) = 0.905$$

$$\mathbf{w}^2 = \begin{bmatrix} 1.905 \\ -2.81 \\ 1.357 \\ 0.5 \end{bmatrix}$$

Subsequent training steps result in weight vector adjustment as below:

Step 2

$$f(net^2) = -0.077$$

$$\mathbf{w}^3 = \begin{bmatrix} 1.828 \\ -2.772 \\ 1.512 \\ 0.616 \end{bmatrix}$$

Step 3

$$f(net^3) = -0.932$$

$$\mathbf{w}^4 = \begin{bmatrix} 1.828 \\ -3.70 \\ 2.44 \\ -0.783 \end{bmatrix}$$

Comparison of learning using discrete and continuous activation functions indicates that the weight adjustments are tapered for continuous $f(net)$ but are generally in the same direction. ■

Perceptron Learning Rule

For the perceptron learning rule, the learning signal is the difference between the desired and actual neuron's response (Rosenblatt 1958). Thus, learning is supervised and the learning signal is equal to

$$r \overset{\Delta}{=} d_i - o_i \tag{2.33}$$

where $o_i = \text{sgn}(\mathbf{w}_i^t \mathbf{x})$, and d_i is the desired response as shown in Figure 2.23. Weight adjustments in this method, $\Delta \mathbf{w}_i$ and Δw_{ij}, are obtained as follows

$$\Delta \mathbf{w}_i = c \left[d_i - \text{sgn}(\mathbf{w}_i^t \mathbf{x}) \right] \mathbf{x} \tag{2.34a}$$

$$\Delta w_{ij} = c \left[d_i - \text{sgn}(\mathbf{w}_i^t \mathbf{x}) \right] x_j, \quad \text{for } j = 1, 2, \ldots, n \tag{2.34b}$$

Note that this rule is applicable only for binary neuron response, and the relationships (2.34) express the rule for the bipolar binary case. Under this rule, weights are adjusted if and only if o_i is incorrect. Error as a necessary condition of learning is inherently included in this training rule. Obviously, since the desired response is either 1 or -1, the weight adjustment (2.34a) reduces to

$$\Delta \mathbf{w}_i = \pm 2c\mathbf{x} \tag{2.35}$$

where a plus sign is applicable when $d_i = 1$, and $\text{sgn}(\mathbf{w}^t\mathbf{x}) = -1$, and a minus sign is applicable when $d_i = -1$, and $\text{sgn}(\mathbf{w}^t\mathbf{x}) = 1$. The reader should notice that the weight adjustment formula (2.35) cannot be used when $d_i = \text{sgn}(\mathbf{w}_i^t\mathbf{x})$. The weight adjustment is inherently zero when the desired and actual responses agree. As we will see throughout this text, the perceptron learning rule is of central importance for supervised learning of neural networks. The weights are initialized at any values in this method.

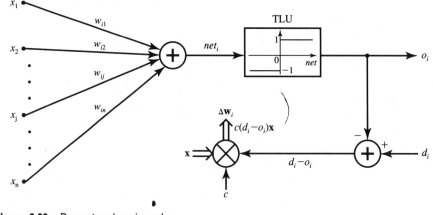

Figure 2.23 Perceptron learning rule.

EXAMPLE 2.5 ▬▬▬▬▬▬▬▬▬▬▬▬▬▬▬▬▬▬

This example illustrates the perceptron learning rule of the network shown in Figure 2.23. The set of input training vectors is as follows:

$$\mathbf{x}_1 = \begin{bmatrix} 1 \\ -2 \\ 0 \\ -1 \end{bmatrix}, \quad \mathbf{x}_2 = \begin{bmatrix} 0 \\ 1.5 \\ -0.5 \\ -1 \end{bmatrix}, \quad \mathbf{x}_3 = \begin{bmatrix} -1 \\ 1 \\ 0.5 \\ -1 \end{bmatrix}$$

and the initial weight vector $\mathbf{w}^1$ is assumed identical as in Example 2.4. The learning constant is assumed to be $c = 0.1$. The teacher's desired responses for $\mathbf{x}_1$, $\mathbf{x}_2$, $\mathbf{x}_3$ are $d_1 = -1$, $d_2 = -1$, and $d_3 = 1$, respectively. The learning according to the perceptron learning rule progresses as follows.

Step 1 Input is $\mathbf{x}_1$, desired output is d_1:

$$net^1 = \mathbf{w}^{1t}\mathbf{x}_1 = \begin{bmatrix} 1 & -1 & 0 & 0.5 \end{bmatrix} \begin{bmatrix} 1 \\ -2 \\ 0 \\ -1 \end{bmatrix} = 2.5$$

Correction in this step is necessary since $d_1 \neq \text{sgn}\,(2.5)$. We thus obtain updated weight vector

$$\mathbf{w}^2 = \mathbf{w}^1 + 0.1(-1 - 1)\mathbf{x}_1$$

Plugging in numerical values we obtain

$$\mathbf{w}^2 = \begin{bmatrix} 1 \\ -1 \\ 0 \\ 0.5 \end{bmatrix} - 0.2 \begin{bmatrix} 1 \\ -2 \\ 0 \\ -1 \end{bmatrix} = \begin{bmatrix} 0.8 \\ -0.6 \\ 0 \\ 0.7 \end{bmatrix}$$

Step 2 Input is $\mathbf{x}_2$, desired output is d_2. For the present weight vector $\mathbf{w}^2$ we compute the activation value net^2 as follows:

$$net^2 = \mathbf{w}^{2t}\mathbf{x}_2 = \begin{bmatrix} 0 & 1.5 & -0.5 & -1 \end{bmatrix} \begin{bmatrix} 0.8 \\ -0.6 \\ 0 \\ 0.7 \end{bmatrix} = -1.6$$

Correction is not performed in this step since $d_2 = \text{sgn}\,(-1.6)$

Step 3 Input is $\mathbf{x}_3$, desired output is d_3, present weight vector is $\mathbf{w}^3$. Computing net^3 we obtain:

$$net^3 = \mathbf{w}^{3t}\mathbf{x}_3 = \begin{bmatrix} -1 & 1 & 0.5 & -1 \end{bmatrix} \begin{bmatrix} 0.8 \\ -0.6 \\ 0 \\ 0.7 \end{bmatrix} = -2.1$$

Correction is necessary in this step since $d_3 \neq$ sgn (-2.1). The updated weight values are

$$\mathbf{w}^4 = \mathbf{w}^3 + 0.1(1 + 1)\mathbf{x}_3$$

or

$$\mathbf{w}^4 = \begin{bmatrix} 0.8 \\ -0.6 \\ 0 \\ 0.7 \end{bmatrix} + 0.2 \begin{bmatrix} -1 \\ 1 \\ 0.5 \\ -1 \end{bmatrix} = \begin{bmatrix} 0.6 \\ -0.4 \\ 0.1 \\ 0.5 \end{bmatrix}$$

This terminates the sequence of learning steps unless the training set is recycled. It is not a coincidence that the fourth component of $\mathbf{x}_1$, $\mathbf{x}_2$, and $\mathbf{x}_3$ in this example is invariable and equal to -1. Perceptron learning requires fixing of one component of the input vector, although not necessarily at the -1 level.

The reader may ask what this training has achieved, if anything. At this point the answer can be very preliminary. The real objectives of training and its significance will require more thorough study later in this text. Our preliminary answer for now is that if the same training set is resubmitted, the respective output error should be, in general, smaller. Since the binary perceptron does not provide fine output error information, we may look at its input. The reader may verify it to see that $net^4 = 0.9$ obtained after three training steps as a response to resubmitted pattern $\mathbf{x}_1$ is closer to $net < 0$ than the initial activation value in the first training step, $net^1 = 2.5$. By observing successive net values for continued training we would see the trend of improving answers. We show in Chapter 3 that, eventually, the network trained in this mode will stop committing any mistakes. ■

Delta Learning Rule

The delta learning rule is only valid for continuous activation functions as defined in (2.3a), (2.4a), and in the supervised training mode. The learning signal for this rule is called *delta* and is defined as follows

$$r \overset{\Delta}{=} [d_i - f(\mathbf{w}_i^t\mathbf{x})]f'(\mathbf{w}_i^t\mathbf{x}) \tag{2.36}$$

The term $f'(\mathbf{w}_i^t\mathbf{x})$ is the derivative of the activation function $f(net)$ computed for $net = \mathbf{w}_i^t\mathbf{x}$. The explanation of the delta learning rule is shown in Figure 2.24. This learning rule can be readily derived from the condition of least squared error between o_i and d_i. Calculating the gradient vector with respect to $\mathbf{w}_i$ of the squared error defined as

$$E \overset{\Delta}{=} \frac{1}{2}(d_i - o_i)^2 \tag{2.37a}$$

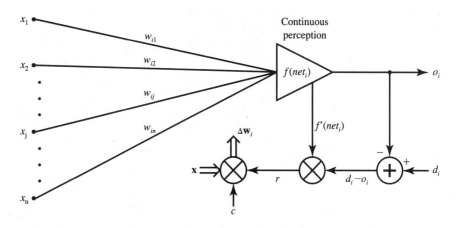

Figure 2.24 Delta learning rule.

which is equivalent to

$$E = \frac{1}{2}\left[d_i - f(\mathbf{w}_i^t\mathbf{x})\right]^2 \tag{2.37b}$$

we obtain the error gradient vector value

$$\nabla E = -(d_i - o_i)f'(\mathbf{w}_i^t\mathbf{x})\mathbf{x} \tag{2.38a}$$

The components of the gradient vector are

$$\frac{\partial E}{\partial w_{ij}} = -(d_i - o_i)f'(\mathbf{w}_i^t\mathbf{x})x_j, \quad \text{for } j = 1, 2, \ldots, n \tag{2.38b}$$

Since the minimization of the error requires the weight changes to be in the negative gradient direction, we take

$$\Delta\mathbf{w}_i = -\eta\nabla E \tag{2.39}$$

where η is a positive constant. We then obtain from Eqs. (2.38a) and (2.39)

$$\Delta\mathbf{w}_i = \eta(d_i - o_i)f'(net_i)\mathbf{x} \tag{2.40a}$$

or, for the single weight the adjustment becomes

$$\Delta w_{ij} = \eta(d_i - o_i)f'(net_i)x_j, \quad \text{for } j = 1, 2, \ldots, n \tag{2.40b}$$

Note that the weight adjustment as in (2.40) is computed based on minimization of the squared error. Considering the use of the general learning rule (2.28) and plugging in the learning signal as defined in (2.36), the weight adjustment becomes

$$\Delta\mathbf{w}_i = c(d_i - o_i)f'(net_i)\mathbf{x} \tag{2.41}$$

Therefore, it can be seen that (2.41) is identical to (2.40), since c and η have been assumed to be arbitrary constants. The weights are initialized at any values for this method of training.

The delta rule was introduced only recently for neural network training (McClelland and Rumelhart 1986). This rule parallels the discrete perceptron training rule. It also can be called the continuous perceptron training rule. The delta learning rule can be generalized for multilayer networks. This will be discussed in more detail in Chapter 3 and extended in Chapter 4.

EXAMPLE 2.6 ■■■■■■■■■■■■■■

This example discusses the delta learning rule as applied to the network shown in Figure 2.24. Training input vectors, desired responses, and initial weights are identical to those in Example 2.5. The delta learning requires that the value $f'(net)$ be computed in each step. For this purpose, we can use the following result derived in Equations (3.48) through (3.51):

$$f'(\text{net}) = \frac{1}{2}(1 - o^2)$$

valid for the bipolar continuous activation function. The result is useful since it expresses the slope of the activation function through the neuron's output signal. Using (2.41) for the arbitrarily chosen learning constant $c = 0.1$, and $\lambda = 1$ for the bipolar continuous acitivation function $f(net)$ as in (2.3a), the delta rule training can be summarized as follows.

Step 1   Input is vector $\mathbf{x}_1$, initial weight vector is $\mathbf{w}^1$:

$$net^1 = \mathbf{w}^{1t}\mathbf{x}_1 = 2.5$$
$$o^1 = f(net^1) = 0.848$$
$$f'(net^1) = \frac{1}{2}[1 - (o^1)^2] = 0.140$$
$$\mathbf{w}^2 = c(d_1 - o^1)f'(net^1)\mathbf{x}_1 + \mathbf{w}^1$$
$$= \begin{bmatrix} 0.974 & -0.948 & 0 & 0.526 \end{bmatrix}^t$$

Step 2   Input is vector $\mathbf{x}_2$, weight vector is $\mathbf{w}^2$:

$$net^2 = \mathbf{w}^{2t}\mathbf{x}_2 = -1.948$$
$$o^2 = f(net^2) = -0.75$$
$$f'(net^2) = \frac{1}{2}[1 - (o^2)^2] = 0.218$$
$$\mathbf{w}^3 = c(d_2 - o^2)f'(net^2)\mathbf{x}_2 + \mathbf{w}^2$$
$$= \begin{bmatrix} 0.974 & -0.956 & 0.002 & 0.531 \end{bmatrix}^t$$

Step 3 Input is x_3, weight vector is $\mathbf{w}^3$:

$$net^3 = \mathbf{w}^{3t}\mathbf{x}_3 = -2.46$$

$$o^3 = f(net^3) = -0.842$$

$$f'(net^3) = \frac{1}{2}[1 - (o^3)^2] = 0.145$$

$$\mathbf{w}^4 = c(d_3 - o^3)f'(net^3)\mathbf{x}_3 + \mathbf{w}^3$$

$$= \begin{bmatrix} 0.947 & -0.929 & 0.016 & 0.505 \end{bmatrix}^t$$

Obviously, since the desired values are ± 1 in this example, the corrections will be performed in each step, since $d_i - f(net_i) \neq 0$ throughout the entire training. This method usually requires small c values, since it is based on moving the weight vector in the weight space in the negative error gradient direction. ■

Widrow-Hoff Learning Rule

The Widrow-Hoff learning rule (Widrow 1962) is applicable for the supervised training of neural networks. It is independent of the activation function of neurons used since it minimizes the squared error between the desired output value d_i and the neuron's activation value $net_i = \mathbf{w}_i^t\mathbf{x}$. The learning signal for this rule is defined as follows

$$r \overset{\Delta}{=} d_i - \mathbf{w}_i^t\mathbf{x} \tag{2.42}$$

The weight vector increment under this learning rule is

$$\Delta\mathbf{w}_i = c(d_i - \mathbf{w}_i^t\mathbf{x})\mathbf{x} \tag{2.43a}$$

or, for the single weight the adjustment is

$$\Delta w_{ij} = c(d_i - \mathbf{w}_i^t\mathbf{x})x_j, \quad \text{for } j = 1, 2, \ldots, n \tag{2.43b}$$

This rule can be considered a special case of the delta learning rule. Indeed, assuming in (2.36) that $f(\mathbf{w}_i^t\mathbf{x}) = \mathbf{w}_i^t\mathbf{x}$, or the activation function is simply the identity function $f(net) = net$, we obtain $f'(net) = 1$, and (2.36) becomes identical to (2.42). This rule is sometimes called the *LMS (least mean square) learning rule*. Weights are initialized at any values in this method.

Correlation Learning Rule

By substituting $r = d_i$ into the general learning rule (2.28) we obtain the correlation learning rule. The adjustments for the weight vector and the single weights, respectively, are

$$\Delta \mathbf{w}_i = c d_i \mathbf{x} \tag{2.44a}$$

$$\Delta w_{ij} = c d_i x_j, \quad \text{for } j = 1, 2, \ldots, n \tag{2.44b}$$

This simple rule states that if d_i is the desired response due to x_j, the corresponding weight increase is proportional to their product. The rule typically applies to recording data in memory networks with binary response neurons. It can be interpreted as a special case of the Hebbian rule with a binary activation function and for $o_i = d_i$. However, Hebbian learning is performed in an unsupervised environment, while correlation learning is supervised. While keeping this basic difference in mind, we can observe that Hebbian rule weight adjustment (2.32a) and correlation rule weight adjustment (2.44a) become identical. Similar to Hebbian learning, this learning rule also requires the weight initialization $\mathbf{w} = \mathbf{0}$.

Winner-Take-All Learning Rule

This learning rule differs substantially from any of the rules discussed so far in this section. It can only be demonstrated and explained for an ensemble of neurons, preferably arranged in a layer of p units. This rule is an example of competitive learning, and it is used for unsupervised network training. Typically, winner-take-all learning is used for learning statistical properties of inputs (Hecht-Nielsen 1987). The learning is based on the premise that one of the neurons in the layer, say the m'th, has the maximum response due to input $\mathbf{x}$, as shown in Figure 2.25. This neuron is declared the *winner*. As a result of this winning event, the weight vector $\mathbf{w}_m$

$$\mathbf{w}_m = \begin{bmatrix} w_{m1} & w_{m2} & \cdots & w_{mn} \end{bmatrix}^t \tag{2.45}$$

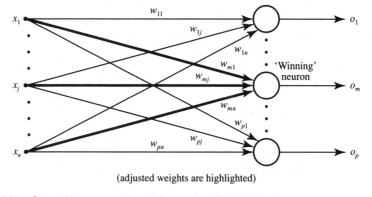

(adjusted weights are highlighted)

Figure 2.25 Competitive unsupervised "winner-take-all" learning rule.

containing weights highlighted in the figure is the only one adjusted in the given unsupervised learning step. Its increment is computed as follows

$$\Delta\mathbf{w}_m = \alpha(\mathbf{x} - \mathbf{w}_m) \tag{2.46a}$$

or, the individual weight adjustment becomes

$$\Delta w_{mj} = \alpha(x_j - w_{mj}), \quad \text{for } j = 1, 2, \ldots, n \tag{2.46b}$$

where $\alpha > 0$ is a small learning constant, typically decreasing as learning progresses. The winner selection is based on the following criterion of maximum activation among all p neurons participating in a competition:

$$\mathbf{w}_m^t\mathbf{x} = \max_{i=1,2,\ldots,p} (\mathbf{w}_i^t\mathbf{x}) \tag{2.47}$$

As shown later in Chapter 7, this criterion corresponds to finding the weight vector that is closest to the input $\mathbf{x}$. The rule (2.46) then reduces to incrementing $\mathbf{w}_m$ by a fraction of $\mathbf{x} - \mathbf{w}_m$. Note that only the winning neuron fan-in weight vector is adjusted. After the adjustment, its fan-in weights tend to better estimate the input pattern in question. In this method, the winning neighborhood is sometimes extended beyond the single neuron winner so that it includes the neighboring neurons. Weights are typically initialized at random values and their lengths are normalized during learning in this method. More detailed justification and application of this rule is provided in Chapter 7.

Outstar Learning Rule

Outstar learning rule is another learning rule that is best explained when neurons are arranged in a layer. This rule is designed to produce a desired response $\mathbf{d}$ of the layer of p neurons shown in Figure 2.26 (Grossberg 1974, 1982). The rule is used to provide learning of repetitive and characteristic properties of input/output relationships. This rule is concerned with supervised learning; however, it is supposed to allow the network to extract statistical properties of the input and output signals. The weight adjustments in this rule are computed as follows

$$\Delta\mathbf{w}_j = \beta(\mathbf{d} - \mathbf{w}_j) \tag{2.48a}$$

or, the individual weight adjustments are

$$\Delta w_{mj} = \beta(d_m - w_{mj}), \quad \text{for } m = 1, 2, \ldots, p \tag{2.48b}$$

Note that in contrast to any learning rule discussed so far, the adjusted weights are fanning out of the j'th node in this learning method and the weight vector in (2.48a) is defined accordingly as

$$\mathbf{w}_j \overset{\Delta}{=} \begin{bmatrix} w_{1j} & w_{2j} & \cdots & w_{pj} \end{bmatrix}^t$$

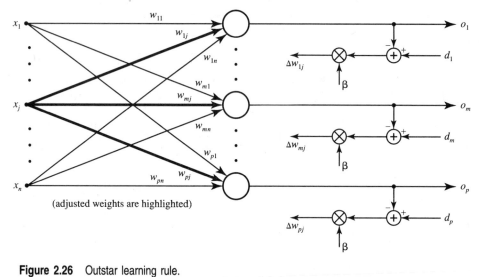

Figure 2.26 Outstar learning rule.

Arbitrarily selectable β is a small positive learning constant decreasing during training. The rule typically ensures that the output pattern becomes similar to the undistorted desired output after repetitively applying (2.48) on distorted output versions. More detailed discussion and application of the outstar learning rule is presented in Chapter 7.

Summary of Learning Rules

Table 2.1 provides the summary of learning rules and of their properties. Seven learning rules are tabulated and compared in terms of the single weight adjustment formulas, supervised versus unsupervised learning mode, weight initialization, and required neuron activation functions. Also, reference is made in the table regarding the conditions of learning. Most learning rules allow for learning of a single, isolated neuron's weight with exception of winner-take-all and outstar rules. Both of these rules require a layer of neurons in order for the weight adaptation to proceed.

So far we have assumed that desired output values are precisely known for each input pattern when a network is trained in the supervised mode. But in some situations fewer details are available. When only partial information is available about the correctness of the network's response, we have so-called reinforcement learning. In the extreme case, only "right" or "wrong" information is available to provide instruction to the network. The amount of feedback received from the environment is very limited in such cases since the teacher's signal is

the learning rules has its meaning and its own mathemat.
applicability. Indeed, neural networks can be trained using th.
useful tasks such as classification, recognition, or association.
the training is as usual for any training: Results are for the most p.
but failures are also sometimes possible; however, they are the exce.
than the rule. The exposition in later chapters provides more detailed a.
questions about why neural networks are capable of learning. We will als.
how the network learning assists in solving problems that otherwise would.
been difficult to solve.

OVERVIEW OF
NEURAL NETWORKS

The review of introductory concepts of artificial neural systems in this
chapter considers the main aspects of neural processing. Performance of neural
networks during recall and their basic learning techniques are studied. We also
address some elementary information processing tasks that neural networks can
solve. The review would not be complete, however, without an overview and
taxonomy of artificial neural systems architectures.

More than a dozen specific architectures are covered in this text. Let us
attempt to group them into classes. There seem to be numerous ways of classifying artificial neural systems for the purposes of study, analysis, understanding,
and utilization. One such way of characterizing neural networks makes use of
the fact that the recall of information can be effected in two ways.

The recall can be performed in the feedforward mode, or from input toward
output, only. Such networks are called feedforward and have no memory. Recall
in such networks is instantaneous, thus the past time conditions are irrelevant
for their computation. Feedforward network's behavior does not depend on what
happened in the past but rather what happens now. Specifically, the network
responds only to its present input.

The second group of networks performs recall computation with feedback
operational. These networks can be considered as dynamical systems, and a certain time interval is needed for their recall to be completed. Feedback networks
are also called recurrent. They interact with their input through the output. As we
have seen, recurrent networks can operate either in a discrete- or continuous-time
mode.

Another meaningful basis for classification is to differentiate neural r
works by their learning mode. As discussed in Sections 2.4 and 2.5, sup.
and unsupervised learning are the main forms of learning. In additior
a large group of networks that does not undergo supervised or .
training, because the complete design information is available
artificial neural memories fall into this category. They are des.
or encoding desired equilibria. We say that such networks a.

TABLE 2.1

Summary of learning rules and their properties.

Learning rule	Single weight adjustment Δw_{ij}	Initial weights	Learning	Neu character.	
Hebbian	$co_i x_j$ $j = 1, 2, \ldots, n$	0	U	Any	
Perceptron	$c\left[d_i - \mathrm{sgn}\,(\mathbf{w}_i^t \mathbf{x})\right] x_j$ $j = 1, 2, \ldots, n$	Any	S	Binary bipolar, or Binary unipolar[*]	
Delta	$c(d_i - o_i) f'(net_i) x_j$ $j = 1, 2, \ldots, n$	Any	S	Continuous	N
Widrow-Hoff	$c(d_i - \mathbf{w}_i^t \mathbf{x}) x_j$ $j = 1, 2, \ldots, n$	Any	S	Any	Neuro
Correlation	$cd_i x_j$ $j = 1, 2, \ldots, n$	0	S	Any	Neuron
Winner-take-all	$\Delta w_{mj} = \alpha(x_j - w_{mj})$ m-winning neuron number $j = 1, 2, \ldots, n$	Random Normalized	U	Continuous	Layer of p neurons
Outstar	$\beta(d_i - w_{ij})$ $i = 1, 2, \ldots, p$	0	S	Continuous	Layer of p neurons

c, α, β are positive learning constants
S — supervised learning, U — unsupervised learning
[*] — Δw_{ij} not shown

rather evaluative than instructive. The reinforcement learning is sometimes called "learning with a critic" as opposed to learning with a teacher (Hertz, Krogh, and Palmer 1991).

The coverage of the seven most important learning rules in this section is by no means exhaustive. Only those rules that are used later in the text have been covered. However, a serious reader may at this point raise a question about validity, convergence, or practical importance of the rules. Fortunately, each of mode. The continuous or discrete data that need to be associated, or hetero-associated, are used for batch mode learning. The weights of such networks remain fixed following the recording. The reader should be aware that because there are few standards for neural network terminology, some authors consider memories trained by recording, or in batch mode, as networks trained with supervision.

Table 2.2 summarizes the taxonomy of the most important artificial neural system architectures. Thirteen different architectures are listed in the first column

TABLE 2.2

Classification of the most important artificial neural networks according to their learning and recall modes.

Network Architecture	Learning Mode S, U, R	Recall Mode FF, REC	Recall Time Domain CT, DT
Single-layer Network of Discrete and Continuous Perceptrons (Figure 1.1)	S	FF	—
Multilayer Network of Discrete and Continuous Perceptrons (EEG spike detectors, ALVINN, Figures 1.3 and 2.9)	S	FF	—
Gradient-type Network (Figures 1.8 and 2.15)	R	REC	CT
Linear Associative Memory	R	FF	—
Autoassociative Memory [Figures 1.5, 1.7, 2.12, and 2.16(a)]	R	REC	DT or CT
Bidirectional Associative Memory [Figure 2.16(b)] (also Multidirectional Associative Memory)	R	REC	DT or CT
Temporal Associative Memory	R	REC	DT or CT
Hamming Network	R	FF	—
MAXNET	R (fixed)	REC	DT or CT
Clustering Network (Figure 2.25)	U	FF	—
Counterpropagation Network (Figure 2.25 and 2.26)	U + S	FF	—
Self-Organizing Neural Array (Figure 1.11)	U	FF	—
Adaptive Resonance Theory 1 Network	U	REC	DT or CT

Learning Mode
S—Supervised
U—Unsupervised
R—Recording (Batch)

Recall Mode
FF—Feedforward
REC—Recurrent

Recall Time Domain (only for recurrent networks)
CT—Continuous-time
DT—Discrete-time

of the table. Only basic network configurations covered in this text are included, therefore the table is by no means exhaustive. To link the discussed architectures with the examples of networks introduced in Chapters 1 and 2, a number of references are provided in the first column.

As stressed before, the learning and recall modes are the most important characteristics of the networks we study. Supervised / unsupervised / recording (batch) learning modes are specified in the table for each network of interest. Feedforward, or recurrent recall mode, is also highlighted. Note that feedforward networks provide instantaneous recall. Additionally, continuous- and discrete-time networks have been marked within the group of recurrent networks.

No judgment or opinion about comparative worth of networks is made here or at any other place in this book. Instead, the focus is on the mathematical and algorithmic principles of each network.

Neural networks can also be characterized in terms of their input and output values as discrete (binary) or continuous. As mentioned earlier in this chapter, diverse neuron models are used in various networks, sometimes even a combination of them. These aspects of artificial neural networks will be highlighted in the sections where they are discussed.

2.7   CONCLUDING REMARKS

At this point it may be desirable to reiterate and expand the introductory remarks made so far concerning the differences between the conventional and neural network computation. Table 2.3 provides a summary overview of the basic aspects of computation for each of the approaches. Inspection of the entries of the table indicates that neural networks represent collective, non-algorithmic, low-precision, nonlinear computing machines that learn during training from examples and are data-controlled. As such they are very different from programmable conventional computers. The reader is encouraged to look at the details provided in Table 2.3.

To gain better understanding of the presented concepts, let us look for analogies between the theory of learning neurons and the theory of learning of organisms. According to psychologists, there are two basic forms of learning. *Operant conditioning* is a form of learning that reinforces only the responses of an organism. The reinforcement is aimed at making the desired responses more likely and ignoring or punishing those that are not desirable. In contrast to this form of learning, *classical conditioning* is based on training for a stimulus-response sequence.

Perceptron or delta training rules are aimed at influencing responses so that they become more desirable when the same input is applied repetitively. These

TABLE 2.3

Comparison of conventional and neural
network computation.

Task or performance aspect	Conventional computation	Neural network computation
Problem solving	Algorithm formulation	Selection of architecture and definition of the set of representative examples
Input data	Numerical form	Numerical, but also perceptual representation allowed
Knowledge acquisition	Programming	Training
Knowledge retrieval	Sequential computation	Recall in the form of collective processing
Computation	High-precision arithmetic	Low-precision, nonlinear mapping
Internal data	Internal representation in control of the ·algorithm	Internal representation in control of input data
Fixed- or intermediate-data storage	ROM, RAM-high-precision binary memories	Interconnecting weights of typically continuous values

rules will thus correspond to operant conditioning. The Hebbian learning rule couples the input and output and involves the relationship between the present stimulus-response pair, or input-output correlation. Thus, this learning rule corresponds to the classical conditioning organism learning.

This chapter treats introductory concepts and definitions used in artificial neural systems. It contains a discussion of relationships between real neural systems and their artificial counterparts. The chapter provides an overview of the fundamental terminology. It also introduces a historical model of the artificial neuron developed by McCulloch and Pitts. Subsequently, a number of other artificial neuron models are discussed.

The basic taxonomy of neural networks as feedforward and recurrent recall systems is provided along with recall analysis examples. The most important features of the learning modes are formulated and discussed in this chapter. The phenomenon of network learning is explained based on the unifying general learning rule and on the so-called learning signal concept. This approach clarifies how neural networks learn. Learning rules for adapting neuron's weights as introduced in this chapter provide the reference framework needed for further study. In subsequent chapters our focus is on what the learning can accomplish, how it happens, and how to use it in the most efficient way.

PROBLEMS

Please note that problems highlighted with an asterisk (*) are typically computationally intensive and the use of programs is advisable to solve them.

P2.1 The logic networks shown in Figure P2.1 use the McCulloch-Pitts model neuron from Figure 2.3. Find the truth tables and the logic functions that are implemented by networks (a), (b), (c), and (d).

P2.2 Use McCulloch-Pitts neurons to design logic networks that implement the following functions. Use a single neuron in (a), and two neurons in cascade for (b) and (c). (A prime denotes a logic complement.)

$$(a)\ \ o^{k+1} = x_1^k x_2^k x_3'^k$$

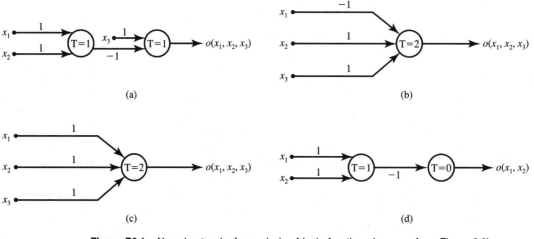

Figure P2.1 Neural networks for analysis of logic functions (neurons from Figure 2.3).

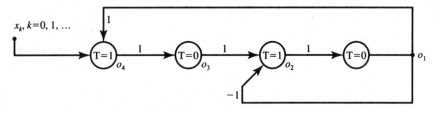

Figure P2.3 Randomizing shift register using neurons from Figure 2.3.

(b) $o^{k+2} = x_1'^k x_2^k x_3'^k$

(c) $o^{k+2} = x_1^k x_2^k$

P2.3 The sequential circuit shown in Figure P2.3 contains a shift register, which processes the incoming impulse sequence and memorizes it using the register cell property of the McCulloch-Pitts neurons. Assume that input data are $x^0 = 1$, $x^1 = 1$, $x^2 = 0$, $x^3 = 1$, $x^4 = x^5 = x^6 = \ldots = 0$. Compute the contents of the register $(o_1^8, o_2^8, o_3^8, o_4^8)$ after eight processing steps have elapsed. Assume all cells have initially cleared outputs at $k = 0$.

P2.4 The feedforward network shown in Figure P2.4 using bipolar binary neurons is mapping the entire plane x_1, x_2 into a binary o value. Find the segment of the x_1, x_2 plane for which $o_4 = 1$, and its complement for which $o_4 = -1$.

P2.5 Each of the two networks shown in Figure P2.5 implements an identical function on unipolar binary vectors in two-dimensional input space. Analyze the networks to show that they are equivalent. Assume

$$f(net) = \begin{cases} 0 & net \le 0 \\ 1 & net > 0 \end{cases}$$

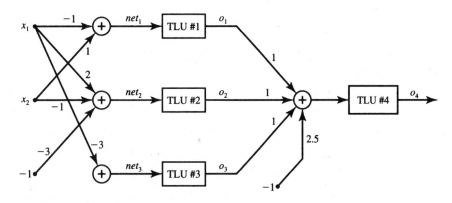

Figure P2.4 Feedforward network for Problem P2.4.

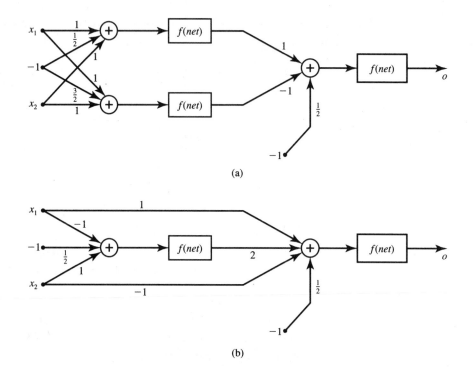

(a)

(b)

Figure P2.5 Feedforward network for analysis in Problem P2.5.

P2.6   The network shown in Figure P2.6 is an analog-to-digital converter and can be used for coding a continuous value x into a 4-bit unipolar binary code (o_3 o_2 o_1 o_0). Analyze the network and find each range of x that is converted in each of the binary codes (0 0 0 0), ..., (1 1 1 1). Assume $-1 \le x \le 16$ and unipolar binary neurons used as in Problem P2.5.

P2.7   The feedforward network shown in Figure P2.7 has been designed to code the grey intensity of a pixel expressed on a continuous scale, $0 \le x \le 1$ (Ramacher 1989). The output binary code is (q_3 q_2 q_1). Analyze the network and find each range of x that is converted into the binary codes (0 0 0), ..., (1 1 1). Assume unipolar binary neurons as in Problem P2.5.

P2.8   The network shown in Figure P2.8 uses neurons with a continuous activation function as in (2.3a) with $\lambda = 1$. The neuron's output has been measured as $o_1 = 0.28$ and $o_2 = -0.73$. Find the input vector $\mathbf{x} = \begin{bmatrix} x_1 & x_2 \end{bmatrix}^t$ that has been applied to the network. Also find the slope values of the activation function at the activations net_1 and net_2.

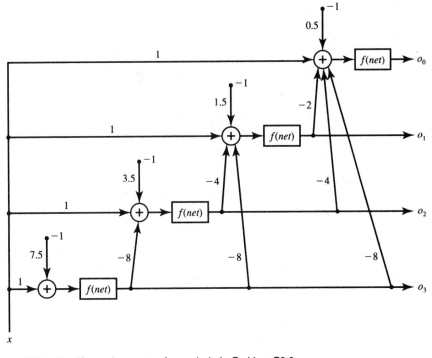

Figure P2.6 Feedforward converter for analysis in Problem P2.6.

P2.9 The network shown in Figure P2.9 using neurons with $f(net)$ as in (2.3a) has been designed to assign input vectors x_1, x_2, x_3 to cluster 1 or 2. The cluster number is identical to the number of the neuron yielding the larger response. Determine the most likely cluster membership for each of the following three vectors. Assume $\lambda = 2$. The input vectors are

$$x_1 = \begin{bmatrix} 0.866 \\ 0.5 \end{bmatrix}, \quad x_2 = \begin{bmatrix} -0.985 \\ -0.174 \end{bmatrix}, \quad x_3 = \begin{bmatrix} 0.342 \\ -0.94 \end{bmatrix}$$

P2.10 The two networks shown in Figure P2.10 implement partitioning of the plane x_1, x_2 and yield $o_1 = \pm 1$ (network *a*, bipolar binary output neuron), and $|o_1| < 1$ (network *b*, bipolar continuous output neuron). The neurons used in both networks are with bipolar characteristics as in (2.3). Assume for network *b* that $\lambda = 1$. For both networks:

(a) Find o_1 as a function of x_1 with $x_2 = +2$.

(b) Draw the line on x_1, x_2 plane separating positive and negative responses for $|x_1| < 5$ and $|x_2| < 5$.

P2.11 The network shown in Figure P2.11 uses neurons with continuous bipolar characteristics with $\lambda = 1$. It implements partitioning of plane x_1, x_2 and

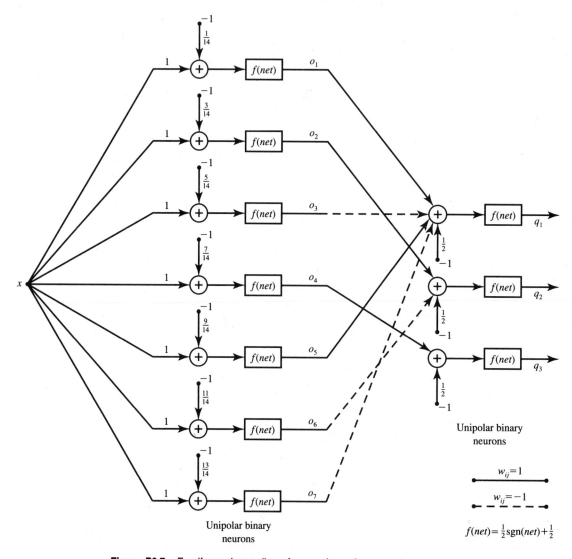

Figure P2.7 Feedforward encoding of an analog value.

maps it into $|o_1| < 1$. Analyze the network and obtain regions on the plane x_1, x_2 with positive and negative responses o_1 for $|x_1| < 5$, $|x_2| < 5$, and $T_1 = T_2 = 0$. Then simulate the network and tabulate the function $o_1(x_1, x_2)$ in the domain of interest.

P2.12 The network shown in Figure P2.12 uses neurons with continuous bipolar characteristics with $\lambda = 5$. It implements mapping of plane x_1, x_2 into

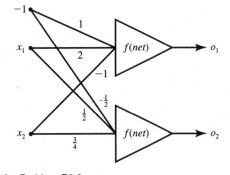

Figure P2.8 Network for Problem P2.8.

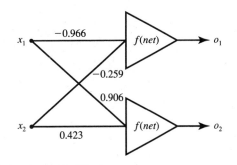

Figure P2.9 Network for cluster identification.

$|o_1| < 1$. Simulate the network and tabulate the function $o_1(x_1, x_2)$ for $|x_1| < 2.5$ and $|x_2| < 2.5$.

P2.13 Assume that the vertices of a three-dimensional bipolar binary cube are used to represent eight states of a recurrent neural network with three bipolar binary neurons. The equilibrium states are $\mathbf{o}_1 = \begin{bmatrix} -1 & -1 & -1 \end{bmatrix}^t$ and $\mathbf{o}_2 = \begin{bmatrix} 1 & 1 & 1 \end{bmatrix}^t$. Sketch the desirable state transitions between the vertices.

P2.14 A discrete-time four-neuron recurrent network as in Figure 2.10 in the text with bipolar binary neurons has the weight matrix

$$\mathbf{W} = \begin{bmatrix} 0 & -1 & -1 & 1 \\ -1 & 0 & 1 & -1 \\ -1 & 1 & 0 & -1 \\ 1 & -1 & -1 & 0 \end{bmatrix}$$

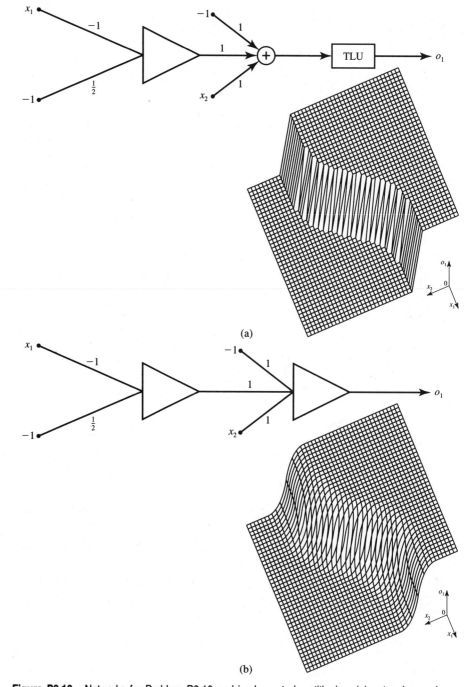

(a)

(b)

Figure P2.10　Networks for Problem P2.10 and implemented partitioning: (a) network *a* and (b) network *b*.

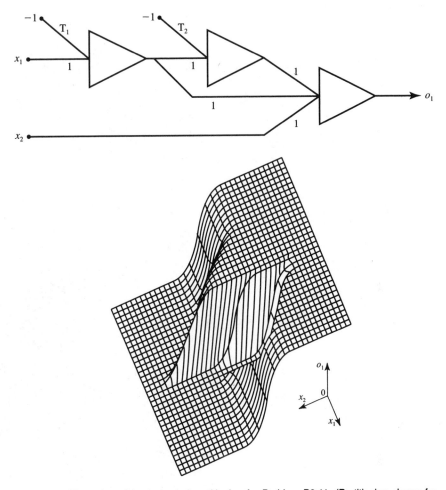

Figure P2.11 Network and implemented partitioning for Problem P2.11. (Partitioning shown for $T_1 \neq 0$ and $T_2 \neq 0$.)

Find the sequence of state transitions after the network has been initialized at $\mathbf{x}^0 = \begin{bmatrix} -1 & -1 & -1 & 1 \end{bmatrix}^t$. Repeat for three other initializing vectors

$$\mathbf{x}^0 = \begin{bmatrix} 1 \\ 1 \\ -1 \\ 1 \end{bmatrix}, \quad \mathbf{x}^0 = \begin{bmatrix} 1 \\ -1 \\ 1 \\ 1 \end{bmatrix}, \quad \mathbf{x}^0 = \begin{bmatrix} 1 \\ -1 \\ -1 \\ -1 \end{bmatrix}$$

P2.15 For the continuous-time network using the bipolar neurons shown in Figure P2.15:

(a) Obtain discretized differential equations.

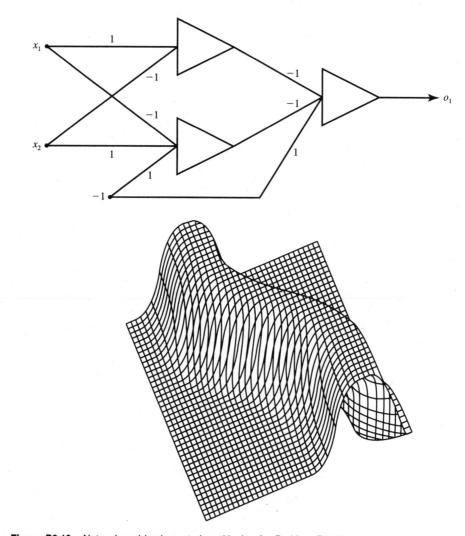

Figure P2.12 Network and implemented partitioning for Problem P2.12.

(b) Perform sample simulations showing that $\mathbf{o}_1 = \begin{bmatrix} 1^- & 1^- & 1^- \end{bmatrix}^t$ and $\mathbf{o}_2 = \begin{bmatrix} -1^+ & -1^+ & -1^+ \end{bmatrix}^t$ are equilibrium points stored in the network shown in the figure.

P2.16 Four steps of Hebbian learning of a single-neuron network as in Figure 2.21 have been implemented starting with $\mathbf{w}^1 = \begin{bmatrix} 1 & -1 \end{bmatrix}^t$ for learning constant $c = 1$ using inputs as follows:

$$\mathbf{x}_1 = \begin{bmatrix} 1 \\ -2 \end{bmatrix}, \quad \mathbf{x}_2 = \begin{bmatrix} 0 \\ 1 \end{bmatrix}, \quad \mathbf{x}_3 = \begin{bmatrix} 2 \\ 3 \end{bmatrix}, \quad \mathbf{x}_4 = \begin{bmatrix} 1 \\ -1 \end{bmatrix}$$

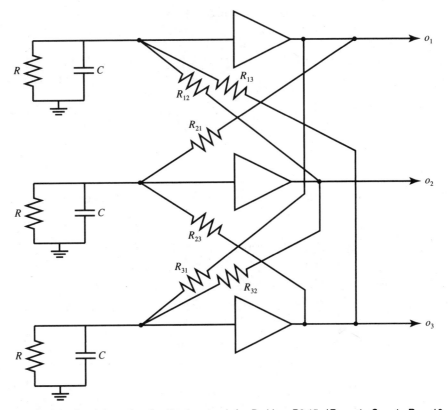

Figure P2.15 Continuous-time feedback network for Problem P2.15. ($R_{ij} = 1$, $C = 1$, $R = 10$, and $\lambda = 2.5$.)

Find final weights for:

(a) bipolar binary $f(net)$

(b) bipolar continuous $f(net)$, $\lambda = 1$.

P2.17 Implement the perceptron rule training of the network from Figure 2.23 using $f(net) = \text{sgn}(net)$, $c = 1$, and the following data specifying the initial weights $\mathbf{w}^1$, and the two training pairs

$$\mathbf{w}^1 = \begin{bmatrix} 0 \\ 1 \\ 0 \end{bmatrix}, \left(\mathbf{x}_1 = \begin{bmatrix} 2 \\ 1 \\ -1 \end{bmatrix}, d_1 = -1 \right), \left(\mathbf{x}_2 = \begin{bmatrix} 0 \\ -1 \\ -1 \end{bmatrix}, d_2 = 1 \right)$$

Repeat the training sequence $(\mathbf{x}_1, d_1)$, $(\mathbf{x}_2, d_2)$ until two correct responses in a row are achieved. List the net^k values obtained during training.

P2.18 A single-neuron network using $f(net) = \text{sgn}(net)$ as in Figure 2.23 has been trained using the pairs of x_i, d_i as shown below:

$$\left(x_1 = \begin{bmatrix} 1 \\ -2 \\ 3 \\ -1 \end{bmatrix}, \quad d_1 = -1 \right), \quad \left(x_2 = \begin{bmatrix} 0 \\ -1 \\ 2 \\ -1 \end{bmatrix}, \quad d_2 = 1 \right),$$

$$\left(x_3 = \begin{bmatrix} -2 \\ 0 \\ -3 \\ -1 \end{bmatrix}, \quad d_3 = -1 \right)$$

The final weights obtained using the perceptron rule are

$$w^4 = \begin{bmatrix} 3 & 2 & 6 & 1 \end{bmatrix}^t$$

Knowing that correction has been performed in each step for $c = 1$, determine the following weights:

(a) w^3, w^2, w^1 by back-tracking the training

(b) w^5, w^6, w^7 obtained for steps 4, 5, and 6 of training by reusing the sequence (x_1, d_1), (x_2, d_2), (x_3, d_3).

P2.19 Perform two training steps of the network as in Figure 2.24 using the delta learning rule for $\lambda = 1$ and $c = 0.25$. Train the network using the following data pairs

$$\left(x_1 = \begin{bmatrix} 2 \\ 0 \\ -1 \end{bmatrix}, \quad d_1 = -1 \right), \quad \left(x_2 = \begin{bmatrix} 1 \\ -2 \\ -1 \end{bmatrix}, \quad d_2 = 1 \right)$$

The initial weights are $w^1 = \begin{bmatrix} 1 & 0 & 1 \end{bmatrix}^t$. [*Hint:* Use $f'(net) = (1/2)(1 - o^2)$ and $f(net)$ as in (2.3a).]

P2.20 A recurrent network with three bipolar binary neurons has been trained using the correlation learning rule with a single bipolar binary input vector in a single training step only. The training was implemented starting at $w^0 = 0$, for $c = 1$. The resulting weight matrix is

$$W = \begin{bmatrix} 1 & -1 & -1 \\ -1 & 1 & 1 \\ -1 & 1 & 1 \end{bmatrix}$$

Find the vectors x and d that have been used for training. (There are two different answers.)

P2.21 Perform two training steps for the network as in Figure 2.24 using the Widrow-Hoff learning rule. Assume the same training data as in Problem P2.19.

P2.22* Write the program for analysis of two-layer feedforward networks. The user-specified parameters should include type of the activation function (2.3a-b), (2.4a-b), λ (if needed), the size of the network, and test input vectors. Verify your program using data from Problems P2.7 and P2.12, and from Example 2.1. Note that each neuron needs to have one fixed input (bias) with an associated weight.

P2.23* Implement the learning algorithms by writing a program that can be used to train weights of a single neuron with up to six inputs. The program should allow the user to specify the learning rule, the type of activation function, λ (if needed), training data, and to perform the specified number of training steps. Rules to include are Hebbian, perceptron, delta, and Widrow-Hoff. Verify your program using data from Problems P2.16, P2.17, P2.19, and P2.21.

REFERENCES

Amari, S. I. 1990. "Mathematical Foundations of Neurocomputing," *IEEE Proc.* 78(9): 1443–1463.

Arbib, M. A. 1987. *Brains, Machines and Mathematics,* 2nd ed. New York: Springer Verlag.

Bernasconi, J. 1988. "Analysis and Comparison of Different Learning Algorithms for Pattern Association Problems," in *Neural Information Processing Systems,* ed. D. Anderson. New York: American Institute of Physics.

Carpenter, G. A. 1989. "Neural Network Models for Pattern Recognition and Associative Memory," *Neural Networks* 2: 243–257.

Dayhoff, J. 1990. *Neural Network Architectures—An Introduction.* New York: Van Nostrand Reinhold.

Durbin, R. 1989. "On the Correspondence Between Network Models and the Nervous System," in *The Computing Neuron,* ed. R. Durbin, C. Miall, G. Mitchison, Reading, Mass.: Addison-Wesley Publishing Co.

Feldman, J. A., M. A. Fanty, and N. Goddard. 1988. "Computing with Structured Neural Networks," *IEEE Computer* (March): 91–103.

Grossberg, S. 1977. *Classical and Instrumental Learning by Neural Networks* in *Progress in Theoretical Biology,* vol. 3. New York: Academic Press, 51–141.

Grossberg, S. 1982. *Studies of Mind and Brain: Neural Principles of Learning Perception, Development, Cognition, and Motor Control.* Boston: Reidell Press.

Hebb, D. O. 1949. *The Organization of Behavior, a Neuropsychological Theory.* New York: John Wiley.

Hecht-Nielsen, R. 1987. "Counterpropagation Networks," *Appl. Opt.* 26(23): 4979–4984.

Hecht-Nielsen, R. 1990. *Neurocomputing.* Reading, Mass.: Addison-Wesley Publishing Co.

Hertz, J., A. Krogh, and R. G. Palmer. 1991. *Introduction to the Theory of Neural Computation.* Redwood City, Calif.: Addison-Wesley Publishing Co.

Hopfield, J. J., and D. W. Tank. 1986. "Computing with Neural Circuits: A Model," *Science* 233: 625–633.

Lerner, A. Ya. 1972. *Fundamentals of Cybernetics.* London: Chapman and Hall Ltd.

Lippmann, R. P. 1987. "An Introduction to Computing with Neural Nets," *IEEE Magazine on Acoustics, Signal and Speech Processing* (April): 4–22.

McClelland, T. L., D. E. Rumelhart, and the PDP Research Group. 1986. *Parallel Distributed Processing.* Cambridge: The MIT Press.

McCulloch, W. S., and W. H. Pitts. 1943. "A Logical Calculus of the Ideas Imminent in Nervous Activity," *Bull Math. Biophy.* 5: 115–133.

Mitchison, G. 1989. "Learning Algorithms and Networks of Neurons," in *The Computing Neuron,* ed. R. Durbin, C. Miall, G. Mitchison. Reading, Mass.: Addison-Wesley Publishing Co.

Poggio, T., and F. Girosi. 1990. "Networks for Approximation and Learning," *Proc. IEEE* 78(9): 1481–1497.

Ramacher, U., Wesseling, M. 1989. "A Geometrical Approach to Neural Network Design," *Proc. of the Joint Neural Networks Conf.,* Washington, D.C., pp. II, 147–152.

Reilly, D. L., and L. N. Cooper. 1990. "An Overview of Neural Networks: Early Models to Real World Systems," in *Introduction of Neural and Electronic Networks.* New York: Academic Press.

Rosenblatt, F. 1958. "The Perceptron: A Probabilistic Model for Information Storage and Organization in the Brain," *Psych. Rev.* 65: 386–408.

Rumelhart, D. E. 1990. "Brain Style Computation: Learning and Generalization," in *Introduction to Neural and Electronic Networks.* New York: Academic Press.

Szu, H. 1990. "Reconfigurable Neural Nets by Energy Convergence Learning Priniciples Based on Extended McCulloch-Pitts Neurons and Synapses," *Proc. IEEE Int. Neural Networks Conf.* pp. I-485–I-496.

Tsypkin, Ya. Z. 1973. *Foundations of the Theory of Learning Systems.* New York: Academic Press.

Wasserman, P. D. 1989. *Neural Computing Theory and Practice.* New York: Van Nostrand Reinhold.

Widrow, B. 1962. "Generalization and Information Storage in Networks of Adaline 'Neurons'," in *Self-Organizing Systems 1962,* ed. M. C. Jovitz, G. T. Jacobi, G. Goldstein. Washington, D.C.: Spartan Books, 435–461.

3

SINGLE-LAYER PERCEPTRON CLASSIFIERS

*A cat that once sat on a hot
stove will never again sit on a
hot stove or on a cold one either.*

M. TWAIN

In this chapter, the foundations of trainable decision-making networks will be formulated. The principal function of a decision-making system is to yield decisions concerning the class membership of the input pattern with which it is confronted. Conceptually, the problem can be described as a transformation of sets, or functions, from the input space to the output space, which is called the classification space. In general, the transformations of input data into class membership are highly complex and noninvertible.

We will develop the expertise gradually. The linear discriminant functions will be introduced first, and the simple correction rule to perform network training will be devised. The training, or network adaptation, will be presented as a sequence of iterative weight adjustments. Strong emphasis will be put on the geometrical interpretation of the training procedure. This will provide the reader with necessary insight and, hopefully, with a better understanding of mathematical methods for neural network-based classifiers.

Starting with the definitions of basic concepts of classification and with examples of two-class classifiers using the hard-limiting thresholding device, the training rules will then be extended to the case of continuous error function minimization. This extension will require the replacement of the summing and hard-limiting thresholding device, or a discrete perceptron, with a continuous perceptron. The chapter will conclude with preliminary discussion of multi-neuron multicategory single-layer networks and their training. The architectures discussed in this chapter are limited to single-layer feedforward networks. The chapter also provides an explanation and justification of perceptron and delta training rules introduced formally but without proof in the previous chapter.

The approach presented in this chapter is introductory and applicable mainly to the classification of linearly separable classes of patterns; thus it may be viewed as having somewhat limited practical importance. However, the same approach can easily be generalized and applied later for different network architectures. As the reader will see, such extension will prove to be much more powerful and useful. The discussion of these more versatile and complex architectures and relevant training approaches will be presented in subsequent chapters.

3.1

CLASSIFICATION MODEL, FEATURES, AND DECISION REGIONS

Our discussion of neural network classifiers and classification issues has so far been rather informal. A simplistic two-class classifier (Figure 1.1) was presented in Section 1.1. Also, classification was introduced in Section 2.3 as a form of neural computation and, specifically, as a form of information recall. This notion was illustrated in Figure 2.17(a). We now approach the classification issues in more detail.

One of the most useful tasks that can be performed by networks of interconnected nonlinear elements introduced in the previous chapter is pattern classification. A *pattern* is the quantitative description of an object, event, or phenomenon. The classification may involve spatial and temporal patterns. Examples of spatial patterns are pictures, video images of ships, weather maps, fingerprints, and characters. Examples of temporal patterns include speech signals, signals vs. time produced by sensors, electrocardiograms, and seismograms. Temporal patterns usually involve ordered sequences of data appearing in time.

The goal of pattern classification is to assign a physical object, event, or phenomenon to one of the prespecified *classes* (also called *categories.)* Despite the lack of any formal theory of pattern perception and classification, human beings and animals have performed these tasks since the beginning of their existence. Let us look at some of the classification examples.

The oldest classification tasks required from a human being have been classification of the human environment into such groups of objects as living species, plants, weather conditions, minerals, tools, human faces, voices, or silhouettes, etc. The interpretation of data has been learned gradually as a result of repetitive inspecting and classifying of examples. When a person perceives a pattern, an inductive inference is made and the perception is associated with some general concepts or clues derived from the person's past experience. The problem of pattern classification may be regarded as one of discriminating the input data within object population via the search for invariant attributes among members of the population.

While some of the tasks mentioned above can be learned easily, the growing complexity of the human environment and technological progress has created classification problems that are diversified and also difficult. As a result, the use of various classifying aids became helpful and in some applications, even indispensable. Reading and processing bank checks exemplifies a classification problem that can be automated. It obviously can be performed by a human worker, however, machine classification can achieve much greater efficiency.

Extensive study of the classification process has led to the development of an abstract mathematical model that provides the theoretical basis for classifier design. Eventually, machine classification came to maturity to help people in their classification tasks. The electrocardiogram waveform, biomedical photograph, or disease diagnosis problem can nowadays be handled by machine classifiers. Other applications include fingerprint identification, patent searches, radar and signal detection, printed and written character classification, and speech recognition.

Figure 3.1(a) shows the block diagram of the recognition and classification system. As mentioned in Section 2.3, recognition is understood here as a class assignment for input patterns that are not identical to the patterns used for training of the classifier. Since the training concept has not been fully explained yet, we will focus first on techniques for classifying patterns.

The classifying system consists of an input transducer providing the input pattern data to the feature extractor. Typically, inputs to the feature extractor are sets of data vectors that belong to a certain category. Assume that each such set member consists of real numbers corresponding to measurement results for a given physical situation. Usually, the converted data at the output of the transducer can be compressed while still maintaining the same level of machine performance. The compressed data are called *features*. The feature extractor at the input of the classifier in Figure 3.1(a) performs the reduction of dimensionality. The feature space dimensionality is postulated to be much smaller than the dimensionality of the pattern space. The feature vectors retain the minimum number of data dimensions while maintaining the probability of correct classification, thus making handling data easier.

An example of possible feature extraction is available in the analysis of speech vowel sounds. A 16-channel filterbank can provide a set of 16-component spectral vectors. The vowel spectral content can be transformed into perceptual quality space consisting of two dimensions only. They are related to tongue height

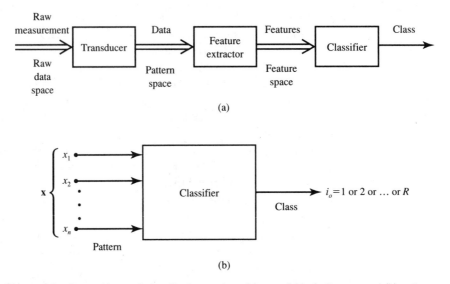

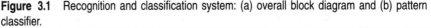

Figure 3.1 Recognition and classification system: (a) overall block diagram and (b) pattern classifier.

and retraction. Another example of dimensionality reduction is the projection of planar data on a single line, reducing the feature vector size to a single dimension. Although the projection of data will often produce a useless mixture, by moving and/or rotating the line it might be possible to find its orientation for which the projected data are well separated. In such a case, two-dimensional data are represented by single-dimensional features denoting the position of the projected points on the line.

It is beyond the scope of this chapter to discuss the selection of measurements or data feature extraction from the input pattern vector. We shall henceforth assume that the sets of extracted feature vectors yield the sets of pattern vectors to be classified and that the extraction, or selection, of input components to the classifier has been done as wisely as possible. Thus, the pattern vector **x** shown in Figure 3.1(b) consists of components that may be features. Chapter 7 covers neural network architectures suitable for separate feature extractions.

However, the n-tuple vectors at the input to the classifier on Figure 3.1(b) may also be input pattern data when separate feature extraction does not take place. In such a case the classifier's function is to perform not only the classification itself but also to internally extract input pattern features. The rationale for this approach in our study is that neural networks can be successfully used for joint classification/recognition tasks and for feature extraction. For such networks, the feature extractor and classifier from Figure 3.1(a) can be considered merged to the single classifier network of Figure 3.1(b). Networks that operate on input data and perform no separate feature extraction when classifying patterns are discussed in Section 8.2.

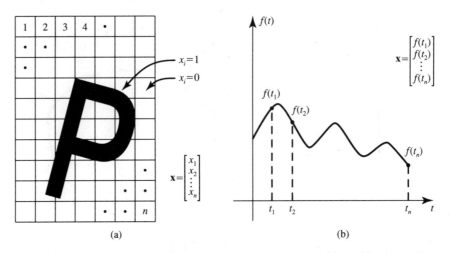

Figure 3.2 Two simple ways of coding patterns into pattern vectors: (a) spatial object and (b) temporal object (waveform).

In further discussion we will represent the classifier input components as a vector $\mathbf{x}$. The classification at the system's output is obtained by the classifier implementing the decision function $i_o(\mathbf{x})$. The discrete values of the response i_o are 1 or 2 or ... or R. The responses represent the categories into which the patterns should be placed. The classification (decision) function of Equation (3.1) is provided by the transformation, or mapping, of the n-component vector $\mathbf{x}$ into one of the category numbers i_o as shown in Figure 3.1(b):

$$i_o = i_o(\mathbf{x}) \tag{3.1}$$

where

$$\mathbf{x} = \begin{bmatrix} x_1 \\ x_2 \\ \vdots \\ x_n \end{bmatrix}$$

Figure 3.2 depicts two simple ways to generate the pattern vector for cases of spatial and temporal objects to be classified. In the case shown in Figure 3.2(a), each component x_i of the vector $\mathbf{x} = \begin{bmatrix} x_1 & x_2 & \cdots & x_n \end{bmatrix}^t$ is assigned the value 1 if the i'th cell contains a portion of a spatial object; otherwise, the value 0 (or -1) is assigned. In the case of a temporal object being a continuous function of time t, the pattern vector may be formed at discrete time instants t_i by letting $x_i = f(t_i)$, for $i = 1, 2, \ldots, n$. This is shown in Figure 3.2(b).

Classification can often be conveniently described in geometric terms. Any pattern can be represented by a point in n-dimensional Euclidean space E^n called the *pattern space*. Points in that space corresponding to members of the pattern

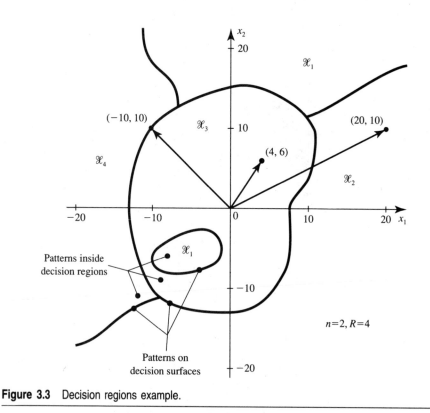

Figure 3.3 Decision regions example.

---

set are n-tuple vectors $\mathbf{x}$. A pattern classifier maps sets of points in E^n space into one of the numbers $i_o = 1, 2, \ldots, R$, as described by the decision function (3.1). The sets containing patterns of classes $1, 2, \ldots, R$ are denoted here by $\mathscr{X}_1, \mathscr{X}_2, \ldots, \mathscr{X}_R$, respectively.

An example case for $n = 2$ and $R = 4$ is illustrated in Figure 3.3 showing disjoint regions $\mathscr{X}_1, \ldots, \mathscr{X}_4$. Let us postulate for simplicity that the classifier's response as in (3.1) should be the class number. We now have the decision function for a pattern of class j yielding the following result:

$$i_o(\mathbf{x}) = j \quad \text{for all } \mathbf{x} \in \mathscr{X}_j, \quad j = 1, 2, 3, 4$$

Thus, the example vector $\mathbf{x} = \begin{bmatrix} 20 & 10 \end{bmatrix}^t$ belongs to $\mathscr{X}_2$ and is of class 2, vector $\mathbf{x} = \begin{bmatrix} 4 & 6 \end{bmatrix}^t$ belongs to $\mathscr{X}_3$ and is of class 3, etc.

The regions denoted $\mathscr{X}_i$ are called *decision regions*. Regions $\mathscr{X}_i$ are separated from each other by so-called *decision surfaces*. We shall assume that patterns located on decision surfaces do not belong to any category. In Figure 3.3 an example of such a pattern located on the boundary is $\mathbf{x} = \begin{bmatrix} -10 & 10 \end{bmatrix}^t$. Note that the decision surfaces in two-dimensional pattern space E^2 are curved lines. For a more general case of space E^n they may be $(n-1)$-dimensional hypersurfaces.

3.2

DISCRIMINANT FUNCTIONS

In this chapter, the assumption is made that both a set of n-dimensional patterns x_1, x_2, ..., x_P and the desired classification for each pattern are known. The size P of the pattern set is finite, and it is usually much larger than the dimensionality n of the pattern space. In many practical cases we will also assume that P is much larger than the number of categories R. Although the assumptions regarding n, P, and R are often valid for practical classification cases, they do not necessarily hold for our study of classification principles, nor do they limit the validity of our final conclusions.

We will first discuss classifiers that use the discriminant functions concept. This discussion will lead to interesting conclusions as to how neural network classifiers should be trained. The study will also explicitly produce some of the training rules introduced in Chapter 2.

Let us assume momentarily, and for the purpose of this presentation, that the classifier has already been designed so that it can correctly perform the classification tasks. During the classification step, the membership in a category needs to be determined by the classifier based on the comparison of R *discriminant functions* $g_1(x)$, $g_2(x)$, ..., $g_R(x)$, computed for the input pattern under consideration. It is convenient to assume that the discriminant functions $g_i(x)$ are scalar values and that the pattern x belongs to the i'th category if and only if

$$g_i(x) > g_j(x), \quad \text{for } i,j = 1, 2, \ldots, R, \, i \neq j \tag{3.2}$$

Thus, within the region $\mathscr{X}_i$, the i'th discriminant function will have the largest value. This maximum property of the discriminant function $g_i(x)$ for the pattern of class i is fundamental, and it will be subsequently used to choose, or assume, specific forms of the $g_i(x)$ functions.

The discriminant functions $g_i(x)$ and $g_j(x)$ for contiguous decision regions $\mathscr{X}_i$ and $\mathscr{X}_j$ define the decision surface between patterns of classes i and j in E^n space. Since the decision surface itself obviously contains patterns x without membership in any category, it is characterized by $g_i(x)$ equal to $g_j(x)$. Thus, the decision surface equation is

$$g_i(x) - g_j(x) = 0 \tag{3.3}$$

Figure 3.4(a) displays six example patterns belonging to one of the two classes, with the simplest example of a decision surface in pattern space x_1, x_2 being here a straight line. The case illustrated here is for $n = R = 2$ and exemplifies the concept of the linear discriminant function. Inspection of the figure indicates that there is an infinite number of discriminant functions yielding correct classification. Let us look at the particulars of the depicted classification task in the following example. This example will also allow the reader to gain better insight into the more formal discussion of classification issues that follows.

EXAMPLE 3.1 ■■■■■■■■■■■■■■■■■

Six patterns in two-dimensional pattern space shown in Figure 3.4(a) need to be classified according to their membership in sets as follows

$$\left\{ [0 \quad 0]', [-0.5 \quad -1]', [-1 \quad -2]' \right\} : \text{ class } 1$$

$$\left\{ [2 \quad 0]', [1.5 \quad -1]', [1 \quad -2]' \right\} : \text{ class } 2$$

Inspection of the patterns indicates that the equation for the decision surface can be arbitrarily chosen as shown in the figure

$$g(\mathbf{x}) = -2x_1 + x_2 + 2 \tag{3.4}$$

Let us note that in the case discussed here we first arbitrarily select the Eq. (3.4) of the decision surface rather than determine the two discriminant functions $g_i(\mathbf{x})$, for $i = 1, 2$. Equation (3.4) represents the straight line dividing the pattern space that is plane x_1, x_2 into the contiguous decision regions $\mathscr{X}_1$, $\mathscr{X}_2$. It is obvious that $g(\mathbf{x}) > 0$ and $g(\mathbf{x}) < 0$ in each of the half-planes containing patterns of class 1 and 2, respectively, and $g(\mathbf{x}) = 0$ for all points on the line. Therefore, the evaluation of the sign of $g(\mathbf{x}) = g_1(\mathbf{x}) - g_2(\mathbf{x})$ can in this case replace the evaluation of the general maximum condition as in (3.2). Specifically, the functions $g_1(\mathbf{x})$ and $g_2(\mathbf{x})$ have not even been searched for in this case. Let us note that following explicitly the maximum condition expressed by (3.2) we would have to find and compare two specific discriminant functions.

The following discussion analyzes classification using original condition (3.2) with two suitably chosen discriminant functions: $g_1(\mathbf{x})$ and $g_2(\mathbf{x})$. Note that according to Equation (3.3), the projection of the intersection of two discriminant functions on the plane x_1, x_2 is the decision surface given by (3.4). The example discriminant functions have been arbitrarily chosen as planes of $g_1(\mathbf{x})$ and $g_2(\mathbf{x})$ shown in Figure 3.4(b). The reader can see that they fulfill the correct classification requirements. Their contour maps are illustrated in Figure 3.4(c). The plane equations are:

$$2x_1 - x_2 + 2g_1(\mathbf{x}) - 4 = 0$$
$$-2x_1 + x_2 + 2g_2(\mathbf{x}) = 0 \tag{3.5a}$$

Note how appropriate plane equations have been produced. We first observe that the decision line given by the equation $-2x_1 + x_2 + 2 = 0$ has two normal vectors. They are planar vectors $[2 \quad -1]'$ and $[-2 \quad 1]'$. The discriminant function $g_1(\mathbf{x})$ can be built by appropriately selecting its 3-tuple unit normal vector $\mathbf{r}_1$. This can be done by augmenting the vector $[2 \quad -1]'$ by a third component of positive value, say equal to 2. The details of the procedure of building this vector are shown in Figure 3.4(d). The resulting normal vector

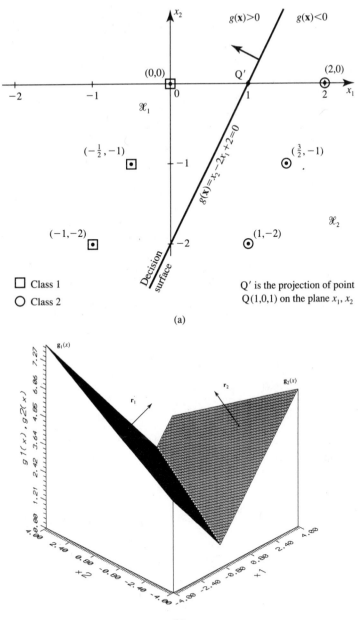

Figure 3.4a,b   Illustration for Example 3.1: (a) pattern display and decision surface, (b) discriminant functions.

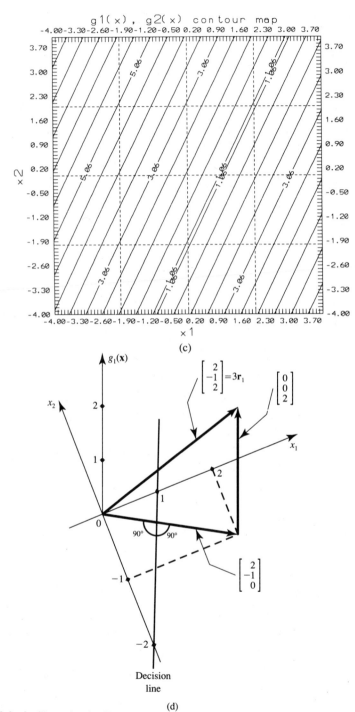

(c)

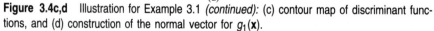

(d)

Figure 3.4c,d   Illustration for Example 3.1 *(continued):* (c) contour map of discriminant functions, and (d) construction of the normal vector for $g_1(\mathbf{x})$.

is $\begin{bmatrix} 2 & -1 & 2 \end{bmatrix}^t$; it thus needs normalization. Similar augmentation can also be carried out for the other planar normal vector $\begin{bmatrix} -2 & 1 \end{bmatrix}^t$ to yield $\mathbf{r}_2$.

The unit normal vectors $\mathbf{r}_1$ and $\mathbf{r}_2$, which provide appropriate plane orientations as shown in Figure 3.4(b) and correct discrimination by the classifier are thus equal (after normalization)

$$\mathbf{r}_1 = \begin{bmatrix} \dfrac{2}{3} \\ -\dfrac{1}{3} \\ \dfrac{2}{3} \end{bmatrix}, \quad \mathbf{r}_2 = \begin{bmatrix} -\dfrac{2}{3} \\ \dfrac{1}{3} \\ \dfrac{2}{3} \end{bmatrix} \tag{3.5b}$$

Let us arbitrarily assume that the discriminant function planes, $g_1(\mathbf{x})$, intersects the point $x_1 = 1$, $x_2 = 0$, $g_1 = 1$. The discriminant function plane $g_2(\mathbf{x})$ has to intersect therefore the same point $x_1 = 1$, $x_2 = 0$, $g_2 = 1$. For each of the planes we have produced their normal vector and the coordinates of the intersecting point represented by a vector $\mathbf{Q} = \begin{bmatrix} 1 & 0 & 1 \end{bmatrix}^t$. Using the normal vector-point equation from the Appendix we obtain for the first and second discriminant functions, respectively

$$\mathbf{r}_1^t \left(\begin{bmatrix} x_1 \\ x_2 \\ g_1 \end{bmatrix} - \begin{bmatrix} 1 \\ 0 \\ 1 \end{bmatrix} \right) = 0$$

$$\mathbf{r}_2^t \left(\begin{bmatrix} x_1 \\ x_2 \\ g_2 \end{bmatrix} - \begin{bmatrix} 1 \\ 0 \\ 1 \end{bmatrix} \right) = 0 \tag{3.5c}$$

The reader can notice that equations (3.5c) are identical with the equations (3.5a).

From (3.5a) we see that the explicit equations yielding the discriminant functions are:

$$g_1(\mathbf{x}) = \begin{bmatrix} -1 & \dfrac{1}{2} \end{bmatrix} \begin{bmatrix} x_1 \\ x_2 \end{bmatrix} + 2 \; ,$$

$$g_2(\mathbf{x}) = \begin{bmatrix} 1 & -\dfrac{1}{2} \end{bmatrix} \begin{bmatrix} x_1 \\ x_2 \end{bmatrix} \tag{3.6}$$

The reader can easily verify that equating $g_1(\mathbf{x})$ to $g_2(\mathbf{x})$ given by Equation (3.6) leads to the decision surface equation (3.4). Let us point out that the decision surface does not uniquely specify the discriminant functions. Vectors $\mathbf{r}_1$ and $\mathbf{r}_2$ as chosen in (3.5b) are also not unique and there are an infinite number of vectors that could be used here. Also, the same arbitrary constant can be added to both $g_1(\mathbf{x})$ and $g_2(\mathbf{x})$ without changing the projection of the $g_1(\mathbf{x})$, $g_2(\mathbf{x})$ intersection on the plane x_1, x_2.

To conclude the example, let us compare the computed values of discriminant functions $g_i(\mathbf{x})$ for selected patterns. The comparison should yield the complete class membership information. Indeed, pattern $[2 \quad 0]^t$ belongs to $\mathcal{X}_2$ since $g_2(2 \quad 0) = 2 > g_1(2 \quad 0) = 0$, pattern $[0 \quad 0]^t$ belongs to $\mathcal{X}_1$ since $g_1(0 \quad 0) = 2 > g_2(0 \quad 0) = 0$, etc. In this example, the decision surface has been determined by inspection of patterns, and the example discriminant functions have been produced and discussed based on inspection of the geometrical conditions in the pattern space.   ■

Assuming that the discriminant functions are known, the block diagram of a basic pattern classifier can now be adopted as in Figure 3.5(a). For a given pattern, the i'th discriminator computes the value of the function $g_i(\mathbf{x})$ called briefly the *discriminant*. The maximum selector implements condition (3.2) and selects the largest of all inputs, thus yielding the response equal to the category number i_o.

The discussion above and the associated example of classification has highlighted a special case of the classifier into R classes for $R = 2$. Such a classifier is called the *dichotomizer*. Although the ancient Greek civilization is rather famous for other interests than decision-making machines, the word *dichotomizer* is of Greek origin. The two separate greek language roots are *dicha* and *tomia* and they mean *in two* and *cut*, respectively. It has been noted that the general classification condition (3.2) for the case of a dichotomizer can now be reduced to the inspection of the sign of the following discriminant function

$$g(\mathbf{x}) \overset{\Delta}{=} g_1(\mathbf{x}) - g_2(\mathbf{x}) \tag{3.7a}$$

Thus, the general classification rule (3.2) can be rewritten for a dichotomizer as follows

$$\begin{aligned} g(\mathbf{x}) > 0 &: \text{ class 1} \\ g(\mathbf{x}) < 0 &: \text{ class 2} \end{aligned} \tag{3.7b}$$

The evaluation of conditions in (3.7b) is easier to implement in practice than the selection of maximum. Subtraction and sign examination has replaced the maximum value evaluation. A single threshold logic unit (TLU) can be used to build such a simple dichotomizer as shown in Figure 3.5(b). As discussed in the previous chapter, the TLU can be considered as a binary (discrete) version of a neuron. The TLU with weights has been introduced in Chapter 2 as the discrete binary perceptron. The responses 1, -1, of the TLU should be interpreted as indicative of categories 1 and 2, respectively. The TLU element simply implements the sign function defined as

$$i_o = \text{sgn}\left[g(\mathbf{x})\right] = \begin{cases} -1 & \text{for } g(\mathbf{x}) < 0 \\ \text{undefined} & \text{for } g(\mathbf{x}) = 0 \\ 1 & \text{for } g(\mathbf{x}) > 0 \end{cases} \tag{3.8}$$

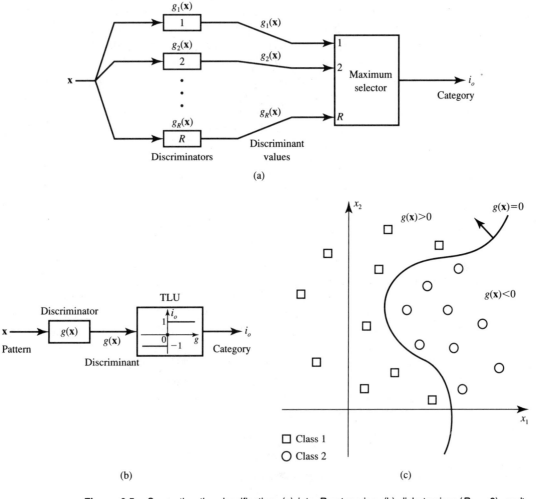

(a)

(b)

(c)

Figure 3.5 Computing the classification: (a) into R categories, (b) dichotomizer ($R = 2$), and (c) decision surface for $n = 2$ and $R = 2$.

Another example of a decision surface for $d = R = 2$ is shown in Figure 3.5(c). Although we can see that the TLU element would probably provide decision about the class membership of the depicted set of patterns, the design of the discriminator for this dichotomizer does not seem as straightforward as in Example 3.1. Let us only notice that the discriminant functions may result as nonlinear functions of x_1, x_2, and let us postpone more detailed discussion of such a case until later in this chapter.

Once a general functional form of the discriminant functions has been suitably chosen, discriminants can be computed using *a priori* information about the classification of patterns, provided that such information is available. In such an approach, the design of a classifier can be based entirely on the computation of decision boundaries as derived from patterns and their membership in classes. Throughout this chapter and most portions of this book, however, we will focus mainly on classifiers whose decision capabilities are generated from training patterns by means of an iterative learning, or training, algorithm. Once a type of discriminant function has been assumed, the algorithm of learning should result in a solution for the initially unknown coefficients of discriminant functions, provided the training pattern sets are separable by the assumed type of decision function. For study of such adaptive, or trainable, classifiers, the following assumptions are made:

1. The training pattern set and classification of all its members are known, thus the training is supervised.

2. The discriminant functions have a linear form and only their coefficients are adjusted in the training procedure.

Under these assumptions, a trainable classifier can be implemented that learns by examples. In this context, we will be interested in input data vectors for which we have *a priori* knowledge of their correct classification. These vectors will be referred to as class prototypes or exemplars. The classification problem will then be one of finding decision surfaces, in n-dimensional space, that will enable correct classification of the prototypes and will afford some degree of confidence in correctly recognizing and classifying unknown patterns that have not been used for training. The only limitation regarding the unknown patterns to be recognized is that they are drawn from the same underlying distributions that have been used for classifier's training.

3.3

LINEAR MACHINE AND MINIMUM DISTANCE CLASSIFICATION

The efficient classifier having the block diagram as shown in Figure 3.5(a) must be described, in general, by discriminant functions that are not linear functions of the inputs $x_1, x_2, \ldots, x_n$. An example of such classification is provided in Figure 3.5(c). As will be shown later, the use of nonlinear discriminant functions can be avoided by changing the classifier's feedforward architecture to the multilayer form. Such an architecture is comprised of more layers of elementary classifiers such as the discussed dichotomizer or the "dichotomizer" providing continuous response between -1 and $+1$. The elementary decision-making discrete, or continuous dichotomizers, will then again be described with the argument $g(\mathbf{x})$ being the basic linear discriminant function.

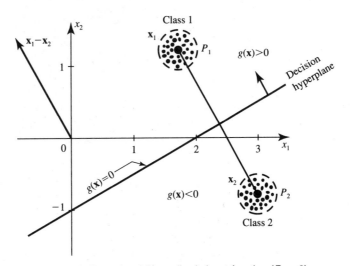

Figure 3.6   Illustration to n-dimensional linear discriminant function ($R = 2$).

Since the linear discriminant function is of special importance, it will be discussed below in detail. It will be assumed throughout that E^n is the n-dimensional Euclidean pattern space. Also, without any loss of generality, we will initially assume that $R = 2$. In the linear classification case, the decision surface is a hyperplane and its equation can be derived based on discussion and generalization of Figure 3.6.

Figure 3.6 depicts two clusters of patterns, each cluster belonging to one known category. The center points of the clusters shown of classes 1 and 2 are vectors x_1 and x_2, respectively. The center, or prototype, points can be interpreted here as centers of gravity for each cluster. We prefer that the decision hyperplane contain the midpoint of the line segment connecting prototype points P_1 and P_2, and it should be normal to the vector $x_1 - x_2$, which is directed toward P_1. The decision hyperplane equation can thus be written in the following form (see Appendix):

$$(x_1 - x_2)^t x + \frac{1}{2} \left(\|x_2\|^2 - \|x_1\|^2 \right) = 0 \tag{3.9}$$

The left side of Equation (3.9) is obviously the dichotomizer's discriminant function $g(x)$. It can also be seen that $g(x)$ implied here constitutes a hyperplane described by the equation

$$w_1 x_1 + w_2 x_2 + \cdots + w_n x_n + w_{n+1} = 0, \text{ or} \tag{3.10a}$$

$$w^t x + w_{n+1} = 0 \tag{3.10b}$$

or, briefly,

$$\begin{bmatrix} w \\ w_{n+1} \end{bmatrix}^t \begin{bmatrix} x \\ 1 \end{bmatrix} = 0 \tag{3.10c}$$

where **w** denotes the weight vector defined as follows:

$$\mathbf{w} \triangleq \begin{bmatrix} w_1 \\ w_2 \\ \vdots \\ w_n \end{bmatrix}$$

The weighting coefficients w_1, w_2, ..., w_{n+1} of the dichotomizer can now be obtained easily from comparing (3.9) and (3.10) as follows:

$$\mathbf{w} = \mathbf{x}_1 - \mathbf{x}_2$$
$$w_{n+1} = \frac{1}{2}\left(\|\mathbf{x}_2\|^2 - \|\mathbf{x}_1\|^2\right) \tag{3.11}$$

It can be seen from Equation (3.11) that the discriminant function becomes explicitly known if prototype points P_1 and P_2 are known. We can also note that unless the cluster center coordinates $\mathbf{x}_1$, $\mathbf{x}_2$ are known, $g(\mathbf{x})$ cannot be determined *a priori* using the method just presented.

The linear form of discriminant functions can also be used for classifications between more than two categories. In the case of R pairwise separable classes, there will be up to $R(R-1)/2$ decision hyperplanes like the one computed in (3.11) for $R = 2$. For $R = 3$, there are up to three decision hyperplanes. For a larger number of classes, some decision regions $\mathcal{X}_i$, $\mathcal{X}_j$ may not be contiguous, thus eliminating some decision hyperplanes. In such cases, the equation $g_i(\mathbf{x}) = g_j(\mathbf{x})$ has no solution. Still, the dichotomizer example just discussed can be considered as a simple case of a multiclass minimum-distance classifier. Such classifiers will be discussed in more detail later in this chapter.

Let us assume that a minimum-distance classification is required to classify patterns into one of the R categories. Each of the R classes is represented by prototype points P_1, P_2, ..., P_R being vectors $\mathbf{x}_1$, $\mathbf{x}_2$, ..., $\mathbf{x}_R$, respectively. The Euclidean distance between input pattern $\mathbf{x}$ and the prototype pattern vector $\mathbf{x}_i$ is expressed by the norm of the vector $\mathbf{x} - \mathbf{x}_i$ as follows:

$$\|\mathbf{x} - \mathbf{x}_i\| = \sqrt{(\mathbf{x} - \mathbf{x}_i)^t(\mathbf{x} - \mathbf{x}_i)} \tag{3.12}$$

A minimum-distance classifier computes the distance from pattern $\mathbf{x}$ of unknown classification to each prototype. Then, the category number of that closest, or smallest distance, prototype is assigned to the unknown pattern. Calculating the squared distances from Equation (3.12) yields

$$\|\mathbf{x} - \mathbf{x}_i\|^2 = \mathbf{x}^t\mathbf{x} - 2\mathbf{x}_i^t\mathbf{x} + \mathbf{x}_i^t\mathbf{x}_i, \quad \text{for } i = 1, 2, \ldots, R \tag{3.13}$$

Obviously, the term $\mathbf{x}^t\mathbf{x}$ is independent of i and shows up in each of the R distances under evaluation in Equation (3.13). Thus, it will suffice to compute only R terms, $2\mathbf{x}_i^t\mathbf{x} - \mathbf{x}_i^t\mathbf{x}_i$, for $i = 1, \ldots, R$, in (3.13), and to determine for which $\mathbf{x}_i$ this term takes the largest of all R values. It can also be seen that choosing the largest of the terms $\mathbf{x}_i^t\mathbf{x} - 0.5\mathbf{x}_i^t\mathbf{x}_i$ is equivalent to choosing the smallest of the distances $\|\mathbf{x} - \mathbf{x}_i\|$. This property can now be used to equate the highlighted term with a discriminant function $g_i(\mathbf{x})$:

$$g_i(\mathbf{x}) = \mathbf{x}_i^t\mathbf{x} - \frac{1}{2}\mathbf{x}_i^t\mathbf{x}_i, \quad \text{for } i = 1, 2, \ldots, R \tag{3.14}$$

It now becomes clear that the discriminant function (3.14) is of the general linear form, which can be expressed as:

$$g_i(\mathbf{x}) = \mathbf{w}_i^t\mathbf{x} + w_{i,n+1}, \quad \text{for } i = 1, 2, \ldots, R \tag{3.15}$$

The discriminant function coefficients that are weights $\mathbf{w}_i$ can be determined by comparing (3.14) and (3.15) as follows:

$$\mathbf{w}_i = \mathbf{x}_i$$
$$w_{i,n+1} = -\frac{1}{2}\mathbf{x}_i^t\mathbf{x}_i, \quad \text{for } i = 1, 2, \ldots, R \tag{3.16}$$

At this point, note that minimum-distance classifiers can be considered as linear classifiers, sometimes called *linear machines*. Since minimum-distance classifiers assign category membership based on the closest match between each prototype and the current input pattern, the approach is also called *correlation classification*. The block diagram of a linear machine employing linear discriminant functions as in Equation (3.15) is shown in Figure 3.7. It can be viewed as a special case of the more general classifier depicted in Figure 3.5. The machine consists of R scalar product computing nodes and of a single maximum selector. During classification, after simultaneously computing all of the R discriminants $g_i(\mathbf{x})$ for a submitted pattern, the output stage of the classifier selects the maximum discriminant and responds with the number of the discriminant having the largest value.

Let us finally notice that the decision surface S_{ij} for the contiguous decision regions $\mathscr{X}_i$, $\mathscr{X}_j$ is a hyperplane given by the equation

$$g_i(\mathbf{x}) - g_j(\mathbf{x}) = 0, \quad \text{or} \tag{3.17a}$$
$$\mathbf{w}_i^t\mathbf{x} + w_{i,n+1} - \mathbf{w}_j^t\mathbf{x} - w_{j,n+1} = 0 \tag{3.17b}$$

It is a widely accepted convention to append formally a 1 as the $n + 1$'th component of each pattern vector. The augmented pattern vector is now denoted by $\mathbf{y}$, it consists of $n + 1$ rows, and is defined as follows:

$$\mathbf{y} \triangleq \begin{bmatrix} \mathbf{x} \\ 1 \end{bmatrix} \tag{3.18}$$

Using the notation of the augmented pattern vector allows for rewriting expression (3.15) for the linear discriminant function to the more compact form of

$$g_i(\mathbf{y}) = \mathbf{w}_i^t\mathbf{y} \tag{3.19}$$

Note, however, that whenever the augmented pattern vector is used, the associated weight vector $\mathbf{w}$ contains $n + 1$ components. The augmenting weight component is $w_{i,n+1}$, for $i = 1, 2, \ldots, R$. For the sake of notational simplicity, the notation

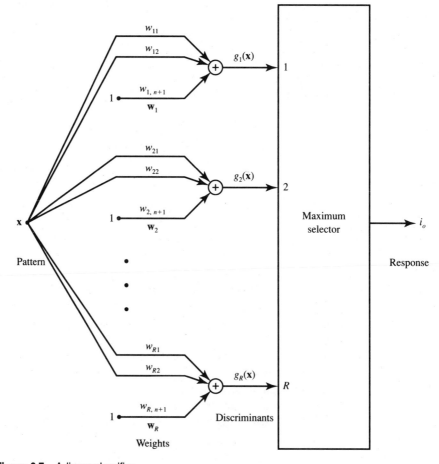

Figure 3.7   A linear classifier.

for both weight vectors and augmented weight vectors are the same throughout the text. Whether or not a pattern or weight vector has been augmented can usually be determined from the context.

EXAMPLE 3.2

In this example a linear (minimum-distance) classifier is designed. Decision lines are generated using *a priori* knowledge about the center of gravity of the prototype points. The assumed prototype points are as shown in Figure 3.8(a) and their coordinates are

$$\mathbf{x}_1 = \begin{bmatrix} 10 \\ 2 \end{bmatrix}, \ \mathbf{x}_2 = \begin{bmatrix} 2 \\ -5 \end{bmatrix}, \ \mathbf{x}_3 = \begin{bmatrix} -5 \\ 5 \end{bmatrix}$$

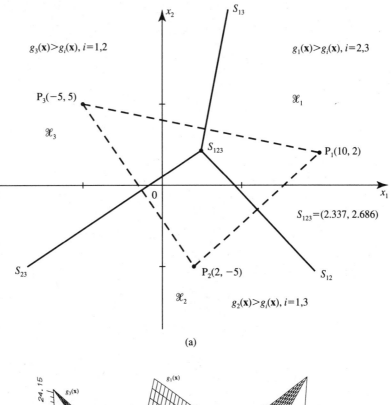

(a)

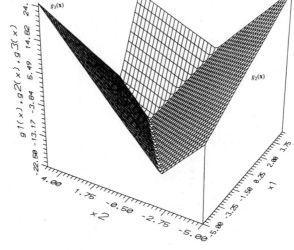

(b)

Figure 3.8a,b Illustration to linear classifier with $n = 2$ and $R = 3$ in Example 3.2: (a) geometrical interpretation, (b) discriminant functions.

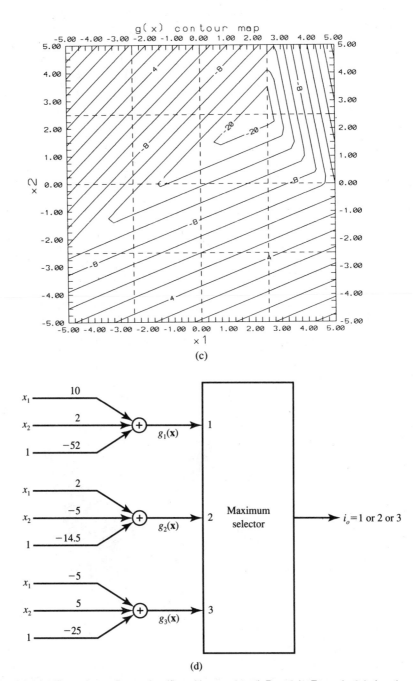

(c)

(d)

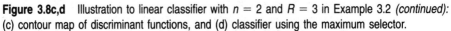

Figure 3.8c,d   Illustration to linear classifier with $n = 2$ and $R = 3$ in Example 3.2 *(continued):* (c) contour map of discriminant functions, and (d) classifier using the maximum selector.

It is also assumed that each prototype point index corresponds to its class number. Using formula (3.16) for $R = 3$, the weight vectors can be obtained as

$$\mathbf{w}_1 = \begin{bmatrix} 10 \\ 2 \\ -52 \end{bmatrix}, \; \mathbf{w}_2 = \begin{bmatrix} 2 \\ -5 \\ -14.5 \end{bmatrix}, \; \mathbf{w}_3 = \begin{bmatrix} -5 \\ 5 \\ -25 \end{bmatrix} \qquad (3.20a)$$

Note that the weight vectors in (3.20a) are augmented. The corresponding linear discriminant functions are

$$\begin{aligned} g_1(\mathbf{x}) &= 10x_1 + 2x_2 - 52 \\ g_2(\mathbf{x}) &= 2x_1 - 5x_2 - 14.5 \\ g_3(\mathbf{x}) &= -5x_1 + 5x_2 - 25 \end{aligned} \qquad (3.20b)$$

The three discriminant functions are shown in Figure 3.8(b), and their contour map in the pattern space x_1, x_2 is illustrated in Figure 3.8(c). Based on the computed discriminant functions, a minimum-distance classifier using the maximum selector can be completed for $R = 3$. The resulting classifier is shown in Figure 3.8(d). Inspecting Figure 3.8(a) reveals that there are three decision lines S_{12}, S_{13}, and S_{23} separating the contiguous decision regions $\mathcal{X}_1, \mathcal{X}_2$; $\mathcal{X}_1, \mathcal{X}_3$; and $\mathcal{X}_2, \mathcal{X}_3$, respectively. These lines are given by the projections on the pattern plane x_1, x_2 of the intersections of the discriminant functions of Figures 3.8(b) and (c). The decision lines can be calculated by using the condition (3.17) and the discriminant functions (3.20b) as

$$\begin{aligned} S_{12}: & \; 8x_1 + 7x_2 - 37.5 = 0 \\ S_{13}: & \; -15x_1 + 3x_2 + 27 = 0 \\ S_{23}: & \; -7x_1 + 10x_2 - 10.5 = 0 \end{aligned} \qquad (3.20c)$$

Substituting the weight vectors (3.20a) directly into the decision function formula (3.17b) also results in the decision lines (3.20c). In this example we have derived the weight vectors and equations for decision surfaces for a three-class classifier. We have also provided insight into the geometrical relationships in the pattern space. ■

The notion of linearly separable patterns is now introduced. Assume that there is a pattern set $\mathcal{X}$. This set is divided into subsets $\mathcal{X}_1, \mathcal{X}_2, \ldots, \mathcal{X}_R$, respectively. If a linear machine can classify the patterns from $\mathcal{X}_i$ as belonging to class i, for $i = 1, 2, \ldots, R$, then the pattern sets are *linearly separable*. Using this property of the linear discriminant functions, the linear separability can be formulated more formally. If R linear functions of $\mathbf{x}$ as in (3.10) exist such that

$$g_i(\mathbf{x}) > g_j(\mathbf{x}) \quad \text{for all } \mathbf{x} \in \mathcal{X}_i, \quad i = 1, 2, \ldots, R; \; j = 1, 2, \ldots, R, \; i \neq j$$

then the pattern sets $\mathcal{X}_i$ are linearly separable.

Figure 3.9 shows the example sets of linearly nonseparable patterns in two- and three-dimensional pattern space. It depicts the parity function $f(x_1, x_2, \ldots, x_n)$

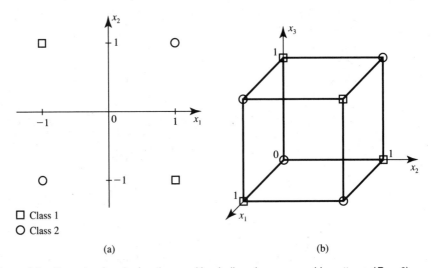

□ Class 1
○ Class 2

(a)   (b)

Figure 3.9 Example of parity function resulting in linearly nonseparable patterns ($R = 2$): (a) $x_1 \oplus x_2$ and (b) $x_1 \oplus x_2 \oplus x_3$.

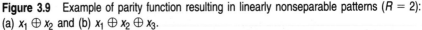

for two and three variables (see Appendix). Figure 3.9(a) exemplifies the bipolar and Figure 3.9(b) the unipolar version of the parity function spanned at the corners of an n-dimensional hypercube. The parity function as defined in Equation (3.21) is often called the *XOR function:*

$$XOR(x_1, x_2, \ldots, x_n) = x_1 \oplus x_2 \oplus \ldots \oplus x_n \tag{3.21}$$

where the symbol $\oplus$ denotes the Exclusive OR Boolean function operator. This function is often convenient to exemplify classification of patterns that are linearly nonseparable.

Geometrically, it can easily be seen that if hyperplanes exist that divide the sets $\mathcal{X}_1, \mathcal{X}_2, \ldots, \mathcal{X}_R$, then the patterns are linearly separable. In contrast to Figures 3.9, 3.3, and 3.5(c) showing examples of linearly nonseparable patterns, Figures 3.4, 3.6, 3.8(a) show classification of patterns that are linearly separable. It can be noticed that decision surfaces for linearly separable patterns define convex decision regions in the pattern space.

3.4
NONPARAMETRIC TRAINING CONCEPT

Thus far our approach to the design of pattern classifiers has been analytical and based on computations of decision boundaries derived from inspection of sample patterns, prototypes, or their clusters. In theoretical considerations and

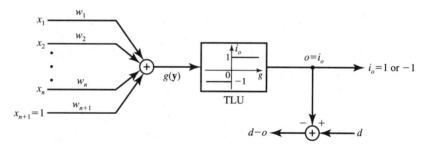

Figure 3.10 Linear dichotomizer using hard-limiting threshold element, or the TLU-based perceptron.

Examples 3.1 and 3.2, we have shown that coefficients of linear discriminant functions called weights can be determined based on *a priori* information about sets of patterns and their class membership.

In this section we will begin to examine neural network classifiers that derive their weights during the learning cycle. The sample pattern vectors x_1, x_2, ..., x_P, called the *training sequence,* are presented to the machine along with the correct response. The response is provided by the teacher and specifies the classification information for each input vector. The classifier modifies its parameters by means of iterative, supervised learning. The network learns from experience by comparing the targeted correct response with the actual response. The classifier structure is usually adjusted after each incorrect response based on the error value generated.

Let us now look again at the dichotomizer introduced and defined in Section 3.2. We will develop a supervised training procedure for this two-class linear classifier. The expanded diagram of the dichotomizer introduced originally in Figure 3.5(b) is now redrawn in Figure 3.10. The dichotomizer shown consists of $n + 1$ weights and the TLU performing as a binary decision element. It is identical to the binary bipolar perceptron from Figure 2.7(a). The TLU itself can be considered a binary response neuron. The input to the binary response neuron is the weighted sum of components of the augmented input vector y.

In the next part of this section, we discuss the adaptive linear binary classifier and derive the perceptron training algorithm based on the originally nonadaptive dichotomizer. Assuming that the desired response is provided, the error signal is computed. The error information can be used to adapt the weights of the discrete perceptron from Figure 3.10. First we examine the geometrical conditions in the augmented weight space. This will make it possible to devise a meaningful training procedure for the dichotomizer under consideration.

From previous considerations we know that the decision surface equation in n-dimensional pattern space is

$$\mathbf{w}^t\mathbf{x} + w_{n+1} = 0 \tag{3.22a}$$

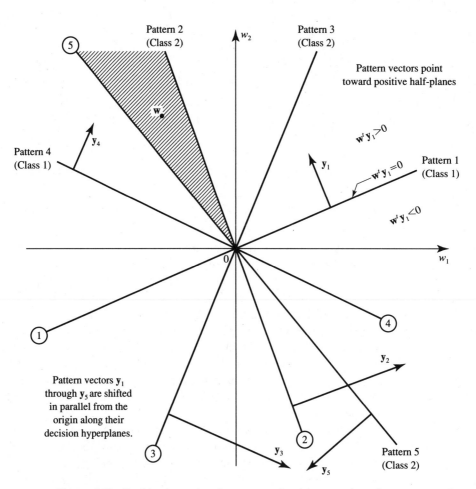

Figure 3.11 Decision hyperplane in augmented weight space for a five pattern set from two classes.

and Equation (3.22a) can be rewritten in the augmented weight space E^{n+1} as

$$\mathbf{w}^t\mathbf{y} = 0 \tag{3.22b}$$

This is a normal vector-point equation and is the first equation in this text considered in the weight space as compared to the earlier equations evaluated in the pattern space. Equation (3.22b) describes a decision hyperplane in augmented weight space. In contrast to the decision hyperplane of Equation (3.22a) in n-dimensional space, this hyperplane always intersects the origin, point $\mathbf{w} = \mathbf{0}$. Its normal vector, which is perpendicular to the plane, is the pattern $\mathbf{y}$. To visualize this, five example decision hyperplanes in the augmented weight space for five prototype patterns of two classes are shown in Figure 3.11.

In further discussion it will be understood that the normal vector will always point toward the side of the space for which $\mathbf{w}^t\mathbf{y} > 0$, called the positive side, or semispace, of the hyperplane. Accordingly, the vector $\mathbf{y}_1$ points toward the positive side of the decision hyperplane $\mathbf{w}^t\mathbf{y}_1 = 0$ in Figure 3.11. The pattern vector orientation is thus fixed toward class 1 decision half-plane. The same remarks also apply to the remaining four patterns $\mathbf{y}_2, \ldots, \mathbf{y}_5$, for which decision hyperplanes and normal vectors have also been shown in the figure. By labeling each decision boundary in the augmented weight space with an arrow pointing into the positive half-plane, we can easily find a region in the weight space that satisfies the linearly separable classification. (This notation using arrows or pattern vectors for pointing positive half-space is used throughout the text.) To find the solution for weights, we will look for the intersection of the positive decision regions due to the prototypes of class 1 and of the negative decision regions due to the prototypes of class 2.

Inspection of the figure reveals that the intersection of the sets of weights yielding all five correct classifications of depicted patterns is in the shaded region of the second quadrant as shown in Figure 3.11. Let us now attempt to arrive iteratively at the weight vector $\mathbf{w}$ located in the shaded weight solution area. To accomplish this, the weights need to be adjusted from the initial value located anywhere in the weight space. This assumption is due to our ignorance of the weight solution region as well as weight initialization. The adjustment discussed, or network training, is based on an error-correction scheme.

As shown below, analysis of geometrical conditions can provide useful guidelines for developing the weight vector adjustment procedure. However, if the dimensionality of the augmented pattern vector is higher than three, our powers of visualization are no longer of assistance in determining the decision or adjustment conditions. Under these circumstances, the only reasonable recourse would be to follow the analytical approach. Fortunately, such an analytical approach can be devised based on geometrical conditions and visualization of decision boundaries for two or three dimensions only of pattern vectors.

Figure 3.12(a) shows a decision surface for the training pattern $\mathbf{y}_1$ in the augmented weight space of the discrete perceptron from Figure 3.10. Assume that the initial weights are $\mathbf{w}^1$ (case A) and that pattern $\mathbf{y}_1$ of class 1 is now input. In such a case, weights $\mathbf{w}^1$ are located in the negative half-plane. Obviously, the pattern is misclassified since we have for the present weights $\mathbf{w}^1$ and pattern $\mathbf{y}_1$ a negative decision due to $\mathbf{w}^{1t}\mathbf{y}_1 < 0$. To increase the discriminant function $\mathbf{w}^{1t}\mathbf{y}_1$, we need to adjust the weight vector, preferably in the direction of steepest increase, which is that of a gradient. The gradient ∇_w can be expressed as follows:

$$\nabla_w(\mathbf{w}^t\mathbf{y}_1) = \mathbf{y}_1 \tag{3.23}$$

Thus, when the pattern of class 1 is misclassified, the adjusted weights should preferably become

$$\mathbf{w}' = \mathbf{w}^1 + c\mathbf{y}_1 \tag{3.24}$$

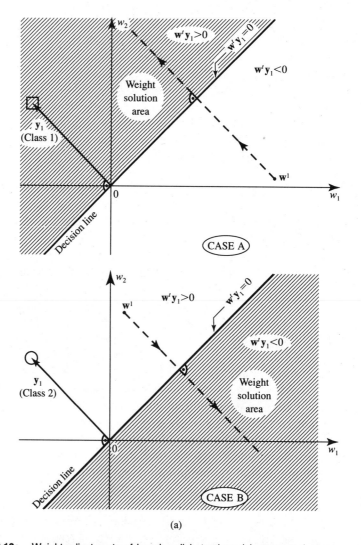

Figure 3.12a Weight adjustments of learning dichotomizer: (a) steepest descent.

where constant $c > 0$ is called the *correction increment,* and a prime is used to denote weights after correction. It can be seen that c controls the size of the adjustment. Repeating the weight adjustment a number of times would bring the weight into the shaded solution region, independent of the chosen correction increment.

Case B in Figure 3.12(a) illustrates a similar misclassification with the initial weights now at $\mathbf{w}^1$ and $\mathbf{y}_1$ of class 2 being input. Since $\mathbf{w}^{1t}\mathbf{y}_1 > 0$ and misclassification occurs also in this case, the discriminant function needs to be changed through weight adjustment, preferably in the steepest decrease, or negative gradient, direction. We thus obtain from Equation (3.23) the following expression

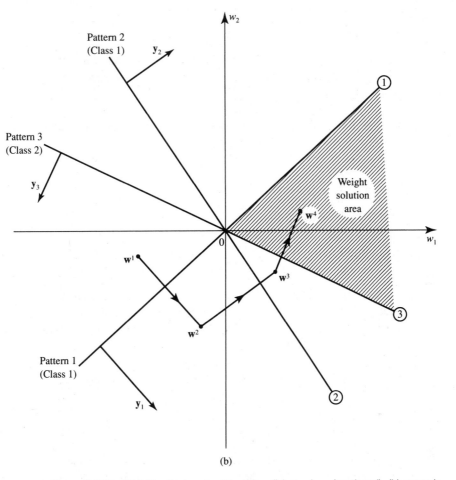

(b)

Figure 3.12b   Weight adjustments of learning dichotomizer *(continued):* (b) example.

for the adjusted weights:

$$\mathbf{w}' = \mathbf{w}^1 - c\mathbf{y}_1 \qquad (3.25)$$

An illustration of a series of weight adjustments in the augmented weight space is shown in Figure 3.12(b). It depicts the weight corrections for an ordered training set of inputs consisting of three augmented pattern vectors $\mathbf{y}_1$, $\mathbf{y}_2$, and $\mathbf{y}_3$. The patterns are numbered here in the sequence as they appear at the input of the classifier. As shown in previous discussion, weights in the shaded region will provide the solution for the augmented weight vector. Three lines labeled ①, ②, and ③ are obviously fixed for variable weight values that result during the training process shown. This is because their normal vectors, patterns $\mathbf{y}_1$, $\mathbf{y}_2$, and $\mathbf{y}_3$, are fixed.

Consider training starting at the initial weight of $\mathbf{w}^1$. During the first step of classification, the first prototype pattern of class 1 is presented and misclassified.

The new augmented weights after correction become

$$\mathbf{w}^2 = \mathbf{w}^1 + c\mathbf{y}_1$$

Similarly, when the second pattern is presented for the current weight vector $\mathbf{w}^2$, it is misclassified, and the corrected weight vector $\mathbf{w}^2$ takes the value

$$\mathbf{w}^3 = \mathbf{w}^2 + c\mathbf{y}_2$$

Since the third pattern belongs to class 2, the misclassification happens again in this step and the new weight vector results as

$$\mathbf{w}^4 = \mathbf{w}^3 - c\mathbf{y}_3$$

Notice that the discussed training procedure with input $\mathbf{y}$ is equivalent to

- increasing the discriminant function $g(\mathbf{y})$ as in (3.19) by $c\|\mathbf{y}\|^2$ if the pattern of class 1 is undetected, and

- decreasing the discriminant function by $c\|\mathbf{y}\|^2$ if the pattern of class 2 is undetected.

Both the increment and decrement of $g(\mathbf{y})$ take place in such a way that the weight vector is displaced in the direction normal to the decision hyperplane. Since this change is in the direction of the shortest path to the correct classification weight area, it is the most appropriate direction.

The supervised training procedure can now be summarized using the following expression for the augmented weight vector $\mathbf{w}'$ after adjustment

$$\mathbf{w}' = \mathbf{w} \pm c\mathbf{y} \tag{3.26}$$

where the positive sign in (3.26) applies for undetected pattern of class 1, and the negative sign applies for undetected pattern of class 2. If a correct classification takes place under this rule, no adjustment of weights is made.

The reader can notice that weight correction formula (3.26) is the same as the perceptron learning rule (2.34–5). Accurate correspondence of both training methods requires that the learning constant in (2.34–5) is a half of the correction increment c in (3.26), and that $\mathbf{x}$ used in (2.34–5) is the augmented pattern vector.

3.5
TRAINING AND CLASSIFICATION USING THE DISCRETE PERCEPTRON: ALGORITHM AND EXAMPLE

Let us look now in more detail at the weight adjustment aspects. Again using the geometrical relationship, we choose the correction increment c so that the weight adjustment step size is meaningfully controlled. The distance p of a point $\mathbf{w}^1$ from the plane $\mathbf{w}^t\mathbf{y} = 0$ in $(n + 1)$-dimensional Euclidean space is computed according to the formula (see Appendix):

$$p = \pm\frac{\mathbf{w}^{1t}\mathbf{y}}{\|\mathbf{y}\|} \tag{3.27a}$$

where the sign in front of the fraction is chosen to be the opposite of the sign of the value of w_{n+1}. A simpler rule is that the sign must be chosen to be identical to the sign of $\mathbf{w}^{1t}\mathbf{y}$. Since p is always a nonnegative scalar by definition of the distance, expression (3.27a) can be rewritten using the absolute value notation as follows:

$$p = \frac{\left|\mathbf{w}^{1t}\mathbf{y}\right|}{\|\mathbf{y}\|} \tag{3.27b}$$

Let us now require that the correction increment constant c be selected such that the corrected weight vector $\mathbf{w}^2$ based on (3.26) dislocates on the decision hyperplane $\mathbf{w}^{1t}\mathbf{y} = 0$, which is the decision hyperplane used for this particular correction step. This implies that

$$\mathbf{w}^{2t}\mathbf{y} = 0, \text{ or}$$
$$(\mathbf{w}^1 \pm c\mathbf{y})^t\mathbf{y} = 0 \tag{3.28}$$

and the required correction increment results for this training step as

$$c = \mp\frac{\mathbf{w}^{1t}\mathbf{y}}{\mathbf{y}^t\mathbf{y}} \tag{3.29a}$$

Since the correction increment c is positive, (3.29a) can be briefly rewritten as

$$c = \frac{\left|\mathbf{w}^{1t}\mathbf{y}\right|}{\mathbf{y}^t\mathbf{y}} \tag{3.29b}$$

The length of the weight adjustment vector $c\mathbf{y}$ can now be expressed as

$$\|c\mathbf{y}\| = \frac{\left|\mathbf{w}^{1t}\mathbf{y}\right|}{\mathbf{y}^t\mathbf{y}}\|\mathbf{y}\| \tag{3.30}$$

Noting that $\mathbf{y}^t\mathbf{y} = \|\mathbf{y}\|^2$ leads to the conclusion that, as required, the distance p from the point $\mathbf{w}^1$ to the decision plane and expressed by (3.27) is identical to the length of the weight increment vector (3.30). For this case the correction increment c is therefore not constant and depends on the current training pattern as expressed by (3.29).

The basic correction rule (3.26) for $c = 1$ leads to a very simple adjustment of the weight vector. Such adjustment alters the weight vector exactly by the pattern vector $\mathbf{y}$. Using the value of the correction increment calculated in (3.29) as a reference, several different adjustment techniques can be devised depending on the length of the weight correction vector $\mathbf{w}^2 - \mathbf{w}^1$. This length is proportional

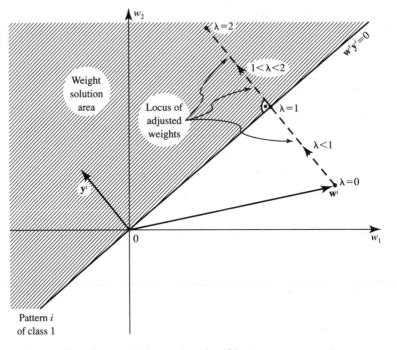

Figure 3.13 Illustration of correction increment value, i'th step.

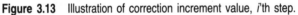

to a coefficient $\lambda > 0$, where

$$c = \lambda \frac{|\mathbf{w}^{1t}\mathbf{y}|}{\mathbf{y}^t\mathbf{y}} \tag{3.31}$$

It follows from the preceding discussion of geometrical terms that λ is the ratio of the distance between the old weight vector $\mathbf{w}^1$ and the new weight vector $\mathbf{w}^2$, to the distance from $\mathbf{w}^1$ to the pattern hyperplane in the weight space.

The different choices for correction increment values c are depicted in Figure 3.13. No weight adjustment in the i'th step takes place for $\lambda = 0$. For $\lambda = 1$ the corrected weights displace exactly onto the decision plane $\mathbf{w}^t\mathbf{y}^i = 0$ as stated before in case (3.30). For $\lambda = 2$, the corrected weights are reflected symmetrically with respect to the decision plane. In the two intermediate cases we have

$$0 < \lambda < 1 \text{ fractional correction rule}$$

$$1 < \lambda < 2 \text{ absolute correction rule}$$

The reader may notice that the fractional correction rule, although it moves $\mathbf{w}^i$ in the right direction, results in another misclassification during the repeated demonstration of the same training pattern, unless the weights have moved to the appropriate side of its decision plane due to the other corrections that might have taken place in the meantime. For the *fixed correction rule* introduced originally with $c = $ const, correction of weights is always the same fixed portion of the current training vector $\mathbf{y}$. Let us also note that the training algorithm based on the computation of distance $\|\mathbf{y}\|$ requires that the initial weight vector be different from $\mathbf{0}$. This is needed to make the denominator of (3.31) of nonzero value.

EXAMPLE 3.3

Let us look at a simple, but nonetheless, instructive example of nonparametric training of a discrete perceptron. The trained classifier should provide the following classification of four patterns x with known class membership d

$$x_1 = 1, \; x_3 = 3, \; d_1 = d_3 = 1 : \text{ class 1}$$
$$x_2 = -0.5, \; x_4 = -2, \; d_2 = d_4 = -1 : \text{ class 2}$$

The single discrete perceptron with unknown weights w_1 and w_2 as shown in Figure 3.14(a) needs to be trained using the augmented input vectors as below

$$\mathbf{y}_1 = \begin{bmatrix} 1 \\ 1 \end{bmatrix}, \; \mathbf{y}_2 = \begin{bmatrix} -0.5 \\ 1 \end{bmatrix}, \; \mathbf{y}_3 = \begin{bmatrix} 3 \\ 1 \end{bmatrix}, \; \mathbf{y}_4 = \begin{bmatrix} -2 \\ 1 \end{bmatrix}$$

Decision lines $\mathbf{w}^t\mathbf{y}_i = 0$, for $i = 1, 2, 3, 4$, have been sketched in the augmented weight space as illustrated in Figure 3.14(b), along with their corresponding normal vectors, which are simply patterns $\mathbf{y}_i$, for $i = 1, 2, 3, 4$. The shaded area in the weight plane represents the anticipated solution region for the given supervised training task. The shaded area of weight solutions is known to us based on the similar considerations as in Figure 3.11. The classifier weights, however, must yet be trained to relocate possibly to the shaded area in this example.

Let us review the training with an arbitrary selection of $c = 1$, and with the initial weights chosen arbitrarily as $\mathbf{w}^1 = \begin{bmatrix} -2.5 & 1.75 \end{bmatrix}^t$. Using (3.26), the weight training with each step 1 through 10 and illustrated in Figure 3.14(b) can be summarized as follows

$$\Delta\mathbf{w}^k = \frac{c}{2}\left[d_k - \text{sgn}\,(\mathbf{w}^{kt}\mathbf{y}_k) \right] \mathbf{y}^k$$

During the training we obtain the following outputs and weight updates.

Step 1   Pattern $\mathbf{y}_1$ is input

$$o_1 = \text{sgn}\left(\begin{bmatrix} -2.5 & 1.75 \end{bmatrix} \begin{bmatrix} 1 \\ 1 \end{bmatrix} \right) = -1$$
$$d_1 - o_1 = 2$$

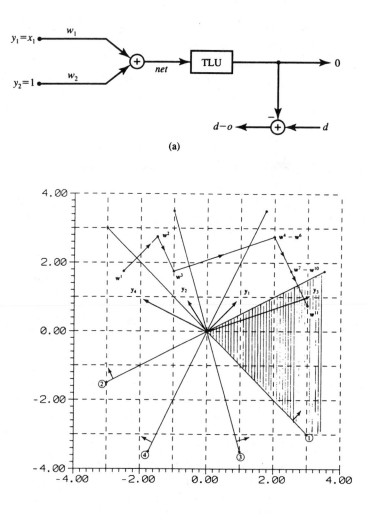

(a)

(b)

Figure 3.14a,b Discrete perceptron classifier training in Example 3.3: (a) network diagram, (b) fixed correction rule training.

Pattern vector $\mathbf{y}^1 = \mathbf{y}_1$ is added to the present weight vector $\mathbf{w}^1$

$$\mathbf{w}^2 = \mathbf{w}^1 + \mathbf{y}^1 = \begin{bmatrix} -1.5 \\ 2.75 \end{bmatrix}$$

Step 2 Pattern $\mathbf{y}_2$ is input

$$o_2 = \mathrm{sgn}\left(\begin{bmatrix} -1.5 & 2.75 \end{bmatrix} \begin{bmatrix} -0.5 \\ 1 \end{bmatrix} \right) = 1$$

$$d_2 - o_2 = -2$$

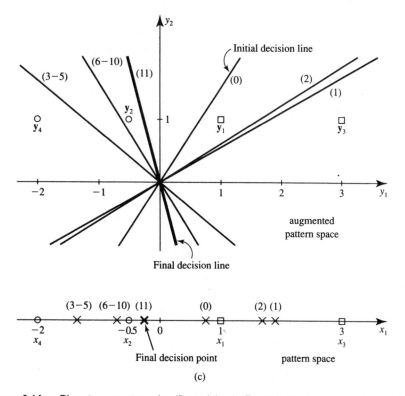

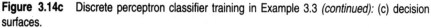

Figure 3.14c Discrete perceptron classifier training in Example 3.3 *(continued)*: (c) decision surfaces.

Pattern vector $\mathbf{y}^2 = \mathbf{y}_2$ is subtracted from the present weight vector $\mathbf{w}^2$

$$\mathbf{w}^3 = \mathbf{w}^2 - \mathbf{y}^2 = \begin{bmatrix} -1 \\ 1.75 \end{bmatrix}$$

Step 3   Pattern $\mathbf{y}_3$ is input

$$o_3 = \text{sgn}\left(\begin{bmatrix} -1 & 1.75 \end{bmatrix} \begin{bmatrix} 3 \\ 1 \end{bmatrix} \right) = -1$$

$$d_3 - o_3 = 2$$

Pattern vector $\mathbf{y}^3 = \mathbf{y}_3$ is added to the present weight vector $\mathbf{w}^3$

$$\mathbf{w}^4 = \mathbf{w}^3 + \mathbf{y}^3 = \begin{bmatrix} 2 \\ 2.75 \end{bmatrix}$$

Since we have no evidence of correct classification for weights $\mathbf{w}^4$, the training set consisting of an ordered sequence of patterns $\mathbf{y}_1$, $\mathbf{y}_2$, and $\mathbf{y}_3$ needs to be recycled. We thus have $\mathbf{y}^4 = \mathbf{y}_1$, $\mathbf{y}^5 = \mathbf{y}_2$, etc. The superscript is used to denote the following training step number.

Steps 4, 5 $\mathbf{w}^6 = \mathbf{w}^5 = \mathbf{w}^4$. (No misclassification, thus no weight adjustment.)

The reader can easily verify that the adjustments following in Steps 6 through 10 are as follows:

$$\mathbf{w}^7 = \begin{bmatrix} 2.5 & 1.75 \end{bmatrix}^t$$
$$\mathbf{w}^{10} = \mathbf{w}^9 = \mathbf{w}^8 = \mathbf{w}^7$$
$$\mathbf{w}^{11} = \begin{bmatrix} 3 & 0.75 \end{bmatrix}^t$$

As indicated, only Steps 6 and 10 have resulted in weight adjustment during continued training with recycled inputs. Since after ten training steps the weight vector $\mathbf{w}^{11}$ ended up in the solution area, $w_1 = 3$, and $w_2 = 0.75$ represent the final weights of the classifier from Figure 3.14(a) and the training terminates. The reader can verify that $\mathbf{w}^{11}$ represents the solution weight vector and provides correct classification for the entire training set.

The training has been so far performed in the augmented weight space as shown in Figure 3.14(b). It should be realized, however, that the original decision surfaces used by the TLU element are generated in the pattern space. Figure 3.14(c) shows the decision surfaces produced for the example training for each of Steps 1 through 10. In the augmented pattern space y_1, y_2, the decision surfaces are the straight lines shown; in the pattern space, the decision surfaces reduce to points on the x_1 axis. ■

We now simulate a fixed-correction training rule for a case of higher dimension. An example with $n = 3$ and $R = 2$ is shown in Figure 3.15. As illustrated in the first eight rows of Figure 3.15(a), eight binary patterns spanned in three-dimensional space and representing one of the two classes are submitted to the input of the classifier in an ascending binary sequence. As listed in the rightmost column, four patterns located on the plane $x_3 = 0$, which is the bottom of the unity side cube in E^3 space, belong to class 2; the remaining four patterns belong to class 1. In the calculations shown, we also assume that the perceptron can respond with zero. Such "no decisive response" is interpreted as a mistake and is followed by a correction.

Accordingly, starting from the initial weight vector $\mathbf{w} = 0$ as shown in the first row of iteration 1, the first corrected weight vector in the second row becomes the difference of the current weight vector $\begin{bmatrix} 0 & 0 & 0 & 0 \end{bmatrix}^t$ and the misclassified pattern vector $\begin{bmatrix} 0 & 0 & 0 & 1 \end{bmatrix}^t$. The *net* values at the input of the TLU expressing scalar products $\mathbf{w}^t\mathbf{y}$ are shown in the rightmost column of the figure. As shown, the training takes only three full sweeps through the set of prototypes, since the patterns are apparently easily separable. The resulting decision plane shown in 3.15(c) is $4x_3 - 1 = 0$. The equation has been obtained by inspection of the last row of the iteration 3 of Figure 3.15(a).

Input data and classes

x_1	x_2	x_3	x_4	d
0	0	0	1	2
0	0	1	1	1
0	1	0	1	2
0	1	1	1	1
1	0	0	1	2
1	0	1	1	1
1	1	0	1	2
1	1	1	1	1

Training Steps				w_1	w_2	w_3	w_4	$net = \mathbf{w}^t\mathbf{y}$
Iteration = 1								
0	0	0	1	0.00	0.00	0.00	0.00	0.00
0	0	1	1	0.00	0.00	0.00	−1.00	−1.00
0	1	0	1	0.00	0.00	1.00	0.00	0.00
0	1	1	1	0.00	−1.00	1.00	−1.00	−1.00
1	0	0	1	0.00	0.00	2.00	0.00	0.00
1	0	1	1	−1.00	0.00	2.00	−1.00	0.00
1	1	0	1	0.00	0.00	3.00	0.00	0.00
1	1	1	1	−1.00	−1.00	3.00	−1.00	0.00
Iteration = 2								
0	0	0	1	0.00	0.00	4.00	0.00	0.00
0	0	1	1	0.00	0.00	4.00	−1.00	3.00
0	1	0	1	0.00	0.00	4.00	−1.00	−1.00
0	1	1	1	0.00	0.00	4.00	−1.00	3.00
1	0	0	1	0.00	0.00	4.00	−1.00	−1.00
1	0	1	1	0.00	0.00	4.00	−1.00	3.00
1	1	0	1	0.00	0.00	4.00	−1.00	−1.00
1	1	1	1	0.00	0.00	4.00	−1.00	3.00
Iteration = 3								
0	0	0	1	0.00	0.00	4.00	−1.00	−1.00
0	0	1	1	0.00	0.00	4.00	−1.00	3.00
0	1	0	1	0.00	0.00	4.00	−1.00	−1.00
0	1	1	1	0.00	0.00	4.00	−1.00	3.00
1	0	0	1	0.00	0.00	4.00	−1.00	−1.00
1	0	1	1	0.00	0.00	4.00	−1.00	3.00
1	1	0	1	0.00	0.00	4.00	−1.00	−1.00
1	1	1	1	0.00	0.00	4.00	−1.00	3.00

The training took 2 iterations.

The final weights are: 0.00   0.00   4.00   −1.00 .

$$\mathbf{x} = \begin{bmatrix} x_1 \\ x_2 \\ x_3 \end{bmatrix} \text{ is pattern vector.}$$

$x_4 = 1$ is augmented pattern component, d is desired class membership.

(a)

Figure 3.15a Example dichotomizer training, $n = 3$: (a) fixed correction rule ($c = 1$).

Input data and classes

x_1	x_2	x_3	x_4	d
0	0	0	1	2
0	0	1	1	1
0	1	0	1	2
0	1	1	1	1
1	0	0	1	2
1	0	1	1	1
1	1	0	1	2
1	1	1	1	1

Training Steps				w_1	w_2	w_3	w_4	$net = \mathbf{w}^t\mathbf{y}$
Iteration = 1								
0	0	0	1	0.00	0.00	0.00	0.00	0.00
0	0	1	1	0.00	0.00	0.00	−1.50	−1.50
0	1	0	1	0.00	0.00	1.13	−0.38	−0.38
0	1	1	1	0.00	0.00	1.13	−0.38	0.75
1	0	0	1	0.00	0.00	1.13	−0.38	−0.38
1	0	1	1	0.00	0.00	1.13	−0.38	0.75
1	1	0	1	0.00	0.00	1.13	−0.38	−0.38
1	1	1	1	0.00	0.00	1.13	−0.38	0.75
Iteration = 2								
0	0	0	1	0.00	0.00	1.13	−0.38	−0.38
0	0	1	1	0.00	0.00	1.13	−0.38	0.75
0	1	0	1	0.00	0.00	1.13	−0.38	−0.38
0	1	1	1	0.00	0.00	1.13	−0.38	0.75
1	0	0	1	0.00	0.00	1.13	−0.38	−0.38
1	0	1	1	0.00	0.00	1.13	−0.38	0.75
1	1	0	1	0.00	0.00	1.13	−0.38	−0.38
1	1	1	1	0.00	0.00	1.13	−0.38	0.75

The training took 1 iteration.

The final weights are: 0.00 0.00 1.13 −0.38 .

$$\mathbf{x} = \begin{bmatrix} x_1 \\ x_2 \\ x_3 \end{bmatrix} \text{ is pattern vector.}$$

$x_4 = 1$ is augmented pattern component, d is desired class membership.

(b)

Figure 3.15b Example dichotomizer training, $n = 3$ *(continued):* (b) absolute correction rule.

Similar results, but produced within only two sweeps through the training set, have been obtained for the absolute correction rule. The resulting plane is $1.13x_3 - 0.38 = 0$ for the weight computation using this rule. The simulated training is shown in Figure 3.15(b), and the resulting decision plane is shown in Figure 3.15(c).

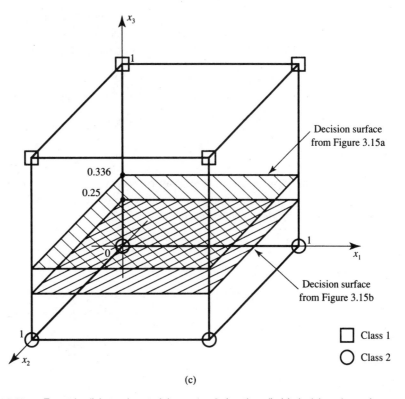

Figure 3.15c Example dichotomizer training, $n = 3$ *(continued):* (c) decision planes for parts (a) and (b).

Let us summarize the classification of linearly separable patterns belonging to two classes only. The training task for the classifier was to find the weight vector **w** such that

$$\begin{aligned} \mathbf{w}'\mathbf{y} > 0 \quad \text{for each } \mathbf{x} \text{ of } \mathscr{X}_1 \\ \mathbf{w}'\mathbf{y} < 0 \quad \text{for each } \mathbf{x} \text{ of } \mathscr{X}_2 \end{aligned} \tag{3.32}$$

Completion of the training with the fixed correction training rule for any initial weight vector and any correction increment constant leads to the following weights

$$\mathbf{w}^* = \mathbf{w}^{k_o} = \mathbf{w}^{k_o+1} = \mathbf{w}^{k_o+2} \cdots \tag{3.33}$$

with **w*** as a solution vector for (3.32). The integer k_o is the training step number starting at which no more misclassification occurs, and thus no weight adjustments take place for $k_o \geq 0$. This theorem, called the *perceptron convergence theorem*, states that a classifier for two linearly separable classes of patterns is always trainable in a finite number of training steps. Below we provide the proof of the theorem.

Assume that the solution weight vector $\mathbf{w}^*$ exists, and is normalized such that $\|\mathbf{w}^*\| = 1$. The existence of hypothetical solution weights $\mathbf{w}^*$ allows rewriting of (3.32) for a small arbitrarily selected constant $0 < \delta < 1$ as follows

$$\begin{aligned} \mathbf{w}^{*t}\mathbf{y} > \delta > 0 \quad \text{for each } \mathbf{x} \in \mathscr{X}_1 \\ \mathbf{w}^{*t}\mathbf{y} < -\delta < 0 \quad \text{for each } \mathbf{x} \in \mathscr{X}_2 \end{aligned} \tag{3.34}$$

Let us evaluate the following function:

$$\phi(\mathbf{w}) \stackrel{\Delta}{=} \frac{\mathbf{w}^{*t}\mathbf{w}}{\|\mathbf{w}\|} \tag{3.35}$$

Since $\phi(\mathbf{w})$ is a scalar product of normalized vectors, $\phi(\mathbf{w}) = \cos \sphericalangle (\mathbf{w}^*, \mathbf{w}) \leq 1$. Rearranging the numerator and denominator of (3.35) we obtain for the k'th learning step, respectively,

$$\mathbf{w}^{*t}\mathbf{w}^{k+1} = \mathbf{w}^{*t}\mathbf{w}^k + \mathbf{w}^{*t}\mathbf{y} > \mathbf{w}^{*t}\mathbf{w}^k + \delta \tag{3.36a}$$

$$\|\mathbf{w}^{k+1}\|^2 = (\mathbf{w}^{kt} + \mathbf{y}^t)(\mathbf{w}^k + \mathbf{y}) < \|\mathbf{w}^k\|^2 + 1 \tag{3.36b}$$

for the normalized pattern used for training and for $c = 1$.

Upon performing the total of k_o training steps (3.36a) and (3.36b) can be rewritten, respectively, as

$$\mathbf{w}^{*t}\mathbf{w}^{k_o+1} > k_o\delta \tag{3.36c}$$

This condition can be rewritten as follows:

$$\|\mathbf{w}^{k_o+1}\|^2 < k_o \tag{3.36d}$$

The function (3.35) now becomes for $\mathbf{w} = \mathbf{w}^{k_o+1}$

$$\phi(\mathbf{w}^{k_o+1}) = \frac{\mathbf{w}^{*t}\mathbf{w}^{k_o+1}}{\|\mathbf{w}^{k_o+1}\|} \tag{3.37a}$$

and from (3.36c) and (3.36d) note that

$$\phi(\mathbf{w}^{k_o+1}) > \sqrt{k_o}\delta \tag{3.37b}$$

Since $\phi(\mathbf{w}^{k_o+1})$ has an upper bound of 1, the inequality (3.37b) would be violated if a solution were not found for $\sqrt{k_o}\delta < 1$. Thus, this concludes the proof that the discrete perceptron training is convergent. The maximum number of learning steps is $k_o = 1/\delta^2$ (Amit 1989). If the value $1/\delta^2$ is not an integer, it should be rounded up to the closest integer.

The number of steps k_o needed to achieve correct classification depends strongly on the c value and on the sequence of training patterns submitted. The theorem can also be extended and proven for R category machines classifying patterns that are linearly separable and trained through submission of such patterns in any sequence (Nilsson 1965).

The perceptron training procedure expressed in (3.26) may be rewritten as

$$\mathbf{w}^{k+1} = \mathbf{w}^k + \frac{c}{2}(d^k - o^k)\mathbf{y}^k \tag{3.38}$$

where k denotes the number of the current training step, o^k is the actual output of the classifier being trained, and d^k is the teacher-submitted desired output for the vector $\mathbf{y}^k$ applied at the input. When $d^k = o^k$, no adjustment of weights is undertaken. When $d^k = 1$ and $o^k = -1$, signifying jointly that the pattern of class 1 was mistakenly not detected, the weight correction becomes

$$\mathbf{w}^{k+1} - \mathbf{w}^k = c\mathbf{y}^k \tag{3.39a}$$

Whenever a pattern of class 2 is not detected, and the classification is resulting in $o^k = 1$ while $d^k = -1$, the weight correction is

$$\mathbf{w}^{k+1} - \mathbf{w}^k = -c\mathbf{y}^k \tag{3.39b}$$

In summary, the training of a single discrete perceptron two-class classifier requires a change of $\mathbf{w}$ if and only if a misclassification occurs. If the reason for misclassification is $\mathbf{w}^t\mathbf{y} < 0$, then all weights w_i are increased in proportion to y_i; if $\mathbf{w}^t\mathbf{y} > 0$, then all weights w_i are decreased in proportion to y_i. The weights are then punished in an appropriate way. If the classification is correct, no punishment takes place, but its absence can be taken as a reward. We can formulate the single discrete perceptron training algorithm as given below.

The error value E used in the algorithm is computed to detect the series of correct classifications within the training cycle and to terminate the training. Left-pointing arrows below indicate the operation of an assignment. By the operation of assignment, the argument on the left side is assigned the value indicated on the right side.

■ *Summary of the Single Discrete Perceptron Training Algorithm (SDPTA)*

Given are P training pairs

$$\{\mathbf{x}_1, d_1, \mathbf{x}_2, d_2, \ldots, \mathbf{x}_P, d_P\}, \quad \text{where}$$
$$\mathbf{x}_i \text{ is } (n \times 1), \, d_i \text{ is } (1 \times 1), \, i = 1, 2, \ldots P.$$

Note that augmented input vectors are used:

$$\mathbf{y}_i = \begin{bmatrix} \mathbf{x}_i \\ 1 \end{bmatrix}, \quad \text{for } i = 1, 2, \ldots, P$$

In the following, k denotes the training step and p denotes the step counter within the training cycle.

Step 1: $c > 0$ is chosen.

Step 2: Weights are initialized at $\mathbf{w}$ at small random values, $\mathbf{w}$ is $(n + 1) \times 1$. Counters and error are initialized:

$$k \leftarrow 1, \, p \leftarrow 1, \, E \leftarrow 0$$

Step 3: The training cycle begins here. Input is presented and output computed:

$$\mathbf{y} \leftarrow \mathbf{y}_p, \, d \leftarrow d_p$$
$$o \leftarrow \text{sgn}(\mathbf{w}^t\mathbf{y})$$

Step 4:   Weights are updated:

$$\mathbf{w} \leftarrow \mathbf{w} + \frac{1}{2}c(d - o)\mathbf{y}$$

Step 5:   Cycle error is computed:

$$E \leftarrow \frac{1}{2}(d - o)^2 + E$$

Step 6:   If $p < P$ then $p \leftarrow p + 1$, $k \leftarrow k + 1$, and go to Step 3; otherwise, go to Step 7.

Step 7:   The training cycle is completed. For $E = 0$, terminate the training session. Output weights and k.

  If $E > 0$, then $E \leftarrow 0$, $p \leftarrow 1$, and enter the new training cycle by going to Step 3.

The training rule expressed by the Equations (3.26) and (3.38) will be extended in the next section to cases where the TLU or the threshold device is no longer the most favored decision computing element. Instead, a continuous perceptron element with sigmoidal activation function will be introduced to facilitate the training of multilayer feedforward networks used for classification and recognition.

3.6 SINGLE-LAYER CONTINUOUS PERCEPTRON NETWORKS FOR LINEARLY SEPARABLE CLASSIFICATIONS

In this section we introduce the concept of an error function in multidimensional weight space. Also, the TLU element with weights will be replaced by the continuous perceptron. This replacement has two main direct objectives. The first one is to gain finer control over the training procedure. The other is to facilitate working with differentiable characteristics of the threshold element, thus enabling computation of the error gradient. Such a continuous characteristic, or sigmoidal activation function, describes the neuron in lieu of the sgn function as discussed in Chapter 2.

According to the training theorem discussed in the last section, the TLU weights are converging to some solution $\mathbf{w}^{k_o}$ for any positive correction increment constant. The weight modification problem could be better solved, however, by minimizing the scalar criterion function. Such a task can possibly be attempted by again using the gradient, or steepest descent, procedure.

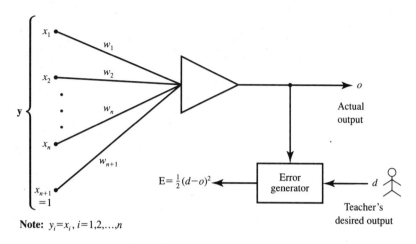

Figure 3.16 Continuous perceptron training using square error minimization.

The basic procedure of descent is quite simple. Starting from an arbitrary chosen weight vector $\mathbf{w}$, the gradient $\nabla E(\mathbf{w})$ of the current error function is computed. The next value of $\mathbf{w}$ is obtained by moving in the direction of the negative gradient along the multidimensional error surface. The direction of negative gradient is the one of steepest descent. The algorithm can be summarized as below:

$$\mathbf{w}^{k+1} = \mathbf{w}^k - \eta \nabla E(\mathbf{w}^k) \tag{3.40}$$

where η is the positive constant called the *learning constant* and the superscript denotes the step number.

Let us define the error E_k in the k'th training step as the squared difference between the desired value d^k at the output of the continuous perceptron and its actual output value o^k computed. As shown in Figure 3.16, the desired value d^k is provided by the teacher.

The expression for classification error to be minimized is

$$E_k = \frac{1}{2}(d^k - o^k)^2, \text{ or} \tag{3.41a}$$

$$E_k = \frac{1}{2}\left[d^k - f(\mathbf{w}^{kt}\mathbf{y}^k)\right]^2 \tag{3.41b}$$

where the coefficient $1/2$ in front of the error expression is intended for convenience in simplifying the expression of the gradient value, and it does not affect the location of the error minimum or the error minimization itself.

Our intention is to achieve minimization of the error function $E(\mathbf{w})$ in $(n+1)$-dimensional weight space. An example of a well-behaving error function is shown in Figure 3.17. The error function has a single minimum at $\mathbf{w} = \mathbf{w}_f$, which can be achieved using the negative-gradient descent starting at the initial weight

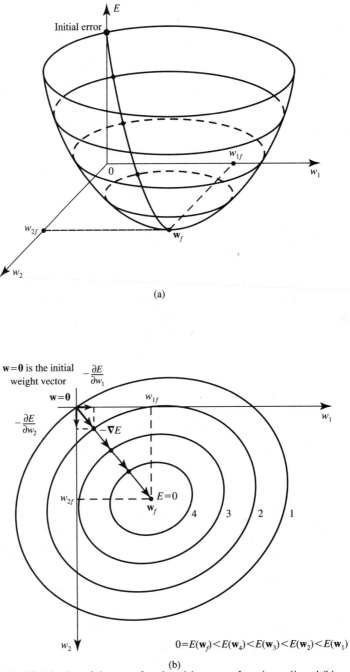

(a)

(b)

Figure 3.17　Minimization of the error function: (a) error surface ($n = 1$) and (b) error contours for determination of the gradient vector ∇E.

vector $\mathbf{0}$ shown in the figure. The vicinity of the point $E(\mathbf{w}_f) = 0$ is shown to be reached within a finite number of steps. The movement of the weight vector can be observed both on the error surface in Figure 3.17(a), or across the error contour lines shown in Figure 3.17(b). In the depicted case, the weights displace from contour 1 through 4 ideally toward the point $E = 0$. By definition of the steepest descent concept, each elementary move should be perpendicular to the current error contour.

Unfortunately, neither error functions for a TLU-based dichotomizer nor those for more complex multiclass classifiers using TLU units result in a form suitable for the gradient descent-based training. The reason for this is that the error function has zero slope in the entire weight space where the error function exists, and it is nondifferentiable on the decision surface itself. This property directly results from calculating any gradient vector component $\nabla E(\mathbf{w})$ using (3.41) with sgn (net) replacing $f(net)$. Indeed, the derivative of the internal function sgn $(\cdot)$ is nonexistent in zero, and of zero value elsewhere.

The error minimization algorithm (3.40) requires computation of the gradient of the error (3.41) as follows:

$$\nabla E(\mathbf{w}) = \frac{1}{2}\nabla\left[d - f(net)\right]^2 \tag{3.42}$$

The training step superscript k in (3.42) has been temporarily skipped for simplicity, but it should be understood that the error gradient computation refers strictly to the k'th training step. In the remaining part of this section, the gradient descent training rule for the single continuous perceptron will be derived in detail.

The $n + 1$-dimensional gradient vector (3.43) is defined as follows:

$$\nabla E(\mathbf{w}) \overset{\Delta}{=} \begin{bmatrix} \dfrac{\partial E}{\partial w_1} \\ \dfrac{\partial E}{\partial w_2} \\ \vdots \\ \dfrac{\partial E}{\partial w_{n+1}} \end{bmatrix} \tag{3.43}$$

Using (3.42) we obtain for the gradient vector

$$\nabla E(\mathbf{w}) = -(d - o)f'(net) \begin{bmatrix} \dfrac{\partial(net)}{\partial w_1} \\ \dfrac{\partial(net)}{\partial w_2} \\ \vdots \\ \dfrac{\partial(net)}{\partial w_{n+1}} \end{bmatrix} \tag{3.44}$$

Since $net = \mathbf{w}^t\mathbf{y}$ we have

$$\frac{\partial(net)}{\partial w_i} = y_i, \quad \text{for } i = 1, 2, \ldots, n + 1 \tag{3.45}$$

and (3.44) can be rewritten as

$$\nabla E(\mathbf{w}) = -(d - o)f'(net)\mathbf{y} \tag{3.46a}$$

or

$$\frac{\partial E}{\partial w_i} = -(d - o)f'(net)y_i \tag{3.46b}$$

which is the training rule of the continuous perceptron. It can be seen that the rule is equivalent to the delta training rule (2.38). The computation of adjusted weights as in (3.40) requires the assumption of η and the specification for the activation function used.

Note that in further considerations we assume trainable weights. Therefore, we will no longer need to use the steepness coefficient λ of the activation function as a variable. The assumption that $\lambda = 1$ is thus as valid as the assumption of any other constant λ value used to scale all the weights in the same proportion.

Let us express $f'(net)$ in terms of continuous perceptron output. Using the bipolar continuous activation function $f(net)$ of the form

$$f(net) = \frac{2}{1 + \exp(-net)} - 1 \tag{3.47}$$

we obtain

$$f'(net) = \frac{2\exp(-net)}{[1 + \exp(-net)]^2} \tag{3.48}$$

A useful identity (3.49) can be applied here:

$$\frac{2\exp(-net)}{[1 + \exp(-net)]^2} = \frac{1}{2}(1 - o^2) \tag{3.49}$$

The identity (3.49) is verified below. Letting $o = f(net)$ as in (3.47) on the right side of (3.49) leads to

$$\frac{1}{2}(1 - o^2) = \frac{1}{2}\left[1 - \left(\frac{1 - \exp(-net)}{1 + \exp(-net)}\right)^2\right] \tag{3.50}$$

The right side of (3.50) reduces after rearrangements to

$$\frac{1}{2}\left[1 - \left(\frac{1 - \exp(-net)}{1 + \exp(-net)}\right)^2\right] = \frac{2\exp(-net)}{[1 + \exp(-net)]^2} \tag{3.51}$$

which completes the verification of (3.49).

The gradient (3.46a) becomes

$$\nabla E(\mathbf{w}) = -\frac{1}{2}(d - o)(1 - o^2)\mathbf{y} \tag{3.52}$$

where $net^k = \mathbf{w}^{kt}\mathbf{y}^k$. Note that for fixed patterns $\mathbf{y}^k = \mathbf{y}_k$, for $k = 1, 2,$ 3, 4, the error can be expressed as a function of two weights only. Thus, we can easily track the error minimization procedure during training in the two-dimensional weight space. The error function in the first training step can be obtained using numerical values of Example 3.3 plugged into the error expression above. For the first pattern being input we have

$$E_1(\mathbf{w}) = \frac{1}{2}\left\{1 - \left[\frac{2}{1 + \exp\left[-\lambda(w_1 + w_2)\right]} - 1\right]\right\}^2$$

Plugging $\lambda = 1$ and reducing the terms simplifies the above expression for error to the form as below

$$E_1(\mathbf{w}) = \frac{2}{[1 + \exp(w_1 + w_2)]^2}$$

for the first training step. Subsequent Steps 2, 3, and 4 need to reduce the training step error values, respectively, as follows:

$$E_2(\mathbf{w}) = \frac{2}{[1 + \exp(0.5w_1 - w_2)]^2}$$

$$E_3(\mathbf{w}) = \frac{2}{[1 + \exp(3w_1 + w_2)]^2}$$

$$E_4(\mathbf{w}) = \frac{2}{[1 + \exp(2w_1 - w_2)]^2}$$

During training, the error E_k in k'th training step is minimized as a function of weights at $\mathbf{w} = \mathbf{w}^k$. The error surfaces E_1 through E_4 are shown in Figure 3.18. It can be seen from the figure that each training step error is monotonically decreasing and it asymptotically reaches 0 at decision regions yielding correct classification.

Although the error surfaces clearly visualize the anticipated displacement of $\mathbf{w}^k$ toward the lower error values using the steepest descent technique, reconstruction of the trajectories of trained weights for the sequence of steps is somewhat complex. Adding errors E_1 through E_4 provides better overall insight into the error minimization process. The total error surface is shown in Figure 3.19(a). The total error monotonically decreases and reaches values near 0 in the shaded region of Figure 3.14(b). A contour map of the total error is depicted in Figure 3.19(b).

The classifier training has been simulated for $\eta = 0.5$ for four arbitrarily chosen initial weight vectors, including the one taken from Example 3.3. The resulting trajectories of 150 simulated training steps are shown in Figure 3.19(c) (each tenth step is shown). In each case the weights converge during training toward the center of the solution region obtained for the discrete perceptron case from Figure 3.14(b). ■

and the complete delta training rule for the bipo
results from (3.40) as

$$\mathbf{w}^{k+1} = \mathbf{w}^k + \frac{1}{2}\eta(d^k - o^k)(1 -$$

where k denotes the reinstated number of the training su

It may be noted that the weight adjustment rule (3.53) ⌐
the same direction as the discrete perceptron learning rule c
in (3.38). The size, or simply length, of the weight correction
difference between the rules of Equations (3.38) and (3.53). ⌐
involve adding or subtracting a fraction of the pattern vector y⌐
difference is the presence of the moderating factor $1 - o^{k2}$. This sca⌐
obviously always positive and smaller than 1. For erroneous respons
close to 0, or a weakly committed perceptron, the correction scaling fₐ
be larger than for those responses generated by a *net* of large magnitude.

Another significant difference between the discrete and continuous pε
tron training is that the discrete perceptron training algorithm always leads ι
solution for linearly separable problems. In contrast to this property, the negatiν
gradient-based training does not guarantee solutions for linearly separable patterns
(Wittner and Denker 1988).

At this point the TLU-based classifier has been modified and consists of a
continuous perceptron element. In the past, the term perceptron has been used to
describe the TLU-based discrete decision element with synaptic weights and a
summing node. Here, we have extended the perceptron concept by replacing the
TLU decision element with a neuron characterized by a continuous activation
function. As in the case of a discrete perceptron, the pattern components arrive
through synaptic weight connections yielding the *net* signal. The *net* signal excites
the neuron, which responds according to its continuous activation function.

EXAMPLE 3.4 ■■■■■■■■■

This example revisits the training of Example 3.3, but it discusses a continuous perceptron rather than a discrete perceptron classifier. The training
pattern set is identical to that of Example 3.3. The example demonstrates
supervised training using the delta rule for a continuous perceptron, which is
shown in Figure 3.16. As has been shown, the training rule (3.53) minimizes
the error (3.41) in each step by following the negative gradient direction.
The error value in step k is

$$E_k = \frac{1}{2}\left\{d^k - \left[\frac{2}{1 + \exp(-\lambda net^k)} - 1\right]\right\}^2$$

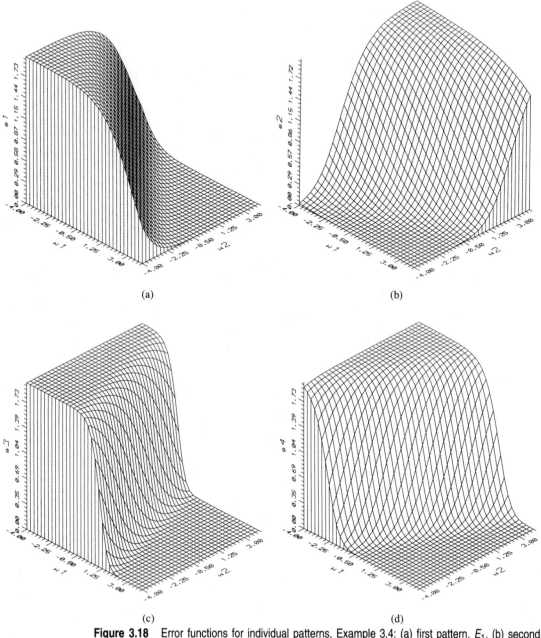

(a)   (b)

(c)   (d)

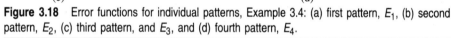

Figure 3.18 Error functions for individual patterns, Example 3.4: (a) first pattern, E_1, (b) second pattern, E_2, (c) third pattern, and E_3, and (d) fourth pattern, E_4.

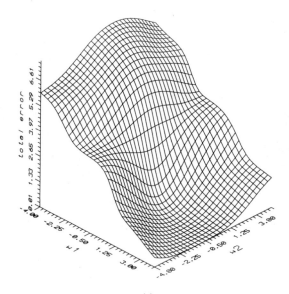

(a)

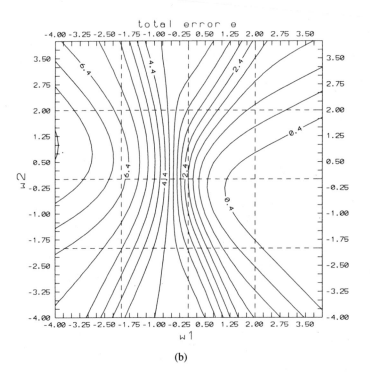

(b)

Figure 3.19a,b   Delta rule training illustration for training in Example 3.4: (a) total error surface, (b) total error contour map.

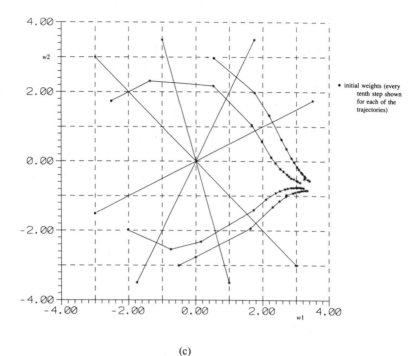

(c)

Figure 3.19c   Delta rule training illustration for training in Example 3.4 *(continued):* (c) trajectories of weight adjustments during training (each tenth step shown).

We can formulate the single continuous perceptron training algorithm as given below.

■   *Summary of the Single Continuous Perceptron Training Algorithm (SCPTA)*

Given the same data as for SDPTA in Section 3.5:

Step 1: $\eta > 0$, $\lambda = 1$, $E_{\max} > 0$ chosen.

Step 2:   Same as SDPTA in Section 3.5.

Step 3:   The training cycle begins here. Input **y** is presented and output computed:

$$\mathbf{y} \leftarrow \mathbf{y}_p, d \leftarrow d_p$$
$$o \leftarrow f(\mathbf{w}^t\mathbf{y}), \text{ with } f(net) \text{ as in (2.3a)}$$

Step 4:   Weights are updated:

$$\mathbf{w} \leftarrow \mathbf{w} + \frac{1}{2}\eta(d - o)(1 - o^2)\mathbf{y}$$

Steps 5,6:   Same as SDPTA in Section 3.5

Step 7:   The training cycle is completed. For $E < E_{max}$ terminate the training session. Output weights, k and E.
If $E \geq E_{max}$, then $E \leftarrow 0$, $p \leftarrow 1$, and enter the new training cycle by going to Step 3.

3.7 MULTICATEGORY SINGLE-LAYER PERCEPTRON NETWORKS

Our approach so far has been limited to training of dichotomizers using both discrete and continuous perceptron elements. In this section we will attempt to apply the error-correcting algorithm to the task of multicategory classification. The assumption needed is that classes are linearly pairwise separable, or that each class is linearly separable from each other class. This assumption is equivalent to the fact that there exist R linear discriminant functions such that

$$g_i(\mathbf{x}) > g_j(\mathbf{x}), \quad \text{for } i, j = 1, 2, \ldots, R, \, i \neq j$$

Let us devise a suitable training procedure for such an R-category classifier. To begin, we need to define the augmented weight vector $\mathbf{w}_q$ as

$$\mathbf{w}_q \overset{\Delta}{=} \begin{bmatrix} w_{q1} & w_{q2} & \cdots & w_{q,n+1} \end{bmatrix}^t$$

Assume that an augmented pattern $\mathbf{y}$ of class i is presented to the maximum selector-based classifier as in Figure 3.7. The R decision functions $\mathbf{w}_1^t\mathbf{y}$, $\mathbf{w}_2^t\mathbf{y}$, ..., $\mathbf{w}_R^t\mathbf{y}$ are evaluated. If $\mathbf{w}_i^t\mathbf{y}$ is larger than any of the remaining $R - 1$ discriminant functions, no adjustment of weight vectors is needed, since the classification is correct. This indicates that

$$
\begin{aligned}
\mathbf{w}_1' &= \mathbf{w}_1 \\
\mathbf{w}_2' &= \mathbf{w}_2 \\
&\vdots \\
\mathbf{w}_R' &= \mathbf{w}_R
\end{aligned}
\tag{3.54a}
$$

The prime is again used to denote the weights after correction. If, however, for some m value we have $\mathbf{w}_i^t\mathbf{y} \leq \mathbf{w}_m^t\mathbf{y}$, then the updated weight vectors become

$$
\begin{aligned}
\mathbf{w}_i' &= \mathbf{w}_i + c\mathbf{y} \\
\mathbf{w}_m' &= \mathbf{w}_m - c\mathbf{y} \\
\mathbf{w}_k' &= \mathbf{w}_k, \quad \text{for } k = 1, 2, \ldots, R, \quad k \neq i, m
\end{aligned}
\tag{3.54b}
$$

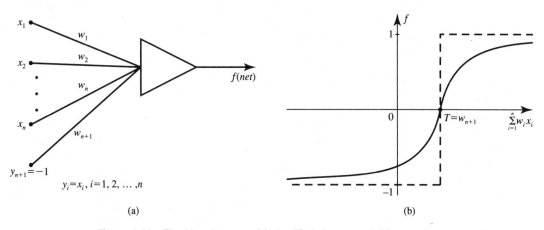

Figure 3.20 The biased neuron: (a) simplified diagram and (b) neuron's response for nonzero threshold.

The matrix formula (3.54b) can be rewritten using the double-subscript notation for the weights used in Figure 3.7 as follows:

$$w'_{ij} = w_{ij} + cy_j \quad \text{for } j = 1, 2, \ldots, n + 1$$
$$w'_{mj} = w_{mj} - cy_j \quad \text{for } j = 1, 2, \ldots, n + 1 \tag{3.54c}$$
$$w'_{kj} = w_{kj} \quad \text{for } k = 1, 2, \ldots, R, \quad k \neq i, m, \; j = 1, 2, \ldots, n + 1$$

It can be seen from Eq. (3.54c) that the weight value of the connection between the i'th output and the j'th component of the input is supplemented with cy_j if the i'th output is too small. The weight value toward the m'th output from the j'th component of the input is reduced by cy_j if the m'th output is excessive.

So far in this chapter we have been dealing with the augmented pattern vector $\mathbf{y}$ with the $(n + 1)$'th component always of fixed value $+1$. It is somewhat instructive to take a different look at this fixed component of the pattern vector to gain better insight into the perceptron's thresholding operation. Figure 3.20(a) shows the perceptron-based dichotomizer in which the augmented pattern component is $y_{n+1} = -1$. Compared with the diagram from Figure 3.16, the weight values w_{n+1} on both figures have to be of opposite values to yield identical decision functions. Since the weights are iteratively chosen during the training process anyway, it is not relevant at all which of the two perceptron diagrams is adopted for the weight training. It becomes thus irrelevant whether y_{n+1} is assumed of value $+1$ or -1.

Let us assume now that the neuron is excited as in Figure 3.20(a). We can now write that

$$net = \mathbf{w}^t \mathbf{x} - w_{n+1} \tag{3.55}$$

Denoting w_{n+1} as the neuron activation threshold, or bias, value equals T

$$T \overset{\Delta}{=} w_{n+1} \tag{3.56}$$

it becomes obvious that the output of the neuron can be expressed as

$$f(net) = \begin{cases} > 0 & \text{for } \mathbf{w}^t\mathbf{x} > T \\ < 0 & \text{for } \mathbf{w}^t\mathbf{x} < T \end{cases} \tag{3.57}$$

The activation function expressed now in the form of $f(\mathbf{w}^t\mathbf{x})$ with $\mathbf{w}^t\mathbf{x}$ as an argument is shown in Figure 3.20(b). The figure shows an activation function of a neuron with the positive threshold value, $T > 0$, and sketched versus nonaugmented activation $\mathbf{w}^t\mathbf{x}$. It is instructive to notice that now the $(n + 1)$'th weight value is equal to the threshold T, and the neuron is excited if the weighted sum of the original, unaugmented pattern exceeds the threshold value T.

Otherwise, the neuron remains inhibited. The nonzero threshold value causes the neuron to behave as a biased device with T being its bias level. It is important to stress again that from the training viewpoint, any value $y_{n+1} = $ const is an appropriate choice. When $y_{n+1} = -1$, however, the w_{n+1} value becomes equal to the actual firing threshold of the neuron with input being the original pattern $\mathbf{x}$. In further considerations we will use $y_{n+1} = -1$ and $w_{n+1} = T$ unless otherwise stated.

So far our discussion has focused on a continuous perceptron performing the dichotomizer-like function. We now show that the continuous perceptron is useful in building any linear classifier. We begin by modifying the minimum distance classifier so that it uses discrete perceptrons and no maximum selector is needed.

Let us now try to eliminate the maximum selector in an R-class linear classifier as in Figure 3.7 and replace it first with R discrete perceptrons. The network generated this way is comprised of R discrete perceptrons as shown in Figure 3.21. The properly trained classifier from Figure 3.7 should respond with $i_o = 1$ when $g_1(\mathbf{x})$ is larger than any of the remaining discriminant functions $g_i(\mathbf{x})$, for $i = 2, 3, \ldots, R$, for all patterns belonging to $\mathcal{X}_1$. Instead of signaling the event by the single-output maximum selector responding with $i_o = 1$, a TLU #1 as in Figure 3.21 may be used. Then, outputs $o_1 = 1$ and $o_2 = o_3 = \ldots = o_R = -1$ should indicate category 1 input.

The adjustment of threshold can be suitably done by altering the value of $w_{1,n+1}$ through adding additional threshold value T_1. Such an adjustment is clearly feasible since $g_1(\mathbf{x})$ exceeds all remaining discriminant values for all $\mathbf{x}$ in $\mathcal{X}_1$. The adjustment is done by changing only the single weight value $w_{1,n+1}$ at the input of the first TLU by T_1. None of the remaining weights is affected during the T_1 setting step with the input of class 1. Applying a similar procedure to the remaining inputs of the maximum selector from Figure 3.7, the classifier using R individual TLU elements as shown in Figure 3.21 can be obtained. For

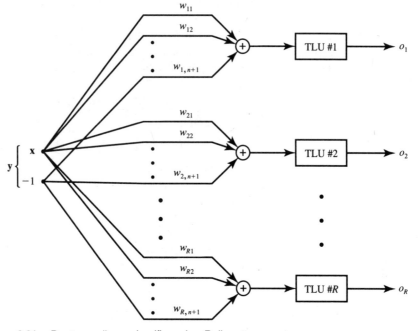

Figure 3.21 *R*-category linear classifier using *R* discrete perceptrons.

this classifier, the k'th TLU response of $+1$ is indicative of class k and all other TLUs respond with -1.

The training procedure outlined in (3.54) uses the maximum selector network which will be covered in Chapter 7 in more detail. For our neural network studies however, architectures with the TLU elements are much more important than those with maximum selectors. As shown in the previous paragraphs, the approach can be used to devise the multicategory perceptron-based classifier by replacing the maximum selector through R threshold logic units. Alternatively, direct supervised training of the network of Figure 3.21 can be performed. The weight adjustment during the k'th step for this network is as follows:

$$\mathbf{w}_i^{k+1} = \mathbf{w}_i^k + \frac{c^k}{2}(d_i^k - o_i^k)\mathbf{y}^k, \quad \text{for } i = 1, 2, \ldots, R \qquad (3.58)$$

where d_i and o_i are the desired and actual responses, respectively, of the i'th discrete perceptron. The formula (3.58) expresses the *R-category discrete perceptron classifier training*. For R-category classifiers with so-called *local representation*, the desired response for the training pattern of the i'th category is

$$d_i = 1, \quad d_j = -1, \quad \text{for } j = 1, 2, \ldots, R, \quad j \neq i \qquad (3.59)$$

For R-category classifiers with so-called *distributed representation*, condition

(3.59) is not required, because as more than a single neuron is allowed to respond +1 in this mode.

We can formulate the R-category discrete perceptron training algorithm as given below. Local representation is assumed, thus indicating that R individual TLU elements are used for this R-category classifier.

■ *Summary of the R-Category Discrete Perceptron Training Algorithm (RDPTA)*

Given are P training pairs

$$\{x_1, d_1, x_2, d_2, \ldots, x_P, d_P\},$$

where x_i is $(n \times 1)$, d_i is $(R \times 1)$, $i = 1, 2, \ldots, P$. Note that augmented input vectors are used:

$$y_i = \begin{bmatrix} x_i \\ -1 \end{bmatrix}, \quad \text{for } i = 1, 2, \ldots, P$$

and k denotes the training step; p denotes the step counter within the training cycle.

Step 1: Same as SDPTA in Section 3.5.

Step 2: Weights are initialized at W at small random values, $W = [w_{ij}]$ is $R \times (n + 1)$.

$$k \leftarrow 1, p \leftarrow 1, E \leftarrow 0$$

Step 3: The training cycle begins here. Input is presented and output computed:

$$y \leftarrow y_p, \quad d \leftarrow d_p$$
$$o_i \leftarrow \text{sgn}(w_i^t y), \quad \text{for } i = 1, 2, \ldots, R$$

where w_i is the i'th row of W

Step 4: Weights are updated:

$$w_i \leftarrow w_i + \frac{1}{2}c(d_i - o_i)y, \quad \text{for } i = 1, 2, \ldots, R$$

Step 5: Cycle error is computed:

$$E \leftarrow \frac{1}{2}(d_i - o_i)^2 + E, \quad \text{for } i = 1, 2, \ldots, R$$

Steps 6, 7: Same as SDPTA in Section 3.5.

The example below demonstrates how a multicategory classifier using a maximum selector is converted so that it uses only discrete perceptrons. Also, the multicategory training procedure for a multi-perceptron classifier is illustrated.

EXAMPLE 3.5 ▬▬▬▬▬▬▬▬▬▬▬▬▬▬▬▬▬

Let us revisit the three-class classifier design problem of Example 3.2. We will modify the classifier from Figure 3.8(d) so that it uses three discrete perceptrons. This will require changing the threshold values of each unit as described earlier in this section.

It is easy to verify from (3.20a) that the discriminant values $g_1(\mathbf{x})$, $g_2(\mathbf{x})$, and $g_3(\mathbf{x})$ for each of the three prototype patterns are as shown below:

	Input		
Discriminant	Class 1 $\begin{bmatrix} 10 & 2 \end{bmatrix}^t$	Class 2 $\begin{bmatrix} 2 & -5 \end{bmatrix}^t$	Class 3 $\begin{bmatrix} -5 & 5 \end{bmatrix}^t$
$g_1(\mathbf{x})$	52	−42	−92
$g_2(\mathbf{x})$	−4.5	14.5	−49.5
$g_3(\mathbf{x})$	−65	−60	25

As required by the definition of the discriminant function, the responses on the diagonal are the largest in each column. Inspection of the discriminant functions (3.20b) yields the thresholds $w_{1,3}$, $w_{2,3}$, and $w_{3,3}$ of values 52, 14.5, and 25, respectively. Let us choose additional threshold $T_1 = -2$. This lowers the weight $w_{1,3}$ from 52 to 50. This will ensure that the TLU #1 only will be responding with +1 for class 1 input. Choosing similarly T_2 and T_3 values of −2 allows for TLU #2 and TLU #3 to respond properly. The resulting three-perceptron classifier is shown in Figure 3.22(a).

Instead of using classifiers which are designed based on the minimum-distance classification for known prototypes and deriving the network with three perceptrons from the form of the discriminant functions, our objective in the following part of the example is to train the network of three perceptrons using expression (3.58). Randomly chosen initial weight vectors are

$$\mathbf{w}_1^1 = \begin{bmatrix} 1 \\ -2 \\ 0 \end{bmatrix}, \quad \mathbf{w}_2^1 = \begin{bmatrix} 0 \\ -1 \\ 2 \end{bmatrix}, \quad \mathbf{w}_3^1 = \begin{bmatrix} 1 \\ 3 \\ -1 \end{bmatrix}$$

Assuming that augmented patterns are presented in the sequence $\mathbf{y}_1$, $\mathbf{y}_2$, $\mathbf{y}_3$, $\mathbf{y}_1$, $\mathbf{y}_2$, ..., and local representation condition (3.59) holds, we obtain (incorrect answers and thus requiring corrections are marked by asterisks)

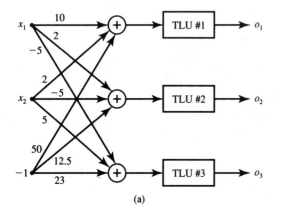

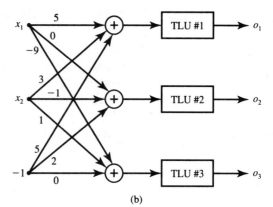

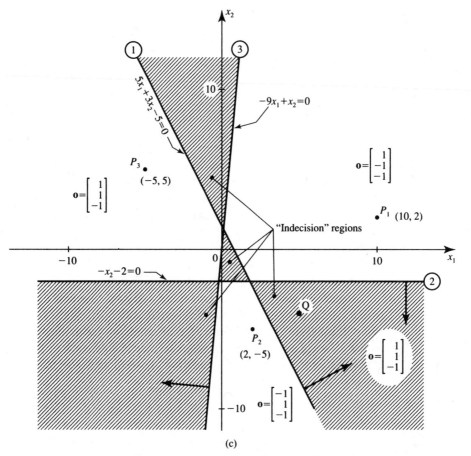

Figure 3.22   Three-class classifier for Example 3.5: (a) three-perceptron classifier from maximum selector, (b) three-perceptron trained classifier, and (c) decision regions for classifier from part (b).

Step 1: y_1 is input:

$$\text{sgn}\left(\begin{bmatrix} 1 & -2 & 0 \end{bmatrix}\begin{bmatrix} 10 \\ 2 \\ -1 \end{bmatrix}\right) = 1$$

$$\text{sgn}\left(\begin{bmatrix} 0 & -1 & 2 \end{bmatrix}\begin{bmatrix} 10 \\ 2 \\ -1 \end{bmatrix}\right) = -1$$

$$\text{sgn}\left(\begin{bmatrix} 1 & 3 & -1 \end{bmatrix}\begin{bmatrix} 10 \\ 2 \\ -1 \end{bmatrix}\right) = 1*$$

Since the only incorrect response is provided by TLU #3, we have for $c = 1$:

$$\mathbf{w}_1^2 = \mathbf{w}_1^1, \quad \mathbf{w}_2^2 = \mathbf{w}_2^1, \quad \mathbf{w}_3^2 = \begin{bmatrix} 1 \\ 3 \\ -1 \end{bmatrix} - \begin{bmatrix} 10 \\ 2 \\ -1 \end{bmatrix} = \begin{bmatrix} -9 \\ 1 \\ 0 \end{bmatrix}$$

Step 2: y_2 is input:

$$\text{sgn}\left(\begin{bmatrix} 1 & -2 & 0 \end{bmatrix}\begin{bmatrix} 2 \\ -5 \\ -1 \end{bmatrix}\right) = 1*$$

$$\text{sgn}\left(\begin{bmatrix} 0 & -1 & 2 \end{bmatrix}\begin{bmatrix} 2 \\ -5 \\ -1 \end{bmatrix}\right) = 1$$

$$\text{sgn}\left(\begin{bmatrix} -9 & 1 & 0 \end{bmatrix}\begin{bmatrix} 2 \\ -5 \\ -1 \end{bmatrix}\right) = -1$$

The weight updates are:

$$\mathbf{w}_1^3 = \begin{bmatrix} 1 \\ 2 \\ 0 \end{bmatrix} - \begin{bmatrix} 2 \\ -5 \\ -1 \end{bmatrix} = \begin{bmatrix} -1 \\ 3 \\ 1 \end{bmatrix}, \quad \mathbf{w}_2^3 = \mathbf{w}_2^2, \quad \mathbf{w}_3^3 = \mathbf{w}_3^2$$

Step 3: y_3 is input:

$$\text{sgn}(\mathbf{w}_1^{3t}\mathbf{y}_3) = 1*$$
$$\text{sgn}(\mathbf{w}_2^{3t}\mathbf{y}_3) = -1$$
$$\text{sgn}(\mathbf{w}_3^{3t}\mathbf{y}_3) = 1$$

The weight updates are:

$$\mathbf{w}_1^4 = \begin{bmatrix} 4 \\ -2 \\ 2 \end{bmatrix}, \quad \mathbf{w}_2^4 = \mathbf{w}_2^3, \quad \mathbf{w}_3^4 = \mathbf{w}_3^3$$

This terminates the first learning cycle and the third step of weight adjustment. The reader may verify easily that the only adjusted weights from now on are those of the first perceptron. The outcome of the subsequent training steps is:

$$\mathbf{w}_1^5 = \mathbf{w}_1^4$$

$$\mathbf{w}_1^6 = \begin{bmatrix} 2 \\ 3 \\ 3 \end{bmatrix}$$

$$\mathbf{w}_1^7 = \begin{bmatrix} 7 \\ -2 \\ 4 \end{bmatrix}$$

$$\mathbf{w}_1^8 = \mathbf{w}_1^7$$

$$\mathbf{w}_1^9 = \begin{bmatrix} 5 \\ 3 \\ 5 \end{bmatrix}$$

This outcome terminates the training procedure since none of the last three pattern presentations require the adjustment of weights. The three-perceptron network obtained as a result of the training is shown in Figure 3.22(b). It performs the following classification:

$$o_1 = \text{sgn}\,(5x_1 + 3x_2 - 5)$$
$$o_2 = \text{sgn}\,(-x_2 - 2)$$
$$o_3 = \text{sgn}\,(-9x_1 + x_2)$$

The resulting decision surfaces are shown in Figure 3.22(c). We may notice that the three-perceptron classifier produces, in fact, triple dichotomization of the plane x_1, x_2. Three decision surfaces produced, which are lines in this case, are

$$5x_1 + 3x_2 - 5 = 0$$
$$-x_2 - 2 = 0$$
$$-9x_1 + x_2 = 0$$

The lines are shown in Figure 3.22(c) along with their corresponding normal vectors directed toward their positive sides. Note that in contrast to the minimum-distance classifier, this method has produced several indecision regions. Indecision regions are regions where no class membership of an input pattern can be uniquely determined based on the response of the classifier. Patterns in shaded areas are not assigned any reasonable classification. One of such patterns may be Q, arbitrarily selected as an example input. The reader can easily verify that the classifier's output for input Q is $\mathbf{o} = \begin{bmatrix} 1 & 1 & -1 \end{bmatrix}^t$. It thus indicates an indecisive response. However, no patterns such as Q have been used for training in the example.   ■

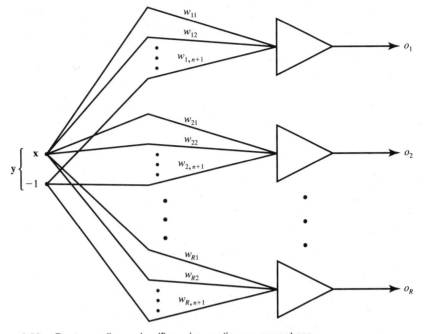

Figure 3.23 *R*-category linear classifier using continuous perceptrons.

The gradient descent training rule derived for $R = 2$ is also applicable to the single-layer continuous perceptron network as shown in Figure 3.23. The figure displays the R class perceptron classifier derived from the TLU-based classifier in Figure 3.21. We can now produce the generalized gradient descent training rule for a single-layer network of any size. To do this, we combine training rule (3.53) with (3.58) as follows:

$$\mathbf{w}_i^{k+1} = \mathbf{w}_i^k + \frac{1}{2}\eta(d_i^k - o_i^k)(1 - o_i^{k2})\mathbf{y}^k \quad \text{for } i = 1, 2, \ldots, R \qquad (3.60)$$

The training rule of Eq. (3.60) is equivalent to individual weight adjustment

$$w_{ij}^{k+1} = w_{ij}^k + \frac{1}{2}\eta(d_i^k - o_i^k)(1 - o_i^{k2})y_j^k$$
$$\text{for } j = 1, 2, \ldots, n + 1, \quad \text{and} \quad i = 1, 2, \ldots, R \qquad (3.61)$$

Expressions (3.60) and (3.61) exemplify the delta training rule for a bipolar continuous activation function as in (2.3a). Since the formula is of paramount importance for the multilayer perceptron network training, it will be covered in the next chapter in more detail. At this point we will only mention that the delta training rule can be used both for networks with single-layer and for multilayer networks, provided that continuous perceptrons are used.

Let us finish with the general diagram of a supervised learning system as shown in Figure 3.24. The discussed training mode can be represented in block

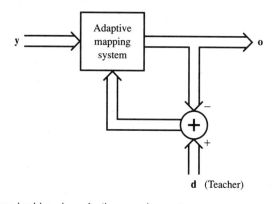

Figure 3.24   Supervised learning adaptive mapping system.

diagram form as illustrated. Both TLU-based and continuous perceptron classifiers discussed in this chapter fall into the diagram of Figure 3.24. The single recall step of the system maps the set in the input space y onto sets in the output space o. The error function $E(\mathbf{d}, \mathbf{o})$ is being used as a criterion to accomplish the supervised learning. Although the definition of error function E is not limited to any particular form, it is widely accepted that is should be dependent on the difference vector $\mathbf{d} - \mathbf{o}$. The error function has been used to modify the internal parameters (called weights) of the adaptive mapping system.

3.8   CONCLUDING REMARKS

The exposition in this chapter has been organized around the assumptions of traditional pattern recognition principles. Although the coverage does not fully take advantage of the potential that is manifested by more complex neural network architectures, it provides a good overall base for the discussion of basic neural network concepts. A list of such concepts includes classification, trainable classifiers, design of dichotomizers and of R category classifiers, linear separability of patterns, perceptron training theorem, negative gradient descent-based training, and others.

In this chapter we have reviewed basic concepts of deterministic pattern classification. Trainable classifiers have been discussed that use gradient descent minimization of the error between the desired and actual response. The gradient descent-based supervised training rules for single-layer neural classifiers have been derived. Both discrete and continuous perceptron single-layer neural classifiers have been discussed and have been designed based on the weight space considerations. The training procedures have been illustrated using the geometrical visualization in the weight space. It has also been shown that replacing the sgn $(\cdot)$ function of the TLU element in a discrete perceptron with the continuous activation function modifies the learning by the factor $f'(net)$.

Material covered in this chapter has been largely based on Nilsson (1965) and other sources, such as Tou and Gonzalez (1974), Sklansky and Wassel (1981), and Young and Calvert (1974). The chapter covers the results of early efforts in machine learning, and it emphasizes the perceptron model of learning. The mathematical concepts that resulted from development of perceptrons continue to play a central role in most feedforward neural network learning and recall. Intuitive geometric explanations and mathematical foundations presented in this chapter can be viewed as fundamental for multilayer neural network learning.

To bridge the traditional learning concept using discrete perceptrons in single-layer networks with multilayer networks, continuous perceptron network learning has been introduced. By replacing the discontinuous threshold operation with a continuous activation function, it is possible to compute the mapping error gradient in multilayer feedforward networks. The multilayer network training algorithm has opened new areas of solutions and applications. It also opened new questions. They will all be introduced in the following chapter.

PROBLEMS

Please note that problems highlighted with an asterisk (*) are typically computationally intensive and the use of programs is advisable to solve them.

P3.1 Write down equations along with the constraint inequalities for the decision planes subdividing the cube into four decision regions $\mathcal{X}_1, \ldots, \mathcal{X}_4$ as shown in Figure P3.1. The pattern vectors' $\mathbf{x}$ memberships in classes are:

$$i_o = 1 \text{ for } \mathbf{x} = \begin{bmatrix} 1 & 0 & 0 \end{bmatrix}^t, \quad \begin{bmatrix} 1 & 1 & 0 \end{bmatrix}^t$$
$$i_o = 2 \text{ for } \mathbf{x} = \begin{bmatrix} 1 & 0 & 1 \end{bmatrix}^t, \quad \begin{bmatrix} 1 & 1 & 1 \end{bmatrix}^t$$
$$i_o = 3 \text{ for } \mathbf{x} = \begin{bmatrix} 0 & 1 & 0 \end{bmatrix}^t, \quad \begin{bmatrix} 0 & 1 & 1 \end{bmatrix}^t$$
$$i_o = 4 \text{ for } \mathbf{x} = \begin{bmatrix} 0 & 0 & 0 \end{bmatrix}^t, \quad \begin{bmatrix} 0 & 0 & 1 \end{bmatrix}^t$$

Note that the faces, edges, and vertices here belong to the pattern space. Whenever the decision surface intersects the edge of the cube, the intersection point should halve that edge (see Appendix for appropriate form of plane equations).

P3.2 A commonly used method for classification is template matching. Templates in this problem are unipolar binary vectors $\mathbf{v}_0$, $\mathbf{v}_1$, $\mathbf{v}_8$, and $\mathbf{v}_9$ corresponding to the digit bit maps shown in Figure P3.2. These vectors are stored as weights within the network. Both template and input vectors contain 42 rows with a 0 entry for white pixels and a 1 entry for black

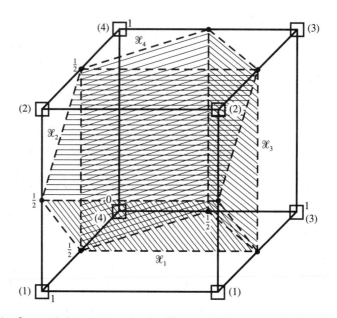

Figure P3.1　Geometric interpretation for classification of cube vertices in three-dimensional space (class numbers in parentheses).

pixels. The measure of matching of an input x to a template $\mathbf{v}$ is the scalar product $\mathbf{v}^t\mathbf{x}$. The product value x_j is proportional to the similarity of input and template.

Since the templates have different numbers of black pixels, each x_j should be multiplied by a coefficient w_j inversely proportional to the number of black pixels in each template to equalize measures of similarity. This simple classification procedure reduces now to the selection of the maximum of the four responses being normalized matching scores $x_j w_j$ and computing i_o denoting the number of the largest input.

Compute and tabulate the normalized matching scores between each pair of the digits 0, 1, 8, 9 shown at the input in Figure P3.2. Inspect the matching scores and for each digit being input find

(a) its nearest neighbor digit with the strongest overlap of the two vectors,

(b) its furthest neighbor digit with the weakest overlap of the two vectors.

Assume now that the input bit maps of digits are randomly distorted. Based on the matching scores calculated determine which is

(c) the most likely misclassification pair among the pairs of digits

(d) the least likely misclassification pair among the pairs of digits.

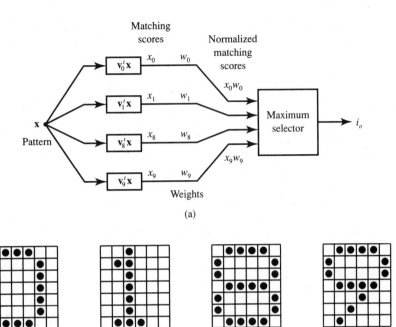

Figure P3.2 Template matching-based digit recognition system for Problem P3.2: (a) classifier and (b) character bit maps used for classification.

P3.3 For the minimum-distance (linear) dichotomizer, the weight and augmented pattern vectors are

$$\mathbf{w} = \begin{bmatrix} 2 \\ -1 \\ 2 \end{bmatrix}, \quad \mathbf{y} = \begin{bmatrix} x_1 \\ x_2 \\ 1 \end{bmatrix}$$

(a) Find the equation of the decision surface in the pattern space.

(b) Find the equation of the decision surface in the augmented pattern space.

(c) Compute the new solution weight vector if the two class prototype points are

$$\mathbf{x}_1 = \begin{bmatrix} 2 & 5 \end{bmatrix}^t \text{ and } \mathbf{x}_2 = \begin{bmatrix} -1 & -3 \end{bmatrix}^t.$$

(d) Sketch the decision surfaces for each case in parts (a), (b), and (c).

P3.4 Compute the solution weight vectors $\mathbf{w}_1$, $\mathbf{w}_2$, $\mathbf{w}_3$, and $\mathbf{w}_4$ needed for the linear machine to classify patterns as indicated in Figure P3.1 and using the decision planes shown. The decision plane equations should be developed in this problem based on inspection of conditions in the pattern space, not on the iterative training procedure.

P3.5 Sketch the example discriminant functions $g_1(\mathbf{x})$ and $g_2(\mathbf{x})$ as in Example 3.1 for the dichotomizer with the following augmented weight and input vectors, respectively:

$$\mathbf{w} = \begin{bmatrix} -1 \\ 2 \\ 1 \end{bmatrix}, \quad \mathbf{y} = \begin{bmatrix} x_1 \\ x_2 \\ 1 \end{bmatrix}$$

knowing that the pattern $\mathbf{y} = \begin{bmatrix} 0 & 0 & 1 \end{bmatrix}^t$ belongs to class 1.

P3.6 A dichotomizer has to be trained to assign $x = 0$ and $x = 2$ to class 1 and 2, respectively. Display the movement of the weight vector on the weight plane starting from the initial weights of $\begin{bmatrix} 1 & 1 \end{bmatrix}^t$ values and follow intermediate steps until weights fall to the solution region

  (a) Use $c = 1$.

  (b) Use $\lambda = 1$, as in (3.31).

  (c) Use $\lambda = 2$, as in (3.31).

  (*Hint:* In the case of $\lambda = 1$, adjusted weights fall on the decision plane. This can also happen for $\lambda \neq 1$ in other training modes. Thus, to achieve the correct classification, the final adjustment must move weights from the decision plane into the decision region.)

P3.7 Prototype points are given as

$$\mathbf{x}_1 = [5 \ 1]^t, \mathbf{x}_2 = [7 \ 3]^t, \mathbf{x}_3 = [3 \ 2]^t, \mathbf{x}_4 = [5 \ 4]^t : \text{ class 1}$$
$$\mathbf{x}_5 = [0 \ 0]^t, \mathbf{x}_6 = [-1 \ -3]^t, \mathbf{x}_7 = [-2 \ 3]^t, \mathbf{x}_8 = [-3 \ 0]^t : \text{ class 2}$$

  (a) Determine if the two classes of patterns are linearly separable.

  (b) Determine the center of gravity for patterns of each class, and find and draw the decision surface in pattern space.

  (c) Using (3.9) or (3.11) design the dichotomizer for the given prototype points and determine how it would recognize the following input patterns of unknown class membership:

$$\mathbf{x} = [4 \ 2]^t, \quad \mathbf{x} = [0 \ 5]^t, \quad \mathbf{x} = \begin{bmatrix} \frac{36}{13} & 0 \end{bmatrix}^t$$

P3.8 Class prototype vectors are known as

$$\mathbf{x}_1 = [-2], \mathbf{x}_2 = \begin{bmatrix} -\frac{2}{3} \end{bmatrix}, \mathbf{x}_3 = [3] : \text{ class 1}$$
$$\mathbf{x}_4 = [1], \mathbf{x}_5 = [2] : \text{ class 2}$$

  (a) Draw patterns in the augmented pattern space.

  (b) Draw separating lines in the augmented weight space for each pattern.

(c) Find the set of weights for the linear dichotomizer, or conclude that this is not a linearly separable classification problem and go to part (d).

(d) Design the dichotomizer using a single discrete perceptron and non-linear discriminant function of quadratic type.

[*Hint:* $g(\mathbf{x})$ needs to be chosen as a quadratic function of $\mathbf{x}$.]

P3.9* Implement the Single Discrete Perceptron Training Algorithm for $c = 1$ for the discrete perceptron dichotomizer, which provides the following classification of six patterns:

$$\mathbf{x} = \begin{bmatrix} 0.8 & 0.5 & 0 \end{bmatrix}^{t}, \begin{bmatrix} 0.9 & 0.7 & 0.3 \end{bmatrix}^{t}, \begin{bmatrix} 1 & 0.8 & 0.5 \end{bmatrix}^{t}: \text{ class 1}$$
$$\mathbf{x} = \begin{bmatrix} 0 & 0.2 & 0.3 \end{bmatrix}^{t}, \begin{bmatrix} 0.2 & 0.1 & 1.3 \end{bmatrix}^{t}, \begin{bmatrix} 0.2 & 0.7 & 0.8 \end{bmatrix}^{t}: \text{ class 2}$$

Perform the training task starting from initial weight vector $\mathbf{w} = \mathbf{0}$ and obtain the solution weight vector.

P3.10* Repeat Problem P3.9 for the user-selectable coefficient λ. Solve the training task for $\lambda = 1$, then for $\lambda = 2$ as in (3.31). Note that the initial weight vector $\mathbf{w} \neq \mathbf{0}$ should be assumed.

P3.11 Derive the continuous perceptron training rule (delta training rule) (3.40) and obtain a formula for $\mathbf{w}^{k+1}$ similar to (3.53). Assume the unipolar activation function of the neuron

$$f(net) = \frac{1}{1 + \exp(-net)}$$

Note that $f'(net)$ should be expressed as function of the neuron's output.

P3.12* Implement the delta training rule as in (3.53) for a single continuous perceptron suitable for the classification task specified in Problem P3.9. Train the network using data from Problem P3.9. Try several different learning constant values and note the speed of weight convergence in each learning simulation.

P3.13 The error function to be minimized has the contour map shown in Figure P3.13 and is given by

$$E(\mathbf{w}) = \frac{1}{2} \left[(w_2 - w_1)^2 + (1 - w_1)^2 \right]$$

(a) Find analytically the gradient vector

$$\nabla E(\mathbf{w}) = \begin{bmatrix} \dfrac{\partial E}{\partial w_1} \\ \dfrac{\partial E}{\partial w_2} \end{bmatrix}$$

(b) Find analytically the weight vector $\mathbf{w}^*$ that minimizes the error function such that $\nabla E(\mathbf{w}) = \mathbf{0}$.

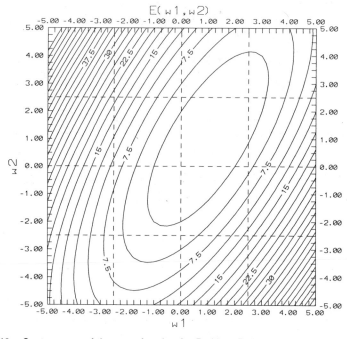

Figure P3.13   Contour map of the error function for Problem P3.13.

(c) Based on part (a) draw the computed gradient vector at three selected weight values. Superimpose the three vectors on Figure P3.13 and check for the consistency of the gradient vectors with the contours' direction and steepness.

P3.14 The multicategory trainable classifier using the maximum selector requires weight adjustment as expressed in (3.54). Implement the sequence of training steps that is needed to classify correctly the three classes as in Example 3.2 and Figure 3.8. Present the patterns in the sequence P_1, P_2, P_3, and start from initial weights $\mathbf{w} = \mathbf{0}$. Assume $c = 1$. The augmented pattern component equals -1.

P3.15* Implement the training procedure (3.54) for a four-class classifier having the prototype points as in Problem P3.1. Use $c = 1$ and obtain weights $\mathbf{w}_1$, $\mathbf{w}_2$, $\mathbf{w}_3$, and $\mathbf{w}_4$, connecting each of the four inputs to the maximum selector as shown in Figure 3.7 for $R = 4$.

Then convert the classifier obtained using the maximum selector with four inputs to the form as in Figure 3.21 so that it uses four discrete perceptrons. Determine the additional threshold values T_1, ..., T_4 if the augmented pattern component is $y_4 = -1$.

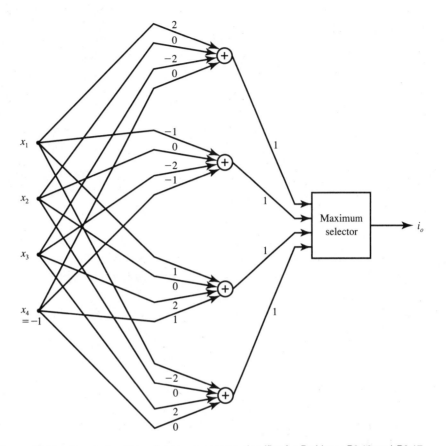

Figure P3.16 A pretrained four-discrete perceptron classifier for Problems P3.16 and P3.17.

P3.16 After the completion of training of the linear machine, its weights have been obtained as in Figure P3.16. The patterns that have been submitted during the supervised training cycle are eight vertices of the three-dimensional cube spanned across $0 \le x_i \le 1$. The augmented pattern component is assumed to be $y_4 = -1$ on the figure. Find the class membership of each of the cube vertices.

P3.17 Convert the classifier shown in Figure P3.16 to the form found in Figure 3.21 and determine the additional threshold values $T_1, \ldots, T_4$ necessary for correct classification.

P3.18 The initial weight vectors for a three-class classifier with discrete bipolar perceptrons performing the classification as in Example 3.5 are selected as $\mathbf{w}_1^1 = \mathbf{w}_2^1 = \mathbf{w}_3^1 = \mathbf{0}$. For patterns presented in the sequence $P_1, P_2, P_3, P_1, P_2, \ldots$, and trained as in (3.58) find

(a) final weights for $c = 1$. Assume $net = 0$ as an incorrect response, thus requiring weight adjustment.

(b) any "indecision" regions of the trained classifier that may be of significance on the x_1, x_2 plane in case of recognition of points that are not identical to the prototypes.

P3.19 Training the weight adjustments as in (3.58) (RDPTA) of a three-class classifier using a three discrete bipolar perceptron network has been completed in three steps with the augmented pattern component of -1 and $c = 1$.

Step 1: presentation of $\mathbf{y}_1$ resulted in adjustment of all weights initialized as

$$\mathbf{w}_1^1 = \mathbf{w}_2^1 = \mathbf{w}_3^1 = \mathbf{0}.$$

Step 2: presentation of $\mathbf{y}_2$ resulted in adjustment of weight $\mathbf{w}_3^2$ only.

Step 3: presentation of $\mathbf{y}_3$ resulted in adjustment of $\mathbf{w}_2^3$ only.

The final weights are

$$\mathbf{w}_1^4 = \begin{bmatrix} 1 \\ 3 \\ -1 \end{bmatrix}, \ \mathbf{w}_2^4 = \begin{bmatrix} 5 \\ -1 \\ -2 \end{bmatrix}, \ \mathbf{w}_3^4 = \begin{bmatrix} 1 \\ -1 \\ 2 \end{bmatrix}$$

Find patterns $\mathbf{x}_1$, $\mathbf{x}_2$, and $\mathbf{x}_3$ used for the training.

P3.20 Assume that the training rule given in (3.38) has been modified to the form

$$\mathbf{w}^{k+1} = \mathbf{w}^k + c_k e^k \frac{\mathbf{y}^k}{\|\mathbf{y}^k\|^2}$$

where c_k is a constant, $0 < c_k < 1$, and the error e^k is defined as

$$e^k = d^k - \mathbf{w}^{kt}\mathbf{y}^k$$

and is equal to the difference between the current desired response d^k and the current value of the neuron's activation net^k [see (2.43) for the learning rule]. Assume that the $(k + 1)$'th step requires weight adaptation. Prove that after the weight correction is made in the k'th step, and again the same input pattern $\mathbf{y}^{k+1} = \mathbf{y}^k$ is presented, the error is reduced $(1 - c_k)$ times. [This is the property of Widrow-Hoff learning rule (Widrow 1962).]

P3.21* Implement the RDPTA training algorithm for the four-category classifier using four bipolar discrete perceptrons and using eight prototype points in three-dimensional input pattern space. Use $c = 1$ and compute weights $\mathbf{w}_1$, $\mathbf{w}_2$, $\mathbf{w}_3$, and $\mathbf{w}_4$ connecting each of the four inputs to the perceptrons 1, 2, 3, and 4, respectively, as a result of the training. Carry out the training using the prototype points as specified in Problem P3.1. Sketch

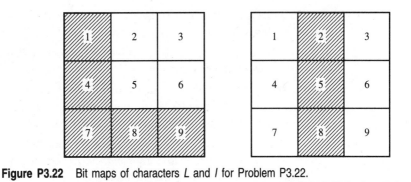

Figure P3.22 Bit maps of characters *L* and *I* for Problem P3.22.

the decision planes produced as a result of the training and verify that the classification is in agreement with specifications.

P3.22[*] Design and train the classifier of printed characters *L* and *I* shown in the bit map form in Figure P3.22. Assign input vector entries 0 and 1 to white and black pixels, respectively. Use a single discrete bipolar perceptron with ten input weights, including the threshold.

P3.23 The three-class classifier from Example 3.5 produces the decision regions as illustrated in Figure 3.22. In addition to three correct classification regions for points used during training, it also produces four "indecision" regions, shaded on the figure. Compute the classifier's response in each of the four "indecision" regions by inspecting the decision surfaces shown in the figure.

REFERENCES

Amit, D. J. 1989. *Modeling Brain Function: The World of Attractor Neural Networks*. Cambridge: Cambridge University Press.

Andrews, H. C. 1972. *Introduction to Mathematical Techniques in Pattern Recognition*. New York: Wiley Interscience.

Nilsson, N. J. 1965. *Learning Machines: Foundations of Trainable Pattern Classifiers*. New York: McGraw Hill Book Co; also republished as *The Mathematical Foundations of Learning Machines*. San Mateo, Calif.: Morgan Kaufmann Publishers.

Rektorys, K. 1969. *Survey of Applicable Mathematics*. Cambridge: The MIT Press.

Rosenblatt, F. 1961. *Principles of Neurodynamics: Perceptrons and the Theory of Brain Mechanisms*. Washington D.C.: Spartan Books.

Sklansky, J. and G. N. Wassel. *Pattern Classifiers and Trainable Machines.* Berlin: Springer-Verlag.

Tou, J. T. and R. C. Gonzalez. 1974. *Pattern Recognition Principles.* Reading, Mass.: Addison-Wesley Publishing Co.

Widrow, B. 1962. "Generalization and Information Storage in Networks of Adaline 'Neurons'," in *Self-Organizing Systems 1962,* ed. M. C. Jovitz, G. T. Jacobi, G. Goldstein. Washington, D.C.: Spartan Books, 435–461.

Wittner, B. S. and S. Denker. 1988. "Strategies for Teaching Layered Networks Classification Tasks," in *Neural Information Processing Systems,* ed. D. L. Anderson. New York: American Institute of Physics, 850–857.

Young, T. Y. and T. W. Calvert. 1974. *Classification, Estimation and Pattern Recognition.* New York: Elsevier Publishing Co.

4

MULTILAYER FEEDFORWARD NETWORKS

*A certain lady claims that, after
tasting a cup of tea with milk, she
can say which is first poured in the
cup—milk or tea. This lady states that
even if she sometimes makes mistakes,
she is more often right than wrong.*

R. FISHER

O ur study thus far has focused on using neural networks for classification with input patterns that are linearly separable. Networks discussed in the previous chapter have been able to acquire experiential knowledge during the supervised training process. Both two- and multicategory classification learning procedures have been formulated for single-layer networks. The experiential knowledge acquisition has been based on the convergent training of single-layer discrete perceptron networks, which can adjust their weights incrementally in order to achieve correct classification of linearly separable sets of patterns.

To this point, we have discussed networks that use a linear combination of inputs with weights being proportionality coefficients. Such networks work with the argument of the nonlinear element simply computed as a scalar product of the weight and input vectors. We may call networks of this type *linear* keeping in mind, however, that the nonlinear operation $f(net)$ is still performed by the decision element on the argument *net* at every computing node.

For training patterns that are linearly separable, the linear neural network introduced in previous chapters must be modified if it is to perform the correct classification. The modification could involve either a departure from the concept of the linear discriminant function or a major change in network architecture. Typical nonlinear discriminant functions are chosen to be quadratic or piecewise linear. The piecewise linear discriminant functions can be implemented by a single-layer linear network employing perceptrons (Nilsson 1965). Our chosen architecture, however, will be that of the multilayer network. Each layer of a multilayer network is composed of a linear network, i.e., it is based on the original concept of the linear discriminant function. As discussed in Section 2.2, multilayer networks are of the feedforward type and are functionally similar to the networks covered in Chapter 3.

Although multilayer learning machines have been known of for more than a quarter of a century, the lack of appropriate training algorithms has prevented their successful applications for practical tasks. Recent developments in the supervised training algorithms of multilayer networks with each layer employing the linear discriminant function have led to their widespread and successful present use. Multilayer networks are often called *layered networks*. They can implement arbitrary complex input/output mappings or decision surfaces separating pattern classes.

The most important attribute of a multilayer feedforward network is that it can learn a mapping of any complexity. The network learning is based on repeated presentations of the training samples, as has been the case for single-layer networks. The trained network often produces surprising results and generalizations in applications where explicit derivation of mappings and discovery of relationships is almost impossible.

In addition to the classification tasks studied in Chapters 3 and 4 to gain insight into the single- and multilayer neural networks, many other tasks can be performed by such networks. Examples include function approximation, handwritten character recognition, speech recognition, dynamical plant control, robot kinematics and trajectory generation, expert systems, and many other applications. We postpone the discussion of applications until Chapter 8 and focus on principles and training methods for layered networks.

Multilayer feedforward network theory and applications have been dominating in the neural network literature for several years now. Researchers have looked for the properties of layered networks and their training methods. Industrial entrepreneurs found a wealth of successful applications, others developed accelerator boards to speed up network simulations on personal computers, and graduate students began to write and sell inexpensive training software. Layered networks seem to be the most widespread neural network architecture at present.

To understand the nature of mapping performed by multilayer feedforward networks and the training of such networks, we must return to the fundamentals. In this chapter we will study trainable layered neural networks employing the input pattern mapping principles. In the case of layered network training, we will see that the mapping error can be propagated into hidden layers so that the output error information passes backward. This mechanism of backward error transmission is used to modify the synaptic weights of internal and input layers. The delta learning rule and its generalization are used throughout the chapter for supervised training of multilayer continuous perceptron networks.

4.1

LINEARLY NONSEPARABLE PATTERN CLASSIFICATION

Expressions (3.32) formulated the condition for linear separability of patterns. This condition can now be briefly restated for the case of linearly nonseparable dichotomization. Assume the two training sets $\mathcal{Y}_1$ and $\mathcal{Y}_2$ of augmented patterns are available for training. If no weight vector $\mathbf{w}$ exists such that

$$\mathbf{y}^t\mathbf{w} > 0 \text{ for each } \mathbf{y} \in \mathcal{Y}_1, \quad \text{and}$$
$$\mathbf{y}^t\mathbf{w} < 0 \text{ for each } \mathbf{y} \in \mathcal{Y}_2$$

then the pattern sets $\mathcal{Y}_1$ and $\mathcal{Y}_2$ are *linearly nonseparable*.

Let us now see how the original *pattern space* can be mapped into the so-called *image space* so that a two-layer network can eventually classify the patterns that are linearly nonseparable in the original pattern space.

Assume initially that the two sets of patterns $\mathcal{X}_1$ and $\mathcal{X}_2$ should be classified into two categories. The example patterns are shown in Figure 4.1(a). Three arbitrary selected partitioning surfaces 1, 2, and 3 have been shown in the pattern space x. The partitioning has been done in such a way that the pattern space now has compartments containing only patterns of a single category. Moreover, the partitioning surfaces are hyperplanes in pattern space E^n. The partitioning shown in Figure 4.1(a) is also nonredundant, i.e., implemented with minimum number of lines. It corresponds to mapping the n-dimensional original pattern space x into the three–dimensional image space o.

Recognizing that each of the decision hyperplanes 1, 2, or 3 is implemented by a single discrete perceptron with suitable weights, the transformation of the pattern space to the image space can be performed by the network as in Figure 4.1(b). As can be seen from the figure, only the first layer of discrete perceptrons responding with o_1, o_2, and o_3 is involved in the discussed space transformation. Let us look at some of the interesting details of the proposed transformation.

The discussion below shows how a set of patterns originally linearly nonseparable in the pattern space can be mapped into the image space where it becomes linearly separable. Realizing that the arrows point toward the positive side of the decision hyperplane in the pattern space, each of the seven compartments from Figure 4.1(a) is mapped into one of the vertices of the $[-1, 1]$

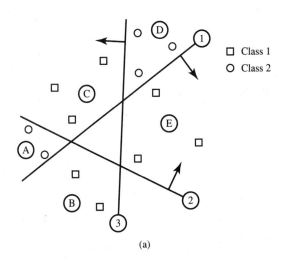

(a)

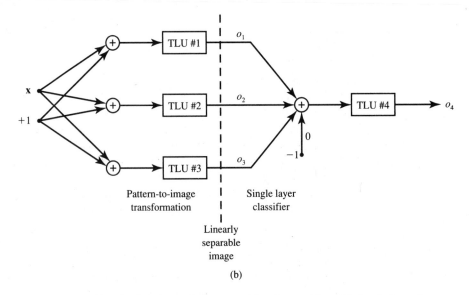

(b)

Figure 4.1a,b Classification of linearly nonseparable patterns: (a) partitioning in the pattern space, (b) layered network implementing the classification from part (a).

cube. The result of the mapping for the patterns from the figure is depicted in Figure 4.1(c) showing the cube in image space o_1, o_2, and o_3 with corresponding compartment labels at corners.

The patterns of class 1 from the original compartments B, C, and E are mapped into vertices $(1, -1, 1)$, $(-1, 1, 1)$, and $(1, 1, -1)$, respectively. In turn,

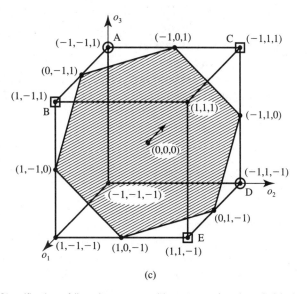

(c)

Figure 4.1c Classification of linearly nonseparable patterns *(continued):* (c) classification in the image space by the output perceptron from part (b).

patterns of class 2 from compartments A and D are mapped into vertices $(-1, -1, 1)$ and $(-1, 1, -1)$, respectively. This shows that in the image space o, the patterns of class 1 and 2 are easily separable by a plane arbitrarily selected, such as the one shown in Figure 4.1(c) having the equation $o_1 + o_2 + o_3 = 0$. The single discrete perceptron in the output layer with the inputs o_1, o_2, and o_3, zero bias, and the output o_4 is now able to provide the correct final mapping of patterns into classes as follows:

$$o_4 = \begin{cases} \text{sgn}\,(o_1 + o_2 + o_3) > 0: & \text{class 1} \\ \text{sgn}\,(o_1 + o_2 + o_3) < 0: & \text{class 2} \end{cases}$$

From the discussion above, we see that the procedure of training, in the case of the layered network, has to produce linearly separable images in the image space. If the pattern parameters and desired responses were completely known, the weight calculation of the two-layer linear machine could be accomplished, as just described, without an experiential knowledge acquisition. In another approach, a single-layer-only machine with the piecewise linear discriminant functions can be employed. Such a classifier with a nonlinear discriminant function would be able to produce appropriate partitioning of the input space and to classify patterns that are linearly nonseparable.

Although both these approaches are feasible, they possess a rather significant disadvantage. Since we favor acquiring experiential knowledge by the layered learning network over the calculation of weights from pattern parameters, we should adopt and use its stepwise supervised learning algorithms. We will also favor employing linear discriminant functions instead of piecewise, quadratic, or any other type of nonlinear function. This preference is based on the premise that the continuous perceptron with *net* in the form of a scalar product is trainable and it offers both mapping and representation advantages. However, no efficient and systematic learning algorithms were known for layered linear machines employing perceptrons until recently (Werbos 1974; McClelland and Rumelhart 1986).

EXAMPLE 4.1 ■

In this example we design a simple layered classifier that is able to classify four linearly nonseparable patterns. The discussion will emphasize geometrical considerations in order to visualize the input-to-image-to-output space mapping during the learning cycle. The classifier is required to implement the XOR function as defined in (3.21) for two variables. The decision function to be implemented by the classifier is:

x_1	x_2	Output
0	0	1
0	1	-1
1	0	-1
1	1	1

The patterns, along with the proposed pattern space partitioning implemented by the first layer consisting of two bipolar discrete perceptrons, are shown in Figure 4.2(a). The arbitrary selected partitioning shown is provided by the two decision lines having equations

$$-2x_1 + x_2 - \frac{1}{2} = 0$$
$$x_1 - x_2 - \frac{1}{2} = 0 \tag{4.1a}$$

For the lines shown, the corresponding unit normal vectors pointing toward the positive side of each line are equal to

$$\mathbf{r}_1 = \frac{1}{\sqrt{5}} \begin{bmatrix} -2 \\ 1 \end{bmatrix}, \quad \mathbf{r}_2 = \frac{1}{\sqrt{2}} \begin{bmatrix} 1 \\ -1 \end{bmatrix} \tag{4.1b}$$

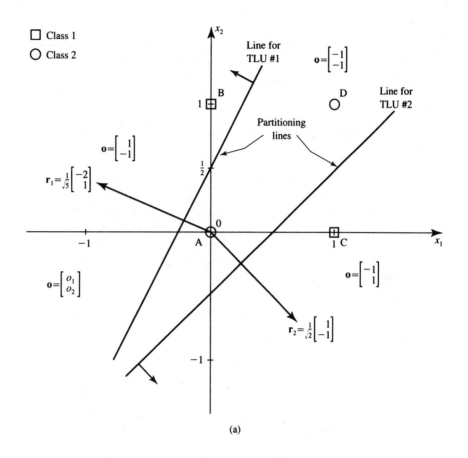

(a)

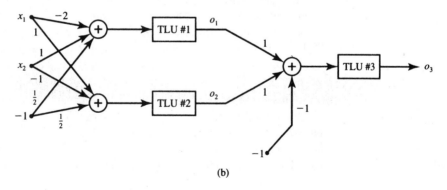

(b)

Figure 4.2 Figure for Example 4.1: (a) pattern to image space transformation and (b) classifier diagram.

Figure 4.2(a) shows that the three compartments produced in the x_1, x_2 plane are mapped through the two first-layer discrete perceptrons with TLU #1 and TLU #2 shown in Figure 4.2(b). The mapping of patterns into the image space is:

$$o_1 = \text{sgn}\left(-2x_1 + x_2 - \frac{1}{2}\right)$$

$$o_2 = \text{sgn}\left(x_1 - x_2 - \frac{1}{2}\right)$$

(4.2a)

The performed mapping is explained in more detail in Figure 4.3. Figure 4.3(a) provides the mapping and classification summary table. As before, the first layer provides an appropriate mapping of patterns into images in the image space. The second layer implements the classification of the images rather than of the original patterns. Note that both input patterns A and D collapse in the image space into a single image $(-1, -1)$. The image space with images of original patterns is shown in Figure 4.3(b). An arbitrary decision line providing the desired classification and separating A,D and B,C in the image space has been selected as

$$o_1 + o_2 + 1 = 0$$

(4.2b)

The TLU #3 implements the decision o_3 as

$$o_3 = \text{sgn}(o_1 + o_2 + 1)$$

(4.2c)

The complete diagram of the classifier is shown in Figure 4.2(b). The output perceptron has weights $w_1 = 1$, $w_2 = 1$, and $w_3 = -1$ to satisfy Eq. (4.2c). Figure 4.4 illustrates the joint mapping between the pattern and output space. Discrete perceptron mapping of plane x_1, x_2 into o_3 is shown in Figure 4.4(a). Figure 4.4(b) presents the contour map $o_3(x_1, x_2)$ for continuous bipolar perceptrons with $\lambda = 6$ used rather than discrete perceptrons. The weight values for the mapping depicted are identical to those in Figure 4.2(b), only the sgn$(\cdot)$ functions have been replaced with functions defined as in (2.3a).

This example provides insight into the parametric design of a layered classifier for linearly nonseparable patterns. The design has used arbitrary but meaningful mapping of inputs into their images and then into outputs, and decision lines suitable for classification of patterns with known parameters have been produced by inspection. The example, however, has not yet involved an experiential training approach needed to design neural network classifiers. ■

Before we derive a formal training algorithm for layered perceptron networks, one additional aspect is worth highlighting. The layered networks develop

Symbol	Pattern Space		Image Space		TLU #3 Input	Output Space	Class Number
	x_1	x_2	o_1	o_2	$o_1 + o_2 + 1$	o_3	
A	0	0	−1	−1	−	−1	2
B	0	1	1	−1	+	+1	1
C	1	0	−1	1	+	+1	1
D	1	1	−1	−1	−	−1	2

(a)

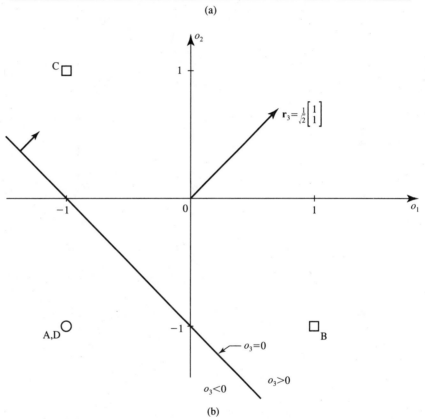

(b)

Figure 4.3 Mapping performed by the output perceptron: (a) classification summary table and (b) decision line.

significant, if not powerful, self-organization and mapping properties during train-ing. The self-organization and mapping do not have to be engineered in advance. Instead, the acquisition of knowledge takes place gradually during the training phase by inspection of mapping examples.

Figure 4.5(a) illustrates the specific case of classification of more involved planar patterns. Both shaded disjoint areas A and B on the figure belong to

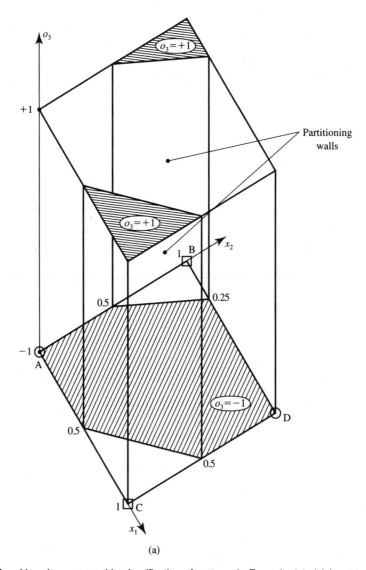

Figure 4.4a　Linearly nonseparable classification of patterns in Example 4.1: (a) input to output mapping using discrete perceptrons.

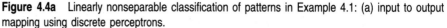

the category 1, and the rest of the pattern space of the plane belongs to the category 2. The classification of the input patterns, or mapping of the input space to classes, can be provided by the network shown in Figure 4.5(b). If the weighted sum of the nonaugmented patterns exceeds the threshold value T, the TLU element responds with $+1$, otherwise with -1.

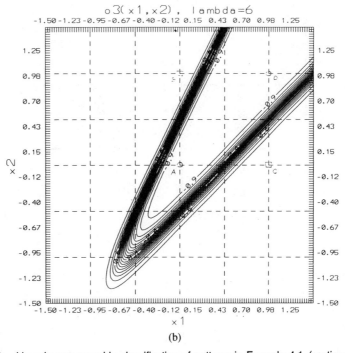

Figure 4.4b Linearly nonseparable classification of patterns in Example 4.1 *(continued):*
(b) input to output mapping using continuous perceptrons ($\lambda = 6$).

It is easy to verify that the input layer provides the following mapping: units #1 and #2 select the vertical strip $a < x_1 < b$, and units #3 and #4 select the strip $c < x_1 < d$. Units #5 with #6 select the horizontal strip $e < x_2 < f$. The output layer unit has the threshold value of 3.5. It responds with $+1$ signifying membership in class 1 when either its weighted input activations from units 1 and 2 at the summing node are both 1, or its weighted input activations from units 3 and 4 are both 1, and, at the same time, its weighted input activations from units 5 and 6 are also both 1. The summed excitatory input value to TLU #7 is thus of value 4 in the case of inputs in either area A or B, which results in a TLU #7 output of $+1$, thus signifying class 1.

The layered networks consisting of discrete perceptrons described in this section are also called "committee" networks (Nilsson 1965). The term committee is used because it takes a number of votes of the first layer to determine the input pattern classification. The inputs in the pattern space are first mapped into the images consisting of vertices of the cube $[-1, 1]$. Up to 2^n images, each image being a vertex of the cube, are available as binary images of n-tuple input vectors. Then, the image space mapping is investigated by the output perceptrons as to its separability and as to the mapped vectors class membership.

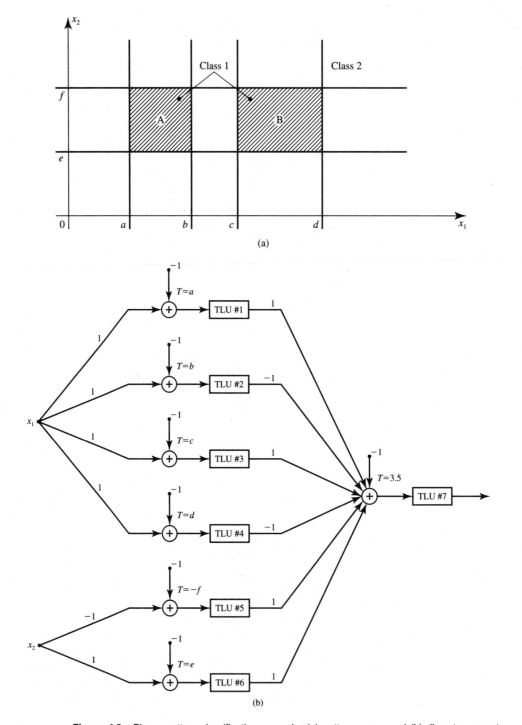

(a)

(b)

Figure 4.5 Planar pattern classification example: (a) pattern space and (b) discrete perceptron classifier network.

4.2

DELTA LEARNING RULE FOR MULTIPERCEPTRON LAYER

The following discussion is focused on a training algorithm applied to the multilayer feedforward networks. The algorithm is called the *error back-propagation training* algorithm. As mentioned earlier in this chapter, the algorithm has reawakened the scientific and engineering community to the modeling of many quantitative phenomena using neural networks.

The back-propagation training algorithm allows experiential acquisition of input/output mapping knowledge within multilayer networks. Similarly, as in simple cases of the delta learning rule training studied before, input patterns are submitted during the back-propagation training sequentially. If a pattern is submitted and its classification or association is determined to be erroneous, the synaptic weights as well as the thresholds are adjusted so that the current least mean-square classification error is reduced. The input/output mapping, comparison of target and actual values, and adjustment, if needed, continue until all mapping examples from the training set are learned within an acceptable overall error. Usually, mapping error is cumulative and computed over the full training set.

During the association or classification phase, the trained neural network itself operates in a feedforward manner. However, the weight adjustments enforced by the learning rules propagate exactly backward from the output layer through the so-called "hidden layers" toward the input layer. To formulate the learning algorithm, the simple continuous perceptron network involving K neurons will be revisited first. Let us take another look at the network shown in Figure 3.23. It is redrawn again in Figure 4.6 with a slightly different connection form and notation, but both networks are identical.

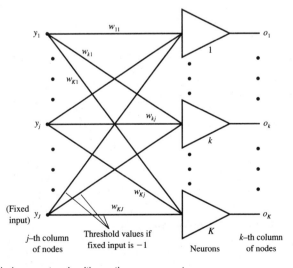

Figure 4.6 Single-layer network with continuous perceptrons.

The input and output values of the network are denoted y_j and o_k, respectively. We thus denote y_j, for $j = 1, 2, \ldots, J$, and o_k, for $k = 1, 2, \ldots, K$, as signal values at the j'th column of nodes, and k'th column of nodes, respectively. As before, the weight w_{kj} connects the output of the j'th neuron with the input to the k'th neuron.

Using the vector notation, the forward pass in the network from Figure 4.6 can be expressed as follows

$$\mathbf{o} = \Gamma[\mathbf{Wy}] \tag{4.3a}$$

where the input and output vector and the weight matrix are, respectively

$$\mathbf{y} = \begin{bmatrix} y_1 \\ y_2 \\ \vdots \\ y_J \end{bmatrix}, \quad \mathbf{o} = \begin{bmatrix} o_1 \\ o_2 \\ \vdots \\ o_K \end{bmatrix}$$

$$\mathbf{W} = \begin{bmatrix} w_{11} & w_{12} & \cdots & w_{1J} \\ w_{21} & w_{22} & \cdots & w_{2J} \\ \vdots & \vdots & \cdots & \vdots \\ w_{K1} & w_{K2} & \cdots & w_{KJ} \end{bmatrix}$$

and the nonlinear diagonal operator $\Gamma[\cdot]$ is

$$\Gamma[\cdot] = \begin{bmatrix} f(\cdot) & 0 & \cdots & 0 \\ 0 & f(\cdot) & \cdots & 0 \\ \vdots & \vdots & \cdots & \vdots \\ 0 & 0 & \cdots & f(\cdot) \end{bmatrix}$$

The desired (target) output vector is

$$\mathbf{d} \triangleq \begin{bmatrix} d_1 \\ d_2 \\ \vdots \\ d_K \end{bmatrix}$$

Observe that the activation vector $\mathbf{net}_k$ of the layer k is contained in the brackets in relationship (4.3a) and it can be expressed as

$$\mathbf{net}_k = \mathbf{Wy} \tag{4.3b}$$

The error expression introduced in (2.37) for a single perceptron is now generalized to include all squared errors at the outputs $k = 1, 2, \ldots, K$

$$E_p = \frac{1}{2} \sum_{k=1}^{K} (d_{pk} - o_{pk})^2 = \frac{1}{2} \|\mathbf{d}_p - \mathbf{o}_p\|^2 \tag{4.4}$$

for a specific pattern p, where $p = 1, 2, \ldots, P$. Let us note that the subscript p in (4.4) refers to a specific pattern that is at the input and produces the output error.

At this point, the delta training rule introduced in (2.36), and later intuitively obtained in (3.55), can be formally derived for a multiperceptron layer. Let us assume that the gradient descent search is performed to reduce the error E_p through the adjustment of weights. For simplicity, it is assumed that the threshold values T_k, for $k = 1, 2, \ldots, K$, are adjustable along with the other weights, and no distinction is made between the weights and thresholds during learning. Now the thresholds T_k are learned exactly in the same manner as the remaining weights. This, of course, implies that

$$w_{kJ} = T_k, \quad \text{for } k = 1, 2, \ldots, K$$

and the fixed input is of value

$$y_J = -1$$

during both the training and feedforward recall phases. Requiring the weight adjustment as in (2.39) we compute individual weight adjustment as follows:

$$\Delta w_{kj} = -\eta \frac{\partial E}{\partial w_{kj}} \tag{4.5a}$$

where the error E is defined in (4.4) with subscript p skipped for brevity. For each node in layer k, $k = 1, 2, \ldots, K$, we can write using (4.3b)

$$net_k = \sum_{j=1}^{J} w_{kj} y_j \tag{4.5b}$$

and further, using (4.3a) the neuron's output is

$$o_k = f(net_k)$$

The *error signal term* δ called *delta* produced by the k'th neuron is defined for this layer as follows

$$\delta_{ok} \overset{\Delta}{=} -\frac{\partial E}{\partial (net_k)} \tag{4.6}$$

It is obvious that the gradient component $\partial E / \partial w_{kj}$ depends only on the net_k of a single neuron, since the error at the output of the k'th neuron is contributed to only by the weights w_{kj}, for $j = 1, 2, \ldots, J$, for the fixed k value. Thus, using the chain rule we may write

$$\frac{\partial E}{\partial w_{kj}} = \frac{\partial E}{\partial (net_k)} \cdot \frac{\partial (net_k)}{\partial w_{kj}} \tag{4.7}$$

The second term of the product of Eq. (4.7) is the derivative of the sum of products of weights and patterns $w_{k1} y_1 + w_{k2} y_2 + \cdots + w_{kJ} y_J$ as in (4.5b). Since the values y_j, for $j = 1, 2, \ldots, J$, are constant for a fixed pattern at the input, we obtain

$$\frac{\partial (net_k)}{\partial w_{kj}} = y_j \tag{4.8}$$

Combining (4.6) and (4.8) leads to the following form for (4.7):

$$\frac{\partial E}{\partial w_{kj}} = -\delta_{ok} y_j \tag{4.9}$$

The weight adjustment formula (4.5a) can now be rewritten using the error signal δ_{ok} term as below

$$\Delta w_{kj} = \eta \delta_{ok} y_j, \quad \text{for } k = 1, 2, \ldots, K \text{ and } j = 1, 2, \ldots, J \tag{4.10}$$

Expression (4.10) represents the general formula for *delta training / learning weight adjustments* for a single-layer network. It can be noted that Δw_{kj} in (4.10) does not depend on the form of an activation function. As mentioned in Chapter 2, the delta value needs to be explicitly computed for specifically chosen activation functions. It also follows from (4.10) that the adjustment of weight w_{kj} is proportional to the input activation y_j, and to the error signal value δ_{ok} at the k'th neuron's output.

To adapt the weights, the error signal term delta δ_{ok} introduced in (4.6) needs to be computed for the k'th continuous perceptron. Note that E is a composite function of net_k, therefore it can be expressed for $k = 1, 2, \ldots, K$, as follows:

$$E(net_k) = E\left[o_k(net_k)\right] \tag{4.11}$$

Thus, we have from (4.6)

$$\delta_{ok} = -\frac{\partial E}{\partial o_k} \cdot \frac{\partial o_k}{\partial(net_k)} \tag{4.12}$$

Denoting the second term in (4.12) as a derivative of the activation function

$$f'_k(net_k) \stackrel{\Delta}{=} \frac{\partial o_k}{\partial(net_k)} \tag{4.13a}$$

and noting that

$$\frac{\partial E}{\partial o_k} = -(d_k - o_k) \tag{4.13b}$$

allows rewriting formula (4.12) as follows

$$\delta_{ok} = (d_k - o_k)f_k'(net_k), \quad \text{for } k = 1, 2, \ldots, K \tag{4.14}$$

Equation (4.14) shows that the error signal term δ_{ok} depicts the local error $(d_k - o_k)$ at the output of the k'th neuron scaled by the multiplicative factor $f_k'(net_k)$, which is the slope of the activation function computed at the following activation value

$$net_k = f^{-1}(o_k)$$

The final formula for the weight adjustment of the single-layer network can now be obtained from (4.10) as

$$\Delta w_{kj} = \eta(d_k - o_k)f_k'(net_k)y_j \tag{4.15a}$$

and it is identical to the delta training rule (2.40). The updated weight values become

$$w'_{kj} = w_{kj} + \Delta w_{kj} \quad \text{for } k = 1, 2, \ldots, K, \text{ and } j = 1, 2, \ldots, J \quad (4.15b)$$

Formula (4.15) refers to any form of the nonlinear and differentiable activation function $f(net)$ of the neuron. Let us examine the two commonly used delta training rules for the two selected typical activation functions $f(net)$.

For the unipolar continuous activation function defined in (2.4a), $f'(net)$ can be obtained as

$$f'(net) = \frac{\exp(-net)}{[1 + \exp(-net)]^2} \quad (4.16a)$$

This can be rewritten as

$$f'(net) = \frac{1}{1 + \exp(-net)} \cdot \frac{1 + \exp(-net) - 1}{1 + \exp(-net)} \quad (4.16b)$$

or, if we use (2.4a) again, it can be rearranged to a more useful form involving output values only

$$f'(net) = o(1 - o) \quad (4.16c)$$

Let us also observe that the delta value of (4.14) for this choice of the activation function becomes

$$\delta_{ok} = (d_k - o_k)o_k(1 - o_k) \quad (4.17)$$

The delta value for the bipolar continuous activation function as in (2.3a) can be expressed as

$$\delta_{ok} = \frac{1}{2}(d_k - o_k)(1 - o_k^2) \quad (4.18a)$$

which uses the following identity for $f'(net)$

$$f'(net) = \frac{1}{2}(1 - o^2) \quad (4.18b)$$

Expression (4.18b) was derived in Section 3.6, see formulas (3.48) through (3.51).

Summarizing the discussion above, the updated individual weights under the delta training rule can be expressed for $k = 1, 2, \ldots, K$, and $j = 1, 2, \ldots, J$, as follows

$$w'_{kj} = w_{kj} + \eta(d_k - o_k)o_k(1 - o_k)y_j \quad (4.19a)$$

for

$$o_k = \frac{1}{1 + \exp(-net_k)}$$

and

$$w'_{kj} = w_{kj} + \frac{1}{2}\eta(d_k - o_k)(1 - o_k^2)y_j \quad (4.19b)$$

for

$$o_k = 2 \left(\frac{1}{1 + \exp(-net_k)} - \frac{1}{2} \right)$$

The updated weights under the delta training rule for the single-layer network shown in Figure 4.6 can be succinctly expressed using the vector notation

$$\mathbf{W}' = \mathbf{W} + \eta \boldsymbol{\delta}_o \mathbf{y}^t \tag{4.20}$$

where the error signal vector $\boldsymbol{\delta}_o$ is defined as a column vector consisting of the individual error signal terms:

$$\boldsymbol{\delta}_o \stackrel{\Delta}{=} \begin{bmatrix} \delta_{o1} \\ \delta_{o2} \\ \vdots \\ \delta_{oK} \end{bmatrix}$$

Error signal vector entries δ_{ok} are given by (4.14) in the general case, or by (4.17) or (4.18a) depending on the choice of the activation function. Noticeably, entries δ_{ok} are local error signals dependent only on o_k and d_k of the k'th neuron. It should be noted that the nonaugmented pattern vector in input space is $J - 1$ dimensional. Input values y_j, for $j = 1, 2, \ldots, J - 1$, are not limited, while y_J is fixed at -1.

The training rule for this single-layer neural network does provide a more diversified response than the network of K discrete perceptrons discussed in Chapter 3. The properly trained network also provides a continuous degree of associations that would have been of the binary form if TLUs alone were used. As such, a continuous perceptron network will be able to provide a more diversified set of responses rather than only binary-valued vectors, which are the natural responses at the classifier's output. These novel aspects of a continuous perceptron network will be discussed later along with introductory examples of its application.

The algorithm for multicategory perceptron training is given below.

■   *Summary of the Multicategory Continuous Perceptron Training Algorithm (MCPTA)*

> Given are P training pairs arranged in the training set
>
> $$\{\mathbf{y}_1, \mathbf{d}_1, \mathbf{y}_2, \mathbf{d}_2, \ldots, \mathbf{y}_P, \mathbf{d}_P\}$$
>
> where $\mathbf{y}_i$ is $(J \times 1)$, $\mathbf{d}_i$ is $(K \times 1)$, and $i = 1, 2, \ldots, P$. Note that the J'th component of each $\mathbf{y}_i$ has the value -1 since input vectors have been augmented. Integer q denotes the training step and p denotes the counter within the training cycle.
>
> **Step 1:** $\eta > 0$, $E_{\max} > 0$ chosen.

Step 2: Weights $\mathbf{W}$ are initialized at small random values; $\mathbf{W}$ is $(K \times J)$:

$$q \leftarrow 1, \, p \leftarrow 1, \, E \leftarrow 0.$$

Step 3: Training step starts here. Input is presented and output computed:

$$\mathbf{y} \leftarrow \mathbf{y}_p, \mathbf{d} \leftarrow \mathbf{d}_p$$
$$o_k \leftarrow f(\mathbf{w}_k^t \mathbf{y}), \quad \text{for } k = 1, 2, \ldots, K$$

where $\mathbf{w}_k$ is the k'th row of $\mathbf{W}$ and $f(net)$ is as defined in (2.3a).

Step 4: Weights are updated:

$$\mathbf{w}_k \leftarrow \mathbf{w}_k + \frac{1}{2}\eta(d_k - o_k)(1 - o_k^2)\mathbf{y}, \quad \text{for } k = 1, 2, \ldots, K$$

where $\mathbf{w}_k$ is the k'th row of $\mathbf{W}$ (See Note at end of list.)

Step 5: Cumulative cycle error is computed by adding the present error to E:

$$E \leftarrow \frac{1}{2}(d_k - o_k)^2 + E, \quad \text{for } k = 1, 2, \ldots, K.$$

Step 6: If $p < P$, then $p \leftarrow p + 1$, $q \leftarrow q + 1$, and go to Step 3; otherwise, go to Step 7.

Step 7: The training cycle is completed.
For $E < E_{\max}$ terminate the training session.
Output weights $\mathbf{W}$, q, and E. If $E > E_{\max}$, then $E \leftarrow 0$, $p \leftarrow 1$, and initiate a new training cycle by going to Step 3.

■ **NOTE:** If formula (2.4a) is used in Step 3, then the weights are updated in Step 4 as follows:

$$\mathbf{w}_k \leftarrow \mathbf{w}_k + \eta(d_k - o_k)o_k(1 - o_k)\mathbf{y}, \quad \text{for } k = 1, 2, \ldots, K$$

4.3   GENERALIZED DELTA LEARNING RULE

We now focus on generalizing the delta training rule for feedforward layered neural networks. The architecture of the two-layer network considered below is shown in Figure 4.7. It has, strictly speaking, two layers of processing neurons. If, however, the layers of nodes are counted, then the network can also be labeled as a three-layer network. The i'th column of signals would be understood in such

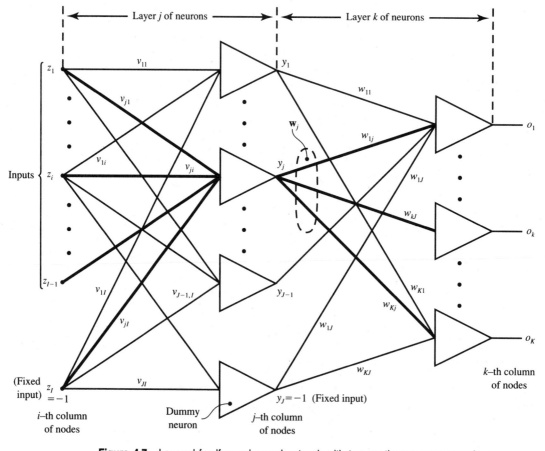

Figure 4.7   Layered feedforward neural network with two continuous perceptron layers.

a case to be an output layer response of a nonexistent (input) layer of neurons. We can thus refer to the architecture in Figure 4.7 as a two-neuron layer network, or three-node layer network.

There is no agreement in technical literature as to which approach is to be used to describe network architectures. In this text we will use the term "layer" in reference to the actual number of existing and processing neuron layers. Therefore, we will not count input terminals as layers. This convention is becoming more frequently adopted and seems more logical since the input nodes play no significant role in processing. Thus, the network of Figure 4.7 is a two-layer network. Let us also note that an N-layer network has $N - 1$ layers of neurons whose outputs are not accessible.

Layers with neurons whose outputs are not directly accessible are called *internal* or *hidden layers*. Thus, all but the output layer are hidden layers. Since the output of layer j of the neurons is not accessible from input and output, the network from Figure 4.7 can be called a single hidden-layer network. In subsequent considerations, we will derive a general expression for the weight increment Δv_{ji} for any layer of neurons that is not an output layer. The reader may notice the change of subscripts. The computed weights lead now from node i toward node j as shown in the figure.

The negative gradient descent formula (4.5a) for the hidden layer now reads

$$\Delta v_{ji} = -\eta \frac{\partial E}{\partial v_{ji}}, \quad \text{for } j = 1, 2, \ldots, J \text{ and } i = 1, 2, \ldots, I \quad (4.21a)$$

and formula (4.7) becomes

$$\frac{\partial E}{\partial v_{ji}} = \frac{\partial E}{\partial(net_j)} \cdot \frac{\partial(net_j)}{\partial v_{ji}} \quad (4.21b)$$

Let us notice that the inputs to the layer are z_i, for $i = 1, 2, \ldots, I$. Based on relation (4.8), the second term in the product (4.21b) is equal to z_i, and we may express the weight adjustment similarly to (4.10) as

$$\Delta v_{ji} = \eta \delta_{yj} z_i \quad (4.21c)$$

where δ_{yj} is the error signal term of the hidden layer having output **y**. This error signal term is produced by the j'th neuron of the hidden layer, where $j = 1, 2, \ldots, J$. The error signal term is equal to

$$\delta_{yj} \stackrel{\Delta}{=} -\frac{\partial E}{\partial(net_j)}, \quad \text{for } j = 1, 2, \ldots, J \quad (4.22)$$

In contrast to the output layer neurons' excitation net_k, which affected the k'th neuron output only, the net_j contributes now to *every* error component in the error sum containing K terms specified in expression (4.4). The error signal term δ_{yj} at the node j can be computed as follows:

$$\delta_{yj} = -\frac{\partial E}{\partial y_j} \cdot \frac{\partial y_j}{\partial(net_j)} \quad (4.23a)$$

where

$$\frac{\partial E}{\partial y_j} = \frac{\partial}{\partial y_j} \left(\frac{1}{2} \sum_{k=1}^{K} \{d_k - f[net_k(\mathbf{y})]\}^2 \right) \quad (4.23b)$$

and, obviously, the second term of (4.23a) is equal to

$$\frac{\partial y_j}{\partial(net_j)} = f_j'(net_j) \quad (4.23c)$$

Routine calculations of (4.23b) result in

$$\frac{\partial E}{\partial y_j} = -\sum_{k=1}^{K} (d_k - o_k) \frac{\partial}{\partial y_j} \{f[net_k(\mathbf{y})]\} \quad (4.24a)$$

Calculation of the derivative in braces of expression (4.24a) yields

$$\frac{\partial E}{\partial y_j} = -\sum_{k=1}^{K} (d_k - o_k) f'(net_k) \frac{\partial(net_k)}{\partial y_j} \quad (4.24b)$$

We can simplify the above expression to the compact form as below by using expression (4.14) for δ_{ok} and (4.5b) for net_k.

$$\frac{\partial E}{\partial y_j} = - \sum_{k=1}^{K} \delta_{ok} w_{kj} \qquad (4.24c)$$

Combining (4.23c) and (4.24c) results in rearranging δ_{yj} expressed in (4.23a) to the form

$$\delta_{yj} = f_j'(net_j) \sum_{k=1}^{K} \delta_{ok} w_{kj}, \quad \text{for } j = 1, 2, \ldots, J \qquad (4.25)$$

The weight adjustment (4.21c) in the hidden layer now becomes

$$\Delta v_{ji} = \eta f_j'(net_j) z_i \sum_{k=1}^{K} \delta_{ok} w_{kj}, \quad \text{for } j = 1, 2, \ldots, J \text{ and} \qquad (4.26a)$$
$$i = 1, 2, \ldots, I$$

where the $f_j'(net_j)$ terms are to be computed either from (4.16d) or from (4.18b) as in case of simple delta rule training. Formula (4.26a) expresses the so-called *generalized delta learning rule*. The adjustment of weights leading to neuron j in the hidden layer is proportional to the weighted sum of all δ values at the adjacent following layer of nodes connecting neuron j with the output. The weights that fan out from node j are themselves the weighting factors. The weights affecting δ_{yj} of the j'th hidden neuron have been highlighted in the output layer in Figure 4.7. All output layer errors $\delta_{ok} w_{kj}$, for $k = 1, 2, \ldots, K$, contribute to the adjustment of highlighted weights v_{ji}, for $i = 1, 2, \ldots, I$, of the hidden layer. The modified weights of the hidden layer can be expressed now as

$$v_{ji}' = v_{ji} + \eta f_j'(net_j) z_i \sum_{k=1}^{K} \delta_{ok} w_{kj}, \quad \text{for } j = 1, 2, \ldots, J \text{ and} \qquad (4.26b)$$
$$i = 1, 2, \ldots, I$$

The hidden layer weight adjustment based on the generalized delta training rule for the network in Figure 4.7 can be succinctly stated in vector notation as

$$\mathbf{V}' = \mathbf{V} + \eta \boldsymbol{\delta}_y \mathbf{z}^t \qquad (4.27)$$

where

$$\mathbf{z} = \begin{bmatrix} z_1 \\ z_2 \\ \vdots \\ z_I \end{bmatrix},$$

$$\mathbf{V} = \begin{bmatrix} v_{11} & v_{12} & \cdots & v_{1I} \\ v_{21} & v_{22} & \cdots & v_{2I} \\ \vdots & \vdots & \cdots & \vdots \\ v_{J1} & v_{J2} & \cdots & v_{JI} \end{bmatrix}$$

and $\boldsymbol{\delta}_y$ is the column vector with entries δ_{yj} given by (4.25).

Defining now the j'th column of matrix $\mathbf{W}$ as $\mathbf{w}_j$, vector $\boldsymbol{\delta}_y$ can be expressed compactly as follows

$$\boldsymbol{\delta}_y = \mathbf{w}_j^t \boldsymbol{\delta}_o \mathbf{f}_y' \qquad (4.28)$$

where $\mathbf{f}_y'$ is the column vector with entries f_{yj}' expressed for each hidden layer neuron $1, 2, \ldots, J$, for unipolar and bipolar activation functions, respectively, as

$$f_{yj}' = y_j(1 - y_j) \qquad (4.29a)$$

$$f_{yj}' = \frac{1}{2}(1 - y_j^2) \qquad (4.29b)$$

Vector $\boldsymbol{\delta}_o$ used in (4.28) is defined as in (4.20).

Comparison of the delta training rule (4.20) for adjusting the output layer weights and the generalized delta training rule (4.27) for adjusting the hidden layer weights indicate that both formulas are fairly uniform. The significant difference is in subscripts referring to the location of weights and input signals, and in the way the error signal vector $\boldsymbol{\delta}$ is computed. The vector $\boldsymbol{\delta}_o$ contains scalar entries (4.17) or (4.18a). Each component of vector $\boldsymbol{\delta}_o$ is simply the difference between the desired and actual output values times the derivative of the activation function. The vector $\boldsymbol{\delta}_y$, however, contains entries that are scalar products $\mathbf{w}_j^t \boldsymbol{\delta}_o f_{yj}'$ expressing the weighted sum of contributing error signals δ_o produced by the following layer. The generalized delta learning rule propagates the error back by one layer, allowing the same process to be repeated for every layer preceding the discussed layer j. In the following section we will formalize the training method for layered neural networks.

4.4   FEEDFORWARD RECALL AND ERROR BACK-PROPAGATION TRAINING

As discussed in the previous section, the network shown in Figure 4.7 needs to be trained in a supervised mode. The training pattern vectors $\mathbf{z}$ should be arranged in pairs with desired response vectors $\mathbf{d}$ provided by the teacher. Let us look at a network feedforward operation, or recall. As a result of this operation the network computes the output vector $\mathbf{o}$.

Feedforward Recall

In general, the layered network is mapping the input vector $\mathbf{z}$ into the output vector $\mathbf{o}$ as follows

$$\mathbf{o} = N\,[\mathbf{z}] \qquad (4.30)$$

where N denotes a composite nonlinear matrix operator. For the two-layer network shown, the mapping $\mathbf{z} \to \mathbf{o}$ as in (4.30) can be represented as a mapping within a mapping, or

$$\mathbf{o} = \Gamma[\mathbf{W}\Gamma[\mathbf{Vz}]], \qquad (4.31a)$$

where the internal mapping is

$$\Gamma[\mathbf{Vz}] = \mathbf{y} \qquad (4.31b)$$

and it relates to the hidden layer mapping $\mathbf{z} \to \mathbf{y}$. Note that the right arrows denote mapping of one space into another. Each of the mappings is performed by a single-layer of the layered network. The operator Γ is a nonlinear diagonal operator with diagonal elements being identical activation functions defined as in (4.3a). The diagonal elements of Γ operate on *net* values produced at inputs of each neuron. It follows from (4.31) that the $f(\cdot)$ arguments here are elements of vectors $\mathbf{net}_j$ and $\mathbf{net}_k$ for the hidden and output layers, respectively.

As can be seen from (4.31b), the assumption of identical and fixed activation functions $f(net)$ leads to the conclusion that the only parameters for mapping $\mathbf{z} \to \mathbf{o}$ so that $\mathbf{o}$ matches $\mathbf{d}$ are weights. Specifically, we have two matrices $\mathbf{V}$ and $\mathbf{W}$ to be adjusted so that the error value proportional to $\|\mathbf{d} - \mathbf{o}\|^2$ is minimized. Thus, we can look at layered neural networks as versatile nonlinear mapping systems with weights serving as parameters (Narendra 1990).

Error Back-propagation Training

Figure 4.8(a) illustrates the flowchart of the error back-propagation training algorithm for a basic two-layer network as in Figure 4.7. The learning begins with the feedforward recall phase (Step 2). After a single pattern vector $\mathbf{z}$ is submitted at the input, the layers' responses $\mathbf{y}$ and $\mathbf{o}$ are computed in this phase. Then, the error signal computation phase (Step 4) follows. Note that the error signal vector must be determined in the output layer first, and then it is propagated toward the network input nodes. The $K \times J$ weights are subsequently adjusted within the matrix $\mathbf{W}$ in Step 5. Finally, $J \times I$ weights are adjusted within the matrix $\mathbf{V}$ in Step 6.

Note that the cumulative cycle error of input to output mapping is computed in Step 3 as a sum over all continuous output errors in the entire training set. The final error value for the entire training cycle is calculated after each completed pass through the training set $\{\mathbf{z}_1, \mathbf{z}_2, \ldots, \mathbf{z}_P\}$. The learning procedure stops when the final error value below the upper bound, $E_{\max}$, is obtained as shown in Step 8.

Figure 4.8(b) depicts the block diagram of the error back-propagation trained network operation and explains both the flow of signal, and the flow of error within the network. The feedforward phase is self-explanatory. The shaded portion of the diagram refers to the feedforward recall. The blank portion of the diagram refers to the training mode of the network. The back-propagation of

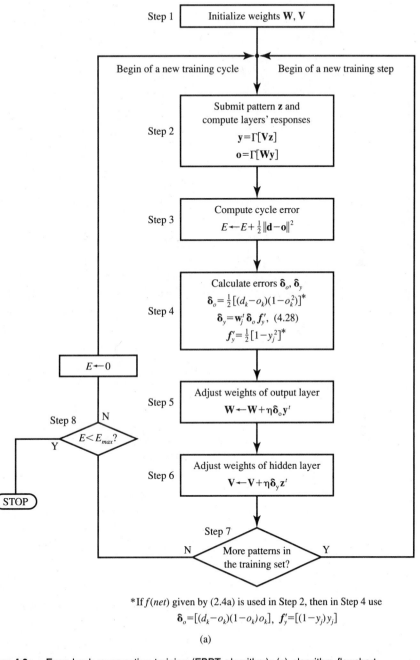

*If $f(net)$ given by (2.4a) is used in Step 2, then in Step 4 use
$$\delta_o=[(d_k-o_k)(1-o_k)o_k], \quad f_y'=[(1-y_j)y_j]$$

(a)

Figure 4.8a Error back-propagation training (EBPT algorithm): (a) algorithm flowchart.

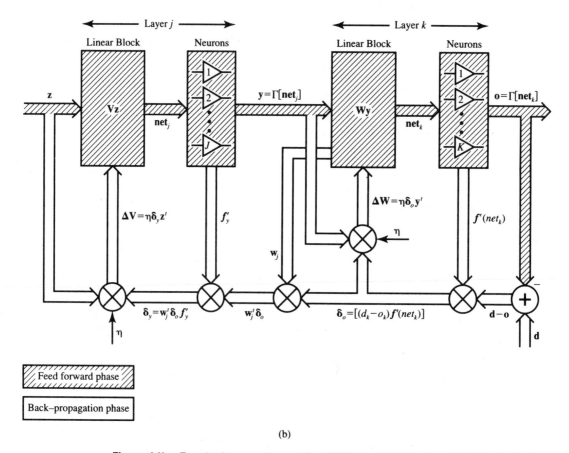

Figure 4.8b Error back-propagation training (EBPT algorithm) *(continued):* (b) block diagram illustrating forward and backward signal flow.

error $\mathbf{d} - \mathbf{o}$ from each output, for $k = 1, 2, \ldots, K$, using the negative gradient descent technique is divided into functional steps such as calculation of the error signal vector $\boldsymbol{\delta}_o$ and calculation of the weight matrix adjustment $\Delta \mathbf{W}$ of the output layer. The diagram also illustrates the calculation of internal error signal vector $\boldsymbol{\delta}_y$ and of the resulting weight adjustment $\Delta \mathbf{V}$ of the input layer.

The algorithm of error back-propagation training is given below.

■ Summary of the Error Back-Propagation Training Algorithm (EBPTA)

Given are P training pairs

$$\{\mathbf{z}_1, \mathbf{d}_1, \mathbf{z}_2, \mathbf{d}_2, \cdots, \mathbf{z}_P, \mathbf{d}_P\},$$

where $\mathbf{z}_i$ is $(I \times 1)$, $\mathbf{d}_i$ is $(K \times 1)$, and $i = 1, 2, \ldots, P$. Note that the I'th component of each $\mathbf{z}_i$ is of value -1 since input vectors have been augmented. Size $J - 1$ of the hidden layer having outputs $\mathbf{y}$ is selected. Note that the J'th component of $\mathbf{y}$ is of value -1, since hidden layer outputs have also been augmented; $\mathbf{y}$ is $(J \times 1)$ and $\mathbf{o}$ is $(K \times 1)$.

Step 1: $\eta > 0$, E_{max} chosen.
Weights $\mathbf{W}$ and $\mathbf{V}$ are initialized at small random values; $\mathbf{W}$ is $(K \times J)$, $\mathbf{V}$ is $(J \times I)$.

$$q \leftarrow 1, p \leftarrow 1, E \leftarrow 0$$

Step 2: Training step starts here (See Note 1 at end of list.)
Input is presented and the layers' outputs computed [$f(net)$ as in (2.3a) is used]:

$$\mathbf{z} \leftarrow \mathbf{z}_p, \mathbf{d} \leftarrow \mathbf{d}_p$$

$$y_j \leftarrow f(\mathbf{v}_j^t \mathbf{z}), \quad \text{for } j = 1, 2, \ldots, J$$

where $\mathbf{v}_j$, a column vector, is the j'th row of $\mathbf{V}$, and

$$o_k \leftarrow f(\mathbf{w}_k^t \mathbf{y}), \quad \text{for } k = 1, 2, \ldots, K$$

where $\mathbf{w}_k$, a column vector, is the k'th row of $\mathbf{W}$.

Step 3: Error value is computed:

$$E \leftarrow \frac{1}{2}(d_k - o_k)^2 + E, \quad \text{for } k = 1, 2, \ldots, K$$

Step 4: Error signal vectors $\boldsymbol{\delta}_o$ and $\boldsymbol{\delta}_y$ of both layers are computed. Vector $\boldsymbol{\delta}_o$ is $(K \times 1)$, $\boldsymbol{\delta}_y$ is $(J \times 1)$. (See Note 2 at end of list.)
The error signal terms of the output layer in this step are

$$\delta_{ok} = \frac{1}{2}(d_k - o_k)(1 - o_k^2), \quad \text{for } k = 1, 2, \ldots, K$$

The error signal terms of the hidden layer in this step are

$$\delta_{yj} = \frac{1}{2}(1 - y_j^2) \sum_{k=1}^{K} \delta_{ok} w_{kj}, \quad \text{for } j = 1, 2, \ldots, J$$

Step 5: Output layer weights are adjusted:

$$w_{kj} \leftarrow w_{kj} + \eta \delta_{ok} y_j, \quad \text{for } k = 1, 2, \ldots, K \text{ and}$$
$$j = 1, 2, \ldots, J$$

Step 6: Hidden layer weights are adjusted:

$$v_{ji} \leftarrow v_{ji} + \eta \delta_{yj} z_i, \quad \text{for } j = 1, 2, \ldots, J \text{ and}$$
$$i = 1, 2, \ldots, I$$

Step 7: If $p < P$ then $p \leftarrow p + 1$, $q \leftarrow q + 1$, and go to Step 2; otherwise, go to Step 8.

Step 8: The training cycle is completed.

For $E < E_{max}$ terminate the training session. Output weights **W**, **V**, q, and E.

If $E > E_{max}$, then $E \leftarrow 0$, $p \leftarrow 1$, and initiate the new training cycle by going to Step 2.

■ **NOTE 1**   For best results, patterns should be chosen at random from the training set (justification follows in Section 4.5).

■ **NOTE 2**   If formula (2.4a) is used in Step 2, then the error signal terms in Step 4 are computed as follows

$$\delta_{ok} = (d_k - o_k)(1 - o_k)o_k, \quad \text{for } k = 1, 2, \ldots, K$$

$$\delta_{yj} = y_j(1 - y_j) \sum_{k=1}^{K} \delta_{ok}w_{kj}, \quad \text{for } j = 1, 2, \ldots, J$$

Several aspects of the error back-propagation training method are noteworthy. The incremental learning of the weight matrix in the output and hidden layers is obtained by the outer product rule as

$$\Delta\mathbf{W} = \eta\boldsymbol{\delta}\mathbf{y}^t$$

where $\boldsymbol{\delta}$ is the error signal vector of a layer and $\mathbf{y}$ is the input signal vector to that layer. Noticeably, the error signal components δ_{ok} at the output layer are obtained as simple scalar products of the output error component $d_k - o_k$ and $f'(net_k)$. In contrast to this mode of error computation, hidden-layer error signal components δ_{yj} are computed with the weight matrix $\mathbf{W}$ seen in the feedforward mode, but now using its columns $\mathbf{w}_j$. As we realize, the feedforward mode involves rows of matrix $\mathbf{W}$ for the computation of the following layer's response.

Another observation can be made regarding linear versus nonlinear operation of the network during training and recall phases. Although the network is nonlinear in the feedforward mode, the error back-propagation is computed using the linearized activation function. The linearization is achieved by extracting the slope $f'(net)$ at each neuron's operating point and using it for back-transmitted error signal scaling.

Example of Error Back-Propagation Training

The following example demonstrates the main features of the error back-propagation training algorithm applied to a simple two-layer network.

EXAMPLE 4.2 ▬▬▬▬▬▬▬▬▬▬▬▬▬▬▬▬

In this example we will perform a single training step for the three-neuron, two-layer network shown in Figure 4.9(a). Let us note that the original network has been augmented in the figure with dummy neurons 1 and 2 to conform to the general network structure as illustrated in Figure 4.7. Obviously, the virtual inputs to the network have to be assigned values o_1 and o_2, which are the responses of the dummy neurons. A single two-component training pattern is assumed to be present at inputs o_1 and o_2. In addition, dummy neuron 0 with a fixed output of -1 has been added to generate the weights w_{30}, w_{40}, and w_{50} corresponding to the thresholds T_3, T_4, and T_5, respectively, for actual neurons 3, 4, and 5. Its only function is to augment the input vectors to each neuron by a fixed bias component.

For the sake of clarity and to avoid identical indices for different weights in this example, the hidden layer neurons in column j have been numbered 3 and 4, and the output neuron has been numbered 5. The learning starts after all weights have been randomly initialized. Inputs o_1 and o_2 are presented and o_3, o_4, and o_5 are computed with $o_0 = -1$. This feedforward recall phase more than likely results in a nonzero error E defined as in (4.4).

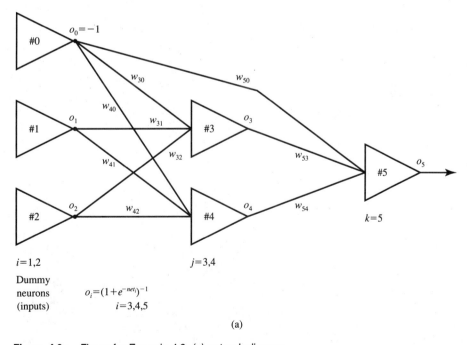

(a)

Figure 4.9a Figure for Example 4.2: (a) network diagram.

The error signal term value δ_5 can now be computed using (4.14), or for the selected activation function using formula (4.17) as follows:

$$\delta_5 = (d_5 - o_5)o_5(1 - o_5)$$

The generalized delta values δ_3 and δ_4 as in (4.25) need to be expressed for hidden layer neurons 3 and 4:

$$\delta_3 = f'_3(net_3) \sum_{k=5}^{5} \delta_k w_{k3}$$

$$\delta_4 = f'_4(net_4) \sum_{k=5}^{5} \delta_k w_{k4}$$

(4.32a)

Using (4.29a) yields the final expressions for δ_3 and δ_4 as

$$\delta_3 = o_3(1 - o_3)\delta_5 w_{53}$$

$$\delta_4 = o_4(1 - o_4)\delta_5 w_{54}$$

(4.32b)

Now the weight vector corrections Δw_{kj} and Δw_{ji} can be computed for the selected η value. Output layer weight adjustments computed from (4.10) are

$$\Delta w_{50} = -\eta \delta_5$$

$$\Delta w_{53} = \eta \delta_5 o_3$$

$$\Delta w_{54} = \eta \delta_5 o_4$$

(4.33a)

The adjustments of hidden-layer weights associated with the neurons 3 and 4 computed from (4.21c) or (4.26a) are, respectively,

$$\Delta w_{30} = -\eta \delta_3$$

$$\Delta w_{31} = \eta \delta_3 o_1$$

$$\Delta w_{32} = \eta \delta_3 o_2$$

(4.33b)

and

$$\Delta w_{40} = -\eta \delta_4$$

$$\Delta w_{41} = \eta \delta_4 o_1$$

$$\Delta w_{42} = \eta \delta_4 o_2$$

(4.33c)

Superposition of the computed weight adjustments (4.33) and of the present weights w_{kj} and w_{ji} results in the updated weight values. This terminates the single supervised learning step based on the single pattern vector from the training set. Subsequently, the next pattern vector is submitted and the training step repeated. The training steps proceed until all patterns in the training set are exhausted. This terminates the complete training cycle understood as the sweep through the sequence of P training steps, where P denotes the number of training patterns in the training set.

The cumulative cycle error is computed for the complete training cycle using expression (4.4). It is then compared with the maximum error allowed.

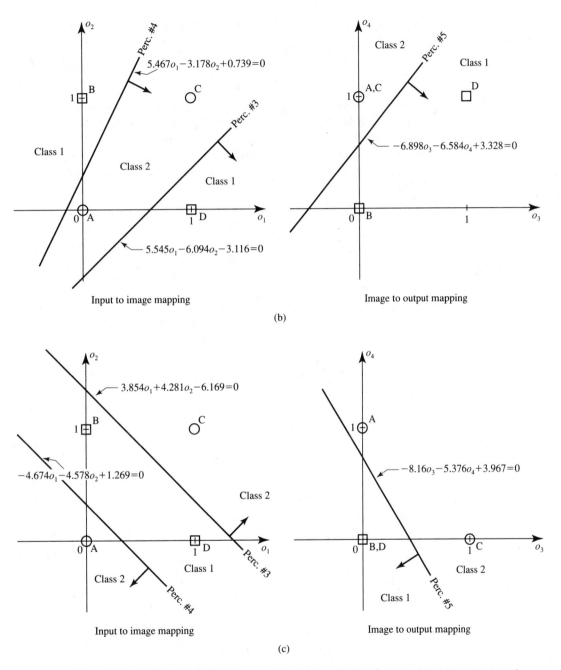

(b)

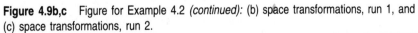

Figure 4.9b,c Figure for Example 4.2 *(continued):* (b) space transformations, run 1, and (c) space transformations, run 2.

The training cycles repeat until the cycle error drops below the specified maximum error value. If the network has failed to learn the training set successfully, the training should be restarted with different initial weights. If this also fails, other remedies need to be taken to meet the training requirements. Such steps are discussed in Section 4.5 in more detail.

The network covered in this example can also be used to demonstrate the classification of linearly nonseparable patterns. Due to its size, it can be used directly to solve the XOR problem for two variables. Network training has been simulated and two sample runs with random initial weight values are summarized below for $\eta = 0.1$. Matrices $\mathbf{W}$ and $\mathbf{V}$ are defined for this network as

$$\mathbf{W} \triangleq \begin{bmatrix} w_{50} & w_{53} & w_{54} \end{bmatrix}$$

$$\mathbf{V} \triangleq \begin{bmatrix} w_{30} & w_{31} & w_{32} \\ w_{40} & w_{41} & w_{42} \end{bmatrix}$$

The resulting weight matrices obtained for run 1 (1244 steps) with random initial weights are:

$$\mathbf{W}_1 = \begin{bmatrix} -3.328 & 6.898 & -6.584 \end{bmatrix}$$

$$\mathbf{V}_1 = \begin{bmatrix} 3.116 & 5.545 & -6.094 \\ -0.739 & 5.467 & -3.178 \end{bmatrix}$$

The resulting weight matrices obtained for run 2 (2128 steps) with another random set of initial weights are:

$$\mathbf{W}_2 = \begin{bmatrix} -3.967 & -8.160 & -5.376 \end{bmatrix}$$

$$\mathbf{V}_2 = \begin{bmatrix} 6.169 & 3.854 & 4.281 \\ -1.269 & -4.674 & -4.578 \end{bmatrix}$$

Since we require that the network from Figure 4.9(a) to function as a classifier with binary outputs, let us preserve all its weights as computed above. Continuous perceptrons used for training, however, need to be replaced with bipolar binary neurons. This will result in a binary-valued response that provides the required class numbers of values 1 or 0 for classes 1 and 2, respectively.

Based on the result obtained, we can analyze the implemented mapping of input-to-image-to-output space. As a result of run 1, perceptrons 3 and 4 implement the following mapping to image space o_1 and o_2, respectively,

$$5.545o_1 - 6.094o_2 - 3.116 = 0$$

$$5.467o_1 - 3.178o_2 + 0.739 = 0$$

The generated decision lines are shown in Figure 4.9(b). The reader can verify that the decision lines are obtained using the rows of computed matrix $\mathbf{V}_1$, and also under the assumption that net_3 and net_4 of zero value determine the respective partitioning lines. In addition, perceptron 5 performs the image-to-output space mapping and the equation of the class decision line is as follows:

$$6.898o_3 - 6.584o_4 + 3.328 = 0$$

The line is also shown in the figure. It can be seen that mapped patterns B,D and A,C are positioned at different sides of the decision line, which is generated by the output perceptron in the image space. This part of the example demonstrates how linearly nonseparable original patterns can be correctly classified by this classifier. Interestingly, these results have been produced as a result of error back-propagation network training.

Inspecting the results of run 2, the reader can easily verify that the decision surfaces generated by perceptrons 3, 4, and 5 are as shown in Figure 4.9(c). Markedly, it can be seen that the results of run 2 are very similar to those obtained in Example 4.1 without training the classifier network. Reviewing the mappings from Figures 4.9(b) and (c), note that they both merge patterns of the same class to the same compartment in the image space. For the decision lines as shown and an activation function with $\lambda = 1$ used for training the network, the output values close to 0 or 1 need to be thresholded to values of 0 or 1 to yield binary classification response. As an alternative, λ can be increased and outputs, in limit, will approach the 0, 1 levels. ■

Training Errors

Every supervised training algorithm covered so far in the text, including the error back-propagation training algorithm, involves the reduction of an error value. For the purpose of weight adjustment in a single training step, the error to be reduced is usually that computed only for a pattern currently applied at the input of the network. For the purpose of assessing the quality and success of the training, however, the joint error must be computed for the entire batch of training patterns. The discussion below addresses the main definitions of errors used for evaluation of neural network training.

Note that the *cumulative error* is computed over the error back-propagation training cycle (Step 3, EBPTA), and it is expressed as a quadratic error

$$E = \frac{1}{2} \sum_{p=1}^{P} \sum_{k=1}^{K} (d_{pk} - o_{pk})^2 \qquad (4.34)$$

This error is a sum of P errors computed for single patterns using formula (4.4). It can be seen that the error of Eq. (4.34) depicts the accuracy of the neural network mapping after a number of training cycles have been implemented. Such definition of error, however, is not very useful for comparison of networks with different numbers of training patterns P and having a different number of output neurons. Networks with the same number of outputs K when trained using large numbers of patterns in the training set will usually produce large cumulative errors (4.34) due to the large number of terms in the sum. For similar reasons, networks with large K trained using the same training set would usually also produce large cumulative errors. Thus, a more adequate error measure can be introduced as in (4.35):

$$E_{\text{rms}} = \frac{1}{PK} \sqrt{\sum_{p=1}^{P} \sum_{k=1}^{K} (d_{pk} - o_{pk})^2} \qquad (4.35)$$

The value E_{rms} has the sense of a *root-mean-square normalized error,* and it seems to be more descriptive than E as in (4.34) when comparing the outcome of the training of different neural networks among each other.

In some applications, the networks' continuous responses are of significance and thus any of the discussed error measures E and E_{rms} bear useful information. The degree of association or the accuracy of mapping can be measured by these continuous error measures. In other applications, however, the neurons' responses are assigned binary values after the thresholding. These applications include classifier networks. For example, all unipolar neurons responding below 0.1 and above 0.9 can be considered as approximating binary responses 0 and 1, respectively.

Assuming that the network is trained as a classifier, usually all the desired output values can be set to zero except for the one corresponding to the class the input pattern is from. That desired output value is set to 1. In such cases, the *decision error,* rather than the continuous response errors, more adequately reflects the accuracy of neural network classifiers. The decision error can be defined as

$$E_d = \frac{N_{\text{err}}}{PK} \qquad (4.36)$$

where N_{err} is the total number of bit errors resulting at K thresholded outputs over the complete training cycle. Note that networks in classification applications may perform as excellent classifiers and exhibit zero decision errors while still yielding substantial E and E_{rms} errors.

Multilayer Feedforward Networks as Universal Approximators

Although classification is a very important form of neural computation, the binary response only of neural networks would seriously limit their mapping potential. Our focus in this section is to study the performance of multilayer feedforward networks as universal approximators. As we discussed early in Section 2.4, the problem of finding an approximation of a multivariable function $h(\mathbf{x})$ can

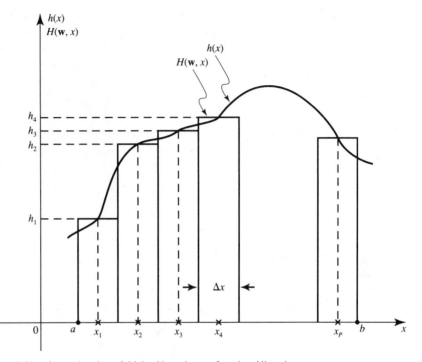

Figure 4.10 Approximation of $h(x)$ with staircase function $H(\mathbf{w}, x)$.

be approached through supervised training of an input-output mapping from a set of examples. The learning proceeds as a sequence of iterative weight adjustments until the solution weight vector $\mathbf{w}^*$ is found that satisfies the minimum distance criterion (2.26).

An example function $h(x)$ to be approximated is illustrated in Figure 4.10. Assume that P samples of the function are known on a set of arguments $\{x_1, x_2, \ldots, x_P\}$. The samples are simply examples of function values in the interval (a, b). It is assumed for simplicity that the example arguments are uniformly distributed between a and b and are Δx apart, i.e.

$$x_{i+1} - x_i = \Delta x = \frac{b-a}{P}, \quad \text{for } i = 1, 2, \ldots, P$$

We note that the interval (a, b) is divided into P equal intervals of length Δx defined as

$$\left(x_i - \frac{\Delta x}{2}, x_i + \frac{\Delta x}{2}\right), \quad \text{for } i = 1, 2, \ldots, P$$

where

$$x_1 - \frac{\Delta x}{2} = a, \quad x_P + \frac{\Delta x}{2} = b$$

The function values $h_i = h(x_i)$ at argument values determine the height of each of the P rectangles depicted on the figure. This way we obtain a staircase approximation $H(\mathbf{w}, x)$ of the continuous-valued function $h(x)$. Let us define a function $\zeta(x)$ such that

$$\zeta(x) = \frac{1}{2}\,\text{sgn}\,x + \frac{1}{2} = \begin{cases} 0 & \text{for } x < 0 \\ \text{undefined} & \text{for } x = 0 \\ 1 & \text{for } x > 0 \end{cases} \tag{4.37}$$

The function $\zeta(x)$ is called the *unit step function*. The staircase approximation can be expressed using the unit step functions as follows

$$H(\mathbf{w}, x) = h_1\left[\zeta\left(x - x_1 + \frac{\Delta x}{2}\right) - \zeta\left(x - x_1 - \frac{\Delta x}{2}\right)\right] + \cdots$$
$$+ h_P\left[\zeta\left(x - x_P + \frac{\Delta x}{2}\right) - \zeta\left(x - x_P - \frac{\Delta x}{2}\right)\right] \tag{4.38a}$$

or, briefly

$$H(\mathbf{w}, x) = \sum_{i=1}^{P} h_i\left[\zeta\left(x - x_i + \frac{\Delta x}{2}\right) - \zeta\left(x - x_i - \frac{\Delta x}{2}\right)\right] \tag{4.38b}$$

We note that each term in brackets in (4.38b) is a unity height window of width Δx centered at x_i as shown by the continuous line in Figure 4.11(a). This window expressed in terms of the sgn ($\cdot$) function using (4.37) can be rewritten as

$$\zeta\left(x - x_i + \frac{\Delta x}{2}\right) - \zeta\left(x - x_i - \frac{\Delta x}{2}\right) = \frac{1}{2}\,\text{sgn}\left(x - x_i + \frac{\Delta x}{2}\right)$$
$$- \frac{1}{2}\,\text{sgn}\left(x - x_i - \frac{\Delta x}{2}\right) \tag{4.39}$$

Figure 4.11(b) illustrates how to implement Equation (4.39) by using two TLU elements with appropriate thresholds and summing their properly weighted responses. It can thus be seen that two binary perceptrons are needed to produce a single window. We may notice that a network with $2P$ individual TLU elements similar to the one shown in Figure 4.11(b) can be used to implement the staircase approximation (4.38). An example of such a network is illustrated in Figure 2.9(a).

Note that the network of Figure 4.11(b) has two constant inputs x_i and -1. Merging them would result in a functionally identical network, which is shown in Figure 4.12(a). Binary response units TLU #1 and TLU #2 are now replaced with the bipolar continuous perceptrons as shown in Figure 4.12(b). As a result, the mapping of input x into output o takes the form of a single bump centered at x_i rather than of the rectangular window. The bump is shown in Figure 4.11(a) by the dashed line. Let us also note that with the increasing steepness factor λ, the dashed line is getting closer to the continuous one, and the bump approaches the rectangular window. In fact, even the increase of λ is not necessary because it can be replaced with scaling the weight up by using the multiplicative factor λ

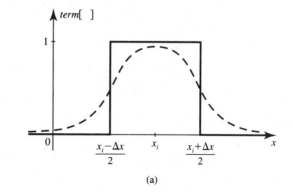

(a)

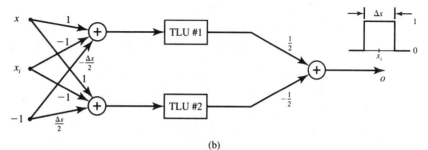

(b)

Figure 4.11 Illustration to staircase function approximation of $h(x)$: (a) elementary window and (b) window implementation using two TLUs.

for the weights shown in Figure 4.12(b). In two or more dimensions, we could add one function producing a bump for each dimension. Figure 2.9(c) provides here an appropriate illustration. We could also combine peaks as in (4.38) for a staircase approximation of a multivariable function $H(\mathbf{w}, \mathbf{x})$. Although the bump approach may not be the best for a particular problem, it is intended only as proof of existence.

The preliminary and rather nonrigorous considerations above indicate that a sufficient number of continuous neurons can implement a finite sum of localized bumps spread over the multidimensional domain of the argument space $\mathbf{x}$. The construction presented indicates that multivariable functions $h(\mathbf{x})$ can be modeled by two-layer networks. Whether or not the approximations are learnable and the approximating weights $\mathbf{w}^*$ can be found by training remains an open question. We also do not know exactly what may be the best network architectures and whether or not the number of $2P$ units in the first layer is adequate or if the number is excessive.

In a more formal approach, networks of the type shown in Figure 4.12 can be used to map R^n into R by using P examples of the function $h(\mathbf{x})$ to be

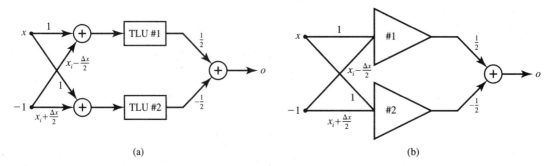

Figure 4.12 Networks implementing the window function of Eq. (4.39): (a) with binary term (4.39) and (b) with continuous neurons [dashed line in Figure 4.11(b)].

approximated by performing the nonlinear mapping with continuous neurons in the first layer as follows

$$\mathbf{y} = \Gamma[\mathbf{V}\mathbf{x}] \tag{4.40a}$$

and by computing the linear combination by the single node of the output layer

$$o = H(\mathbf{x}) = \mathbf{w}^t\mathbf{y} \tag{4.40b}$$

Although the concept of nonlinear mapping (4.40a) followed by linear mapping (4.40b) pervasively demonstrates the approximating potential of neural networks, most theoretical and practical technical reports deal with the second layer also providing the nonlinear mapping (Poggio and Girosi 1990; Funanashi 1989; Hornik, Stinchcombe, and White 1989).

The general network architecture performing the nested nonlinear scheme was shown earlier in Figure 4.7. It consists of a single hidden layer and it implements K mappings, each mapping being the component of $\mathbf{o}_k$

$$\mathbf{o}_k = \Gamma\big[\mathbf{W}\Gamma[\mathbf{V}\mathbf{o}]\big] \tag{4.41}$$

This standard class of neural networks architecture can approximate virtually any multivariable function of interest, provided sufficiently many hidden neurons are available. The studies of Funanashi (1989), Hornik, Stinchcombe, and White (1989) prove that multilayer feedforward networks perform as a class of universal approximators. The results also provide a fundamental basis for establishing the ability of multilayer feedforward networks to learn the connection strengths that achieve the desired accuracy of the approximation. The reader is referred to the specialized literature for more details (Hornik, Stinchcombe, and White 1989; Funanashi 1989; Poggio and Girosi 1990).

Failures in approximation application can, in general, be attributed to inadequate learning. The reasons for failure quoted in the literature are an inadequate (too low or too high) number of hidden neurons, or the lack of a deterministic relationship between the input and target output values used for training. If functions to be approximated are not bounded and $h(\mathbf{x})$ cannot be properly scaled, the use of the linear mapping by the second layer as in (4.40b) may offer the solution. Rather than assuming the ordinary 'signoidal' activation functions, simple identity activation functions of the output neurons can be used in such cases.

The function values that need to be used as desired output values during training of the network from Figure 4.7 with neurons' response bounded must also be bounded. The range of function values is $(-1, 1)$ for bipolar continuous activation functions and $(0, 1)$ for unipolar continuous activation functions. Several practical demonstrations of neural network approximation capability are presented in Chapter 8 in relation to their applications to robotics and control systems. The example below discusses the main features of the function approximation issues.

EXAMPLE 4.3

In this example we will review an application of a three-neuron network for approximation of a two-variable function. The network to be trained has the architecture shown in Figure 4.9(a). Bipolar continuous activation functions are used for the network training. Weight matrices $\mathbf{W}$ and $\mathbf{V}$ are defined as in Example 4.2.

Let us attempt to train the network to compute the length of a planar vector with components o_1 and o_2. This yields the desired value for o_5 as follows:

$$d = \sqrt{o_1^2 + o_2^2} \tag{4.42}$$

Using (4.41) we can write

$$o_5 = \Gamma[\mathbf{W}\Gamma[\mathbf{V}\mathbf{o}]] \tag{4.43}$$

where

$$\mathbf{o} = \begin{bmatrix} -1 & o_1 & o_2 \end{bmatrix}^t$$

The weights w_{kj} and v_{ji} need to be adjusted during training. The input domain for training has been chosen to be the first quadrant of the plane o_1, o_2 with $0 < o_i < 0.7$, for $i = 1, 2$.

In the first experiment only 10 training points have been selected. They have been uniformly spread only in the lower half of the first quadrant. The network has reached an acceptable error level established at 0.01 after 2080 training steps with $\eta = 0.2$. Matrices $\mathbf{W}$ and $\mathbf{V}$ obtained from the simulation are

$$\mathbf{W} = \begin{bmatrix} 0.03 \\ 3.66 \\ 2.73 \end{bmatrix}$$

$$\mathbf{V} = \begin{bmatrix} -1.29 & -3.04 & -1.54 \\ 0.97 & 2.61 & 0.52 \end{bmatrix} \tag{4.44}$$

To check how the network has learned the examples from the training set, the complete surface constructed by the trained network has been generated. The magnitude of the mapping error computed as $|d - o_5|$ is illustrated in Figure 4.13(a). Magnitudes of error associated with each training pattern are also shown on the surface.

The results produced by the network indicate that the mapping of the function has been learned much better within the training domain than outside it. Thus, any generalization provided by the trained network beyond the training domain remains questionable. This is particularly vivid for the left upper corner of the quadrant where the discrepancy between the accurate function value and its approximation reaches 0.45. Also, patterns that are clustered in the training domain are mapped more accurately. Therefore, the recall of the training patterns that are at the borders of the training area does not yield as low an error as recalled patterns, which are located inside it.

Figure 4.13(b) provides more detailed insight into the mapping property of this network. It displays the error $d - o_5$ in a form of the contour map. The map indicates that an ideal approximation contour for $d = o_5$ would be located somewhere between the contours -0.02 and 0.01. Note that the 10 training points are marked as circles on the graph.

The training experiment was then repeated for the same architecture but with 64 training points now densely covering the entire quadrant domain. The network has reached an error level of value 0.02 after 1200 training steps with $\eta = 0.4$. The weights obtained as a result of training are

$$\mathbf{W} = \begin{bmatrix} -3.47 & -1.8 & 2.07 \end{bmatrix}$$

$$\mathbf{V} = \begin{bmatrix} -2.54 & -3.68 & 0.61 \\ 2.76 & 0.07 & 3.83 \end{bmatrix} \tag{4.45}$$

The mapping performed by the network is shown in Figure 4.14(a). This figure shows the result of the surface reconstruction and has been obtained as a series of numerous recalls for points o_1 and o_2 densely covering the first quadrant, which is our domain of interest. Figure 4.14(b) provides the detailed contour error map of the error $d - o_5$ for the designed network. The training points for this experiment have been selected at the intersection of the mesh. The mapping is reasonably accurate in the entire domain; however, it tends to get worse for points approaching the boundaries of the training domain.

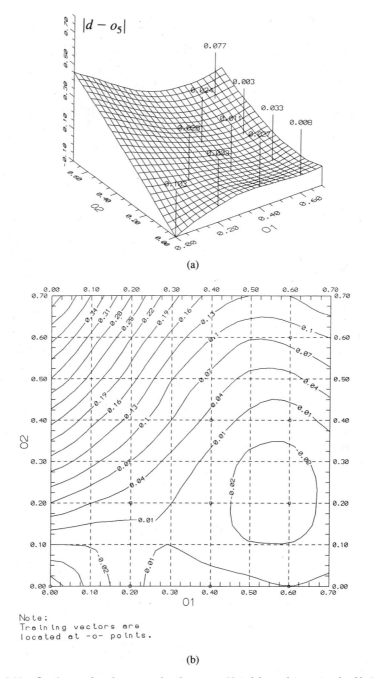

Note:
Training vectors are
located at -o- points.

(b)

Figure 4.13 Continuous function approximation error, 10 training points, network with three neurons: (a) $|d - o_5|$ training points shown and (b) contour map of $d - o_5$.

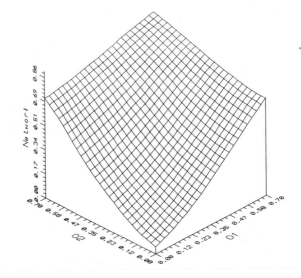

(a)

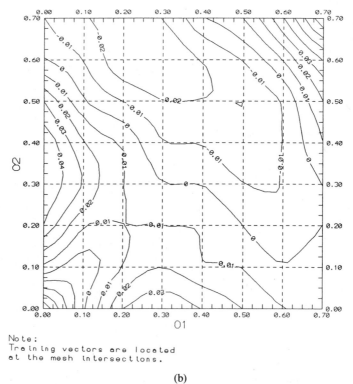

Note:
Training vectors are located
at the mesh intersections.

(b)

Figure 4.14　Continuous function network approximation, 64 training points, network with three neurons: (a) resulting mapping and (b) contour map of $d - o_5$.

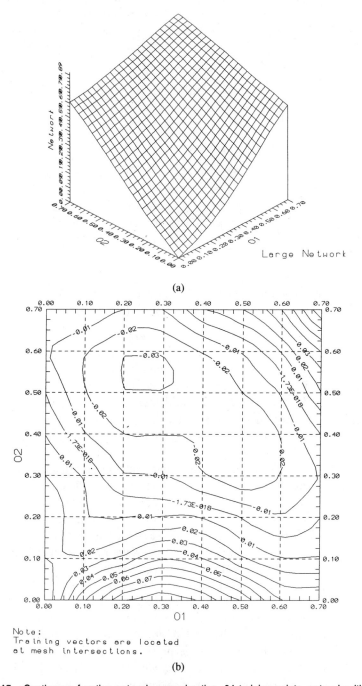

(a)

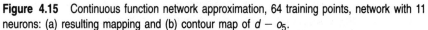

Note:
Training vectors are located
at mesh intersections.

(b)

Figure 4.15 Continuous function network approximation, 64 training points, network with 11 neurons: (a) resulting mapping and (b) contour map of $d - o_5$.

As the last in a series of computational experiments, the architecture of the network has been changed to contain 10 hidden neurons ($J = 10$). The same set of 64 training points has been used. The network has reached a desired error level of value 0.015 after 1418 training steps with $\eta = 0.4$. Weights obtained are

$$\mathbf{W} = [\, -2.22 \quad -0.30 \quad -0.30 \quad -0.47 \quad 1.49 \quad -0.23 \quad 1.85$$
$$-2.07 \quad -0.24 \quad 0.79 \quad -0.15\,] \tag{4.46}$$

$$\mathbf{V} = \begin{bmatrix} 0.57 & 0.66 & -0.10 & -0.53 & 0.14 & 1.06 & -0.64 & -3.51 & -0.03 & 0.01 \\ 0.64 & -0.57 & -1.13 & -0.11 & -0.12 & -0.51 & 2.94 & 0.11 & -0.58 & -0.89 \end{bmatrix}$$

The mapping obtained in this case is displayed in Figure 4.15(a), and the respective error contour map is provided in Figure 4.15(b). The overall quality of the mapping is comparable to that shown in Figure 4.14(b). However, the network training required much more CPU time than for the case of two neurons only in the hidden layer. ■

4.5 ■■■■■■■■■■■■■■■■■■■■■■

LEARNING FACTORS

The back-propagation learning algorithm in which synaptic strengths are systematically modified so that the response of the network increasingly approximates the desired response can be interpreted as an optimization problem. The generic criterion function optimization algorithm is simply negative gradient descent with a fixed step size. The output error function (4.4), which serves as an objective function, is defined in the overall weight space, which has $J(I + K)$ dimensions. The learning algorithm modifies the weight matrices so that the error value decreases.

The essence of the error back-propagation algorithm is the evaluation of the contribution of each particular weight to the output error. This is often referred to as the problem of credit assignment. Since the objective function of a neural network contains continuously differentiable functions of the weights, the evaluation of credit assignment can be easily accomplished numerically. As a reminder, note that this evaluation would not have been possible without replacing the discrete perceptrons with continuous perceptrons.

It might appear that the error back-propagation algorithm has made a breakthrough in supervised learning of layered neural networks. In practice, however, implementation of the algorithm may encounter different difficulties. The difficulties are typical of those arising in other multidimensional optimization approaches. One of the problems is that the error minimization procedure may produce only a *local minimum* of the error function. Figure 4.16 shows a typical cross section of an error space in a single weight dimension. It can be seen that the error is a nonnegative function of the weight variable. The ideal mapping would reduce E_{rms} to zero.

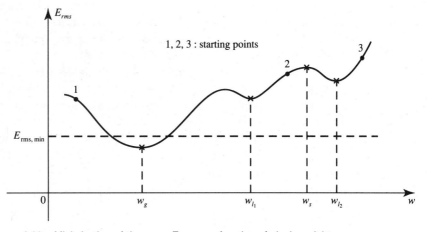

Figure 4.16 Minimization of the error E_{rms} as a function of single weight.

In practice, however, the learning would be considered successful for E_{rms} below an acceptable minimum E_{rms} value. The error function shown in Figure 4.16 possesses one global minimum below the min E_{rms} value, but it also has two local minima at w_{l1} and w_{l2}, and one stationary point at w_s. The learning procedure will stop prematurely if it starts at point 2 or 3; thus the trained network will be unable to produce the desired performance in terms of its acceptable terminal error. To ensure convergence to a satisfactory minimum the starting point should be changed to 1. Moreover, there is a question of how long it might take a network to learn. An appropriate choice of the learning parameters should guarantee that a good quality solution is found within a reasonable period of computing time.

Although the negative gradient descent scheme and all other optimization techniques can become stuck in local minima of the error function, local minima have not been much of a problem in many of the training cases studied. Since these minima are not very deep, inserting some form of *randomness to the training* may be sufficient to get out.

However, a more convincing explanation for reasons why the local minima are not a major problem in this training procedure has its background in the stochastic nature of the algorithm. The square error surfaces produced are random. The larger the neural network, the better should be the training outcome. In fact, the error back-propagation technique has been found to be equivalent to a form of stochastic approximation explored in the early 1960s (Tsypkin 1973). The major novel aspect of the algorithm is that it is computationally efficient for the empirical study of stochastic approximation techniques (White 1989).

One of the factors that usually improves the convergence of training is the statistical nature of inputs and outputs, which may be realizations of two somewhat related random processes. Also, even when inputs are purely deterministic, superposition of noise with the zero mean value can increase the efficiency of the training process. However, in absence of solid theories, the neural network modeler should often rely on experimentation and on understanding of basic network principles to achieve satisfactory results.

The discussion below continues to address the issue of convergence of the back-propagation algorithm. We will also focus on several main aspects and some practical properties of the algorithm. The most important of these are initial weights, cumulative weight adjustment, the form of the neuron's activation function, and selection of the learning constant and momentum term. We will also discuss selected aspects of the network architecture that are relevant for successful training.

Initial Weights

The weights of the network to be trained are typically initialized at small random values. The initialization strongly affects the ultimate solution. If all weights start out with equal weight values, and if the solution requires that unequal weights be developed, the network may not train properly. Unless the network is disturbed by random factors or the random character of input patterns during training, the internal representation may continuously result in symmetric weights.

Also, the network may fail to learn the set of training examples with the error stabilizing or even increasing as the learning continues. In fact, many empirical studies of the algorithm point out that continuing training beyond a certain low-error plateau results in the undesirable drift of weights. This causes the error to increase and the quality of mapping implemented by the network decreases. To counteract the drift problem, network learning should be restarted with other random weights. The choice of initial weights is, however, only one of several factors affecting the training of the network toward an acceptable error minimum.

Cumulative Weight Adjustment versus Incremental Updating

As stated before, the error back-propagation learning based on the single pattern error reduction (4.4) requires a small adjustment of weights which follows each presentation of the training pattern. This scheme is called *incremental updating*. As shown by McClelland and Rumelhart (1986), the back-propagation learning also implements the gradient-like descent minimization of the overall error function as defined in (4.34) computed over the complete cycle of P presentations, provided the learning constant η is sufficiently small.

The advantage of minimization of the current and single pattern error as illustrated in the flowchart of Figure 4.8 and summarized in the EBPT algorithm of Section 4.4 is that the algorithm implements a true gradient descent downhill of the error surface. Moreover, during the computer simulation, the weight adjustments determined by the algorithm do not need to be stored and gradually compounded over the learning cycle consisting of P joint error signal and weight adjustment computation steps. The network trained this way, however, may be skewed toward the most recent patterns in the cycle. To counteract this specific problem, either a small learning constant η should be used or cumulative weight changes imposed as follows

$$\Delta w = \sum_{p=1}^{P} \Delta w_p$$

for both output and hidden layers. The weight adjustment in this scheme is implemented at the conclusion of the complete learning cycle. This may also have an averaging effect on the training, however. Provided that the learning constant is small enough, the cumulative weight adjustment procedure can still implement the algorithm close to the gradient descent minimization.

Although both cumulative weight adjustment after each completed training cycle or incremental weight adjustment after each single pattern presentation can bring satisfactory solutions, attention should be paid to the fact that the training works best under random conditions. It would thus seem advisable to use the incremental weight updating after each pattern presentation, but choose patterns in a random sequence from a training set. This introduces much-needed noise into the training and alleviates the problems of averaging and skewed weights which would tend to favor the most recent training patterns.

Steepness of the Activation Function

As introduced in Chapter 2, the neuron's continuous activation function $f(net, \lambda)$ is characterized by its steepness factor λ. Also, the derivative $f'(net)$ of the activation function serves as a multiplying factor in building components of the error signal vectors δ_o and δ_y. Thus, both the choice and shape of the activation function would strongly affect the speed of network learning.

The derivative of the activation function (2.3a) can be easily computed as follows:

$$f'(net) = \frac{2\lambda \exp(-\lambda net)}{\left[1 + \exp(-\lambda net)\right]^2} \tag{4.47}$$

and it reaches a maximum value of $\frac{1}{2}\lambda$ at $net = 0$. Figure 4.17 shows the slope function of the activation function and it illustrates how the steepness λ affects the learning process. Since weights are adjusted in proportion to the value

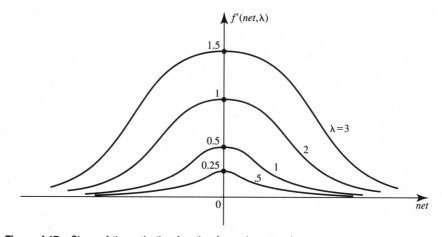

Figure 4.17　Slope of the activation function for various λ values.

$f'(net)$, the weights that are connected to units responding in their midrange are changed the most. The weights of uncommitted neurons with uncertain responses are thus affected more strongly than of those neurons that are already heavily turned on or turned off. Since the local signal errors δ_{ok} and δ_{yj} are computed with $f'(net)$ as a multiplier, the transmitted components of the back-propagating error are large only for neurons in steep thresholding mode.

The other feature apparent from Figure 4.17 is that for a fixed learning constant all adjustments of weights are in proportion to the steepness coefficient λ. This particular observation leads to the conclusion that using activation functions with large λ may yield results similar as in the case of large learning constant η. It thus seems advisable to keep λ at a standard value of 1, and to control the learning speed using solely the learning constant η, rather than controlling both η and λ.

Learning Constant

The effectiveness and convergence of the error back-propagation learning algorithm depend significantly on the value of the learning constant η. In general, however, the optimum value of η depends on the problem being solved, and there is no single learning constant value suitable for different training cases. This problem seems to be common for all gradient-based optimization schemes. While gradient descent can be an efficient method for obtaining the weight values that minimize an error, error surfaces frequently possess properties that make the procedure slow to converge.

When broad minima yield small gradient values, then a larger value of η will result in a more rapid convergence. However, for problems with steep and narrow minima, a small value of η must be chosen to avoid overshooting the solution. This leads to the conclusion that η should indeed be chosen experimentally for each problem. One should also remember that only small learning constants guarantee a true gradient descent. The price of this guarantee is an increased total number of learning steps that need to be made to reach the satisfactory solution. It is also desirable to monitor the progress of learning so that η can be increased at appropriate stages of training to speed up the minimum seeking.

Although the choice of the learning constant depends strongly on the class of the learning problem and on the network architecture, the values ranging from 10^{-3} to 10 have been reported throughout the technical literature as successful for many computational back-propagation experiments. For large learning constants, the learning speed can be drastically increased; however, the learning may not be exact, with tendencies to overshoot, or it may never stabilize at any minimum.

Even though the simple gradient descent can be efficient, there are situations when moving the weights within a single learning step along the negative gradient vector by a fixed proportion will yield a minor reduction of error. For flat error surfaces for instance, too many steps may be required to compensate for the small gradient value. Furthermore, the error contours may not be circular and the gradient vector may not point toward the minimum. Some heuristics for improving the rate of convergence are proposed below based on the observations just discussed.

Momentum Method

The purpose of the momentum method is to accelerate the convergence of the error back-propagation learning algorithm. The method involves supplementing the current weight adjustments (4.5) and (4.21a) with a fraction of the most recent weight adjustment. This is usually done according to the formula

$$\Delta w(t) = -\eta \nabla E(t) + \alpha \Delta w(t - 1) \qquad (4.48a)$$

where the arguments t and $t - 1$ are used to indicate the current and the most recent training step, respectively, and α is a user-selected positive momentum constant. The second term, indicating a scaled most recent adjustment of weights, is called the *momentum term*. For the total of N steps using the momentum method, the current weight change can be expressed as

$$\Delta w(t) = -\eta \sum_{n=0}^{N} \alpha^n \nabla E(t - n) \qquad (4.48b)$$

Typically, α is chosen between 0.1 and 0.8. Figure 4.18 illustrates the momentum method heuristics and provides the justification for its use.

Let us initiate the gradient descent procedure at point A'. The consecutive derivatives $\partial E / \partial w_1$ and $\partial E / \partial w_2$ at training points A', A'', ..., are of the same sign. Obviously, combining the gradient components of several adjacent steps

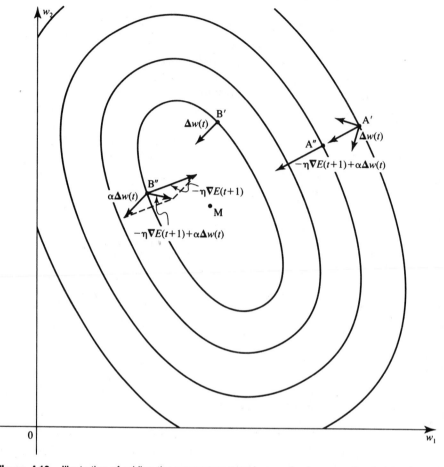

Figure 4.18 Illustration of adding the momentum term in error back-propagation training for a two-dimensional case.

would result in convergence speed-up. If the error surface has a smooth variation along a certain axis, the learning rate along this particular component should thus be increased. By adding the momentum term, the weight adjustment in A'' is enhanced by the fraction of the adjustment of weights at A'.

After starting the gradient descent procedure at B', the two derivatives $\partial E / \partial w_1$ and $\partial E / \partial w_2$, initially negative at B', both alter their signs at B''. The figure indicates that the negative gradient does not provide an efficient direction of weight adjustment because the desired displacement from B'' should be more toward the minimum M, or move the weight vector along the valley rather than across it. As seen from the figure, the displacement $\eta \nabla E(t+1)$ at B'' would move the weights by a rather large magnitude almost across the valley and near the starting point B'. Moving the weights by $-\eta \nabla E(t+1) + \alpha \Delta w(t)$, however, reduces the magnitude of weight adjustment and points the resulting vector $\Delta w(t+1)$

more along the valley. One can thus infer that if the gradient components change signs in two consecutive iterations, the learning rate along this axis should be decreased. This discussion thus indicates that the momentum term typically helps to speed up convergence, and to achieve an efficient and more reliable learning profile (Jacobs 1988).

To gain some further insight into the momentum method, let us look at the comparison of the performance of the error back-propagation technique without and with the momentum term. The comparative study of both techniques has been carried out using the scalar valued function of two-dimensional weight vector as follows:

$$E(\mathbf{w}) = (aw_1)^2 + w_2^2$$

By varying a in the error expression above, it is possible to shape the error surface. Values of a that are close to unity ensure circular error contours in contrast to small values, which produce a narrow valley. For $a = 0.02$, different angles of rotation of the valley axis relative to the w_1 axis can be generated through a simple rotational transform. The basic error back-propagation technique without and with the momentum method has been used to seek the minimum of $E(\mathbf{w})$ with the final error below 10^{-3} and for initial weights of $(100, 2)$. The following table summarizes the number of computational steps for different values of η and α (Silva and Almeida 1990).

Rotation		0°	10°	20°	30°	45°
EBPT, $\eta = 0.5$				10367		
EBPT with momentum						
$\alpha = 0.5$	$\eta = 0.5$			5180		
$\alpha = 0.9$	$\eta = 0.5$			1007		
$\alpha = 0.9$	$\eta = 0.05$			10339		

We see that a twofold and even tenfold increase of training speed has been observed. The result shows that the inclusion of the momentum term can considerably speed up convergence when comparable η and α are employed compared to the regular error back-propagation technique. Although this discussion has only used w as symbol of weight adjusted using the momentum method, both weights v_{ji} and w_{kj} can be adapted using this method. Thus, the momentum term technique can be recommended for problems with convergence that occur too slowly or for cases when learning is difficult to achieve.

Network Architectures Versus Data Representation

One of the most important attributes of a layered neural network design is choosing the architecture. In this section we will study networks with a single hidden layer of J neurons, and with an output layer consisting of K neurons. In accordance with Figure 4.7, the network has I input nodes. Let us try to determine the guidelines for selection of network sizes expressed through I, J, and K. The number of input nodes is simply determined by the dimension, or size, of the input vector to be classified, generalized or associated with a certain output quantity. The input vector size usually corresponds to the number of distinct features of the input pattern. In this discussion the input vector is considered as nonaugmented.

In the case of planar images, the size of the input vector is sometimes made equal to the total number of pixels in the evaluated image. In another approach, however, it may be a vector of size two only. In such cases, a trade-off usually exists between the number of training patterns P needed to create the training set and the dimension I of the input pattern vector. To illustrate this with an example, assume three planar training images, characters C, I, and T, represented on a 3×3 grid. Using the first of the two approaches, nine pixels can be used to depict each of the characters as shown in Figure 4.19. On the figure, pixels of character C are represented using this approach. Assuming that the size of the input pattern vector is nine, we have $P = 3$ and the following three training vectors in the training pattern set $\{\mathbf{x}_1, \mathbf{x}_2, \mathbf{x}_3\}$:

$$\mathbf{x}_1 = \begin{bmatrix} 1 & 1 & 1 & 1 & 0 & 0 & 1 & 1 & 1 \end{bmatrix}^t : \text{class C}$$

$$\mathbf{x}_2 = \begin{bmatrix} 0 & 1 & 0 & 0 & 1 & 0 & 0 & 1 & 0 \end{bmatrix}^t : \text{class I}$$

$$\mathbf{x}_3 = \begin{bmatrix} 1 & 1 & 1 & 0 & 1 & 0 & 0 & 1 & 0 \end{bmatrix}^t : \text{class T}$$

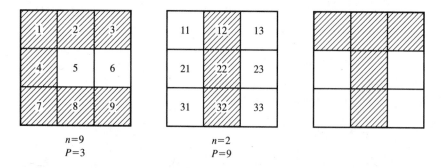

$$n=9 \qquad\qquad n=2$$
$$P=3 \qquad\qquad P=9$$

Figure 4.19   Illustration for trade-off between the size of the pattern vector and the number of necessary training patterns.

assuming that white and black pixels correspond to vector components 0, 1, respectively.

Alternatively, the dimensionality of the planar input images can be preserved as equal to only two. In such a case, however, the number of training patterns P has to be made equal to the number of pixels. Pixels of character I on the figure are labeled according to this method of pattern representation. It can now be seen that we have $P = 9$. Without any feature extraction or compression of original training data, the training pattern set can be written now as $\{x_1, x_2, \ldots, x_9\}$, where

$$x_1 = \begin{bmatrix} 1 & 1 \end{bmatrix}^t : \text{class C, T}$$
$$x_2 = \begin{bmatrix} 1 & 2 \end{bmatrix}^t : \text{class C, I, T}$$
$$\cdots$$
$$x_9 = \begin{bmatrix} 3 & 3 \end{bmatrix}^t : \text{class C}$$

The reader may also notice that relaxation of the requirements for dimensionality of input patterns leads to further interesting conclusions. Why not, for instance, represent the three patterns from Figure 4.19 as a set of $P = 27$ patterns, each of them considered to be of single dimension? We now have arrived at three different input representations, each of them being as sensible as the other for this simple problem. Lacking the guidelines regarding the choices and trade-offs between P and n, we may have to approach the problem of input representation with flexibility and be ready to experiment.

As discussed in Chapter 3, n-dimensional pattern vectors can be handled by the network with $I = n + 1$ input nodes, where the augmentation from n to $n + 1$ input nodes is required for single- and multilayer feedforward networks trained in a supervised mode. Thus, the choice of the input pattern dimensionality uniquely imposes the size of the input layer of the network to be designed. Understandably, the choice of input representation has rather significant consequences on the properties of the input patterns. As will be shown later, patterns that are difficult to classify in low-dimensional space often become easily separable after dimensionality expansion.

Let us look at conditions for selecting the number of output neurons. The number of neurons in the output layer, K, can be made equal to the dimension of vectors to be associated if the network is employed as an associator of input to output vectors. If the network works as an auto-associator, which associates the distorted input vector with the undistorted class prototype, then we obviously have $I = K$. In the case of a network functioning as a classifier, K can be made equal to the number of classes. In such cases, described earlier in Section 3.7 as local representation, the network would also perform as a class decoder, which responds with only one output value different than all the remaining outputs. The network can be trained in this output representation to indicate the class number as equal to the active output number.

The number of output neurons K can sometimes be lowered if no class decoding is required. Binary-coded or other encoded class numbers can be postulated for such a classifier for the purpose of its training. This is called the *distributed representation* case as described in Section 3.7. For example, a four-class classifier can be trained using only two output neurons having outputs, after thresholding, of 00, 01, 10, and 11, for classes 0, 1, 2, and 3, respectively. For the same reason, alphabet character classifiers would need at least five neurons in the output layer since there are 26 classes to be identified.

We can easily note that the number of output neurons in a K-class classifier can be any integer value from $\log_2 K$ through K, including these boundaries. These numbers correspond to the local and distributed representation of classifiers' output data, respectively. It is, however, somewhat likely and intuitively plausible that shrinking the network and the compression of the output layer below the number of K neurons will affect the length of the training itself, and the robustness of the final network.

Necessary Number of Hidden Neurons

The size of a hidden layer is one of the most important considerations when solving actual problems using multilayer feedforward networks. The problem of the size choice is under intensive study with no conclusive answers available thus far for many tasks. The exact analysis of the issue is rather difficult because of the complexity of the network mapping and due to the nondeterministic nature of many successfully completed training procedures. In this section we will look at some guidelines that may assist a neural network modeler with a number of useful hints.

Single-hidden layer networks can form arbitrary decision regions in n-dimensional input pattern space. There exist certain useful solutions as to the number J of hidden neurons needed for the network to perform properly. The solutions also determine the lower bound on the number of different patterns P required in the training set. As will be shown, the number of hidden neurons depends on the dimension n of the input vector and on the number of separable regions in n-dimensional Euclidean input space.

Let us assume that the n-dimensional nonaugmented input space is linearly separable into M disjoint regions with boundaries being parts of hyperplanes. Each of the M regions in the input space can be labeled as belonging to one of the R classes, where $R \leq M$. Figure 4.20 shows an example separation for $n = 2$, $M = 7$, and $R = 3$. Intuitively, it is obvious that the number of separable regions M indicates the lower bound on the size P of the set required for meaningful training of the network to be designed. Thus, we must have $P \geq M$.

Choosing $P = M$ would indicate the coarsest possible separation of input space into M regions using parts of partitioning hyperplanes. Clearly, in such a

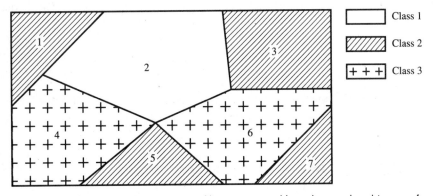

Figure 4.20 Two-dimensional input space with seven separable regions assigned to one of three classes.

case when one training pattern per region is available, granularity of the proposed classification is not fine at all. The more curved the contours of separated decision regions and involved pattern space partitioning are, the higher should be the ratio of $P/M \geq 1$. Choosing $P/M \gg 1$ would hopefully allow the network to discriminate pattern classes using fine piecewise hyperplane partitioning.

There exists a relationship between M, J, and n allowing for calculation of one of the three parameters, given the other two of them. As shown by Mirchandini and Cao (1989), the maximum number of regions linearly separable using J hidden neurons in n-dimensional input space is given by the relationship

$$M(J,n) = \sum_{k=0}^{n} \binom{J}{k}, \quad \text{where} \quad \binom{J}{k} = 0 \text{ for } J < k \qquad (4.49a)$$

Using formula (4.49a) allows the estimation of the hidden layer size J given n and M. A simple computation shows that the network providing the classification illustrated in Figure 4.20 should have three hidden layer neurons provided input patterns are of dimensionality two, or $n = 2$. Let us consider the case of input patterns of large dimension assuming that the expected, or estimated, size of the hidden nodes is small. For large-size input vectors compared to the number of hidden nodes, or when $n \geq J$, we have from (4.49a)

$$M = \binom{J}{0} + \binom{J}{1} + \binom{J}{2} + \cdots + \binom{J}{J} = 2^J \qquad (4.49b)$$

It follows from (4.49b) that the hidden neuron layer with three nodes would be capable of providing classification into up to eight classes; but since $n \geq J$, the size of the input vector has to be larger than three.

The formulas (4.49) can be inverted to find out how many hidden layer neurons J need to be used to achieve classification into M classes in n-dimensional pattern space. This number constitutes the solution of the equation

$$M = 1 + J + \frac{J(J-1)}{2!}$$
$$+ \frac{J(J-1)(J-2)}{3!} + \frac{J(J-1)\cdots(J-n+1)}{n!}, \quad \text{for } J > n \tag{4.50a}$$

For the case $J \leq n$ we have for J from (4.49b) simply

$$J = \log_2 M \tag{4.50b}$$

EXAMPLE 4.4 ■■■■■■■■■■■■■■■■■■■■

In this example we will use the discussed guidelines to propose suitable network architectures for the solution of the two-dimensional XOR problem. Assuming $J \leq n$ and $n = 2$, we obtain from (4.50b) that $M = 4$ for $J = 2$.

The corresponding partitioning of the two-dimensional input space is shown in Figure 4.21(a) along with an example network implementation using a single hidden layer architecture. The reader can verify that the network provides an appropriate classification by replacing continuous neurons with TLU elements and analyzing the mapping performed by each unit. Alternatively, the same two-dimensional XOR problem can be considered in three-dimensional space. It is possible to add the third dimension x_3 indicating, if equal to 1, the conjunction of both inputs x_1 and x_2 being 1; otherwise, x_3 remains zero.

Now, a single plane can partition the cube as simply as shown in Figure 4.21(b). It can be seen that neuron 1 performs the mapping of x_1 and x_2 to yield an appropriate x_3 value. Neuron 2 implements the decision plane as shown. Indeed, noting that $n = 3$ and $M = 2$, the formula (4.50b) yields $J = 1$. Thus, a single hidden layer unit as shown in Figure 4.21(b) can be used to solve alternatively the XOR problem using a total number of two neurons instead of three as in Figure 4.21a. The size of the hidden layer has been reduced by 1, or 33%, at no cost. This example has shown how to select the size of the hidden layer to solve a specific classification problem. ■

Another way of optimizing the architecture is related to *pruning of feedforward multilayer network*. Pruning is done as network trimming within the assumed initial architecture. The network can be trimmed by removal of unimportant weights. This can be accomplished by estimating the sensitivity of the total error to the exclusion of each weight in the network (Karnin 1990). The weights which are insensitive to error changes can be discarded after each step of incremental training. Unimportant neurons can also be removed (Sietsma and

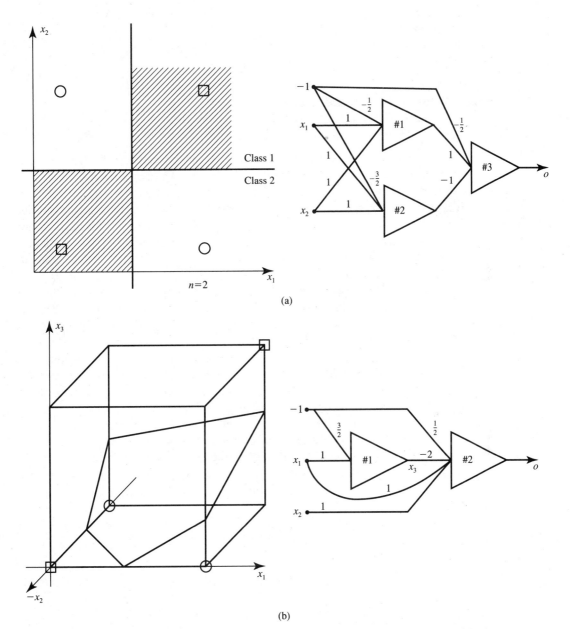

Figure 4.21 Basic architectures implementing the XOR function: (a) two hidden layer neurons and (b) single hidden layer neuron.

Dow 1988). In either case it is advisable to retrain the network with the modified architecture. The trimmed network is of smaller size and is likely to train faster than before its trimming.

4.6 CLASSIFYING AND EXPERT LAYERED NETWORKS

Multilayer feedforward neural networks can be successfully applied to a variety of classification and recognition problems. The application of such networks represents a major change in the traditional approach to problem solution. It is not necessary to know a formal mathematical model of the classification or recognition problem to train and then recall information from the feedforward neural systems. Instead, if a sufficient training set and a suitable network architecture are devised, then the error back-propagation algorithm can be used to adapt network parameters to obtain an acceptable solution (Cybenko 1990). The solution is obtained through experimentation and simulation rather than through rigorous and formal approach to the problem. As such, neural network computation offers techniques that are in the middle ground, somewhere between the traditional engineering and the artificial intelligence approach.

Although it is not yet clear from the technical literature what constitutes an adequate training pattern set and network architecture, a number of successful applications ranging from speech recognition to sonar signal processing have been reported (Sejnowski and Rosenberg 1987; Gorman and Sejnowski 1988). A number of technical reports describe other successful phonetic classification and speech experiments (Leung and Zue 1989; Waibel 1989; Bengio et al. 1989). More detailed exposition of multilayer feedforward network applications for practical tasks is provided in Chapter 8. The discussion below is mainly to enhance the principles, to illustrate the main features of the training, and to discuss example results.

Let us summarize the task the error back-propagation network needs to solve. Given are the training data in the form of P vector pairs $(\mathbf{z}_p, \mathbf{d}_p)$, or the training set

$$\{(\mathbf{z}_p, \mathbf{d}_p), \quad p = 1, 2, \ldots, P\} \tag{4.51}$$

For a given pattern p the network maps $\mathbf{z}_p$ into $\mathbf{o}_p$ using the highly nonlinear operation of Equation (4.31a) as follows:

$$\mathbf{o}_p = \Gamma[\mathbf{W}\Gamma[\mathbf{V}\mathbf{z}_p]] \tag{4.52}$$

The goal of the training has been to produce $\mathbf{o}_p$ such that it replicates $\mathbf{d}_p$, or $\mathbf{o}(\mathbf{z}_p) \cong \mathbf{d}_p$. The quality of approximation is determined by the error

$$E = \sum_{p=1}^{P} \|\mathbf{o}(\mathbf{W}, \mathbf{V}, \mathbf{z}_p) - \mathbf{d}_p\|^2 \tag{4.53}$$

Minimization of error (4.53) can be interpreted as a classical interpolation and estimation problem—given data, we seek parameters w and v that approximate data for a class of functions selected as in (4.52).

Character Recognition Application

Let us look at a typical application of the error back-propagation algorithm for handwritten character recognition, details of which are covered in Chapter 8 (Burr 1988). An input character is first normalized so that .it extends to the full height and width of the bar mask. The handwritten alphabet character is then encoded into 13 line segments arranged in a template as in Figure 4.22(a). The encoding takes the form of shadow projection. A shadow projection operation is defined as simultaneously projecting a point of the character into its three closest vertical, horizontal, and diagonal bars. After all points are projected, shaded encoded bars are obtained.

Each of the 13 segments shown in Figure 4.22(b) is now represented by the shadow code ranging from 0 to 50. The shadow codes for the bars representing character S from top to bottom, left to right are: 50, 46, 4, 14, 50, 24, 14, 6, 43, 42, and 50. The shadow codes can be understood as extracted pattern features. The shadow codes need to be normalized to within the 0, 1, which is the range for unipolar neurons used in the network. This enables the use of the activation

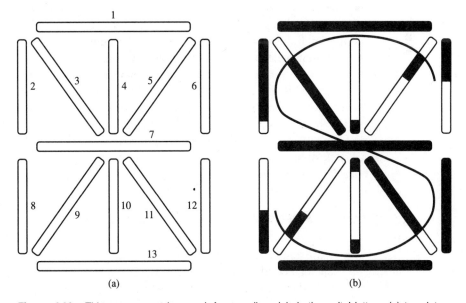

Figure 4.22 Thirteen-segment bar mask for encoding alphabetic capital letters: (a) template and (b) encoded S character. [Adapted from Burr (1988), © IEEE; reprinted with permission.]

function in its region of high slope and makes the training easier and more efficient. The network thus has 13 real valued inputs between 0 and 1, and 26 outputs, one for each alphabetic character. The convention used has been that the output corresponding to a letter should be 1 if the character is detected, and 0 otherwise.

Thus, the network is of size $I = 14$ (including one fixed input) and $K = 26$. The network has been tested with 12, 16, 20, and 24 hidden-layer neurons. Networks with 20 or 24 hidden-layer neurons usually trained faster with $\eta = 0.3$ and 2.0. The training data consisted of 104 handprinted uppercase characters, 4 for each letter scaled and centered in the template as in Figure 4.22. After training, the network performed at levels of 90 to 95% accuracy for the new 104 written samples provided to test the generalization.

In a related experiment of handwritten digit recognition, a seven-segment template has been used for shadow code computation. The template has been obtained by removing bars 3-5 and 9-11 from the 13-bar template of Figure 4.22(a). A similar projection method has been employed to obtain shadow codes for 100 handwritten numerals 0 through 9. Fifty vectors have been used to train the network, 50 remaining vectors were needed for test purposes. The architecture was trained with 7 inputs and 10 output neurons. The best results have been reported by Burr (1988) for the 6 to 16 hidden-layer neurons for $\eta = 2$ and $\alpha = 0.9$ used for training. The accuracy of recognition achieved using this method was between 96 and 98% correct answers on the test set.

For the experiment with letter recognition, there was a total of $14 \times 12 + 13 \times 26 = 506$ weights for the 12 hidden nodes of the network. We may thus consider that the network had 506 degrees of freedom. As observed by Cybenko (1990), the number of degrees of freedom in many successful applications exceeds the number of training samples used to train the network. This, in turn, contradicts the common belief that the estimation problems should be overdetermined, and that there should be more data points than parameters to be estimated. This, in particular, is the case in linear regression and other conventional data fitting approaches. Neural networks of the class discussed in both the example covered as well as in other applications typically seem to solve underdetermined problems (Cybenko 1990). One of the possible explanations is that the true network dimensionality is not determined by the number of its weights, but is considerably smaller.

EXAMPLE 4.5 ▬▬▬▬▬▬▬▬▬

This example demonstrates network training using the error back-propagation technique for the bit-map classification of a single-hidden layer network. The task is to design a network that can classify the simplified bit maps of three characters as shown in Figure 4.23(a). Assuming that the

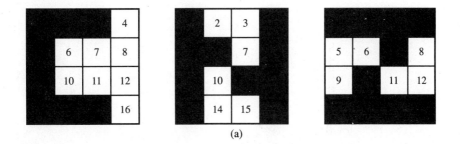

(a)

For $\eta = 1.000$
Total iterations $= 144$
Final error $= 0.00995$

$$
\mathbf{V}^t = \begin{array}{ccccccccc}
-0.225 & 0.646 & 0.488 & -0.317 & 0.707 & -0.608 & -0.954 & 0.896 & 0.540 \\
-0.198 & 0.734 & -0.159 & 0.503 & 1.004 & -0.497 & 1.033 & -0.922 & 0.503 \\
-0.877 & 1.129 & 0.826 & -0.485 & -0.471 & -0.801 & -0.143 & -0.591 & -0.731 \\
0.646 & 0.185 & -1.356 & 0.376 & -1.003 & 0.596 & 0.214 & 0.509 & -0.064 \\
0.261 & 0.323 & 0.425 & 0.343 & 1.357 & -0.299 & -1.521 & 1.405 & -0.264 \\
0.770 & -0.823 & 0.210 & -0.855 & -0.320 & -0.659 & -0.263 & 0.545 & 0.160 \\
-0.817 & 0.018 & -0.809 & -0.855 & -1.350 & -0.279 & 0.966 & -0.603 & -0.916 \\
0.693 & -0.766 & -0.316 & -0.713 & -0.038 & -0.294 & -1.151 & 0.039 & 0.891 \\
-0.507 & -0.799 & -0.238 & 0.893 & 0.314 & -0.798 & 0.101 & 0.667 & 0.599 \\
-0.197 & -0.027 & -0.724 & 0.177 & -0.161 & 1.044 & 1.544 & -0.131 & -0.016 \\
0.823 & 0.040 & -0.371 & 0.229 & -0.472 & -0.336 & -0.511 & 0.541 & -0.293 \\
1.033 & -0.920 & -0.235 & -0.225 & -1.029 & -0.212 & -0.499 & 0.198 & -0.564 \\
-0.186 & -0.312 & -1.030 & -0.135 & 0.174 & 0.551 & 0.632 & -0.535 & -0.026 \\
-1.193 & 0.339 & 0.901 & -0.804 & 0.332 & 0.793 & -0.564 & -0.931 & -0.618 \\
0.513 & 0.479 & 0.906 & -0.077 & 0.185 & -0.152 & -0.433 & 0.075 & -0.893 \\
-0.303 & -0.184 & -0.955 & 0.061 & -1.696 & 1.188 & 0.578 & -0.544 & 0.102 \\
-0.324 & -0.101 & 0.123 & 0.493 & -0.745 & 0.002 & -0.188 & -0.325 & 0.954
\end{array}
$$

$$
\mathbf{W}^t = \begin{array}{ccc}
-1.402 & 1.500 & -0.350 \\
0.011 & -1.709 & 1.046 \\
2.202 & -1.346 & -0.491 \\
0.156 & -0.060 & -0.598 \\
2.659 & -1.062 & -2.063 \\
-1.371 & -0.635 & 0.617 \\
-1.043 & -1.260 & 2.460 \\
-0.395 & 2.172 & -2.264 \\
-1.249 & -0.106 & -0.571
\end{array}
$$

(b)

Figure 4.23a,b Figure for Example 4.5: (a) bit maps for classification, (b) resulting weight matrices, 16 nonaugmented inputs, eight hidden layer neurons, three output neurons.

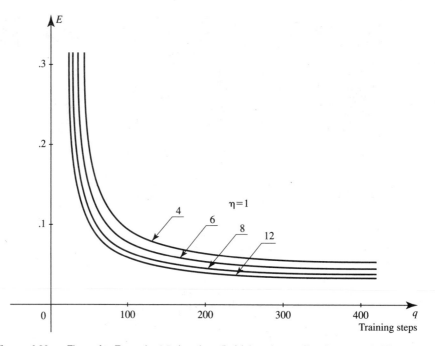

Figure 4.23c Figure for Example 4.5 *(continued):* (c) learning profiles for several different hidden layer sizes.

dimensionality of the nonaugmented input pattern is 16, we have $P = 3$ for the following input/desired output training data:

Character C: $\mathbf{z}_1 = [\,1\ 1\ 1\ -1\ 1\ -1\ -1\ -1\ 1\ -1\ -1\ -1\ 1\ 1\ 1\ -1\,]^t$
Class number: $\mathbf{d}_1 = \begin{bmatrix} 1 & 0 & 0 \end{bmatrix}^t$
Character N: $\mathbf{z}_2 = [\,1\ -1\ -1\ 1\ 1\ 1\ -1\ 1\ 1\ -1\ 1\ 1\ 1\ -1\ -1\ 1\,]^t$
Class number: $\mathbf{d}_2 = \begin{bmatrix} 0 & 1 & 0 \end{bmatrix}^t$
Character Z: $\mathbf{z}_3 = [\,1\ 1\ 1\ 1\ -1\ -1\ 1\ -1\ -1\ 1\ -1\ -1\ 1\ 1\ 1\ 1\,]^t$
Class number: $\mathbf{d}_3 = \begin{bmatrix} 0 & 0 & 1 \end{bmatrix}^t$

The readers may notice that black and white pixels are coded as 1 and -1, respectively, and that the local representation is used for detecting the class membership.

The program listed in the Appendix has been used to train the network with eight hidden neurons with $\eta = 1$ and $\lambda = 1$. Due to the necessary augmentation of inputs and of the hidden layer by one fixed input, the trained network has 17 input nodes, nine hidden neurons, and three output neurons with an architecture like that of Figure 4.7. Error E has been defined as in (4.4) or as in the EBPT algorithm of Section 4.4. Since this is a rather simple classification task, the training takes only 144 iterations, which is an equivalent of 48 incremental training cycles consisting of three patterns each. The resulting weight matrices $\mathbf{W}$ and $\mathbf{V}$ are shown in Figure 4.23(b).

The typical output vectors recalled by the trained network with input vectors equal to $\mathbf{z}_1$, $\mathbf{z}_2$, and $\mathbf{z}_3$ are, respectively,

$$\mathbf{o}_1 = \begin{bmatrix} 0.901 & 0.050 & 0.078 \end{bmatrix}^t$$
$$\mathbf{o}_2 = \begin{bmatrix} 0.011 & 0.984 & 0.013 \end{bmatrix}^t \qquad (4.54)$$
$$\mathbf{o}_3 = \begin{bmatrix} 0.014 & 0.013 & 0.984 \end{bmatrix}^t$$

Simple thresholding of the computed vector entries of (4.54) provides the desired binary classification. It has been observed that using a value of 0.2 for η has increased the number of training steps to 722 for the same error $E_{\max} = 0.01$. Using values of 5 and 10 for η has reduced the number of training steps to 37 and 16, respectively. However, drastic changes of E in both directions for large η values have also been observed. Thus, to achieve moderately fast and reliable learning, the learning constant of value $\eta = 1$ has been used.

Different sizes of hidden layers have been attempted during training with $\eta = 1$. Learning profiles for 4, 6, 8, and 12 (nonaugmented) hidden nodes are shown in Figure 4.23(c). Increasing the number of hidden nodes has allowed for training to converge in fewer training steps. It takes longer, however, to train the large network. In addition, the network hardware becomes more expensive. The increase in the number of hidden nodes from 8 to 16 produced marginal reduction of the training from 144 to 106 steps. It has therefore been concluded that the suitable number of hidden nodes for this type of problem is between 4 and 8. ■

Expert Systems Applications

In the previous sections of this chapter, we introduced the supervised learning techniques of layered feedforward networks. Let us again consider such layered networks, which respond with outputs that can be represented as variables assuming one of several possible values, or continuum of values. Let us note that considering more than two output values of a neuron, or even continuous outputs, would make it possible to handle uncertainties. The degree of belief in a certain response can be determined using such fine quantized outputs.

The conventional approach to building an expert system requires a human expert to formulate the rules by which the input data can be analyzed. The number of rules needed to drive an expert system may be large. Further, the lack of rigorous analysis, or even a lack of understanding of the knowledge domain, often makes formulation of such rules difficult. The rule formulation may become particularly complex with large sets of input data. Realizing that layered networks can be trained without encapsulating the knowledge into the rules, let us look at how they can be applied as an alternative to conventional rule-based expert systems.

Neural networks for diagnosis, fault detection, predictions, pattern recognition and association solve essentially various classification, association, and generalization problems. Such networks can acquire knowledge without extracting IF-THEN rules from a human expert provided that the number of training vector pairs is sufficient to suitably form all decision regions. Thus, neural networks would be able to ease the knowledge acquisition bottleneck that is hampering the creation and development of conventional expert systems. After training, even with a data-rich situation, neural networks will have the potential to perform like expert systems. What would often be missing, however, in neural expert system performance is their explanation function. Neural network expert systems are typically unable to provide the user with the reasons for the decisions made. The applications of neural networks for large-scale expert systems will be discussed in more detail in Chapter 8. This section covers only basic application concepts for layered diagnostic networks that are trainable using the error back-propagation technique. We will call such networks *connectionist expert systems.*

Let us take another look at the training and recall phases of error back-propagation-trained networks. Assume that a feedforward layered network is trained using the training vector pairs $(\mathbf{z}_1, \mathbf{d}_1), (\mathbf{z}_2, \mathbf{d}_2), \ldots, (\mathbf{z}_P, \mathbf{d}_P)$. In the test, or recall, phase, the network described by Equation (4.52) performs the recognition task if it is tested with the input being a vector $\mathbf{z}_i$ $(1 \leq i \leq P)$ corrupted by noise. The network is expected to reproduce $\mathbf{o}_i$ at its output in spite of the presence of noise. If no noise has been added, the network performs either a simple classification or association task.

If the trained neural network is tested with an input substantially different from any of the training set members, the expected response is supposed to solve the generalization problem. The generalization of the knowledge of the domain, which the network has learned during training, should cause it to respond correctly to any unseen before new input vector. Typical examples of generalization are diagnosis and prediction. The classification task may also be performed as a generalization operation but only in cases for which the domain models are partially defined. Examples of such classifications are medical and most technical diagnoses.

Let us consider first how a connectionist expert system for medical diagnosis can be built (Gallant 1988; Hripcsak 1988). A block diagram of an example expert system is shown in Figure 4.24. Input nodes take the information about the

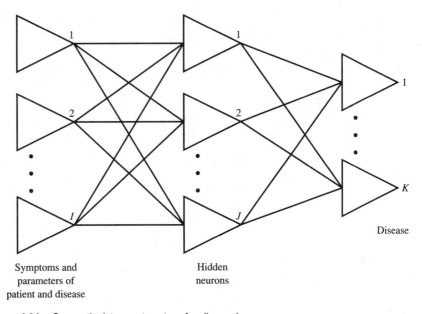

Figure 4.24 Connectionist expert system for diagnosis.

selected symptoms and their parameters. These can be numerical values assigned to symptoms, test results, or a relevant medical history for the patient. In the simplest version, input signals may be the binary value 1, if the answer to the symptom question is yes, or -1, if the answer is no. The "unknown" answer should thus be made 0 to eliminate the effect of the missing parameter on the conclusion. With I input nodes, the network is capable of handling that many binary or numerical disease or patient data. The number of identifiable diseases can be made equal to the number of output nodes K.

In conventional automated medical diagnosis, a substantial obstacle is the formulation and entry of many rules by an expert. In contrast to a rule-driven system, a connectionist expert system can learn from currently accepted diagnoses. Diagnoses are generated from available hospital or doctor databases. As disease patterns and the art of diagnosis change, the connectionist expert system for diagnosis needs only be retrained or trained incrementally on a new set of data. In the case of major changes in diagnostic techniques, however, the expert system's numbers of input and hidden nodes and its architecture may also have to be changed.

As mentioned before, special care needs to be taken when choosing the number of hidden nodes. Too low a number of hidden nodes J can cause difficulties in mapping of I inputs into K outputs; too large a value for J will increase unnecessarily the learning and diagnosis times and/or cause uncertainty of the

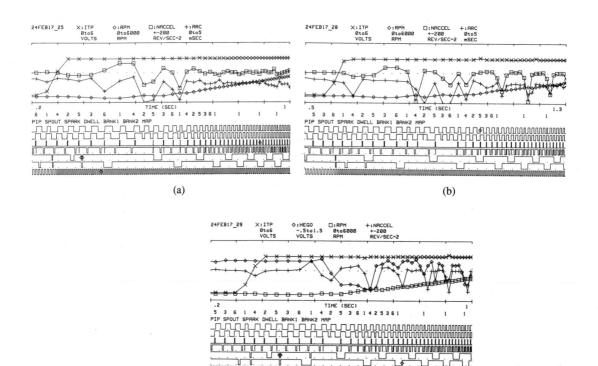

(a)   (b)

(c)

Figure 4.25 Automobile engine diagnostic data: (a) no-fault engine, (b) defective spark plug 4, and (c) defective fuel injector. [Source: Marko et al. (1989). © IEEE; reprinted with permission.]

training objective. In general, for J larger than needed, weights become more difficult to estimate reliably from the training data.

Let us review an example of a connectionist expert system for fault diagnosis of an automobile engine (Marko et al. 1989). The input and output data are controlled and monitored by an electronic engine control computer. Waveforms of analog/digital data such as those shown in Figure 4.25(a) are obtained first from an engine without faults, which is accelerated in neutral against the inertial load. These multichannel data serve as a reference and they are used for training of the expert system modeling the fault-free operation of an engine. Although a skilled engineer can analyze the complex engine output data shown in the figure, most technical personnel would find the interpretation of them rather difficult.

The practical identification of a fault becomes more complicated and time-consuming when signal anomalies are small and distributed over several signals that are time functions. This can be observed in Figures 4.25(b) and (c), which show a set of input/output signals for a faulted engine. Figure 4.25(b) displays signals with a defective spark plug on cylinder 4, which causes a misfire at this cylinder in each engine cycle. Figure 4.25(c) displays the data from an engine with a defective fuel injector. In particular in this case, the fault can only be identified from simultaneous comparison of many of the traces of data.

The task of defective engine diagnosis has been successfully solved by a back-propagation trained single-hidden layer network. The connectionist expert system for engine diagnosis makes it possible to identify 26 different faults such as a shorted plug, an open plug, a broken fuel injector, etc. The training set consists of 16 sets of data for each failure, each of the sets representing a single engine cycle. A total of 16×26 data vectors with 52 elements in each vector has been used for training.

The described neural network-based expert system needs 10 minutes of training time on the NESTOR NDS-100 computer. It attains 100% fault recognition accuracy on the test data set. Low learning rates, a number of hidden units equal to twice the number of inputs, and a randomized presentation order within the training set have been used in the initial development phase. To improve the learning speed, the number of hidden units was then decreased to less than the number of input units. As a result, the learning time decreased five times while maintaining 100% accuracy on the test set.

Learning Time Sequences

A number of practical applications require neural networks that respond to a sequence of patterns. Figure 3.2(b) exemplifies a case of a temporal pattern consisting of waveform samples. The neural network should produce a particular output in response to a particular sequence of inputs. Speech signals, measured waveform data, and control signals are examples of waves that are considered as discrete-time sequences rather than as unordered data.

One simple way to use the conventional training methods for mapping of training data sequences is to turn the temporal sequence into a spatial input pattern. When this is accomplished, we may consider that the given set of samples in a sequence is fed simultaneously to the network. This case is illustrated in Figure 4.26. It can be seen that a series connection of delay elements provides the solution to the problem. Inputs to the network are samples $x_i = x(t - i\Delta)$, for $i = 0, 1, \ldots, n$. The network with tapped delay lines is called a *time-delay network*. The figure shows a single-channel temporal sequence. We may note that for handling multidimensional data sequences, the series connection of delay elements and tapping must be implemented through an appropriate expansion of the input node layer.

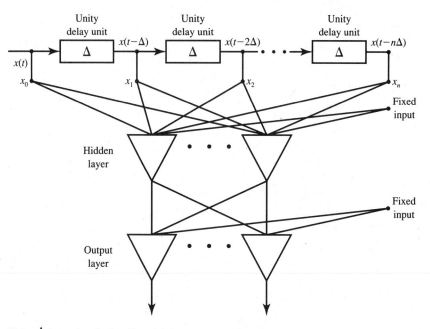

Note: Δ is equal to the sampling period

Figure 4.26 A time-delay neural network converting a data sequence into the single data vector (single variable sequence shown).

4.7 FUNCTIONAL LINK NETWORKS

Earlier discussion in this chapter focused on two-layer mapping networks and their training. The hidden layer of neurons provides an appropriate pattern to image transformation, and the output layer yields the final mapping. Instead of carrying out a two-stage transformation, input/output mapping can also be achieved through an artificially augmented single-layer network. The separating hyperplanes generated by such a network are defined in the extended input space. Since the network has only one layer, the mapping can be learned using the simple delta learning rule instead of the generalized delta rule. The concept of training an augmented and expanded network leads to the so-called *functional link network* as introduced by Pao (1989). Functional link networks are single-layer neural networks that are able to handle linearly nonseparable tasks due to the appropriately enhanced input representation.

The key idea of the method is to find a suitably enhanced representation of the input data. Additional input data that are used in the scheme incorporate

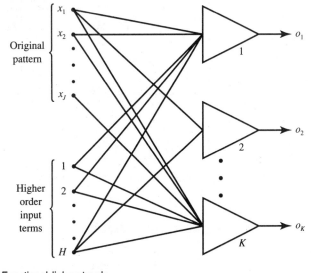

Figure 4.27 Functional link network.

higher order effects and artificially increase the dimension of the input space. The expanded input data are then used for training instead of the actual input data. The block diagram of a functional link network is shown in Figure 4.27. The network uses an enhanced representation of input patterns composed now of $J + H$ components. The higher order input terms applied at H bottom inputs of the functional link network from Figure 4.27 are to be produced in a linearly independent manner from the original pattern components. Although no new information is explicitly inserted into the process, the input representation has been enhanced and the linear separability can be achieved in the extended space. The discussion below covers two methods of extending the dimensionality of the input space for functional link network design.

Assume that the original data are represented by J-tuple vectors. In the so-called *tensor model,* suitable for handling input patterns in the form of vectors, the additional input terms are obtained for each J-dimensional input pattern as the products $x_i x_j$ for all $1 \leq i$ and $j \leq J$ such that $i < j \leq J$ (case A). A number of product terms generated is shown in Figure 4.28. Alternatively, the products can be computed as in case A and augmented with $x_i x_j x_k$ terms for all $1 \leq i, j, k \leq J$ such that $i < j < k \leq J$ (case B). This discussion shows that the number of additional inputs required for the functional link method grows very quickly. The increment H in the size of input vector is also given in Figure 4.28. The figure also lists several first new product terms generated in each of the cases A and B. The following example revisits Example 4.1 and vividly demonstrates the power of the functional link approach.

J	H		Terms generated in Case A	Additional terms generated in Case B
	Case A	Case B		
2	1	1	$x_1 x_2$	None
3	3	4	$x_1 x_2, x_1 x_3, x_2 x_3$	$x_1 x_2 x_3$
4	6	10	$x_1 x_2, x_1 x_3, x_1 x_4,$ $x_2 x_3, x_2 x_4, x_3 x_4$	$x_1 x_2 x_3, x_1 x_3 x_4,$ $x_2 x_3 x_4, x_1 x_2 x_4$
5	10	20	$x_1 x_2, x_1 x_3, x_1 x_4,$ $\dots$	$x_1 x_2 x_3, x_1 x_3 x_4,$ $\dots$

Figure 4.28 Increase in input vector size and example additional terms for vector input patterns.

EXAMPLE 4.6

Let us discuss a simple solution of the two-dimensional XOR problem with the functional link network. Both cases A or B yield the single product $x_1 x_2$ as the third input. We thus have $H = 1$. The new, extended input space representation using coordinates $\{x_1, x_2, x_1 x_2\}$ of extended XOR input data is shown in Figure 4.29(a). The training set in the new input space consists of four patterns $\{-1 \ -1 \ 1, \ -1 \ 1 \ -1, \ 1 \ -1 \ -1, \ 1 \ 1 \ 1\}$ and the ordered set output of target values is $\{-1, 1, 1, -1\}$.

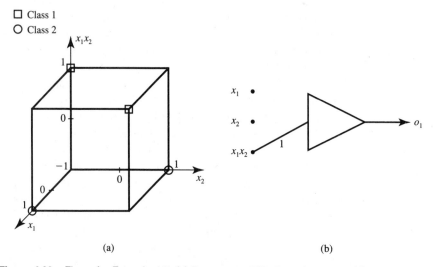

Figure 4.29 Figure for Example 4.6: (a) linear separability through ennanced input representation and (b) network diagram.

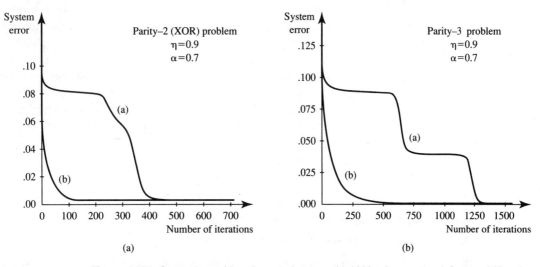

Figure 4.30 Comparison of learning rate between the hidden layer network [curves (a)] and functional link network [curves (b)]: (a) two-variable XOR problem and (b) three-variable XOR problem. [Source: Pao (1989). ©1989 Addison-Wesley; reprinted with permission.]

We now see that the enhanced input patterns are linearly separable. An example equation defining the weights is

$$x_1 x_2 = 0 \tag{4.55}$$

The horizontal plane as in (4.55) passing through the origin provides one of the infinite number of solutions. The related functional link network diagram is shown in Figure 4.29(b).

The learning rates of functional link networks are reportedly significantly better for two- and three-variable XOR problems than those of two-layer networks. Curves (b) of Figure 4.30 obtained for the functional link approach show the dramatic improvement of learning speed over the conventional back-propagation-trained two-layer networks [curves (a)]. ■

In the so-called *functional model* of a functional link network, the higher order input terms are generated using the orthogonal basis functions. Functions such as $\sin \pi x$, $\cos \pi x$, $\sin 2\pi x$, $\cos 2\pi x$, ..., can be used to enhance the representation of input x. A function $f(x)$ of a single variable can also be learned in a single-layer network. Obviously, there is a question about how many of the terms need to be retained to achieve efficient learning of function approximation. Excellent results have been reported by Pao (1989) with learning of an example function $f(x)$ using its 20 sample point pairs x, $f(x)$. The terms that needed to be generated have been x, $\sin \pi x$, $\cos \pi x$, $\sin 2\pi x$, $\cos 2\pi x$, and $\sin 4\pi x$.

The reader has certainly noticed that the network with a single-layer, or so-called "flat" neural network based on the concept of a functional link does not strictly belong to the class of layered networks discussed in this chapter. It has only one layer of neurons. However, due to its intrinsic mapping properties, the functional link network performs very similarly to the multilayer network. The linearly nonseparable patterns acquire an enhanced input representation, so that mapping can be performed through a single layer. The distinct advantage of the functional link network is apparently easier training; however, more research needs to be done to compare conclusively the functional link approach with the error back-propagation alternative.

4.8 CONCLUDING REMARKS

The material in this chapter describes the principal concepts of multilayer feedforward artificial neural networks. Appropriate input space mapping properties are developed starting with the simple prototype point space partitioning and its mapping to the linearly separable image space. The scheme, originally introduced for discrete perceptron networks and visualized in low-dimensional space, is then extended to multilayer neural networks using continuous perceptrons and formulated in terms of network training.

The delta rule and generalized delta rule training algorithms have been developed. It has been illustrated that the back-propagation algorithm solves the training task of an artificial layered neural network to perform potentially arbitrary input-output mappings defined by training examples. The algorithm uses the least mean square error minimization strategy. The gradient of error resulting for the current value of the input pattern is computed. A step in the weight space is then taken along the negative gradient to reduce the current error value. The advantage of the method is that each adjustment step is computed quickly, without presentation of all the patterns and without finding an overall direction of the descent for the training cycle. The discussion of learning parameters has been provided to enhance the understanding of error back-propagation learning performance. Due to the randomness of the minimum search during training, the error back-propagation technique is based on stochastic approximation theory. As such, it provides accurate input-output mapping in a statistical sense.

The basic concepts underlying the idea of classification applications and of intelligent layered neural networks have also been outlined in this chapter. We have seen how back-propagation-trained networks can perform like rule-based expert systems. Application examples of diagnostic layered networks show the feasibility of the neural network approach for the selected practical tasks of classification of characters and engine fault diagnosis. An alternative approach to the generalized delta rule using layered network training has also been presented.

The functional link method is able to implement arbitrary input-output mappings due to the proper expansion of input data representation. It merely requires simple delta rule training since it employs a single-layer network.

PROBLEMS

Please note that problems highlighted with an asterisk (*) are typically computationally intensive and the use of programs is advisable to solve them.

P4.1   The linearly nonseparable patterns $x_1, \ldots, x_{10}$ listed below have to be classified in two categories using a layered network and an appropriate pattern-image space transformation. Design a two-layer classifier with the bipolar discrete perceptrons based on the appropriate space mapping.

$$\mathbf{x}_1 = \begin{bmatrix} 1 \\ 3 \end{bmatrix}, \mathbf{x}_2 = \begin{bmatrix} 3 \\ 3 \end{bmatrix}, \mathbf{x}_3 = \begin{bmatrix} 1 \\ 2 \end{bmatrix}, \mathbf{x}_4 = \begin{bmatrix} 2 \\ 2 \end{bmatrix}, \mathbf{x}_5 = \begin{bmatrix} 3 \\ 2 \end{bmatrix},$$

$$\mathbf{x}_6 = \begin{bmatrix} 2 \\ 1.5 \end{bmatrix}, \mathbf{x}_7 = \begin{bmatrix} -2 \\ 0 \end{bmatrix}, \mathbf{x}_8 = \begin{bmatrix} 1 \\ 0 \end{bmatrix}, \mathbf{x}_9 = \begin{bmatrix} 3 \\ 0 \end{bmatrix}, \mathbf{x}_{10} = \begin{bmatrix} 5 \\ 0 \end{bmatrix}$$

$\mathbf{x}_4, \mathbf{x}_6, \mathbf{x}_7, \mathbf{x}_8, \mathbf{x}_9$: class 1; remaining patterns: class 2.

P4.2   Linearly nonseparable patterns as shown in Figure P4.2 have to be classified in two categories using a layered network. Construct the separating planes in the pattern space and draw patterns in the image space. Calculate all weights and threshold values of related TLU units. Use the minimum number of threshold units to perform the classification.

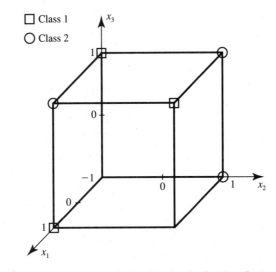

Figure P4.2   Patterns for layered network classification for Problem P4.2.

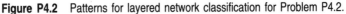

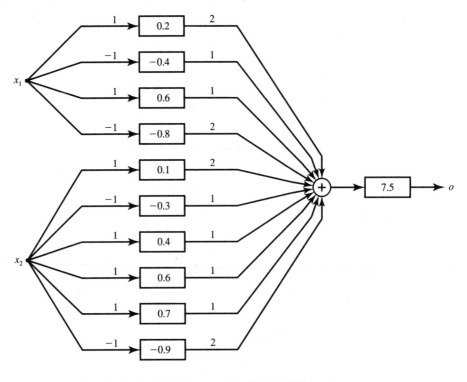

Note: threshold values marked within the TLU as below

Figure P4.3   Layered discrete perceptron network for Problem P4.3.

P4.3   The layered bipolar perceptron network as shown in Figure P4.3 implements a concave partition of space x_1, x_2. The values inside TLU elements are their respective thresholds T. Find the subset $\mathscr{X}$ that results in the response $o = 1$ and draw it on the x_1, x_2 plane.

P4.4   Two planar input pattern regions of class 1 and 2 are shown in Figure P4.4. Note that since one decision region is concave, the dichotomization shown is linearly nonseparable. Using the layered bipolar discrete perceptron network with TLU elements, design the dichotomizer to separate pattern classes as shown. Solve the problem for Figure P4.4(a) using two hidden layers and for (b) using a single hidden layer by appropriate input to image space mapping.

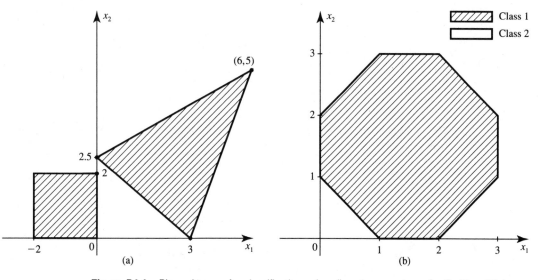

Figure P4.4 Planar images for classification using discrete perceptrons for Problem P4.4.

P4.5 Note that the TLU networks producing a unit step function defined as

$$i_0(\mathbf{w}^t\mathbf{x}) = \begin{cases} 1 & \text{for } \mathbf{w}^t\mathbf{x} > T \\ 0 & \text{for } \mathbf{w}^t\mathbf{x} < T \end{cases}$$

can implement Boolean functions. Find the diagrams of networks consisting of discrete perceptrons and appropriate weights. The networks should realize the following functions (a prime denotes the logic complement operation):

(a) $F(x_1, x_2, x_3) = x_1 x_2 x_3$

(b) $F(x_1, x_2, x_3) = x_1 + x_2 + x_3$

(c) $F(x_1, x_2, x_3) = x_1(x_2 + x_3)$

(d) $F(x_1, x_2, x_3) = x_1'x_2' + x_1'x_2x_3' + x_1(x_2'x_3' + x_2x_3)$

knowing that x_1, x_2, and x_3 are Boolean variables 0 and 1, and that the positive logic is used.

P4.6 A layered TLU network employing a single hidden unipolar TLU as defined in Problem P4.5 and a single output unipolar TLU can be used to implement the XOR function defined in Example 4.1. Partial design of the network is shown in Figure P4.6. Specify all missing weights of the network including the threshold value of the output unit. Note that the image and input pattern data are combined in this case in an attempt to achieve proper response o_4.

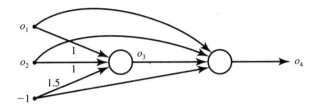

Figure P4.6 Dichotomizer using two unipolar TLU elements for solution of the XOR problem from Problem P4.6.

P4.7   The network shown in the Figure P4.7 and employing unipolar TLU elements similar to those used in Problem P4.5 has been trained to classify all eight three-bit pattern vectors that are vertices of a three-dimensional cube. The training set is $\{o_i\} = \{0 \quad 0 \quad 0, \cdots, 1 \quad 1 \quad 1\}$. Analyze the network and find the function it implements in terms of the inputs o_1, o_2, and o_3.

P4.8   You are presented with the prototypes in augmented form:

$$\mathbf{x}_1 = \begin{bmatrix} 3 \\ 1 \\ 1 \end{bmatrix}, \ \mathbf{x}_2 = \begin{bmatrix} 4 \\ 0 \\ 1 \end{bmatrix}, \ \mathbf{x}_3 = \begin{bmatrix} 4 \\ -1 \\ 1 \end{bmatrix}, \ \mathbf{x}_4 = \begin{bmatrix} 5 \\ 2 \\ 1 \end{bmatrix}$$

$$\mathbf{x}_5 = \begin{bmatrix} 5 \\ 3 \\ 1 \end{bmatrix}, \ \mathbf{x}_6 = \begin{bmatrix} 3 \\ 3 \\ 1 \end{bmatrix}, \ \mathbf{x}_7 = \begin{bmatrix} 2 \\ 0 \\ 1 \end{bmatrix}, \ \mathbf{x}_8 = \begin{bmatrix} 1 \\ 1 \\ 1 \end{bmatrix}$$

A layered machine with two discrete bipolar perceptrons in the hidden layer and a single discrete bipolar output perceptron needs to classify the prototypes so that only $\mathbf{x}_1$, $\mathbf{x}_2$, and $\mathbf{x}_3$ belong to class 1, with the remaining prototypes belonging to class 2.

(a)   Check whether weight vectors

$$\mathbf{w}_1 = \begin{bmatrix} 2 \\ 1 \\ 5 \end{bmatrix}, \quad \mathbf{w}_2 = \begin{bmatrix} 0 \\ 1 \\ -2 \end{bmatrix}$$

would provide the linear separation of patterns as required.

(b)   Repeat part (a) for the new weight vectors:

$$\mathbf{w}_1 = \begin{bmatrix} 0 \\ -1 \\ 1.5 \end{bmatrix}, \quad \mathbf{w}_2 = \begin{bmatrix} 1 \\ 0 \\ -2.5 \end{bmatrix}$$

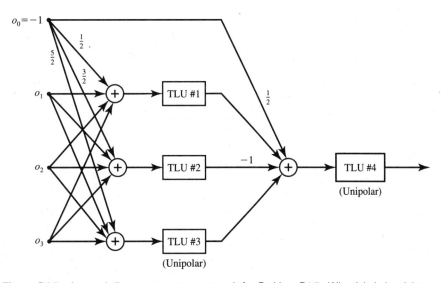

$o_0 = -1$

$\frac{1}{2}$

$\frac{5}{2}$

$\frac{3}{2}$

o_1

TLU #1

$\frac{1}{2}$

o_2

TLU #2

-1

TLU #4

(Unipolar)

o_3

TLU #3

(Unipolar)

Figure P4.7 Layered discrete perceptron network for Problem P4.7. (All unlabeled weights are of unity value.)

(c) Complete the design of the classifier by using the results from either part (a) or (b), and compute the weights of the single perceptron at the output.

P4.9 Prove that for $n = 2$, the number of hidden layer neurons J needed for hyperplane partition into M regions is

$$J = \frac{1}{2}\left(\sqrt{8M-7}-1\right)$$

P4.10 Assume that a two-class classification problem of a planar pattern $(n = 2)$ is solved using a neural network architecture with $J = 8$ and $K = 2$. Determine the lower bound on P, which is the number of vectors in the planar training set. This number is equal to the number of separable regions M.

P4.11 Assume that a two-class classification problem for $n = 60$ needs to be solved using $J = 7$ and $K = 2$. Determine the lower bound on P, which is the number of vectors in the training set. Assume that P is equal to the number of separable regions M.

P4.12 Planar input patterns of four classes are shown in Figure P4.12. Using the layered network of bipolar discrete perceptrons, design the classifier for the linearly nonseparable classes shown. Use three perceptrons in the output layer; when none of the three perceptrons responds $+1$, this indicates class 4.

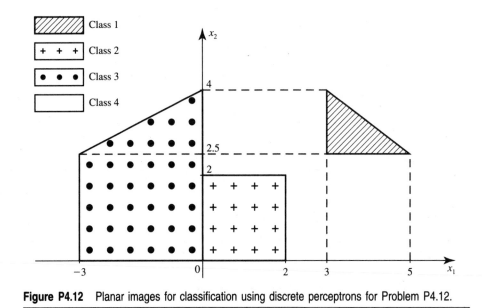

Figure P4.12 Planar images for classification using discrete perceptrons for Problem P4.12.

*P4.13** Implement the delta training rule algorithm for a four continuous bipolar perceptron network and a four-dimensional augmented pattern vector. The network trained is supposed to provide classification into four categories of *P* patterns. Perform the training of the network for pattern data as in Problem P3.1. (The number of training patterns is $P = 8$.) Use local representation, assume $\lambda = 1$ for training.

P4.14 The network shown in Figure P4.14, when properly trained, should respond with

$$\begin{bmatrix} o_1 \\ o_2 \end{bmatrix} = \begin{bmatrix} 0.95 \\ 0.05 \end{bmatrix}$$

to the augmented input pattern

$$\begin{bmatrix} z_1 \\ z_2 \\ -1 \end{bmatrix} = \begin{bmatrix} 1 \\ 3 \\ -1 \end{bmatrix}$$

The network weights have been initialized as shown in the figure. Analyze a single feedforward and back-propagation step for the initialized network by doing the following:

(a) Find weight matrices **V** and **W**.

(b) Calculate $\mathbf{net}_j$, **y**, $\mathbf{net}_k$, and **o**.

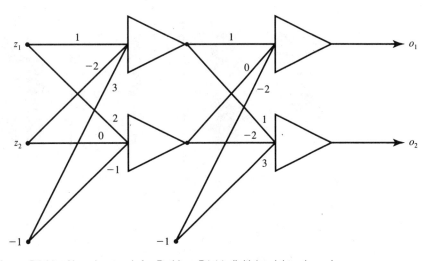

Figure P4.14 Neural network for Problem P4.14. (Initial weights shown.)

(c) Calculate slopes $\mathbf{f}'(net_j)$ and $\mathbf{f}'(net_k)$.

(d) Compute error signals δ_o and δ_y.

(e) Compute $\Delta\mathbf{V}$ and $\Delta\mathbf{W}$.

(f) Find updated weights.

For computations assume $f(net) = [1 + \exp(-net)]^{-1}$ and $\eta = 1$.

P4.15* Write a program implementing the error back-propagation training algorithm (EBPTA) for user-selectable I, J, and K values for a single hidden layer network. The flowchart of the algorithm is outlined in Section 4.4. Learning constant η should be user-selectable; no momentum term is needed. The initial weights for the network should be selected at random. Provisions for specification of input pattern(s) and the desired response(s) should be made in order to initiate and carry out the training. Use bipolar continuous perceptrons.

P4.16* (This problem requires the use of a back-propagation training program written by the student in Problem P4.15, or available from other sources.)

Implement the classifier of three printed characters A, I, and O as shown in Figure P4.16. Set an appropriate E_{rms} value such that an error-free classification is assured. Assume no momentum term; try different η values. Evaluate the number of training cycles for comparable η values for two different architectures. The target values should be selected as $(1 \quad -1 \quad -1)$ for A, $(-1 \quad 1 \quad -1)$ for I, and $(-1 \quad -1 \quad 1)$ for O.

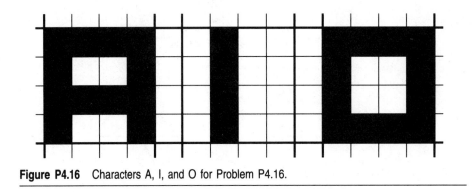

Figure P4.16 Characters A, I, and O for Problem P4.16.

Assume two different input representations according to the following guidelines:

(a) 16 pixels, three input vectors in the training set, $n = 16$ ($I = 17$, $J = 9$, and $K = 3$)

(b) two coordinates of each pixel, 16 input vectors in the training set, $n = 2$ ($I = 3$, $J = 9$, and $K = 3$).

P4.17 The network shown in Figure P4.17 has been trained to classify correctly a number of two-dimensional, two-class inputs.

(a) Draw the separating lines between the two classes on the x_1, x_2 plane assuming that the neurons operate with the discrete bipolar activation function.

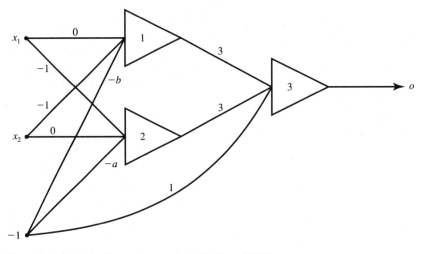

Figure P4.17 Trained neural network for Problem P4.17.

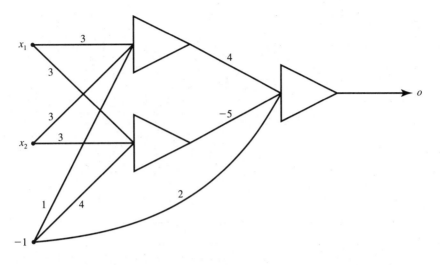

Figure P4.18 Trained neural network for Problem P4.18.

(b) Assume the bipolar continuous activation function of neurons. Now, the thresholding above and below certain levels of output can be used to assert the membership in classes. Generate equations for the region of uncertainty in classification on both sides of the borderline analyzed in part (a) if the following criterion for indecision is used: $o > 0.9$, class 1; $o < -0.9$, class 2. Perform computations assuming for simplicity $a = b = 0$.

P4.18 The network shown in Figure P4.18 has been trained to classify correctly a set of two-dimensional, two-class patterns.

(a) Identify the function performed by the classifier, assuming initially that the neurons have unipolar discrete activation function. Draw the resulting separating lines between the two classes on the x_1, x_2 plane.

(b) Generate 36 points of the test inputs within the $[0, 1]$ square on the x_1, x_2 plane by incrementing each of the coordinates by 0.2. By performing recall for each of the test patterns, find the responses for the network with continuous perceptrons assuming the unipolar activation function $o = [1 + \exp(-net)]^{-1}$.

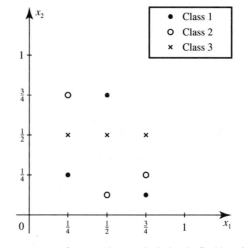

Figure P4.19 Training pattern set for neural network design in Problem P4.19.

P4.19 Design a feedforward network for the example training set containing linearly nonseparable patterns of three classes shown in Figure P4.19.

　　(a) Select a suitable number of neurons in the hidden layer of the network using $n = 2$. Use $K = 3$ so that the target vectors are $[1 \ -1 \ -1]^t$, $[-1 \ 1 \ -1]^t$, and $[-1 \ -1 \ 1]^t$ for classes 1, 2, and 3, respectively.

　　*(b)** Train the network as selected in part (a) by using the nine vectors of the set shown. Select the E_{rms} value that assures an error-free classification. Assume no momentum term, try different η values. (This part of the problem requires the use of a back-propagation training program written by the student in Problem P4.15 or available from other sources.)

P4.20 The network consisting of unipolar discrete perceptrons responding 0 for negative input, or otherwise 1, and shown in Figure P4.20 has been designed to detect one of the aircraft fault modes (Passino, Sartori, and Antsaklis 1989). Quantities Θ (deg) and q (deg/s) denote the aircraft's pitch angle and pitch rate, respectively.

　　(a) Find the decision regions in coordinates Θ, q indicating the specific failure by analyzing the network diagram.

　　(b) Simplify the network architecture, if possible, by reducing the number of hidden nodes J.

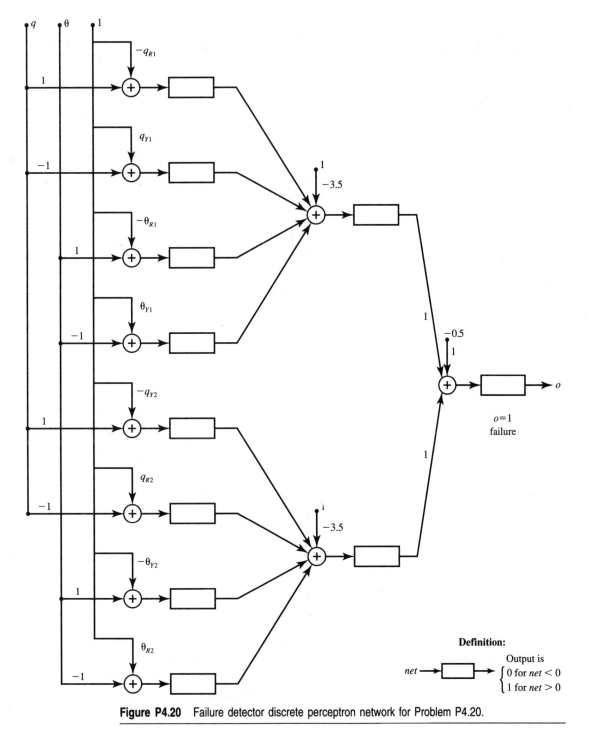

Figure P4.20   Failure detector discrete perceptron network for Problem P4.20.

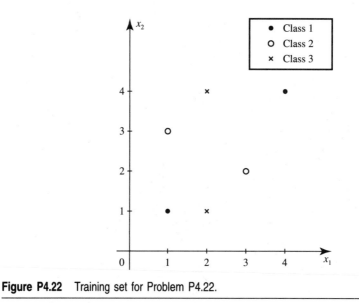

Figure P4.22 Training set for Problem P4.22.

P4.21 A functional link network based on the tensor model has been trained with the following extended input vectors

$$\begin{bmatrix} 8 \\ -8 \\ -64 \end{bmatrix}, \begin{bmatrix} -7 \\ 5 \\ -35 \end{bmatrix} \quad \text{of class 1, and}$$

$$\begin{bmatrix} 6 \\ 12 \\ 72 \end{bmatrix}, \begin{bmatrix} 10 \\ 8 \\ 80 \end{bmatrix}, \begin{bmatrix} 1 \\ -2 \\ -2 \end{bmatrix}, \begin{bmatrix} -3 \\ -5 \\ 15 \end{bmatrix} \quad \text{of class 2.}$$

(a) Determine whether the training patterns in the original space are linearly separable.

(b) Derive the set of weights of functional link network using the single TLU that would satisfy the required classification.

P4.22 Design a functional link classifier using the tensor model for a set of training patterns as shown in Figure P4.22. Use the delta learning rule for training of the single-layer network.

P4.23 Figure P4.23(a) shows the network that approximates a continuous function of a single variable t. The network uses bipolar continuous perceptrons, has 10 hidden layer units, and a single output unit. Knowing that the network weights are as listed in Figure P4.23(b),

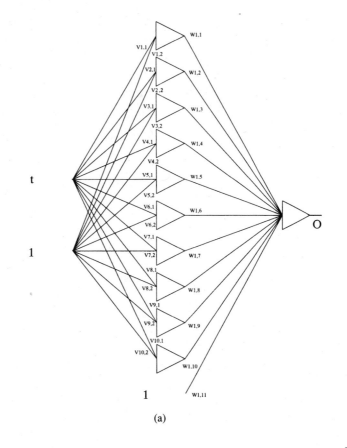

(a)

$$\mathbf{V}^t = \begin{bmatrix} 1.12 & 2.46 & 6.11 & -1.08 & 0.96 & -1.03 & -0.58 & -1.11 & 1.13 & 1.05 \\ 0.36 & 0.27 & 0.09 & 0.28 & 0.24 & -0.29 & 0.12 & -0.34 & 0.05 & 0.06 \end{bmatrix}$$

$$\mathbf{W} = \begin{bmatrix} -1.35 & 0.14 & 4.26 & 1.18 & -1.02 & 1.20 & 0.55 & 1.33 & -1.27 & -1.20 & 0.45 \end{bmatrix}$$

(b)

Figure P4.23 Network for function approximation: (a) network diagram and (b) weight matrices.

find numerically the function implemented by the network by performing recall of selected test patterns in the range $-1 \le t \le 1$.

P4.24* Figure P4.24 illustrates an accurate function $h(x)$ (dashed line):

$$h(x) = 0.8 \sin \pi x, \quad \text{for } -1 \le x \le 1$$

and its neural network approximation $o(x)$ (continuous line). It can be seen that the training conditions have been $P = 11$, $\eta = 0.4$, and

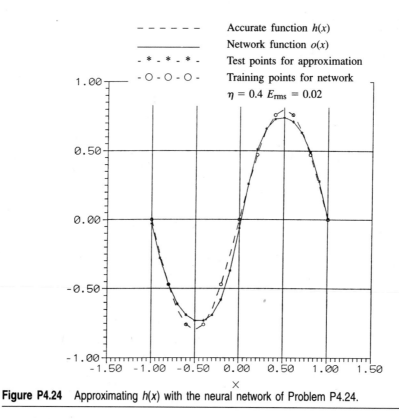

Figure P4.24   Approximating $h(x)$ with the neural network of Problem P4.24.

$E_{rms} = 0.02$. It can also be seen that 21 test points uniformly covering the range $[-1, 1]$ have been used.

Using the simulation conditions for training and testing the network as illustrated on the figure, find a neural network that performs the required approximation. Use single hidden-layer network and bipolar continuous perceptrons.

REFERENCES

Bengio, Y., R. Cardio, R. DeMori, and P. Cosi. 1989. "Use of Multilayered Networks for Coding Speech with Multi-Phonetic Speeches," in *Advances in Neural Information Processing Systems,* vol. 1, ed. D. S. Touretzky. San Mateo, Calif.: Morgan Kaufmann Publishers, pp. 224–231.

Burr, D. 1988. "Experiments on Neural Net Recognition of Spoken and Written Text," *IEEE Trans. Acoustics, Speech, and Signal Proc.* 36: 1162–1168.

Cybenko, G. 1990. "Complexity Theory of Neural Networks and Classification Problems," in *Neural Networks EURASIP Workshop Proc.,* ed. L. B. Almeida, C. J. Wellekens. Sesimbra, Portugal, February 1990, pp. 24–44.

Dietz, W. E., E. L. Kiech, and M. Ali. 1989. "Jet and Rocket Engine Fault Diagnosis in Real Time," *J. Neural Network Computing* (Summer): 5–18.

Funanashi, K. I. 1989. "On the Approximate Realization of Continuous Mappings by Neural Networks," *Neural Networks* 2: 183–192.

Gallant, S. I. 1988. "Connectionist Expert Systems," *Comm. ACM* 31(2): 152–169.

Gorman, R., and T. Sejnowski. 1988. "Learned Classification of Sonar Targets Using a Massively Parallel Network," *IEEE Trans. Acoustics, Speech, and Signal Proc.* 36: 1135–1140.

Hornik, K., M. Stinchcombe, and H. White. 1989. "Multilayer Feedforward Networks Are Universal Approximators," *Neural Networks* 2: 359–366.

Hripcsak, G. 1988. "Problem-Solving Using Neural Networks," San Diego, Calif.: SAIC Communication.

Jacobs, R. A. 1988. "Increased Rates of Convergence Through Learning Rate Adaptation," *Neural Networks* 1:295–307.

Karin, E. D. 1990. "A Simple Procedure for Pruning Back-Propagation Trained Neural Networks," *IEEE Trans. on Neural Networks* 1(2): 239–242.

Leung, H. C., and V. W. Zue. 1989. "Applications of Error Back-Propagation to Phonetic Classification," in *Advances in Neural Information Processing Systems,* vol. 1, ed. D. S. Touretzky. San Mateo, Calif.: Morgan Kaufmann Publishers, pp. 206–214.

Marko, K. A., J. James, J. Dosdall, and J. Murphy. 1989. "Automotive Control System Diagnostics Using Neural Nets for Rapid Pattern Classification of Large Data Sets," in *Proc. 2nd Int. IEEE Joint Conf. on Neural Networks,* Washington, D.C., June 18–22, pp. 13–17.

McClelland, T. L., D. E. Rumelhart, and the PDP Research Group. 1986. *Parallel Distributed Processing.* Cambridge: The MIT Press.

Mirchandini, G., and W. Cao. 1989. "On Hidden Nodes in Neural Nets," *IEEE Trans. Circuits and Systems* 36(5): 661–664.

Narendra, K. S., and K. Parthasarathy. 1990. "Identification and Control of Dynamical Systems using Neural Networks," *IEEE Trans. on Neural Networks* 1(1): 4–21.

Nilsson, N. J. 1965. *Learning Machines: Foundations of Trainable Pattern Classifiers.* New York: McGraw Hill Book Co.; also republished as *The Mathematical Foundations of Learning Machines.* San Mateo, Calif.: Morgan Kaufmann Publishers.

Pao, Y. H. 1989. *Adaptive Pattern Recognition and Neural Networks.* Reading, Mass.: Addison-Wesley Publishing Co.

Passino, K. M., M. A. Sartori, and P. J. Antsaklis. 1989. "Neural Computing for Numeric-to-Symbolic Conversion in Control Systems," *IEEE Control Systems Magazine,* (April): 44–51.

Poggio, T., and F. Girosi. 1990. "Networks for Approximation and Learning," *Proc. IEEE* 78(9): 1481–1497.

Sejnowski, T., and C. Rosenberg. 1987. "Parallel Networks that Learn to Pronounce English Text," *Complex Systems* 1: 145–168.

Sietsma, J., and R. J. F. Dow. 1988. "Neural Network Pruning—Why and How," in *Proc. 1988 IEEE Int. Conf. on Neural Networks,* San Diego, California, vol. I, pp. 325–333.

Silva, F. M., and L. B. Almeida. 1990. "Acceleration Technique for the Back Propagation Algorithm," in *Neural Networks EURASIP Workshop Proc.,* ed. L. B. Almeida, C. J. Wellekens. Sesimbra, Portugal, February 1990, pp. 110–119.

Tsypkin, Ya. Z. 1973. *Foundations of the Theory of Learning Systems.* New York: Academic Press.

Waibel, A. 1989. "Consonant Recognition by Modular Construction of Large Phonemic Time-Delay Networks," in *Advances in Neural Information Processing Systems,* vol. 1, ed. D. S. Touretzky. San Mateo, Calif.: Morgan Kaufmann Publishers, pp. 215–223.

Werbos, P. 1974. "Beyond Regression: New Tools for Prediction and Analysis in the Behavioral Sciences," Ph.D. diss., Harvard University.

White, H. 1989. "Learning in Artificial Neural Networks: A Statistical Perspective," *Neural Computation* 1(4): 425–469.

Wieland, A., and R. Leighton. 1988. "Geometric Analysis of Neural Network Capabilities," MP-88 W 00022. McLean, Va.: Mitre Corporation.

SINGLE-LAYER
FEEDBACK NETWORKS

Who errs and mends, to
God himself commends.

CERVANTES

The neural networks introduced in this chapter represent dynamical systems evolving in time in either a continuous, or discrete, output space. The movement of the network is usually characterized by many degrees of freedom. It is also dissipative in the sense that the movement is in the direction of lower so-called computational energies exhibited by the system. As will be shown, transition in a dynamical neural network is toward an asymptotically stable solution that is a local minimum of a dissipated energy function.

The feedforward networks presented in Chapters 3 and 4 have no feedback activity during the information recall phase. Let us look in more detail at the role and presence of feedback in feedforward networks. As discussed in earlier chapters, the feedback interactions in single- and multilayer perceptron-type networks occurred during their learning, or training, phase. The adjustment of weights during training gradually reduced the overall output error. The error reduction embedded in one of the supervised training algorithms provided that feedback-type interaction. Noticeably, that interaction was teacher-enforced rather than spontaneous, and externally imposed rather than occurring within the system. Feedback interactions within the network ceased once the training had been completed.

The single-layer neural networks discussed in this chapter are inherently feedback-type nonlinear networks. Neurons with either a hard-limiting activation function or with a continuous activation function can be used in such systems. As discussed in Chapter 2, recall of data from within the dynamical system requires time. To recall information stored in the network, an input pattern is applied, and the network's output is initialized accordingly. Next, the initializing pattern is removed and the initial output forces the new, updated input through feedback connections. The first updated input forces the first updated output. This, in turn, produces the second updated input and the second updated response. The process of sequential updating continues, and the activity of outputs for a properly designed, or stable, network becomes less frequent. The transition process continues until no new updated responses are produced and the network has reached its equilibrium.

In the case of a *discrete-time operation,* also called recursive, *single-layer feedback networks* can be termed as *recurrent.* A recurrent network is a discrete-time dynamical system, which, at any given instant of time, is characterized by a binary output vector. Examples of such networks are illustrated in Figures 2.10, 2.11, and 2.12. The recurrent networks' sequential updating process described in the preceding paragraph can be considered either discrete synchronous or discrete asynchronous in time. A more extensive analysis of recurrent single-layer feedback networks with discrete neurons and an explanation of their update dynamics will be pursued in Chapter 6 in the framework of associative memory architectures.

The discussion of single-layer feedback networks in this chapter focuses on networks operating in *continuous time* and with continuous output vector values. Accordingly, continuous activation functions are assumed for such networks and the updating is simply continuous in time at every network output. Noticeably, network outputs are also neuron outputs since the network is with single layer.

Examples of continuous-time single-layer feedback networks are shown in Figures 2.14 and 2.15. In this chapter we will look at the relevant facets, such as dynamics, design, and updating schemes, of single-layer neural systems that store knowledge in their stable states. These networks fulfill certain assumptions that make the class of networks stable and useful, and their behavior predictable in most cases.

Remember, however, that fully coupled single-layer neural networks represent nonlinear feedback systems. Such systems are known, in general, to possess rather complex dynamics. Fortunately, single-layer feedback networks represent a class of networks that allows for great reduction of the complexity. As a result, their properties can be controlled and solutions utilized by neural network designers. This presents possibilities for solving optimization problems and applying such networks to modeling of technological and economical systems.

The networks discussed here are based on the seminal papers of Hopfield (1984, 1985, 1986). However, many years of development in the areas of continuous- and discrete-time systems have contributed to the existing state-of-the-art single-layer feedback networks. As we will see, the networks can be useful in many ways. They can provide associations or classifications, optimization problem solution, restoration of patterns, and, in general, as with perceptron networks, they can be viewed as mapping networks. Despite some unsolved problems and limitations of the fully coupled single-layer networks, their impressive performance has been documented in the technical literature. Both hardware implementations and their numerical simulations indicate that single-layer feedback networks provide a useful alternative to traditional approaches for pattern recognition, association, and optimization problems.

5.1 BASIC CONCEPTS OF DYNAMICAL SYSTEMS

The neural networks covered in this chapter are dynamical systems. As such, they process the initial condition information over time while moving through a sequence of states. Let us look at a classical problem of recognition of a distorted alphanumerical character. Characters shown in bit map form can be represented as vectors consisting of the binary variables 0 and 1. Specific example letters to be recognized are presented in Figure 3.2(a), Figure 4.19, and in Example 4.5, Figure 4.23(a). Taking a different perspective than in Chapter 4, we will now design a dynamical system so that its states of equilibrium correspond to the set of selected character vectors.

Let us consider several basic concepts before we examine their definitions more closely in Chapter 6. An *attractor* is a state toward which the system evolves in time starting from certain initial conditions. Each attractor has its set of initial conditions, which initiates the evolution terminating in that attractor. This set of conditions for an attractor is called the *basin of attraction.* If an attractor is a unique point in state space, then it is called a *fixed point.* However, an attractor may consist of a periodic sequence of states, in which case it is called the *limit cycle,* or it may have a more complicated structure.

Using the concept and properties of single-layer feedback networks, a dynamical system can be postulated and designed so that it has three vectors representing the letters C, I, and T from Figure 4.19 as fixed points. Moreover, the system can have its basins of attractions shaped in such a way that it will evolve toward an appropriate character vector even if the initializing vector does not exactly resemble the original character. Thus, a certain amount of noise or distortion of the character vector not only can be tolerated by the system, but even removed under the appropriate conditions. In our approach we are more interested in the conclusions that systems can reach than in the transient evolutions from any initial conditions that are provided to initialize the transients. However, to enhance the understanding of dynamical network performance, a study of both aspects is necessary.

Let us note that the information about the stationary point of a dynamical system must be coded in its internal parameters and not in its initial conditions. A nontrivial recognition or association task will obviously require a large amount of information to be stored in system parameters, which are its weights. Therefore, dynamical neural networks need to have their numerous parameters selected carefully. Accordingly, their state sequences will evolve toward suitable attractors in multidimensional space. In addition, the system will have to be inherently nonlinear to be useful.

The learning of parameters of a dynamical system is dependent on the network model adopted. A variety of learning methods is applied to store information in single-layer feedback networks. Although correlation or Hebbian learning is primarily used, many applications would require a highly customized learning approach. Typically, the learning of dynamical systems is accomplished without a teacher. The adjustment of system parameters, which are functions of patterns or associations to be learned, does not depend on the difference between the desired and actual output value of the system during the learning phase.

One of the inherent drawbacks of dynamical systems is their very limited explanation capability. The solutions offered by the networks are hard to track back or to explain and are often due to random factors. This can make it difficult to accept the conclusion, but it does not reduce the networks' levels of performance. However, it should be stressed that the dynamical systems approach to cognitive tasks is still in an early development stage. The application of the dynamical models to real-size optimization or association problems beyond their present scope will require a great deal of further scientific development.

5.2 MATHEMATICAL FOUNDATIONS OF DISCRETE-TIME HOPFIELD NETWORKS

The attention given currently to this class of networks and to their mathematical model is due to their very interesting intrinsic properties. Following the development of the theory of this class of networks in the early and mid-1980s, modern microelectronic and optoelectronic technology has made it possible to fabricate microsystems based on the formulated network model (Howard, Jackel, and Graf 1988; Alspector et al. 1988). This section reviews the main properties of the continuous-time dynamical system model. A discussion of feedback network implementation issues is provided in Chapter 9.

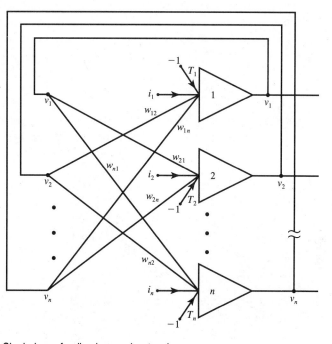

Figure 5.1 Single-layer feedback neural network.

Following the postulates of Hopfield, the single-layer feedback neural network is assumed as shown in Figure 5.1. It consists of n neurons having threshold values T_i. The feedback input to the i'th neuron is equal to the weighted sum of neuron outputs v_j, where $j = 1, 2, \ldots, n$. Denoting w_{ij} as the weight value connecting the output of the j'th neuron with the input of the i'th neuron, we can express the total input net_i of the i'th neuron as

$$net_i = \sum_{\substack{j=1 \\ j \neq i}}^{n} w_{ij}v_j + i_i - T_i, \quad \text{for } i = 1, 2, \ldots, n \tag{5.1a}$$

Note that this notation is consistent with the double subscript notation used in Chapters 2, 3, and 4. The external input to the i'th neuron has been denoted here as i_i. Introducing the vector notation for synaptic weights and neuron output, Equation (5.1a) can be rewritten as

$$net_i = \mathbf{w}_i^t \mathbf{v} + i_i - T_i, \quad \text{for } i = 1, 2, \ldots, n \tag{5.1b}$$

where

$$\mathbf{w}_i \overset{\Delta}{=} \begin{bmatrix} w_{i1} \\ w_{i2} \\ \vdots \\ w_{in} \end{bmatrix}$$

is the weight vector containing weights connected to the input of the i'th neuron, and

$$\mathbf{v} \triangleq \begin{bmatrix} v_1 \\ v_2 \\ \vdots \\ v_n \end{bmatrix}$$

is the neural network output vector, also called the output vector. The complete matrix description of the linear portion of the system shown in Figure 5.1 is given by

$$\mathbf{net} = \mathbf{W}\mathbf{v} + \mathbf{i} - \mathbf{t} \tag{5.2}$$

where

$$\mathbf{net} \triangleq \begin{bmatrix} net_1 \\ net_2 \\ \vdots \\ net_n \end{bmatrix}, \quad \mathbf{i} \triangleq \begin{bmatrix} i_1 \\ i_2 \\ \vdots \\ i_n \end{bmatrix}$$

are vectors containing activations and external inputs to each neuron, respectively. The threshold vector $\mathbf{t}$ has been defined here as

$$\mathbf{t} \triangleq \begin{bmatrix} T_1 \\ T_2 \\ \vdots \\ T_n \end{bmatrix}$$

Matrix $\mathbf{W}$, sometimes called the *connectivity matrix,* is an $n \times n$ matrix containing network weights arranged in rows of vectors $\mathbf{w}_i^t$ as defined in (5.1b) and it is equal to

$$\mathbf{W} = \begin{bmatrix} \mathbf{w}_1^t \\ \mathbf{w}_2^t \\ \vdots \\ \mathbf{w}_n^t \end{bmatrix}$$

In the expanded form this matrix becomes

$$\mathbf{W} = \begin{bmatrix} 0 & w_{12} & w_{13} & \cdots & w_{1n} \\ w_{21} & 0 & w_{23} & \cdots & w_{2n} \\ w_{31} & w_{32} & 0 & \cdots & w_{3n} \\ \vdots & \vdots & \vdots & \cdots & \vdots \\ w_{n1} & w_{n2} & w_{n3} & \cdots & 0 \end{bmatrix}$$

Note that we assume the weight matrix $\mathbf{W}$ in this model that is symmetrical, i.e., $w_{ij} = w_{ji}$, and with diagonal entries equal explicitly to zero, i.e., $w_{ii} = 0$. (See Figure 5.1; no connection exists from any neuron back to itself). Physically, this condition is equivalent to the lack of the self-feedback in the nonlinear dynamical system of Figure 5.1. Summarizing, the j'th neuron output is connected to each of the neurons' inputs through a multiplicative synaptic weight w_{ij}, for $i = 1, 2, \ldots, n$, but it is not connected to its own input.

Let us assume momentarily that the neuron's activation function is sgn $(\cdot)$, like this of a TLU element. This causes the following response, or update, of the i'th neuron excited as in (5.1) or (5.2):

$$v_i \rightarrow -1 \text{ if } net_i < 0$$
$$v_i \rightarrow +1 \text{ if } net_i > 0 \tag{5.3}$$

Transitions indicated by right arrows based on the update rule of (5.3) are taking place at certain times. If the total input to a particular neuron gathered additively as a weighted sum of outputs plus the external input applied is below the neuron's threshold, the neuron will have to move to, or remain in, the inhibited state. The *net* value as in (5.1a) exceeding zero would result in the excitatory state $+1$ immediately after the update. Let us note that the resulting state $+1$ of the i'th neuron is either preceded by the transition or not.

The rule (5.3) of interrogating the neurons' weighted outputs and updating the output of the i'th neuron is applied in an *asynchronous* fashion. This means that for a given time, only a single neuron is allowed to update its output, and only one entry in vector $\mathbf{v}$ as in (5.1b) is allowed to change. The next update in a series uses the already updated vector $\mathbf{v}$. In other words, under asynchronous operation of the network, each element of the output vector is updated separately, while taking into account the most recent values for the elements that have already been updated and remain stable. This mode of update realistically models random propagation delays and random factors such as noise and jitter. Such phenomena would indeed be likely to occur in an artificial neural network using high-gain neurons described with an activation function close to sgn (net).

Formalizing the update algorithm (5.3) for a discrete-time recurrent network and using (5.1), we can obtain the following update rule:

$$v_i^{k+1} = \text{sgn}\left(\mathbf{w}_i^t \mathbf{v}^k + i_i - T_i\right), \quad \text{for } i = 1, 2, \ldots, n \text{ and } k = 0, 1, \ldots \tag{5.4a}$$

where superscript k denotes the index of recursive update.

The update scheme in (5.4a) is understood to be asynchronous, thus taking place only for one value of i at a time. Note that the right arrow in (5.3) has been replaced by the delay between the right and left sides of (5.4a). The update superscript of v_i^{k+1} refers here to the discrete-time instant, and it could be replaced with $v_i[(k + 1)t]$, or simply with $v_i(k + 1)$, where t denotes the neurons' update interval assumed here of unity value. The recursion starts at $\mathbf{v}^0$, which is the output vector corresponding to the initial pattern submitted. The first iteration for $k = 1$ results in v_i^1, where the neuron number, i, is random. The other updates are also for random node number j, resulting in updates v_j^1, $j \neq i$, until all updated elements of the vector $\mathbf{v}^1$ are obtained based on vector $\mathbf{v}^0$. This particular update algorithm is referred to as an *asynchronous stochastic recursion* of the Hopfield model network.

The matrix equation (5.2) can be used as an alternative to express the recursive update algorithm (5.3). In such a case we have

$$\mathbf{v}^{k+1} = \Gamma \left[\mathbf{W}\mathbf{v}^k + \mathbf{i} - \mathbf{t} \right], \quad \text{for } k = 0, 1, \ldots, \tag{5.4b}$$

where sgn($\cdot$) operates on every scalar row of the bracketed matrix. However, caution should now be exercised since formula (5.4b) describes the synchronous, or parallel, update algorithm. Under this update mode, all n neurons of the layer, rather than a single one, are allowed to change their output simultaneously. Indeed, starting at vector $\mathbf{v}^0$, entries of vector $\mathbf{v}^1$ are concurrently computed according to (5.4b) based on the originally initialized $\mathbf{v}^0$ value, then $\mathbf{v}^2$ is computed using $\mathbf{v}^1$, etc.

The asynchronous update scheme requires that once an updated entry of vector $\mathbf{v}^{k+1}$ has been computed for a particular step, this update is substituted for the current value $\mathbf{v}^k$ and used to calculate its subsequent update. This process should continue until all entries of $\mathbf{v}^{k+1}$ have been updated. The recursive computation continues until the output node vector remains unchanged with further iterations. It thus can be said that when using formula (5.4b), each of the recursion steps for $k = 0, 1, \ldots$ should be divided into n individual, randomly sequenced single neuron updates.

It is rather illustrative to visualize the vector of neuron outputs $\mathbf{v}$ in n-dimensional space. The output vector is one of the vertices of the n-dimensional cube $[-1, 1]$ in E^n space. The vector moves during recursions (5.4) from vertex to vertex, until it stabilizes in one of the 2^n vertices available. Note that the movement is from a vertex to an adjacent vertex since the asynchronous update mode allows for a single-component update of an n-tuple vector at a time. The final position of $\mathbf{v}^k$, as $k \to \infty$, is determined by weights, thresholds, inputs, and the initial vector $\mathbf{v}^0$. It is also determined by the order of transitions.

Some of the open questions are whether the system has any attractors, and whether it stabilizes, which we have assumed so far without proof; and, if so, is there any link between the initial pattern $\mathbf{v}^0$ and its final value $\mathbf{v}^k, k \to \infty$. Further, it is interesting to see how the equilibrium is reached and how many attractors can be stored, if any, in the system discussed. Finally, we will be understandably interested to see how networks of this type can be designed and their weights computed to suit specific mapping needs.

To evaluate the stability property of the dynamical system of interest, let us study a so-called *computational energy function*. This is a function usually defined in n-dimensional output space v^n. The motivation for such choice of space is that system specifications are given most often in terms of its desired outputs and are usually available in output space as opposed to the neuron input space, which is the state space. Also, the space v^n is bounded to within the $[-1, 1]$ hypercube, including its walls, edges, and vertices. If the increments of a certain bounded positive-valued computational energy function under the algorithm (5.3) are found to be nonpositive, then the function can be called a *Liapunov function*, and the system would be asymptotically stable (see the Appendix).

The scalar-valued energy function for the discussed system is a quadratic form (see the Appendix) and has the matrix form

$$E \triangleq -\frac{1}{2}\mathbf{v}'\mathbf{W}\mathbf{v} - \mathbf{i}'\mathbf{v} + \mathbf{t}'\mathbf{v} \tag{5.5a}$$

or, in the expanded form, it is equal to

$$E \triangleq -\frac{1}{2}\sum_{\substack{i=1 \\ i \neq j}}^{n}\sum_{j=1}^{n} w_{ij}v_iv_j - \sum_{i=1}^{n} i_iv_i + \sum_{i=1}^{n} t_iv_i \tag{5.5b}$$

Let us study the changes of the energy function for the system which is allowed to update. Assume that the output node i has been updated at the k'th instant so that $v_i^{k+1} - v_i^k = \Delta v_i$. Since only the single neuron computes, the scheme is one of asynchronous updates. Let us determine the related energy increment in this case. Computing the energy gradient vector, we obtain from (5.5a) (see the Appendix)

$$\nabla E = -\frac{1}{2}(\mathbf{W}^t + \mathbf{W})\mathbf{v} - \mathbf{i}^t + \mathbf{t}^t \tag{5.6a}$$

which reduces for symmetrical matrix $\mathbf{W}$ for which $\mathbf{W}^t = \mathbf{W}$ to the form

$$\nabla E = -\mathbf{W}\mathbf{v} - \mathbf{i}^t + \mathbf{t}^t \tag{5.6b}$$

The energy increment becomes equal:

$$\Delta E = (\nabla E)^t \Delta \mathbf{v} \tag{5.6c}$$

Since only the i'th output is updated, we have

$$\Delta \mathbf{v} \triangleq \begin{bmatrix} 0 \\ \vdots \\ \Delta v_i \\ \vdots \\ 0 \end{bmatrix}$$

and the energy increment (5.6c) reduces to the form

$$\Delta E = (-\mathbf{w}_i^t\mathbf{v} - i_i^t + t_i)\Delta v_i \tag{5.6d}$$

This can be rewritten as:

$$\Delta E = -\left(\sum_{j=1}^{n} w_{ij}v_j + i_i - t_i\right)\Delta v_i, \quad \text{for } j \neq i \tag{5.6e}$$

or briefly

$$\Delta E = -net_i\Delta v_i$$

Inspecting the update rule (5.3), we see that the expression in parentheses in (5.6d) and (5.6e), which is equal to net_i, and the current update value of the output node, Δv_i, relate as follows:

(a) when $net_i < 0$, then $\Delta v_i \leq 0$, and

(b) when $net_i > 0$, then $\Delta v_i \geq 0$

$$(5.7)$$

The observations stated here mean that under the update algorithm discussed, the product term $net_i \Delta v_i$ is always nonnegative. Thus, any corresponding energy changes ΔE in (5.6d) or (5.6e) are nonpositive. We therefore can conclude that the neural network undergoing transitions will either decrease or retain its energy E as a result of each individual update.

We have shown that the nonincreasing property of the energy function E is valid only when $w_{ij} = w_{ji}$. Otherwise, the proof of nonpositive energy increments does not hold entirely. Indeed, if no symmetry of weights is imposed, the corresponding energy increments under the algorithm (5.3) take on the following value:

$$\Delta E = - \left[\sum_{j=1}^{n} \frac{1}{2}(w_{ij} + w_{ji})v_j + i_i - t_i \right] \Delta v_i \qquad (5.8a)$$

and the term in brackets of (5.8a) is different from net_i. Therefore, the energy increment [(5.6d) and (5.6e)] becomes nonpositive under rule (5.3) if $w_{ij} = w_{ji}$ without any further conditions on the network. The asymmetry of the weight matrix $\mathbf{W}$, however, may lead to the modified neural networks, which are also stable (Roska 1988). Since the performance of the modified and original symmetric networks remains similar and it is much easier to design a symmetric network, we will focus further consideration on the symmetric connection model. The additional condition $w_{ii} = 0$ postulated for the discussed network will be justified later in this chapter when the performance of the continuous-time model performance network is discussed. For the asynchronous update scheme, one of the network's stable states which acts as an attractor is described by the solution

$$\mathbf{v}^{k+1} = \lim_{k \to \infty} \text{sgn}(\mathbf{W}\mathbf{v}^k + \mathbf{i} - \mathbf{t}) \qquad (5.8b)$$

We have found so far that the network computing rule (5.3) results in a nonincreasing energy function. However, we must now show that the energy function indeed has a minimum, otherwise the minimization of the energy function would not be of much use. Let us note that since the weight matrix $\mathbf{W}$ is indefinite because of its zero diagonal, then the energy function E has neither a minimum nor maximum in unconstrained output space. This is one of the properties of quadratic forms such as (5.5). However, the function E is obviously bounded in n-dimensional space consisting of the 2^n vertices of n-dimensional cube. Thus, the energy function has to reach its minimum finally under the update algorithm (5.3).

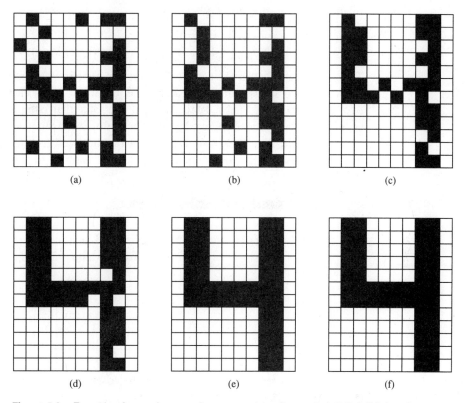

Figure 5.2 Example of recursive asynchronous update of corrupted digit 4: (a) $k = 0$, (b) $k = 1$, (c) $k = 2$, (d) $k = 3$, (e) $k = 4$, and (f) $k = 5$.

Example snapshots of neural network transitions were given in Figure 1.8. Another example of convergence of a 10×12 neuron network is illustrated in Figure 5.2. It shows the 10×12 bit map of black and white pixels representing the digit 4 during the update as defined in (5.3). Figure 5.2(a) has been made for $k = 0$, and it shows the initial, distorted digit 4 with 20% of the pixels randomly reversed. Consecutive responses are shown in Figure 5.2(b) through (f). It can be seen that the updates continue until $k = 4$ as in Figure 5.2(e), and for $k \geq 5$ no changes are produced at the network output since the system arrived into one of its stable states (5.8b).

It has been shown in the literature that the synchronous state updating algorithm can lead to persisting cyclic states that consist of two complementary patterns (Kamp and Hasler 1990). Consider the 2×2 weight matrix with zero diagonal and off-diagonal entries of -1, and the synchronous updates of the output vector $\mathbf{v}^0 = \begin{bmatrix} -1 & -1 \end{bmatrix}^t$. By processing the signal $\mathbf{v}^0$ once we obtain

$$\mathbf{v}^1 = \Gamma \begin{bmatrix} 0 & -1 \\ -1 & 0 \end{bmatrix} \begin{bmatrix} -1 \\ -1 \end{bmatrix} = \begin{bmatrix} \text{sgn}\,(1) \\ \text{sgn}\,(1) \end{bmatrix} = \begin{bmatrix} 1 \\ 1 \end{bmatrix}$$

In the following update of $\mathbf{v}^1$ we obtain

$$\mathbf{v}^2 = \Gamma \begin{bmatrix} 0 & -1 \\ -1 & 0 \end{bmatrix} \begin{bmatrix} 1 \\ 1 \end{bmatrix} = \begin{bmatrix} \operatorname{sgn}(-1) \\ \operatorname{sgn}(-1) \end{bmatrix} = \begin{bmatrix} -1 \\ -1 \end{bmatrix}$$

Thus we obtain the same vector as $\mathbf{v}^0$, and the synchronous update has produced a cycle of two states rather than a single equilibrium state. The cycle consists of two complementary states. Also, we will see later that complementary patterns correspond to identical energy levels. The following example of a discrete-time neural network illustrates how the energy function and the update scheme (5.3) are related while network is undergoing asynchronous updating.

EXAMPLE 5.1 ■■■■■■■■■■■■

Let us look at the energy distribution and output updating process of the fully coupled single-layer network from Example 2.2. Recall that its weight matrix is

$$\mathbf{W} = \begin{bmatrix} 0 & 1 & 1 & -1 \\ 1 & 0 & 1 & -1 \\ 1 & 1 & 0 & -1 \\ -1 & -1 & -1 & 0 \end{bmatrix} \tag{5.9a}$$

For the threshold and external inputs assumed zero, the energy function (5.5) becomes

$$E(\mathbf{v}) = -\frac{1}{2} \begin{bmatrix} v_1 & v_2 & v_3 & v_4 \end{bmatrix} \begin{bmatrix} 0 & 1 & 1 & -1 \\ 1 & 0 & 1 & -1 \\ 1 & 1 & 0 & -1 \\ -1 & -1 & -1 & 0 \end{bmatrix} \begin{bmatrix} v_1 \\ v_2 \\ v_3 \\ v_4 \end{bmatrix} \tag{5.9b}$$

and after rearrangements we obtain

$$E(\mathbf{v}) = -v_1(v_2 + v_3 - v_4) - v_2(v_3 - v_4) + v_3 v_4 \tag{5.9c}$$

The system produces discrete energy levels of value -6, 0, and 2 for bipolar binary neurons used in this example. The reader can verify this statement by analyzing the energy levels (5.9c) for each binary vector starting at $\begin{bmatrix} -1 & -1 & -1 & -1 \end{bmatrix}^t$ and ending at $\begin{bmatrix} 1 & 1 & 1 & 1 \end{bmatrix}^t$. Figure 5.3 shows the energy levels computed for each of the 2^4 binary vectors, which are vertices of the four-dimensional cube that the four-neuron network can represent.

Each edge of the state diagram depicts the single asynchronous state transition. As can be seen from the figure, which shows energy values marked at each cube vertex, the transitions under rule (5.3) indeed displace the state vector toward a lower energy value. Since the energy value decreases at each transition, the network seeks the energy minimum of -6,

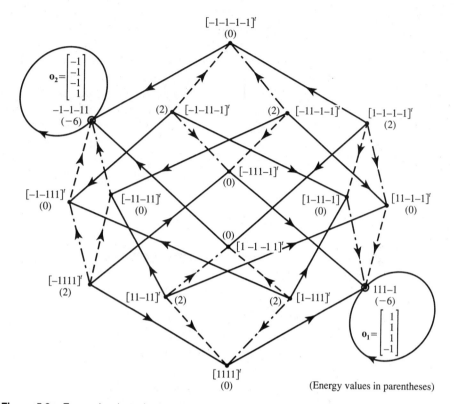

Figure 5.3 Energy levels and state transitions for the network of Example 5.1.

which is either at $\mathbf{o}_1 = \begin{bmatrix} 1 & 1 & 1 & -1 \end{bmatrix}^t$ or at $\mathbf{o}_2 = \begin{bmatrix} -1 & -1 & -1 & 1 \end{bmatrix}^t$. Therefore, the example network always stabilizes at energy level $E = -6$ provided transitions are asynchronous.

Note that synchronous transitions, which were originally considered in Example 2.2, neither minimize the energy function nor are they stable. The reader may easily verify that starting at $\mathbf{v}^0 = \begin{bmatrix} 1 & -1 & 1 & 1 \end{bmatrix}^t$, the first synchronous transition results in

$$\mathbf{v}^1 = \begin{bmatrix} -1 \\ 1 \\ -1 \\ -1 \end{bmatrix}$$

and then the network starts oscillating between $\mathbf{v}^0$ and $\mathbf{v}^1$ since

$$\mathbf{v}^2 = \begin{bmatrix} 1 \\ -1 \\ 1 \\ 1 \end{bmatrix} = \mathbf{v}^0$$

Thus, the energy stabilizes at the nonminimum level of 2 associated with each of the two complementary states.

In contrast to the observed phenomena, asynchronous transitions always lead to one of the energy minima. Moreover, under the asynchronous and random updating algorithm, the convergence to a minimum of E is essentially unique and nonrepetitive. Specifically, the sequence of updating bits determines to which of the equilibrium state minima the network converges. Indeed, let us look at the movement of the network starting at $\mathbf{v}^0 = \begin{bmatrix} -1 & 1 & 1 & 1 \end{bmatrix}^t$. Inspecting the transition map of Figure 5.3 we see that if the updates begin with the first bit, then the transitions have to end up at $\mathbf{o}_1$. If, however, the second bit of $\mathbf{v}^0$ is allowed to update first, the transitions end up at $\mathbf{o}_2$.   ■

5.3
MATHEMATICAL FOUNDATIONS OF GRADIENT-TYPE HOPFIELD NETWORKS

Gradient-type neural networks are generalized Hopfield networks in which the computational energy decreases continuously in time. Time is assumed to be a continuous variable in gradient-type networks. Such networks represent a generalization of the discrete-time networks introduced in the preceding section. As discussed in Chapter 2, the discrete-time networks introduced in the previous section can be viewed as the limit case of continuous-time networks. For a very high gain λ of the neurons, continuous-time networks perform similarly to discrete-time networks. In the limit case, $\lambda \to \infty$, they will perform identically. The *continuous-time single-layer feedback networks,* also called *gradient-type networks,* are discussed in this section.

Specifically, gradient-type networks converge to one of the stable minima in the state space. The evolution of the system is in the general direction of the negative gradient of an energy function. Typically, the network energy function is made equivalent to a certain objective (penalty) function that needs to be minimized. The search for an energy minimum performed by gradient-type networks corresponds to the search for a solution of an optimization problem. Gradient-type neural networks are examples of nonlinear, dynamical, and asymptotically stable systems. The concept, fundamentals, and examples of such networks will be discussed below. In the discussion of their properties, we will again use the scalar energy function $E[\mathbf{v}(t)]$ in the n-dimensional output space v^n.

Although single-layer feedback networks can be completely described by a set of ordinary nonlinear differential equations with constant coefficients, modeling of such a set of equations by a physical system provides us with better

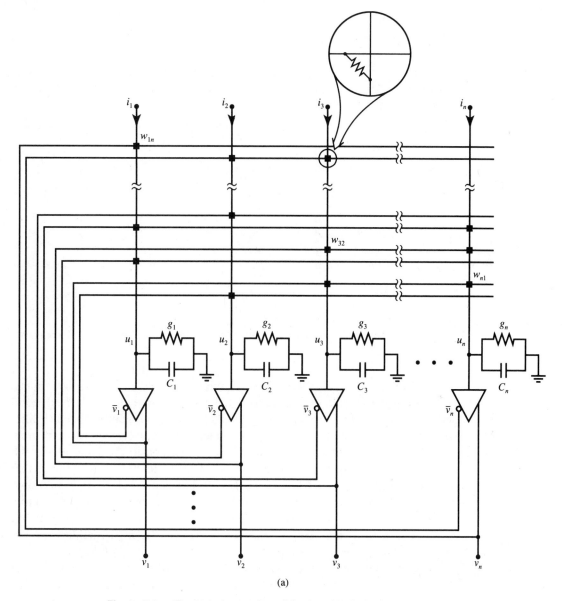

Figure 5.4a The neural network model using electrical components: (a) diagram.

insight into such networks' behavior. It also provides the link between the theory and implementation. The model of a gradient-type neural system using electrical components is shown in Figure 5.4(a). It consists of n neurons, each mapping its input voltage u_i into the output voltage v_i through the activation function $f(u_i)$, which is the common static voltage transfer characteristic (VTC) of the neuron.

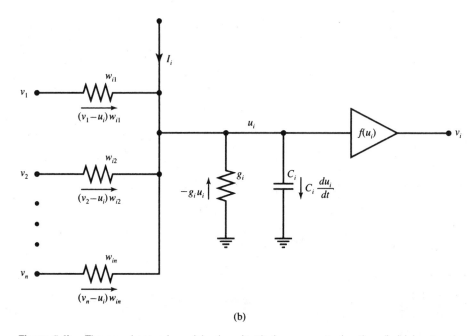

(b)

Figure 5.4b The neural network model using electrical components *(continued):* (b) input node of the *i*'th neuron.

To preserve the original notation of seminal Hopfield's papers, the variable u is used for this network to denote a neuron's activation; for other neural networks the symbol *net* is adopted in this text. Any high-gain voltage amplifier with saturation could be used in this model as a replacement for a neuron. Conductance w_{ij} connects the output of the *j*'th neuron to the input of the *i*'th neuron. The inverted neuron outputs $\bar{v}_i$ are usually tapped at inverting rather than noninverting outputs to avoid negative conductance values w_{ij} connecting, in inhibitory mode, the output of the *j*'th neuron to the input of the *i*'th neuron. Note that the postulated network is required to be symmetric, i.e., $w_{ij} = w_{ji}$. Also, since it has been assumed that $w_{ii} = 0$, the outputs of neurons are not connected back to their own inputs.

Let us note that the electrical model of the Hopfield network shown in the figure has conductance g_i between the *i*'th neuron input and ground. It represents the nonzero input conductance of the *i*'th neuron. With the conductance extracted, the neuron can be considered as a parasitic-free voltage amplifier absorbing no current. Similarly, C_i represents the nonzero input capacitance of the *i*'th neuron. Capacitances C_i, for $i = 1, 2, \ldots, n$, are responsible for the dynamics of the transients in this model.

Let us derive mathematical description of this network. The input of the *i*'th neuron is shown in Figure 5.4(b). The KCL equation for the input node having potential u_i can be obtained as

$$i_i + \sum_{\substack{j=1 \\ j \neq i}}^{n} w_{ij}v_j - u_i \left(\sum_{\substack{j=1 \\ j \neq i}}^{n} w_{ij} + g_i \right) = C_i \left(\frac{du_i}{dt} \right) \tag{5.10}$$

The left side of Equation (5.10) represents the total current entering the capacitance C_i. It is a sum of $n - 1$ currents of value $(v_j - u_i)w_{ij}$, for $j = 1$, 2, ..., n, $j \neq i$, the current i_i, and the current $-g_iu_i$. For the sake of clarity, all the branch currents involved in the summation at the left side of (5.10) have been marked in Figure 5.4(b). The reader can easily notice that the feedback current term $\sum_{j=1}^{n}(v_j - u_i)w_{ij}$, $j \neq i$, has been split in (5.10) to properly group terms with time variables. Since the weights w_{ij} transform the voltage $v_j - u_j$ into currents, they have dimensions of conductances and are expressed in this example in mhos. Denoting the total conductance connected to the neuron's input node i as G_i, where

$$G_i \overset{\Delta}{=} \sum_{j=1}^{n} w_{ij} + g_i,$$

Equation (5.10) can be simplified to the form of a single state equation as

$$i_i + \sum_{j=1}^{n} w_{ij}v_j - u_iG_i = C_i \left(\frac{du_i}{dt} \right) \tag{5.11}$$

Let us now introduce the matrices $\mathbf{C}$ and $\mathbf{G}$ defined as

$$\mathbf{C} \overset{\Delta}{=} \text{diag}[C_1, C_2, \ldots, C_n] \text{ and } \mathbf{G} \overset{\Delta}{=} \text{diag}[G_1, G_2, \ldots, G_n]$$

and arrange $u_i(t)$, $v_i(t)$, and i_i in n-dimensional column state vector $\mathbf{u}(t)$, output vector $\mathbf{v}(t)$, and the bias current vector $\mathbf{i}$. The final equations of the entire model network consisting of the *state equation* (5.12a) and the *output equation* (5.12b) written in matrix form can now be expressed from (5.11) for $i = 1, 2, \ldots, n$ as

$$\mathbf{C}\frac{d\mathbf{u}(t)}{dt} = \mathbf{W}\mathbf{v}(t) - \mathbf{G}\mathbf{u}(t) + \mathbf{i} \tag{5.12a}$$

$$\mathbf{v}(t) = \mathbf{f}[\mathbf{u}(t)] \tag{5.12b}$$

Let us study the stability of the system described by the ordinary nonlinear differential equations (5.12). The stability of the equations can be evaluated using a generalized computational energy function $E[\mathbf{v}(t)]$. The function $E[\mathbf{v}(t)]$ has not yet been determined in our discussion. We do not know the form of the function; however, we assume that it exists. It is obviously, as before, a scalar-valued function of output vector $\mathbf{v}$. The time derivative of $E[\mathbf{v}(t)]$ can easily be obtained using the chain rule as

$$\frac{dE[\mathbf{v}(t)]}{dt} = \sum_{i=1}^{n} \frac{\partial E(\mathbf{v})}{\partial v_i} \dot{v}_i \tag{5.13a}$$

where

$$\dot{v}_i = \frac{d}{dt} v_i$$

This may be written compactly as a scalar product of the vectors

$$\frac{dE[\mathbf{v}(t)]}{dt} = \nabla E^t(\mathbf{v}) \, \dot{\mathbf{v}} \tag{5.13b}$$

where $\nabla E(\mathbf{v})$ denotes the gradient vector

$$\nabla E(\mathbf{v}) \overset{\Delta}{=} \begin{bmatrix} \dfrac{\partial E(\mathbf{v})}{\partial v_1} \\[2mm] \dfrac{\partial E(\mathbf{v})}{\partial v_2} \\[2mm] \vdots \\[2mm] \dfrac{\partial E(\mathbf{v})}{\partial v_n} \end{bmatrix}$$

Note that the computational energy function $E[\mathbf{v}(t)]$ is defined in n-dimensional output space v^n where the designed neural system specifications are usually known. The corresponding energy function in the state space u^n of an asymptotically stable system would be the system's Liapunov function. If its time derivative is found to be negative, then the energy function in the output space also has a negative derivative, since Equation (5.12b) describes a monotonic mapping of space u^n into space v^n. The formal verification of this property will be presented below.

The suitable energy function for the system in Figure 5.4 has the following form:

$$E(\mathbf{v}) = -\frac{1}{2} \mathbf{v}^t \mathbf{W} \mathbf{v} - \mathbf{i}^t \mathbf{v} + \sum_{i=1}^{n} G_i \int_0^{v_i} f_i^{-1}(z) \, dz \tag{5.14}$$

where $f_i^{-1}(z)$ is the inverse of the activation function f_i. Although the time argument has been omitted in (5.14), for notational convenience, it is understood that vector $\mathbf{v}$ represents $\mathbf{v}(t)$. Let us see why and how the energy function (5.14) can provide us with insight into the system of Equation (5.11).

First, the threshold term of (5.5a) has for simplicity been absorbed into the $\mathbf{i}^t \mathbf{v}$ term in (5.14). Also, the third term of the energy expression containing the integral of the inverse of the activation function has been introduced in (5.14) to account for the property of continuous activation function of neurons. We may now evaluate how the energy function (5.14) varies with time. Calculating the rate of change of energy for symmetric $\mathbf{W}$ using the chain rule and the property

$$\frac{d}{dv_i} \left(G_i \int_0^{v_i} f_i^{-1}(z) \, dz \right) = G_i u_i$$

yields the following result for the time derivative of the energy (see the Appendix):

$$\frac{\mathrm{d}E}{\mathrm{d}t} = (-\mathbf{W}\mathbf{v} - \mathbf{i} + \mathbf{G}\mathbf{u})^t \, \dot{\mathbf{v}} \tag{5.15}$$

Noticeably, the expression for the gradient vector has now resulted within the parentheses of (5.15) before the transpose. The state equation (5.12a) can now be rewritten using the gradient symbol:

$$-\nabla E(\mathbf{v}) = \mathbf{C}\frac{\mathrm{d}\mathbf{u}}{\mathrm{d}t} \tag{5.16}$$

From (5.16) we see that the negative gradient of the energy function $E(\mathbf{v})$ is directly proportional to the speed of the state vector $\mathbf{u}$, with the capacitance C_i being the proportionality coefficient of the state vector's i'th component. The appropriate changes of u_i are in the general direction of the negative gradient component $\partial E / \partial v_i$. The velocity $\mathrm{d}\mathbf{u}/\mathrm{d}t$ of the state vector is not strictly in the negative gradient direction, but always has a positive projection on it (see the Appendix). This is illustrated in Figure 5.5(a), which shows the equipotential, or equal energy, lines in v^2 space of an example neural network consisting of two neurons. Other examples of this class of networks and its properties will be discussed in more detail later in this chapter.

It is now interesting to see how the energy E of this system varies with time. Combining (5.13) and (5.15) yields

$$\frac{\mathrm{d}E}{\mathrm{d}t} = - \left(\mathbf{C}\frac{\mathrm{d}\mathbf{u}}{\mathrm{d}t} \right)^t \frac{\mathrm{d}\mathbf{v}}{\mathrm{d}t} \tag{5.17}$$

Using the inverse activation function $f^{-1}(v_i)$ of the neuron's VTC, the individual directions of changes of the output vector $\mathbf{v}(t)$, or velocities, can now be computed as follows:

$$C_i\frac{\mathrm{d}u_i}{\mathrm{d}t} = C_i f^{-1'}(v_i)\frac{\mathrm{d}v_i}{\mathrm{d}t} \tag{5.18}$$

Since $f^{-1'}(\mathbf{v}_i) > 0$, it can be noticed that $\mathrm{d}u_i/\mathrm{d}t$ and $\mathrm{d}v_i/\mathrm{d}t$ have identical signs. But, as stated previously in (5.16), the values of $\mathrm{d}u_i/\mathrm{d}t$ are of the same sign as the negative gradient components $\partial E / \partial v_i$. It follows thus that the changes of E, in time, are in the general direction toward lower values of the energy function in v^n space. The changes in time, however, do not exactly follow the direction of the gradient itself, since the term $C_i f^{-1'}(v_i)$ provides here such scaling that

$$\frac{\mathrm{d}v_i}{\mathrm{d}t} = \frac{\mathrm{d}E / \mathrm{d}v_i}{C_i f^{-1'}(v_i)} \tag{5.19}$$

This energy minimization property of the system discussed here motivates the name of a gradient-type system. The property of energy minimization makes it possible to replace the evaluation of rather complex convergence *to the minimum of E versus time,* like it really occurs in an artificial neural system, with the

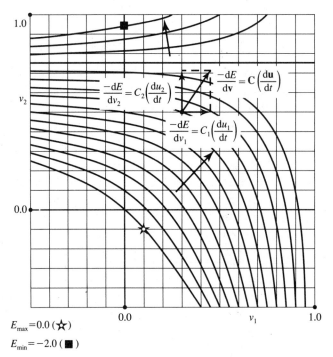

$$\frac{-dE}{dv_2}=C_2\left(\frac{du_2}{dt}\right)$$

$$\frac{-dE}{dv}=C\left(\frac{du}{dt}\right)$$

$$\frac{-dE}{dv_1}=C_1\left(\frac{du_1}{dt}\right)$$

$E_{\text{max}}=0.0\ (\bigstar)$

$E_{\text{min}}=-2.0\ (\blacksquare)$

(a)

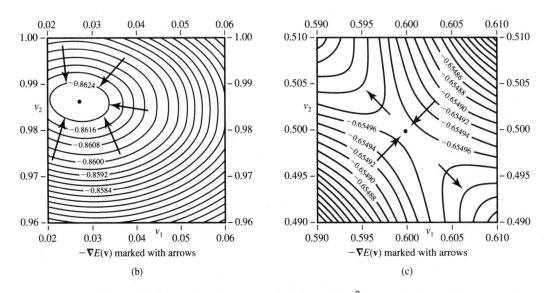

$-\nabla E(\mathbf{v})$ marked with arrows

(b)

$-\nabla E(\mathbf{v})$ marked with arrows

(c)

Figure 5.5 Illustration of energy gradient descent in v^2 space: (a) descent along a negative gradient, (b) minimum point, and (c) saddle point.

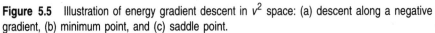

convergence *to the minimum of* $E(\mathbf{v})$ in the output space. It can also be noticed that such a solution for the minimum $E(\mathbf{v})$ results from solving the nonlinear, but purely algebraic, equations describing the nondynamic system, i.e., the system as shown in Figure 5.4(b) but with the capacitors removed.

It is interesting to note that the E function also has the meaning of the so-called cocontent function (Kennedy and Chua 1988). Remarkably, the stationary point of the system's dynamics may be examined by finding the zero value of the system's energy gradient vector $\nabla E(\mathbf{v})$. Since $dE/dt \leq 0$, the energy function decreases in time, unless $dE/dt = 0$. At the network's attractor, where the condition $dE/dt = 0$ holds, we also have $du_i/dt = 0$, for $i = 1, 2, \ldots, n$, as can be seen from (5.17). The attractor of the network must be a point so that any oscillations or cycles are excluded, and the network is totally stable.

As the system comes to rest at the minimum of $E(\mathbf{v})$ after it has moved toward a minimum in the output space, it has also reached equilibrium in the neuron's input, or state, space u. This can be seen from expression (5.19). Because the system seeks out one of its energy minima, it is instructive to see the relationship between the weight matrix $\mathbf{W}$ and the minima of the system's energy function. Below, we discuss the conditions of existence of such minima.

As derived in previous paragraphs, finding an equilibrium point for the dynamic network with continuous activation function neurons corresponds to finding the solution $\mathbf{v}^*$ of the following algebraic equation

$$\nabla E(\mathbf{v}) = \mathbf{0} \tag{5.20a}$$

Speaking more precisely, an equilibrium point $\mathbf{v}^*$ is called the *stationary point*. The stationary point can be a maximum, minimum, or saddle. The case of a minimum is illustrated on the contour map of the energy function of Figure 5.5(b). Figure 5.5(c) shows the stationary point which is the saddle. Although the gradient vector vanishes at the saddle point, the dynamical system does not stabilize there. On the figure shown, the system will tend to move toward the upper left or bottom right corner of the map.

Let us find the stationary points of the energy function. Using the gradient vector value computed from (5.14), Equation (5.20a) can be rewritten as

$$-\mathbf{W}\mathbf{v} - \mathbf{i} + \mathbf{G}\mathbf{u} = 0 \tag{5.20b}$$

The additional relationship (5.12b) is mapping the state space into the output space, $u^n \rightarrow v^n$, and along with (5.20b) they can be used for finding $\mathbf{v}^*$, which are the stationary points of the energy function.

Solving Equation (5.20) without consideration of the constraints on the solution as belonging to the v^n hypercube yields

$$\mathbf{W}\mathbf{v} = -\mathbf{i} \tag{5.21a}$$

and the solution $\mathbf{v}^*$ is obtained as

$$\mathbf{v}^* = -\mathbf{W}^{-1}\mathbf{i} \tag{5.21b}$$

The additional assumption has been made in (5.21) of high-gain neurons, which eliminates the last term in (5.20b). It can be also noted in such cases that the Hessian matrix (see the Appendix) of the unconstrained system using high-gain neurons is

$$\nabla^2 E(\mathbf{v}) = \nabla\,[-\mathbf{Wv} - \mathbf{i}] \qquad (5.22\text{a})$$

which yields

$$\nabla^2 E(\mathbf{v}) = -\mathbf{W}. \qquad (5.22\text{b})$$

By having previously chosen $w_{ii} = 0$ for the discussed neural network model, the Hessian matrix of the energy function equal to $-\mathbf{W}$ has been made neither positive definite nor negative definite (see the Appendix). This is resulting from our previous assumption that the postulated system has no self-feedback. In fact, symmetric matrix $\mathbf{W}$ with zero diagonal produces scalar-valued energy function of quadratic form $(-\frac{1}{2})\mathbf{v}^t\mathbf{Wv} - \mathbf{i}^t\mathbf{v}$, which has neither minima nor maxima since $\mathbf{W}$ is neither positive nor negative definite. Thus, the energy function $E(\mathbf{v})$ possesses no unconstrained minima. This, in turn, means that in the case of limitation of the output space of the system to a $[-1, 1]$ hypercube, the constrained minima of $E(\mathbf{v})$ must be located somewhere at the hypercube's boundary, or in other words, on the edges or faces of the cube. If a solution $\mathbf{v}^*$ of the constrained system within the cube $[-1, 1]$ exists, then it must be a saddle point. Clearly, this solution does not represent an attractor for the discussed dynamical system (Park 1989).

Let us try to examine the locations of the stationary points of a high-gain neural network. The energy function (5.14) without its third term, and evaluated on the faces and on the edges simplifies to the following expressions, respectively,

$$E = -\frac{1}{2}(w_{ij}v_iv_j + w_{ji}v_jv_i) - k_iv_i - k_jv_j \qquad (5.23\text{a})$$

$$E = -k_iv_i + c \qquad (5.23\text{b})$$

where k_i is constant. Indices i and j, for $i, j = 1, 2, \ldots, n$, in Equation (5.23) determine the face (i, j) or the edge (i), of the n-dimensional cube. Since the Hessian matrix for the two-variable function $E(v_i, v_j)$ as in (5.23a) has again a zero diagonal, no minima can exist on any of the faces of the cube. Further, since (5.23b) is a monotonic and linear function of a single variable v_i, the minima may not occur on the edges of the cube either. Thus, the minima, if they exist, must be confined to the vertices of the cube.

We have shown that the assumption of high-gain neurons resulting in neglecting the last term of energy in (5.14) enforces the constrained minima to be exactly in the vertices of the $[-1, 1]$ cube having a total of 2^n vertices. The high-gain network that approaches, in the limit case, the discrete-time system is expected to have its energy minima in the cube corners. The convergence observed in actual gradient-type network hardware should result in one such cube corner solution.

The gradient-type network with finite neuron gain values also evolves in the continuous-time mode to one of the minima of $E(\mathbf{v})$. However, the minima are now within the cube and are attractors of the system. Such minima are usually desirable if they are as close to the vertices of the hypercube as possible. Understandably, they will always be within the $[-1, 1]$ cube, and for $\lambda \to \infty$ they will reach the cube corners.

Concluding this discussion of stationary points of energy function for single-layer feedback networks we notice that the solutions of Equations (5.20) and (5.12b) always represent either the constrained minimum or saddle of the energy function. There is, in general, more than one solution to (5.20) and (5.12b). The solution reached by an actual neural network is dependent on network parameters and on the initial condition within the network. Some of the solutions produced by neural networks of this class are useful, so they will be desirable. Other solutions will be less useful and may even be erroneous, although sometimes hard to avoid. This property applies both to discrete-time and continuous-time rules of convergence. We have considered a number of properties of single-layer feedback neural networks that will bring in a number of interesting results and applications. While these results and applications will be studied later, the example below will highlight some of the aspects just discussed.

EXAMPLE 5.2 ▬▬▬▬▬▬▬▬▬▬▬▬▬▬▬▬

In this example we design a simple continuous-time network using the concept of computational energy function and also evaluate stationary solutions of the network. The A/D converter circuit discussed below was first proposed in Tank and Hopfield (1986).

Let us assume that the analog input value x is to be converted by a two-neuron network as in Figure 5.1 or 5.4(a) to its binary representation. In this example it will be assumed that the activation function $f(u_i)$ is continuous unipolar and defined between 0 and 1. The A/D conversion error E_c can be considered here as an energy function. We can thus express it by the following formula

$$E_c = \frac{1}{2}\left(x - \sum_{i=0}^{1} v_i 2^i\right)^2 \tag{5.24a}$$

where the $v_0 + 2v_1$ is the decimal value of the binary vector $\begin{bmatrix} v_1 & v_0 \end{bmatrix}^t$ and it corresponds to the analog x value.

The reason for this choice of the energy function is that minimizing the energy will simultaneously minimize the conversion error. Our objective is to find matrix $\mathbf{W}$ and the input current vector $\mathbf{i}$ for a network minimizing the error E_c. Evaluation of the error (5.24a) indicates, however, that it contains terms v_0^2 and v_1^2, thus making the w_{ii} terms equal to 2^{2i} instead of equal to zero as postulated by the network definition. Therefore, a supplemental error term E_a, as in (5.24b), will be added. In addition to eliminating the diagonal entries of $\mathbf{W}$, this term will be minimized close to the corners of the $[0, 1]$ square on v_0, v_1 plane. A suitable choice for E_a is therefore

$$E_a = -\frac{1}{2} \sum_{i=0}^{1} 2^{2i} v_i(v_i - 1) \tag{5.24b}$$

Indeed, if we note that E_a is nonnegative we can see that it has the lowest value for $v_i = 0$ or $v_i = 1$. Thus, combining E_a and E_c, chosen as in (5.24), results in the following total energy function, which is minimized by the neural network A/D converter:

$$E = \frac{1}{2}\left(x - \sum_{i=0}^{1} v_i 2^i\right)^2 - \frac{1}{2} \sum_{i=0}^{1} 2^{2i} v_i(v_i - 1) \tag{5.25a}$$

This expression for energy should be equated to the general formula for energy as in (5.14), which is equal in this high-gain neuron case:

$$E = -\frac{1}{2} \sum_{i=0}^{1} \sum_{\substack{j=0 \\ j \neq i}}^{1} w_{ij} v_i v_j - \sum_{i=0}^{1} i_i v_i \tag{5.25b}$$

Note that the energy function (5.14) in the high-gain case retains only two terms, and the term with the integral vanishes because of the high-gain neurons used. Routine rearrangements of the right side of the energy expression (5.25a) yield

$$E = \frac{1}{2}x^2 + \frac{1}{2} \sum_{i=0}^{1} \sum_{\substack{j=0 \\ i \neq j}}^{1} 2^{i+j} v_i v_j + \sum_{i=0}^{1} \left(2^{2i-1} - 2^i x\right) v_i \tag{5.26}$$

When the analog input x is fixed, the term $(\frac{1}{2})x^2$ is an additive constant in (5.26), and it is irrelevant for the minimization of E given by (5.26) on the v_0, v_1 plane; therefore, it will be omitted. Comparing the like coefficients of v_0 and v_1 on the right side of energy functions (5.25b) and (5.26) results in the following network parameters:

$$
\begin{aligned}
w_{01} = w_{10} &= -2 \\
i_0 &= x - \frac{1}{2} \\
i_1 &= 2x - 2
\end{aligned}
\tag{5.27}
$$

The resulting two-bit A/D converter network is the special case of the general network from Figure 5.4(a) and is designed according to specifications (5.27). The network diagram is shown in Figure 5.6(a). The two

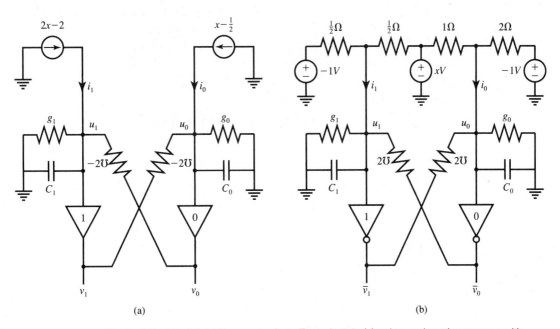

Figure 5.6 Two-bit A/D converter from Example 5.2: (a) using noninverting neurons with activation function $f(net)$ and (b) using inverting neurons with activation function $-f(net)$ and voltage sources producing i_0 and i_1.

current sources produce the biasing currents i_0 and i_1 and the weights are of $-0.5\,\Omega$ values. Let us note that the KCL equations (5.11) for nodes $i = 0$ and $i = 1$ can be obtained by inspection of Figure 5.6(a) as follows:

$$C_0 \frac{du_0}{dt} = x - \frac{1}{2} + (-2)v_1 - u_0(-2 + g_0)$$

$$C_1 \frac{du_1}{dt} = 2x - 2 + (-2)v_0 - u_1(-2 + g_1)$$

(5.28)

As we have already mentioned, the last term of the expression for energy (5.14) vanishes for high-gain neurons since the products u_iG_i become negligibly small. This assumption remains valid for large-gain λ values yielding small activation values u_i, unless the solution is very far from the square's vertices. Under this assumption, the converter diagram from Figure 5.6(a) can be redrawn as shown in Figure 5.6(b). An explicit assumption made for this figure is that $u_0 \cong u_1 \cong 0$, so that currents i_0 and i_1 as in (5.27) can be produced by a voltage source having voltage x combined with the reference voltage source, which delivers the voltage of value -1 V.

An additional change introduced in Figure 5.6(b) compared to Figure 5.6(a) for the sake of practicality has been the replacement of neurons with activation function $f(net)$ by neurons with its negative activation function $-f(net)$. Neurons with inverting properties can be called *inverting neurons*. Their outputs are now denoted $\bar{v}_0$ and $\bar{v}_1$. As a result of this modification, the previously negative conductances w_{01} and w_{10} of value -2 become positive, as desired. It is left to the reader to verify that Equations (5.28) now can be rewritten as follows

$$
\begin{aligned}
C_0 \frac{du_0}{dt} &= x - \frac{1}{2} + 2\bar{v}_1 - u_0(2 + g_0) \\
C_1 \frac{du_1}{dt} &= 2x - 2 + 2\bar{v}_0 - u_1(2 + g_1)
\end{aligned}
\tag{5.29a}
$$

Equation (5.29a) can be arranged in matrix form as in (5.12a):

$$
\begin{bmatrix} C_0 & 0 \\ 0 & C_1 \end{bmatrix}
\begin{bmatrix} \dfrac{du_0}{dt} \\ \dfrac{du_1}{dt} \end{bmatrix}
=
\begin{bmatrix} 0 & 2 \\ 2 & 0 \end{bmatrix}
\begin{bmatrix} \bar{v}_0 \\ \bar{v}_1 \end{bmatrix}
$$

$$
- \begin{bmatrix} 2 + g_0 & 0 \\ 0 & 2 + g_1 \end{bmatrix}
\begin{bmatrix} u_0 \\ u_1 \end{bmatrix}
+ \begin{bmatrix} x - \dfrac{1}{2} \\ 2x - 2 \end{bmatrix}
\tag{5.29b}
$$

The condition $w_{ij} \geq 0$ ensures the realizability of the network using resistive interconnections of values R_{ij}. The conductance matrix $\mathbf{W}$ now has positive valued elements $w_{ij} = 1/R_{ij}$. ■

5.4　TRANSIENT RESPONSE OF CONTINUOUS-TIME NETWORKS

Equation (5.11) or (5.12) describes the discussed nonlinear dynamical system in the form of its state equations. Because analytical methods for solving such equations in closed form do not exist, suitable numerical approaches need to be devised for obtaining transients $\mathbf{v}(t)$ and the stationary solution thereof $\lim_{t \to \infty} \mathbf{v}(t)$.

A number of numerical integration methods allow for computing the dynamic solution for $\mathbf{v}(t)$ starting at initial condition $\mathbf{v}(t_0)$. Also, steady-state solutions for the stationary points may be obtained by a number of methods for solving static nonlinear equations. In this section we will address only those among the many numerical approaches that are particularly useful in providing additional insight into network dynamics pattern.

Let us see first how the *vector field method* can be used to illustrate the real-time phenomena in networks with finite gain neurons. The method allows the transients of the nonlinear dynamical system to be captured. The vector field obtained by using this method involves all possible network trajectories in E^n space.

To obtain the vector field expression of the network of interest, Eq. (5.11) needs to be normalized using the C_i value as a divisor. Thus, the description of the system is given by n equations below:

$$\frac{du_i}{dt} = \frac{1}{C_i}\left(i_i - G_i u_i + \sum_{j=1}^{n} w_{ij}v_j\right), \quad \text{for } i = 1, 2, \dots, n \qquad (5.30)$$

Our vector field analysis objective is to transform the description of the system, originally as in (5.30), to the following form:

$$\frac{dv_i}{dt} = \psi_i[\mathbf{v}(t)], \quad \text{for } i = 1, 2, \dots, n \qquad (5.31)$$

where ψ_i are functions that should be found. These functions are vector field components. Subsequently, after discretizing differential equations [Equations (5.31)], values $\psi_1(\mathbf{v})$, $\psi_2(\mathbf{v}), \dots, \psi_n(\mathbf{v})$ are numerically computed at each point of the space v. As a result, we obtain the vector field diagram, which clearly indicates complete trajectories of the system's dynamics and shows how it evolves in time during transients. While the solution is somewhat more qualitative and the produced vectors contain no explicit time component, the vector field provides complete information about basins of attractions for any given initial point, as well as about the stationary solutions.

To be able to use the vector field method, we note that the specific form of the activation function should be assumed in order to produce Equation (5.31). For the discussion below it has been chosen as

$$v = f(u) = \frac{1}{1 + \exp(-\lambda u)} \qquad (5.32a)$$

Simple differentiation of (5.32a) leads to

$$\frac{dv}{du} = \lambda(v - v^2) \qquad (5.32b)$$

The increments of v_i as functions of increments of u_i can now be expressed as

$$dv_i = \lambda(v_i - v_i^2)du_i \qquad (5.32c)$$

Inserting the result of Equation (5.32c) into (5.30) leads to

$$\frac{dv_i}{dt} = \frac{\lambda(v_i - v_i^2)}{C_i}\left(i_i - G_i f^{-1}(v_i) + \sum_{j=1}^{n} w_{ij}v_j\right), \quad \text{for } i = 1, 2, \dots, n \quad (5.33)$$

Equation (5.33) is a specific form of the general vector field expression (5.31) for which we have been looking. Vector field components ψ_i are equal to the right side of (5.33). To trace the movement of the system within the output space, the components of ψ must be computed for the entire cube $v \in [0, 1]$ as follows:

$$\psi_i(\mathbf{v}) = \frac{\lambda(v_i - v_i^2)}{C_i} \left(i_i - G_i f^{-1}(v_i) + \sum_{j=1}^{n} w_{ij} v_j \right), \text{ for } i = 1, 2, \ldots, n \quad (5.34)$$

It is interesting to observe that the trajectories depend on the selected λ values, if they are finite, and also on the values of capacitances C_i. In addition to these factors, the steady state, or equilibrium solution may be reached along one of the many trajectories dependent on the initial conditions. The example below will provide more insight into the transient performance of a network with finite λ_i values.

EXAMPLE 5.3 ■■■■■■■■■■■■■■

In this example we will evaluate stationary points and discuss the time-domain behavior of the continuous-time example two-bit A/D neural converter designed in Example 5.2. In particular, we will trace the behavior of the converter output versus time and inspect the energy minimization property during the evolution of the system.

Substituting the weights and current values as calculated in (5.27) we can express the truncated energy function given by (5.25b) for very high gains λ_i as follows:

$$E = -\frac{1}{2} \sum_{\substack{i=0 \\ i \neq j}}^{1} \sum_{j=0}^{1} (-2) v_i v_j - \left(x - \frac{1}{2} \right) v_0 - (2x - 2) v_1 \quad (5.35a)$$

Expanding the double sum and rearranging terms leads to the value for E:

$$E = 2 v_0 v_1 + \frac{v_0}{2} + 2 v_1 - x(v_0 + 2 v_1) \quad (5.35b)$$

Figure 1.10 displays two cases of the truncated energy function of Equation (5.35) for analog input $x = 0$ and $x = 1$. As shown in the figure, the only stationary points are appropriate minima, $v_0 = v_1 = 0$ for $x = 0$, and $v_0 = 1$ and $v_1 = 0$ for $x = 1$. Figure 5.7(a) shows the energy function for $x = 0.5$ and it can be seen that, in contrast to previous cases, the minimum of the energy function exists for $0 < v_0 < 1, v_1 = 0$. It is thus spread over the entire range of output variable v_0. Indeed, an absence of a definite response by the network is caused by the fact that no digital conversion of the analog input $x = 0.5$ exists that would minimize the conversion error (5.24a).

Another interesting case of energy function behavior occurs for $1 < x < 2$. The energy functions (5.35) are illustrated for $x = 1.25$ and $x = 1.5$ on Figures 5.7(b) and (c), respectively. Inspection of both functions reveals that they both have (1) a desirable minimum at $v_0 = 1$ and $v_1 = 0$, (2) an undesirable minimum at $v_0 = 0$ and $v_1 = 1$, and (3) a saddle point somewhere inside the unity square.

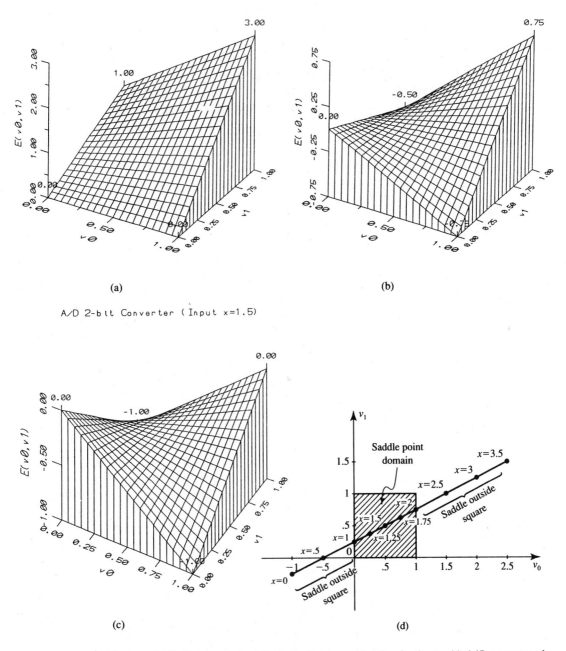

Figure 5.7 Stationary points of the truncated energy function for the two-bit A/D converter of Example 5.3: (a) energy function ($x = 0.5$), (b) energy function ($x = 1.25$), (c) energy function ($x = 1.5$), and (d) saddle point locus ($0 < x < 2.5$).

The discussion below focuses on more detailed analysis of the energy function so that the equilibrium points of the system can be investigated based on the evaluation of the energy function. This should provide us with much insight into the behavior of the system, but even more importantly, will perhaps eliminate the need for solution of differential equations (5.11) and replace it with inspection of the energy function minima.

Let us evaluate the truncated energy function (5.35b). The energy gradient $\nabla E(\mathbf{v})$ can be computed from (5.35b) and equated to zero for the fixed value of x to determine possible high-gain minima at $\mathbf{v}^*$:

$$\nabla E(\mathbf{v}) = \begin{bmatrix} 2v_1 + \dfrac{1}{2} - x \\ 2v_0 + 2 - 2x \end{bmatrix} \tag{5.36a}$$

To find the type of stationary points of the network, it is helpful to see that the Hessian matrix $\mathbf{H}$ of the energy function (5.35b) becomes

$$\mathbf{H} = \nabla^2 E(\mathbf{v}) = \begin{bmatrix} 0 & 2 \\ 2 & 0 \end{bmatrix} \tag{5.36b}$$

Result (5.36b) indicates that the Hessian matrix is not positive definite. The energy function has therefore no unconstrained minima. Stationary points $\mathbf{v}^*$ may still be maxima and/or saddles. We can also see that Hessian matrix determinants are

$$\det H_{11} = 0$$

$$\det H_{22} = \begin{bmatrix} 0 & 2 \\ 2 & 0 \end{bmatrix} = -4$$

Thus, the Hessian matrix is not negative definite either. Thus, whatever solutions $\mathbf{v}^*$ are identified within the cube $(0, 1)$ such that

$$\nabla E(\mathbf{v}^*) = \mathbf{0} \tag{5.36c}$$

will be the saddle points of the $E(\mathbf{v})$ function. This coincides with our conclusions related to Equation (5.22) and (5.23) that the minima of the truncated energy function (5.35b) are at cube vertices, and the saddle points may be located anywhere inside it.

The solution for a saddle point of the energy function (5.35b) results directly from (5.36a) and (5.36c) as

$$v_1 = \frac{1}{2}v_0 + \frac{1}{4} \tag{5.37}$$

The saddle point locus is shown in Figure 5.7(d). The saddle point exists within the unity square $0 < v_i < 1$, for $i = 0, 1$, and only for $1 < x < 2$. The cases $0 < x < 1$ and $2 < x < 3.5$ are characterized by a monotonic energy function and the absence of a saddle point within the square of interest. However, there exists a saddle point outside the square and thus outside the domain of definition of vector $\mathbf{v}$. ■

Let us see how the study of the energy function and the properties of the converter's vector field can be merged to provide insight into the network behavior. Examples of selected vector field diagrams produced from Equation (5.34) for the discussed converter are shown in Figure 5.8. The figure illustrates four different cases of convergence to the equilibrium point for selected gain values of $\lambda = 10$ and 100. The remaining convergence parameters of interest are the input conductances g_i of the neurons and the capacitance ratio C_1/C_0. The convergence has been evaluated for inputs $x = 0$ [Figures 5.8(a) and (b)] and $x = 1.8$ [Figures 5.8(c) and (d)]. The energy function contours, or equipotential lines, have also been marked as background lines. The energy contour maps displayed are for the case of very high-gain neurons and a truncated energy expression as in (5.35b) (Zurada, Kang, and Aronhime 1990).

Unless the terms u_0G_0 and u_1G_1 are excessive, the system evolves in time toward lower values of the truncated energy function as shown. Otherwise, the system minimizes the complete energy function as in (5.14), involving therefore the third term. In any of the cases, the evolution of the system in time is not exactly in the energy function negative gradient direction. It can be seen that for a high value of gain λ and small input conductances g_i of neurons (note that these are the conditions which make a network free from parasitic phenomena) the equilibrium solution approaches one of the corners shown in Figures 5.8(a) and (c). As shown in Figure 5.8(b), for large input conductances $g_0 = g_1 = 10\,\Omega^{-1}$, the convergence does not end at any of the corners. The truncated energy function contours do not exactly describe now the evolution of the network in the case of large g_iu_i terms. The stationary point M in Figure 5.8(b) is not in the truncated energy function minimum; however, it is a minimum of the complete energy function involving its last term. It is also the endpoint of all relevant trajectories indicating the dynamics of the network. Point M is the minimum of the complete energy function (5.14), which for this case becomes

$$E_{\text{tot}} = E + E_3 \tag{5.38a}$$

Energy E is given by (5.35b) and the term E_3 can be obtained from (5.14) as

$$E_3 = \sum_{i=0}^{1} G_i \int_{1/2}^{v_i} f(\lambda, z)^{-1}\, dz \tag{5.38b}$$

where the inverse of the activation function (5.32a) can be expressed

$$f(\lambda, z)^{-1} = \frac{1}{\lambda} \ln\left(\frac{z}{1-z}\right)$$

This yields the explicit value of the third term of energy as

$$E_3 = \sum_{i=0}^{1} \frac{G_i}{\lambda_i} \left[v_i \ln v_i + (1 - v_i)\ln(1 - v_i) + \ln 2\right] \tag{5.38c}$$

It should be noted that the total energy function E_{tot} now has minima within the cube. Indeed, when neurons are of finite gains λ, then the minimum of the energy function must exist within the cube, since no walls, edges, or corners

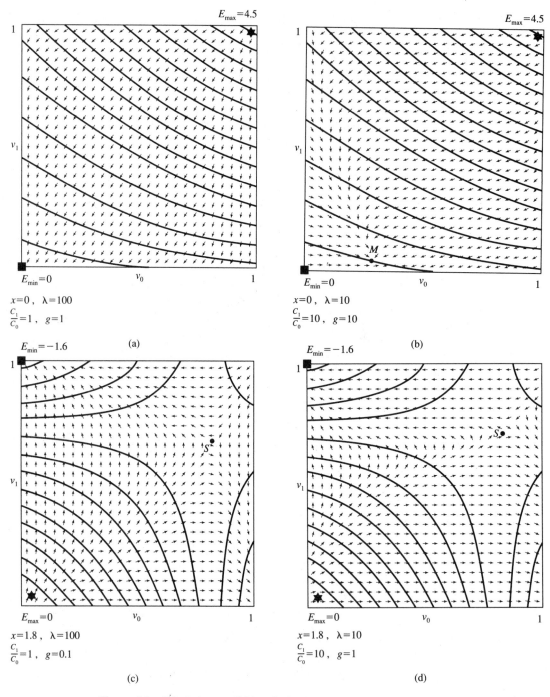

Figure 5.8 Selected vector field method solutions for dynamic behavior of two-bit A/D converter: (a) $x = 0$, $\lambda = 100$, $C_1/C_0 = 1$, $g = 1$, (b) $x = 0$, $\lambda = 10$, $C_1/C_0 = 10$, $g = 10$, (c) $x = 1.8$, $\lambda = 100$, $C_1/C_0 = 1$, $g = 0.1$, and (d) $x = 1.8$, $\lambda = 10$, $C_1/C_0 = 10$, $g = 1$.

are the domain of vector **v**. This is in contrast to the case of the truncated energy function for which minima have been confined to vertices and edges of the cube. We can see that the total energy (5.38c) has no truncation error and more realistically characterizes the properties of actual networks for which λ is of finite value. The reader may refer to Problem P5.19 for more illustrations related to the total energy function.

Let us see how we can utilize the vector field trajectories to visualize the phenomena occurring in the network. By comparing the vector fields of Figures 5.8(a) and (b), we can see that the trajectories become horizontally skewed for large C_1/C_0. This condition promotes movement of the system with slowly varying v_1 and faster varying v_0. This asymmetry of motion is due to the fact that C_1 holds the majority of charge and the voltage u_1 has to change more slowly than u_0 in this otherwise symmetric network.

In addition, the vector field provides valuable insight for the case of an energy function saddle, as has been shown in Figures 5.8(c) and (d). The analog input which needs to be converted is of value $x = 1.8$. It can be computed from (5.36a) that the saddle point S denoted as **v*** is at (0.8, 0.65). It can also be seen that the trajectories indicate that either of the solutions $v_0 = 0$ and $v_1 = 1$ or $v_0 = 1$ and $v_1 = 0$ can be reached by the network depending on the initial condition selected. Comparison of convergence with zero initial conditions at $\mathbf{v} = \begin{bmatrix} 0.5 & 0.5 \end{bmatrix}^t$ indicates that the right solution for converting the analog input $x = 1.8$ is reached in the case of equal capacitances C_1 and C_0 in Figure 5.8(a). The case shown in Figure 5.8(d) depicts the incorrect solution due to the horizontally biased movement of the system toward the right.

In conclusion, the vector field method provides detailed insight into the transients and stability conditions of the actual network. Although the method can be illustrated by trajectories and provides insight only for cases of networks with up to three neurons, it can be applied for any value of n. In addition, one of the many numerical integration formula can be used for numerical analysis of dynamic performance of continuous-time networks (DiZitti et al. 1989). Selected exercises at the end of the chapter are devoted to this approach.

5.5   RELAXATION MODELING IN SINGLE-LAYER FEEDBACK NETWORKS

The discussion in the preceding sections of this chapter has shown that the gradient-type single-layer network converges, in time, to one of the minima of $E(\mathbf{v})$ located within the hypercube $[-1, 1]$. This assumption is valid for bipolar continuous neurons with outputs defining the components of n-dimensional vector **v**. Whether simulated, or reached in actual gradient-type hardware network, the solution may or may not be satisfactory. The solution may not even be the desired one due to the existence of a much better solution.

Let us devise an efficient numerical approach for finding the solution of differential equations (5.12). As stated before, the solution of differential equations (5.12) can be replaced by solving the purely algebraic equation (5.20b) with the additional nonlinear mapping condition (5.12b). Let us notice that (5.20b) is equivalent to n algebraic equations written as

$$\sum_{j=1}^{n} w_{ij}v_j + i_i = G_i u_i, \quad \text{for } i = 1, 2, \ldots, n \tag{5.39a}$$

Using (5.12b), the above expression can be rewritten in the form involving the nonlinear mapping $v = f(u)$ as follows:

$$v_i = f\left[\frac{1}{G_i}\left(\sum_{j=1}^{n} w_{ij}v_j + i_i\right)\right], \quad \text{for } i = 1, 2, \ldots, n \tag{5.39b}$$

The numerical solution of (5.39b) for v_i can be modeled by the fixed-point iteration method as follows:

$$v_i^{k+1} = f\left[\frac{1}{G_i}\left(\sum_{j=1}^{n} w_{ij}v_j^k + i_i\right)\right], \quad \text{for } i = 1, 2, \ldots, n \tag{5.40a}$$

where superscript k denotes the index of numerical recursion, $k = 0, 1, \ldots$. Equation (5.40a) can be briefly rewritten in the vector form as

$$\mathbf{v}^{k+1} = \mathbf{f}\left[\mathbf{G}^{-1}(\mathbf{W}\mathbf{v}^k + \mathbf{i})\right] \tag{5.40b}$$

Equation (5.40b) represents the computational model for recursive numerical calculations of vector $\mathbf{v}^{k+1}$. First, an initial output vector $\mathbf{v}^0$ is submitted to the network to initialize it, then the response $\mathbf{v}^1$ is computed and is used to replace the value $\mathbf{v}^0$ on the right side of (5.40b). The algorithm of Equations (5.40) is referred to in literature as the *relaxation,* or method of successive approximation, *algorithm.* As we can see, the algorithm is static, and it represents the solution of a system *without* its dynamic components. Indeed, it is remarkable that the solution (5.40b) does not involve network capacitances. Although the relaxation algorithm is computationally simple, it does not provide any insight into the network dynamics. In addition, the algorithm shown below is numerically stable only under certain conditions.

The recursive computation of $\mathbf{v}^{k+1}$ using fixed-point iterations (5.40) is convergent only under certain conditions, which are discussed in more detail and derived in Zurada and Shen (1990). A sufficient condition for convergence of the relaxation algorithm is

$$\lambda < \min_{i=1,2,\ldots,n}\left\{\frac{4}{n}\left|\frac{G_i}{w_{ij}}\right|\right\}, \quad \text{for } j = 1, 2, \ldots, n, \quad j \neq i \tag{5.40c}$$

It can be seen from (5.40c) that to assure unconditional convergence of the

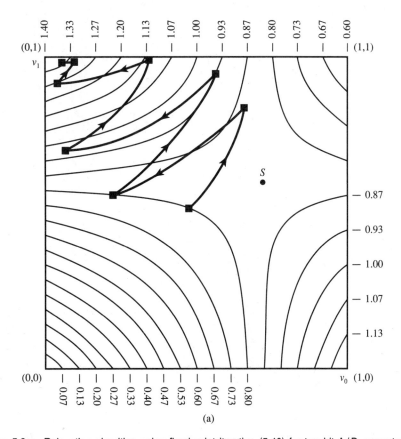

Figure 5.9a Relaxation algorithm using fixed-point iteration (5.40) for two-bit A/D converter, $x = 1.7$: (a) $\lambda = 3.5$, stable numerical solution.

algorithm, λ must be kept below an upper bound value on the right side of the inequality. An illustration of the relaxation algorithm for the two-bit A/D converter is shown in Figure 5.9 for the input $x = 1.7$. Figure 5.9(a) shows stable recursive calculations using (5.40) for $\lambda = 3.5$. The recursive calculations become oscillatory, however, for the λ value of 5, as shown in Figure 5.9(b). Note that both cases from Figure 5.9 originate at zero initial conditions of $\mathbf{v}^0 = \begin{bmatrix} 0.5 & 0.5 \end{bmatrix}^t$. This corresponds to the network without an initial energy and starting at a neutral initial point. Specifically, the network capacitances hold no initial charge and provide no initial bias.

In summary, the vector $\mathbf{v}(t)$ converges, in time, to one of the minima of $E(\mathbf{v})$ constrained to within the $[0, 1]$ cube, and transients are dependent on the initial condition $\mathbf{v}(0) = \mathbf{f}[\mathbf{u}(0)]$. The system settles there according to its dynamics, and the capacitors and other components determine the actual rate of convergence

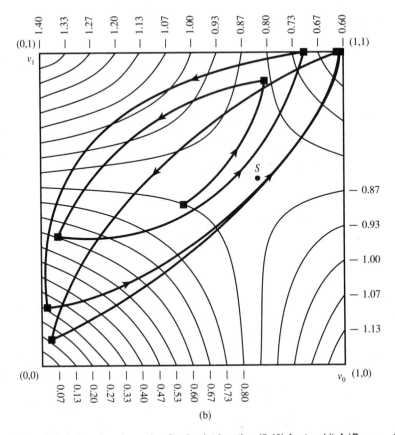

Figure 5.9b   Relaxation algorithm using fixed-point iteration (5.40) for two-bit A/D converter, $x = 1.7$ *(continued):* (b) $\lambda = 5$, unstable numerical solution.

toward the minimum of $E(\mathbf{v})$. The computational relaxation model (5.38), although entirely based on the resistive portion of the network, captures one of the time-domain, or transient, solutions at which the gradient vector vanishes.

It should also be noted that the relaxation algorithm, or any other static algorithm that solves the equation (5.20b) based on zeroing of the gradient vector, should be used for finding stationary points rather than for finding minima only. Indeed, since $\nabla E(\mathbf{v}) = \mathbf{0}$ both at saddle points and at minima, the numerical solutions for cases as shown in Figure 5.9 also produce the saddle point S.

Similar results can be obtained from analysis of single-layer feedback networks using the Newton-Raphson algorithm to solve (5.20b). The Newton-Raphson algorithm is unconditionally stable; however, it is very sensitive to the initial conditions. More insight into application of this algorithm for neural network numerical solutions is available to the reader in Problem P5.18.

EXAMPLE SOLUTIONS OF OPTIMIZATION PROBLEMS

In this section, two comprehensive examples of continuous-time single-layer feedback networks will be covered. The discussion will emphasize understanding and practical integration of most of the concepts introduced earlier in the chapter. Both examples present the solution of optimization problems modeled with fully coupled single-layer network. The first example covers the design of an electronic network that performs the conversion of a multidimensional analog signal into a four-dimensional binary unipolar vector using the least squared error criterion. The presentation of the first example involves all stages of the design, and is followed by the detailed performance study of the network. The second example approaches a classical and more general optimization problem solution known in technical literature as the *traveling salesman problem*. The presentation of this second example focuses on formulating the most suitable objective function that would need to be substituted for an energy function.

Summing Network With Digital Outputs

The network is based on the concept presented earlier in Example 4.2. The adder/converter discussed in this section and the simple two-bit A/D converter in Example 4.2 belong to the same class of optimization networks. They both attempt to solve specific optimization problems of error minimization between analog input values and their digital output representation using Boolean vectors. Note that the problem essentially reduces to finding a mapping of various input signals into an n-dimensional binary vector such that the mapping objective function, defined as quadratic error, is minimized. To design the network, appropriate responses need to be encoded as its equilibrium states.

Assume that the circuit shown in Figure 5.4 needs to compute the sum of N analog voltages x_k with corresponding weighting coefficients a_k. A digital representation of the output sum using n bits is required, thus $v_i = 0, 1$, for $i = 0, 1, \ldots, n - 1$. Let us momentarily assume that the accurate analog sum of the signals is x, thus:

$$x = \sum_{k=0}^{N-1} a_k x_k \tag{5.41}$$

This value has to be approximated by a binary n-component vector. The computational energy that needs to be minimized for this circuit behaving as an n-bit A/D converter can be expressed in terms of the squared error

$$E_c = \frac{1}{2} \left(x - \sum_{i=0}^{n-1} v_i 2^i \right)^2 \tag{5.42a}$$

Expansion of the sum indicates that (5.42a) contains square terms $(v_i 2^i)^2$, thus making the w_{ii} terms equal to 2^{2i}, instead of equal to zero as required. Similarly, as in Example 5.2, a supplemental energy term E_a (5.42b) should be added that, in addition to eliminating diagonal entries of the weight matrix $\mathbf{W}$, will have minima at v_i equal to 0 or 1.

$$E_a = -\frac{1}{2} \sum_{i=0}^{n-1} 2^{2i} v_i (v_i - 1) \tag{5.42b}$$

Let us sum E_c and E_a and use the truncated energy function (5.14) which is allowed in case of high-gain neurons. We can now require equality between the specific energy function value on the left side of Equation (5.43) and its general form shown on the right side of (5.43):

$$\frac{1}{2}\left(x - \sum_{i=0}^{n-1} v_i 2^i\right)^2 - \frac{1}{2}\sum_{i=0}^{n-1} 2^{2i} v_i(v_i - 1) = -\frac{1}{2}\mathbf{v}^t\mathbf{W}\mathbf{v} - \mathbf{i}^t\mathbf{v} \tag{5.43}$$

Comparing coefficients on both sides of (5.43) yields the conductance matrix and bias current vector entries of the designed neural network as follows

$$w_{ij} = -2^{i+j} \tag{5.44a}$$

$$i_i = -2^{2i-1} + 2^i x \tag{5.44b}$$

In the case of a four-bit A/D converter, the results of Equations (5.44) can be written in matrix form as follows:

$$\mathbf{W} = -\begin{bmatrix} 0 & 2 & 4 & 8 \\ 2 & 0 & 8 & 16 \\ 4 & 8 & 0 & 32 \\ 8 & 16 & 32 & 0 \end{bmatrix}, \quad \mathbf{i} = -\begin{bmatrix} \frac{1}{2} - x \\ 2 - 2x \\ 8 - 4x \\ 32 - 8x \end{bmatrix} \tag{5.44c}$$

Due to the simplification introduced in (5.41), these are only preliminary answers. To complete the design and to obtain the full diagram of the summing and converting circuit, the value of x as in (5.41) should be plugged into the left side of formula (5.43). This yields the modified energy function in the following form:

$$E = \frac{1}{2}\left(\sum_{k=0}^{N-1} a_k x_k - \sum_{i=0}^{n-1} v_i 2^i\right)^2 - \frac{1}{2}\sum_{i=0}^{n-1} 2^{2i} v_i(v_i - 1) \tag{5.45a}$$

Rearranging the above expression results in the energy function for the summing circuit being equal to

$$E = -\frac{1}{2}\sum_{\substack{i=0 \\ i \neq j}}^{n-1}\sum_{j=0}^{n-1} -2^{i+j} v_i v_j - \sum_{i=0}^{n-1}\left(-2^{2i-1} + 2^i \sum_{k=0}^{N-1} a_k x_k\right) v_i$$

$$+ \frac{1}{2}\left(\sum_{k=0}^{N-1} a_k x_k\right)^2 \tag{5.45b}$$

Comparing Equation (5.45b) with the right side of Equation (5.43) allows the calculation of the conductance matrix elements w_{ij} and the neuron input currents i_i of network S as

$$w_{ij} = -2^{i+j} \tag{5.46a}$$

$$i_i = -2^{2i-1} + 2^i \sum_{k=0}^{N-1} a_k x_k \tag{5.46b}$$

Figure 5.10 shows the resulting network with appropriate conductance values labeled. The network consists of two parts. The bottom part replicates the fully coupled single-layer network of Figure 5.4a. This is a "neural" part of the network with synaptic weights as in (5.46a). Note that the originally negative signs of the conductance values have been absorbed by the feedback signal derived from inverted neuron outputs. The top part of the network denoted S produces appropriate bias currents by computing the expression (5.41) as indicated by the sum on the right side of (5.46b). Conductances connect voltage sources x_j and a voltage source -1 V with inputs of neurons to produce current according to formula (5.46b).

The approach presented in the preceding paragraphs can be extended to the case of binary addition. For binary coded values of signals x and y, the corresponding energy function similar to that obtained in (5.45a) becomes

$$E = \frac{1}{2}\left(\sum_{k=0}^{n-1} 2^k x_k + \sum_{k=0}^{n-1} 2^k y_k - \sum_{i=0}^{n} v_i 2^i\right)^2 - \frac{1}{2}\sum_{i=0}^{n} 2^{2i} v_i(v_i - 1) \tag{5.47}$$

Rearrangement of (5.47) leads to an expression for the values w_{ij} identical to (5.46a). The new conductance values of network S performing the binary addition are now the only difference between the originally considered converting circuit and the joint summing and converting circuit. The input currents to the neurons are specified by the following expression:

$$i_i = -2^{2i-1} + 2^i \left(\sum_{k=0}^{n-1} 2^k x_k + \sum_{k=0}^{n-1} 2^k y_k\right), \quad \text{for } i = 0, 1, \ldots, n \tag{5.48}$$

The binary adder network S generating the bias current vector $\mathbf{i}$ consists now of the total of $(2N + 1)(n + 1)$ conductances. The "neural" part of the adder remains unchanged and identical as in previous cases of an A/D converter and an analog signal adder.

To illustrate the theoretical considerations involved in this design, the performance of an electronic network model has been simulated. The convergence of transients for the hardware model has been evaluated for nine different initial conditions. The neurons have been designed using NMOS transistors (Zurada and Kang 1989). For the simple two-dimensional case, contour maps of truncated energy functions, as in (5.35b), have been computed and convergence versus time evaluated for $x = 0, 1, 2$, and 3. The resulting trajectories obtained from an electronic circuit simulator program SPICE2G1.6 are shown in Figure 5.11.

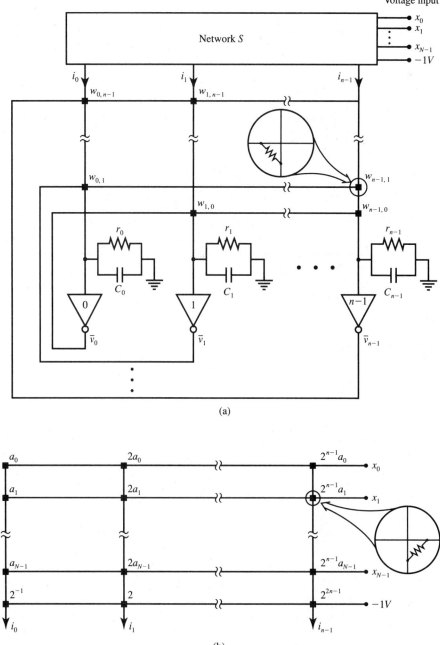

(a)

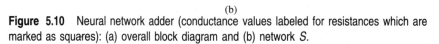

(b)

Figure 5.10 Neural network adder (conductance values labeled for resistances which are marked as squares): (a) overall block diagram and (b) network S.

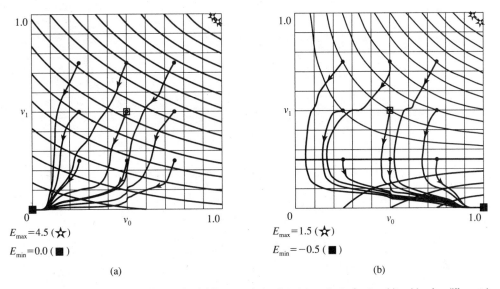

$E_{max}=4.5\ (\bigstar)$

$E_{min}=0.0\ (\blacksquare)$

$E_{max}=1.5\ (\bigstar)$

$E_{min}=-0.5\ (\blacksquare)$

(a)   (b)

Figure 5.11a,b Equipotential lines and simulated transients for two-bit adder for different inputs (• denotes initial point, □ denotes zero initial conditions point): (a) $x = 0$, (b) $x = 1$.

The distance between each of the two neighboring energy contour lines shown is equal to $1/16$ of the energy difference within the cube. As expected, none of the energy functions has local minima within the cube. Transitions in time take place toward one of the constrained minima and they are generally not in the negative gradient direction.

In the cases of $x = 1.3$ and 1.8, the corresponding energy functions have a saddle point and two minima at 01 and 10, respectively. The convergence of transients is to the correct minimum in both cases for $C_0 = C_1$ if zero initial conditions are chosen. For other choices of initial conditions, the transients may decay while yielding an incorrect final response at the output of this neural-type A/D converter. The erroneous response case is depicted in Figures 5.11(e) and (f), which show three trajectories ending up at the incorrect minimum.

For small slopes of the energy surface, the convergence is expected to be slow. This has actually been observed in Figures 5.11(b) and (c) for curves leaving the initial points most distant from the correct solutions, which are 01 and 10, respectively. The trajectories indicate rather slowly varying transients near $v_1 = 0.25$ [Figure 5.11(b)] and $v_1 = 0.75$ [Figure 5.11(c)], respectively. Slight discontinuities on all curves of Figure 5.11 are also noticeable. They are due to the shape of the voltage transfer characteristics near $u = 0$ for the actual electronic neuron models.

The results of transient simulations at the circuit level using the SPICE2G1.6 program for a four-bit summing network with zero initial conditions have been correct for 145 of 155 simulated cases. Input x applied to a four-bit summing

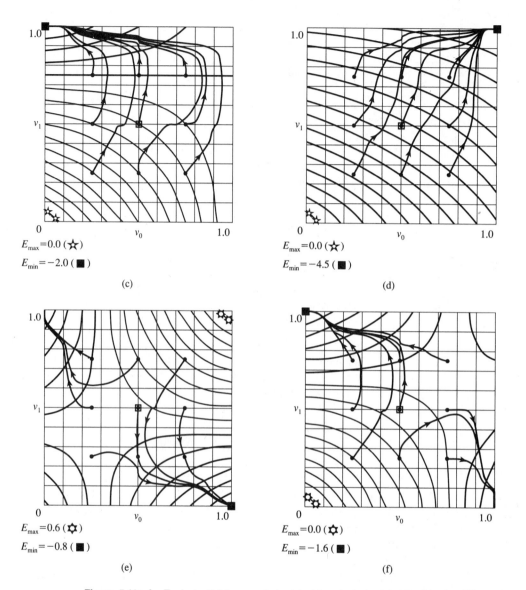

Figure 5.11c–f Equipotential lines and simulated transients for two-bit adder for different inputs (• denotes initial point, □ denotes zero initial conditions point) *(continued):* (c) $x = 2$, (d) $x = 3$, (e) $x = 1.3$, and (f) $x = 1.8$.

network is varied in the range between 0 and 15.5 with a step of 0.1. In all 10 cases of erroneous convergence, however, the settled binary output is adjacent to the correct answer, thus making the resulting response error bounded. Results of the transient circuit analysis and subsequent thresholding of **v** are shown in Table 5.1.

TABLE 5.1

Simulation results for input x from the interval [0, 15.5], four-bit adder.

Input Integer Part	Input Decimal Part									
	0	0.1	0.2	0.3	0.4	0.5	0.6	0.7	0.8	0.9
0	0	0	0	0	0	0.5	1	1	1	1
1	1	1	1	1	1	1	1	2	2	2
2	2	2	2	2	2	2.5	3	3	3	3
3	3	3	3	3	3	3	3	3	3	4
4	4	4	4	4	4	4.5	5	5	5	5
5	5	5	5	5	5	6	6	6	6	6
6	6	6	6	6	6	6.5	7	7	7	7
7	7	7	7	7	7	8	8	8	8	8
8	8	8	8	8	8	8.5	9	9	9	9
9	9	9	9	9	9	9	9	10	10	10
10	10	10	10	10	10	10.5	11	11	11	11
11	11	11	12	12	12	12	12	12	12	12
12	12	12	12	12	12	12.5	13	13	13	13
13	13	13	14	14	14	14	14	14	14	14
14	14	14	14	14	14	14.5	15	15	15	15
15	15	15	15	15	15					

Interesting results have been observed for simulation of the case when the integer answer for the sum, or A/D conversion problem solution, does not exist because it is exactly equidistant from the adjacent integers. The v_0 bit has remained undetermined and has settled very close to 0.5 for 8 of 15 such cases. Evaluation of the energy value (5.14) shows flat minima spread between adjacent integers. The case is reminiscent to the one depicted in Figure 5.7(a) for the truncated energy function of the two-neuron network.

Sample actual transients illustrating such cases are shown in Figure 5.12, which shows for case $x = 0.5$ that the truncated energy function is monotonic, it has no saddle point within the cube, and the least significant output bit of the network converges to near 0.5. On the other side if $x = 1.5$, the convergence is somewhat erroneous as shown in Figure 5.12(b), because the saddle point at $v_0 = v_1 = 0.5$ divides symmetrically the two monotonic subsurfaces of the error surface E. This case was depicted earlier in Figure 5.7(c) showing the truncated energy surface for $x = 1.5$.

Inspection of corresponding energy surfaces has also shown that for the erroneous results listed in Table 5.1 for the four-dimensional case, the network outputs have converged to erroneous shallow minima. It has also been observed that the convergence to correct minima is usually more reliable when initiated

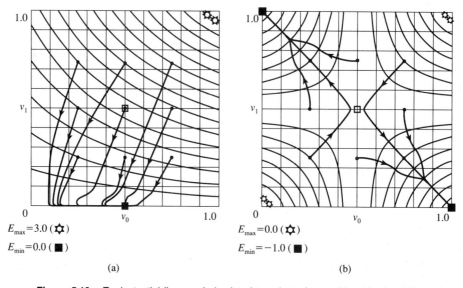

$E_{max}=3.0$ (✿) $E_{max}=0.0$ (✿)

$E_{min}=0.0$ (■) $E_{min}=-1.0$ (■)

(a)   (b)

Figure 5.12 Equipotential lines and simulated transients for two-bit adder for different inputs (• denotes initial points, □ denotes zero initial conditions point): (a) $x = 0.5$ and (b) $x = 1.5$.

from a higher initial energy level. It has also been found that the network unmistakably rejected all obviously incorrect suggestions. Additions with negative results have all been rounded to the lowest sum 00, ..., 0. Additions with overflow sums have been rounded by the network to the highest sum 11, ..., 1.

Minimization of the Traveling Salesman Tour Length

The traveling salesman problem of minimization of the tour length through a number of cities with only one visit in each city is one of the classic optimization problems. The objective of the problem is to find a closed tour through n cities such that the tour length is minimized. The problem is NP-complete (nondeterministic polynomial time).

Typically, an optimization problem of size n may have many possible solutions. However, only one of the solutions minimizes the cost, or error, function. Optimization problems of this kind are called *combinational optimization problems*. They are often divided into classes according to the time needed to solve them.

If an algorithm exists that is able to solve the problem in a time that increases polynomially with the size n of the problem, the problem is said to be polynomial (*P*). NP-complete problems are a class within the *P* class. Such

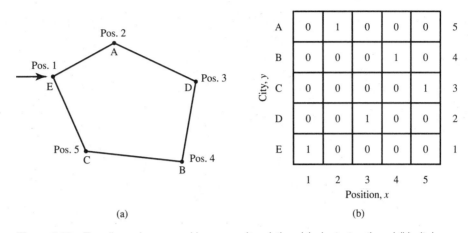

Figure 5.13 Traveling salesman problem example solution: (a) shortest path and (b) city/position matrix.

problems can be tested in polynomial time whether or not a guessed solution of the problem is correct. To solve an NP problem in practice, it usually takes time of order $\exp(n)$. Thus, the traveling salesman problem solution using the conventional combinational optimization approach grows exponentially with the number of cities n. We consider a solution for the problem using continuous-time gradient-type neural networks (Hopfield and Tank 1985).

An example of the cities and the proposed tour is shown in Figure 5.13(a) for $n = 5$. The distances between cities are assumed to be constant for a given set of visited cities. The reader can verify that there are $n!$ tours that can be produced in an n city problem. Among them, $2n$ closed paths are originating at different n cities and going in both directions; therefore, they are of identical lengths. Thus, there are $(n-1)!/2$ distinct paths that have to be evaluated as far as total tour length minimization is concerned.

A network consisting of n^2 unipolar continuous neurons can be designed to solve this problem. Let us arrange the neurons in an $n \times n$ array. The suggested representation for the $n \times n$ neuron array can be arranged in the form of a matrix, where the j'th row in the $n \times n$ matrix corresponds to a city y_j, and the i'th column in the matrix corresponds to a city position x_i. We thus have city rows and position columns. One example solution of the problem is shown in Figure 5.13(b) for $n = 5$. It has the form of a city/position matrix with 0, 1 entries representing the best tour shown in Figure 5.13(a). Since each city can only be visited once and no simultaneous visits are allowed, the solution matrix can have only a single 1 in each column and a single 1 in each row. The neuron turned on, or with output 1, in the square array of neurons indicates a particular position of a particular city.

Note that the example of Figure 5.13 introduced specific notation. The row subscript corresponds to a city name, and the column subscript indicates a position in the tour. Using the correspondence between the neuron's array and the solution matrix, we may say that a valid solution of the problem would have only a single neuron in each column and only a single neuron in each row on. Thus, a total of n of n^2 neurons is distinctly turned on. Accordingly, we will assume high-gain neurons for the network modeling this problem. Note that the truncated energy function as in (5.14), with the third term omitted for simplicity, can be rewritten as follows:

$$E = -\frac{1}{2}\sum_{Xi}\sum_{Yj} w_{Xi,Yj} v_{Xi} v_{Yj} - \sum_{Xi} i_{Xi} v_{Xi} \tag{5.49}$$

Let us observe that the domain of vectors $\mathbf{v}$ where the function E is minimized is the $2^{n \times n}$ corners of the n^2-dimensional hypercube $[0, 1]$.

Let us attempt to find the suitable expression for the energy function solving this problem (Hopfield and Tank 1985). Our objective is to find weights and currents that are coefficients of the quadratic form of the energy function (5.49) such that the objective function is minimized. The goal of the optimization is to select the shortest tours. Also, the matrix of responses has to be penalized for more than a single "on" neuron per row and per column. In addition, the matrix has to be penalized for trivial solutions of all entries being zero. Let us quantitatively express each of the optimization conditions just spelled out qualitatively by using four following terms of the energy function, each fulfilling a separate role:

$$E_1 = A\sum_{X}\sum_{i}\sum_{j} v_{Xi} v_{Xj}, \quad \text{for } i \neq j \tag{5.50a}$$

$$E_2 = B\sum_{i}\sum_{X}\sum_{Y} v_{Xi} v_{Yi}, \quad \text{for } X \neq Y \tag{5.50b}$$

$$E_3 = C\left(\sum_{X}\sum_{i} v_{Xi} - n\right)^2 \tag{5.50c}$$

$$E_4 = D\sum_{X}\sum_{Y}\sum_{i} d_{XY} v_{Xi}\left(v_{Y,i+1} + v_{Y,i-1}\right), \quad X \neq Y \tag{5.50d}$$

Let us discuss the term E_1, as in (5.50a), of the energy function. A matrix with 0 and 1 entries has no more than one 1 in each row if and only if all possible column-by-column dot products within the matrix are zero. The double internal sum of (5.50a) expresses the $N - 1$ dot products of a column having position X times the remaining columns. Performing the leftmost summation operation (in 5.50a) yields the required sum of all column dot products, which ideally should all be zero. The zero value of E_1 would guarantee that each city will be visited only once. Note that the penalty will progress and become larger if more than a single 1 is contained in one or more rows.

The energy term E_2 proposed as in (5.50b) can be substantiated in a similar way, and it contains a progressive penalty for two or more ones in each column of the matrix. This penalty takes a form of positive value for this term of the energy function and is for simultaneous visits in more than a single city. The justification for this term is similar to that above for E_1, however, it applies to controlling the number of ones within columns of the city/position matrix.

Note that penalties E_1 and E_2 are also of zero value for trivial solutions containing no ones, or less ones than required within the city/position matrix. Therefore the term E_3, as in (5.50c), is required to ensure that the matrix does not simply contain all zeroes. In addition, this term penalizes the objective function for having more or less than n ones in the matrix. The energy function $E_1 + E_2 + E_3$ has minima of value 0 for all matrices that have exactly one 1 per row per column, and all other responses of neurons produce higher energy values. Minimization of the energy function $E_1 + E_2 + E_3$ ensures, or better, favors, that one of the valid tours can be generated.

The discussion of the energy function has focused on formulating constraints and has not yet involved the true goal of tour optimization. The term E_4, as in (4.50d), needs to be added and minimized for the shortest tours. Simply summing the distance of the tour is a natural choice for E_4, since minimizing the tour length is the goal. However, denoting the intercity distances as d_{XY}, we want to make sure that only the distances between adjacent cities are counted. To include end effects like the adjacency of city $n-1$ and 1, the subscripts for summations have to be understood as summed modulo n. This term is numerically equal to the length of the path of the tour.

The resulting weight matrix and bias currents can now be obtained by equating the sum of energies E_1 through E_4 specified by (5.50) with the total energy value as in (5.49). The weights computed in this problem are (Hopfield and Tank 1985):

$$W_{Xi,Yj} = -2A\delta_{XY}(1 - \delta_{ij}) - 2B\delta_{ij}(1 - \delta_{XY})$$
$$- 2C - 2Dd_{XY}(\delta_{j,i+1} + \delta_{j,i-1}) \tag{5.51a}$$

where δ_{ij} is the Kronecker delta function defined as $\delta_{ij} = 1$, for $i = j$, and $\delta_{ij} = 0$, for $i \neq j$. Positive constants A, B, C, and D are selected heuristically to build an appropriate sum of terms E_1 through E_4. The constants are responsible for weighting the relative validity of each of the four penalty terms in the overall energy function E to be minimized. The external bias currents are

$$i_{Xi} = 2Cn \tag{5.51b}$$

Observe that the four separate terms of the weight matrix (5.51a) have been generated by the four parts of the energy function as in Equations (5.50a) through (5.50d), respectively. The term E_1 leads to inhibitory (negative) connection of value $-A$ within each row. The term E_2 causes identical inhibitory connections within each column. The term E_3 results in global inhibition provided by each weight, and the term E_4 contains the city distances data weight contribution. Finally, the external input currents are set at an excitation bias level as in (5.51b).

The problem formulated as shown above has been solved numerically for the continuous activation function defined in (2.4a) with $\lambda = 50$, $A = B = D = 250$, and $C = 100$, for $10 \leq n \leq 30$ (Hopfield and Tank 1985). The normalized city maps were randomly generated within the unity square to initialize each computational experiment using a simulated neural network. The equations solved numerically were

$$\frac{du_{X_i}}{dt} = -\frac{u_{Xi}}{\tau} - 2A \sum_{j \neq i} v_{Xj} - 2B \sum_{Y \neq X} v_{Yi}$$

$$- 2C \left(\sum_X \sum_j v_{Xj} - n \right) - 2D \sum_Y d_{XY}(v_{Y,i+1} + v_{Y,i-1}) \tag{5.52}$$

where the time constant τ was selected as 1. For $n = 10$, 50% of the trials produced the two best paths among 181440 distinct paths. For $n = 30$, there exists about 4.4×10^{30} possible paths. The simulations of the solutions for this size of problem have routinely produced paths shorter than 7. Statistical evaluation of all paths shows that there are only 10^8 paths shorter than 7. Although no optimal solution has been reported when using this approach, the bad path rejection ratio by the network has been impressive. In numerical experiments by Hopfield and Tank (1985), the bad path rejection ratio was between 10^{-23} and 10^{-22}.

There are practical limitations of the discussed approach. The method becomes more difficult to apply for larger problems, typically larger than 10 cities. However, the example of the traveling salesman problem illustrates that a class of optimization tasks can be approached using the dynamical system model presented in this chapter. Many other possible applications of the model have been reported in the literature. Typical problems solved have been of the resource allocation type, which are subject to different constraints. Job shop scheduling optimization has been reported by Foo and Takefuji (1988). In another application, the concentrator-to-sites assignment problem was mapped onto the single-layer network model by associating each neuron with the hypothesis that a given site should be assigned a particular concentrator (Tagliarini and Page 1988).

Fully coupled single-layer networks can be applied to a variety of other technical problems. Networks of this class are capable of handling optimal routing of calls through a three-stage interconnection network (Melsa, Kenney, and Rohrs 1990). The solution uses a discrete neuron network that seeks a minimum of an energy function for cases in which an open path exists through the interconnection network. When no such path is available, the energy function minimization performed by the network terminates at a null state indicating that the interconnection network is blocked.

Another successful application of energy minimizing networks is for routing communication traffic within a multinode network consisting of many nodes and links. The solution of such a problem requires finding the best of multilink paths for node-to-node traffic to minimize loss. The loss is represented by expected delay or some other traffic inconvenience. The minimization procedure has been implemented using a modification of the traveling salesman problem solution (Rauch and Winarske 1988). Reasonable convergence for a 16-node network has been reported for up to four links from origin to destination.

Other applications of this class of neural networks involve microelectronic circuit module placement on the chip that minimizes the total interconnecting wire length (Sriram and Kang 1990). The two-dimensional problem has been decomposed into two coupled one-dimensional placement problems. The performance of the designed neural network on problems involving placement with up to 64 modules has been very encouraging, with the network being able to find the globally optimal or near-optimal solutions in many cases.

Single-layer networks have also been successfully applied to general linear and nonlinear programming tasks. Nonlinear programming is a basic tool in systems where a set of design parameters is optimized subject to inequality constraints. Both experimental and theoretical results have been presented for completely stable solutions of specific linear and nonlinear programming problems (Kennedy and Chua 1988; Maa and Shanblatt 1989). An economic power dispatch problem has also been solved by using the linear programming network with linear equality and inequality constraints (Maa, Chin, and Shanblatt 1990). A linear programming problem formulation and solution is also demonstrated in Section 8.1.

5.7 CONCLUDING REMARKS

In this chapter we have introduced the basic properties of single-layer feedback neural networks. Neurocomputing algorithms producing convergence toward solutions for both discrete-time and continuous-time networks have been reviewed. The discussion emphasized the dynamical principles of single-layer continuous-time feedback networks. Also, several network design examples have been presented to illustrate the basic concepts of system evolution toward its attractors. Throughout the chapter, the concept of energy function has been stressed. This had two goals in mind: to demonstrate the inherent stability of the networks and the suitability of the networks for producing solutions of certain optimization tasks.

In addition to many questions that have been answered about the performance of this neural network model, some problems still remain open. Let us raise some of the remaining open questions. The stationary solution reached in the time domain does not represent, in general, a global optimum solution to the problem of energy function minimization. This is due to the often highly complex shape of the multidimensional energy function $E(\mathbf{v})$. This limitation is somewhat mitigated by the fact that global solutions of real large-scale minimization problems of $E(\mathbf{v})$ are often mathematically very hard to track anyway, and for large-scale problems cannot be found with certainty.

One of the difficult tasks faced by the designer at the beginning of the design process is the translation of the optimization problem into the energy function minimization. Here, the general energy function must be matched by the criterion function which is specific for the problem being solved. Given the restrictions on the connectivity matrix imposed by the model, these functions may not match easily. Therefore, problem-specific energy functions are usually hard to find. We have been able to discuss several choices of $E(\mathbf{v})$, but the general solution to the problem does not exist. The only energy form known is the general one stated as in (5.5) or (5.14). Following simplifying modification can often be applied here: If high-gain neurons are used, the third term of the energy expression can be skipped. Also, when no external bias input $\mathbf{i}$ is needed, the second energy term vanishes and network weights only need to be computed.

It often takes much of the network designer's ingenuity to devise a meaningful energy function in the neurons output space $\mathbf{v}$ and to find its coefficients w_{ij} and i_i. In fact, our ignorance concerning possibly existing energy functions that solve a number of optimization problems creates one of the bottlenecks that makes the use of the gradient-type networks not as simple. For certain classes of systems, such as associative memories, however, $E(\mathbf{v})$ and w_{ij} are easy to find in an explicit form. This will be discussed in the next chapter.

As we have seen, the convergence toward an attractor being a solution for single-layer feedback neural networks corresponds to the transient behavior of a nonlinear dynamical system. Although the concept of a time constant is not directly applicable to nonlinear networks, the transient analysis shows that the convergence of a neural network typically requires several time constants as defined for the network's linear portion. This property is often reported based on numerous experiments both involving actual hardware and numerical simulations.

Figure 5.14 illustrates the procedure for solving optimization problems using single-layer feedback networks. Basic steps that need to be followed by the designer are summarized on the diagram. The problem modeling procedure terminates by implementing transients within the network and accepting the solution produced. In easy optimization tasks, each of the generated solutions is usually correct. This has been the case for A/D conversion networks for low n values. For harder optimization problems such as the traveling salesman problem for large n ($n \geq 30$), the produced solutions are often good but not strictly optimal. This is due to the presence of many local minima in n-dimensional space which are responsible for trapping the evolution of the transients. It should be realized that this class of networks for large n values yields solutions which are not necessarily optimal but acceptable in a statistical sense, i.e., over a population of experiments rather than for a single transient event.

An additional limitation existing within the networks discussed concerns their capacity. There is a limit on the total number of correct solutions that can be stored and expected from the network as its output. Although this number cannot be set precisely, heuristic evaluations of gradient-type networks show that the number of encoded solution vectors that can be retrieved satisfactorily is only a small fraction of the total number of neurons n. The network capacity issues and others related to network performance will be discussed in more detail in the following chapter.

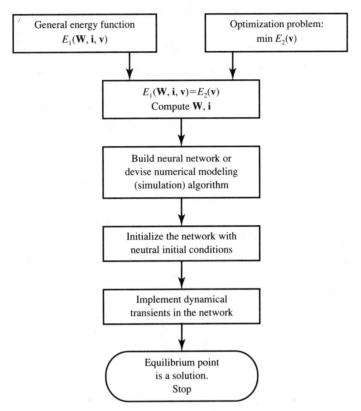

Figure 5.14 Flowchart of producing solutions of optimization problems using fully coupled feedback networks.

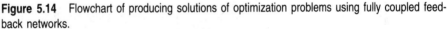

PROBLEMS

Please note that problems highlighted with an asterisk (*) are typically computationally intensive and the use of programs is advisable to solve them.

P5.1 The weight matrix **W** for a network with bipolar discrete binary neurons is given as

$$\mathbf{W} = \begin{bmatrix} 0 & 1 & -1 & -1 & -3 \\ 1 & 0 & 1 & 1 & -1 \\ -1 & 1 & 0 & 3 & 1 \\ -1 & 1 & 3 & 0 & 1 \\ -3 & -1 & 1 & 1 & 0 \end{bmatrix} \Omega^{-1}$$

Knowing that the thresholds and external inputs of neurons are zero, compute the values of energy for $\mathbf{v} = \begin{bmatrix} -1 & 1 & 1 & 1 & 1 \end{bmatrix}^t$ and $\mathbf{v} = \begin{bmatrix} -1 & -1 & 1 & -1 & -1 \end{bmatrix}^t$.

P5.2   Figure P5.2 shows a discrete-time recurrent network with high-gain bipolar neurons.

(*a*) Find the weight matrix of the network by inspecting the connections.

(*b*) Analyze asynchronous updates from the following initial states:

$$\mathbf{v}^0 = \begin{bmatrix} -1 \\ -1 \\ 1 \\ 1 \\ 1 \end{bmatrix}, \mathbf{v}^0 = \begin{bmatrix} -1 \\ -1 \\ 1 \\ 1 \\ -1 \end{bmatrix}, \mathbf{v}^0 = \begin{bmatrix} -1 \\ -1 \\ -1 \\ 1 \\ -1 \end{bmatrix}, \mathbf{v}^0 = \begin{bmatrix} -1 \\ 1 \\ -1 \\ 1 \\ -1 \end{bmatrix}, \mathbf{v}^0 = \begin{bmatrix} 1 \\ -1 \\ 1 \\ 1 \\ -1 \end{bmatrix}$$

Assume that the updates take place in natural order starting with the first neuron, i.e., 1, 2, ...

(*c*) Identify any stable equilibrium state(s) of the network based on part (b).

(*d*) Compute the energy value at the stable equilibrium state(s) evaluated in part (c). (Use the truncated energy function.)

P5.3* Assuming the weight matrix and other input conditions from Problem P5.1, compute the energy values for all 32 bipolar binary vectors (there are five energy levels here). Identify the potential attractors that may have been encoded in the system described by the specified matrix **W** by comparing the energy values at each of the $[-1, +1]$ cube vertices. Implement five sample asynchronous discrete-time transitions from high- to low-energy vertices.

P5.4   The weight matrix **W** for a single-layer feedback network with three neurons is given as

$$\mathbf{W} = \begin{bmatrix} 0 & -1 & -1 \\ -1 & 0 & 1 \\ -1 & 1 & 0 \end{bmatrix} \Omega^{-1}$$

Calculate the gradient vector, $\nabla E(\mathbf{v})$, for the energy function in three-dimensional output space and its Hessian matrix, $\nabla^2 E(\mathbf{v})$. Prove that the Hessian matrix is not positive definite (see the Appendix).

P5.5   For the two-neuron continuous-time single-layer feedback network shown in Figure P5.5 with high-gain neurons, find the following:

(*a*) state equations

(*b*) the weight (conductance) matrix, **W**

(*c*) the truncated energy function, $E(\mathbf{v})$

(*d*) the gradient vector of the truncated energy function, $\nabla E(\mathbf{v})$.

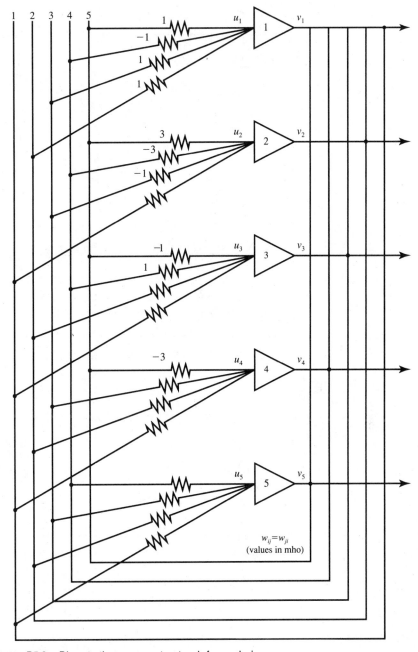

Figure P5.2 Discrete-time recurrent network for analysis.

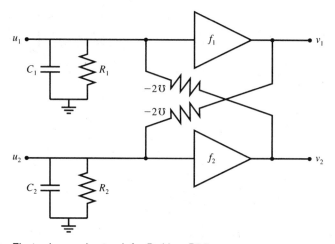

Figure P5.5   Electronic neural network for Problem P5.5.

P5.6   For the continuous-time single-layer feedback network shown in Figure P5.6 with high-gain neurons, find the following:

(*a*)   state equations

(*b*)   the weight (conductance) matrix, **W**

(*c*)   the current vector, **i**

(*d*)   the truncated energy function, $E(\mathbf{v})$

(*e*)   the gradient vector of the truncated energy function, $\nabla E(\mathbf{v})$.

P5.7   Find the weight matrix **W** for the four high-gain neuron network shown in Figure P5.7. The network uses inverting neurons and four positive-valued conductances of value $2\,\Omega^{-1}$ each. Then find the energy values for outputs $\mathbf{v}_1$, $\mathbf{v}_2$, and $\mathbf{v}_3$ given as below:

$$\mathbf{v}_1 = [-1\ {-1}\ \ 1\ \ 1]^t,\ \mathbf{v}_2 = [-1\ {-1}\ {-1}\ \ 1]^t,\ \mathbf{v}_3 = [-1\ {-1}\ {-1}\ {-1}]^t.$$

P5.8   Sketch the appropriate conductances connecting outputs of inverting and noninverting neurons in a network having the overall diagram as shown in Figure P5.7 knowing that

$$\mathbf{W} = \begin{bmatrix} 0 & -1 & -1 \\ -1 & 0 & 1 \\ -1 & 1 & 0 \end{bmatrix}\Omega^{-1},\quad \mathbf{i} = \mathbf{0}$$

Evaluate the truncated energy function produced by the network for $v_i = \pm 1$, for $i = 1, 2, 3$, and identify possible attractors of the discrete-time network with high-gain neurons.

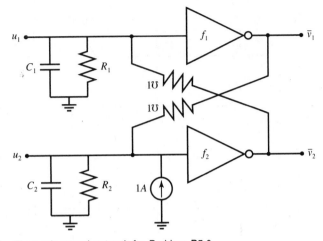

Figure P5.6 Electronic neural network for Problem P5.6.

P5.9 The truncated energy function, $E(\mathbf{v})$, of a certain two-neuron network is specified as

$$E(\mathbf{v}) = -\frac{1}{2}\left(v_1^2 + 2v_1v_2 + 4v_2^2 + v_1\right)$$

Assuming high-gain neurons:

(a) Find the weight matrix $\mathbf{W}$ and the bias current vector $\mathbf{i}$.

(b) Determine whether single-layer feedback neural network postulates (symmetry and lack of self-feedback) are fulfilled for $\mathbf{W}$ and $\mathbf{i}$ computed in part (a).

P5.10 Assuming the energy functions and other conditions as in Problem P5.9, find

(a) the gradient vector of the energy function, $\nabla E(\mathbf{v})$

(b) the Hessian matrix of the energy function, $\nabla^2 E(\mathbf{v})$

(c) any unconstrained minima or maxima $\mathbf{v}^*$ the energy function may have.

P5.11 The truncated energy function of a certain three-neuron single-layer network is known as

$$E(\mathbf{v}) = v_1^2 - v_2^2 + v_3^2 - 2v_1v_3 - v_2v_3 + 4v_1 + 12$$

Find the following:

(a) the gradient vector, $\nabla E(\mathbf{v})$

(b) the Hessian matrix, $\nabla^2 E(\mathbf{v})$

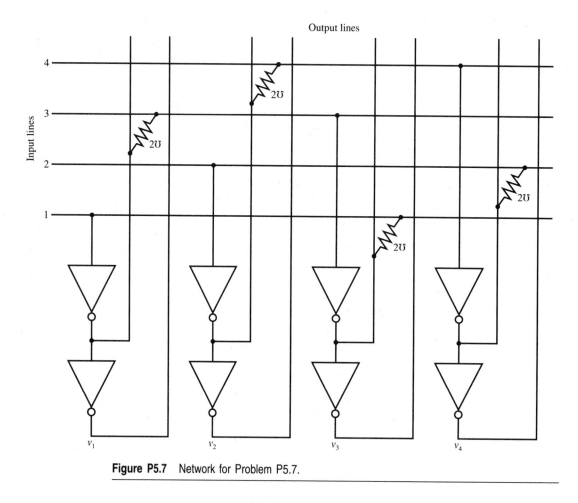

Figure P5.7 Network for Problem P5.7.

(c) any minima, maxima, or saddle points the energy function may have. What are they?

P5.12 The high-gain neuron continuous-time network is shown in Figure P5.12. By evaluating its energy function, find analytically any minima, maxima, or saddle points the function has within the $[-1, 1]$ three-dimensional cube. Use the truncated energy expression containing no third term. Then compute numerical energy values at each of the cube's eight vertices.

P5.13 The energy function $E(\mathbf{v})$ for the two-bit A/D converter discussed in Example 5.3 is specified by Equation (5.35b). It has been derived under the assumption of infinite gain neurons. Calculate the accurate energy function at $\mathbf{v} = \begin{bmatrix} 0.01 & 0.01 \end{bmatrix}^t$ using the accurate expression for energy (5.14) which, in addition to (5.35b), involves the additional integral term

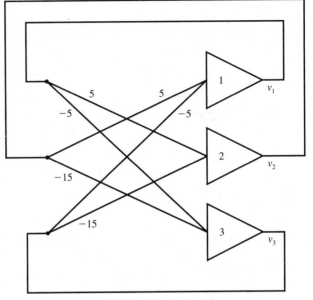

(Weight values in mhos)

Figure P5.12 High-gain neuron network for Problem P5.12.

(5.38c). This term is equal to

$$\sum_{i=0}^{1} G_i \int_{0.5}^{v_i} f_i^{-1}(z)\, dz$$

Assume the converter as in Figure 5.6(b) with $g_0 = g_1 = 1\,\Omega^{-1}$, $x = 1.7$, and

$$v_i = f_i(u_i) = \frac{1}{1 + \exp(-10u_i)}$$

P5.14 Calculate the truncated energy function $E(v_0, v_1, v_2)$ for a three-bit A/D converter that uses high-gain neurons. Then calculate the point v^* for which $\nabla E(v^*) = \mathbf{0}$. Based on the evaluation of the Hessian matrix, $\nabla^2 E(v^*)$, determine what is the type of point v^* computed.

P5.15 A single-layer feedback neural network is described by the nonlinear differential equations, which must be solved numerically

$$\frac{du_i}{dt} = \frac{1}{C_i}\left(\sum_{j=1}^{n} w_{ij}v_j - u_iG_i + i_i \right), \quad \text{for } i = 1, 2, \ldots, n$$

and

$$v_i = f(u_i)$$

(a) Derive the forward Euler numerical integration formula to find u_i, for $i = 1, 2, \ldots, n$.

(b) Derive the backward Euler numerical integration formula to find u_i, for $i = 1, 2, \ldots, n$.

P5.16* Implement the backward Euler numerical integration formula derived in Problem P5.15 to solve for $\mathbf{v}(t)$. Obtain the solution for a simple two-bit A/D converter as in Figure 5.6. Assume $C_0 = C_1 = 1\,F$, $g_0 = g_1 = 1\,\Omega^{-1}$, $x = 0$, and

$$v_i = f(u_i) = \frac{1}{1 + \exp(-10u_i)}, \quad \text{for } i = 0, 1$$

Test the program for the following initial conditions: $\mathbf{v}_0 = \begin{bmatrix} 0.25 & 0.25 \end{bmatrix}^t$, $\mathbf{v}_0 = \begin{bmatrix} 0.5 & 0.5 \end{bmatrix}^t$, and $\mathbf{v}_0 = \begin{bmatrix} 0.75 & 0.75 \end{bmatrix}^t$.

P5.17 Rearrange the nonlinear differential equations (5.28) describing the simple two-bit A/D converter to the form (5.34) so that the vector field components ψ_0, and ψ_1

$$\frac{dv_0}{dt} = \psi_0(v_0, v_1)$$

$$\frac{dv_1}{dt} = \psi_1(v_0, v_1)$$

can be explicitly computed for known values of x_i, g_i, C_i, and λ_i ($i = 0, 1$). Find $\psi_0(v_0, v_1)$ and $\psi_1(v_0, v_1)$ for the activation function $v_i = [1 + \exp(-\lambda u_i)]^{-1}$.

P5.18 The stationary point solution of Equations (5.28) describing the simple two-bit A/D converter can be obtained using the Newton-Raphson method by solving the nonlinear algebraic equation $\mathbf{F}(\mathbf{u}) = \mathbf{0}$, where

$$\mathbf{F}(\mathbf{u}) = \begin{bmatrix} -2v_1 + x - 0.5 - (g_0 - 2)u_0 \\ -2v_0 + 2x - 2 - (g_1 - 2)u_1 \end{bmatrix}$$

The iterative solution is obtained in this method as shown:

$$\begin{bmatrix} u_0^{k+1} \\ u_1^{k+1} \end{bmatrix} = \begin{bmatrix} u_0^k \\ u_1^k \end{bmatrix} - [\mathbf{J}(\mathbf{u})]^{-1} \begin{bmatrix} F_0(\mathbf{u}^k) \\ F_1(\mathbf{u}^k) \end{bmatrix}$$

where the Jacobian matrix is defined

$$\mathbf{J} \triangleq \begin{bmatrix} \dfrac{\partial F_0}{\partial u_0} & \dfrac{\partial F_0}{\partial u_1} \\ \dfrac{\partial F_1}{\partial u_0} & \dfrac{\partial F_1}{\partial u_1} \end{bmatrix}$$

Find the closed form for the iterative solution of the equation $\mathbf{F}(\mathbf{u}) = \mathbf{0}$, including the Jacobian matrix entries (no matrix inversion required). The

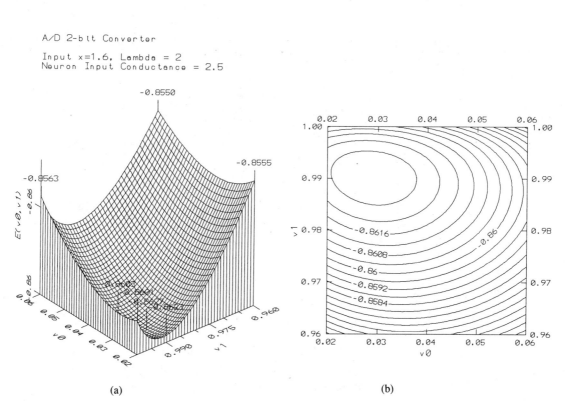

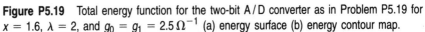

(a)   (b)

Figure P5.19   Total energy function for the two-bit A/D converter as in Problem P5.19 for $x = 1.6$, $\lambda = 2$, and $g_0 = g_1 = 2.5\,\Omega^{-1}$ (a) energy surface (b) energy contour map.

activation function to be assumed is

$$v_i = \left[1 + \exp\left(-\lambda u_i\right)\right]^{-1}, \quad \text{for } i = 0, 1$$

P5.19 Figure P5.19 illustrates the energy surface and the energy contour map near the upper left corner of the unity square. The graphs shown are made for the two-bit A/D converter and the following conditions: $x = 1.6$, $\lambda = 2$, and $g_0 = g_1 = 2.5\,\Omega^{-1}$. The displayed energy function expresses the total energy of the network, thus it involves the integral term (5.38c) additive with the truncated energy function (5.35b). Compute the numerical value of the total energy function at the energy minimum located approximately at

$$v_0^* \cong 0.03, \quad v_1^* \cong 0.99$$

P5.20 Figure P5.20 illustrates two cases of vector fields for the two-bit A/D converter. Each of the continuous lines drawn within the fields are for the condition $\partial v_0/\partial t = 0$ and $\partial v_1/\partial t = 0$. Obviously, stationary points are

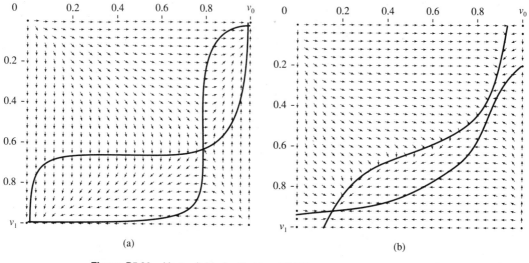

Figure P5.20   Vector fields for Problem P5.20.

located at the intersections of the lines, since both $\partial v_0 / \partial t = \partial v_1 / \partial t = 0$ there. By analyzing the vector field determine the following conditions:

(a) What are the types of the stationary points displayed in each of the figures?

(b) What is the approximate analog input value for the vector field of Figure P5.20(a)?

REFERENCES

Alspector, J., R. B. Allen, V. Hu, S. Satyanarayana. 1988. "Stochastic Learning Networks and Their Electronic Implementation," in *Neural Information Processing Systems,* ed. D. Z. Anderson, New York: American Institute of Physics, pp. 9–21.

DiZitti, E., et al. 1989. "Analysis of Neural Algorithms for Parallel Architectures," in *Proc. 1989 IEEE Int. Symp. Circuits and Systems,* Portland, Ore., May 9–12, 1989. New York: IEEE, pp. 2187–2190.

Hopfield, J. J. 1984. "Neurons with Graded Response Have Collective Computational Properties Like Those of Two State Neurons," *Proc. National Academy of Sciences* 81: 3088–3092.

Hopfield, J. J., and D. W. Tank. 1985. "Neural" Computation of Decisions in Optimization Problems," *Biolog. Cybern.* 52: 141–154.

Hopfield, J. J., and D. W. Tank. 1986. "Computing with Neural Circuits: A Model," *Science* 233: 625–633.

Howard, R. E., L. D. Jackel, and H. P. Graf. 1988. "Electronic Neural Networks," *AT&T Tech. J.* (May): 58–64.

Kamp, Y., and M. Hasler. 1990. *Recursive Neural Networks for Associative Memory,* Chichester, U.K.: John Wiley & Sons.

Kennedy, M. P., and L. O. Chua. 1988. "Neural Networks for Nonlinear Programming," *IEEE Trans. Circuits and Systems* CAS-35(5): 554–562.

Maa, C. Y., and M. A. Shanblatt. 1989. "Improved Linear Programming Neural Networks," in *Proc. 31st Midwest Symp. on Circuits and Systems,* Urbana, Ill., August 1989, New York, IEEE, pp. 748–751.

Maa, C. Y., C. Chin, and M. A. Shanblatt. 1990. "A Constrained Optimization Neural Net Techniques for Economic Power Dispatch," in *Proc. 1990 IEEE Int. Symp. on Circuits and Systems,* New Orleans, La., May 1–3, 1990. New York: IEEE, pp. 2945–2948.

Melsa, P. J., J. B. Kenney, and C. E. Rohrs. 1990. "A Neural Network Solution for Routing in Three Stage Interconnection Network," in *Proc. 1990 IEEE Int. Symp. on Circuits and Systems,* New Orleans, La., May 1–3, 1990. New York: IEEE, pp. 482–485.

Park, S. 1989. "Signal Space Interpretation of Hopfield Neural Network for Optimization," in *Proc. 1989 IEEE Int. Symp. Circuits and Systems,* Portland, Ore., May 9–12, 1989. New York: IEEE, pp. 2181–2184.

Rauch, H. E., and T. Winarske. 1988. "Neural Networks for Routing Communications Traffic," *IEEE Control Systems Magazine* (April): 26–31.

Roska, T. 1988. "Some Qualitative Aspects of Neural Computing Circuits," *in Proc. 1988 IEEE Int. Symp. on Circuits and Systems,* Helsinki. New York: IEEE, pp. 751–754.

Sriram, M., and S. M. Kang. 1990. "A Modified Hopfield Network for Two-dimensional Module Placement," in *Proc. 1990 IEEE Int. Symp. on Circuits and Systems,* New Orleans, La., May 1–3, 1990. New York: IEEE, pp. 1663–1666.

Tagliarini, G. A., and E. W. Page. 1988. "A Neural Network Solution to the Concentrator Assignment Problem," in *Neural Information Processing Systems,* ed. D. Z. Anderson, New York: American Institute of Physics, pp. 775–782.

Tank, D. W., and J. J. Hopfield. 1986. "Simple 'Neural' Optimization Networks: An A/D Converter, Signal Decision Circuit and a Linear Programming Circuit," *IEEE Trans. Circuits and Systems* CAS-33(5): 533–541.

Zurada, J. M., and M. J. Kang. 1988. "Summing Networks Using Neural Optimization Concept," *Electron. Lett.* 24(10): 616-617.

Zurada, J. M., and M. J. Kang. 1988. "Computational Circuits Using Neural Optimization Concept," *Int. J. Electron.* 67(3): 311–320.

Zurada, J. M., M. J. Kang, and P. B. Aronhime. 1990. "Vector Field Analysis of Single Layer Feedback Neural Networks," in *Proc. Midwest Symp. on Circuits and Systems,* Calgary, Canada, August 12–14, 1990 IEEE, New York: 22–24.

Zurada, J. M., and W. Shen. 1990. "Sufficient Condition for Convergence of Relaxation Algorithm in Neural Optimization Circuits," *IEEE Trans. Neural Networks* 1(4): 300-303.

Zurada, J. M. 1992. "Gradient-Type Neural Systems for Computation and Decision-Making," to appear in *Progress in Neural Networks,* ed. O. M. Omidvar. Vol. II. Norwood, New Jersey, Ablex Publishing Company.

6

ASSOCIATIVE MEMORIES

The clock upbraids me
with a waste of time.
SHAKESPEARE

n the preceding chapter we were concerned with dynamical systems that can be used in information processing systems. As we have shown, their dynamic behavior exhibits stable states that act as attractors during the system's evolution in time. Our discussion of dynamical systems thus far has been primarily oriented toward solving optimization problems. In this chapter, we will interpret the system's evolution as a movement of an input pattern toward another stored pattern, called a *prototype* or *stored memory.* Specifically, we will look at building associations for pattern retrieval and restoration. We will also study the dynamics of the discrete-time convergence process. Neural networks of this class are called *associative memories* and are presented in this chapter.

An efficient associative memory can store a large set of patterns as memories. During recall, the memory is excited with a *key pattern* (also called the *search argument*) containing a portion of information about a particular member of a stored pattern set. This particular stored prototype can be recalled through association of the key pattern and the information memorized. A number of architectures and approaches have been devised in the literature to solve effectively the problem of both memory recording and retrieval of its content. While most of our discussion in this chapter will involve dynamical systems using fully coupled feedback networks from Chapter 5, feedforward memory architectures that employ no feedback will also be discussed. Since feedforward memories were the first developed, their study seems to be both informative and provides insight into the fundamental concepts of neural memories.

Associative memories belong to a class of neural networks that learns according to a certain recording algorithm. They usually acquire information *a priori,* and their connectivity (weight) matrices most often need to be formed in advance. Writing into memory produces changes in the neural interconnections. Reading of the stored information from memory, introduced in Chapter 2 as recall, can be considered as the transformation of the input signals by the network. No usable addressing scheme exists in an associative memory since all memory information is spatially distributed and superimposed throughout the network.

Let us review the expectations regarding associative memory capabilities. The memory should have as large a capacity as possible or a large *p* value, which denotes the number of stored prototypes. At the same time the memory should be able to store data in a robust manner, so that local damage to its structure does not cause total breakdown and inability to recall. In addition, the ideal memory should truly associate or regenerate stored pattern vectors and do so by means of specific similarity criteria. Another very desirable feature of memory would be its ability to add and eliminate associations as storage requirements change.

Associative memory usually enables a parallel search within a stored data file. The purpose of the search is to output either one or all stored items that match the given search argument, and to retrieve it either entirely or partially. It is also believed that biological memory operates according to associative memory principles. No memory locations have addresses; storage is distributed over a large, densely interconnected, ensemble of neurons. What exactly is meant by that network of interconnections is seldomly defined for biological systems. The operating principles of artificial neural memory models are sometimes also very involved, and their presentation in this chapter is by no means exhaustive. The intention is to provide an understanding of basic associative memory concepts and of the potential benefits, applications, and limitations.

6.1

BASIC CONCEPTS

Figure 6.1 shows a general block diagram of an associative memory performing an associative mapping of an input vector $\mathbf{x}$ into an output vector $\mathbf{v}$. The system shown maps vectors $\mathbf{x}$ to vectors $\mathbf{v}$, in the pattern space $\mathbb{R}^n$ and output space $\mathbb{R}^m$, respectively, by performing the transformation

$$\mathbf{v} = M[\mathbf{x}] \tag{6.1}$$

The operator M denotes a general nonlinear matrix-type operator, and it has

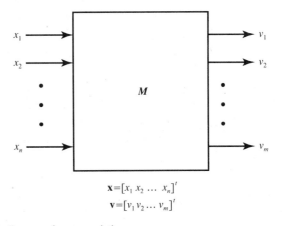

$$\mathbf{x} = [x_1 \ x_2 \ \dots \ x_n]^t$$
$$\mathbf{v} = [v_1 v_2 \dots v_m]^t$$

Figure 6.1   Block diagram of an associative memory.

different meaning for each of the memory models. Its form, in fact, defines a specific model that will need to be carefully outlined for each type of memory. The structure of M reflects a specific neural memory paradigm. For dynamic memories, M also involves time variable. Thus, $\mathbf{v}$ is available at memory output at a later time than the input has been applied.

For a given memory model, the form of the operator M is usually expressed in terms of given prototype vectors that must be stored. The algorithm allowing the computation of M is called the *recording* or *storage algorithm*. The operator also involves the nonlinear mapping performed by the ensemble of neurons. Usually, the ensemble of neurons is arranged in one or two layers, sometime intertwined with each other.

The mapping as in Equation (6.1) performed on a key vector $\mathbf{x}$ is called a *retrieval*. Retrieval may or may not provide a desired solution prototype, or an undesired prototype, but it may not even provide a stored prototype at all. In such an extreme case, erroneously recalled output does not belong to the set of prototypes. In the following sections we will attempt to define mechanisms and conditions for efficient retrieval of prototype vectors.

Prototype vectors that are stored in memory are denoted with a superscript in parenthesis throughout this chapter. As we will see below, the storage algorithm can be formulated using one or two sets of prototype vectors. The storage algorithm depends on whether an autoassociative or a heteroassociative type of memory is designed.

Let us assume that the memory has certain prototype vectors stored in such a way that once a key input has been applied, an output produced by the memory and associated with the key is the memory response. Assuming that there are p stored pairs of associations defined as

$$\mathbf{x}^{(i)} \rightarrow \mathbf{v}^{(i)}, \quad \text{for } i = 1, 2, \dots, p \tag{6.2a}$$

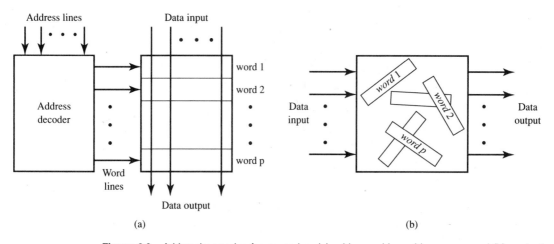

Figure 6.2 Addressing modes for memories: (a) address-addressable memory and (b) content-addressable memory.

and $\mathbf{v}^{(i)} \neq \mathbf{x}^{(i)}$, for $i = 1, 2, \ldots, p$, the network can be termed as *heteroassociative memory*. The association between pairs of two ordered sets of vectors $\{\mathbf{x}^{(1)}, \mathbf{x}^{(2)}, \ldots, \mathbf{x}^{(p)}\}$ and $\{\mathbf{v}^{(1)}, \mathbf{v}^{(2)}, \ldots, \mathbf{v}^{(p)}\}$ is thus heteroassociative. An example of heteroassociative mapping would be a retrieval of the missing member of the pair $(\mathbf{x}^{(i)}, \mathbf{v}^{(i)})$ in response to the input $\mathbf{x}^{(i)}$ or $\mathbf{v}^{(i)}$. If the mapping as in (6.2a) reduces to the form

$$\mathbf{x}^{(i)} \rightarrow \mathbf{v}^{(i)}\big|_{\mathbf{v}^{(i)} = \mathbf{x}^{(i)}}, \quad \text{for } i = 1, 2, \ldots, p \tag{6.2b}$$

then the memory is called *autoassociative*. Autoassociative memory associates vectors from within only one set, which is $\{\mathbf{x}^{(1)}, \mathbf{x}^{(2)}, \ldots, \mathbf{x}^{(p)}\}$. Obviously, the mapping of a vector $\mathbf{x}^{(i)}$ into itself as suggested in (6.2b) cannot be of any significance. A more realistic application of an autoassociative mapping would be the recovery of an undistorted prototype vector in response to the distorted prototype key vector. Vector $\mathbf{x}^{(i)}$ can be regarded in such case as stored data and the distorted key serves as a search key or argument.

Associative memory, which uses neural network concepts, bears very little resemblance to digital computer memory. Let us compare their two different addressing modes which are commonly used for memory data retrieval. In digital computers, data are accessed when their correct addresses in the memory are given. As can be seen from Figure 6.2(a), which shows a typical memory organization, data have input and output lines, and a word line accesses and activates the entire word row of binary cells containing word data bits. This activation takes place whenever the binary address is decoded by the address decoder. The addressed word can be either "read" or replaced during the "write" operation. This is called *address-addressable* memory.

In contrast with this mode of addressing, associative memories are *content-addressable*. The words in this memory are accessed based on the content of the key vector. When the network is excited with a portion of the stored data $\mathbf{x}^{(i)}$, $i = 1, 2, \ldots, p$, the efficient response of the autoassociative network is the complete $\mathbf{x}^{(i)}$ vector. In the case of heteroassociative memory, the content of vector $\mathbf{x}^{(i)}$ should provide the stored response $\mathbf{v}^{(i)}$. However, there is no storage for prototype $\mathbf{x}^{(i)}$ or $\mathbf{v}^{(i)}$, for $i = 1, 2, \ldots, p$, at any location within the network. The entire mapping (6.2) is distributed in the associative network. This is symbolically depicted in Figure 6.2(b). The mapping is implemented through dense connections, sometimes involving feedback, or a nonlinear thresholding operation, or both.

Associative memory networks come in a variety of models. The most important classes of associative memories are static and dynamic memories. The taxonomy is based entirely on their recall principles. Static networks recall an output response after an input has been applied in one feedforward pass, and, theoretically, without delay. They were termed *instantaneous* in Chapter 2. Dynamic memory networks produce recall as a result of output/input feedback interaction, which requires time. Respective block diagrams for both memory classes are shown in Figure 6.3. The static networks implement a feedforward operation of mapping without a feedback, or recursive update, operation. As such they are sometimes also called *non-recurrent*. Static memory with the block diagram shown in Figure 6.3(a) performs the mapping as in Equation (6.1), which can be reduced to the form

$$\mathbf{v}^k = M_1[\mathbf{x}^k] \tag{6.3a}$$

where k denotes the index of recursion and M_1 is an operator symbol. Equation (6.3a) represents a system of nonlinear algebraic equations. Examples of static networks will be discussed in the next section.

Dynamic memory networks exhibit dynamic evolution in the sense that they converge to an equilibrium state according to the recursive formula

$$\mathbf{v}^{k+1} = M_2\left[\mathbf{x}^k, \mathbf{v}^k\right] \tag{6.3b}$$

provided the operator M_2 has been suitably chosen. The operator operates at the present instant k on the present input $\mathbf{x}^k$ and output $\mathbf{v}^k$ to produce the output in the next instant $k + 1$. Equation (6.3b) represents, therefore, a system of nonlinear difference equations. The block diagram of a recurrent network is shown in Figure 6.3(b). The delay element in the feedback loop inserts a unity delay Δ, which is needed for cyclic operation. Autoassociative memory based on the Hopfield model is an example of a recurrent network for which the input $\mathbf{x}^0$ is used to initialize $\mathbf{v}^0$, i.e., $\mathbf{x}^0 = \mathbf{v}^0$, and the input is then removed. The vector retrieved at the instant k can be computed with this initial condition as shown:

$$\mathbf{v}^{k+1} = M_2[\mathbf{v}^k] \tag{6.3c}$$

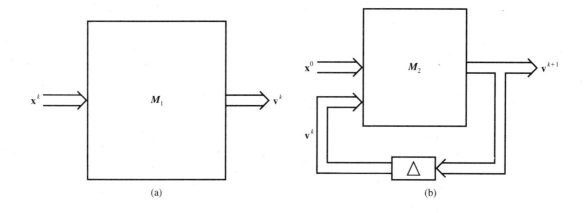

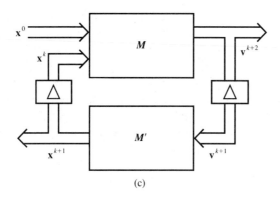

Figure 6.3 Block diagram representation of associative memories: (a) feedforward network, (b) recurrent autoassociative network, and (c) recurrent heteroassociative network.

Figure 6.3(c) shows the block diagram of a recurrent heteroassociative memory that operates with a cycle of 2Δ. The memory associates pairs of vectors $(\mathbf{x}^{(i)}, \mathbf{v}^{(i)})$, $i = 1, 2, \ldots, p$, as given in (6.2a).

Figure 6.4 shows Hopfield autoassociative memory without the initializing input $\mathbf{x}_0$. The figure also provides additional details on how the recurrent memory network implements Equation (6.3c). Operator M_2 consists of multiplication by a weight matrix followed by the ensemble of nonlinear mapping operations $v_i = f(net_i)$ performed by the layer of neurons. The details of processing were discussed in earlier chapters.

There is a substantial resemblance of some elements of autoassociative recurrent networks with feedforward networks discussed in Section 4.5 covering the back propagation network architecture. Using the mapping concepts proposed in (4.30c) and (4.31) we can rewrite expression (6.3c) in the following

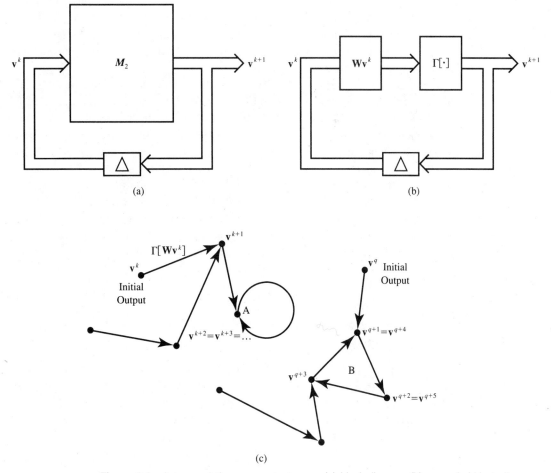

Figure 6.4 Autoassociative recurrent memory: (a) block diagram, (b) expanded block diagram, and (c) example state transition map.

customary form:

$$\mathbf{v}^{k+1} = \Gamma[\mathbf{W}\mathbf{v}^k] \tag{6.4}$$

where $\mathbf{W}$ is the weight matrix of a single layer as defined throughout Chapter 4 or 5. The operator $\Gamma[\cdot]$ is a nonlinear matrix operator with diagonal elements that are hard-limiting (binary) activation functions $f(\cdot)$:

$$\Gamma[\cdot] = \begin{bmatrix} \operatorname{sgn}(\cdot) & 0 & \cdots & 0 \\ 0 & \operatorname{sgn}(\cdot) & \cdots & 0 \\ \vdots & \vdots & \cdots & \vdots \\ 0 & 0 & \cdots & \operatorname{sgn}(\cdot) \end{bmatrix} \tag{6.5}$$

The expanded block diagram of the memory is shown in Figure 6.4(b). Although mappings performed by both feedforward and feedback networks are similar, recurrent memory networks respond with bipolar binary values, and operate in a cyclic, recurrent fashion. Their time-domain behavior and properties will therefore no longer be similar.

Regarding the vector $\mathbf{v}(k + 1)$ as the state of the network at the $(k + 1)$'th instant, we can consider recurrent Equation (6.4) as defining a mapping of the vector $\mathbf{v}$ into itself. The memory state space consists of 2^n n-tuple vectors with components ± 1. The example state transition map for a memory network is shown in Figure 6.4(c). Each node of the graph is equivalent to a state and has one and only one edge leaving it. If the transitions terminate with a state mapping into itself, as is the case of node A, then the equilibrium A is the fixed point. If the transitions end in a cycle of states as in nodes B, then we have a limit cycle solution with a certain period. The period is defined as the length of the cycle. The figure shows the limit cycle B of length three.

Let us begin with a review of associative memory networks beginning with static networks.

6.2   LINEAR ASSOCIATOR

Traditional associative memories are of the feedforward, instantaneous type. As defined in (6.2a), the task required for the associative memory is to learn the association within p vector pairs $\{\mathbf{x}^{(i)}, \mathbf{v}^{(i)}\}$, for $i = 1, 2, \ldots, p$. For the *linear associative memory,* an input pattern $\mathbf{x}$ is presented and mapped to the output by simply performing the matrix multiplication operation

$$\mathbf{v} = \mathbf{W}\mathbf{x} \tag{6.6a}$$

where $\mathbf{x}, \mathbf{v}, \mathbf{W}$ are matrices of size $n \times 1$, $m \times 1$, and $m \times n$, respectively. Thus, the general nonlinear mapping relationship (6.3a) has been simplified to the linear form (6.6a), hence the memory name. The linear associative network diagram can be drawn as in Figure 6.5. Only the customary weight matrix $\mathbf{W}$ is used to perform the mapping. Noticeably, the network does not involve neuron elements, since no nonlinear or delay operations are involved in the linear association. If, however, the use of neurons is required for the reason of uniform perspective of all neural networks, then the mapping (6.3a) can be rewritten as

$$\mathbf{v} = M_1[\mathbf{W}\mathbf{x}] \tag{6.6b}$$

where $M_1[\cdot]$ is a dummy linear matrix operator in the form of the $m \times m$ unity matrix. This observation can be used to append an output layer of dummy neurons with identity activation functions $v_i = f(net_i) = net_i$. The corresponding network extension is shown within dashed lines in Figure 6.5.

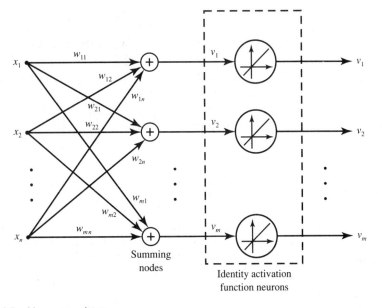

Figure 6.5 Linear associator.

Let us assume that p associations need to be stored in the linear associator. Given are pairs of vectors $\{\mathbf{s}^{(i)}, \mathbf{f}^{(i)}\}$, for $i = 1, 2, \ldots, p$, denoting the stored memories, called *stimuli,* and forced responses, respectively. Since this memory is strictly unidirectional, these terms are self-explanatory. We thus have for n-tuple stimuli and m-tuple response vectors of the i'th pair:

$$\mathbf{s}^{(i)} = \left[s_1^{(i)} \quad s_2^{(i)} \ldots \quad s_n^{(i)} \right]^t, \quad \text{and} \tag{6.6c}$$

$$\mathbf{f}^{(i)} = \left[f_1^{(i)} \quad f_2^{(i)} \ldots \quad f_m^{(i)} \right]^t \tag{6.6d}$$

In practice, $\mathbf{s}^{(i)}$ can be patterns and $\mathbf{f}^{(i)}$ can be information about their class membership, or their images, or any other pairwise assigned association with input patterns. The objective of the linear associator is to implement the mapping (6.6a) as follows

$$\mathbf{f}^{(i)} + \mathbf{\eta}^i = \mathbf{W}\mathbf{s}^{(i)}$$

or, using the mapping symbol

$$\mathbf{s}^{(i)} \rightarrow \mathbf{f}^{(i)} + \mathbf{\eta}^i, \quad \text{for } i = 1, 2, \ldots, p \tag{6.7}$$

such that the length of the *noise term vector* denoted as $\mathbf{\eta}^i$ is minimized. In general, the solution for this problem aimed at finding the memory weight matrix $\mathbf{W}$ is not very straightforward. First of all, matrix $\mathbf{W}$ should be found such that the Euclidean norm $\sum_i \|\mathbf{\eta}^i\|$, is minimized for a large number of observations of mapping (6.7). This problem is dealt with in the mathematical regression analysis and will not be covered here. The general solution of the problem of optimal mapping (6.7) can be found in references on early associative memories (Kohonen 1977; Kohonen et al. 1981). We will find below, however, partial solutions to the general mapping problem expressed by Equation (6.7) that will also prove to be useful later in this chapter.

Below we focus on finding the matrix $\mathbf{W}$ that allows for efficient storage of data within the memory. Let us apply the Hebbian learning rule in an attempt to train the linear associator network. The weight update rule for the i'th output node and j'th input node can be expressed as

$$w'_{ij} = w_{ij} + f_i s_j, \quad \text{for } i = 1, 2, \ldots, m \quad \text{and} \quad j = 1, 2, \ldots, n \qquad (6.8a)$$

where f_i and s_j are the i'th and j'th components of association vectors $\mathbf{f}$ and $\mathbf{s}$ and w_{ij} denotes the weight value before the update. The reader should note that the vectors to be associated, $\mathbf{f}$ and $\mathbf{s}$, must be members of the pair. To generalize formula (6.8a) so it is valid for a single weight matrix entry update to the case of the entire weight matrix update, we can use the outer product formula. We then obtain

$$\mathbf{W}' = \mathbf{W} + \mathbf{fs}^t \qquad (6.8b)$$

where $\mathbf{W}$ denotes the weight matrix before the update. Initializing the weights in their unbiased position $\mathbf{W}_0 = \mathbf{0}$, we obtain for the outer product learning rule:

$$\mathbf{W}' = \mathbf{f}^{(i)} \mathbf{s}^{(i)t} \qquad (6.9a)$$

Expression (6.9a) describes the first learning step and involves learning of the i'th association among p distinct paired associations. Since there are p pairs to be learned, the superposition of weights can be performed as follows

$$\mathbf{W}' = \sum_{i=1}^{p} \mathbf{f}^{(i)} \mathbf{s}^{(i)t} \qquad (6.9b)$$

The memory weight matrix $\mathbf{W}'$ above has the form of a *cross-correlation matrix*. An alternative notation for $\mathbf{W}'$ is provided by the following formula:

$$\mathbf{W}' = \mathbf{FS}^t \qquad (6.9c)$$

where $\mathbf{F}$ and $\mathbf{S}$ are matrices containing vectors of forced responses and stimuli and are defined as follows:

$$\mathbf{F} \triangleq \begin{bmatrix} \mathbf{f}^{(1)} & \mathbf{f}^{(2)} & \ldots & \mathbf{f}^{(p)} \end{bmatrix}$$

$$\mathbf{S} \triangleq \begin{bmatrix} \mathbf{s}^{(1)} & \mathbf{s}^{(2)} & \ldots & \mathbf{s}^{(p)} \end{bmatrix}$$

where the column vectors $\mathbf{f}^{(i)}$ and $\mathbf{s}^{(i)}$ were defined in (6.6c) and (6.6d). The resulting cross-correlation matrix $\mathbf{W}'$ is of size $m \times n$. Integers n and m denote sizes of stimuli and forced responses vectors, respectively, as introduced in (6.6c) and (6.6d). We should now check whether or not the weight matrix $\mathbf{W}$ provides noise-free mapping as required by expression (6.7). Let us attempt to perform an associative recall of the vector $\mathbf{f}^{(i)}$ when $\mathbf{s}^{(i)}$ is applied as a stimulus. If one of the stored vectors, say $\mathbf{s}^{(j)}$, is now used as key vector at the input, we obtain from the retrieval formula [(6.6a) and (6.6b)]:

$$\mathbf{v} = \left(\sum_{i=1}^{p} \mathbf{f}^{(i)} \mathbf{s}^{(i)t} \right) \mathbf{s}^{(j)} \tag{6.10a}$$

Expanding the sum of p terms yields

$$\mathbf{v} = \mathbf{f}^{(1)} \mathbf{s}^{(1)t} \mathbf{s}^{(j)} + \ldots + \mathbf{f}^{(j)} \mathbf{s}^{(j)t} \mathbf{s}^{(j)} + \ldots + \mathbf{f}^{(p)} \mathbf{s}^{(p)t} \mathbf{s}^{(j)} \tag{6.10b}$$

According to the mapping criterion (6.7), the ideal mapping $\mathbf{s}^{(j)} \rightarrow \mathbf{f}^{(j)}$ such that no noise term is present would require

$$\mathbf{v} = \mathbf{f}^{(j)} \tag{6.10c}$$

By inspecting (6.10b) and (6.10c) it can be seen that the ideal mapping can be achieved in the case for which

$$\mathbf{s}^{(i)t} \mathbf{s}^{(j)} = 0, \quad \text{for } i \neq j$$
$$\mathbf{s}^{(j)t} \mathbf{s}^{(j)} = 1 \tag{6.11}$$

Thus, the orthonormal set of p input stimuli vectors $\{ \mathbf{s}^{(1)}, \mathbf{s}^{(2)}, \ldots, \mathbf{s}^{(p)} \}$ ensures perfect mapping (6.10c). Orthonormality is the condition on the inputs if they are to be ideally associated. However, the condition is rather strict and may not always hold for the set of stimuli vectors.

Let us evaluate the retrieval of associations evoked by stimuli that are not originally encoded. Consider the consequences of a distortion of pattern $\mathbf{s}^{(j)}$ submitted at the memory input as $\mathbf{s}^{(j)'}$ so that

$$\mathbf{s}^{(j)'} = \mathbf{s}^{(j)} + \mathbf{\Delta}^{(j)} \tag{6.12}$$

where the distortion term $\mathbf{\Delta}^{(j)}$ can be assumed to be statistically independent of $\mathbf{s}^{(j)}$, and thus it can be considered as orthogonal to it. Substituting (6.12) into formula (6.10a), we obtain for orthonormal vectors originally encoded in the memory

$$\mathbf{v} = \mathbf{f}^{(j)} \mathbf{s}^{(j)t} \mathbf{s}^{(j)} + \mathbf{f}^{(j)} \mathbf{s}^{(j)t} \mathbf{\Delta}^{(j)} + \sum_{i \neq j}^{p} (\mathbf{f}^{(i)} \mathbf{s}^{(i)t}) \mathbf{\Delta}^{(j)} \tag{6.13a}$$

Due to the orthonormality condition this further reduces to

$$\mathbf{v} = \mathbf{f}^{(j)} + \sum_{i \neq j}^{p} (\mathbf{f}^{(i)} \mathbf{s}^{(i)t}) \mathbf{\Delta}^{(j)} \tag{6.13b}$$

It can be seen that the memory response contains the desired association $\mathbf{f}^{(j)}$ and an additive component, which is due to the distortion term $\mathbf{\Delta}^{(j)}$. The second term in the expression above has the meaning of *cross-talk noise* and is caused by the distortion of the input pattern and is present due to the vector $\mathbf{\Delta}^{(j)}$. The term contains, in parentheses, almost all elements of the memory cross-correlation matrix weighted by a distortion term $\Delta^{(j)}$. Therefore, even in the case of stored orthonormal patterns, the cross-talk noise term from all other patterns remains additive at the memory output to the originally stored association. We thus see that the linear associator provides no means for suppression of the cross-talk noise term is of limited use for accurate retrieval of the originally stored association.

Finally, let us notice an interesting property of the linear associator for the case of its autoassociative operation with p distinct n-dimensional prototype patterns $s^{(i)}$. In such a case the network can be called an *autocorrelator*. Plugging $f^{(i)} = s^{(i)}$ in (6.9b) results in the *autocorrelation matrix* W':

$$W' = \sum_{i=1}^{p} s^{(i)}s^{(i)t} \tag{6.14a}$$

This result can also be expressed using the S matrix from (6.9c) as follows

$$W' = SS^t \tag{6.14b}$$

The autocorrelation matrix of an autoassociator is of size $n \times n$. Note that this matrix can also be obtained directly from the Hebbian learning rule. Let us examine the attempted regeneration of a stored pattern in response to a distorted pattern $s^{(j)'}$ submitted at the input of the linear autocorrelator. Assume again that input is expressed by (6.12). The output can be expressed using (6.10b), and it simplifies for orthonormal patterns $s^{(j)}$, for $j = 1, 2, \ldots, p$, to the form

$$v = s^{(j)} + \sum_{i \neq j}^{p} s^{(i)}s^{(i)t}\Delta^{(j)} \tag{6.15a}$$

This becomes equal

$$v = s^{(j)} + (p - 1)\Delta^{(j)} \tag{6.15b}$$

As we can see, the cross-talk noise term again has not been eliminated even for stored orthogonal patterns. The retrieved output is the stored pattern plus the distortion term amplified $p - 1$ times. Therefore, linear associative memories perform rather poorly when retrieving associations due to distorted stimuli vectors.

Linear associator and autoassociator networks can also be used when linearly independent vectors $s^{(1)}, s^{(2)}, \ldots, s^{(p)}$, are to be stored. The assumption of linear independence is weaker than the assumption of orthogonality and it allows for consideration of a larger class of vectors to be stored. As discussed by Kohonen (1977) and Kohonen et al. (1981), the weight matrix W can be expressed for such a case as follows:

$$W = F(S'S)^{-1}S^t \tag{6.16}$$

The weight matrix found from Equation (6.16) minimizes the squared output error between $f^{(j)}$ and $v^{(j)}$ in the case of linearly independent vectors $s^{(j)}$ (see Appendix). Because vectors to be used as stored memories are generally neither orthonormal nor linearly independent, the linear associator and autoassociator may not be efficient memories for many practical tasks.

Linear auto- and heteroassociative memory networks are in a certain limited sense similar to dynamic associative memories. In particular, both memories have similar recording algorithms. However, as shown, linear associators do not provide solutions for the suppression of the noise term in expressions (6.13b) and (6.15). We will show that other memory models utilize a thresholding operation to suppress the noise component present in an output signal. The recurrent autoassociative memory presented in the following section are examples of such memory models.

6.3 BASIC CONCEPTS OF RECURRENT AUTOASSOCIATIVE MEMORY

Discussion of the linear associative memory has pointed out the need for suppressing the output noise at the memory output. This can be done by thresholding the output and by recycling of the output to input in order to produce an improved association. The repetitive process of recycling of the output followed by a feedforward pass through the network can be performed by a recurrent neural network. Such a network is similar to the linear associative memory, however, it has feedback, nonlinear mapping in the form of thresholding, and is dynamical.

Recurrent autoassociative memory has already been introduced as an example of dynamic associative network in Figure 6.4. The reader should by now be familiar with the general theory of such a network. The memory is essentially a single-layer feedback network covered in Section 5.2 as a discrete-time network originally proposed by Hopfield (1982, 1984). In this section, a more detailed view of the model and its performance as an associative memory will be presented. Our focus is mainly on the dynamical performance of recurrent autoassociative memories. In contrast to continuously updating single-layer feedback networks discussed throughout Chapter 5, associative memories are updated in discrete time.

An expanded view of the Hopfield model network from Figure 6.4 is shown in Figure 6.6. Figure 6.6(a) depicts *Hopfield's autoassociative memory*. Under the asynchronous update mode, only one neuron is allowed to compute, or change state, at a time, and then all outputs are delayed by a time Δ produced by the unity delay element in the feedback loop. This symbolic delay allows for the time-stepping of the retrieval algorithm embedded in the update rule of (5.3) or (5.4). Figure 6.6(b) shows a simplified diagram of the network in the form that is often found in the technical literature. Note that the time step and the neurons' thresholding function have been suppressed on the figure. The computing neurons represented in the figure as circular nodes need to perform summation and bipolar thresholding and also need to introduce a unity delay. Note that the recurrent autoassociative memories studied in this chapter provide node responses

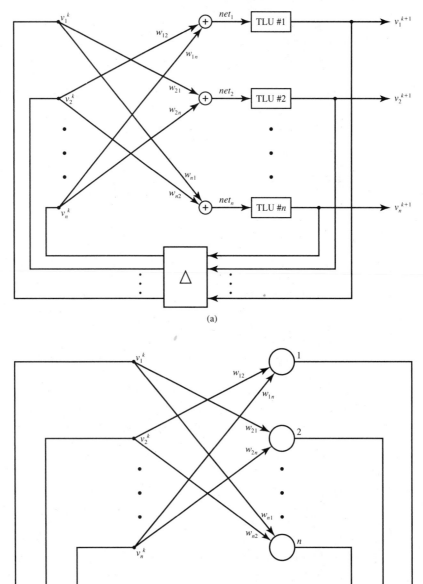

(a)

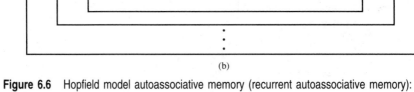

(b)

Figure 6.6 Hopfield model autoassociative memory (recurrent autoassociative memory):
(a) expanded view and (b) simplified diagram.

of discrete values ± 1. The domain of the n-tuple output vectors in $\mathbb{R}^n$ are thus vertices of the n-dimensional cube $[-1, 1]$.

Retrieval Algorithm

Based on the discussion in Section 5.2 the output update rule for Hopfield autoassociative memory can be expressed in the form

$$v_i^{k+1} = \text{sgn} \left(\sum_{j=1}^{n} w_{ij} v_j^k \right) \tag{6.17}$$

where k is the index of recursion and i is the number of the neuron currently undergoing an update. The update rule (6.17) has been obtained from (5.4a) under the simplifying assumption that both the external bias i_i and threshold values T_i are zero for $i = 1, 2, \ldots, n$. These assumptions will remain valid for the remainder of this chapter. In addition, the asynchronous update sequence considered here is random. Thus, assuming that recursion starts at $\mathbf{v}^0$, and a random sequence of updating neurons $m, p, q, \ldots$ is chosen, the output vectors obtained are as follows

$$\text{First update:} \quad \mathbf{v}^1 = \left[v_1^0 \; v_2^0 \; \ldots \; v_m^1 \; \ldots \; v_p^0 \; \ldots \; v_q^0 \; \ldots \; v_n^0 \right]^t$$

$$\text{Second update:} \quad \mathbf{v}^2 = \left[v_1^0 \; v_2^0 \; \ldots \; v_m^1 \; \ldots \; v_p^2 \; \ldots \; v_q^0 \; \ldots \; v_n^0 \right]^t \tag{6.18}$$

$$\text{Third update:} \quad \mathbf{v}^3 = \left[v_1^0 \; v_2^0 \; \ldots \; v_m^1 \; \ldots \; v_p^2 \; \ldots \; v_q^3 \; \ldots \; v_n^0 \right]^t$$

$$\vdots$$

Considerable insight into the Hopfield autoassociative memory performance can be gained by evaluating its respective energy function. The energy function (5.5) for the discussed memory network simplifies to

$$E(\mathbf{v}) = -\frac{1}{2} \mathbf{v}^t \mathbf{W} \mathbf{v} \tag{6.19a}$$

We consider the memory network to evolve in a discrete-time mode, for $k = 1, 2, \ldots$, and its outputs are one of the 2^n bipolar binary n-tuple vectors, each representing a vertex of the n-dimensional $[-1, +1]$ cube. We also discussed in Section 5.2 the fact that the asynchronous recurrent update never increases energy (6.19a) computed for $\mathbf{v} = \mathbf{v}^k$, and that the network settles in one of the local energy minima located at cube vertices.

We can now easily observe that the complement of a stored memory is also a stored memory. For the bipolar binary notation the complement vector of $\mathbf{v}$ is equal to $-\mathbf{v}$. It is easy to see from (6.19a) that

$$E(-\mathbf{v}) = -\frac{1}{2} \mathbf{v}^t \mathbf{W} \mathbf{v} \tag{6.19b}$$

and thus both energies $E(\mathbf{v})$ and $E(-\mathbf{v})$ are identical. Therefore, a minimum of $E(\mathbf{v})$ is of the same value as a minimum of $E(-\mathbf{v})$. This provides us with an important conclusion that the memory transitions may terminate as easily at $\mathbf{v}$ as at $-\mathbf{v}$. The crucial factor determining the convergence is the "similarity" between the initializing output vector, and $\mathbf{v}$ and $-\mathbf{v}$.

Storage Algorithm

Let us formulate the information storage algorithm for the recurrent autoassociative memory. Assume that the bipolar binary prototype vectors that need to be stored are $\mathbf{s}^{(m)}$, for $m = 1, 2, \ldots, p$. The *storage algorithm* for calculating the weight matrix is

$$\mathbf{W} = \sum_{m=1}^{p} \mathbf{s}^{(m)}\mathbf{s}^{(m)t} - p\mathbf{I} \qquad (6.20a)$$

or

$$w_{ij} = \left(1 - \delta_{ij}\right) \sum_{m=1}^{p} s_i^{(m)} s_j^{(m)} \qquad (6.20b)$$

where, as before, δ_{ij} denotes the usual Kronecker function $\delta_{ij} = 1$ if $i = j$, and $\delta_{ij} = 0$ if $i \neq j$. The weight matrix $\mathbf{W}$ is very similar to the autocorrelation matrix obtained using Hebb's learning rule for the linear associator introduced in (6.14). The difference is that now $w_{ii} = 0$. Note that the system does not remember the individual vectors $\mathbf{s}^{(m)}$ but only the weights w_{ij}, which basically represent correlation terms among the vector entries.

Also, the original Hebb's learning rule does not involve the presence of negative synaptic weight values, which can appear as a result of learning as in (6.20). This is a direct consequence of the condition that *only bipolar binary vectors $\mathbf{s}^{(m)}$ are allowed for building the autocorrelation matrix* in (6.20). Interestingly, additional autoassociations can be added at any time to the existing memory by superimposing new, incremental weight matrices. Autoassociations can also be removed by respective weight matrix subtraction. The storage rule (6.20) is also invariant with respect to the sequence of storing patterns.

The information storage algorithm for unipolar binary vectors $\mathbf{s}^{(m)}$, for $m = 1, 2, \ldots, p$, needs to be modified so that a -1 component of the vectors simply replaces the 0 element in the original unipolar vector. This can be formally done by replacing the entries of the original unipolar vector $\mathbf{s}^{(m)}$ with the entries $2s_i^{(m)} - 1$, $i = 1, 2, \ldots, n$. The memory storage algorithm (6.20b) for the unipolar binary vectors thus involves scaling and shifting and takes the form

$$w_{ij} = (1 - \delta_{ij}) \sum_{m=1}^{p} (2s_i^{(m)} - 1)(2s_j^{(m)} - 1) \qquad (6.21)$$

Notice that the information storage rule is invariant under the binary complement

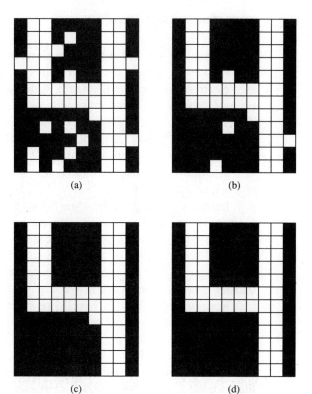

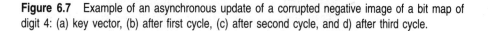

Figure 6.7 Example of an asynchronous update of a corrupted negative image of a bit map of digit 4: (a) key vector, (b) after first cycle, (c) after second cycle, and d) after third cycle.

operation. Indeed, storing complementary patterns $\mathbf{s}'^{(m)}$ instead of original patterns $\mathbf{s}^{(m)}$ results in the weights as follows:

$$w'_{ij} = (1 - \delta_{ij}) \sum_{m=1}^{p} (2s'^{(m)}_i - 1)(2s'^{(m)}_j - 1) \qquad (6.22)$$

The reader can easily verify that substituting

$$s'^{(m)}_i = 1 - s^{(m)}_i \qquad (6.23)$$

into (6.22) results in $w'_{ij} = w_{ij}$. Figure 6.7 shows four example convergence steps for an associative memory consisting of 120 neurons with a stored binary bit map of digit 4. Retrieval of a stored pattern initialized as shown in Figure 6.7(a) terminates after three cycles of convergence as illustrated in Figure 6.7(d). It can be seen that the recall has resulted in the true complement of the bit map originally stored. The reader may notice similarities between Figures 5.2 and 6.7.

EXAMPLE 6.1 ■■■■■■■■■■■

In this example we will discuss the simplest recurrent associative memory network known, which at the same time, seems to be the most commonly used electronic network in the world. Although the network has been popular for more than half a century, we will take a fresh look at it and investigate its performance as of a neural memory. The bistable flip-flop is the focus of our discussion. In fact, most digital computers use this element as a basic memory cell and as a basic computing device.

The flip-flop network is supposed to find and indefinitely remain in one of the two equilibrium states: $\mathbf{s}^{(1)} = \begin{bmatrix} 1 & -1 \end{bmatrix}^t$ or $\mathbf{s}^{(2)} = \begin{bmatrix} -1 & 1 \end{bmatrix}^t$.

Before we design a bistable flip-flop using the associative memory concept, let us review its basic physical properties. The network as shown in Figure 6.8(a) consists of two cascaded inverting neurons. Consider the feedback loop switch K to be open initially. Each of the neurons represented by amplifiers with saturation is characterized by the two identical voltage transfer characteristics as shown in Figures 6.8(b) and (c).

Resistances R_1 and R_2 have to be positive, but their values are of no significance since the ideal neurons absorb no input current. By connecting two neurons in cascade, the output $\bar{v}_2$ is a function of $\bar{v}_1$, and v_1 is a function of v_0. Thus, $\bar{v}_2$ can be expressed as a composite function of v_0. The cascade of two amplifiers has a composed characteristic $\bar{v}_2[\bar{v}_1(v_0)]$ as illustrated in Figure 6.8(d). When the switch K closes and enforces the condition $\bar{v}_2 = v_0$ represented by the unity-slope straight line on the figure, the circuit immediately starts evolving toward one of the equilibrium points. Note that the three potential equilibrium points are A, B, and S.

The origin S of the coordinates here is an unstable equilibrium point. If any perturbation arises in either direction with the network momentarily at S, it is going to be magnified by the positive feedback within the network so the transition will finally end in either A or B. Thus, the physical memory network will never stabilize at S, which is supposedly the saddle point of its energy function. Note that the equilibrium states for high-gain amplifiers are, for points A and B, respectively:

$$\begin{bmatrix} v_1 \\ v_2 \end{bmatrix} \cong \begin{bmatrix} 1 \\ -1 \end{bmatrix}, \begin{bmatrix} v_1 \\ v_2 \end{bmatrix} \cong \begin{bmatrix} -1 \\ 1 \end{bmatrix} \tag{6.24}$$

The dynamics of the equilibrium search, which is essential for the network's physical operation during the transition period, has been suppressed in this description for simplicity. The issue of dynamics was extensively discussed in Chapter 5. A trace of capacitance and neuron input conductance is, in fact, indispensable for this circuit to respond. The associative memory discussed here performs the input/output mapping, and discrete-time formalism is used only to characterize it. The physical output update process, however,

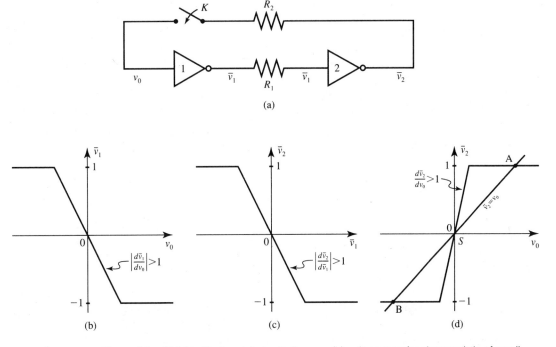

Figure 6.8 Bistable flip-flop: (a) circuit diagram, (b) voltage transfer characteristic of amplifier 1, (c) voltage transfer characteristic of amplifier 2, and (d) joint characteristics and equilibrium states.

follows the continuous-time behavior of the model, which uses the continuous activation function of the neurons.

Knowing now the basic physical principles of the network, we can approach the problem of a bistable neural memory design with better understanding. Since the learning (storage) rule is invariant under the binary complement operation, it is sufficient to store either of the two patterns $\mathbf{s}^{(1)}$ and $\mathbf{s}^{(2)}$ only. From (6.20a) we obtain the weight matrix

$$\mathbf{W} = \begin{bmatrix} 0 & -1 \\ -1 & 0 \end{bmatrix} \tag{6.25}$$

This results in the bistable flip-flop circuit shown in Figure 6.9(a) with weights of $w_{12} = w_{21} = -1\,\Omega$. The circuit has negative resistances, which are difficult to implement. It has, however, noninverting neurons. By transforming noninverting neurons into inverting neurons and by changing the signs of the resistances, an equivalent circuit is obtained as shown in Figure 6.9(b). Although the equivalency is valid strictly for a hard-limiting activation function and zero input conductance of the neurons, both circuits of

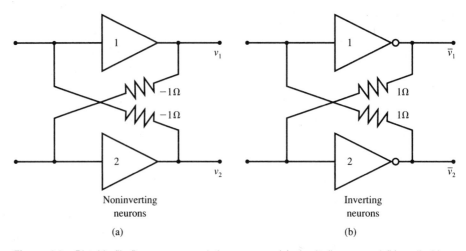

Figure 6.9 Bistable flip-flop as an associative memory: (a) circuit diagram and (b) realizable circuit diagram.

Figure 6.9 can be considered equivalent for all practical purposes. As we can see, the memory circuit obtained is identical to the basic flip-flop circuit configuration introduced earlier in Figure 6.8(a).

To complete our study of the network, let us consider its energy function. Substituting (6.25) into (6.19), the energy function of this memory network is obtained as

$$E = v_1 v_2 \qquad (6.26)$$

The energy function is shown in Figure 6.10(a). It consists of two surfaces monotonically decreasing toward $\mathbf{s}^{(1)}$ and $\mathbf{s}^{(2)}$, where $\mathbf{s}^{(1)} = \begin{bmatrix} 1 & -1 \end{bmatrix}^t$ and $\mathbf{s}^{(2)} = \begin{bmatrix} -1 & 1 \end{bmatrix}^t$. The ridge of the function is at $v_1 = v_2$. It can easily be seen that for the initial condition $v_1^0 < v_2^0$, the update process will result in stable output pattern $\mathbf{s}^{(2)}$. For $v_1^0 > v_2^0$, the network will stabilize at output $\mathbf{s}^{(1)}$. The figure shows that this network has a virtually perfect recall ability to the closer of the two memories stored. These properties refer to the update by the continuous-time network employing neurons with the continuous activation function.

Let us inspect the performance of the memory operating in the discrete-time mode. The memory cell now employs two bipolar binary neurons. In Section 5.2 we considered the recurrent memory network with the weight matrix as in (6.25). We then showed that the synchronous transitions of the network were oscillations between $\begin{bmatrix} -1 & -1 \end{bmatrix}^t$ and $\begin{bmatrix} 1 & 1 \end{bmatrix}^t$, provided the updates originated at one of these outputs. The transition map for this case is depicted in Figure 6.10(b). It can be seen from the map that the energy

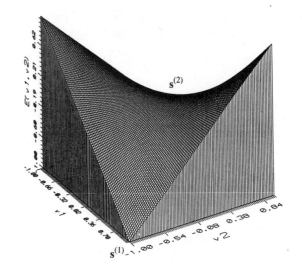

(a)

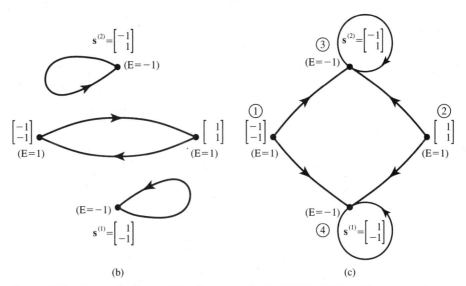

(b)   (c)

Figure 6.10 Energy function and transition maps for the bistable flip-flop: (a) energy surface, (b) transition map for synchronous update, and (c) transition map for asynchronous update.

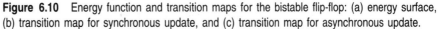

minimization property does not hold for the synchronous update mode since there are lower energy levels that cannot be reached. This is the case for oscillatory updates between the energy levels of value 1 never reaching the lower value of -1.

Consider now the asynchronous updates for this circuit. Starting at each of the first four initial vectors $\mathbf{v}^0$ we obtain in a single update step:

1. For $\mathbf{v}^0 = \begin{bmatrix} -1 & -1 \end{bmatrix}^t$ and the first neuron allowed to update

$$\mathbf{v}^1 = \Gamma \begin{bmatrix} 0 & -1 \\ -1 & 0 \end{bmatrix} \begin{bmatrix} -1 \\ -1 \end{bmatrix} = \begin{bmatrix} 1 \\ -1 \end{bmatrix} = \mathbf{s}^{(1)}$$

Energy has dropped from 1 to -1 as a result of the update and the network has settled at $\mathbf{s}^{(1)}$. Starting again at $\mathbf{v}^0$ as above but with the second neuron allowed to update, we obtain

$$\mathbf{v}^1 = \begin{bmatrix} 0 & -1 \\ -1 & 0 \end{bmatrix} \begin{bmatrix} -1 \\ -1 \end{bmatrix} = \begin{bmatrix} -1 \\ 1 \end{bmatrix} = \mathbf{s}^{(2)}$$

and we have the same energy drop from 1 to -1 while the network settled at $\mathbf{s}^{(2)}$.

2. For $\mathbf{v}^0 = \begin{bmatrix} 1 & 1 \end{bmatrix}^t$ and the first neuron allowed to update

$$\mathbf{v}^1 = \Gamma \begin{bmatrix} 0 & -1 \\ -1 & 0 \end{bmatrix} \begin{bmatrix} 1 \\ 1 \end{bmatrix} = \begin{bmatrix} -1 \\ 1 \end{bmatrix} = \mathbf{s}^{(2)}$$

Energy has dropped from 1 to -1 as a result of this update. Allowing the second neuron to update, we obtain

$$\mathbf{v}^1 = \Gamma \begin{bmatrix} 0 & -1 \\ -1 & 0 \end{bmatrix} \begin{bmatrix} 1 \\ 1 \end{bmatrix} = \begin{bmatrix} 1 \\ -1 \end{bmatrix} = \mathbf{s}^{(1)}$$

and we have the same energy drop from 1 to -1.

3. For $\mathbf{v}^0 = \begin{bmatrix} -1 & 1 \end{bmatrix}^t$ we obtain

$$\mathbf{v}^1 = \Gamma \begin{bmatrix} 0 & -1 \\ -1 & 0 \end{bmatrix} \begin{bmatrix} -1 \\ 1 \end{bmatrix} = \begin{bmatrix} -1 \\ 1 \end{bmatrix} = \mathbf{s}^{(2)}$$

independent of the update sequence. The energy value remains at the lowest level of -1.

4. For $\mathbf{v}^0 = \begin{bmatrix} 1 & -1 \end{bmatrix}^t$ we obtain

$$\mathbf{v}^1 = \Gamma \begin{bmatrix} 0 & -1 \\ -1 & 0 \end{bmatrix} \begin{bmatrix} 1 \\ -1 \end{bmatrix} = \begin{bmatrix} 1 \\ -1 \end{bmatrix} = \mathbf{s}^{(1)}$$

independent of the update sequence. As in step 3, energy remains at the lowest level of -1.

The summary of the transitions in the asynchronous mode for this simple associative memory is illustrated in Figure 6.10(c). The figure shows the discussed transitions between the four vertices of the graph. Case numbers correspond to initial node numbers which are circled on the figure.　■

Because of the network size, the presented example has been more educational than of any practical value. The practical importance of recurrent associative memory is for larger size networks. In fact, many of its attractive properties related to recall and noise suppression are valid under statistical independence of stored vectors and for large n values. As stated before, the network is able to produce correct stored states when an incomplete or noisy version of the stored vector is applied at the input and after the network is allowed to update its output asynchronously.

■ *Summary of the Recurrent Associative Memory Storage and Retrieval Algorithm (RAMSRA)*

Given are p bipolar binary vectors:

$\left\{ \mathbf{s}^{(1)}, \mathbf{s}^{(2)}, \ldots, \mathbf{s}^{(p)} \right\}$, where $\mathbf{s}^{(m)}$ is $(n \times 1)$, for $m = 1, 2, \ldots, p$

Initializing vector $\mathbf{v}^0$ is $(n \times 1)$

Storage

Step 1: Weight matrix $\mathbf{W}$ is $(n \times n)$:

$$\mathbf{W} \leftarrow \mathbf{0}, \quad m \leftarrow 1$$

Step 2: Vector $\mathbf{s}^{(m)}$ is stored:

$$\mathbf{W} \leftarrow \mathbf{s}^{(m)}\mathbf{s}^{(m)t} - \mathbf{I}$$

Step 3: If $m < p$ then $m \leftarrow m + 1$, and go to Step 2, otherwise, go to Step 4.

Step 4: Recording of vectors is completed. Output weights $\mathbf{W}$.

Recall

Step 1: Cycle counter k is initialized, $k \leftarrow 1$. Update counter i within cycle is initialized, $i \leftarrow 1$ and the network is initialized, $\mathbf{v} \leftarrow \mathbf{v}^0$.

Step 2: Integers $1, 2, \ldots, n$, are arranged in an ordered random sequence $\alpha_1, \alpha_2, \ldots, \alpha_n$ for this cycle. (See note at end of list.)

Step 3: Neuron i is updated by computing $vnew_{\alpha_i}$

$$net_{\alpha_i} = \sum_{j=1}^{n} w_{\alpha_i j} v_j$$

$$vnew_{\alpha_i} = \text{sgn}\,(net_{\alpha_i})$$

Step 4: If $i < n$, then $i \leftarrow i + 1$, and go to Step 3; otherwise, go to Step 5.

Step 5: If $vnew_{\alpha_i} = v_{\alpha_i}$, for $i = 1, 2, \ldots, n$, then no updates occur in this cycle; thus, recall is complete; output k and $vnew_1, vnew_2, \ldots, vnew_n$; otherwise $k \leftarrow k + 1$ and go to Step 2.

■ NOTE: Recall is much simpler to implement without randomizing the update sequence. In such case, Step 2 of the algorithm is eliminated and we have $\alpha_1 = 1$, $\alpha_2 = 2, \ldots, \alpha_n = n$, or simply $\alpha_i = i$ at each update cycle. Elimination of Step 2 can, however, result in reduced efficiency of retrieval.

Performance Considerations

Hopfield autoassociative memory is often referred to in the literature as an error correcting decoder in that, given an input vector that is equal to the stored memory plus random errors, it produces as output the original memory that is closest to the input. The reason why the update rule proposed by Hopfield can reconstruct a noise-corrupted or incomplete pattern can be understood intuitively. The memory works best for large n values and this is our assumption for further discussion of memory's performance evaluation. Let us assume that a pattern $\mathbf{s}^{(m')}$ has been stored in the memory as one of p patterns. This pattern is now at the memory input. The activation value of the i'th neuron for the update rule (6.17) for retrieval of pattern $\mathbf{s}^{(m')}$ has the following form:

$$net_i^{(m')} = \sum_{j=1}^{n} w_{ij} s_j^{(m')} \tag{6.27a}$$

or, using (6.20b) and temporarily neglecting the contribution coming from the nullification of the diagonal, we obtain

$$net_i^{(m')} \cong \sum_{j=1}^{n} \sum_{m=1}^{p} s_i^{(m)} s_j^{(m)} s_j^{(m')} \tag{6.27b}$$

Thus, we can write

$$net_i^{(m')} \cong \sum_{m=1}^{p} s_i^{(m)} \sum_{j=1}^{n} s_j^{(m)} s_j^{(m')} \tag{6.27c}$$

If terms $s_j^{(m)}$ and $s_j^{(m')}$, for $j = 1, 2, \ldots, n$, were totally statistically independent or unrelated for $m = 1, 2, \ldots, p$, then the average value of the second sum resulted in zero. Note that the second sum is the scalar product of two n-tuple vectors and if the two vectors are statistically independent (also when orthogonal) their product vanishes. If, however, any of the stored patterns $\mathbf{s}^{(m)}$, for $m = 1, 2, \ldots, p$, and vector $\mathbf{s}^{(m')}$ are somewhat overlapping, then the value of the second sum becomes positive. Note that in the limit case the second sum would reach n for both vectors being identical, understandably so since we have here the scalar product of two identical n-tuple vectors with entries of value ± 1. Thus for the major overlap case, the sign of entry $s_i^{(m')}$ is expected to be the same as that of $net_i^{(m')}$, and we can write

$$net_i^{(m')} \cong s_i^{(m')}n, \quad \text{for } i = 1, 2, \dots, n \tag{6.27d}$$

This indicates that the vector $\mathbf{s}^{(m')}$ does not produce any updates and is therefore stable.

Assume now that the input vector is a distorted version of the prototype vector $\mathbf{s}^{(m')}$, which has been stored in the memory. The distortion is such that only a small percentage of bits differs between the stored memory $\mathbf{s}^{(m')}$ and the initializing input vector. The discussion that formerly led to the simplification of (6.27c) to (6.27d) still remains valid for this present case with the additional qualification that the multiplier originally equal to n in (6.27d) may take a somewhat reduced value. The multiplier becomes equal to the number of overlapping bits of $\mathbf{s}^{(m')}$ and of the input vector.

It thus follows that the impending update of node i will be in the same direction as the entry $s_i^{(m')}$. Negative and positive bits of vector $\mathbf{s}^{(m')}$ are likely to cause negative and positive transitions, respectively, in the upcoming recurrences. We may say that the majority of memory initializing bits is assumed to be correct and allowed to take a vote for the minority of bits. The minority bits do not prevail, so they are flipped, one by one and thus asynchronously, according to the will of the majority. This shows vividly how bits of the input vector can be updated in the right direction toward the closest prototype stored. The above discussion has assumed large n values, so it has been more relevant for real-life application networks.

A very interesting case can be observed for the stored orthogonal patterns $\mathbf{s}^{(m)}$. The activation vector $\mathbf{net}$ can be computed as

$$\mathbf{net} = \left(\sum_{m=1}^{p} \mathbf{s}^{(m)}\mathbf{s}^{(m)t} - p\mathbf{I} \right) \mathbf{s}^{(m')} \tag{6.28a}$$

The orthogonality condition, which is $\mathbf{s}^{(i)t}\mathbf{s}^{(j)} = 0$, for $i \neq j$, and $\mathbf{s}^{(i)t}\mathbf{s}^{(j)} = n$, for $i = j$, makes it possible to simplify (6.28a) to the following form

$$\mathbf{net} = (n - p)\mathbf{s}^{(m')} \tag{6.28b}$$

Assuming that under normal operating conditions the inequality $n > p$ holds, the network will be in equilibrium at state $\mathbf{s}^{(m')}$. Indeed, computing the value of the energy function (6.19) for the storage rule (6.20b) we obtain

$$E(\mathbf{v}) = -\frac{1}{2}\mathbf{v}^t \left(\sum_{m=1}^{p} \mathbf{s}^{(m)}\mathbf{s}^{(m)t} \right) \mathbf{v} + \frac{1}{2}\mathbf{v}^t p\mathbf{I}\mathbf{v} \tag{6.29a}$$

For every stored vector $\mathbf{s}^{(m')}$ which is orthogonal to all other vectors the energy value (6.29a) reduces to

$$E\left(\mathbf{s}^{(m')}\right) = -\frac{1}{2} \sum_{m=1}^{p} \left(\mathbf{s}^{(m')t}\mathbf{s}^{(m)}\right)\left(\mathbf{s}^{(m)t}\mathbf{s}^{(m')}\right) + \frac{1}{2}\mathbf{s}^{(m')t}p\mathbf{I}\mathbf{s}^{(m')} \qquad (6.29b)$$

and further to

$$E\left(\mathbf{s}^{(m')}\right) = -\frac{1}{2}(n^2 - pn) \qquad (6.29c)$$

The memory network is thus in an equilibrium state at every stored prototype vector $\mathbf{s}^{(m')}$, and the energy assumes its minimum value expressed in (6.29c).

Considering the simplest autoassociative memory with two neurons and a single stored vector ($n = 2$, $p = 1$), Equation (6.29c) yields the energy minimum of value -1. Indeed, the energy function (6.26) for the memory network of Example 6.1 has been evaluated and found to have minima of that value.

For the more general case, however, when stored patterns $\mathbf{s}^{(1)}, \mathbf{s}^{(2)}, \ldots, \mathbf{s}^{(p)}$ are not mutually orthogonal, the energy function (6.29b) does not necessarily assume a minimum at $\mathbf{s}^{(m')}$, nor is the vector $\mathbf{s}^{(m')}$ always an equilibrium for the memory. To gain better insight into memory performance let us calculate the activation vector **net** in a more general case using expression (6.28a) without an assumption of orthogonality:

$$\mathbf{net} = n\mathbf{s}^{(m')} - p\mathbf{s}^{(m')} + \sum_{m \neq m'}^{p} (\mathbf{s}^{(m)}\mathbf{s}^{(m)t})\mathbf{s}^{(m')} \qquad (6.30a)$$

This resulting activation vector can be viewed as consisting of an equilibrium state term $(n - p)\mathbf{s}^{(m')}$ similar to (6.28b). In this case discussed before, either full statistical independence or orthogonality of the stored vectors was assumed. If none of these assumptions is valid, then the sum term in (6.30a) is also present in addition to the equilibrium term. The sum term can be viewed as a "noise" term vector $\boldsymbol{\eta}$ which is computed as follows

$$\boldsymbol{\eta} = \left(\mathbf{W} - \mathbf{s}^{(m')}\mathbf{s}^{(m')t} + \mathbf{I}\right)\mathbf{s}^{(m')} \qquad (6.30b)$$

Expression (6.30b) allows for comparison of the noise terms relative to the equilibrium term at the input to each neuron. When the magnitude of the i'th component of the noise vector is larger than $(n - p)s_i^{(m')}$ and the term has the opposite sign, then $s_i^{(m')}$ will not be the network's equilibrium. The noise term obviously increases for an increased number of stored patterns, and also becomes relatively significant when the factor $(n - p)$ decreases.

As we can see from the preliminary study, the analysis of stable states of memory can become involved. In addition, firm conclusions are hard to derive unless statistical methods of memory evaluation are employed. The next section will focus on the performance analysis of autoassociative recurrent memories.

6.4

PERFORMANCE ANALYSIS
OF RECURRENT
AUTOASSOCIATIVE MEMORY

In this section relationships will be presented that relate the size of the memory n to the number of distinct patterns that can be efficiently recovered. These also depend on the degree of similarity that the initializing key vector has to the closest stored vector and on the similarity between the stored patterns. We will look at example performance and capacity, as well as the fixed points of associative memories.

As mentioned, associative memories recall patterns that display a degree of "similarity" to the search argument. To measure this "similarity" precisely, the quantity called the *Hamming distance* (HD) is often used. Strictly speaking, the Hamming distance is proportional to the dissimilarity of vectors. It is defined as an integer equal to the number of bit positions differing between two binary vectors of the same length.

For two n-tuple bipolar binary vectors $\mathbf{x}$ and $\mathbf{y}$, the Hamming distance is equal:

$$\text{HD}(\mathbf{x}, \mathbf{y}) \overset{\Delta}{=} \frac{1}{2} \sum_{i=1}^{n} |x_i - y_i| \tag{6.31}$$

Obviously, the maximum HD value between any vectors is n and is the distance between a vector and its complement. Let us also notice that the asynchronous update allows for updating of the output vector by HD = 1 at a time. The following example depicts some of the typical occurrences within the autoassociative memory and focuses on memory state transitions.

EXAMPLE 6.2

Let us look at the design and convergence properties of an autoassociative memory that stores the following two vectors $\mathbf{s}^{(1)}$, $\mathbf{s}^{(2)}$:

$$\mathbf{s}^{(1)} = \begin{bmatrix} -1 & -1 & 1 & 1 \end{bmatrix}^t$$
$$\mathbf{s}^{(2)} = \begin{bmatrix} -1 & 1 & 1 & -1 \end{bmatrix}^t$$

The weight matrix computed according to (6.20) results:

$$\mathbf{W} = \begin{bmatrix} 0 & 0 & -2 & 0 \\ 0 & 0 & 0 & -2 \\ -2 & 0 & 0 & 0 \\ 0 & -2 & 0 & 0 \end{bmatrix}$$

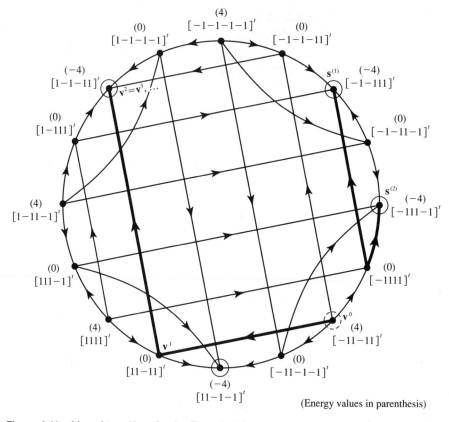

(Energy values in parenthesis)

Figure 6.11 Map of transitions for the Example 6.2.

The energy function computed from (6.19) is readily obtainable as

$$E(\mathbf{v}) = 2(v_1 v_3 + v_2 v_4)$$

When the network is allowed to update, it evolves through certain states, which are shown on the state transition diagram in Figure 6.11. States are vertices of the four-dimensional cube. The figure shows all possible asynchronous transitions and their directions. Only transitions between states have been marked on the graph; the self-sustaining or stable state transitions have been omitted for clarity of the picture. Since only asynchronous transitions are allowed for autoassociative recurrent memory, every vertex is connected by an edge only to the neighboring vertex differing by a single bit. Thus, there are only four transition paths connected to every state. The paths indicate directions of possible transitions. As explained earlier, transitions for the update rule (6.17) are toward lower energy values. The energy values for each state have been marked in parentheses at each vertex.

Let us review several sample transitions. Starting at $\mathbf{v}^0 = [-1\ 1\ -1\ 1]^t$, and with nodes updating asynchronously in ascending order, we have the state sequence

$$\mathbf{v}^1 = \begin{bmatrix} 1 & 1 & -1 & 1 \end{bmatrix}^t$$
$$\mathbf{v}^2 = \begin{bmatrix} 1 & -1 & -1 & 1 \end{bmatrix}^t$$
$$\mathbf{v}^3 = \mathbf{v}^4 = \ldots = \begin{bmatrix} 1 & -1 & -1 & 1 \end{bmatrix}^t$$

as it has been marked on the state diagram. The actual convergence is toward a negative image of the stored pattern $\mathbf{s}^{(2)}$. This result should have been expected. The initial pattern had no particular similarity to any of the stored patterns and apparently did not fall into any closeness category of patterns discussed in the previous section. In fact, the selected initializing pattern $\mathbf{v}^0$ has an HD value of 2 to each of the stored patterns. As such, the HD value is equal to half of the input vector dimension and the memory does not recover any of the stored vectors $\mathbf{s}^{(1)}$ or $\mathbf{s}^{(2)}$.

Let us look at a regeneration of a key vector $\mathbf{v}^0 = \begin{bmatrix} -1 & 1 & 1 & 1 \end{bmatrix}^t$ which is at HD = 1 to both $\mathbf{s}^{(1)}$ and $\mathbf{s}^{(2)}$. The transition starting in ascending order leads to $\mathbf{s}^{(1)}$ in single step

$$\mathbf{v}^1 = \mathbf{v}^0$$
$$\mathbf{v}^2 = \begin{bmatrix} -1 & -1 & 1 & 1 \end{bmatrix}^t$$
$$\mathbf{v}^3 = \mathbf{v}^2$$
$$\mathbf{v}^4 = \mathbf{v}^3, \quad \text{etc.}$$

The reader can verify that by carrying out the transitions initialized at $\mathbf{v}^0$, but carried out in descending node order, pattern $\mathbf{s}^{(2)}$ can be recovered. ■

The reader has certainly noticed that the example autoassociative memory just discussed has a number of problems, the most serious of them being uncertain recovery. Indeed, the memory in this example has been heavily overloaded since p/n is 50%. Overloaded memory by design does not provide error-free or efficient recovery of stored patterns. Another problem encountered in the memory is its unplanned stable states. Evaluation of similar examples of slightly larger memories would make it possible to find out that stable states exist that are not the stored memories. Such purposely not encoded but physically existent states of equilibrium are called spurious memories. *Spurious memories* are caused by the minima of the energy function that are additional to the ones we want. We could also find examples of convergence that are not toward the closest memory as measured with the HD value (see Problem P6.10). These are further drawbacks of the original model since the memories may not all be fixed points. These issues become particularly important near or above the memory capacity.

Energy Function Reduction

The energy function (6.19) of the autoassociative memory decreases during the memory recall phase. The dynamic updating process continues until a local energy minimum is found. Similar to continuous-time systems, the energy is minimized along the following gradient vector direction:

$$\nabla_v E(\mathbf{v}) = -\mathbf{W}\mathbf{v} \tag{6.32a}$$

As we will see below, the gradient (6.32a) is a linear function of the Hamming distance between $\mathbf{v}$ and each of the p stored memories (Petsche 1988). By substituting (6.20a) into the gradient expression (6.32a), it can be rearranged to the form

$$\nabla_v E(\mathbf{v}) = -\sum_{m=1}^{p} \mathbf{s}^{(m)} \left[n - 2\mathrm{HD}\left(\mathbf{s}^{(m)}, \mathbf{v}\right) \right] + p\mathbf{v} \tag{6.32b}$$

where the scalar product $\mathbf{s}^{(m)t}\mathbf{v}$ has been replaced by the expression in brackets (see Appendix). The components of the gradient vector, $\nabla_{v_i} E(\mathbf{v})$, can be obtained directly from (6.32b) as

$$\frac{\partial E(\mathbf{v})}{\partial v_i} = -n \sum_{m=1}^{p} s_i^{(m)} + 2 \sum_{m=1}^{p} s_i^{(m)} \mathrm{HD}(\mathbf{s}^{(m)}, \mathbf{v}) + p v_i \tag{6.32c}$$

Expression (6.32c) makes it possible to explain why it is difficult to recover patterns $\mathbf{v}$ at a large Hamming distance from any of the stored patterns $\mathbf{s}^{(m)}$, $m = 1, 2, \ldots, p$.

When bit i of the output vector, v_i, is erroneous and equals -1 and needs to be corrected to $+1$, the i'th component of the energy gradient vector (6.32c) must be negative. This condition enables appropriate bit update while the energy function value would be reduced in this step. From (6.32c) we can notice, however, that any gradient component of the energy function is linearly dependent on $\mathrm{HD}\left(\mathbf{s}^{(m)}, \mathbf{v}\right)$, for $m = 1, 2, \ldots, p$. The larger the HD value, the more difficult it is to ascertain that the gradient component indeed remains negative due to the large potential contribution of the second sum term to the right side of expression (6.32c). Similar arguments against large HD values apply for correct update of bit $v_i = 1$ toward -1 which requires positive gradient component $\partial E(\mathbf{v})/\partial v_i$.

Let us characterize the local energy minimum $\mathbf{v}^*$ using the energy gradient component. For autoassociative memory discussed, $\mathbf{v}^*$ constitutes a local minimum of the energy function if and only if the condition holds that $v_i^*(\partial E / \partial v_i)|_{\mathbf{v}^*} < 0$ for all $i = 1, 2, \ldots, n$. The energy function as in (6.19) can

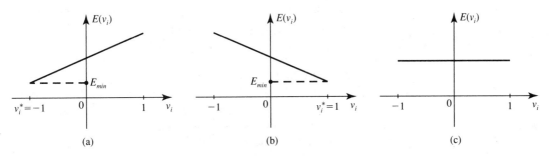

Figure 6.12 Three possible energy function cross sections along the v_i axis: (a) positive slope, minimum at -1, (b) negative slope, minimum at 1, and (c) zero slope, no unique minimum.

be expressed as

$$E(\mathbf{v}) = -v_i \sum_{\substack{j=1 \\ j \neq i}}^{n} w_{ij}v_j - \frac{1}{2} \sum_{k=1}^{n} \sum_{\substack{j=1 \\ j \neq k, j \neq i}}^{n} w_{kj}v_kv_j \qquad (6.33a)$$

where the first term of (6.33a) is linear in v_i and the second term is constant. Therefore, the slope of $E(v_i)$ is a constant that is positive, negative, or zero. This implies that one of the three conditions applies at the minimum $\mathbf{v}^*$

$$\left. \frac{\partial E}{\partial v_i} \right|_{\mathbf{v}^*} > 0, \quad v_i^* = -1 \qquad (6.33b)$$

$$\left. \frac{\partial E}{\partial v_i} \right|_{\mathbf{v}^*} < 0, \quad v_i^* = 1 \qquad (6.33c)$$

$$\left. \frac{\partial E}{\partial v_i} \right|_{\mathbf{v}^*} = 0, \quad v_i^* = \pm 1 \qquad (6.33d)$$

The three possible cases are illustrated in Figure 6.12. The energy function is minimized for $v_i^* = -1$ (case a) or for $v_i^* = 1$ (case b). Zero slope of the energy, or gradient component equal to zero (case c), implies no unique minimum at either $+1$ or -1.

Capacity of Autoassociative Recurrent Memory

One of the most important performance parameters of an associative memory is its capacity. Detailed studies of memory capacity have been reported in by McEliece et al. (1987) and Komlos and Paturi (1988). A state vector of the memory is considered to be *stable* if $\mathbf{v}^{k+1} = \Gamma[\mathbf{W}\mathbf{v}^k]$ provided that $\mathbf{v}^{k+1} = \mathbf{v}^k$.

Note that the definition of stability is not affected by synchronous versus asynchronous transition mode; rather, the stability concept is independent from the transition mode.

A useful measure for memory capacity evaluation is the *radius of attraction* ρ, which is defined in terms of the distance ρn from a stable state **v** such that every vector within the distance ρn eventually reaches the stable state **v**. It is understood that the distance ρn is convenient if measured as a Hamming distance and therefore is of integer value. For the reasons explained earlier in the chapter the radius of attraction for an autoassociative memory is somewhere between $1/n$ and $1/2$, which corresponds to the distance of attraction between 1 and $n/2$.

For the system to function as a memory, we require that every stored memory $\mathbf{s}^{(m)}$ be stable. Somewhat less restrictive is the assumption that there is at least a stable state at a small distance εn from the stored memory where ε is a positive number. In such a case it is then still reasonable to expect that the memory has an error correction capability. For example, when recovering the input key vector at a distance ρn from stored memory, the stable state will be found at a distance εn from it. Note that this may still be an acceptable output in situations when the system has learned too many vectors and the memory of each single vector is faded. Obviously, when $\varepsilon = 0$, the stored memory is stable within a radius of ρ.

The discussion above indicates that the error correction capability of an autoassociative memory can only be evaluated if stored vectors are not too close to each other. Therefore, each of the p distinct stored vectors used for a capacity study are usually selected at random. The asymptotic capacity of an autoassociative memory consisting of n neurons has been estimated in by McEliece et al. (1987) as

$$c = \frac{(1 - 2\rho)^2 n}{4 \ln n} \tag{6.34a}$$

When the number of stored patterns p is below the capacity c expressed as in (6.34a), then all of the stored memories, with probability near 1, will be stable. The formula determines the number of key vectors at a radius ρ from the stored memory that are correctly recallable to one of the stable, stored memories. The simple stability of the stored memories, with probability near 1, is ensured by the upper bound on the number p given as

$$c = \frac{n}{4 \ln n} \tag{6.34b}$$

For any radius between 0 and $1/2$ of key vectors to the stored memory, almost all of the c stored memories are attractive when c is bounded as in (6.34b). If a small fraction of the stored memories can be tolerated as unrecoverable, and not stable, then the capacity boundary c can be considered twice as large compared to c computed from (6.34b). In summary, it is appropriate to state that regardless of the radius of attraction $0 < \rho < 1/2$ the capacity of the Hopfield memory is bounded as follows

$$\frac{n}{4 \ln n} < c < \frac{n}{2 \ln n} \tag{6.34c}$$

To offer a numerical example, the boundary values for a 100-neuron network computed from (6.34c) are about 5.4, with 10.8 memory vectors.

Assume that the number of stored patterns p is kept at the level αn, for $0 < \alpha < 1$, and n is large. It has been shown that the memory still functions efficiently at capacity levels exceeding those stated in (6.34c) (Amit, Gutfreund, and Sompolinsky 1985). When $\alpha \cong 0.14$, stable states are found that are very close to the stored memories at a distance $0.03n$. As α decreases to zero, this distance decreases as $\exp(-(1/2)\alpha)$. Hence, the memory retrieval is mostly accurate for $p \le 0.14n$. A small percentage of error must be tolerated though if the memory operates at these upper capacity levels.

The study by McEliece et al. (1987) also reveals the presence of spurious fixed points, which are not stored memories. They tend to have rather small basins of attraction compared to the stored memories. Therefore, updates terminate in them if they start in their vicinity.

Although the number of distinct pattern vectors that can be stored and perfectly recalled in Hopfield's memory is not large, the network has found a number of practical applications. However, it is somewhat peculiar that the network can recover only c memories out of the total of 2^n states available in the network as the cube corners of n-dimensional hypercube.

Memory Convergence versus Corruption

To supplement the study of the original Hopfield autoassociative memory, it is worthwhile to look at the actual performance of an example memory. Of particular interest are the convergence rates versus memory parameters discussed earlier. Let us inspect the memory performance analysis curves shown in Figure 6.13 (Desai 1990). The memory performance on this figure has been evaluated for a network with $n = 120$ neurons. As pointed out earlier in this section, the total number of stored patterns, their mutual Hamming distance and their Hamming distance to the key vector determine the success of recovery. Figure 6.13(a) shows the percentage of correct convergence as a function of key vector corruption compared to the stored memories. Computation shown is for a fixed HD between the vectors stored of value 45. It can be seen that the correct convergence rate drops about linearly with the amount of corruption of the key vector. The correct convergence rate also reduces as the number of stored patterns increases for a fixed distortion value of input key vectors. The network performs very well at $p = 2$ patterns stored but recovers rather poorly distorted vectors at $p = 16$ patterns stored.

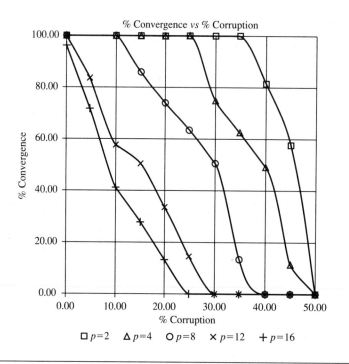

%. Convergence *vs* %. Corruption

□ p=2   △ p=4   O p=8   × p=12   + p=16

Convergence vs. Corruption

Network Type: Hopfield Memory

Network Parameters: Dimension—n (120)
                    Threshold—Hard Limited
                    @ Hamming Distance HD = 45

Curve Parameters: Patterns P

Features: 20 samples per point.

Comments: As can be seen from the curves the performance is of good quality for corruption levels up to 25% with a capacity of 0.04 × n only. The noise tolerance becomes poor as the number of patterns approaches the capacity of 18.

(a)

Figure 6.13a Memory convergence versus corruption of key vector: (a) for a different number of stored vectors, HD = 45.

Figure 6.13(b) shows the percentage of correct convergence events as a function of key vector corruption for a fixed number of stored patterns equal to four. The HD between the stored memories is a parameter for the family of curves shown on the figure. The network exhibits high noise immunity for large and very large Hamming distances between the stored vectors. A gradual

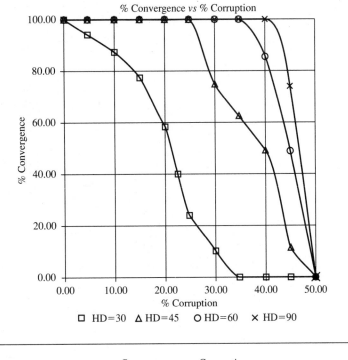

□ HD=30 △ HD=45 ○ HD=60 ✕ HD=90

Convergence vs. Corruption

Network Type: Hopfield Memory

Network Parameters: Dimension—n (120)
                    Threshold—Hard Limited
                    Patterns $p = 4$

Curve Parameters: Hamming Distance

Features: 20 samples per point.

Comments: This network shows excellent performance and is extremely insensitive to noise
          for corruption levels as high as 35% at a Hamming Distance of 60 between
          the stored prototypes. An abrupt degradation in performance is observed for
          prototypes having more than three quarter of their bits in common.

(b)

Figure 6.13b Memory convergence versus corruption of key vector *(continued):* (b) for different HD values, four vectors stored.

---

degradation of initially excellent recovery can be seen as stored vectors become more overlapping. For stored vectors that have 75% of the bits in common, the recovery of correct memories is shown to be rather inefficient.

To determine how long it takes for the memory to suppress errors, the number of update cycles has also been evaluated for example recurrences for

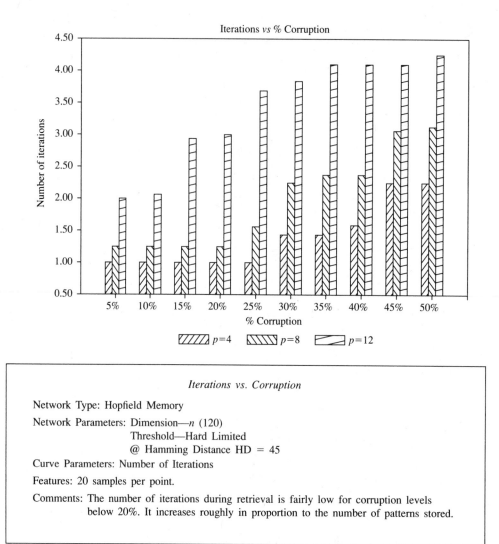

Figure 6.13c   Memory convergence versus corruption of key vector *(continued):* (c) the number of sweep cycles for different corruption levels.

the discussed memory example. The update cycle is understood as a full sweep through all of the *n* neuron outputs. The average number of measured update cycles has been between 1 and 4 as illustrated in Figure 6.13(c). This number increases roughly linearly with the number of patterns stored and with the percent corruption of the key input vector.

Fixed Point Concept

We now look in more detail at the convergence of recurrent autoassociative networks. Since the energy function $E(\mathbf{v})$ of Equation (6.19) is bounded from below, the network evolves under the asynchronous dynamics toward $E(\mathbf{v}^{k+1})$ such that

$$E(\mathbf{v}^{k+1}) \leq E(\mathbf{v}^k) \tag{6.35a}$$

Since vectors $\mathbf{v}^{k+1}$ and $\mathbf{v}^k$ differ during the memory transitions by at most a single component (bit), the stabilization of $E(\mathbf{v}^{k+1})$ means that

$$E(\mathbf{v}^{k+1}) = E(\mathbf{v}^k) \quad \text{for } k > k_0 \tag{6.35b}$$

The transitions stop at the energy minimum, which also implies that

$$\mathbf{v}^{k+1} = \mathbf{v}^k \tag{6.35c}$$

Thus the network reaches its fixed point $\mathbf{v}^k$, or stable state, at the energy minimum $E(\mathbf{v}^k)$. We also know from the energy function study that the only attractors of the discussed network are its fixed points. Limit cycles such as B shown in Figure 6.4(c) are thus excluded in these type of networks.

It is instructive to devote more attention to the fixed-point concept, because it sheds more light on memory performance. Let us begin with a discussion of the one-dimensional recurrent system shown in Figure 6.14. For the output at $t = k + 1$ we have

$$\mathbf{v}^{k+1} = f(w, \mathbf{v}^k) \tag{6.36a}$$

The fixed point is defined at $v*$ if the following relationship holds:

$$v* = f(v*) \tag{6.36b}$$

where it has been assumed that network parameter w in (6.36a) is constant. In geometrical terms the fixed point is found at the intersection of function $f(v)$ and v. Whether or not this point is the solution of recursive Equation (6.36a) remains, however, an open question. In terms of the recursive formula (6.36a), the fixed point is said to be stable if

$$\lim_{k \to \infty} v^k = v*, \quad \text{or} \tag{6.37a}$$

$$\cdot \lim_{k \to \infty} e^{k+1} = 0 \tag{6.37b}$$

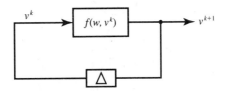

Figure 6.14   One-dimensional recurrent network.

where e is the recursion error defined as

$$e^{k+1} \triangleq |v^{k+1} - v^*|$$

The recursion error can be expressed using (6.36a) as

$$e^{k+1} = |f(v^k) - v^*| \tag{6.38a}$$

and further rearranged to the form

$$e^{k+1} = \left| \frac{f\left[v^* + (v^k - v^*)\right] - f(v^*)}{v^k - v^*} \right| e^k \tag{6.38b}$$

For a differentiable function f responsible for network's feedforward processing, this further reduces to

$$e^{k+1} \cong |f'(v^*)| \, e^k \tag{6.38c}$$

Now the condition (6.38c) translates to the form

$$|f'(v)| < 1 \tag{6.39}$$

which is the sufficient condition for the existence of a stable fixed point in the neighborhood where condition (6.39) holds. We have derived the condition for stable fixed-point existence in a simple one-dimensional case.

Let us look at an example of two systems and analyze the existence of stable fixed points. Figure 6.15(a) depicts a curve (Serra and Zanarini 1990) that serves as an example:

$$f(v) = w \left(1 - 2 \left| \frac{1}{2} - v \right| \right) \tag{6.40}$$

The curve is called a *triangular map* and is made for the parameter $w = 1/3$, $0 \le v \le 1$. The function has only a single stable fixed point, $v^* = 0$. The several successive recursions shown indicate this clearly. Moreover, condition (6.39) is also fulfilled for the entire neighborhood $0 \le v \le 1$.

Another triangular map made for a different value of the triangular map parameter, $w = 2$, is shown in Figure 6.15(b). Two unstable fixed points are found for this case. They are at $v = 0$ and $v = 2/3$. The fixed point instability can be noticed from displayed recursive movements of the solution starting at v^0 and $\bar{v}^0$. The reader can verify that performing recursions

$$v^{k+1} = f(v^k) = 2 \left(1 - 2 \left| \frac{1}{2} - v^k \right| \right)$$

starting either at v^0 or at $\bar{v}^0$, the recursive updates are not converging to any of the solutions that clearly exist at $v = 0$ and $v = 2/3$.

As we have seen, even a simple one-dimensional recurrent network exhibits interesting properties. The network from Figure 6.14 may be looked at as a single

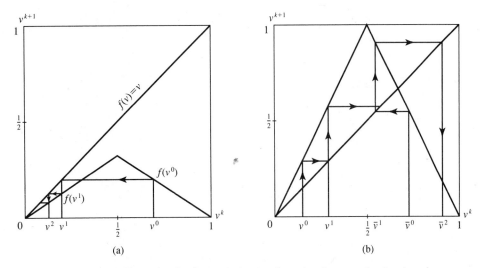

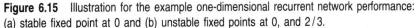

Figure 6.15   Illustration for the example one-dimensional recurrent network performance: (a) stable fixed point at 0 and (b) unstable fixed points at 0, and 2/3.

computing node, which illustrates the discussion of the one-dimensional case just concluded. The recurrent progression of outputs in a multidimensional recurrent network is much more complex than shown. There are, however, fixed-point attractors in such memories similar to the ones discussed.

Figure 6.16 shows a single-neuron recurrent memory that has two stable fixed points at A and B, and one unstable stationary point at the origin. Although this network does have self-feedback, it operates with a continuous activation function, and thus it does not totally qualify as an associative memory by our criteria. However, it is useful for understanding fixed-point recursion mechanisms, which make stable or unstable neural networks. In limit case of high feedforward gain, the network shown in Figure 6.16 but using a hard-limiting activation function would stabilize at output $+1$ or -1. Note that the network from Figure 6.16(a) is a disguised bistable flip-flop from Figure 6.8(a). It employs a single non-inverting neuron rather than two inverting ones in cascade. Their operating principle concept, behavior and final outcome are the same.

Modified Memory Convergent Toward Fixed Points

Recall from the previous section that in several basic cases of memory studies we have been able to show that **net** $= c\mathbf{s}^{(m')}$, where c is a positive constant and $\mathbf{s}^{(m')}$ is one of the stored patterns. With respect to the discussion of

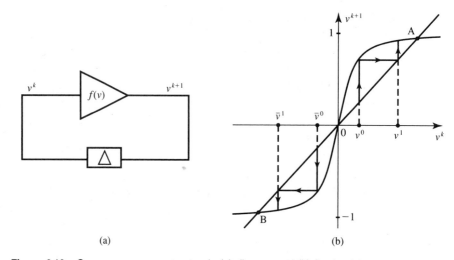

Figure 6.16 One-neuron recurrent network: (a) diagram and (b) fixed points.

stable fixed points, these cases could be understood as stable recurrent solutions for fixed points such that

$$\lim_{k \to \infty} \mathbf{v}^{k+1} = \mathbf{s}^{(m')} \tag{6.41}$$

Assume that only a single pattern $\mathbf{s}^{(m')}$ has been stored in an autoassociative memory. The recurrent update of the i'th node requires that

$$v_i^{k+1} = \sum_{j=1}^{n} s_i^{(m')} s_j^{(m')t} s_j^{(m')} - s_i^{(m')} \tag{6.42a}$$

and it reduces to

$$v_i^{k+1} = (n - 1)s_i^{(m')} \tag{6.42b}$$

Thus, the vector $\mathbf{s}^{(m')}$ can be considered a stable fixed point in the memory.

When the network has been taught more than a single pattern, the patterns stored remain as fixed points, but a new stable state might also appear. In the case for which the number of stored patterns exceeds two, it is not even possible to guarantee that they, in fact, remain as fixed points (Serra and Zanarini 1990). The substantiation of the property is rather tedious, however, and is thus omitted.

The discussion below provides some additional insight into complex recurrent processes within the discussed class of memory networks. Realizing the limitations of the original model for autoassociative memory, the original Hebbian learning rule with the diagonal nullification used throughout Sections 6.3 and 6.4 can be modified. This modification results in a memory with improved properties. A memory recording method is presented below that makes each of the patterns an independent equilibrium point.

Observe that a pattern $\mathbf{s}^{(m')}$ is a fixed point if and only if the following inequality holds:

$$\left(\sum_{j=1}^{n} w_{ij} s_j^{(m')} \right) s_i^{(m')} \geq 0, \quad \text{for } i = 1, 2, \ldots, n \tag{6.43}$$

An alternative design procedure for the memory can be devised based on (6.43). To implement the condition that each of the p patterns be a fixed point, $n \times p$ inequalities such as (6.43) must be fulfilled. Note that (6.43) holds when the following condition holds:

$$\mathbf{W}\mathbf{s}^{(m)} = \mathbf{s}^{(m)}, \quad \text{for } m = 1, 2, \ldots, p \tag{6.44a}$$

Condition (6.44a) can be written compactly as a single matrix expression

$$\mathbf{W}\mathbf{S} = \mathbf{S} \tag{6.44b}$$

where

$$\mathbf{S} \triangleq \begin{bmatrix} \mathbf{s}^{(1)} & \mathbf{s}^{(2)} & \cdots & \mathbf{s}^{(p)} \end{bmatrix}$$

To accomplish the modified memory design, we are interested in finding the matrix $\mathbf{W}$ that fulfills (6.44b). The matrix equation (6.44b) is actually a system of np linear equations for solving n^2 unknowns which are entries of the $\mathbf{W}$ matrix. Note that for memory that is not overloaded, p should always be smaller than n. The linear system (6.44b) is thus underdetermined, so there is a solution for $\mathbf{W}$ that approximates (6.44b). One of the possible solutions to (6.44) has been presented by Personnaz, Guyon, and Dreyfus (1986) and it is reviewed below. The resulting solution weight matrix is

$$\mathbf{W} = \mathbf{S}\mathbf{S}^+ \tag{6.45}$$

where $\mathbf{S}^+$ is the Moore-Penrose pseudoinverse matrix (see Appendix). For linearly independent vectors $\mathbf{s}^m$, the matrix $\mathbf{S}^+$ can be expressed as

$$\mathbf{S}^+ \triangleq (\mathbf{S}^t\mathbf{S})^{-1}\mathbf{S}^t$$

It can be seen that since the matrix $\mathbf{S}$ is of size $n \times p$, the computation of $\mathbf{W}$ as in (6.45) involves the inversion of a $p \times p$ matrix. The method presented is called the *projection learning rule* and it departs from the conventional Hebb's learning rule for weight matrix entries (Michel and Farrell 1990). Interestingly, formula (6.45) simplifies to the Hebbian learning rule for orthogonal vectors to be stored. Indeed, using the orthogonality condition we have

$$\mathbf{S}^t\mathbf{S} = \mathbf{I} \tag{6.46}$$

which yields from (6.45)

$$\mathbf{W} = \mathbf{S}\mathbf{S}^t \tag{6.47}$$

This result for the weight matrix exactly coincides with Hebbian learning rule

(6.14b). In conclusion, the projection learning rule offers an improvement over the Hebbian rule in the sense that each of the stored memories is a stable fixed point. Thus, the method guarantees that the stored vectors correspond to stable solutions. Note that both learning rules lead to symmetric matrices $\mathbf{W}$. The disadvantage of the projection learning rule is that the regions of attraction for each pattern become significantly smaller for a larger number of patterns p stored within a given size network. For p approaching $n/2$, the decrease of memory convergence quality is rather drastic.

Advantages and Limitations

Theoretical considerations and examples of memory networks discussed in this chapter point out a number of advantages and limitations. As we have seen, recurrent associative memories, whether designed by the Hebbian learning rule or by a modified rule, suffer from substantial capacity limitations. Capacity limitation causes diversified symptoms. It can amount to convergence to spurious memories and difficulties with recovery of stored patterns if they are close to each other in the Hamming distance sense. Overloaded memory may not be able to recover data stored or may recall spurious outputs. Another inherent problem is the memory convergence to stored pattern complements.

In spite of all these deficiencies, the Hopfield network demonstrates the power of recurrent neural processing within a parallel architecture. The recurrences through the thresholding layer of processing neurons tend to eliminate gradually noise superimposed on the initializing input vector. This coerces the incorrect pattern bits toward one of the stored memories. The network's computational ability makes it possible to apply it in speech processing, database retrieval, image processing, pattern classification and other fields. The electronic implementations of Hopfield's associative memories will be discussed in Chapter 9.

6.5

BIDIRECTIONAL ASSOCIATIVE MEMORY

Bidirectional associative memory is a heteroassociative, content-addressable memory consisting of two layers. It uses the forward and backward information flow to produce an associative search for stored stimulus-response association (Kosko 1987, 1988). Consider that stored in the memory are p vector association pairs known as

$$\left\{ \left(\mathbf{a}^{(1)}, \mathbf{b}^{(1)} \right), \left(\mathbf{a}^{(2)}, \mathbf{b}^{(2)} \right), \ldots, \left(\mathbf{a}^{(p)}, \mathbf{b}^{(p)} \right) \right\} \qquad (6.48)$$

When the memory neurons are activated, the network evolves to a stable state of two-pattern reverberation, each pattern at output of one layer. The stable reverberation corresponds to a local energy minimum. The network's dynamics involves two layers of interaction. Because the memory processes information in time and involves bidirectional data flow, it differs in principle from a linear associator, although both networks are used to store association pairs. It also differs from the recurrent autoassociative memory in its update mode.

Memory Architecture

The basic diagram of the bidirectional associative memory is shown in Figure 6.17(a). Let us assume that an initializing vector $\mathbf{b}$ is applied at the input to the layer A of neurons. The neurons are assumed to be bipolar binary. The input is processed through the linear connection layer and then through the bipolar threshold functions as follows:

$$\mathbf{a}' = \Gamma[\mathbf{Wb}] \tag{6.49a}$$

where $\Gamma[\cdot]$ is a nonlinear operator defined in (6.5). This pass consists of matrix multiplication and a bipolar thresholding operation so that the i'th output is

$$a_i' = \operatorname{sgn}\left(\sum_{j=1}^{m} w_{ij} b_j\right), \quad \text{for } i = 1, 2, \ldots, n \tag{6.49b}$$

Assume that the thresholding as in (6.49a) and (6.49b) is synchronous, and the vector $\mathbf{a}'$ now feeds the layer B of neurons. It is now processed in layer B through similar matrix multiplication and bipolar thresholding but the processing now uses the transposed matrix $\mathbf{W}^t$ of the layer B:

$$\mathbf{b}' = \Gamma[\mathbf{W}^t \mathbf{a}'] \tag{6.49c}$$

or for the j'th output we have

$$b_j' = \operatorname{sgn}\left(\sum_{i=1}^{n} w_{ij} a_i'\right), \quad \text{for } j = 1, 2, \ldots, m \tag{6.49d}$$

From now on the sequence of retrieval repeats as in (6.49a) or (6.49b) to compute $\mathbf{a}''$, then as in (6.49c) or (6.49d) to compute $\mathbf{b}''$, etc. The process continues until further updates of $\mathbf{a}$ and $\mathbf{b}$ stop. It can be seen that in terms of a recursive update mechanism, the retrieval consists of the following steps:

First Forward Pass: $\qquad\qquad \mathbf{a}^1 = \Gamma[\mathbf{Wb}^0]$

First Backward Pass: $\qquad\quad\; \mathbf{b}^2 = \Gamma[\mathbf{W}^t \mathbf{a}^1]$

Second Forward Pass: $\qquad\;\; \mathbf{a}^3 = \Gamma[\mathbf{Wb}^2]$ $\qquad\qquad\qquad$ (6.50)

$$\vdots$$

k/2'th Backward Pass: $\qquad\; \mathbf{b}^k = \Gamma[\mathbf{W}^t \mathbf{a}^{k-1}]$

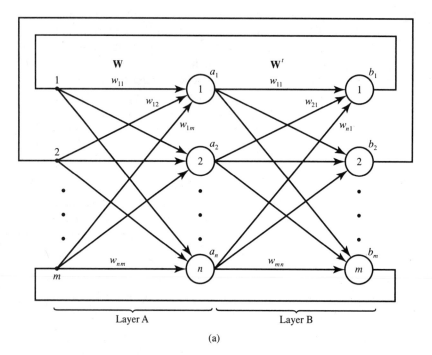

(a)

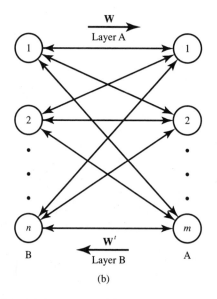

(b)

Figure 6.17 Bidirectional associative memory: (a) general diagram and (b) simplified diagram.

Ideally, this back-and-forth flow of updated data quickly equilibrates usually in one of the fixed pairs $(\mathbf{a}^{(i)}, \mathbf{b}^{(i)})$ from (6.48). Let us consider in more detail the design of the memory that would achieve this aim.

Figure 6.17(b) shows the simplified diagram of the bidirectional associative memory often encountered in the literature. Layers A and B operate in an alternate fashion—first transferring the neurons' output signals toward the right by using matrix $\mathbf{W}$, and then toward the left by using matrix $\mathbf{W}^t$, respectively.

The bidirectional associative memory maps bipolar binary vectors $\mathbf{a} = [a_1 \, a_2 \ldots a_n]^t$, $a_i = \pm 1$, $i = 1, 2, \ldots, n$, into vectors $\mathbf{b} = [b_1 \, b_2 \ldots b_m]^t$, $b_i = \pm 1$, $i = 1, 2, \ldots, m$, or vice versa. The mapping by the memory can also be performed for unipolar binary vectors. The input-output transformation is highly nonlinear due to the threshold-based state transitions.

For proper memory operation, the assumption needs to be made that no state changes are occurring in neurons of layers A and B at the same time. The data between layers must flow in a circular fashion: $A \rightarrow B \rightarrow A$, etc. The convergence of memory is proved by showing that either synchronous or asynchronous state changes of a layer decrease the energy. The energy value is reduced during a single update, however, only under the update rule (5.7). Because the energy of the memory is bounded from below, it will gravitate to fixed points. Since the stability of this type of memory is not affected by an asynchronous versus synchronous state update, it seems wise to assume synchronous operation. This will result in larger energy changes and, thus, will produce much faster convergence than asynchronous updates which are serial by nature and thus slow.

Figure 6.18 shows the diagram of discrete-time bidirectional associative memory. It reveals more functional details of the memory such as summing nodes, TLUs, unit delay elements, and it also introduces explicitly the index of recursion k. The figure also reveals a close relationship between the memory shown and the single-layer autoassociative memory discussed in Section 6.4. If the weight matrix is square and symmetric so that $\mathbf{W} = \mathbf{W}^t$, then both memories become identical and autoassociative.

Association Encoding and Decoding

The coding of information (6.48) into the bedirectional associative memory is done using the customary outer product rule, or by adding p cross-correlation matrices. The formula for the weight matrix is

$$\mathbf{W} = \sum_{i=1}^{p} \mathbf{a}^{(i)} \mathbf{b}^{(i)t} \tag{6.51a}$$

where $\mathbf{a}^{(i)}$ and $\mathbf{b}^{(i)}$ are bipolar binary vectors, which are members of the i'th pair. As shown before in (6.8), (6.51a) is equivalent to the Hebbian learning rule

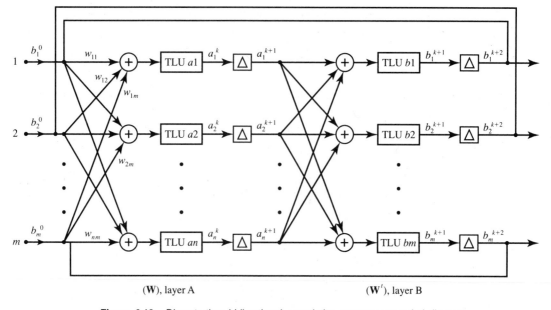

Figure 6.18 Discrete-time bidirectional associative memory expanded diagram.

yielding the following weight values:

$$w_{ij} = \sum_{m=1}^{p} a_i^{(m)} b_j^{(m)} \tag{6.51b}$$

Suppose one of the stored patterns, $\mathbf{a}^{(m')}$, is presented to the memory. The retrieval proceeds as follows from (6.49a)

$$\mathbf{b} = \Gamma \left[\sum_{m=1}^{p} \left(\mathbf{b}^{(m)} \mathbf{a}^{(m)t} \right) \mathbf{a}^{(m')} \right] \tag{6.52a}$$

which further reduces to

$$\mathbf{b} = \Gamma \left[n\mathbf{b}^{(m')} + \sum_{m \neq m'}^{p} \mathbf{b}^{(m)} \mathbf{a}^{(m)t} \mathbf{a}^{(m')} \right] \tag{6.52b}$$

The $\mathbf{net}_b$ vector inside brackets in Equation (6.52b) contains a signal term $n\mathbf{b}^{(m')}$ additive with the noise term $\boldsymbol{\eta}$ of value

$$\boldsymbol{\eta} = \sum_{m \neq m'}^{p} \mathbf{b}^{(m)} \left(\mathbf{a}^{(m)t} \mathbf{a}^{(m')} \right) \tag{6.53}$$

Assuming temporarily the orthogonality of stored patterns $\mathbf{a}^{(m)}$, for $m = 1$, $2, \ldots, p$, the noise term $\boldsymbol{\eta}$ reduces to zero. Therefore, immediate stabilization and exact association $\mathbf{b} = \mathbf{b}^{(m')}$ occurs within only a single pass through layer B. If the input vector is a distorted version of pattern $\mathbf{a}^{(m')}$, the stabilization at $\mathbf{b}^{(m')}$

is not imminent, however, and depends on many factors such as the HD between the key vector and prototype vectors, as well as on the orthogonality or HD between vectors $\mathbf{b}^{(i)}$, for $i = 1, 2, \ldots, p$.

To gain better insight into the memory performance, let us look at the noise term $\boldsymbol{\eta}$ as in (6.53) as a function of HD between the stored prototypes $\mathbf{a}^{(m)}$, for $m = 1, 2, \ldots, p$. Note that two vectors containing ± 1 elements are orthogonal if and only if they differ in exactly $n/2$ bits. Therefore, HD $\left(\mathbf{a}^{(m)}, \mathbf{a}^{(m')}\right) = n/2$, for $m = 1, 2, \ldots, p$, $m \neq m'$, then $\boldsymbol{\eta} = 0$ and perfect retrieval in a single pass is guaranteed.

If $\mathbf{a}^{(m)}$, for $m = 1, 2, \ldots, p$, and the input vector $\mathbf{a}^{(m')}$ are somewhat similar so that HD $\left(\mathbf{a}^{(m)}, \mathbf{a}^{(m')}\right) < n/2$, for $m = 1, 2, \ldots, p$, $m \neq m'$, the scalar products in parentheses in Equation (6.53) tend to be positive, and a positive contribution to the entries of the noise vector $\boldsymbol{\eta}$ is likely to occur. For this to hold, we need to assume the statistical independence of vectors $\mathbf{b}^{(m)}$, for $m = 1, 2, \ldots, p$. Pattern $\mathbf{b}^{(m')}$ thus tends to be positively amplified in proportion to the similarity between prototype patterns $\mathbf{a}^{(m)}$ and $\mathbf{a}^{(m')}$. If the patterns are dissimilar rather than similar and the HD value is above $n/2$, then the negative contributions in parentheses in Equation (6.53) are negatively amplifying the pattern $\mathbf{b}^{(m')}$. Thus, a complement $-\mathbf{b}^{(m')}$ may result under the conditions described.

Stability Considerations

Let us look at the stability of updates within the bidirectional associative memory. As the updates in (6.50) continue and the memory comes to its equilibrium at the k'th step, we have $\mathbf{a}^k \to \mathbf{b}^{k+1} \to \mathbf{a}^{k+2}$, and $\mathbf{a}^{k+2} = \mathbf{a}^k$. In such a case, the memory is said to be *bidirectionally stable*. This corresponds to the energy function reaching one of its minima after which any further decrease of its value is impossible. Let us propose the energy function for minimization by this system in transition as

$$E(\mathbf{a}, \mathbf{b}) \stackrel{\Delta}{=} -\frac{1}{2}\mathbf{a}^t\mathbf{W}\mathbf{b} - \frac{1}{2}\mathbf{b}^t\mathbf{W}^t\mathbf{a} \tag{6.54a}$$

The reader may easily verify that this expression reduces to

$$E(\mathbf{a}, \mathbf{b}) = -\mathbf{a}^t\mathbf{W}\mathbf{b} \tag{6.54b}$$

Let us evaluate the energy changes during a single pattern recall. The summary of thresholding bit updates for the outputs of layer A can be obtained from (6.49b) as

$$\Delta a_i \Big|_{i=1,2,\ldots,n} = \begin{cases} 2 & > 0 \\ 0 \text{ for } \sum\limits_{j=1}^{m} w_{ij}b_j & = 0 \\ -2 & < 0 \end{cases} \tag{6.55a}$$

and for the outputs of layer B they result from (6.49d) as

$$\Delta b_i \Big|_{j=1,2,\dots,m} = \begin{cases} 2 & > 0 \\ 0 \text{ for } \sum_{i=1}^{n} w_{ij}a_i & = 0 \\ -2 & < 0 \end{cases} \qquad (6.55b)$$

The gradients of energy (6.54b) with respect to $\mathbf{a}$ and $\mathbf{b}$ can be computed, respectively, as

$$\nabla_a E(\mathbf{a}, \mathbf{b}) = -\mathbf{W}\mathbf{b} \qquad (6.56a)$$

$$\nabla_b E(\mathbf{a}, \mathbf{b}) = -\mathbf{W}^t \mathbf{a} \qquad (6.56b)$$

The bitwise update expressions (6.55) translate into the following energy changes due to the single bit increments Δa_i and Δb_j:

$$\Delta E_{ai}(\mathbf{a}, \mathbf{b}) = -\left(\sum_{j=1}^{m} w_{ij}b_j \right) \Delta a_i, \quad \text{for } i = 1, 2, \dots, n \qquad (6.57a)$$

$$\Delta E_{bj}(\mathbf{a}, \mathbf{b}) = -\left(\sum_{i=1}^{n} w_{ij}a_i \right) \Delta b_j, \quad \text{for } j = 1, 2, \dots, m \qquad (6.57b)$$

Inspecting the right sides of Equations (6.57) and comparing them with the ordinary update rules as in (6.55) lead to the conclusion that $\Delta E \leq 0$. As with recurrent autoassociative memory, the energy changes are nonpositive. Since E is a bounded function from below according to the following inequality:

$$E(\mathbf{a}, \mathbf{b}) \geq - \sum_{i=1}^{n} \sum_{j=1}^{m} |w_{ij}| \qquad (6.58)$$

then the memory converges to a stable point. The point is a local minimum of the energy function, and the memory is said to be bidirectionally stable. Moreover, no restrictions exist regarding the choice of matrix $\mathbf{W}$, so any arbitrary real $n \times m$ matrix will result in bidirectionally stable memory. Let us also note that this discussion did not assume the asynchronous update for energy function minimization. In fact, the energy is minimized for either asynchronous or synchronous updates.

Memory Example and Performance Evaluation

EXAMPLE 6.3 ■■■■■■■■■■■■■■■■■

In this example we demonstrate coding and retrieval of pairs of patterns. The memory to be designed needs to store four pairs of associations. Four 16-pixel bit maps of letter characters need to be associated to 7-bit binary vectors as shown in Figure 6.19(a). The respective training pairs of vectors $(\mathbf{a}^{(i)}, \mathbf{b}^{(i)})$, $i = 1, 2, 3, 4$ are:

$$\mathbf{a}^{(1)} = [\,1\ 1\ 1\ -1\ 1\ -1\ -1\ -1\ 1\ -1\ -1\ -1\ 1\ 1\ 1\ -1\,]^t,$$
$$\mathbf{b}^{(1)} = [\,1\ -1\ -1\ -1\ -1\ 1\ 1\,]^t$$
$$\mathbf{a}^{(2)} = [\,1\ -1\ -1\ 1\ 1\ 1\ -1\ 1\ 1\ -1\ 1\ 1\ 1\ -1\ -1\ 1\ 1\,]^t,$$
$$\mathbf{b}^{(2)} = [\,1\ -1\ -1\ 1\ 1\ 1\ -1\,]^t$$
$$\mathbf{a}^{(3)} = [\,1\ 1\ 1\ 1\ -1\ -1\ 1\ -1\ -1\ 1\ -1\ -1\ 1\ 1\ 1\ 1\,]^t, \qquad (6.59)$$
$$\mathbf{b}^{(3)} = [\,1\ -1\ 1\ 1\ -1\ 1\ -1\,]^t$$
$$\mathbf{a}^{(4)} = [\,-1\ -1\ -1\ -1\ -1\ -1\ -1\ 1\ 1\ 1\ 1\ 1\ -1\ -1\ -1\ 1\ 1\,]^t,$$
$$\mathbf{b}^{(4)} = [\,-1\ 1\ 1\ -1\ 1\ -1\ 1\,]^t$$

The weight matrix can be obtained from (6.51) as

$$\mathbf{W} = \begin{bmatrix}
4. & -4. & -2. & 2. & -2. & 4. & -2. \\
2. & -2. & 0. & 0. & -4. & 2. & 0. \\
2. & -2. & 0. & 0. & -4. & 2. & 0. \\
2. & -2. & 0. & 4. & 0. & 2. & -4. \\
2. & -2. & -4. & 0. & 0. & 2. & 0. \\
0. & 0. & -2. & 2. & 2. & 0. & -2. \\
0. & 0. & 2. & 2. & -2. & 0. & -2. \\
-2. & 2. & 0. & 0. & 4. & -2. & 0. \\
0. & 0. & -2. & -2. & 2. & 0. & 2. \\
-2. & 2. & 4. & 0. & 0. & -2. & 0. \\
-2. & 2. & 0. & 0. & 4. & -2. & 0. \\
-2. & 2. & 0. & 0. & 4. & -2. & 0. \\
4. & -4. & -2. & 2. & -2. & 4. & -2. \\
2. & -2. & 0. & 0. & -4. & 2. & 0. \\
2. & -2. & 0. & 0. & -4. & 2. & 0. \\
0. & 0. & 2. & 2. & 2. & 0. & -2.
\end{bmatrix} \qquad (6.60)$$

Assume now that the key vector $\mathbf{a}^1$ at the memory input is a distorted prototype of $\mathbf{a}^{(2)}$ as shown in Figure 6.19(b) so that HD $(\mathbf{a}^{(1)}, \mathbf{a}^1) = 4$.

$$\mathbf{a}^1 = [\,-1\ -1\ -1\ 1\ 1\ -1\ 1\ -1\ 1\ 1\ -1\ 1\ 1\ -1\ -1\ 1\ 1\,]^t$$

The memory response, $\mathbf{b}_2$, is computed from (6.50):

$$\mathbf{b}^2 = \Gamma\,[\,-16\quad 16\quad 0\quad 0\quad 32\quad -16\quad 0\,]^t$$

and the thresholding by the operator Γ yields

$$\mathbf{b}^2 = [\,-1\quad 1\quad 0\quad 0\quad 1\quad -1\quad 0\,]^t$$

Continuing the retrieval process until the bidirectional stability is reached

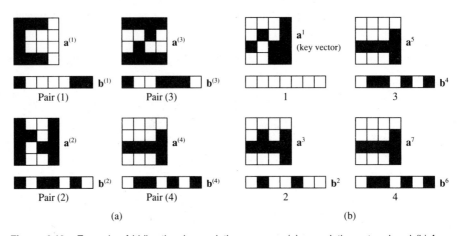

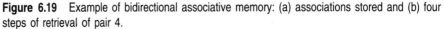

Figure 6.19 Example of bidirectional associative memory: (a) associations stored and (b) four steps of retrieval of pair 4.

within this memory, the updates are computed of following value:

$$\mathbf{a}^3 = \Gamma \left[-14 \ -10 \ -10 \ -6 \ -6 \ 2 \ -2 \ 10 \ 2 \ 6 \ 10 \ 10 \ -14 \ -10 \ -10 \ 2 \right]^t$$

$$\mathbf{a}^3 = \left[-1 \ -1 \ -1 \ -1 \ -1 \ 1 \ -1 \ 1 \ 1 \ 1 \ 1 \ 1 \ -1 \ -1 \ 1 \right]^t$$

$$\mathbf{b}^4 = \Gamma \left[-28 \ \ 28 \ \ 8 \ \ -8 \ \ 40 \ \ -28 \ \ 8 \right]^t$$

$$\mathbf{b}^4 = \left[-1 \ \ 1 \ \ 1 \ \ -1 \ \ 1 \ \ -1 \ \ 1 \right]^t$$

$$\mathbf{a}^5 = \Gamma \left[-20 \ \ -10 \ \ -10 \ \ -14 \ \ -10 \ \ -4 \ \ -4 \right.$$
$$\left. 10 \ \ 4 \ \ 10 \ \ 10 \ \ 10 \ \ -20 \ \ -10 \ \ -10 \ \ 0 \right]^t$$

$$\mathbf{a}^5 = \left[-1 \ -1 \ -1 \ -1 \ -1 \ -1 \ -1 \ 1 \ 1 \ 1 \ 1 \ 1 \ -1 \ -1 \ -1 \ 1 \right]^t$$

$$\mathbf{b}^6 = \mathbf{b}^4$$

$$\mathbf{a}^7 = \mathbf{a}^5$$

The corresponding sequence of patterns is shown in Figure 6.19(b). The figure shows four first steps of retrieval. Interestingly, $\mathbf{a}^1$ has converged to the prototype pair $\left(\mathbf{a}^{(4)}, \mathbf{b}^{(4)} \right)$. Let us note, however, that the HD between $\mathbf{a}^1$ and $\mathbf{a}^{(4)}$ is

$$\text{HD} \left(\mathbf{a}^1, \mathbf{a}^{(4)} \right) = 4$$

We can also notice that other HD values of interest for our case are

$$\text{HD} \left(\mathbf{a}^1, \mathbf{a}^{(1)} \right) = 12$$

$$\text{HD} \left(\mathbf{a}^1, \mathbf{a}^{(2)} \right) = 4$$

$$\text{HD} \left(\mathbf{a}^1, \mathbf{a}^{(3)} \right) = 10$$

We, therefore, can conclude that the memory has converged to one of the two closest prototypes in the Hamming distance sense. ■

Kosko (1988) has shown that the upper limit on the number p of pattern pairs which can be stored and successfully retrieved is $\min(n, m)$. The substantiation for this estimate is rather heuristic. It can be statistically expected that if $p > n$, the noise term $\boldsymbol{\eta}$ of Equation (6.53) exceeds the signal term. Similarly, for processing of a signal and noise mixture by layer B, it is expected that the dominance of the signal term over the noise component is maintained for $p < m$. Hence, a rough and heuristic estimate on memory storage capacity is

$$p \leq \min(m, n) \tag{6.61a}$$

A more conservative heuristic capacity measure (6.61b) is also used in the literature

$$p = \sqrt{\min(m, n)} \tag{6.61b}$$

Like the autoassociative recurrent memory, the performance of bidirectional associative memory depends on the properties of the stored patterns, and its performance varies vastly for different prototype pairs. Figure 6.20 shows the simulated convergence versus corruption curves for a bidirectional associative memory with $n = 25$ and $m = 9$. Randomly generated training patterns $a^{(i)}$ had an average HD $= 11$ between them. The figure shows four curves for different storage levels. The results of the experiment indicate that the memory performance obviously decreases with the increase of p, and also with the increase in search argument distortion. But as can be seen from the figure for $p = 8$, the memory filled near its capacity routinely fails to identify or recall its true memories stored, even with the association argument undistorted.

In addition, the curves show that a memory of this size and under the conditions described is susceptible to noise in general. Indeed, excellent recall is shown for corruption levels limited to below 10%. This is relatively lower noise immunity than for the autoassociative recurrent memory with good recall properties as shown in Figures 6.12(a) and (b) for levels of distortion up to 25%. Although it is difficult to make comparisons between the two different memory architectures and different network sizes, the input vector noise sensitivity of the bidirectional associative memory makes it rather applicable for low-noise situations.

Improved Coding of Memories

The generic bidirectional associative memory described in this section suffers from certain limitations of error-free retrieval of stored pairs. Let us see whether the memory performance can be improved by possibly reshaping its energy function. During the decoding, the energy (6.54b) remains stable or

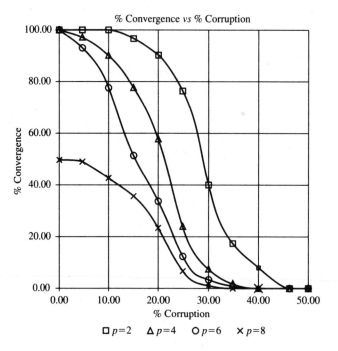

□ p=2   △ p=4   ○ p=6   ✕ p=8

Convergence vs. Corruption

Network Type: Bidirectional Associative Memory (BAM)

Network Parameters: Dimension—$n \times m$ (25×9)
Threshold—Hard Limited
@ Hamming Distance HD = 45

Curve Parameters: Pattern Pairs p

Features: 20 samples per point.

Comments: The upper limit on the number of patterns that can be stored in the memory is min(n, m). This network is fairly insensitive to noise for corruption levels kept below 10% at half of its upper limit. Serious deterioration is observed at near full capacity where the networks fail to converge even to "true" memories.

Figure 6.20 Convergence versus corruption in a BAM for a different number of stored association pairs p.

decreases until it reaches the minimum at $(\mathbf{a}^f, \mathbf{b}^f)$, which is of the following value:

$$E(\mathbf{a}, \mathbf{b}) = -\mathbf{a}^{ft} \mathbf{W} \mathbf{b}^f \tag{6.62}$$

The energy E has a local minimum at $(\mathbf{a}^f, \mathbf{b}^f)$ when none of the vectors at

HD = 1 from $\mathbf{a}^f$ or $\mathbf{b}^f$ will yield a lower energy value than (6.62). Consequently, when the energy (6.54b) for one of the trained p pairs (6.48) does not constitute a local minimum, then the association between a pair of stored vectors cannot be recalled even if the search argument is a member of a stored pair. This would mean in practice that there are unrecoverable stored associations [see Problem P6.20(a) for case studies]. The reason for this deficiency of bidirectional memory is that the coding formula (6.51) does not ensure that stored pairs correspond to local energy minima.

Indeed, inspection of the gradient of the energy function (6.56a) and (6.56b) reveals that at the m'th association pair its gradient $\nabla_a E$ is equal:

$$\nabla_a E \left(\mathbf{a}^{(m)}, \mathbf{b}^{(m)} \right) = - \sum_{i=1}^{p} \mathbf{a}^{(i)} \mathbf{b}^{(i)t} \mathbf{b}^{(m)} \tag{6.63a}$$

Note that the gradient (6.63a) is computed at the m'th association pair, specifically at $\mathbf{b}^{(m)}$. This implies that if the k'th bit $a_k^{(m)}$ of the vector $\mathbf{a}^{(m)}$ changes by $\Delta a_k^{(m)}$, the corresponding energy change ΔE_{ak} is equal to

$$\Delta E_{ak} \left(\mathbf{a}^{(m)}, \mathbf{b}^{(m)} \right) = - \left(\sum_{i=1}^{p} \mathbf{a}^{(i)} \mathbf{b}^{(i)t} \mathbf{b}^{(m)} \right) \Delta a_k^{(m)} \tag{6.63b}$$

Assumption of a local minimum $E \left(\mathbf{a}^{(m)}, \mathbf{b}^{(m)} \right)$ now requires the proof that the expression in parentheses of (6.63b) and $\Delta a_k^{(m)}$ be of different signs so that $\Delta E_{ak} \left(\mathbf{a}^{(m)}, \mathbf{b}^{(m)} \right)$ is positive. This condition, however, is not guaranteed, since the update value is $\Delta a_k^{(m)} = \pm 2$, and the sign of the expression in parenthesis does not alternate with the k'th bit changing sign. Therefore, the retrieval of the association $\mathbf{a}^{(m)}$, $\mathbf{b}^{(m)}$ is not guaranteed for the simple outer product encoding method as in (6.51).

To ensure that the local minima of energy (6.62) are $E(\mathbf{a}^{(m)}, \mathbf{b}^{(m)})$, the *multiple encoding strategy* has been proposed (Wang 1990). For multiple training of order q for the $\left(\mathbf{a}^{(m)}, \mathbf{b}^{(m)} \right)$ pair, one augments the matrix $\mathbf{W}$ from (6.51) by an additional term

$$\Delta \mathbf{W} = (q - 1) \mathbf{a}^{(m)} \mathbf{b}^{(m)t} \tag{6.64}$$

This indicates that the pair is encoded q times rather than one time; thus its energy minimum is enhanced. The coding of the m'th pair among the p existing pairs is thus enhanced through amplification of local minima $E \left(\mathbf{a}^{(m)}, \mathbf{b}^{(m)} \right)$.

Using multiple coding (6.64) to produce a distinct energy minimum at $\left(\mathbf{a}^{(m)}, \mathbf{b}^{(m)} \right)$ however, may produce another pair, or pairs, of vectors in the training set that becomes nonrecoverable. This situation can be remedied by further multiple training. The multiple training method guarantees that eventually all training pairs will be recalled. Indeed, the weight matrix obtained using q-tuple training of the m'th pair can be written as

$$\mathbf{W} = q \mathbf{a}^{(m)} \mathbf{b}^{(m)t} + \sum_{\substack{i \neq m}}^{p} \mathbf{a}^{(i)} \mathbf{b}^{(i)t} \tag{6.65a}$$

For large q, the first term in (6.65a) dominates $\mathbf{W}$ so

$$\mathbf{W} \cong q\mathbf{a}^{(m)}\mathbf{b}^{(m)t} \tag{6.65b}$$

Then the recall according to (6.50) proceeds for input $\mathbf{b}^{(m)}$ as

$$\mathbf{a}^1 \cong q\Gamma\left[\mathbf{a}^{(m)}(\mathbf{b}^{(m)t}\mathbf{b}^{(m)})\right] \tag{6.66}$$

Since $\mathbf{b}^{(m)t}\mathbf{b}^{(m)} = m > 0$, $\mathbf{a}^{(m)}$ is perfectly recalled in this pass. A similar single-step recall would be guaranteed if $\mathbf{a}^{(m)}$ were used as the search argument in the q-tuple training case of the m'th pair.

The multiple training method has been tested for randomly generated sizes of memory $4 \le n$, and $m \le 256$ with a random p value such that $2 \le p \le 16$, and with limiting of the memory load to $p \le \sqrt{\min(n,m)}$ (Wang 1990). The simulation of memory performance resulted in 98.5% of correct recalls for the multiple training method versus 90% of correct recalls for the original bipolar associative memory recording algorithm. The multiple training method has also increased network capacity by 20 to 40%. Capacity notion is understood here as an estimate of the number of recallable training pairs p with a recall success of 90%. The number of training pairs for capacity simulation was selected at four to eight times larger than p to seek the canceling effects of the noise term.

The probability of correct convergence versus the number of stored pairs is shown in Figure 6.21(a) for $n = m = 100$. Curves 1 and 2 correspond to unipolar binary vectors used for training the bidirectional associative memory in the single training and multiple training modes, respectively. Curves 3 and 4 are for the respective training modes using bipolar binary vectors for recording. Although the multiplicity q of the training has not been explicitly stated in the literature, it is known that it has been kept above the value $p(2/n)$.

To guarantee the recall of all training pairs, a method of *dummy augmentation* of training pairs may be used (Wang 1990). The idea of dummy augmentation is to deepen the energy minima at $(\mathbf{a}^{(i)}, \mathbf{b}^{(i)})$, for $i = 1, 2, \ldots, p$, without adding any risk of false decoding, which normally increases as p increases. This can be accomplished by generating a noise-free training set obtained through the generation of augmented vectors containing dummy vector elements. The noise-free training set concept can be understood based on the noise expression (6.53) in terms of the Hamming distance between vectors. The pairs $(\mathbf{a}^{(i)}, \mathbf{a}^{(j)})$ or $(\mathbf{b}^{(i)}, \mathbf{b}^{(j)})$ are called noise-free if for $i = 1, 2, \ldots, p, j = 1, 2, \ldots, p$

$$\begin{aligned} \text{HD}\left(\mathbf{a}^{(i)}, \mathbf{a}^{(j)}\right) &= \frac{n}{2} \\ \text{HD}\left(\mathbf{b}^{(i)}, \mathbf{b}^{(j)}\right) &= \frac{m}{2} \end{aligned} \tag{6.67}$$

For a noise-free training set used to create the memory weight matrix $\mathbf{W}$, the recall of data would be immediate and error free. The training involving the dummy augmentation strategy, however, requires augmenting both vectors $\mathbf{a}^{(i)}$

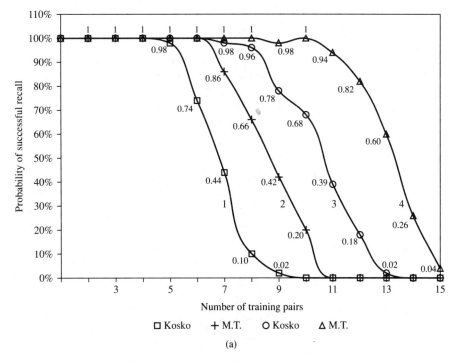

Figure 6.21a Illustration of improved coding strategies for bipolar heteroassociative memory: (a) convergence versus number of encoded pairs. (Adapted from Wang (1990). © IEEE; with permission.)

and $\mathbf{b}^{(i)}$, for $i = 1, 2, \ldots, p$, with additional data (Wang 1990). An example of a noise-free training set is shown in Figure 6.21(b). Notice the dummy augmentation data present in the two bottom rows of the augmented training patterns $\mathbf{a}^{(i)}$, $i = 1, 2, 3$. The bottom rows data do not belong to the original pattern. Their addition to the original training vectors makes the augmented vectors orthogonal according to (6.67). Thus, the dummy augmentation training method corresponds to artificial orthogonalization of stored vectors that were originally nonorthogonal.

The concepts of multiple training and dummy augmentation of training pairs offer significant advantages over the original recording algorithm for discrete-time bidirectional associative memory. They improve the percentage of correct recalls for cases in which the search arguments are both the members of the training set or their distorted counterparts. Dummy augmentation can be guaranteed to produce recall of all training pairs if attaching the dummy data to the training pairs is possible and allowable. One disadvantage though is that the memory size needs to be increased to handle the storage and retrieval of augmented vectors.

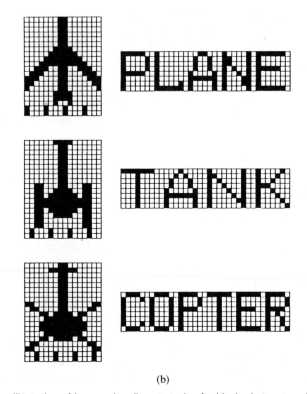

(b)

Figure 6.21b Illustration of improved coding strategies for bipolar heteroassociative memory *(continued):* (b) training pairs for dummy augmentation method. (Adapted from Wang (1990). © IEEE; with permission.)

Multidirectional Associative Memory

Bidirectional associative memory is a two-layer nonlinear recurrent network that accomplishes a two-way associative search for stored stimulus-response associations $(\mathbf{a}^{(i)}, \mathbf{b}^{(i)})$, for $i = 1, 2, \ldots, p$. The bidirectional model can be generalized to enable multiple associations $(\mathbf{a}^{(i)}, \mathbf{b}^{(i)}, \mathbf{c}^{(i)}, \ldots)$, $i = 1, 2, \ldots, p$. The *multiple association memory* is called *multidirectional* (Hagiwara 1990) and is shown schematically in Figure 6.22(a) for the five-layer case. Layers are interconnected with each other by weights that pass information between them. When one or more layers are activated, the network quickly evolves to a stable state of multipattern reverberation. The reverberation which ends in a stable state corresponds to a local energy minimum.

The concept of the multidirectional associative memory will be illustrated with the three-layer network example shown in Figure 6.22(b). Let $(\mathbf{a}^{(i)}, \mathbf{b}^{(i)}, \mathbf{c}^{(i)})$,

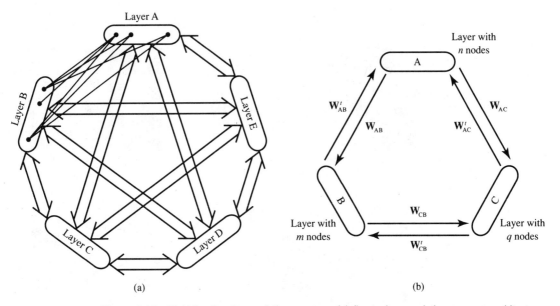

Figure 6.22 Multidirectional associative memory: (a) five-tuple association memory architecture and (b) information flow for triple association memory.

for $i = 1, 2, \ldots, p$, be the bipolar vectors of associations to be stored. Generalization of formula (6.51a) yields the following weight matrices:

$$\mathbf{W}_{AB} = \sum_{i=1}^{p} \mathbf{a}^{(i)}\mathbf{b}^{(i)t}$$

$$\mathbf{W}_{CB} = \sum_{i=1}^{p} \mathbf{c}^{(i)}\mathbf{b}^{(i)t} \qquad (6.68)$$

$$\mathbf{W}_{AC} = \sum_{i=1}^{p} \mathbf{a}^{(i)}\mathbf{c}^{(i)t}$$

where the first and second subscript of matrices denote the destination and source layer, respectively. With the associations encoded as in (6.68) in directions $B \rightarrow A$, $B \rightarrow C$, $C \rightarrow A$, and reverse direction associations obtained through the respective weight matrix transposition, the recall proceeds as follows: Each neuron independently and synchronously updates its output based on its total input sum from all other layers:

$$\mathbf{a}' = \Gamma \left[\mathbf{W}_{AB}\mathbf{b} + \mathbf{W}_{AC}\mathbf{c} \right]$$
$$\mathbf{b}' = \Gamma \left[\mathbf{W}_{CB}^{t}\mathbf{c} + \mathbf{W}_{AB}^{t}\mathbf{a} \right] \qquad (6.69)$$
$$\mathbf{c}' = \Gamma \left[\mathbf{W}_{CB}\mathbf{b} + \mathbf{W}_{AC}^{t}\mathbf{c} \right]$$

The neurons' states change synchronously according to (6.69) until a multidirectionally stable state is reached.

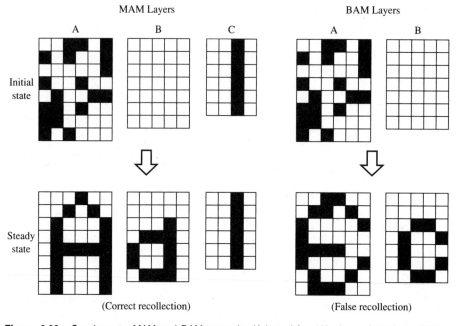

Figure 6.23 Synchronous MAM and BAM example. (Adapted from Hagiwara (1990). © IEEE; with permission.)

Figure 6.23 displays snapshots of the synchronous convergence of three- and two-layer memories. The bit map of the originally stored letter *A* has been corrupted with a probability of 44% to check the recovery. With the initial input as shown, the two-layer memory does not converge correctly. The three-directional memory using additional input to layer *C* recalls the character perfectly as a result of a multiple association effect. This happens as a result of the joint interaction of layers *A* and *B* onto layer *C*. Therefore, additional associations enable better noise suppression. In the context of this conclusion, note also that the bidirectional associative memory is a special, two-dimensional case of the multidirectional network.

6.6

ASSOCIATIVE MEMORY OF SPATIO-TEMPORAL PATTERNS

The bidirectional associative memory concept can be used not only for storing *p* spatial patterns in the form of equilibria encoded in the weight matrix;

it can also be used for storing sequences of patterns in the form of dynamic state transitions. Such patterns are called *temporal* and they can be represented as an ordered set of vectors or functions. We assume all temporal patterns are bipolar binary vectors given by the ordered set, or sequence, S containing p vectors:

$$S \triangleq \left\{ \mathbf{s}^{(1)}, \mathbf{s}^{(2)}, \dots, \mathbf{s}^{(p)} \right\} \tag{6.70}$$

where column vectors $\mathbf{s}^{(i)}$, for $i = 1, 2, \dots, p$, are n-dimensional. The neural network is capable of memorizing the sequence S in its dynamic state transitions such that the recalled sequence is

$$\mathbf{s}^{(i+1)} = \Gamma[\mathbf{W}\mathbf{s}^{(i)}] \tag{6.71}$$

where Γ is the nonlinear operator as in (6.5) and the superscript summation is computed modulo $p + 1$. Starting at the initial state of $\mathbf{x}(0)$ in the neighborhood of $\mathbf{s}^{(i)}$, the sequence S is recalled as a cycle of state transitions. This model was proposed in Amari (1972) and its behavior was mathematically analyzed. The memory model discussed in this section can be briefly called *temporal associative memory*.

To encode a sequence such that $\mathbf{s}^{(1)}$ is associated with $\mathbf{s}^{(2)}$, $\mathbf{s}^{(2)}$ with $\mathbf{s}^{(3)}$, ..., and $\mathbf{s}^{(p)}$ with $\mathbf{s}^{(1)}$, encoding can use the cross-correlation matrices $\mathbf{s}^{(i+1)}\mathbf{s}^{(i)t}$. Since the pair of vectors $\mathbf{s}^{(i)}$ and $\mathbf{s}^{(i+1)}$ can be treated as heteroassociative, the bidirectional associative memory can be employed to perform the desired association. The sequence encoding algorithm for temporal associative memory can thus be formulated as a sum of p outer products as follows

$$\mathbf{W} = \sum_{i=1}^{p-1} \mathbf{s}^{(i+1)}\mathbf{s}^{(i)t} + \mathbf{s}^{(1)}\mathbf{s}^{(p)t}, \quad \text{or} \tag{6.72a}$$

$$\mathbf{W} = \sum_{i=1}^{p} \mathbf{s}^{(i+1)}\mathbf{s}^{(i)t} \tag{6.72b}$$

where the superscript summation in (6.72b) is modulo $p + 1$. Note that if the unipolar vectors $\mathbf{s}^{(i)}$ are to be encoded, they must first be converted to bipolar binary vectors to create correlation matrices as in (6.72), as has been the case for regular bidirectional memories encoding.

A diagram of the temporal associative memory is shown in Figure 6.24(a). The network is a two-layer bidirectional associative memory modified in such a way that both layers A and B are now described by identical weight matrices $\mathbf{W}$. We thus have recall formulas

$$\mathbf{a} = \Gamma[\mathbf{W}\mathbf{b}] \tag{6.73a}$$

$$\mathbf{b} = \Gamma[\mathbf{W}\mathbf{a}] \tag{6.73b}$$

where it is understood that layers A and B update nonsimultaneously and in an alternate circular fashion. To check the proper recall of the stored sequence,

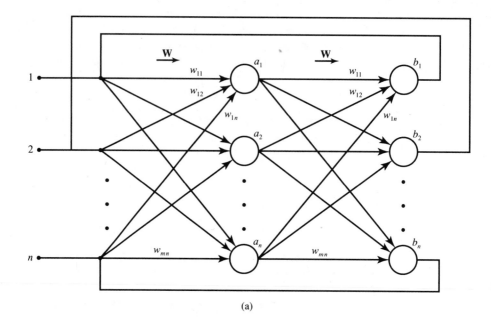

(a)

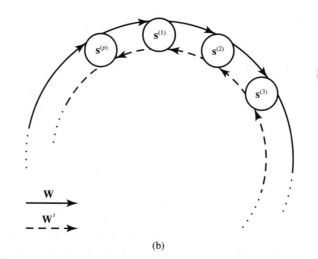

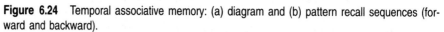

(b)

Figure 6.24 Temporal associative memory: (a) diagram and (b) pattern recall sequences (forward and backward).

vector $\mathbf{s}^{(k)}$, $k = 1, 2, \ldots, p$, is applied to the input of the layer A as in (6.73a). We thus have

$$\mathbf{a} = \Gamma \left[\left(\mathbf{s}^{(2)}\mathbf{s}^{(1)t} + \ldots + \mathbf{s}^{(k+1)}\mathbf{s}^{(k)t} + \ldots + \mathbf{s}^{(1)}\mathbf{s}^{(p)t} \right) \mathbf{s}^{(k)} \right] \tag{6.74}$$

The vector $\mathbf{net}_a$ in brackets of Equation (6.74) contains a signal term $n\mathbf{s}^{(k+1)}$ and the remainder, which is the noise term $\boldsymbol{\eta}$

$$\boldsymbol{\eta} = \sum_{i \neq k}^{p} \mathbf{s}^{(i+1)} \left(\mathbf{s}^{(i)t} \mathbf{s}^{(k)} \right) \tag{6.75}$$

where the superscript summation is modulo $p + 1$. Assuming the orthogonality of the vectors within the sequence S, the noise term is exactly zero and the thresholding operation on vector $n\mathbf{s}^{(k+1)}$ results in $\mathbf{s}^{(k+1)}$ being the retrieved vector. Therefore, immediate stabilization and exact association of the appropriate member vector of the sequence occurs within a single pass within layer A. Similarly, vector $\mathbf{s}^{(k+1)}$ at the input to layer B will result in recall of $\mathbf{s}^{(k+2)}$. The reader may verify this using (6.73b) and (6.72). Thus, input of any member of the sequence set S, say $\mathbf{s}^{(k)}$, results in the desired circular recalls as follows: $\mathbf{s}^{(k+1)} \rightarrow \mathbf{s}^{(k+2)} \rightarrow \dots \rightarrow \mathbf{s}^{(p)} \rightarrow \mathbf{s}^{(1)} \rightarrow \dots$. This is illustrated in Figure 6.24(b), which shows the forward recall sequence.

The reader may easily notice that reverse order recall can be implemented using the transposed weight matrices in both layers A and B. Indeed, transposing (6.72b) yields

$$\mathbf{W}^t = \sum_{i=1}^{p} \mathbf{s}^{(i)} \mathbf{s}^{(i+1)t} \tag{6.76}$$

When the signal term due to the input $\mathbf{s}^{(k)}$ is $n\mathbf{s}^{(k-1)}$, the recall of $\mathbf{s}^{(k-1)}$ will follow.

Obviously, if the vectors of sequence S are not mutually orthogonal, the noise term $\boldsymbol{\eta}$ may not vanish, even after thresholding. Still, for vectors stored at a distance $HD \ll n$, the thresholding operation in layer A or B should be expected to result in recall of the correct sequence.

This type of memory will undergo the same limitations and capacity bounds as the bidirectional associative memory. The storage capacity of the temporal associative memory can be estimated using expression (6.61a). Thus, we have the maximum length sequence to be bounded according to the condition $p < n$. More generally, the memory can be used to store k sequences of length $p_1, p_2, \dots, p_k$. Together they include:

$$p = \sum_{i=1}^{k} p_i \tag{6.77}$$

patterns. In such cases, the total number of patterns as in (6.77) should be kept below the n value.

The temporal associative memory operates in a synchronous serial fashion similar to a single synchronous update step of a bidirectional associative memory. The stability of the memory can be proven by generalizing the theory of stability of the bidirectional associative memory. The temporal memory energy function is defined as

$$E = - \sum_{i=1}^{p} \mathbf{s}^{(i+1)} \mathbf{W} \mathbf{s}^{(i)} \tag{6.78}$$

Calculation of the energy increment due to changes of $\mathbf{s}^{(k)}$ produces the following equation:

$$E = -\mathbf{s}^{(k+1)}\mathbf{W}\mathbf{s}^{(k)} - \mathbf{s}^{(k)}\mathbf{W}\mathbf{s}^{(k-1)} - \sum_{\substack{i \neq k \\ i \neq k-1}}^{p} \mathbf{s}^{(i+1)}\mathbf{W}\mathbf{s}^{(i)} \qquad (6.79)$$

The gradient of energy with respect to $\mathbf{s}^k$ becomes

$$\nabla_s E = -\mathbf{W}^t \mathbf{s}^{(k+1)} - \mathbf{W}\mathbf{s}^{(k-1)} \qquad (6.80)$$

Considering bitwise updates due to increments $\Delta s_i^{(k)}$ we obtain

$$\Delta_s E_i = -\left(\sum_{j=1}^{n} w_{ji} s_j^{(k+1)} + \sum_{i=1}^{n} w_{ij} s_j^{(k-1)} \right) \Delta s_i^{(k)} \qquad (6.81)$$

Each of the two sums in parentheses in Equation (6.81) agree in sign with $\Delta s_i^{(k)}$ under the sgn (net_i) update rule. The second sum corresponds to net_i due to the input $\mathbf{s}^{(k-1)}$, which retrieves $\mathbf{s}^{(k)}$ in the forward direction. The first sum corresponds to net_i due to the input $\mathbf{s}^{(k+1)}$, which again retrieves $\mathbf{s}^{(k)}$ in the reverse direction. Thus, the energy increments are negative during the temporal sequence retrieval $\mathbf{s}^{(1)} \rightarrow \mathbf{s}^{(2)} \rightarrow \ldots \rightarrow \mathbf{s}^{(p)}$. As shown by Kosko (1988), the energy increases stepwise, however, at the transition $\mathbf{s}^{(p)} \rightarrow \mathbf{s}^{(1)}$, and then it continues to decrease within the complete sequence of $p - 1$ retrievals to follow.

EXAMPLE 6.4 ■

In this example temporal associative memory is designed for the vector sequence consisting of vectors $\mathbf{s}^{(1)}$, $\mathbf{s}^{(2)}$, $\mathbf{s}^{(3)}$ arranged in sequence S:

$$S = \{[\,1 \ -1 \ -1 \ 1 \ -1\,]^t, [\,1 \ 1 \ -1 \ -1 \ 1\,]^t, [\,1 \ -1 \ 1 \ -1 \ 1\,]^t\} \qquad (6.82)$$

The memory weight matrix $\mathbf{W}$ is obtained from (6.72) as

$$\mathbf{W} = \mathbf{s}^{(2)}\mathbf{s}^{(1)t} + \mathbf{s}^{(3)}\mathbf{s}^{(2)t} + \mathbf{s}^{(1)}\mathbf{s}^{(3)t} \qquad (6.83a)$$

Substituting the temporal vectors specified, the weight matrix (6.83) becomes

$$\mathbf{W} = \begin{bmatrix} 3 & -1 & -1 & -1 & 1 \\ -1 & -1 & -1 & 3 & -3 \\ -1 & 3 & -1 & -1 & 1 \\ -1 & -1 & 3 & -1 & 1 \\ 1 & 1 & -3 & 1 & -1 \end{bmatrix} \qquad (6.83b)$$

Now evaluate recall of the encoded sequence S. With input $\mathbf{s}^{(1)}$, the layer response is

$$\Gamma[\mathbf{W}\mathbf{s}^{(1)}] = \Gamma[\,3 \ \ 7 \ \ -5 \ \ -5 \ \ 5\,]^t \qquad (6.84)$$

which yields the desired vector $\mathbf{s}^{(2)}$ after thresholding. It is interesting to note from (6.74) and (6.75) that the noise vector $\boldsymbol{\eta}_1$ for the computed transition is

$$\boldsymbol{\eta}_1 = \begin{bmatrix} 3 \\ 7 \\ -5 \\ -5 \\ 5 \end{bmatrix} - 5\mathbf{s}^{(2)} \tag{6.85a}$$

which reduces to

$$\boldsymbol{\eta}_1 = \begin{bmatrix} -2 & 2 & 0 & 0 & 0 \end{bmatrix}^t \tag{6.85b}$$

The magnitude of each component of $\boldsymbol{\eta}_1$ is smaller than the magnitude of the corresponding component of $5\mathbf{s}^{(2)}$; thus, recall is correct in this step due to the sufficient value of the signal-to-noise ratio. Further updates of the memory yield

$$\Gamma[\mathbf{W}\mathbf{s}^{(2)}] = \Gamma\begin{bmatrix} 5 & -7 & 5 & -3 & 3 \end{bmatrix}^t \tag{6.86}$$

and thus recall of $\mathbf{s}^{(3)}$ as required, with the noise term

$$\boldsymbol{\eta}_2 = \begin{bmatrix} 0 & -2 & 0 & 2 & -2 \end{bmatrix}^t \tag{6.87}$$

Finally, $\mathbf{s}^{(1)}$ is recalled due to the thresholding operation

$$\Gamma[\mathbf{W}\mathbf{s}^{(3)}] = \Gamma\begin{bmatrix} 5 & -7 & -3 & 5 & -5 \end{bmatrix}^t \tag{6.88}$$

with the noise vector

$$\boldsymbol{\eta}_3 = \begin{bmatrix} 0 & 2 & 2 & 0 & 0 \end{bmatrix}^t \tag{6.89}$$

This terminates the recall of the sequence $\mathbf{s}^{(2)}$, $\mathbf{s}^{(3)}$, $\mathbf{s}^{(1)}$. ■

6.7 CONCLUDING REMARKS

The associative memories studied in this chapter are a class of artificial neural networks capable of implementing complex associative mapping in a space of vector information. The domain of such mapping is a set of memory vectors, usually having binary values. Recording, or learning, algorithms are used to encode the required mapping between the memory input and output. In addition to coded memories, however, stable false attractors may often result as a side effect of the coding algorithm.

Interesting observations can be drawn from the comparison of the artificial neural memory architectures just studied to the capacity of the human brain. Biological studies have estimated the number of neurons in a human cortex to be of order of 10^{11} (Amit 1989). According to our conclusions in Section 6.4, a fully connected cortex with 10^{11} synapses could store $\alpha 10^{11}$ patterns, where α is the proportionality constant having a lower bound on its estimated value of 0.14. Each of the patterns can be understood at a first glance as a 10^{11}-tuple pattern not correlated with any other pattern in the cortex. This results in a number of $\alpha 10^{22}$ bits of storage space apparently available in the brain. As tentative as this rough estimate is, just its order of magnitude indicates an information pressure to which any brain model relates.

But since the nerve network of the cortex is not fully connected, the above assumption does not hold. According to neurobiological research estimates, each neuron has only about 10^4 synapses. The cortex can thus be viewed as a system of 10^7 elementary networks each comprising 10^4 fully connected neurons. Such a system can store and retrieve $\alpha 10^4$ patterns of 10^4 bits each. Thus, the total informational capacity is $\alpha 10^7 \times 10^4 \times 10^4$, which is equal to $\alpha 10^{15}$ bits. A similar order of magnitude capacity results if we consider a network of 10^{11} neurons to be a uniformly connected network with a mean of 10^4 synapses per neuron (Amit 1989).

The estimate of the number of information bits that can penetrate the central nervous system in a human lifetime through the sensory organs is 10^{20} bits. This estimate, from von Neumann (1958), is based on the neurobiologically determined mean rate of neural activity $(14/s)$, the number of input channels equal to the estimated number of binary neurons in the brain (10^{10}), and the mean length of human life $(10^9 \ s)$.

There is still a five order of magnitude difference between the number of information bits penetrating the natural human memory (10^{20} bits) and its inherent capacity ($\alpha 10^{15}$ bits). The explanation of this discrepancy can be examined by considering the correlation between the ensuing information clusters. Once the network organizes, there are no reasons for independent storage of related patterns. Correlated patterns are storable within their basins of attractions. Therefore, any significant correlations between learned patterns reduce the number of neurons required for storage.

The following are the most important quality criteria for design of neural associative memories with an auto- or heteroassociative processing capability (Hassoun and Youssef 1989):

1. a large capacity

2. an immunity to noisy or partial input

3. few false states which are pseudomemories

4. no memory limit cycles which are oscillatory states

5. implementation of the HD criterion or some other similar measure of neighborhood.

A number of recording algorithms and memory architectures have been covered in this chapter. More approaches have been proposed in the literature. As a result, improved recording techniques have been proposed to optimize the association process. The reader is referred to the specialized literature for further reading on the topic. A high-performance recording technique based on the Ho-Kashyap algorithm is given by Hassoun and Youssef (1989) and Hassoun (1989). Another approach involves a hidden layer of neurons, which increases the orthogonality of the stored patterns so that, similar to a Hopfield memory, the stored patterns are easier to retrieve (Hoffman and Davenport 1990). Higher order learning rules are also introduced by involving higher order correlations between the stored patterns (Chen et al. 1986). Despite applications of various configurations and recording methods, however, none of the associative memories has yet been designed to be perfect and fault-free.

Due to the parallel processing mode, associative memories can be successfully applied if correctly designed. An important design aspect should involve accounting for a safe memory operation margin. This should include the study of existing possible trade-offs between the memory size and the numbers of stored patterns or their pairs. The study should also involve the expected noise tolerance, distances between stored patterns, etc.

Neural associative memories are potentially useful in a wide range of applications such as content-addressable storage, search-and-retrieve tasks, optimization computing, image restoration, pattern recognition, classification, and code correcting (Grant and Sage 1986). Other applications include storage of words and of continuous speech. In optical signal processing, associative memories are used for code filtering, code mapping, code joining, code shifting, and projecting.

PROBLEMS

Please note that problems highlighted with an asterisk (*) are typically computationally intensive and the use of programs is advisable to solve them.

P6.1 The linear associator has to associate the following pairs of vectors:

$$\mathbf{s}^{(1)} = \begin{bmatrix} \frac{1}{2} & \frac{1}{2} & \frac{1}{2} & \frac{1}{2} \end{bmatrix}^t \rightarrow \mathbf{f}^{(1)} = \begin{bmatrix} 0 & 1 & 0 \end{bmatrix}^t$$

$$\mathbf{s}^{(2)} = \begin{bmatrix} \frac{1}{2} & -\frac{5}{6} & \frac{1}{6} & \frac{1}{6} \end{bmatrix}^t \rightarrow \mathbf{f}^{(2)} = \begin{bmatrix} 1 & 0 & 1 \end{bmatrix}^t$$

$$\mathbf{s}^{(3)} = \begin{bmatrix} \frac{1}{2} & \frac{1}{6} & \frac{1}{6} & -\frac{5}{6} \end{bmatrix}^t \rightarrow \mathbf{f}^{(3)} = \begin{bmatrix} 0 & 0 & 0 \end{bmatrix}^t$$

(a) Verify that vectors $\mathbf{s}^{(1)}$, $\mathbf{s}^{(2)}$, and $\mathbf{s}^{(3)}$ are orthonormal.

(b) Create partial weight matrices for each desired association.

(c) Compute the total weight matrix.

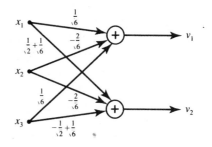

Figure P6.2 Linear associator network.

(d) Verify the association performed by the network for one of the specified patterns $\mathbf{s}^{(i)}$.

(e) Distort $\mathbf{s}^{(i)}$ by setting one of its components to zero and compute the resulting noise vector.

P6.2   The linear associator shown in Figure P6.2 has been trained to associate three unipolar binary output vectors to the following input vectors:

$$\mathbf{s}^{(1)} = \left[\frac{1}{\sqrt{3}} \quad \frac{1}{\sqrt{3}} \quad \frac{1}{\sqrt{3}} \right]^t$$

$$\mathbf{s}^{(2)} = \left[\frac{1}{\sqrt{2}} \quad 0 \quad -\frac{1}{\sqrt{2}} \right]^t$$

$$\mathbf{s}^{(3)} = \left[\frac{1}{\sqrt{6}} \quad -\frac{2}{\sqrt{6}} \quad \frac{1}{\sqrt{6}} \right]^t$$

Find the weight matrix $\mathbf{W}$. Then compute vectors $\mathbf{f}^{(1)}$, $\mathbf{f}^{(2)}$, and $\mathbf{f}^{(3)}$, which have been encoded in the network.

P6.3   Assume that a linear associator has been designed using the cross-correlation matrix for heteroassociative association of p orthonormal patterns. Subsequently, another orthonormal pattern $\mathbf{s}^{(p+1)}$ associated with $\mathbf{f}^{(p+1)}$ must be stored. An incremental change in the weight matrix needs to be performed using the cross-correlation concept. Prove that the association $\mathbf{s}^{(p+1)} \rightarrow \mathbf{f}^{(p+1)}$ results in no noise term present at the output.

P6.4   The linear autoassociator needs to associate distorted versions of vectors $\mathbf{s}_1$, $\mathbf{s}_2$, and $\mathbf{s}_3$ with their undistorted prototypes specified in Problem P6.1. Calculate the weight matrix for the linear autoassociator network.

P6.5   A two-neuron recurrent autoassociative memory has one stable state. Its energy function is of the form $E = -\frac{1}{2}\mathbf{v}^t\mathbf{W}\mathbf{v} - \mathbf{i}^t\mathbf{v}$, so it includes the bias term. The energy function for the circuit is shown in Figure P6.5. Compute elements of $\mathbf{W}$ and $\mathbf{i}$ and draw the network diagram.

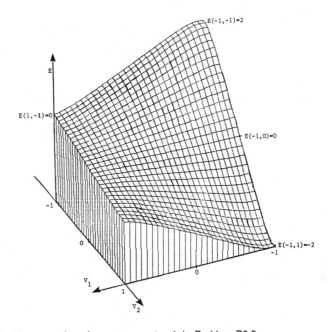

Figure P6.5   Energy surface for memory network in Problem P6.5.

P6.6   The memory recording algorithm expressing the Hebbian learning rule with subsequent nullification of the diagonal matrix

$$\mathbf{W} = \sum_{m=1}^{p} \mathbf{s}^{(m)}\mathbf{s}^{(m)t} - p\mathbf{I}$$

can also be used for unipolar binary vector storage. Prove that this mode of coding is invariant under the complement operation $\mathbf{s}^{(m)} = \mathbf{s}'^{(m)}$, i.e., it leads to identical weight matrices in both cases.

P6.7   A three-bit autoassociative recurrent memory updating under asynchronous rule stores a single vector $\mathbf{s}^{(1)} = \begin{bmatrix} 1 & 1 & -1 \end{bmatrix}^{t}$. Prepare a state transition map using a three-dimensional cube with the energy values assigned to each vertex, and with the direction of all possible transitions assigned to each edge of the cube. Then evaluate all transitions using each vertex as an initial condition.

P6.8   A blank state transition map for a recurrent autoassociative memory with asynchronous update is shown in Figure P6.8. Assume that $\mathbf{s}^{(1)} = \begin{bmatrix} 1 & 1 & -1 & 1 \end{bmatrix}^{t}$ and $\mathbf{s}^{(2)} = \begin{bmatrix} 1 & -1 & 1 & -1 \end{bmatrix}^{t}$ need to be stored.

(a)   Compute $E(\mathbf{v})$.

(b)   Mark energy values at each node of the map.

(c)   Label all possible transitions on the state diagram.

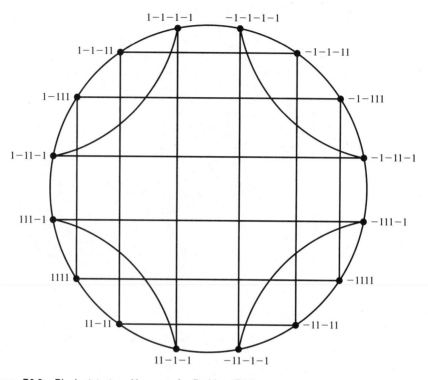

Figure P6.8 Blank state transition map for Problem P6.8.

   (d) Identify whether or not any initial conditions occur that lead to final states that are either spurious memories or that are true memories but are nonoptimal in the Hamming distance sense.

P6.9 A four-neuron Hopfield autoassociative memory has been designed for $\mathbf{s}^{(1)} = \begin{bmatrix} 1 & -1 & -1 & 1 \end{bmatrix}^t$. Assume that the recall is performed synchronously, i.e. all four memory outputs update at the same time.

   (a) Draw the state transition map for this recall mode assuming that any of the 16 states can be considered to be the initial one.

   (b) Compute $E(\mathbf{v})$.

   (c) Determine if the energy value decreases in this update mode.

P6.10 The following vectors need to be stored in a recurrent autoassociative memory:

$$\mathbf{s}^{(1)} = \begin{bmatrix} 1 & 1 & 1 & 1 & 1 \end{bmatrix}^t$$
$$\mathbf{s}^{(2)} = \begin{bmatrix} 1 & -1 & -1 & 1 & -1 \end{bmatrix}^t$$
$$\mathbf{s}^{(3)} = \begin{bmatrix} -1 & 1 & 1 & 1 & 1 \end{bmatrix}^t$$

   (a) Compute the weight matrix $\mathbf{W}$.

(b) Apply the input vector $\mathbf{v}^0 = \begin{bmatrix} 1 & -1 & -1 & 1 & 1 \end{bmatrix}^t$ and allow for asynchronous convergence in ascending node order starting at node 1.

(c) With the same input vector as in part (b) allow for asynchronous convergence in descending node order starting at node 5.

(d) Comment as to whether Hopfield memory provides an optimal solution in terms of the Hamming distance criterion. [The results may be surprising since this is an overloaded memory. Assume sgn (0) = +1 for update purposes in this problem.]

P6.11 The following unipolar binary vectors must be stored in the recurrent autoassociative memory using the outer product method with the nullification of the diagonal:

$$\mathbf{s}^{(1)} = \begin{bmatrix} 1 & 0 & 0 & 1 & 0 \end{bmatrix}^t$$
$$\mathbf{s}^{(2)} = \begin{bmatrix} 0 & 1 & 1 & 0 & 1 \end{bmatrix}^t$$
$$\mathbf{s}^{(3)} = \begin{bmatrix} 1 & 1 & 0 & 1 & 0 \end{bmatrix}^t$$

(a) Compute matrix $\mathbf{W}$.

(b) Find the analytical expression for the energy function that the memory is minimizing.

P6.12 Assume that the recurrent autoassociative memory has been designed for $p < n$ orthogonal patterns encoded in its weight matrix. Show that presenting the key pattern $\mathbf{s}^{(p+1)}$, which is orthogonal to the encoded patterns $\mathbf{s}^{(1)}, \mathbf{s}^{(2)}, \ldots, \mathbf{s}^{(p)}$, but has not been stored, results in the initial energy value $E(\mathbf{s}^{(p+1)}) = +\frac{1}{2}np$. Then compute the energy minima values for this memory for each of the stored vectors $\mathbf{s}^{(1)}, \mathbf{s}^{(2)}, \ldots, \mathbf{s}^{(p)}$.

P6.13 Compute the energy values for all 16 bipolar binary key vectors for a five-bit autoassociative recurrent memory having the following weight matrix (complement vectors need not be checked):

$$\mathbf{W} = \begin{bmatrix} 0 & 0 & 2 & 0 & -2 \\ 0 & 0 & 0 & -2 & 0 \\ 2 & 0 & 0 & 0 & -2 \\ 0 & -2 & 0 & 0 & 0 \\ -2 & 0 & -2 & 0 & 0 \end{bmatrix}$$

By comparing the energy levels, prepare a hypothesis regarding the two stored vectors. Then verify your hypothesis by comparing the computed weight matrix with the matrix $\mathbf{W}$ specified above.

P6.14 Vectors $\mathbf{a}^{(1)} = \begin{bmatrix} 1 & -1 & 1 & 1 \end{bmatrix}^t$ and $\mathbf{a}^{(2)} = \begin{bmatrix} -1 & 1 & -1 & 1 \end{bmatrix}^t$ represent the bit maps shown in Figure P6.14. They need to be autoassociated for input vectors at HD = 1 from the prototypes stored. Design the following two autoassociators:

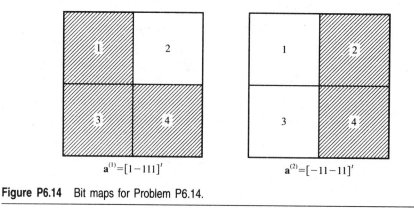

Figure P6.14　Bit maps for Problem P6.14.

(a) a linear autoassociator in the form of a linear associative memory with added thresholding element (TLU) at the output, if needed, but no feedback

(b) a recurrent autoassociative memory with asynchronous updating.

Compare the performance of both networks by evaluating responses to eight input vectors at HD = 1 from $\mathbf{a}^{(1)}$ and $\mathbf{a}^{(2)}$. The nodes of the memory designed in part (b) should be updated in ascending order starting at node 1.

P6.15 A recurrent autoassociative memory has been designed to store $\mathbf{s}^{(1)} = \begin{bmatrix} 1 & -1 & 1 & 1 & 1 \end{bmatrix}^t$ and $\mathbf{s}^{(2)} = \begin{bmatrix} -1 & 1 & 1 & -1 & 1 \end{bmatrix}^t$. The energy values have been computed and marked on the map of state transitions for this memory as shown in Figure P6.15. By analyzing the memory state diagram for all transitions at HD = 1, determine if this memory has any false spurious terminal states. If yes, what are they and what are the input vectors that could possibly be associating with the false memories?

*P6.16** Design the autoassociative recurrent memory to store the bit maps of the characters *A*, *I*, and *O* as specified in Figure P6.16. List the resulting **W** matrix. Implement the asynchronous retrieval algorithm starting at the upper leftmost pixel of the map, moving left to right during the update. Simulate the asynchronous convergence of the memory toward each of the characters stored in the following cases of key vectors:

(a) left upper pixel of each character reversed

(b) four center column pixels of the character field reversed.

Provide the retrieved vectors in each of six cases and note the number of recursion cycles. (Each recursion cycle consists here of a sequence of 16 updates.)

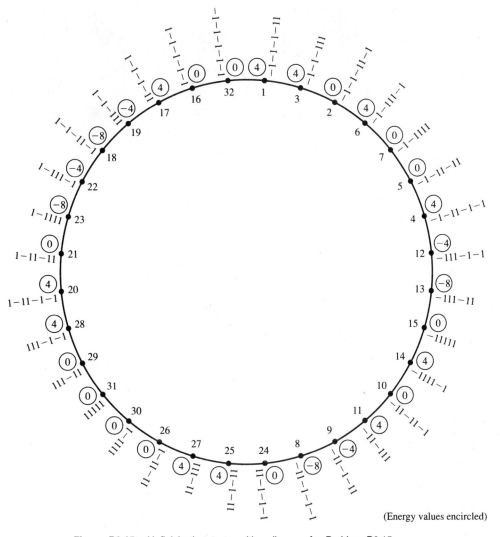

Figure P6.15 Unfinished state transition diagram for Problem P6.15.

P6.17 Analyze graphically the recurrent network with one neuron as shown in Figure 6.15 for the two cases of neuron activation functions as shown in Figure P6.17a,b. Determine whether points *A*, *B*, *C*, and *D* are stable or unstable fixed points, or cyclic solutions.

P6.18 The table here lists three scalar energy functions *E*(**x**) that are often encountered in the studies of associative memory. Their respective expressions for gradient vectors ∇*E*(**x**) are also listed. Derive the expressions for

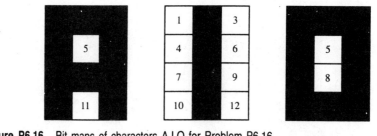

Figure P6.16 Bit maps of characters A,I,O for Problem P6.16.

gradient vectors for the energy functions listed in the left column. Assume $\mathbf{W}$ is $(n \times n)$ and $\mathbf{i}$ and $\mathbf{x}$ are $(n \times 1)$.

Case	$E(\mathbf{x})$	$\nabla E(\mathbf{x})$
1	$\mathbf{i}'\mathbf{x}$	$\mathbf{i}$
2	$\mathbf{x}'\mathbf{W}\mathbf{i}$	$\mathbf{W}\mathbf{i}$
3	$\mathbf{x}'\mathbf{W}\mathbf{x} + \mathbf{i}'\mathbf{x}$	$(\mathbf{W}^t + \mathbf{W})\mathbf{x} + \mathbf{i}$

*P6.19** Design the bidirectional associative memory that associates characters (A, C), (I, I), and (O, T) designed using the bit maps of A, I, and O from Problem P4.16 and of C, I, and T from Figure 4.19.

(a) Compute $\mathbf{W}$.

(b) Check associations within stored pairs using search arguments as the stored characters.

*P6.20** Given are the three following training pairs $(\mathbf{a}^{(i)}, \mathbf{b}^{(i)})$, for $i = 1, 2, 3$, for bidirectional associative memory:

$$\left(\mathbf{a}^{(1)}, \mathbf{b}^{(1)}\right) = \left([1 \quad -1 \quad -1 \quad 1 \quad 1 \quad 1 \quad -1 \quad -1 \quad -1]^t,\right.$$
$$\left.\{1 \quad 1 \quad 1 \quad -1 \quad -1 \quad -1 \quad -1 \quad 1 \quad -1]^t\right)$$

$$\left(\mathbf{a}^{(2)}, \mathbf{b}^{(2)}\right) = \left([-1 \quad 1 \quad 1 \quad 1 \quad -1 \quad -1 \quad 1 \quad 1 \quad 1]^t,\right.$$
$$\left.[1 \quad -1 \quad -1 \quad -1 \quad -1 \quad -1 \quad -1 \quad -1 \quad 1]^t\right)$$

$$\left(\mathbf{a}^{(3)}, \mathbf{b}^{(3)}\right) = \left([1 \quad -1 \quad 1 \quad -1 \quad 1 \quad 1 \quad -1 \quad 1 \quad 1]^t,\right.$$
$$\left.[-1 \quad 1 \quad -1 \quad 1 \quad -1 \quad -1 \quad 1 \quad -1 \quad 1]^t\right)$$

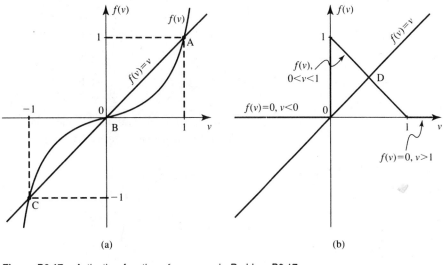

Figure P6.17 Activation functions for neuron in Problem P6.17.

Find the weight matrix $\mathbf{W}$ for the associative memory. Then:

(a) Determine that the input $\mathbf{a}^{(2)}$ does not result in retrieval of $\mathbf{b}^{(2)}$; find $\mathbf{b}^{(f)}$ retrieved instead of $\mathbf{b}^{(2)}$.

(b) Find $E(\mathbf{a}^{(f)}, \mathbf{b}^{(f)})$ and $E(\mathbf{a}^{(2)}, \mathbf{b}^{(2)})$ and compare their values.

(c) Determine whether or not $E(\mathbf{a}^{(2)}, \mathbf{b}^{(2)})$ is a local minimum. This can be done by evaluating $E(\mathbf{a}^{(2)}, \mathbf{b}^{(2)})$ and comparing it with the energy values at points that are at HD = 1 from $\mathbf{a}^{(2)}$ and then from $\mathbf{b}^{(2)}$.

P6.21 Prove the following theorem: If a training pair $(\mathbf{a}^{(m)}, \mathbf{b}^{(m)})$ is a local minimum of the energy function as in (6.54b), then the recovery is guaranteed since

$$\Gamma[\mathbf{W}\mathbf{b}^{(m)}] = \mathbf{a}^m \quad \text{and} \quad \Gamma[\mathbf{W}\mathbf{a}^{(m)}] = \mathbf{b}^{(m)}$$

[*Hint:* Examine the condition for local minimum

$$-\mathbf{a}^{(m)}\mathbf{W}\mathbf{b}^{(m)t} < -\mathbf{a}'^{(m)}\mathbf{W}\mathbf{b}^{(m)}$$

where $\mathbf{a}'^{(m)}$ is defined as differing by HD = 1 from $\mathbf{a}^{(m)}$. Repeat for $\mathbf{b}'^{(m)}$ differing by HD = 1 from $\mathbf{b}^{(m)}$.]

P6.22* Some of the three training pairs in Problem P6.20 coded according to (6.51) are not recoverable when training of multiplicity 1 is used. However, a multiple training method can be used to guarantee the recovery. Apply the multiple training method to obtain the weight matrix with guaranteed recovery for each member of the training pair. Try multiplicity of 2 or 3 in order to test the encoding of each pair. Devise the lowest multiplicity of training for each pair that would guarantee recovery.

P6.23 A temporal associative memory needs to be designed for recall of the following sequence:

$$\mathbf{s}^{(1)} = \begin{bmatrix} 1 \\ -1 \\ -1 \\ 1 \\ -1 \end{bmatrix}, \quad \mathbf{s}^{(2)} = \begin{bmatrix} -1 \\ 1 \\ 1 \\ -1 \\ -1 \end{bmatrix}, \quad \mathbf{s}^{(3)} = \begin{bmatrix} -1 \\ 1 \\ 1 \\ 1 \\ -1 \end{bmatrix}$$

Compute the weight matrix **W** and check the recall of patterns in the forward and backward directions. Assume a bipolar binary activation function.

P6.24 The weight matrix of the temporal associative memory is known as

$$\mathbf{W} = \begin{bmatrix} -1 & 3 & -1 & -1 & -1 \\ -1 & -1 & -1 & -1 & 3 \\ -1 & -1 & 3 & -1 & -1 \\ -1 & 3 & -1 & -1 & -1 \\ 3 & -1 & -1 & 3 & 1 \end{bmatrix}$$

Knowing that a vector $\mathbf{s}^{(1)} = \begin{bmatrix} -1 & 1 & -1 & -1 & 1 \end{bmatrix}^t$ belongs to a sequence, find the remaining vectors of the sequence. Having found the full sequence, verify that encoding it actually yields the weight matrix **W** as specified in the problem. Calculate the noise term vectors generated at each recall step and determine that they are suppressed during the thresholding operation.

REFERENCES

Amari, S. I. 1972. "Learning Patterns and Pattern Sequences by Self-Organizing Nets," *IEEE Trans. Computers* (21), pp. 1197–1206.

Amit, D. J., G. Gutfreund, and H. Sompolinsky. 1985. "Spin-glass Models of Neural Networks," *Phys. Rev. A* 32: 1007–1018.

Amit, D. J. 1989. *Modeling Brain Function: The World of Attractor Neural Networks.* Cambridge: Cambridge University Press.

Carpenter, G. A. 1989. "Neural Network Models for Pattern Recognition and Associative Memory," *Neural Networks* 2: 243–257.

Chen, H. H., Y. C. Lee, G. Z. Sun, and H. Y. Lee. 1986. "Higher Order Correlation Model for Associative Memory," in *Neural Networks for Computing,* ed. J. S. Denker. New York: American Institute of Physics, pp. 86–99.

Desai, M. S. 1990. "Noisy Pattern Retrieval Using Associative Memories," MSEE thesis, University of Louisville, Kentucky.

Grant, P. M., and J. P. Sage. 1986. "A Comparison of Neural Network and Matched Filter Processing for Detecting Lines in Images," in *Neural Networks for Computing,* ed. J. S. Denker. New York: American Institute of Physics, pp. 194–199.

Hagiwara, M. 1990. "Multidimensional Assocciative Memory," in *Proc. 1990 IEEE Joint Conf. on Neural Networks,* Washington, D.C., January 15–19, 1990. New York: IEEE, Vol. I, pp. 3–6.

Hassoun, M. H., and A. M. Youssef. 1989. "High Performance Recording Algorithm for Hopfield Model Associative Memories," *Opt. Eng.* 28(1): 46–54.

Hassoun, M. H. 1989. "Dynamic Heteroassociative Memories," *Neural Networks,* 2: 275–287.

Hoffman, G. W., and M. R. Davenport. 1990. "A Network that Uses the Outer Product Rule, Hidden Neurons, and Peaks in the Energy Landscape," in *Proc. 1990 IEEE Int. Symp. on Circuits and Systems,* New Orleans, La., May 1–3, 1990. New York: IEEE, pp. 196–199.

Hopfield, J. J. 1982. "Neural Networks and Physical Systems with Emergent Collective Computational Abilities," *Proc. National Academy of Sciences* 79: 2554–2558.

Hopfield, J. J. 1984. "Neurons with Graded Response Have Collective Computational Properties Like Those of Two State Neurons," *Proc. National Academy of Sciences* 81: 3088–3092.

Jong, T. L., and H. M. Tai. 1988. "Associative Memory Based on the Modified Hopfield Neural Net Model," in *Proc. 30th Midwest Symp. on Circuits and Systems,* St. Louis, Mo., August 1988. pp. 748–751.

Kamp, Y., and M. Hasler. 1990. *Recursive Neural Networks for Associative Memory,* Chichester, U.K.: John Wiley & Sons.

Kohonen, T. 1977. *Associative Memory: A System-Theoretical Approach,* Berlin: Springer-Verlag.

Kohonen, T., et al. 1981. "Distributed Associative Memory," in *Parallel Models of Distributed Memory Systems,* ed. G. E. Hinton and J. A. Anderson. Hillsdale, New Jersey: Lawrence Erlbaum Associates.

Kohonen, T. 1987. "Adaptive, Associative, and Self-Organizing Functions in Neural Computing," *Appl. Opt.* 26(23): 4910–4918.

Komlos, J., and R. Paturi. 1988. "Convergence Results in an Associative Memory Model," *Neural Networks* 1: 239–250.

Kosko, B. 1987. "Adaptive Bidirectional Associative Memories," *Appl. Opt.* 26(23): 4947–4959.

Kosko, B. 1988. "Bidirectional Associative Memories," *IEEE Trans. Systems, Man, and Cybernetics* 18(1): 49–60.

McEliece, R. J., E. C. Posner, E. R. Rodemich, and S. V. Venkatesh. 1987. "The Capacity of the Hopfield Associative Memory," *IEEE Trans. Information Theory* IT-33(4): 461–482.

Michel, A. N., and J. A. Farrell. 1990. "Associative Memories via Artificial Neural Networks," *IEEE Control Systems Magazine* (April): 6–17.

Personnaz, L., I. Guyon, and G. Dreyfus. 1986. "Collective Computational Properties of Neural Networks: New Learning Mechanism," *Phys. Rev. A* 34(5): 4217–4228.

Petsche, T. 1988. "Topics in Neural Networks," Ph.D. diss., Princeton University, New Jersey.

Petsche, T., and B. W. Dickinson. 1990. "Trellis Codes, Receptive Fields, and Fault-Tolerant Self-Repairing Neural Networks," *IEEE Trans. Neural Networks* 1(2): 154–166.

Serra, R., and G. Zanarini. 1990. *Complex Systems and Cognitive Processes,* Berlin: Springer-Verlag.

von Neumann, J. 1958. *The Computer and the Brain.* New Haven, Conn.: Yale University Press, p. 87.

Wang, Y. F., J. B. Cruz, and J. H. Mulligan. 1990. "Two Coding Strategies for Bidirectional Associative Memory," *IEEE Trans. Neural Networks* 1(1): 81–92.

Wang, Y. F., J. B. Cruz, and J. H. Mulligan. 1990. "On Multiple Training for Bidirectional Associative Memory," *IEEE Trans. Neural Networks,* 1(5): 275–276.

Wang, Y. F., J. B. Cruz, and J. H. Mulligan. 1991. "Guaranteed Recall of All Training Pairs for Bidirectional Associative Memory," *IEEE Trans. Neural Networks,* 2(6): 559–567.

7

MATCHING AND SELF-ORGANIZING NETWORKS

*New opinions are always suspected,
and usually opposed, without any
other reason, but because they are
not already common.*

J. LOCKE

The neural networks covered in previous chapters represent a number of distinct network classes. We studied single-layer and multilayer perceptron networks, which are essentially feedforward recall architectures trained with supervision. Continuous- and discrete-time single-layer networks with recurrent recall form another separate architectural group of networks. Associative memories can also be treated as a distinct class of neural networks. Despite somewhat diversified architectures, associative memories exhibit a common learning mode based on auto- and cross-correlation between stored vectors. Although other learning techniques exist, memories are typically designed with fixed weights by using the technique of batch learning, or recording.

The networks we discuss in this chapter represent a combination of the architectures and recall modes studied thus far. One novel aspect is the networks' learning mode. Our purpose in this chapter is to present networks that learn neither by the familiar correlation rule, nor by the perceptron or gradient descent techniques we have studied. In fact, no feedback from the environment will be provided during learning. The network must discover for itself any relationships of interest that may exist in the input data. Our interest is in designing networks that are able to translate the discovered relationships into outputs. We will see in this chapter that discovery of patterns, features, regularities, or categories can be learned without a teacher.

Networks trained without a teacher usually learn by matching certain explicit familiarity criteria. These networks can produce output that tells us how familiar it is with the present pattern. This is done by comparing the present pattern with typical patterns seen in the past. Consider that the present pattern is evaluated for "similarity" with typical patterns from the past. One important measure of similarity used for learning studied in this chapter is the maximum value of the scalar product of the weights and input vector. Using the scalar product metric, weights can be trained in an unsupervised mode to resemble frequent input patterns, or better, pattern clusters. Another often used measure of similarity is the topological neighborhood, or distance, between the responding neurons arranged in regular geometrical arrays.

Our objective in this chapter is to explore the unsupervised training algorithms of neural networks so that their weights can sensibly adapt during the process called *self-organization*. Networks trained in this mode will not only react to values of inputs but also to their statistical parameters. In this chapter we will assume that both inputs and their probability density will affect the training. Rare inputs will have less impact for learning than those occurring frequently. Sometimes, training inputs will need to be applied in their natural sequence of occurrence.

Unsupervised learning may seem at first impossible to accomplish. Indeed, at the beginning of the learning process, the network's responses may be implausible. The lack of a teacher's input forces the network to learn gradually by itself which features need to be considered in classification or recognition and thus need to be reinforced. At the same time, other less important features can be neglected or suppressed based on the mapping criteria that underlie the unsupervised learning algorithms. The proximity measures allow the computation of important indicators of how to differentiate between more and less important features during the unsupervised learning. What is very peculiar to this learning mode is that the indicators have to be created based on the history of learning experience.

Unsupervised learning can only be implemented with redundant input data. Redundancy provides knowledge about statistical properties of input patterns. In fact, there are close connections between statistical approaches to pattern classification and the neural network techniques discussed here (Duda and Hart 1973).

In the absence of target responses or guidelines provided directly by the teacher, the network can, for example, build classification/recognition/mapping performance during the process devised in Chapter 2 as competitive learning. The winning output node will receive the only reward during learning in the form of a weight adjustment. In some cases, the extension of rewards for the node's neighborhood will also be allowed. Strengthening the winning weights gradually builds into the network a history of what has been seen in the past. Such networks are termed *networks with history sensitivity.*

The neural network architectures covered in this chapter include the Hamming network, MAXNET, the clustering Kohonen layer, the Grossberg outstar learning layer, a counterpropagation network, self-organizing feature mapping networks, and an adaptive resonance network for cluster discovery and classification of binary vectors.

7.1 HAMMING NET AND MAXNET

In this section a two-layer classifier of binary bipolar vectors will be covered. The block diagram of the network is shown in Figure 7.1. It is a minimum Hamming distance classifier, which selects the stored classes that are at a minimum HD value to the noisy or incomplete argument vector presented at the input. This selection is essentially performed solely by the *Hamming network.* The Hamming network is of the feedforward type and constitutes the first layer of the classifier. The p-class Hamming network has p output neurons. The strongest response of a neuron is indicative of the minimum HD value between the input and the category this neuron represents. The second layer of the classifier is called *MAXNET* and it operates as a recurrent recall network in an auxiliary mode. Its only function is to suppress values at MAXNET output nodes other than the initially maximum output node of the first layer (Lippmann 1987).

As stated, the proper part of the classifier is the Hamming network responsible for matching of the input vector with stored vectors. The expanded diagram of the Hamming network for classification of bipolar binary n-tuple input vectors

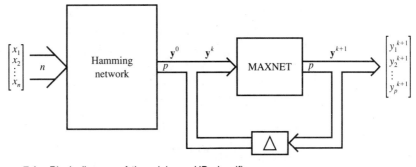

Figure 7.1 Block diagram of the minimum HD classifier.

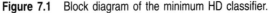

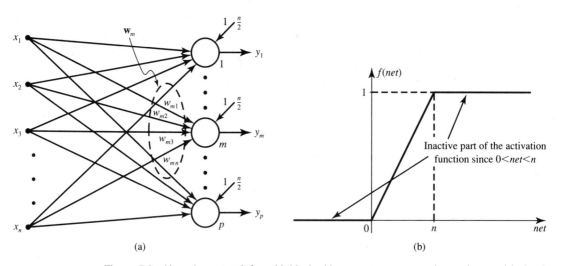

Figure 7.2 Hamming network for n-bit bipolar binary vectors representing p classes: (a) classifier network and (b) neurons' activation function.

is shown in Figure 7.2(a). The purpose of the layer is to compute, in a feed-forward manner, the values of $(n - \text{HD})$, where HD is the Hamming distance between the search argument and the encoded class prototype vector. Assume that the n-tuple prototype vector of the m'th class is $\mathbf{s}^{(m)}$, for $m = 1, 2, \ldots, p$, and the n-tuple input vector is $\mathbf{x}$. Note that the entries of the weight vector $\mathbf{w}_m$ defined as

$$\mathbf{w}_m = \begin{bmatrix} w_{m1} & w_{m2} & \ldots & w_{mn} \end{bmatrix}^t, \quad \text{for } m = 1, 2, \ldots, p$$

connect inputs to the m'th neuron, which performs as the class indicator.

Before we express the value of the Hamming distance by means of the scalar product of $\mathbf{x}$ and $\mathbf{s}^{(m)}$, let us formalize the metric introduced here. A vector classifier with p outputs, one for each class, can be conceived such that the m'th output is 1 if and only if $\mathbf{x} = \mathbf{s}^{(m)}$. This would require that the weights be $\mathbf{w}_m = \mathbf{s}^{(m)}$. The classifier outputs are $\mathbf{x}^t \mathbf{s}^{(1)}, \mathbf{x}^t \mathbf{s}^{(2)}, \ldots, \mathbf{x}^t \mathbf{s}^{(m)}, \ldots, \mathbf{x}^t \mathbf{s}^{(p)}$. When $\mathbf{x} = \mathbf{s}^{(m)}$, only the m'th output is n, provided the classes differ from each other, and assuming ± 1 entries of $\mathbf{x}$. The scalar product of vectors has been used here as an obvious measure for vector matching.

The scalar product $\mathbf{x}^t \mathbf{s}^{(m)}$ of two bipolar binary n-tuple vectors can be written as the total number of positions in which the two vectors agree minus the number of positions in which they differ. Note that the number of different bit positions is the HD value. Understandably, the number of positions in which two vectors agree is $n - \text{HD}$. The equality is written

$$\mathbf{x}^t \mathbf{s}^{(m)} = \left(n - \text{HD}(\mathbf{x}, \mathbf{s}^{(m)}) \right) - \text{HD}(\mathbf{x}, \mathbf{s}^{(m)}) \tag{7.1a}$$

This is equivalent to

$$\frac{1}{2}\mathbf{x}^t\mathbf{s}^{(m)} = \frac{n}{2} - \mathrm{HD}(\mathbf{x}, \mathbf{s}^{(m)}) \tag{7.1b}$$

We can now see that the weight matrix $\mathbf{W}_H$ of the Hamming network can be created by encoding the class vector prototypes as rows in the form as below

$$\mathbf{W}_H = \frac{1}{2} \begin{bmatrix} s_1^{(1)} & s_2^{(1)} & \cdots & s_n^{(1)} \\ s_1^{(2)} & s_2^{(2)} & \cdots & s_n^{(2)} \\ \vdots & \vdots & \cdots & \vdots \\ s_1^{(p)} & s_2^{(p)} & \cdots & s_n^{(p)} \end{bmatrix} \tag{7.2}$$

where the ½ factor is convenient for scaling purposes. Now the network with input vector $\mathbf{x}$ yields the value of $(½)\mathbf{x}^t\mathbf{s}^{(m)}$ at the input to the node m, for $m = 1$, $2, \ldots, p$. Adding the fixed bias value of $n/2$ to the input of each neuron results in the total input net_m

$$net_m = \frac{1}{2}\mathbf{x}^t\mathbf{s}^{(m)} + \frac{n}{2}, \quad \text{for } m = 1, 2, \ldots, p \tag{7.3a}$$

Using the identity (7.1b), net_m can be expressed as

$$net_m = n - \mathrm{HD}(\mathbf{x}, \mathbf{s}^{(m)}) \tag{7.3b}$$

Let us apply neurons in the Hamming network with activation functions as in Figure 7.2(b). The neurons need to perform only the linear scaling of (7.3b) such that $f(net_m) = (1/n)net_m$, for $m = 1, 2, \ldots, p$. Since inputs are between 0 and n, we obtain the outputs of each node scaled down to between 0 and 1. Furthermore, the number of the node with the highest output indeed indicates the class number to which $\mathbf{x}$ is at the smallest HD. A perfect match of input vector to class m, which is equivalent to the condition HD = 0, is signaled by $f(net_m) = 1$. An input vector that is the complement of the prototype of class m would result in $f(net_m) = 0$. The response of the Hamming network essentially terminates the classification in which only the first layer of network from Figure 7.1 computes the relevant matching score values. As seen, the classification by the Hamming network is performed in a feedforward and instantaneous manner.

MAXNET needs to be employed as a second layer only for cases in which an enhancement of the initial dominant response of the m'th node is required. As a result of MAXNET recurrent processing, the m'th node responds positively, as opposed to all remaining nodes whose responses should have decayed to zero. As shown in Figure 7.3(a), MAXNET is a recurrent network involving both excitatory and inhibitory connections. The excitatory connection within the network is implemented in the form of a single positive self-feedback loop with a weighting coefficient of 1. All the remaining connections of this fully coupled feedback network are inhibitory. They are represented as $M - 1$ cross-feedback synapses with coefficients $-\varepsilon$ from each output. The second layer weight matrix

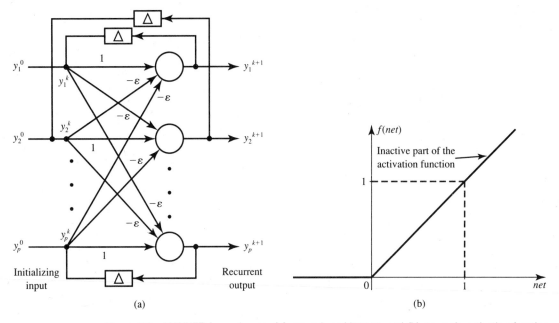

Figure 7.3 MAXNET for p classes: (a) network architecture and (b) neuron's activation function.

$\mathbf{W}_M$ of size $p \times p$ is thus of the form (Pao 1989)

$$\mathbf{W}_M = \begin{bmatrix} 1 & -\varepsilon & -\varepsilon & \cdots & -\varepsilon \\ -\varepsilon & 1 & -\varepsilon & \cdots & -\varepsilon \\ -\varepsilon & & & & \\ \vdots & & & \ddots & \vdots \\ -\varepsilon & -\varepsilon & & -\varepsilon & 1 \end{bmatrix} \tag{7.4}$$

where ε must be bounded $0 < \varepsilon < 1/p$. The quantity ε can be called the *lateral interaction coefficient*. With the activation function as shown in Figure 7.3(b) and the initializing inputs fulfilling conditions

$$0 \le y_i^0 \le 1, \quad \text{for } i = 1, 2, \dots, p$$

the MAXNET network gradually suppresses all but the largest initial network excitation. When initialized with the input vector $\mathbf{y}^0$, the network starts processing it by adding positive self-feedback and negative cross-feedback. As a result of a number of recurrences, the only unsuppressed node will be the one with the largest initializing entry y_m^0. This means that the only nonzero output response node is the node closest to the input vector argument in HD sense. The recurrent processing by MAXNET leading to this response is

$$\mathbf{y}^{k+1} = \Gamma[\mathbf{W}_M \mathbf{y}^k] \tag{7.5a}$$

where Γ is a nonlinear diagonal matrix operator with entries $f(\cdot)$ given below:

$$f(net) = \begin{cases} 0, & net < 0 \\ net, & net \geq 0 \end{cases} \qquad (7.5b)$$

Each entry of the updated vector $\mathbf{y}^{k+1}$ decreases at the k'th recursion step of (7.5a) under the MAXNET update algorithm, with the largest entry decreasing slowest. This is due to the conditions on the entries of matrix $\mathbf{W}_M$ as in (7.4), specifically, due to the condition $0 < \varepsilon < 1/p$.

Assume that $y_m^0 > y_i^0$, $i = 1, 2, \ldots, p$ and $i \neq m$. During the first recurrence, all entries of $\mathbf{y}^1$ are computed on the linear portion of $f(net)$. The smallest of all $\mathbf{y}^0$ entries will first reach the level $f(net) = 0$, assumed at the k'th step. The clipping of one output entry slows down the decrease of y_m^{k+1} in all forthcoming steps. Then, the second smallest entry of $\mathbf{y}^0$ reaches $f(net) = 0$. The process repeats itself until all values except for one, at the output of the m'th node, remain at nonzero values. The example below explains the design and operation of the discussed classifier.

EXAMPLE 7.1 ■■■■■■■■■■■■■■■■■

Let us design the minimum Hamming distance classifier for three characters C, I, and T as shown in Figure 4.19 for which the bipolar binary class prototype vectors are

$$\begin{aligned} \mathbf{s}^{(1)} &= \begin{bmatrix} 1 & 1 & 1 & 1 & -1 & -1 & 1 & 1 & 1 \end{bmatrix}^t \\ \mathbf{s}^{(2)} &= \begin{bmatrix} -1 & 1 & -1 & -1 & 1 & -1 & -1 & 1 & -1 \end{bmatrix}^t \\ \mathbf{s}^{(3)} &= \begin{bmatrix} 1 & 1 & 1 & -1 & 1 & -1 & -1 & 1 & -1 \end{bmatrix}^t \end{aligned} \qquad (7.6a)$$

The weight matrix $\mathbf{W}_H$ of the Hamming network obtained from (7.2) is

$$\mathbf{W}_H = \begin{bmatrix} 1 & 1 & 1 & 1 & -1 & -1 & 1 & 1 & 1 \\ -1 & 1 & -1 & -1 & 1 & -1 & -1 & 1 & -1 \\ 1 & 1 & 1 & -1 & 1 & -1 & -1 & 1 & -1 \end{bmatrix} \qquad (7.6b)$$

Note that the matrix of Equation (7.6b) determines the bipolar binary values of weights w_{ij}. Using formula (7.3a), the input vector **net** is expressed as follows:

$$\mathbf{net} = \frac{1}{2} \begin{bmatrix} 1 & 1 & 1 & 1 & -1 & -1 & 1 & 1 & 1 \\ -1 & 1 & -1 & -1 & 1 & -1 & -1 & 1 & -1 \\ 1 & 1 & 1 & -1 & 1 & -1 & -1 & 1 & -1 \end{bmatrix} \mathbf{x} + \begin{bmatrix} \frac{9}{2} \\ \frac{9}{2} \\ \frac{9}{2} \end{bmatrix} \qquad (7.6c)$$

Selecting $\varepsilon = 0.2 < \frac{1}{3}$ terminates the design process of both layers. The

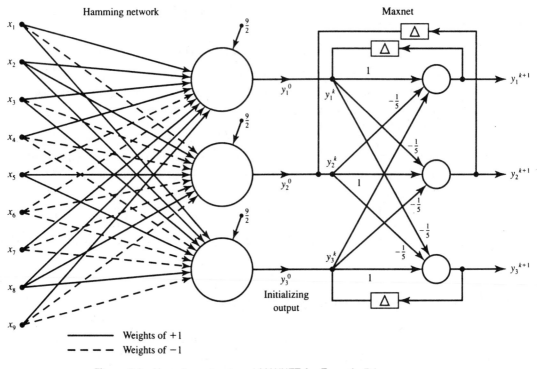

Figure 7.4 Hamming network and MAXNET for Example 7.1.

designed network is shown in Figure 7.4. Let us look at sample responses of both layers of the network. Assume the test input vector to be

$$\mathbf{x} = \begin{bmatrix} 1 & 1 & 1 & 1 & 1 & 1 & 1 & 1 & 1 \end{bmatrix}^t$$

For the Hamming layer neurons' activation and responses, respectively, we obtain from (7.3a) with this input

$$\mathbf{net} = \begin{bmatrix} 7 \\ 3 \\ 5 \end{bmatrix}$$

$$\Gamma[\mathbf{net}] = \begin{bmatrix} \dfrac{7}{9} \\ \dfrac{1}{3} \\ \dfrac{5}{9} \end{bmatrix}$$

Since the computed output, $\Gamma[\mathbf{net}]$, is the input vector to MAXNET, we thus have $\Gamma[\mathbf{net}] = \mathbf{y}^0$. The MAXNET recurrent formula (7.5a) yields the following activation:

$$\mathbf{net}^k = \begin{bmatrix} net_1^k \\ net_2^k \\ net_3^k \end{bmatrix}$$

$$= \begin{bmatrix} 1 & -\dfrac{1}{3} & -\dfrac{1}{3} \\ -\dfrac{1}{3} & 1 & -\dfrac{1}{3} \\ -\dfrac{1}{3} & -\dfrac{1}{3} & 1 \end{bmatrix} \begin{bmatrix} y_1^k \\ y_2^k \\ y_3^k \end{bmatrix}$$

and the following response computed from (7.5b)

$$\mathbf{y}^{k+1} = \begin{bmatrix} f(net_1^k) \\ f(net_2^k) \\ f(net_3^k) \end{bmatrix}$$

In the recurrences $k = 0, 1, 2, 3$, the network produces the following activations and responses, respectively:

Step 1: $k = 0$:

$$\mathbf{net}^0 = \begin{bmatrix} 1 & -0.2 & -0.2 \\ -0.2 & 1 & -0.2 \\ -0.2 & -0.2 & 1 \end{bmatrix} \begin{bmatrix} 0.777 \\ 0.333 \\ 0.555 \end{bmatrix} \begin{bmatrix} 0.599 \\ 0.067 \\ 0.333 \end{bmatrix},$$

$$\mathbf{y}^1 = \begin{bmatrix} 0.599 \\ 0.067 \\ 0.333 \end{bmatrix}$$

Step 2: $k = 1$:

$$\mathbf{net}^1 = \begin{bmatrix} 0.520 \\ -0.120 \\ 0.120 \end{bmatrix}, \quad \mathbf{y}^2 = \begin{bmatrix} 0.520 \\ 0 \\ 0.120 \end{bmatrix}$$

Step 3: $k = 2$:

$$\mathbf{net}^2 = \begin{bmatrix} 0.480 \\ -0.14 \\ 0.096 \end{bmatrix}, \quad \mathbf{y}^3 = \begin{bmatrix} 0.480 \\ 0 \\ 0.096 \end{bmatrix}$$

Step 4: $k = 3$:

$$\mathbf{net}^3 = \begin{bmatrix} 0.461 \\ -0.115 \\ -10^{-7} \end{bmatrix}, \quad \mathbf{y}^4 = \begin{bmatrix} 0.461 \\ 0 \\ 0 \end{bmatrix}$$

This terminates the recursion, since for further recurrences all values of $\mathbf{y}^{k+1} = \mathbf{y}^4$, for $k > 3$. Notice that the thresholding began in Step 2 due to the conditions at the second neuron of the MAXNET. The activation value $net_2^1 = -0.12$ has resulted in the output $y_2^2 = 0$ in this step. This has obviously slowed down the rate of decrease of other nonzero outputs and, more importantly, of y_1. The result computed by the network after four recurrences indicates that the vector $\mathbf{x}$ presented at the input for the minimum Hamming distance classification has been at the smallest HD from $\mathbf{s}^{(1)}$ and, therefore, it represents the distorted character C. ■

Let us summarize the benefits of the discussed neural network architecture. As stated, the Hamming net and MAXNET jointly implement the optimum minimum bit error classification. Let us compare the size of this classifier with its Hopfield autoassociator network counterpart. Assume that a classifier needs to classify a 50-tuple vector belonging to one of the five classes. The Hamming network requires a total of 255 connections to 5 neurons. For comparison, a Hopfield autoassociative memory would involve 2450 connections to 50 neurons. In addition, Hopfield memory is sensitive to the HD parameter within the set of stored patterns. As a result of a random search for the minimum of the energy, Hopfield network may produce spurious responses. Also, the network has rather stringent capacity limits.

This comparison indicates that the Hamming network looks somewhat advantageous as a minimum HD classifier. Moreover, the network is rather straightforward to build and, excluding its MAXNET stage, is of the simple feedforward type. However, the Hamming network retrieves only the closest class index and not the entire prototype vector. The Hamming network is therefore not able to restore any of the key pattern vector entries, if input is a corrupted version of the stored prototype, but can only provide the closest similarity measure of the input to the set of prototypes. We should thus realize that the Hamming network is only a pure classifier and not an autoassociative memory. It provides passive classification and has no built-in data restoration mechanisms. Such mechanisms are naturally embedded, however, in recurrent autoassociative architectures.

The reader has undoubtedly noticed that Hamming network and MAXNET weights are designed by recording rather than through incremental learning, whether supervised or unsupervised. We decided to study Hamming networks in the chapter dealing with unsupervised learning networks, however, because Hamming distance classifiers use the same similarity measure as many of the neural networks that learn in an unsupervised environment. Namely, the network detects the match between the stored prototype and the key vector by computing and comparing their scalar product. This is accomplished by encoding the prototype vector into respective weights of the neurons being the class indicator for this specific prototype.

7.2

UNSUPERVISED LEARNING OF CLUSTERS

Our discussion thus far has focused on the classification, recognition, and association tasks performed by neural networks that have been previously trained. The training has been either supervised, or network parameters have been explicitly computed based on the design requirements in lieu of training. We have consistently assumed the existence of a training set containing both inputs and required responses. In this section we present unsupervised classification learning. The learning is based on clustering of input data. No *a priori* knowledge is assumed to be available regarding an input's membership in a particular class. Rather, gradually detected characteristics and a history of training will be used to assist the network in defining classes and possible boundaries between them.

Such unsupervised classification, called *clustering,* can possibly be thought of as primary compared to a classification of membership in classes that have already been formed. In fact, evolutionary learning by humans must have originated thousands of years ago in an unsupervised form, since there were no teachers, instructions, templates, or books then. Over the years, all known living things, for example, have first been classified as belonging to certain clusters according to their observable characteristics. The single and sensible criterion used has been the objects' similarities within a cluster. As a result of this grouping, clusters were labeled with appropriate names that best reflect their characteristics. Later on, objects were given names following more detailed classification criteria that were developed within clusters.

The objective of clustering neural networks discussed in this section is to categorize or cluster data. The classes must first be found from the correlations of an input data stream. Since the network actually deals with unlabeled data, the clustering should be followed by labeling clusters with appropriate category names or numbers. This process of providing the category of objects with a label is usually termed as *calibration.*

Clustering and Similarity Measures

Clustering is understood to be the grouping of similar objects and separating of dissimilar ones. Suppose we are given a set of patterns without any information as to the number of classes that may be present in the set. The clustering problem in such a case is that of identifying the number of classes according to a certain criterion, and of assigning the membership of the patterns in these classes. The clustering technique presented below assumes that the number of classes is known *a priori.* The pattern set $\{\mathbf{x}_1, \mathbf{x}_2, \ldots, \mathbf{x}_N\}$ is submitted to the

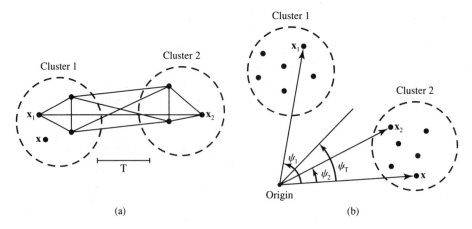

Figure 7.5 Measures of similarity for clustering data: (a) distance and (b) a normalized scalar product.

input to determine decision functions required to identify possible clusters. Since no information is available from the teacher as far as the desired classifier's responses, we will use the similarity of incoming patterns as the criterion for clustering.

To define a cluster, we need to establish a basis for assigning patterns to the domain of a particular cluster. The most common similarity rule, already used in Chapter 3, is the Euclidean distance between two patterns $\mathbf{x}$, for $\mathbf{x}_i$ defined as

$$\|\mathbf{x} - \mathbf{x}_i\| = \sqrt{(\mathbf{x} - \mathbf{x}_i)^t(\mathbf{x} - \mathbf{x}_i)} \tag{7.7}$$

This rule of similarity is simple: the smaller the distance, the closer the patterns. Using (7.7), the distances between all pairs of points are computed. A distance T can then be chosen to discriminate clusters. The value T is understood as the maximum distance between patterns within a single cluster. Figure 7.5(a) shows an example of two clusters with a T value chosen to be greater than the typical within-cluster distance but smaller than the between-cluster distance.

Another similarity rule is the cosine of the angle between $\mathbf{x}$ and $\mathbf{x}_i$:

$$\cos \psi = \frac{\mathbf{x}^t\mathbf{x}_i}{\|\mathbf{x}\| \cdot \|\mathbf{x}_i\|} \tag{7.8}$$

This rule is particularly useful when clusters develop along certain principal and different axes as shown in Figure 7.5(b). For $\cos \psi_2 < \cos \psi_1$, pattern $\mathbf{x}$ is more similar to $\mathbf{x}_2$ than to $\mathbf{x}_1$. It would thus be natural to group it with the second of the two apparent clusters. To facilitate this decision, the threshold angle ψ_T can be chosen to define the minimum angular cluster distance. It should be noted, however, that the measure defined in (7.8) should be used according to certain additional qualifications. If the angular similarity criterion (7.8) is to be efficient, vectors $\mathbf{x}_1$, $\mathbf{x}_2$, and $\mathbf{x}$ should be of comparable, or better, identical lengths.

A number of traditional cluster search algorithms such as maximum-distance, K-means, and isodata, are used in pattern recognition techniques (Tou and Gonzalez 1974; Duda and Hart 1973). In our presentation, we will focus on techniques that involve weight training and employ connectionist algorithms for building clusters rather than on conventional clustering methods.

Winner-Take-All Learning

The network discussed in this section classifies input vectors into one of the specified number of p categories according to the clusters detected in the training set $\{\mathbf{x}_1, \mathbf{x}_2, \ldots, \mathbf{x}_N\}$. The training is performed in an unsupervised mode, and the network undergoes the self-organization process. During the training, dissimilar vectors are rejected, and only one, the most similar, is accepted for weight building. As mentioned, it is impossible in this training method to assign network nodes to specific input classes in advance. It is equally impossible to predict which neurons will be activated by members of particular clusters at the beginning of the training. This node to cluster assignment is, however, easily done by calibrating the network after training.

The network to be trained is called the *Kohonen network* (Kohonen 1988) and is shown in Figure 7.6(a). The processing of input data $\mathbf{x}$ from the training set $\{\mathbf{x}_1, \mathbf{x}_2, \ldots, \mathbf{x}_N\}$, which represents p clusters, follows the customary expression

$$\mathbf{y} = \Gamma[\mathbf{W}\mathbf{x}] \tag{7.9}$$

with diagonal elements of the operator Γ being continuous activation functions operating componentwise on entries of vector $\mathbf{W}\mathbf{x}$. The processing by the layer of neurons is instantaneous and feedforward. To analyze network performance, we rearrange the matrix $\mathbf{W}$ to the following form:

$$\mathbf{W} = \begin{bmatrix} \mathbf{w}_1^t \\ \mathbf{w}_2^t \\ \vdots \\ \mathbf{w}_p^t \end{bmatrix}$$

where

$$\mathbf{w}_i = \begin{bmatrix} w_{i1} \\ w_{i2} \\ \vdots \\ w_{in} \end{bmatrix}, \quad \text{for } i = 1, 2, \ldots, p$$

is the column vector equal to the i'th row of the weight matrix $\mathbf{W}$. Component weights of $\mathbf{w}_m$ are highlighted in Figure 7.6(a) showing a winner-take-all learning network. The learning algorithm treats the set of p weight vectors as variable

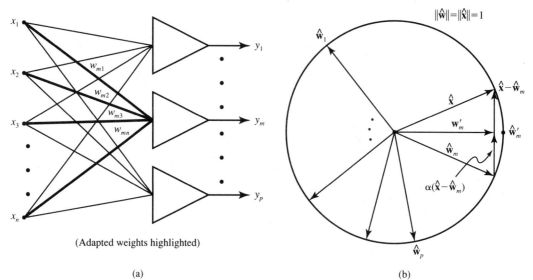

(Adapted weights highlighted)

(a)

$$\|\hat{\mathbf{w}}\|=\|\hat{\mathbf{x}}\|=1$$

(b)

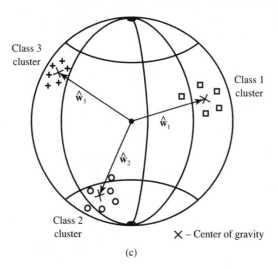

$\times$ – Center of gravity

(c)

Figure 7.6 Winner-take-all learning rule: (a) learning layer, (b) vector diagram, and (c) weight vectors on a unity sphere for $p = n = 3$.

vectors that need to be learned. Prior to the learning, the normalization of all weight vectors is required:

$$\hat{\mathbf{w}}_i \triangleq \frac{\mathbf{w}_i}{\|\mathbf{w}_i\|}, \quad \text{for } i = 1, 2, \ldots, p$$

The weight adjustment criterion for this mode of training is the selection of $\hat{\mathbf{w}}_i$

such that

$$\|\mathbf{x} - \hat{\mathbf{w}}_m\| = \min_{i=1,2,\dots,p} \{\|\mathbf{x} - \hat{\mathbf{w}}_i\|\} \tag{7.10}$$

The index m denotes the winning neuron number corresponding to the vector $\hat{\mathbf{w}}_m$, which is the closest approximation of the current input $\mathbf{x}$. Let us see how this learning should proceed in terms of weight adjustments. The left side of Equation (7.10) can be rearranged to the form

$$\|\mathbf{x} - \hat{\mathbf{w}}_m\| = (\mathbf{x}^t\mathbf{x} - 2\hat{\mathbf{w}}_m^t\mathbf{x} - 1)^{1/2} \tag{7.11}$$

It is obvious from (7.11) that searching for the minimum of p distances as on the right side of (7.10) corresponds to finding the maximum among the p scalar products

$$\hat{\mathbf{w}}_m^t\mathbf{x} = \max_{i=1,2,\dots,p} (\hat{\mathbf{w}}_i^t\mathbf{x}) \tag{7.12}$$

The left side of Equation (7.12) is the activation value of the "winning" neuron which has the largest value net_i, $i = 1, 2, \dots, p$. When using the scalar product metric of similarity as in (7.12), the synaptic weight vectors should be modified accordingly so that they become more similar to the current input vector. With the similarity criterion being $\cos \psi$ as in (7.8), the weight vector lengths should be identical for this training approach. However, their directions should be modified. Intuitively, it is clear that a very long weight vector could lead to a large output of its neuron even if there were a large angle between the weight vector and the pattern. This explains the need for weight normalization.

After the winning neuron has been identified and declared a winner, its weights must be adjusted so that the distance (7.10) is reduced in the current training step. Thus, $\|\mathbf{x} - \mathbf{w}_m\|$ must be reduced, preferably along the gradient direction in the weight space $w_{m1}, w_{m2}, \dots, w_{mn}$

$$\nabla_{\mathbf{w}_m} \|\mathbf{x} - \mathbf{w}_m\|^2 = -2(\mathbf{x} - \mathbf{w}_m) \tag{7.13a}$$

Since vectors $\mathbf{x}$ have a certain probability distribution within a cluster and we are dealing with a single adjustment step due to the single realization of the input, only a fraction of the increment in (7.13a) should be involved in producing the sensible weight adjustments. It seems reasonable to reward the weights of the winning neuron with an increment of weight in the negative gradient direction, thus in the direction $\mathbf{x} - \mathbf{w}_m$. We thus have

$$\Delta\hat{\mathbf{w}}_m' = \alpha(\mathbf{x} - \hat{\mathbf{w}}_m) \tag{7.13b}$$

where α is a small learning constant selected heuristically, usually between 0.1 and 0.7. The remaining weight vectors $\hat{\mathbf{w}}_i$, $i \neq m$, are left unaffected. Note that the rule is identical to Equation (2.46) introduced in Chapter 2 in the framework of learning rules.

Using a superscript to index the weight updates and restating the update criterion (7.10), the learning rule (7.13b) in the k'th step can be rewritten in a more formal way as follows:

$$\hat{\mathbf{w}}_m^{k+1} = \hat{\mathbf{w}}_m^k + \alpha^k(\mathbf{x} - \hat{\mathbf{w}}_m^k) \tag{7.13c}$$

$$\hat{\mathbf{w}}_i^{k+1} = \hat{\mathbf{w}}_i^k, \quad \text{for } i \neq m \tag{7.13d}$$

where α^k is a suitable learning constant and m is the number of the winning neuron selected based on the scalar product comparison as in (7.12). While learning continues and clusters are developed, the network weights acquire similarity to input data within clusters. To prevent further unconstrained growth of weights, α is usually reduced monotonically and the learning slows down.

Learning according to Equations (7.12) and (7.13) is called *"winner-take-all" learning,* and it is a common competitive and unsupervised learning technique. The winning node with the largest net_i is rewarded with a weight adjustment, while the weights of the others remain unaffected.

This mode of learning is easy to implement as a computer simulation; one merely searches for the maximum response and rewards the winning weights only. In a real network it is possible to implement a winner-take-all layer by using units with lateral inhibition to the other neurons in the form of inhibitory connections. At the same time, the neuron should possess excitatory connections to itself like in the MAXNET network. Since all the weights must, in addition to providing stable operation of the layer, be modifiable as a result of combined excitatory/inhibitory interactions, such layers may not be easy to develop as a physical neural network capable of meaningful learning.

Let us look at the impact of the learning rule (7.13c) and (7.13d) on the performance of the network. The rule should increase the chances of winning by the m'th neuron as in (7.12) for repetition of the same input pattern using the updated weights. If the requirement holds, then inequality (7.14a) should be valid for the new weights $\hat{\mathbf{w}}_m'$

$$\hat{\mathbf{w}}_m^t \mathbf{x} < (\hat{\mathbf{w}}_m^t + \Delta\hat{\mathbf{w}}_m^t)\mathbf{x} \tag{7.14a}$$

Using (7.13) we obtain

$$\Delta\mathbf{w}_m^t \mathbf{x} > 0 \tag{7.14b}$$

or

$$\mathbf{x}^t \mathbf{x} - \hat{\mathbf{w}}_m^t \mathbf{x} > 0 \tag{7.14c}$$

which is equivalent to

$$\|\mathbf{x}'\| \cdot \|\mathbf{x}\| \cos 0 - \|\hat{\mathbf{w}}_m^t\| \cdot \|\mathbf{x}\| \cos \psi > 0 \tag{7.14d}$$

Assuming normalized vectors $\hat{\mathbf{x}} = \mathbf{x}$ reduces (7.14d) to

$$1 - \cos \psi > 0 \tag{7.14e}$$

where $\psi = \angle(\hat{\mathbf{w}}, \hat{\mathbf{x}})$. Since (7.14e) is always true, the winner-take-all learning rule produces an update of the weight vector in the proper direction.

It is instructive to observe the geometrical interpretation of the rule. Consider that weights are represented as vectors in Figure 7.6(b). Assume that in this step the normalized input vector denoted as $\hat{\mathbf{x}}$ and the vector $\hat{\mathbf{w}}_m$ yield the maximum scalar product $\hat{\mathbf{w}}_i^t \hat{\mathbf{x}}$, for $i = 1, 2, \ldots, p$. Next, a difference vector $\hat{\mathbf{x}} - \hat{\mathbf{w}}_m$ is created as shown. To implement the rule of (7.13c) and (7.13d) for $\mathbf{x} = \hat{\mathbf{x}}$, an increment of the weight vector is computed as a fraction of $\hat{\mathbf{x}} - \hat{\mathbf{w}}_m$. The result of weight adjustment in this training step is mainly the rotation of the weight vector $\hat{\mathbf{w}}_m$ toward the input vector without a significant length change. The adjusted weight vector results as $\mathbf{w}_m'$ and is of a length below unity. To begin with the new training step, $\mathbf{w}_m'$ must be renormalized. Let us notice that another input belonging to the m'th cluster would make the vector $\mathbf{w}_m$ even more representative of the cluster m.

In the long term this learning mode leads to the weight vectors that approximate the ensembles of past winning input vectors. However, since the weights are adjusted in proportion to the number of events that end up with weight adjustments, this network reacts to the probability of occurrence of inputs. In this context, the network may be used as a clustering network for the particular probability of training vectors coming from each cluster. After the learning is completed, each $\hat{\mathbf{w}}_i$ represents the centroid of an i'th decision region, $i = 1, 2, \ldots, p$, created in the n-dimensional space of the pattern data. On the other side, the network possesses an interesting feature sensitivity, which will be discussed later in this chapter in more detail. In summary, vectors $\hat{\mathbf{w}}$ after training will become organized much like the set of example vectors $\hat{\mathbf{x}}$ used for training.

Note that the neurons' activation function is of no relevance for this learning mode. Figure 7.6(c) illustrates an example of three weight vectors of unity length that have acquired the direction of an average pattern cluster. The case shown is for three clusters and three-dimensional input patterns. It can be seen that the normalized weights approximate the centers of gravity of their respective clusters, which are represented each by a point on the surface of a unit sphere and marked by a cross.

Another learning extension is possible for this network when the proper class for some patterns is known *a priori* (Simpson 1990). Although this means that the encoding of data into weights is then becoming supervised, this information accelerates the learning process significantly. Weight adjustments are computed in the supervised mode as in (7.13b) and only for correct classifications. For improper clustering responses of the network, the weight adjustment carries the opposite sign compared to formula (7.13b). We may thus notice that $\alpha > 0$ for proper node responses, and $\alpha < 0$ otherwise, in the supervised learning mode for the Kohonen layer.

Another modification of the winner-take-all learning rule is that both the winners' and losers' weights are adjusted in proportion to their level of responses. This may be called *leaky competitive learning* and should provide more subtle learning in the cases for which clusters may be hard to distinguish.

Recall Mode

The network trained in the winner-take-all mode responds instantaneously during feedforward recall at all p neuron outputs. The response is computed according to (7.9). Note that the layer now performs as a filter of the input vectors such that the largest output neuron is found as follows

$$y_m = \max{(y_1, y_2, \ldots, y_p)}$$

and the input is identified as belonging to cluster m. In general, the neurons' activation functions should be continuous in this network. For some applications, however, $y_m = 1$ and $y_i = 0$, $i \neq m$, must be set in the recall mode of the clustering layer. In this way, for example, the weights of the following layer can be fanned out from the activated node of this previous layer while other nodes remain suppressed.

Before a one-to-one vector-to-cluster mapping can be made after the network is trained in the unsupervised mode, it needs to be calibrated in a supervised environment. The calibration involves the teacher applying a sequence of p best matching class/cluster inputs and labeling the output nodes 1, 2, ..., p, respectively, according to their observed responses. Obviously, the calibrating labels assigned to the physical neurons of the layer would vary from training to training depending on the sequence of data within the training set, the training parameters, and the initial weights. Once the clustering network is labeled, it can perform as a cluster classifier in a local representation.

Initialization of Weights

As stated before, preferably random initial weight vectors would be used for this training. This indicates that initial weights should be uniformly distributed on the unity hypersphere in n-dimensional pattern space. Self-organization of the network using the described training concept suffers from some limitations, however. One obvious deficiency related to a single-layer architecture is that linearly nonseparable patterns cannot be efficiently handled by this network. The second limitation is that network training may not always be successful even for linearly separable patterns. Weights may get stuck in isolated regions without forming adequate clusters. In such cases the training must be reinitialized with new initial weights, or noise superimposed on weight vectors during the training. After the weights have been trained to provide coarse clustering, the learning constant α should be reduced to produce finer adjustments. This often results in finer weight tuning within each cluster.

One of the weight selection methods developed for training the network is called *convex combination* (Hecht-Nielsen 1987). In this method all weight vectors are initialized at the value

$$\mathbf{w}_i^0 = \frac{1}{\sqrt{n}} \begin{bmatrix} 1 & 1 & \dots & 1 \end{bmatrix}^t, \quad \text{for } i = 1, 2, \dots, p$$

The learning starts at the weights as above and proceeds as in expression (7.13c) and (7.13d) with a very low α value. This forces the weight vectors at the beginning of learning to be close to the input vectors and to have equal lengths. As learning progresses, α is slowly increased. This allows for the gradual separation of weights according to the input clusters used for training. This procedure improves the chances for successful training, but does slow down the process.

The simple winner-take-all training algorithm activates only one output neuron for each input vector; it thus provides local representation. The training approach can be modified, however, to a form in which K winners in the competition are considered and awarded weight increases accordingly. Such learning is called *multiple-winner unsupervised learning*. The winning K neurons would be the ones best matching the input vector, instead of a single one as in the winner-take-all mode. The outputs of winning neurons can be set so that they sum to unity. This interpolation process usually leads to an increased mapping accuracy in applications using the winner-take-all layer as the first layer. A network using this approach is said to be operating in an interpolative mode (Hecht-Nielsen 1987).

EXAMPLE 7.2

We present here an example of a two-cluster case and provide a simple geometrical interpretation of winner-take-all network training based on the criterion of Equation (7.12). The iterative weight adjustment is unsupervised. The patterns are from a normalized example training set:

$$\{\mathbf{x}_1, \mathbf{x}_2, \mathbf{x}_3, \mathbf{x}_4, \mathbf{x}_5\} = \left\{ \begin{bmatrix} 0.8 \\ 0.6 \end{bmatrix}, \begin{bmatrix} 0.1736 \\ -0.9848 \end{bmatrix}, \begin{bmatrix} 0.707 \\ 0.707 \end{bmatrix}, \right. $$
$$\left. \begin{bmatrix} 0.342 \\ -0.9397 \end{bmatrix}, \begin{bmatrix} 0.6 \\ 0.8 \end{bmatrix} \right\} \tag{7.15a}$$

The set of test vectors is shown in Figure 7.7(a). Two output neurons, $p = 2$, have been selected to identify two possible clusters. The normalized initial weights selected at random are

$$\mathbf{w}_1^0 = \begin{bmatrix} 1 \\ 0 \end{bmatrix}, \mathbf{w}_2^0 = \begin{bmatrix} -1 \\ 0 \end{bmatrix}$$

The inputs are submitted in ascending sequence from the set as in (7.15a) and recycled $\mathbf{x}_1, \mathbf{x}_2, \dots, \mathbf{x}_5, \mathbf{x}_1, \mathbf{x}_2 \dots$. Let us evaluate the adjustments of weight vectors during learning. The reader can verify that for $\alpha = \frac{1}{2}$ we

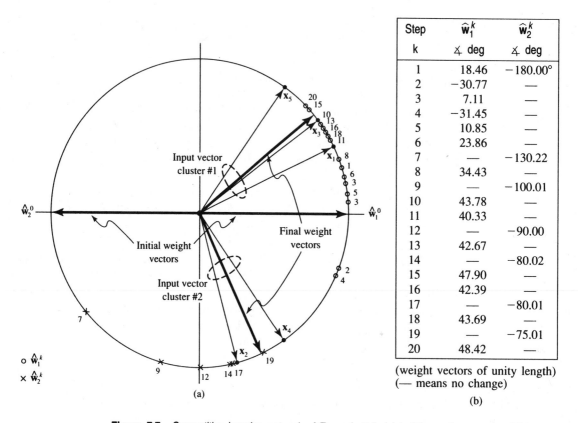

Step	$\hat{\mathbf{w}}_1^k$	$\hat{\mathbf{w}}_2^k$
k	∡ deg	∡ deg
1	18.46	−180.00°
2	−30.77	—
3	7.11	—
4	−31.45	—
5	10.85	—
6	23.86	—
7	—	−130.22
8	34.43	—
9	—	−100.01
10	43.78	—
11	40.33	—
12	—	−90.00
13	42.67	—
14	—	−80.02
15	47.90	—
16	42.39	—
17	—	−80.01
18	43.69	—
19	—	−75.01
20	48.42	—

(weight vectors of unity length)
(— means no change)

(b)

Figure 7.7 Competitive learning network of Example 7.2: (a) training patterns and weight assignments and (b) weight learning, Steps 1 through 20.

obtain from (7.13b) and (7.13c) after renormalization

$$\hat{\mathbf{w}}_1^1 = \begin{bmatrix} 0.948 \\ 0.316 \end{bmatrix}, \quad \mathbf{w}_2^1 = \begin{bmatrix} -1 \\ 0 \end{bmatrix}$$

This is because the first neuron becomes the winner with $\mathbf{x}_1$ as input. For convenience we convert the training set (7.15a) to the polar form as follows:

$$\{\mathbf{x}_1, \mathbf{x}_2, \mathbf{x}_3, \mathbf{x}_4, \mathbf{x}_5\} = \{1∡36.87°, 1∡−80°, 1∡45°,$$
$$1∡−70°, 1∡53.13°\} \tag{7.15b}$$

Since $\hat{\mathbf{w}}_1^1 = 1∡18.46°$, it can be seen that $\hat{\mathbf{w}}_1$ has moved from its initial position $1∡0°$ toward the potential first quadrant cluster. Note that the weights of the second neuron, $\hat{\mathbf{w}}_2$, are unaffected in the first training step. The next training step with input $\mathbf{x}_2$ produces $\hat{\mathbf{w}}_1^2 = 1∡−30.77°$, and $\hat{\mathbf{w}}_2^2 = 1∡180°$, since node 1 is again the winner. The iterative weight adjustments continue. Figure 7.7(b) shows the tabulated results of weight iterations for $k \leq 20$.

Analysis of two data clusters produced by the network indicates that $\mathbf{x}_1$, $\mathbf{x}_3$, and $\mathbf{x}_5$ belong to the first quadrant cluster with the center at

$$\frac{\mathbf{x}_1 + \mathbf{x}_3 + \mathbf{x}_5}{3} = 1 \angle 45°$$

Similarly, $\mathbf{x}_2$ and $\mathbf{x}_4$ form another cluster in the fourth quadrant located at

$$\frac{\mathbf{x}_2 + \mathbf{x}_4}{2} = 1 \angle -75°$$

For large k, weight vectors tend to become stabilized as follows: the first neuron weights center around $1 \angle 45°$ and the second neuron weights center around $1 \angle -75°$. The geometrical interpretation of weight vector displacement during learning shown on the unity circle of Figure 7.7(b) also indicates that the learning has been successful. Weight vectors $\hat{\mathbf{w}}^1$, $\hat{\mathbf{w}}^2$, ... are marked in the unity circle as points indexed 1, 2, 3, ... 20. We may notice, however, that the first neuron won all of the first six competitions in a row and initially started representing both data clusters at the same time. Despite that initial takeover, during the second training cycle, the cluster containing $\mathbf{x}_2$ and $\mathbf{x}_4$ has been detected and identified by the second neuron. Its respective weights were later reinforced during cycles 3 and 4. Finally, the weight values of the second neuron were organized by acquiring the values of second cluster inputs.   ■

Separability Limitations

We now see that winner-take-all learning can successfully produce single-layer clustering/classifying networks. However, the networks will only be trainable using the criterion of Equation (7.12) if classes/clusters of patterns are linearly separable from other classes by hyperplanes passing through origin. This is illustrated in Figure 7.8(a), which shows an example of three-class classification in the pattern space as generated by the trained network.

In the case shown, three distinct clusters can be identified and classified. The weights responsible for clustering are marked $\mathbf{w}_1^f$, $\mathbf{w}_2^f$, and $\mathbf{w}_3^f$. The scalar product metric-based clustering is impossible, however, for patterns distributed as shown in Figure 7.8(b). Since only a single neuron has the strongest response, the winner-take-all rule precludes that the same neuron would at the same time respond if patterns are on the negative side of the partitioning hyperplane. Adding trainable thresholds to neurons' inputs may improve separability conditions. Even then, however, the two neuron network will not be able to learn the solution of an XOR problem, or similar linearly nonseparable tasks. An excessive number of neurons created in the winner-take-all layer could certainly also be of significance when learning difficult clustering.

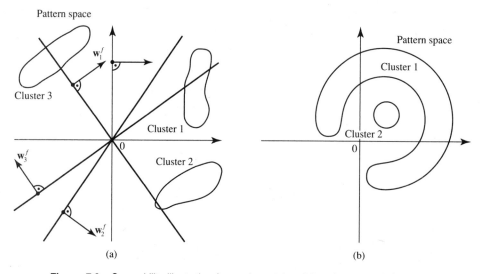

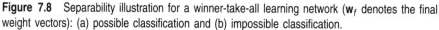

Figure 7.8 Separability illustration for a winner-take-all learning network ($\mathbf{w}_f$ denotes the final weight vectors): (a) possible classification and (b) impossible classification.

To ensure the separability of clusters with *a priori* unknown numbers of training clusters, the unsupervised training can be performed with an excessive number of neurons, which provides a certain separability safety margin. During the training, some neurons are likely not to develop their weights, and if their weights change chaotically, they will not be considered as indicative of clusters. Therefore, such weights can be omitted during the recall phase, since their outputs do not provide any essential clustering information. The weights of the remaining neurons should settle at values that are indicative of clusters.

7.3

COUNTERPROPAGATION NETWORK

The counterpropagation network is a two-layer network consisting of two feedforward layers. The network was introduced by Hecht-Nielsen (1987, 1988). In its simplest version, it is able to perform vector-to-vector mapping similar to heteroassociative memory networks. Compared to bidirectional associative memory, there is no feedback and delay activated during the recall operation mode. The advantage of the counterpropagation network is that it can be trained to perform associative mappings much faster than a typical two-layer network. The counterpropagation network is useful in pattern mapping and associations, data compression, and classification.

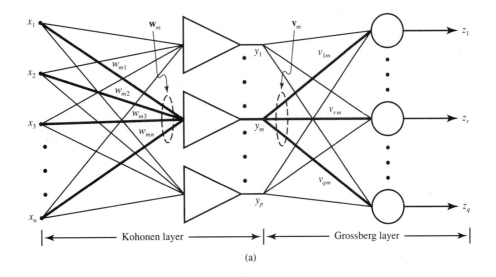

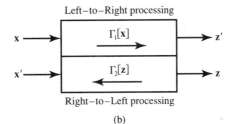

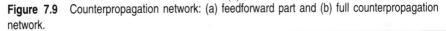

Figure 7.9 Counterpropagation network: (a) feedforward part and (b) full counterpropagation network.

The network is essentially a partially self-organizing look-up table that maps $\mathbb{R}^n$ into $\mathbb{R}^q$ and is taught in response to a set of training examples. The objective of the counterpropagation network is to map input data vectors $\mathbf{x}_i$ into bipolar binary responses $\mathbf{z}_i$, for $i = 1, 2, \ldots, p$. We assume that data vectors can be arranged into p clusters, and that the training data are noisy versions of vectors $\mathbf{x}_i$. The essential part of the counterpropagation network structure is shown in Figure 7.9. It resembles, at first glance, the class of layered feedforward networks covered in Chapter 4. However, counterpropagation combines two different, novel learning strategies, and neither of them is the gradient descent technique. The network's recall operation is also different than for any previously seen architecture.

The first layer of the network is the Kohonen layer, which is trained in the unsupervised winner-take-all mode described in the previous section. Each of the Kohonen layer neurons represents an input cluster, or pattern class, so if the layer works in local representation, this particular neuron's input and response are the largest. Similar input vectors belonging to the same cluster activate the same m'th neuron of the Kohonen layer among all p neurons available in this layer. Note that first-layer neurons are assumed with continuous activation function during learning. However, during recall they respond with the binary unipolar values 0 and 1. Specifically, when recalling with input representing a cluster, for example, m, the output vector $\mathbf{y}$ of the Kohonen layer becomes

$$\begin{bmatrix} y_1 & y_2 & \cdots & y_m & \cdots & y_p \end{bmatrix} = \begin{bmatrix} 0 & 0 & \cdots & 1 & \cdots & 0 \end{bmatrix} \qquad (7.16)$$

Such a response can be generated as a result of lateral inhibitions within the layer which would need to be activated during recall in a physical system. The second layer is called the *Grossberg layer* due to its outstar learning mode (Grossberg 1974, 1982) as discussed in Chapter 2. The Grossberg layer, with weights v_{ij}, functions in a familiar manner

$$\mathbf{z} = \Gamma[\mathbf{Vy}] \qquad (7.17)$$

with diagonal elements of the operator Γ being a sgn $(\cdot)$ function operating componentwise on entries of the vector $\mathbf{Vy}$. Let us denote the column vectors of the weight matrix $\mathbf{V}$ as $\mathbf{v}_1, \mathbf{v}_2, \ldots, \mathbf{v}_m, \ldots, \mathbf{v}_p$. Now, each weight vector $\mathbf{v}_m$ for $i = 1, 2, \ldots, p$, contains entries that are weights fanning out from the m'th neuron of the Kohonen layer. Substituting (7.16) into (7.17) results in

$$\mathbf{z} = \Gamma[\mathbf{v}_m] \qquad (7.18)$$

$$\text{where } \mathbf{v}_m = \begin{bmatrix} v_{1m} & v_{2m} & \cdots & v_{qm} \end{bmatrix}^t$$

As can be seen, the operation of this layer with bipolar binary neurons is simply to output $z_i = 1$ if $v_{im} > 0$, and $z_i = -1$ if $v_{im} < 0$, for $i = 1, 2, \ldots, q$. By assigning just any positive and negative values for weights v_{im} highlighted in Figure 7.9, a desired vector-to-vector mapping $\mathbf{x} \rightarrow \mathbf{y} \rightarrow \mathbf{z}$ can be implemented by this architecture. This is done under the assumption that the Kohonen layer responds as expressed in (7.16). The target vector $\mathbf{z}$ for each cluster must be available for learning so that the weight components of $\mathbf{v}_m$ can be appropriately made equal to $+1$ or -1 according to

$$\mathbf{v}_m = \mathbf{z} \qquad (7.19)$$

However, this is a somewhat oversimplified weight learning rule for this layer. This rule, which is of the batch type rather than incremental, would be appropriate if no statistical relationship existed between input and output vectors within the training pairs $(\mathbf{x}, \mathbf{z})$. In practice, such relationships often exist and they also would need to be established in the network during training.

    As discussed in the previous section, the training rule for the Kohonen layer has involved the adjustment of weight vectors in proportion to the probability of the occurrence and distribution of winning events. Using the outstar learning rule of Equation (7.17) incrementally and not binarily as in (7.19) permits us to treat a stationary additive noise in output $\mathbf{z}$ in a manner similar to the way we considered distributed clusters during the training of the Kohonen layer with "noisy" inputs. The outstar learning rule makes use of the fact that the learning of vector pairs, denoted by the set of mappings $\{(\mathbf{x}_1, \mathbf{z}_1), \dots, (\mathbf{x}_p, \mathbf{z}_p)\}$, will be done gradually and thus involve eventual statistical balancing within the weight matrix $\mathbf{V}$. The supervised learning rule for this layer in such a case becomes incremental and takes the form of the outstar learning rule defined in (2.48):

$$\Delta \mathbf{v}_m = \beta(\mathbf{z} - \mathbf{v}_m) \tag{7.20}$$

where β is set to approximately 0.1 at the beginning of learning and is gradually reduced during the training process (Wasserman 1989). Index m denotes the number of the winning neuron in the Kohonen layer. Vectors $\mathbf{z}_i$, $i = 1, 2, \dots, p$, used for training are stationary random process vectors with statistical properties that make the training plausible.

Note that the supervised outstar rule learning according to (7.20) starts after completion of the unsupervised training of the first layer. Also, as indicated, the weight of the Grossberg layer is adjusted if and only if it fans out from a winning neuron of the Kohonen layer. As training progresses, the weights of the second layer tend to converge to the average value of the desired outputs. Let us also note that the unsupervised training of the first layer produces active outputs at indeterminate positions. The second layer introduces ordering in the mapping so that the network becomes a desirable look-up memory table. During the normal recall mode, the Grossberg layer outputs weight values $\mathbf{z} = \mathbf{v}_m$ connecting each output node to the winning first layer neuron. No processing, except for addition and sgn (net) computation, is performed by the output layer neurons if outputs are binary bipolar vectors.

The network discussed and shown in Figure 7.9(a) is simply feedforward and does not refer to the counterflow of signals for which the original network was named. The full version of the counterpropagation network makes use of bidirectional signal flow. The entire network consists of the doubled network from Figure 7.9(a). It can be simultaneously both trained and operated in the recall mode in an arrangement such as that shown in Figure 7.9(b). This makes it possible to use it as an autoassociator according to the formula

$$\begin{bmatrix} \mathbf{z}' \\ \mathbf{x}' \end{bmatrix} = \begin{bmatrix} \Gamma_1[\mathbf{x}] \\ \Gamma_2[\mathbf{z}] \end{bmatrix} \tag{7.21}$$

Input signals generated by vector $\mathbf{x}$, input, and by vector $\mathbf{z}$, desired output, propagate through the bidirectional network in opposite directions. Vectors $\mathbf{x}'$ and $\mathbf{z}'$ are respective outputs that are intended to be approximations, or autoassociations, of $\mathbf{x}$ and $\mathbf{z}$, respectively.

Let us summarize the main features of this architecture in its simple feedforward version. The counterpropagation network functions in the recall mode as a nearest match look-up table. The input vector $\mathbf{x}$ finds the weight vector $\mathbf{w}_m$ that is its closest match among p vectors available in the first layer. Then the weights that are entries of vector $\mathbf{v}_m$, and are fanning out from the winning m'th Kohonen's neuron, after $\text{sgn}\,(\cdot)$ computation, become binary outputs. Due to the specific training of the counterpropagation network, it outputs the statistical averages of vector $\mathbf{z}$ associated with input $\mathbf{x}$. In practice, the network performs as well as a look-up table can do to approximate vector matching.

Counterpropagation can also be used as a continuous function approximator. Assume that the training pairs are $(\mathbf{x}_i, \mathbf{z}_i)$ and $\mathbf{z}_i = g(\mathbf{x}_i)$, where g is a continuous function on the set of input vectors $\{\mathbf{x}\}$. The mean square error of approximation can be made as small as desired by choosing a sufficiently large number p of Kohonen's layer neurons. However, for the continuous function approximation, the network is not as efficient as error back-propagation trained networks, since it requires many more neurons for comparable accuracy (Hecht-Nielsen 1990). Counterpropagation networks can be used for rapid prototyping of a mapping and to speed up system development, since they typically require orders of magnitude fewer training cycles than is usually needed in error back-propagation training.

The counterpropagation can use a modified competitive training condition for the Kohonen layer. Thus far we have assumed that the winning neuron, for which weights are adjusted as in (7.13c) and (7.13d), is the one fulfilling condition (7.12) of yielding the maximum scalar product of the weights and the training pattern vector. Another alternative for training is to choose the winning neuron of the Kohonen layer such that instead of (7.12), the minimum distance criterion (7.10) is used directly according to the formula

$$\|\mathbf{x} - \mathbf{w}_m\| = \min_{i=1,2,\ldots,p} \{\|\mathbf{x} - \mathbf{w}_i\|\} \tag{7.22}$$

The remaining aspects of weight adaptation and of the training and recall mode would remain as described in the previous section for criterion (7.12). The only difference is that the weights do not have to be renormalized after each step in this training procedure.

7.4   ▬▬▬▬▬▬▬▬▬▬

FEATURE MAPPING

In this section we focus on the feature mapping capabilities of neural networks. Special attention is devoted to mappings that can be arranged in geometrically regular self-organizing arrays. As discussed in Section 3.1, feature extraction is an important task both for classification or recognition and is often necessary as a preprocessing stage of data. In this way data can be transformed from high-dimensional pattern space to low-dimensional feature space. Our goal in this section is to identify neural architectures that can learn feature mapping

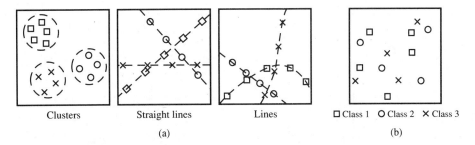

Clusters   Straight lines   Lines   □ Class 1 ○ Class 2 ✕ Class 3

(a)   (b)

Figure 7.10 Pattern structure: (a) natural similarity and (b) no natural similarity.

without supervision. Before introducing such architectures we will first reexamine the concept of features and their extraction.

The patterns in the pattern space can be distributed in two different structures. Although it is hard to define these precisely, we can say the that patterns in Figure 7.10(a) have a certain "natural" structure while the patterns in Figure 7.10(b) do not. The natural structure is often related to pattern clustering or their mutual location in the original pattern space. The natural pattern structure apparently makes the perception of them by a human observer easier. In contrast to the harmonious perception of such classes that show common features, a chaotic mixture of patterns is much more difficult to separate, memorize or classify in any way. The basic difference in identifying "natural" versus "unnatural" patterns structure is that the pattern space may be similar to our human perception space, or they may be different. The mismatch between the pattern space and our perception space is causing the apparent lack of pattern similarity or lack of their natural structure.

In our discussion we are interested in two aspects of mapping features. It is important to reduce the dimensionality of vectors in pattern space when representing these vectors in feature space. To facilitate perception, it is equally important to provide as natural a structure of features as possible. We are interested in easy perception of low-dimension patterns no matter how "unnatural" their distribution may be in the original pattern space.

Some patterns exhibit inherently smaller dimensionality that can be perceived by superficial inspection. The inherent dimensionality reduction results from the explicit relationship that may exist between variables or the correlation between data. The number of degrees of freedom in such relationships can be lower than perceived initially. Figure 7.11 shows an example of constrained freedom pattern data. It depicts the longitudinal displacement d of a point moving with constant acceleration a. Assume that the pattern space is defined as speed v and distance d from the origin. Since the movement parameters are related as $d = v^2/(2a)$, the $d(v)$, motion equation, can be considered one-dimensional in pattern space v, d. This limitation of dimensionality is due to the physical restriction of this motion on the number of degrees of freedom. Most often we

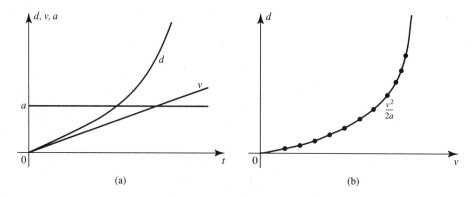

Figure 7.11 Reduction of degree of freedom: (a) movement parameters versus time and (b) pattern space.

are interested in reducing the dimensionality of patterns in feature space in more involved cases when no analytical relationships such as the one documented in Figure 7.11 can be established.

Patterns in multidimensional space, which often can be clustered in one-, two- or three-dimensional feature space, may have a much more complicated structure in the original pattern space. Our goal is to find a self-organizing neural array that consists of neurons arranged in a virtual one-dimensional segment or in a two-dimensional array. Such an array is typically a rectangle or triangle, or a spatial lattice-type connection of neurons within a three-dimensional cuboid. The neurons of such an array are connected to the input vector as shown in Figure 7.12(a) for an example two-dimensional array. Note that each component in the input vector $\mathbf{x}$ is connected to each of the nodes, and the weight w_{ij} transmits the input x_j toward the i'th node of the feature array.

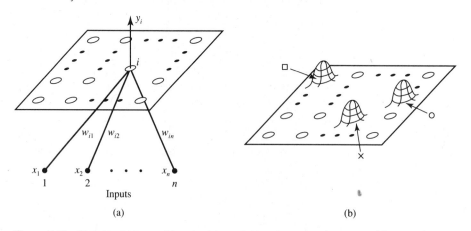

Figure 7.12 Mapping features of input $\mathbf{x}$ into a rectangular array of neurons: (a) general diagram and (b) desirable response peaks for Figure 7.10(b).

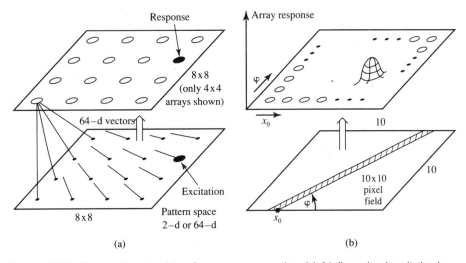

Figure 7.13 Planar pattern to planar feature space mapping: (a) 64-dimensional excitation in pattern space and (b) translation of intercept and angle to planar feature array. [Adapted from Tattershall (1989). © Chapman & Hall; with permission.]

The output y_i of a neuron within the array is a function of similarity S between the input vector $\mathbf{x}$ and $\mathbf{w}_i$ defined as

$$y_i = f\left(S(\mathbf{x}, \mathbf{w}_i)\right) \tag{7.23}$$

We studied in Section 7.2 a simplified version of the unsupervised training of clusters using as the scalar product a similarity metric. Before we exploit similarity metrics any further, let us look at certain interesting aspects of dimensionality reduction.

It seems desirable to filter the input data onto feature space so that the patterns in the image space, as shown in Figure 7.10(b), are mapped into one of the easy to perceive clustering formats. An acceptable arrangement would be that of the leftmost square of Figure 7.10(a). Using the extraction of features architecture of Figure 7.12(a), the planar layer of neurons, called the *feature array,* should possibly display distinct peaks when excited with original patterns. Thus, inputs from classes 1, 2, and 3 should preferably result in perceptually separated excitation peaks as shown in Figure 7.12(b). In the example case illustrated, we map a two-dimensional pattern space into a two-dimensional feature space.

A question arises about the dimensionality of the original planar data. Assume that a number of pattern points are given on the plane or in two-dimensional pattern space. A computational experiment has been designed in which a two-dimensional top array of neurons has been trained using planar input data from the bottom plane (Tattershall 1989). As shown in Figure 7.13(a), the input patterns' dimensionality has been made equal to the number of actual planar inputs.

In the experiment reported, planar data coded as 64-dimensional input vectors from the bottom plane have been used for training of the 8×8 top planar neuron layer shown.

After training, the single excitations of point inputs highlighted on the figure have been successfully mapped into single peaks of neuron responses at positions directly above the excitations. Thus, the one-to-one geometrical mapping of peak responses generated just above excitations indicates that the dimensionality of any pattern data taken from a two-dimensional space is actually only two. The dimensionality of the pattern representation has no significance. Therefore, the described projection of planar data always results in two-dimensional images.

In a related experiment (Tattershall 1989) illustrated in Figure 7.13(b), a straight line within a square 10×10 pixel field has been mapped into a 100-neuron feature array arranged in a square. Since the line has 2 degrees of freedom, two line parameters, which are the intercept with axis and slope, have been produced by the top network trained with 100-dimensional input vectors. The application of a large number of training lines encoded as 100-tuple input vectors causes the feature array to self-organize. Subsequently, an input line forces the output to peak at the corresponding coordinates of intercept and angle. Obviously, calibration of line parameters on the top neural array would also be required after training. The parameter readings can then be made for the performed mapping.

In the following discussion we will look at the details of how regularly shaped neuron layers can arrange and regularize the data from the original pattern space based on a similarity metric. Mappings will be discussed that are at the same time able to preserve pattern space relationships and to reduce the dimensionality of the representation space. The key concept here is the self-organization within a regular array of neurons. This self-organization is demonstrated below based on the lateral feedback concept.

Let us begin by looking for clues about self-organization that may exist in living biological systems. Many biological neural networks in the brain are found to be essentially two-dimensional layers of processing neurons densely interconnected by lateral feedback synapses as shown in Figure 7.14(a). The figure shows a linear array, which is a cross section of a planar array cutting through the neuron i. The biological neurons of the layer have lateral connection strengths that depend on the distance as illustrated in Figure 7.14(b). The immediate neighborhood of the 50- to 100-μm radius is characterized by short-range lateral excitatory connections. The self-feedback produced by each biological neuron connecting to itself is positive. It is expressed by the feedback coefficient value $\gamma > 0$ as shown in the figure. The excitatory area is surrounded by a ring of weaker inhibitory connections of 200- to 500-μm radius (Kohonen 1984). The feedback connections' weights are shaped like a Mexican hat. It is therefore often mentioned in the literature that the layer Figure 7.14(a) displays the "Mexican hat" type of lateral interaction.

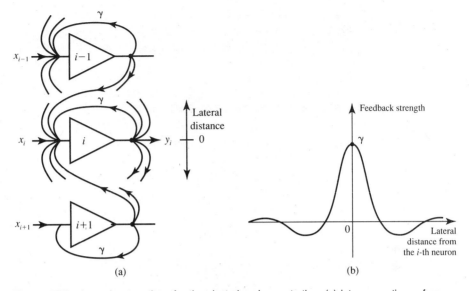

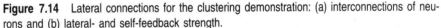

Figure 7.14 Lateral connections for the clustering demonstration: (a) interconnections of neurons and (b) lateral- and self-feedback strength.

It is interesting to observe the response of a planar array of neurons with lateral connections. A two-dimensional layer of neurons responds with an "activity bubble" produced at a location where the input is maximum. The center of the "activity bubble" is the center of the excitation, too. The typical planar array response pattern is shown in Figure 7.15 displaying circular arrays of activated neurons. Reducing positive lateral feedback of individual neurons results

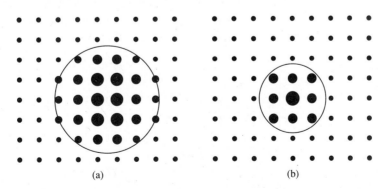

Figure 7.15 Planar activity formation for various strengths of lateral interaction: (a) strong positive feedback and (b) weak positive feedback. [Adapted from Kohonen (1984). © Springer Verlag; with permission.]

in a smaller radius for an activated array. This can be seen from comparison of Figures 7.15(a) and (b). These phenomena are due to the self-organization process. The example below explains and illustrates the observed phenomena in more detail.

EXAMPLE 7.3 ■

Let us look at the self-organization of a linear array of n neurons arranged as shown in Figure 7.16(a). The linear array, or row, of neurons can be thought of as representing an arbitrary cross section through the center of an activity bubble of the planar array, examples of which are presented in Figure 7.15.

The response of the i'th neuron in a linear array can be expressed as

$$y_i(t + 1) = f\left(x_i(t + 1) + \sum_{k=-k_o}^{k_o} y_{i+k}(t)\gamma_k\right) \tag{7.24}$$

The recursive form of Equation (7.24) is due to the small delay in feeding signals $y(t)$ back to the input; the delay value has been normalized here to unity for computational convenience. The feedback coefficients γ_k are shown in Figure 7.16(b) as a function of interneuronal distance. The coefficients represent a discretized feedback strength function that can be thought of as an envelope for γ_k. They are represented as a function of discrete variable k denoting the linear distance rather than as a lateral feedback function defined versus continuous lateral distance. Notice that the neuron's index refers now to the neuron's location in a row. The excitation function for the experiment has been arbitrarily selected with maxima for the fifth and sixth neurons and is defined below in (7.25a). This choice of excitation produces peak local activity formation for the spatial neighborhoods of neurons 5 and 6. Conditions for the simulation experiments are chosen as

$$x_i(t) = 0.5\sin^3\left[\frac{\pi(i + 3)}{17}\right], \quad \text{for } i = 1, 2, \ldots, 10 \tag{7.25a}$$

The neuron's activation function and positive and negative feedback coefficients are, respectively,

$$f(net) \triangleq \begin{cases} 0, & net \leq 0 \\ net, & 0 < net < 2 \\ 2, & net \geq 2 \end{cases} \tag{7.25b}$$

$$b = 0.4, \, c = 0.2$$

Fifteen recursive computational steps (7.24) have been performed for the row of 10 neurons. The results are listed in Figure 7.17(a). The first row

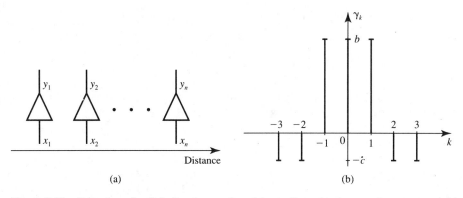

Figure 7.16 Formation of activity in cross section: (a) one-dimensional array of neurons and (b) example lateral feedback.

of the table contains excitation values as in (7.25a). It can be seen that neurons 5 and 6 formed peak and saturated responses after 15 recursions. They attained a constant level of 2 which is the maximum response of the node. The responses of neurons 1, 2, 3, 8, 9, and 10 have been laterally attenuated to zero for all cases studied. The response formation took place gradually over the iterations, as can be seen by comparing rows of the table and by inspecting the four curves shown.

The impact of the lateral feedback coefficients b and c on the response of the linear array is shown in Figure 7.17(b). It can be seen that increasing the positive feedback coefficients from 0.4 to 0.5 substantially widens the radius of maximum response. Increase of negative feedback coefficients from 0.2 to 0.25 narrows the transition activity regions between the maximum and normal response. Values of c that are too small can also increase the region of maximum responses.   ■

We have observed how activity clusters within contiguous regions are generated in a linear array of neurons. The observations and conclusions from this computational experiment can be helpful in formalizing an algorithm that would implement meaningful unsupervised learning within the self-organizing array. Since the center of activity is at the center of excitation, the weight adaptation algorithm should find the point of maximum activity and activate its respective spatial neighborhood. In this way adaptive weight vectors can be tuned to the input variable. Although we only considered an example of the linear array, a simple generalization provides the formation of localized activity to more dimensions.

y_1	y_2	y_3	y_4	y_5	y_6	y_7	y_8	y_9	y_{10}	Step
0.15	0.25	0.36	0.44	0.49	0.49	0.45	0.36	0.25	0.15	0
0.15	0.37	0.55	0.69	0.78	0.78	0.69	0.55	0.37	0.16	1
0.11	0.39	0.66	0.86	0.96	0.96	0.86	0.66	0.39	0.11	2
0.05	0.36	0.71	0.97	1.09	1.09	0.97	0.72	0.36	0.05	3
0.00	0.29	0.73	1.06	1.20	1.20	1.06	0.73	0.29	0.00	4
0.00	0.21	0.71	1.13	1.32	1.32	1.13	0.71	0.21	0.00	5
0.00	0.13	0.65	1.18	1.45	1.45	1.18	0.65	0.13	0.00	6
0.00	0.04	0.56	1.20	1.60	1.60	1.21	0.56	0.04	0.00	7
0.00	0.00	0.44	1.22	1.78	1.78	1.22	0.44	0.00	0.00	8
0.00	0.00	0.31	1.22	1.99	1.99	1.22	0.31	0.00	0.00	9
0.00	0.00	0.18	1.21	2.00	2.00	1.21	0.18	0.00	0.00	10
0.00	0.00	0.11	1.16	2.00	2.00	1.16	0.12	0.00	0.00	11
0.00	0.00	0.07	1.12	2.00	2.00	1.12	0.07	0.00	0.00	12
0.00	0.00	0.03	1.09	2.00	2.00	1.10	0.04	0.00	0.00	13
0.00	0.00	0.01	1.08	2.00	2.00	1.08	0.01	0.00	0.00	14
0.00	0.00	0.00	1.06	2.00	2.00	1.07	0.00	0.00	0.00	15

Positive feedback coefficient $b = .4$
Negative feedback coefficient $c = .2$

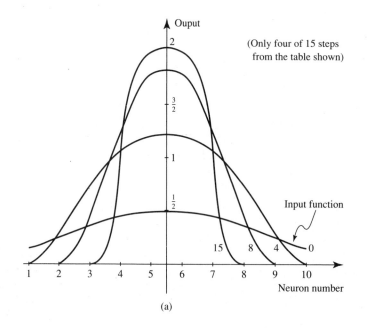

Figure 7.17a Clustering of activity within a cross section: (a) neuron outputs for Steps 0 through 15.

y_1	y_2	y_3	y_4	y_5	y_6	y_7	y_8	y_9	y_{10}	Step
0.00	0.00	0.00	0.88	2.00	2.00	0.88	0.00	0.00	0.00	15
Positive feedback coefficient $b = .4$										
Negative feedback coefficient $c = .25$										
0.00	0.38	1.49	2.00	2.00	2.00	2.00	1.49	0.39	0.00	15
Positive feedback coefficient $b = .5$										
Negative feedback coefficient $c = .2$										
0.00	0.00	0.16	1.39	2.00	2.00	1.41	0.17	0.00	0.00	15
Positive feedback coefficient $b = .5$										
Negative feedback coefficient $c = .25$										
0.00	0.00	0.00	1.06	2.00	2.00	1.06	0.00	0.00	0.00	15
Positive feedback coefficient $b = .5$										
Negative feedback coefficient $c = .3$										
0.00	0.00	0.00	0.88	2.00	2.00	0.88	0.00	0.00	0.00	15
Positive feedback coefficient $b = .5$										
Negative feedback coefficient $c = .35$										

(b)

Figure 7.17b Clustering of activity within a cross section *(continued):* (b) steady-state activity for different feedback coefficients.

7.5 ■■■■■■■■

SELF-ORGANIZING FEATURE MAPS

The feature mapping algorithm is supposed to convert patterns of arbitrary dimensionality into the responses of one- or two-dimensional arrays of neurons. The time-domain recursion illustrated in Example 7.3 needs to be replaced by a self-organizing weight learning rule. ·

First we discuss simple one-dimensional mapping. Assume that a set of input patterns $\{x_i, i = 1, 2, \ldots\}$ has been arranged in an ordering relation with respect to a single feature within the set. One of the simplest systems thought to produce localized responses is a linear array of neurons that receive the same set of input signals in parallel. The linear array system is defined by Kohonen (1982) as the one producing one-dimensional topology-preserving mapping for $i_1 > i_2 > i_3 \ldots$ when

$$y_{i1} = \max_i \{y_i(x_1), \quad i = 1, 2, \ldots, n\}$$
$$y_{i2} = \max_i \{y_i(x_2), \quad i = 1, 2, \ldots, n\}$$
$$y_{i3} = \max_i \{y_i(x_3), \quad i = 1, 2, \ldots, n\} \tag{7.26}$$

$$\vdots$$

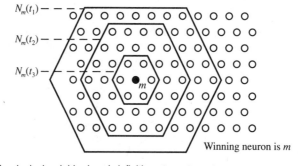

Figure 7.18   Topological neighborhood definition, $t_1 < t_2 < t_3 \ldots$.

This definition can be generalized for two or three dimensions. The topological ordering of output is understood in any mapping case as the one preserving the neighborhood. The input ordering need not be specific and can follow arbitrary metrics and orders. Also, the dimensionality of the input space vectors is not restricted. The basic network on which most of the discussion in this section is based is shown in Figure 7.12(a) with feature mapping from an original input space into a two-dimensional rectangular neuron array.

Learning within self-organizing feature maps results in finding the best matching neuron cells which also activate their spatial neighbors to react to the same input. Such collective and cooperative learning tunes the network in an orderly fashion by defining some feature coordinates over the trained network. After learning, each input causes a localized response having a position on the neurons' array that reflects the dominant feature characteristics of the input.

The feature mapping can be thought of as a nonlinear projection of the input pattern space on the neurons' array that represents features. The projection makes the topological neighborhood relationship geometrically explicit in low-dimensional feature space. Following the formation of self-organized internal representation for existing implicit relationships between original data, the same implicit input space relationships become explicit on the spatial neuron map.

The self-organizing feature map algorithm outlined below has evolved as a result of a long series of simulations. The rigorous mathematical analysis of the dynamics of the self-organization algorithm and the algorithm's proof remain yet to be discovered (Kohonen 1990). Thus, our focus in this section is on formulation of the algorithm, its intuitive interpretation, and sample applications.

The algorithm is explained below for a planar array of neurons with hexagonal neighborhoods (Kohonen 1990) as shown in Figure 7.18. As illustrated in Figure 7.12(a), input **x** is applied simultaneously to all nodes. Instead of using the scalar product metric of similarity, the spatial neighborhood N_m is used here as a more adequate measure S of similarity between **x** and $\mathbf{w}_i$. The weights affecting the currently winning neighborhood, N_m, undergo adaptation at the current learning step, other weights remain unaffected. The neighborhood N_m is found around the best matching node m selected such that

$$\|\mathbf{x} - \mathbf{w}_m\| = \min_i \{\|\mathbf{x} - \mathbf{w}_i\|\} \qquad (7.27)$$

The radius of N_m should be decreasing as the training progresses, $N_m(t_1) > N_m(t_2) > N_m(t_3)\ldots$, where $t_1 < t_2 < t_3 \ldots$. The radius can be very large as learning starts, since it may be needed for initial global ordering of weights. The local ordering within the global order would gradually follow thereafter. Toward the end of training, the neighborhood may involve no cells other than the central winning one. As we realize, this learning neighborhood eventually becomes identical to the neighborhood of the simple competitive learning rule of Kohonen's layer used for cluster learning covered in Section 7.2.

The reader can notice that no explicit lateral interactions of the Mexican hat type are present in the weight adjustment algorithm. However, the mechanism of lateral interaction is embedded in the definition of localized neighborhoods and in the subsequent weight adaptation within the neighborhood.

The weight updating rule for self-organizing feature maps is defined as

$$\Delta \mathbf{w}_i(t) = \alpha \left[\mathbf{x}(t) - \mathbf{w}_i(t) \right] \quad \text{for } i \in N_m(t) \qquad (7.28a)$$

where $N_m(t)$ denotes the current spatial neighborhood. Since learning constant α depends both on training time and the size of the neighborhood, (7.28a) can be rewritten in a more detailed expression as follows:

$$\Delta \mathbf{w}_i(t) = \alpha(N_i, t) \left[\mathbf{x}(t) - \mathbf{w}_i(t) \right] \text{ for } i \in N_m(t) \qquad (7.28b)$$

where α is a positive-valued learning function, $0 < \alpha(N_i, t) < 1$. Because α needs to decrease as learning progresses, it is often convenient to express it as a decreasing function of time. In addition, α can be expressed as a function of the neighborhood radius. An example of a function yielding good practical results in a series of simulations (Kohonen 1990) is

$$\alpha(N_i, t) = \alpha(t) \exp \left[-\|\mathbf{r}_i - \mathbf{r}_m\| / \sigma^2(t) \right] \qquad (7.29)$$

where $\mathbf{r}_m$ and $\mathbf{r}_i$ are the position vectors of the winning cell and of the winning neighborhood nodes, respectively, and $\alpha(t)$ and $\sigma(t)$ are suitably decreasing functions of learning time t.

It seems that the main conditions for the self-organization of the Kohonen's feature map are as follows: (1) The neurons are exposed to a sufficient number of inputs; (2) only the weights leading to an excited neighborhood of the map are affected; and (3) the adjustment is in proportion to the activation received by each neuron within the neighborhood. As a result, the weight adaptation rule tends to enhance the same responses to a sufficiently similar subsequent input.

As a result of weight adjustment algorithm implementation, a planar neuron map is obtained with weights coding the stationary probability density function $p(x)$ of the pattern vectors used for training. The ordered image of patterns forms the weights w_{ij}.

	Item																															
Attribute	A	B	C	D	E	F	G	H	I	J	K	L	M	N	O	P	Q	R	S	T	U	V	W	X	Y	Z	1	2	3	4	5	6
x_1	1	2	3	4	5	3	3	3	3	3	3	3	3	3	3	3	3	3	3	3	3	3	3	3	3	3	3	3	3	3	3	3
x_2	0	0	0	0	0	1	2	3	4	5	3	3	3	3	3	3	3	3	3	3	3	3	3	3	3	3	3	3	3	3	3	3
x_3	0	0	0	0	0	0	0	0	0	0	1	2	3	4	5	6	7	8	3	3	3	3	6	6	6	6	6	6	6	6	6	6
x_4	0	0	0	0	0	0	0	0	0	0	0	0	0	0	0	0	0	0	0	1	2	3	4	1	2	3	4	2	2	2	2	2
x_5	0	0	0	0	0	0	0	0	0	0	0	0	0	0	0	0	0	0	0	0	0	0	0	0	0	0	1	2	3	4	5	6

(a)

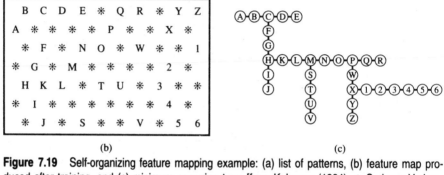
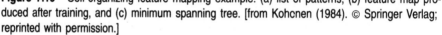

(b) (c)

Figure 7.19 Self-organizing feature mapping example: (a) list of patterns, (b) feature map produced after training, and (c) minimum spanning tree. [from Kohonen (1984). © Springer Verlag; reprinted with permission.]

An interesting example of the mapping of five-dimensional data vectors is shown in Figure 7.19 (Kohonen 1984). Figure 7.19(a) lists 32 different five-dimensional input vectors labeled *A* through 6. The rectangular array of features consists of 70 neurons, each connected by five weights with pattern components x_1, x_2, x_3, x_4, and x_5. The array has been trained using vectors $\mathbf{x}_A \ldots \mathbf{x}_6$ selected at random from the training set. After 10,000 training steps the weights stabilized and then the obtained network was calibrated. Calibration was performed by supervised labeling of array neurons in response to a specific known vector from the training set. Thus, when vector *B* was input, the upper left corner neuron from Figure 7.19(b) produced the strongest response in the entire array. It was therefore labeled *B*, etc. As seen from the figure, 32 neurons are provided with labels and 38 neurons remained uncommitted. Let us analyze the meaning of the obtained map.

Inspection of the similarity of the training vectors reveals that vectors $\mathbf{x}_1 \ldots \mathbf{x}_6$ can be arranged in a so-called *minimum spanning tree* as illustrated in Figure 7.19(c). The minimum spanning tree is a technique for investigating clustering or neighborhoods of data (Andrews 1972). The approach results from a graph theoretical analysis of an arbitrary data set. The minimum spanning tree is defined as a planar tree connecting all points in the data set to their closest neighbors such that the total tree length is minimized. Each vertex of the graph corresponds to only one element from the data set. If we assign a number to each graph edge that is equal to the distance between the vertices that the edge connects, then the minimum spanning tree of a set is that spanning tree which has the sum of the edges of the tree of minimum value.

By inspecting the data $\mathbf{x}_A \ldots \mathbf{x}_6$, the distance between $\mathbf{x}_A$ and $\mathbf{x}_B$ is determined to be

$$\|\mathbf{x}_A - \mathbf{x}_B\| = 1 < \|\mathbf{x}_A - \mathbf{x}_i\|, \quad \text{for } i = C, \ldots, 6$$

Thus the edge connecting A and B should probably belong to the minimum spanning tree. Further, since we have

$$\|\mathbf{x}_B - \mathbf{x}_C\| = 1 < \|\mathbf{x}_B - \mathbf{x}_i\|, \quad \text{for } i = D, \ldots, 6$$

then the edge connecting B and C will probably be part of the tree. Since the distances both between $\mathbf{x}_C$ and $\mathbf{x}_D$, and $\mathbf{x}_C$ and $\mathbf{x}_F$ are both of unity value, the tree would be likely to include the edges CD and CF. The reader can continue generating the minimum spanning tree by inspecting distances between the data and growing branch after branch of the planted tree.

The feature map produced through self-organization has the same structure as the minimum spanning tree. Each piece of data corresponds to a single neuron cell, namely to the best matching one. Thus, the neuron represents its image on the feature array. The data at minimum distances in original five-dimensional space are arranged into topological neighborhoods in two-dimensional feature space. The distances between the vectors $\mathbf{x}_\alpha$ and $\mathbf{x}_\beta$, defined in the original pattern space as the norm

$$\|\mathbf{x}_\alpha - \mathbf{x}_\beta\| = \sqrt{\sum_{i=1}^{5} (x_{\alpha,i} - x_{\beta,i})^2}$$

are preserved in the feature space where they become planar distances. Planar distances are perceptually very pervasive when compared with five-dimensional space distances. As can be seen from the map, distances within multidimensional space between 32 data items are now flattened on the plane. By connecting the topological neighbors on the plane, we obtain the minimum spanning tree. The obtained map of features is somewhat squeezed into the minimum space, but the topological relations are preserved on the map with some parts of the minimum spanning tree lightly bent on the map.

EXAMPLE 7.4 ■■■■■■■■■■■■■■■

In this example, a linear array of 10 neurons is trained using one-dimensional data x distributed uniformly between 0 and 1. The data with equal probability

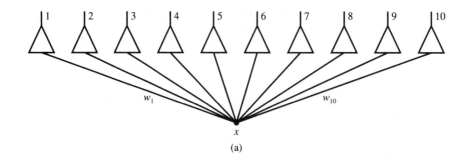

(a)

Weights w_1 - w_{10} (unordered) after 1000 training steps									
0.859	0.961	0.753	0.052	0.181	0.297	0.541	0.398	0.469	0.637
0.041	0.124	0.429	0.315	0.223	0.646	0.736	0.544	0.845	0.952
0.528	0.778	0.707	0.623	0.323	0.872	0.963	0.433	0.069	0.210
0.169	0.064	0.690	0.481	0.879	0.960	0.790	0.275	0.385	0.583
0.049	0.152	0.590	0.651	0.721	0.954	0.833	0.498	0.257	0.372
0.061	0.182	0.265	0.707	0.521	0.596	0.357	0.450	0.814	0.937
0.073	0.202	0.436	0.933	0.798	0.669	0.497	0.552	0.378	0.302
0.920	0.975	0.837	0.610	0.724	0.501	0.315	0.402	0.202	0.067
0.052	0.165	0.684	0.471	0.366	0.274	0.752	0.942	0.835	0.583
0.061	0.265	0.163	0.782	0.853	0.949	0.617	0.707	0.497	0.387

(b)

Figure 7.20a,b Linear array for Example 7.4: (a) network diagram, (b) weights after training, 10 experiments.

of occurrence are thus mapped from one-dimensional pattern space to ten-neuron, one-dimensional linear feature space.

The network arrangement is shown in Figure 7.20(a). Initial weights are random and centered around 0.5 with 0.05 radius. The initial neighborhood radius of one node has been reduced to zero nodes after 300 training steps. The results of 1000 iterations are tabulated in Figure 7.20(b). Each of the 10 rows lists final weights. Each of the 10 computational training experiments started at different initial values and was performed with data submitted in different random sequences. As can be seen, the initially unordered weights can be ordered to become approximately linear. This can be done by cali-brating the trained network through applying known inputs between 0 and 1 that are equally spaced in this range. The average value for a weight matrix obtained in the series of 10 simulations can be computed as

$$\mathbf{W} \cong \frac{1}{100} \begin{bmatrix} 6 & 17 & 28 & 39 & 47 & 57 & 66 & 75 & 85 & 95 \end{bmatrix}^t$$

The weights obtained in the experiment are close to the empirical cumulative

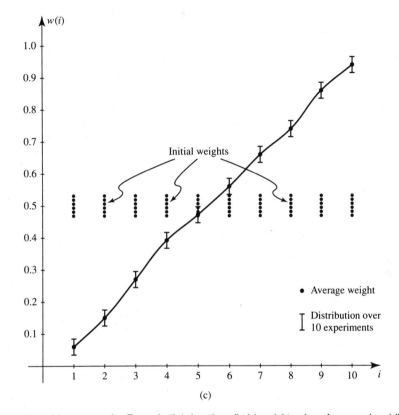

Figure 7.20c Linear array for Example 7.4 *(continued):* (c) weight values for an ordered linear array.

distribution function of a uniform sample of numbers from the range $[0, 1]$. Figure 7.20(c) shows that weights become similarly organized to the training patterns. ■

When applying the self-organizing feature mapping algorithm, formulas (7.27) and (7.28) alternate. Input **x**, even if deterministic and defined, is treated as having a probability density of occurrence. The weight adjustments under Kohonen's algorithm reflect this probability of occurrence. In fact, this learning algorithm summarizes the history of the input data along with their topological relationships in the original pattern space. Moreover, in real-world training situations, input **x** should involve patterns in their natural sequence of occurrence.

Numerous technical reports have been written about successful applications of the feature map algorithm (Kohonen 1984). The algorithm has been applied in sensory mapping, robot control, vector quantization, and speech recognition. One explanatory example of feature mapping is shown in Figure 7.21. The figure

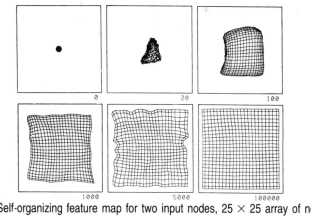

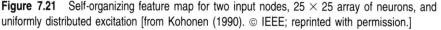

Figure 7.21   Self-organizing feature map for two input nodes, 25 × 25 array of neurons, and uniformly distributed excitation [from Kohonen (1990). © IEEE; reprinted with permission.]

shows the initial and intermediate phases of self-organization of a square feature map for a two-dimensional input vector. The training has been performed on random independent inputs uniformly distributed over the unity square shown in each of the six boxes. In fact, each of the boxes displays the distribution of weights during training. The initial weights are selected to be random and close to the values of 0.5 and 0.5. The final weights, w_{i1} and w_{i2}, of the square array are shown after 100 000 training iterations in the last of the six boxes. The horizontal and vertical coordinates of the plots are the resulting values w_{i1} and w_{i2}, respectively, for an array of 25 × 25 neurons. Line intersections of the maps specify weight values for a single i'th neuron. Lines between the nodes on the graph merely connect weight points for neurons that are topological nearest neighbors.

In practical applications of self-organizing feature maps, input vectors are often high dimensional. In speech recognition, for example, there are typically 15-tuple input pattern vectors. During the initial processing of the speech signal, the microphone signal is first converted into a 15-channel fast Fourier transform (FFT) spectral signal covering the range of frequencies from 200 hertz to 5 kilohertz. Each phoneme of speech tends to occupy one segment of the 15-dimensional spectral signal space. Although spectra of different phonemes partially overlap and 100 percent accurate discrimination is not completely achievable by any method of phoneme classification, an array of properly trained neurons is able to extract most phoneme features and project them on the plane as described below.

The planar neural array has been trained on spectral signals generated every 9.83 ms during the continuous speech (Kohonen 1988). The spectral FFT samples have been used for the weight adaptation algorithm (7.27) and (7.28) in their natural order of occurrence. During training, various neurons become sensitized

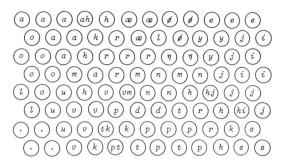

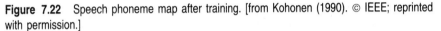

Figure 7.22 Speech phoneme map after training. [from Kohonen (1990). © IEEE; reprinted with permission.]

to spectra of different phonemes. As a result, the trained feature array shown in Figure 7.22 has been generated. The figure displays a phoneme map of natural Finnish speech. The initially unlabeled map was subsequently calibrated using standard reference phoneme spectra. As can be seen, most cells that learned a phoneme have acquired a unique phoneme characterization. Some cells indicate responses to two different phonemes. Discrimination of overlapping phonemes k, p, and t has not worked too reliably and would need an additional phoneme map discrimination.

The map facilitates the planar visualization of complex multidimensional waveforms of speech. The visualization of speech phonemes may be useful for speech therapy or training, but the ultimate goal of speech phoneme processing is automatic speech recognition. Let us note that Figure 7.22, showing the phoneme map, can be thought of as the keyboard of a "phonetic" typewriter (Kohonen 1988). The reader may also refer to Figure 1.11 showing visualization of continuous speech signals on phoneme maps in the form of word trajectories. Generation of word trajectories points out another very interesting application of Kohonen's feature map.

It is often reported in the technical literature that the self-organizing map's successful training depends on the initial weights and the selection of training parameters. Several practical conditions are of importance for the user attempting the implementation of the algorithm. They are discussed below (Kohonen 1990).

The number of weight adjustment steps should be expected to be reasonably large since the learning here is a statistical process. A rule of thumb is that, for good statistical accuracy, the number of steps should be at least 500 times larger than the number of array neurons. Note that although 100 000 training steps are not uncommon, the algorithm is rather simple computationally. Also, intermediate results may be recycled, in particular when the set of training samples is not large.

For approximately 1000 initial steps, the learning function $\alpha(t)$ in (7.29) should be kept close to unity, then it should start decreasing at $t = t_p$. Linear or exponential decreases are exemplified below. The learning function $\alpha(t)$ can be specified for the discussed choices as follows:

$$\alpha(t) = \alpha_0, \quad \text{for } t < t_p \tag{7.30a}$$

and for $t > t_p$ we have linear decrease

$$\alpha(t) = \alpha_0 \left(1 - \frac{t - t_p}{t_q} \right) \tag{7.30b}$$

or, alternatively, exponential decrease

$$\alpha(t) = \alpha_0 \exp \left[(-t - t_p)/t_q \right] \tag{7.30c}$$

where t_q is the time length responsible for the rate of $\alpha(t)$ decay. Its value should be suitably chosen by the user. After the initial map ordering for large α values, $\alpha(t)$ should be kept to a small positive value in the range of 0.01 over an extended period of training. This would suggest that a decelerated decay of α originally chosen as in (7.30b) and (7.30c) may be suitable in many cases.

The criteria for selection of the controlled neighborhood radius was introduced in (7.29). At the beginning of training, the radius of the neighborhood can cover the entire network. After the gradual reduction of the neighborhood radius, the network should be continuously trained in the fine weight adjustment mode with nearest neighbors only. Then, the neighborhood should shrink to zero and only include the neuron itself.

7.6 CLUSTER DISCOVERY NETWORK (ART1)

The network covered in this section was developed by Carpenter and Grossberg (1987, 1988) and is called an *adaptive resonance theory 1* (ART1) network. It serves the purpose of cluster discovery. Similar to networks using a single Kohonen layer with competitive learning neurons covered in Section 7.2, this network learns clusters in an unsupervised mode. The novel property of the ART1 network is the controlled discovery of clusters. In addition, the ART1 network can accommodate new clusters without affecting the storage or recall capabilities for clusters already learned.

The network produces clusters by itself, if such clusters are identified in input data, and stores the clustering information about patterns or features without *a priori* information about the possible number and type of clusters. Essentially the network "follows the leader" after it originates the first cluster with the first input pattern received. It then creates the second cluster if the distance of the second pattern exceeds a certain threshold, otherwise the pattern is clustered with the first cluster. This process of pattern inspection followed by either new cluster

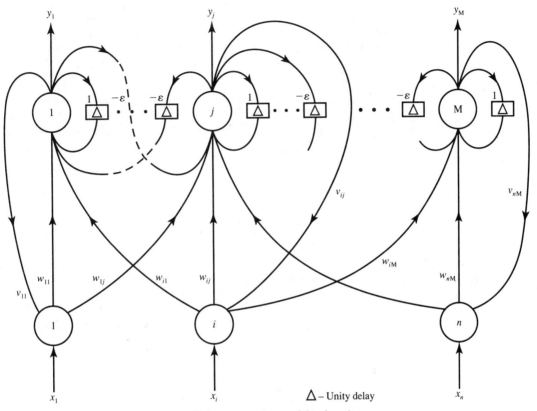

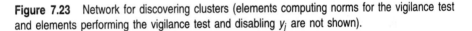

(Only some top–down weights shown)

Figure 7.23 Network for discovering clusters (elements computing norms for the vigilance test and elements performing the vigilance test and disabling y_j are not shown).

origination or acceptance of the pattern to the old cluster is the main step of ART1 network production. A more detailed description of the training and its algorithm is given below.

The central part of the ART1 network computes the matching score reflecting the degree of similarity of the present input to the previously encoded clusters. This is done by the topmost layer of the network in Figure 7.23 performing bottom-to-top processing. This part of the network is functionally identical to the Hamming network and MAXNET from Figure 7.1(a). The initializing input to the m'th node of MAXNET is the familiar scalar product similarity measure between the input $\mathbf{x}$ and the vector $\mathbf{w}_m$. We thus have the initial matching scores of values

$$y_m^0 = \mathbf{w}_m^t\mathbf{x}, \quad \text{for } m = 1, 2, \ldots, M \tag{7.31}$$

where $\mathbf{w}_m = \begin{bmatrix} w_{1m} & w_{2m} & \ldots & w_{nm} \end{bmatrix}^t$. Note that the double subscript convention for weights w_{ij} in this section (and local for only this section of the text) is not followed. The first weight index denotes input node number "from," the second index denotes node number "to." This is to conform with common notation used in the technical literature for this network. The activation function $f(net)$ for the MAXNET neuron is shown in Figure 7.3(b) and given by (7.5b). It is also assumed that a unity delay element stores each MAXNET neuron output signal during the unity time Δ during recursions, before it arrives back at the top-layer node input. The input of the topmost layer is initialized with vector $\mathbf{y}^0$, entries of which are computed as matching scores (7.31), and thereafter the layer undergoes recurrent updates as expressed in (7.5a). We thus have for this portion of the network

$$\mathbf{y}^{k+1} = \Gamma[\mathbf{W}_M \mathbf{y}^k] \tag{7.32}$$

where the weight matrix $\mathbf{W}_M$ is defined as in (7.4) and fulfills all related conditions of the MAXNET weight matrix as stated in Section 7.1. The initializing matching scores vector $\mathbf{y}^0 = \mathbf{net}^0$ for (7.32) and for the top-layer recurrences is given by the simple feedforward mapping

$$\mathbf{y}^0 = \mathbf{W}\mathbf{x} \tag{7.33}$$

where $\mathbf{W}$ is the bottom-to-top processing weight matrix containing entries w_{ij} as follows

$$\mathbf{W} = \begin{bmatrix} w_{11} & w_{21} & \cdots & w_{n1} \\ w_{12} & w_{22} & \cdots & w_{n2} \\ \vdots & \vdots & \cdots & \vdots \\ w_{1M} & w_{2M} & \cdots & w_{nM} \end{bmatrix}$$

As for the MAXNET network, the single nonzero output for a large enough recursion index k, y_j^{k+1}, is produced by the j'th top-layer neuron. For this winning neuron we have

$$y_j^0 = \sum_{i=1}^{n} w_{ij} x_i = \max_{m=1,2,\ldots,M} \left(\sum_{i=1}^{n} w_{im} x_i \right) \tag{7.34}$$

The above discussion is pertinent to the matching score computation of the cluster discovery algorithm. Formulas (7.32), (7.33), and (7.34) are used for calculation of the subscript associated with the largest value y_m^0, $m = 1, 2, \ldots, M$. This is equivalent to the search for the winning node of the top layer. After recursions in the top layer have stabilized, the number of the node with the nonzero output, say j, is the potential cluster number. As we have realized by now, this part of computation also provides the identification of the weight vector $\mathbf{w}_j$ that best matches the input vector $\mathbf{x}$ of all vectors $\mathbf{w}_1, \mathbf{w}_2, \ldots, \mathbf{w}_M$, in the scalar product metric.

The top-down part of the network checks the similarity of the candidate cluster with the stored cluster reference data and performs the vigilance test on normalized $\sum_{i=1}^{n} v_{ij} x_i$ entries as described below. The vigilance threshold δ,

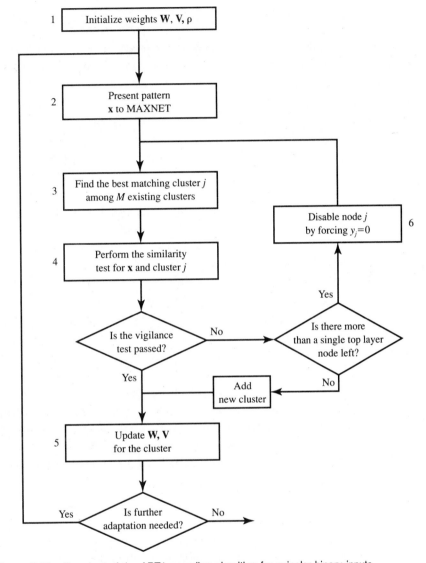

Figure 7.24 Flowchart of the ART1 encoding algorithm for unipolar binary inputs.

$0 < \delta < 1$, sets the degree of required similarity, or "match," between a cluster or pattern already stored in the ART1 network and the current input in order for this new pattern to resonate with the encoded one. If the match between the input vector and j'th cluster is found, the network is said to be in resonance. Let us review the steps of the learning algorithm for cluster discovery (Lippmann 1987; Pao 1989). The cluster encoding algorithm flowchart that we follow below is shown in Figure 7.24.

■ *Summary of the Adaptive Resonance Theory 1 Network Algorithm (ART 1)*

Step 1: The vigilance threshold ρ is set, and for the n-tuple input vectors and M top-layer neurons the weights are initialized. The matrices $\mathbf{W}$, $\mathbf{V}$ are $(M \times n)$ and each is initialized with identical entries:

$$\mathbf{W} = \left[\frac{1}{1+n} \right] \tag{7.35a}$$

$$\mathbf{V} = [1] \tag{7.35b}$$

$$0 < \rho < 1 \tag{7.35c}$$

Step 2: Binary unipolar input vector $\mathbf{x}$ is presented at input nodes, $x_i = 0, 1$, for $i = 1, 2, \ldots, n$.

Step 3: All matching scores are computed from (7.31) or (7.33) as follows:

$$y_m^0 = \sum_{i=1}^{n} w_{im} x_i, \quad \text{for } m = 1, 2, \ldots, M \tag{7.36}$$

In this step, selection of the best matching existing cluster, j, is performed according to the maximum criterium (7.34) as follows:

$$y_j^0 = \max_{m=1,2,\ldots,M} (y_m^0) \tag{7.37}$$

[A practical note is that the recurrences of (7.32) done by MAXNET may be skipped in a discrete-time learning simulation since their only consequence of importance is suppressing to zero all upper node outputs but the j'th one.]

Step 4: The similarity test for the winning neuron j is performed as follows:

$$\frac{1}{\|\mathbf{x}\|} \sum_{i=1}^{n} v_{ij} x_i > \rho \tag{7.38}$$

where ρ is the vigilance parameter and the norm $\|\mathbf{x}\|$ is defined for the purpose of this algorithm as follows:

$$\|\mathbf{x}\| \overset{\Delta}{=} \sum_{i=1}^{n} |x_i| \tag{7.39}$$

If the test (7.38) is passed, the algorithm goes to Step 5.

If the test has failed, the algorithm goes to Step 6 only if the top layer has more than a single active node left. Otherwise, the algorithm goes to Step 5.

Step 5: Entries of the weight matrices are updated for index j passing the test of Step 4. The updates are only for entries (i,j), where $i = 1, 2, \ldots, M$, and are computed as follows:

$$w_{ij}(t + 1) = \frac{v_{ij}(t)x_i}{0.5 + \sum_{i=1}^{n} v_{ij}(t)x_i} \qquad (7.40a)$$

$$v_{ij}(t + 1) = x_i v_{ij}(t) \qquad (7.40b)$$

This updates the weights of the j'th cluster (newly created or the existing one). The algorithm returns to Step 2.

Step 6:   The node j is deactivated by setting y_j to 0. Thus, this mode does not participate in the current cluster search. The algorithm goes back to Step 3 and it will attempt to establish a new cluster different than j for the pattern under test.

In Step 4, the vigilance test is performed on the input vector by comparing the scalar product of the best matching cluster weights $\mathbf{v}_j$ with the input vector divided by the number of bits equal to 1 of the input vector. If the ratio is less than the vigilance threshold, the input is considered to be different from previously stored cluster exemplars. If, at the same time, there are no cluster nodes left for disabling, a new cluster is added. Addition of a new cluster exemplar requires adding one new node and $2n$ new connections.

The vigilance threshold ρ is typically a fraction indicating how close an input must be to a stored cluster prototype to provide a desirable match. A value close to 1 indicates that a close match is required; smaller values indicate that a poorer match is acceptable. Thus, for lower values of ρ, the same set of input patterns may result in a smaller number of clusters being discovered by the ART1 network.

The cluster j is stored in the form of weight vector $\mathbf{w}_j$ as defined in (7.31). These encoded vectors constitute so-called *long-term network memory*. In comparison, weights v_{ij} used for verification of cluster exemplar proximity can be considered to be the short-term memory of the network. In summary, the ART1 network learning algorithm described performs an off-line search through the encoded cluster exemplars and is trying to find a sufficiently close match. If no match is found, a new class is created.

The recall of stored patterns by this network can be interpreted as identical to learning; however, the vigilance test is always passed and no weight updates are performed. A complete description of discrete-time recall in the ART1 network involves complex difference equations, since the system involves numerous feedback loops of which only autonomous competitive top-layer recurrences were taken into account in this discussion. The name of the system comes from the resonance that the system finds in Step 4 when the pattern possibly resonates with one of the patterns, say of class j, and reinforces the storage for this class.

EXAMPLE 7.5 ■■■■■■■■■■■■■■■■■■

This example illustrates stages of discrete-time learning of an example ART1 network with four category neurons indicating the potential for four clusters and a 25-dimensional input vector with entries 0, 1 (Stork 1989). We assume here that the **W** and **V** matrices are of size (25 × 4). Although we are not sure initially whether or not four top-layer cluster neurons are all needed, we consider the choice $M = 4$ as the only reasonable network initialization. If the number of clusters results after training as smaller than the number of input vectors, the actual number of cluster neurons needed in the top layer would reduce accordingly. Simulations of learning with two different vigilance values are shown in Figure 7.25. The vectors representing the bit maps of input patterns are arranged in column vectors in the sequence in which they are presented, left to right.

Consider first the high-vigilance case shown in Figure 7.25(a) of $\rho = 0.7$. Weights are initialized as

$$w_{ij} = \frac{1}{26}$$

$$v_{ij} = 1, \quad i = 1, \ldots, 25, \quad j = 1, 2, 3, 4$$

Step 1: When pattern A is presented, one of the four top-layer neurons has the largest output. It is arbitrarily denoted as neuron number 1. The vigilance test is unconditionally passed since the left side of (7.38) is of unity value in the first pass. This results in unconditional definition of the first cluster. The result of the weight adjustment computed from (7.40a) is that all weights w_{i1} connecting inputs having $x_i = 1$ with the top-level node 1 are increased to $2/11$. Also, top-down weights v_{i1} adjusted according to (7.40b) remain at unity value as initialized if $x_i = 1$; otherwise they are set to 0.

Figure 7.26 shows the ART1 network after completion of the first training step. Note that from among $25 \times 4 = 100$ weights that process raw input from the bottom to the top, w_{ij}, only 5 have changed. From among 100 top-to-bottom weights, v_{ij}, 5 are set to the unity value and 19 are zeroed. All the remaining weights remain as initialized and are not shown in the figure.

Summary of first pass of algorithm, pattern A is input:

$$w_{1,1} = w_{7,1} = w_{13,1} = w_{19,1} = w_{25,1} = \frac{2}{11}$$

The remaining weights $w_{i1} = 1/26$ as initialized.

$$v_{1,1} = v_{7,1} = v_{13,1} = v_{19,1} = v_{25,1} = 1 \text{ as initialized.}$$

The remaining weights are recomputed as $v_{i1} = 0$.

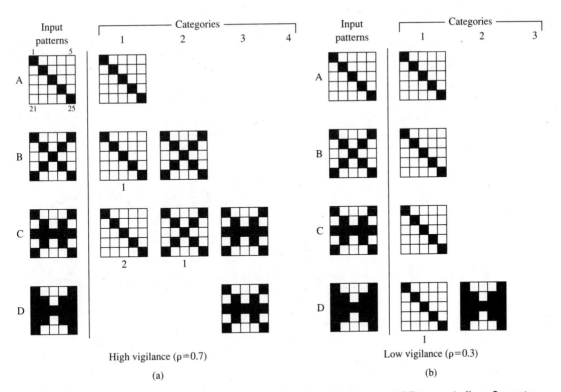

Figure 7.25 Discrete-time learning simulation of an example ART1 network. [from Carpenter and Grossberg (1987). © Academic Press; reprinted with permission.]

Step 2: During the presentation of input pattern B there is no top-layer node competing for clustering, since the only active node is 1. The vigilance test results in

$$\frac{1}{\|\mathbf{x}\|} \sum_{i=1}^{25} v_{i1}x_i = 5\left(\frac{1}{9}\right) < 0.7$$

Due to the failure of the vigilance test and the absence of other nodes for further evaluation and for potential disabling, pattern B is treated as a new cluster. The cluster is therefore represented by another neuron, arbitrarily numbered 2. Its connecting weights are recomputed as w_{i2} and v_{j2}.

Summary of second pass of algorithm, pattern B is input:

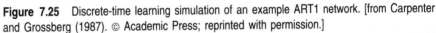

$$w_{1,2} = w_{5,2} = w_{7,2} = w_{9,2} = w_{13,2} = w_{17,2}$$
$$= w_{19,2} = w_{21,2} = w_{25,2} = \frac{2}{19}$$

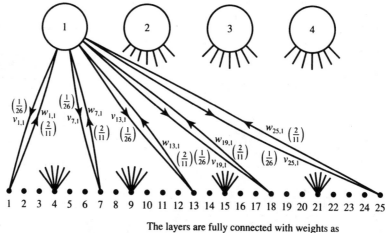

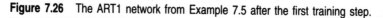

The layers are fully connected with weights as
initialized, with the exception of $i_1 = 0$, $i \neq 1, 7, 13, 19, 25$

Figure 7.26   The ART1 network from Example 7.5 after the first training step.

The remaining weights $w_{i2} = 1/26$.

$$v_{1,2} = v_{5,2} = v_{7,2} = v_{9,2} = v_{13,2} = v_{17,2} = v_{19,2} = v_{21,2} = v_{25,2} = 1$$

The remaining weights $v_{i2} = 0$.

Step 3:   During the presentation of pattern C we have the following matching scores computed from (7.34):

$$y_1^0 = 5\left(\frac{2}{11}\right) + 8\left(\frac{1}{26}\right) = 1.217$$

$$y_2^0 = 9\left(\frac{2}{19}\right) + 4\left(\frac{1}{26}\right) = 1.101$$

Thus, neuron 1 results as a winner. However, the vigilance test is not passed since

$$\frac{1}{\|\mathbf{x}\|} \sum_{i=1}^{25} v_{i1} x_i = \frac{5}{13} < 0.7$$

Node 1 is then disabled and, consequently, node 2 emerges as a winner because of the absence of a competitor node. The vigilance test yields

$$\frac{1}{\|\mathbf{x}\|} \sum_{i=1}^{25} v_{i2} x_i = \frac{9}{13} < 0.7$$

and it fails again, indicating therefore inadequate similarity between the input C and any of the two existing clusters.

Thus, top-layer neuron numbered 3 is added as a new category and weights w_{i3} and v_{i3} are updated accordingly. In contrast to the recent rejection of existing clusters, pattern D is classified to category 3 because of the similarity with pattern C. This is due to the fact that the vigilance test was passed and to the resonance of pattern D within the existing category 3. Notice that the weights computed originally within the third pass of the algorithm and connecting to and from top-layer neuron 3 have been affected in the fourth pass. After patterns A, B, C, and D have been categorized and recorded, when subsequently presented to the network, each of them will access the appropriate category neuron of the top layer and resonate with it. Noticeably, raising the vigilance level to 0.9 or 0.95 will entirely prevent the network from recoding within existing clusters. Therefore, using the training algorithm with this value of the vigilance level enables pattern recall.

The results of ART1 network learning with low vigilance set at 0.3 are shown in Figure 7.25(b). Just two categories are formed in this case. If the vigilance is set at 0.8, however, four categories are produced, one for each pattern. Lowering it to 0.2 would cause only one diffuse category to be formed based on the pattern set A, B, C, and D. All of the four patterns would be categorized as of the same category.   ■

The ART1 network discussed here is a simplified version of the network working only with unipolar binary inputs. The network performs very well with perfect input patterns, but even a small amount of noise superimposed on training patterns can cause problems (Lippmann 1987). With no noise, the vigilance threshold can be set such that two patterns that are somewhat similar but do differ are considered to be different by the network. However, for training using noisy patterns, they can become categorized under noisy conditions. Under no noise conditions, the algorithm shows good performance in both learning and recall. It is reported to be stable and reliable for clustering and classifying unipolar binary input vectors.

EXAMPLE 7.6 ■■■■■■■■■

This example demonstrates the storage of patterns under noisy conditions. The ART1 network is developed using the ANS program from the Appendix. Assume that there are four noise-free unipolar binary pattern vectors representing bit maps of the characters A, B, C, and D, which are shown in Figure 7.27(a). The bit maps are of size 5×5, like those in the previous example.

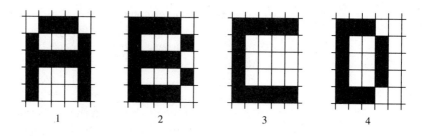

(a)

Input pattern number	Clustering			Desired resonance cluster
	Vigilance level			
	0.95	0.90	0.85	
1	1	1	1	1
2	2	2	2	2
3	3	3·	3	3
4	4	4	4	4
5	5	5	1	1
6	6	6	5	1
7	7	7	2	2
8	8	7	6	2
9	7	7	3	3
10	3	3	3	3
11	9	8	4	4
12	8	7	4	4

(b)

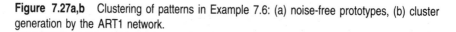

Figure 7.27a,b Clustering of patterns in Example 7.6: (a) noise-free prototypes, (b) cluster generation by the ART1 network.

Training of the network is performed with patterns 1 through 4 first. As a result, four clusters are expected to be built and encoded in the network, one cluster for each respective character. As can be seen from Figure 7.27(b), for each of the three vigilance levels selected for this experiment equal to 0.95, 0.9, and 0.85, four clusters are appropriately generated.

Consider that a distorted version of character A shown in Figure 7.27(c) is submitted as input to the network as the fifth pattern. From the fifth row of the table of Figure 7.27(b) it can be seen that the input fails to cluster it with the previously encoded character *A* unless the vigilance level is lowered to 0.85. When the sixth pattern representing another distorted version of character *A* is input, however, the network fails to cluster it with node 1 under any of the three vigilance levels used for clustering of the fifth

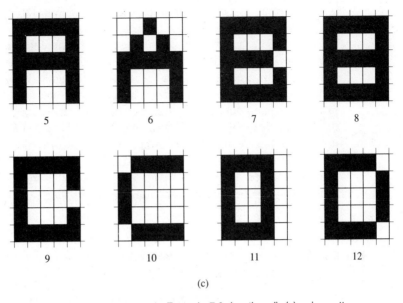

(c)

Figure 7.27c   Clustering of patterns in Example 7.6 *(continued):* (c) noisy patterns.

character. It creates therefore another category that is either number 5 or 6, dependent on the vigilance level previously used for the fifth character's processing.

The seventh and eighth input characters represent distorted versions of character *B* associated with the cluster neuron 2. They both define the new clusters for the highest vigilance level. For the lowest of the vigilance levels, the seventh input character resonates properly with the second node, however, another new cluster is built for the eighth input. The reader can see the tabulated results of clustering for the remaining patterns numbered 9 through 12 from the figure. Note that the network is unable to cluster all noisy versions of patterns under the appropriate category number, but it can do this for some of them. If, however, the vigilance level is lowered below 0.85, then original patterns 1 through 4 used to develop the network do not all form separate categories in the first four training steps. This example illustrates what limitations can be encountered by the user when training the ART1 with noisy versions of the prototype vectors.   ▬

The reader has probably noticed that most of the neural networks studied thus far have the property that learning a new pattern, or association, influences the recall of existing or previously stored information in the network. When a fully trained network must learn a new mapping in a supervised mode, it may be even required to relearn from the beginning. Similarly, when a new pattern is added to the associative or autoassociative memory, this may affect the recall of all previously stored data.

The ART1 network explores a radically different configuration. Note that the network works with a finite supply of output units, M. They are not used, however, until needed to indicate a cluster, and can be considered as waiting for a potential cluster to be defined. The network, therefore, exhibits a degree of plasticity when acquiring new cluster data. At the same time, the recall of the data already learned is not affected, and the weights for clusters already stored are not modifiable. Although the formal mathematical description and convergence proofs of the model have been omitted in our presentation, the basic concepts of learning and recall provided should enable both the understanding and practical use of this important neurocomputing algorithm.

7.7 CONCLUDING REMARKS

Our focus in this chapter has been on networks that learn in an unsupervised mode based on the specified proximity criterion. Except for Hamming network, all networks learned either the similarity between inputs or their input/output mapping without supervision. The proximity, or similarity measures, are embedded in an unsupervised learning algorithm to enable differentiation between similar and dissimilar inputs. In addition, the differentiation capability has been gradually developed within the network based on the learning experience.

We discussed for the most part self-organization, which uses the scalar product similarity measure for developing clusters. We also covered self-organization of patterns into such images in geometrically regular neuron arrays that it reflects the input patterns' mutual structure. Self-organizing arrays have been able to translate clusters in n-dimensional input pattern space into clustering in low-dimensional feature, or image, space. Such self-organizing has preserved and enhanced the topological relationships present in the original input space.

The response of a self-organizing neural network can be used to encode input in fewer dimensions while keeping as much of the vital input information as possible. We have seen that a drastic dimensionality reduction of input data can take place in situations of simultaneous clustering and feature mapping. Indeed, a space with a high dimensionality of input data is generally expected to be mostly empty, and the nonempty parts of the space can be identified and projected into regular array of neurons responding with images that are easy to perceive.

As we have seen, the competitive learning rule enables the unsupervised training process to work. Winner-take-all learning and an adjustable neighborhood definition have been used for weight formation. In addition, extensive lateral inhibition equivalent to mixed positive and negative feedback has provided the mechanism for selecting the winning neuron in regularly shaped feature arrays.

Most networks in this chapter operate through discrimination of the weight to pattern similarity. The input/output mapping is typically implemented by activating only those neurons whose weights exhibit learned similarity to the present input. Based on this detected similarity, the network output is generated, sometimes directly by the receiving layer, but often by the following layer.

The networks covered in this chapter have found many applications. They include minimum-distance vector classification, vector quantization, auto- and heteroassociative memory, classification of noisy vectors into clusters, and cluster synthesis. The class of unsupervised learning neural networks is particularly well suited to applications that require data quantization. Examples where the capability of data quantization is useful include statistical analysis, codebook communication, and transmission and data compression. The idea of data quantization is to categorize a given set of random input vectors through a finite number of classes. The index of the class is found as a number of the output neuron that fires. We then can transmit or store the index of the class rather than complete data. This, however, requires a list of codes, or codebook, that has been agreed upon. Such a codebook must be available at the receiving end of the information transmission system, since the data encoded by the network at the transmitter side must now be decoded.

Finally, self-organizing feature maps can be applied for extracting the hidden features of multi-dimensional input patterns and their probability of occurrence. The inputs are mapped to the line or plane of output units so that neighborhood relations are transferred from the input space to the neuron output space. This is especially useful for detection of hidden relationships that are difficult to group, organize or categorize in a sensible manner. One of the interesting applications of the map is for human language study and is presented in Section 8.6.

PROBLEMS

Please note that problems highlighted with an asterisk (*) are typically computationally intensive and the use of programs is advisable to solve them.

P7.1 Design the Hamming network for the three following class prototype vectors:

$$\mathbf{s}^{(1)} = \begin{bmatrix} 1 & -1 & 1 & -1 & 1 & -1 \end{bmatrix}^t,$$
$$\mathbf{s}^{(2)} = \begin{bmatrix} -1 & -1 & -1 & -1 & -1 & 1 \end{bmatrix}^t,$$
$$\mathbf{s}^{(3)} = \begin{bmatrix} 1 & 1 & 1 & -1 & -1 & 1 \end{bmatrix}^t$$

(a) Compute the weight matrix.

(b) Find net_m, for $m = 1, 2, 3$, for the input vector $\mathbf{x} = [1\ 1\ 1\ 1\ 1\ 1]$ and verify that the HD parameter computed by the network agrees with the actual HD.

(c) Find the normalized responses $f(net_m)$ at the output of each node of the Hamming network.

P7.2 MAXNET with four input nodes has been designed for $\varepsilon = 0.1$. After the two initial recurrences completed, the following network output resulted:

$$\mathbf{y}^2 = \begin{bmatrix} 0.186 & 0.307 & 0.428 & 0.549 \end{bmatrix}^t$$

Based on these data:

(a) Find the initializing vector $\mathbf{y}^0$ that has been applied initially, prior to recurrences.

(b) Knowing that $\mathbf{y}^0$ is the output vector of the Hamming network, determine the HD value between the closest 10-bit prototype and the Hamming network input vector originally applied to yield the computed $\mathbf{y}^0$.

P7.3 The MAXNET with four output nodes, $p = 4$, receives the input vector

$$\mathbf{y}^0 = \begin{bmatrix} 0.5 & 0.6 & 0.7 & 0.8 \end{bmatrix}^t$$

(a) Find the ε value that would be required to suppress the output of the weakest node exactly to the zero value after the first cycle.

(b) Find subsequent responses of the network, $\mathbf{y}^1$ and $\mathbf{y}^2$, for the computed value of ε.

P7.4* Design the Hamming network and the associated MAXNET network to provide optimum classification of bipolar binary vectors representing characters *A*, *I*, and *O* in Problem P4.16 in terms of their minimum Hamming distance.

P7.5 Assume that the following condition holds for the vector initializing a MAXNET network with p nodes:

$$0 \le y_1^0 < y_2^0 < \ldots < y_{p-1}^0 < y_p^0 \le 1$$

Prove that the following increment condition holds during recurrences in the linear mode:

$$\left| y_p^{k+1} - y_p^k \right| < \left| y_{p-1}^{k+1} - y_{p-1}^k \right| < \ldots < \left| y_1^{k+1} - y_1^k \right|$$

P7.6 Given are three cluster centers as

$$\mathbf{x}_1 = \begin{bmatrix} 10 \\ 2 \\ 5 \end{bmatrix}^t , \quad \mathbf{x}_2 = \begin{bmatrix} 5 \\ 1 \\ -2 \end{bmatrix}^t , \quad \mathbf{x}_3 = \begin{bmatrix} -3 \\ -4 \\ 0 \end{bmatrix}^t$$

Compute the weights of the network that has three cluster detecting neurons. Perform a computation based on the requirement that weights must match such patterns. Assume that the normalized weight values of the three neurons have initially been tuned to the normalized values $\mathbf{x}_1$, $\mathbf{x}_2$, and $\mathbf{x}_3$, and then denormalized in inverse proportion to each pattern's distance from the origin. Calculate the responses of each neuron in the recall mode for $f(net) = \frac{2}{1+\exp(-net)} - 1$ with inputs $\mathbf{x}_1$, $\mathbf{x}_2$, and $\mathbf{x}_3$.

P7.7 Perform the first learning cycle using the following normalized pattern set: $\{\mathbf{x}_1, \mathbf{x}_2, \mathbf{x}_3, \mathbf{x}_4\} = \{1 \angle 45°, 1 \angle -135°, 1 \angle 90°, 1 \angle -180°\}$ and $\alpha = 0.5$, using the winner-take-all training rule for two cluster neurons. Draw the resulting separating hyperplanes. Initial weights are to be assumed $\hat{\mathbf{w}}_1^0 = \begin{bmatrix} 1 & 0 \end{bmatrix}^t$ and $\hat{\mathbf{w}}_2^0 = \begin{bmatrix} 0 & -1 \end{bmatrix}^t$.

P7.8 Solve Problem P7.7 graphically using vector subtraction/addition, and renormalization, if needed. Then reduce α to 0.25 and analyze the impact of reduced learning constant α on the initial phase of training.

P7.9* Implement the winner-take-all learning algorithm of the Kohonen layer for clustering noisy characters C, I, and T shown in Figure 4.19 into each of the respective three classes. Assume that the noisy training characters are at distance HD = 1 from the noise-free prototypes. Compute the final weight vectors $\mathbf{w}_C$, $\mathbf{w}_I$, and $\mathbf{w}_T$. During the recall operation, compute the responses $f(net_C)$, $f(net_I)$, and $f(net_T)$ of each neuron with continuous unipolar activation function. Use inputs that are respective bipolar binary vectors as specified in Section 4.5. Assume $\lambda = 1$.

P7.10 Analyze the following counterpropagation network for which the feedforward part is only operational. The network is shown in Figure P7.10. Assume the bipolar binary input and output vectors. Provide results for three- and two-dimensional cubes indicating cluster centers, which the network is supposed to detect and subsequently map into output vectors.

P7.11 The feedforward part of a counterpropagation network is shown in Figure P7.11(a). It is designed to map two bit maps represented by vectors $\mathbf{x}_1$ and $\mathbf{x}_2$ shown in Figure P7.11(b) into two three-tuple vectors, $\mathbf{z}_1$ and $\mathbf{z}_2$. Identify vectors $\mathbf{z}_1$ and $\mathbf{z}_2$ by analyzing the network. Also, complete the design of the Kohonen layer.

P7.12 The objective in this problem is to design a so-called Gray code converter of bipolar binary numbers using the feedforward part processing of the counterpropagation network. The Gray code converter has the property that when $\mathbf{x}_i$ indices increase as 0, 1, 2, 3, only a single output bit of $\mathbf{z}_i$ changes.

(a) Design the first layer of the converter as a Kohonen layer, which converts four two-bit input vectors

$$\mathbf{x}_0 = \begin{bmatrix} -1 \\ -1 \end{bmatrix}, \; \mathbf{x}_1 = \begin{bmatrix} -1 \\ 1 \end{bmatrix}, \; \mathbf{x}_2 = \begin{bmatrix} 1 \\ -1 \end{bmatrix}, \; \mathbf{x}_3 = \begin{bmatrix} 1 \\ 1 \end{bmatrix}$$

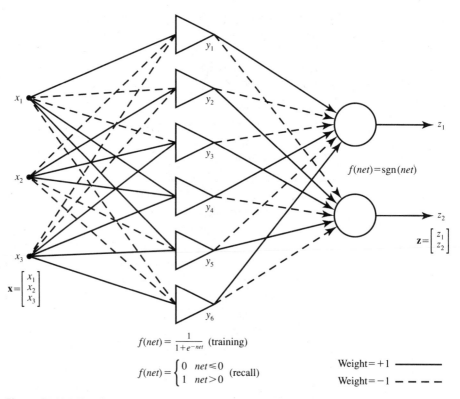

$$f(net) = \frac{1}{1+e^{-net}} \text{ (training)}$$

$$f(net) = \begin{cases} 0 & net \le 0 \\ 1 & net > 0 \end{cases} \text{ (recall)}$$

Weight $= +1$ ———
Weight $= -1$ – – – –

Figure P7.10 Feedforward network for analysis in Problem P7.10.

into, respectively,

$$\mathbf{y}_0 = \begin{bmatrix} 0 \\ 0 \\ 0 \\ 1 \end{bmatrix}, \ \mathbf{y}_1 = \begin{bmatrix} 0 \\ 0 \\ 1 \\ 0 \end{bmatrix}, \ \mathbf{y}_2 = \begin{bmatrix} 0 \\ 1 \\ 0 \\ 0 \end{bmatrix}, \ \mathbf{y}_3 = \begin{bmatrix} 1 \\ 0 \\ 0 \\ 0 \end{bmatrix}$$

(b) Design the second layer of the converter as a Grossberg layer of the feedforward counterpropagation network. Find $\mathbf{V}$ such that the corresponding converter outputs are

$$\mathbf{z}_0 = \begin{bmatrix} 1 \\ 1 \end{bmatrix}, \ \mathbf{z}_1 = \begin{bmatrix} 1 \\ -1 \end{bmatrix}, \ \mathbf{z}_2 = \begin{bmatrix} -1 \\ 1 \end{bmatrix}, \ \mathbf{z}_3 = \begin{bmatrix} -1 \\ -1 \end{bmatrix}$$

Use the explicit design equation (instead of training on noisy input data) to implement mapping and to obtain $\mathbf{W}$ and $\mathbf{V}$.

P7.13 Design the feedforward part of the counterpropagation network that performs the operation XOR (x_1, x_2, x_3) such that $\mathbf{z} = x_1 \oplus x_2 \oplus x_3$ as shown in Figure 3.9(b). Use the explicit design equation instead of training the network on noisy data to obtain $\mathbf{W}$ and $\mathbf{V}$. Assume $x_i = \pm 1$ and $z_i = \pm 1$.

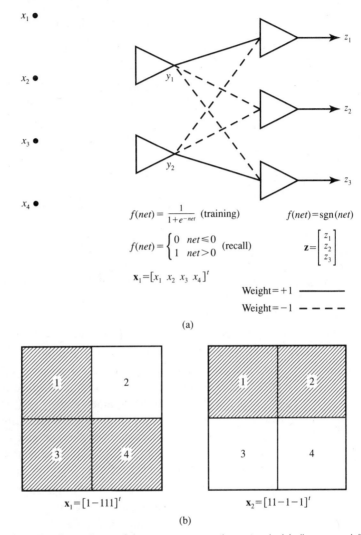

$$f(net) = \frac{1}{1+e^{-net}} \text{ (training)} \qquad f(net) = \text{sgn}(net)$$

$$f(net) = \begin{cases} 0 & net \le 0 \\ 1 & net > 0 \end{cases} \text{ (recall)} \qquad \mathbf{z} = \begin{bmatrix} z_1 \\ z_2 \\ z_3 \end{bmatrix}$$

$$\mathbf{x}_1 = [x_1 \ x_2 \ x_3 \ x_4]^t$$

Weight $= +1$ ———

Weight $= -1$ – – – –

(a)

$$\mathbf{x}_1 = [1-111]^t \qquad \mathbf{x}_2 = [11-1-1]^t$$

(b)

Figure P7.11 Feedforward part of the counterpropagation network: (a) diagram and (b) input vector bit maps.

P7.14 Design the feedforward part of the counterpropagation network that associates the binary bipolar vectors representing bit maps of character pairs (A, C), (I, I), (O, T) as specified in Problem P6.19. Use the explicit design formulas to find $\mathbf{W}$ and $\mathbf{V}$ instead of training the network on noisy data.

P7.15* Solve Problem P7.14 by using noisy training data for all six characters specified. Assume that the noisy vectors are at the distance HD $= 1$ from the undistorted prototypes. Train the network in the three following modes:

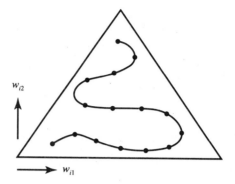

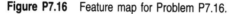

Figure P7.16 Feature map for Problem P7.16.

(a) noisy input vectors only at HD = 1 from input prototypes, outputs are undistorted

(b) noisy output vectors only at HD = 1 from output prototypes, inputs are undistorted

(c) both input and output distorted so that each is at HD = 1 from respective prototypes (random bits distorted, no input/output correlation)

P7.16 The Figure P7.16 shows the final weights of a self-organizing feature map that has been trained for the following conditions (Kohonen 1984): two-dimensional input vectors have been uniformly distributed over the triangular area and the self-organizing array consisted of 15 neurons. Lines between points connect topological neighbors only; points indicate weight coordinates. Sketch the diagram of the network that, in your opinion, has undergone self-organization. Label inputs, neurons, and weights for the computational experiment, results of which are reported on the figure. Suggest the initial weight values that may have been used.

P7.17 A set of five four-dimensional vectors is given

$$\mathbf{x}_1 = \begin{bmatrix} 1 \\ 0 \\ 0 \\ 0 \end{bmatrix}, \mathbf{x}_2 = \begin{bmatrix} 1 \\ 1 \\ 0 \\ 0 \end{bmatrix}, \mathbf{x}_3 = \begin{bmatrix} 1 \\ 1 \\ 1 \\ 0 \end{bmatrix}, \mathbf{x}_4 = \begin{bmatrix} 0 \\ 1 \\ 0 \\ 0 \end{bmatrix}, \mathbf{x}_5 = \begin{bmatrix} 1 \\ 1 \\ 1 \\ 1 \end{bmatrix}$$

Implement the self-organizing feature map algorithm to map the given vectors onto a 5 × 5 array of neurons. Hexagonal neighborhoods should be formed for the array training as shown in Figure P7.17. Decrease α linearly from 0.5 to 0.04 for the first 1000 steps, then decrease it for steps 1000 to 10 000 from 0.04 to 0. Decrease the neighborhood radius from covering the entire array initially (radius of 2 units) to the radius of zero value after 1000 steps. Then calibrate the computed map and draw the produced minimum spanning tree for inputs $\mathbf{x}_1, \ldots, \mathbf{x}_5$. Compare the

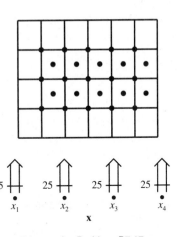

Figure P7.17 Hexagonal map and inputs for Problem P7.17.

computed results produced by the network with the predicted minimum spanning tree.

P7.18 Perform three steps of the discrete-time learning algorithm of the ART1 network for $n = 9$ and $M = 3$ assuming that the training vectors are:

$$\mathbf{x}_1 = \begin{bmatrix} 1 & 0 & 0 & 0 & 1 & 0 & 0 & 0 & 1 \end{bmatrix}^t$$
$$\mathbf{x}_2 = \begin{bmatrix} 1 & 1 & 0 & 0 & 1 & 0 & 0 & 1 & 1 \end{bmatrix}^t$$
$$\mathbf{x}_3 = \begin{bmatrix} 1 & 0 & 1 & 0 & 1 & 0 & 1 & 0 & 1 \end{bmatrix}^t$$

Select an appropriate vigilance threshold ρ so that all three patterns are clustered separately when the sequence $\mathbf{x}_1$, $\mathbf{x}_2$, and $\mathbf{x}_3$ is presented. Compute the final weights $\mathbf{W}$, and $\mathbf{V}$ of the trained network.

P7.19 Figure 7.25(a) shows the simulation steps of discrete-time learning in the ART1 network for $n = 25$ and $M = 4$. The bits of the training vectors are 1 and 0 for black and white bit-map pixels, respectively. Find the following values of the learning network:

(a) the lowest value of ρ that enables definition of a new cluster when pattern B is at the input

(b) the matching scores y_1^0, y_2^0, and y_3^0 of neurons when pattern D is at the input

(c) the lowest value of ρ that enables definition of a new cluster when pattern D is at the input.

P7.20 Figure 7.25(b) shows the simulation results of discrete-time learning in the ART1 network for $n = 25$ and $M = 4$. The bits of the training vectors are 1 and 0 for black and white pixels, respectively. Find the vigilance threshold preventing the occurrence of the second cluster when pattern D is at the input. Assume that patterns A, B, and C have already been clustered together as shown.

*P7.21*Implement the learning and recall algorithm of the adaptive resonance theory network ART1 for the following conditions:

$$M = 4, n = 25, \text{ and user-specified } \rho.$$

Perform the algorithm and program tests by learning the cluster prototypes as shown in Example 7.5. Test the learning and recall phases for the different vigilance levels.

REFERENCES

Andrews, H. C. 1972. *Introduction to Mathematical Techniques in Pattern Recognition.* New York: Wiley Interscience.

Carpenter, G. A., and S. Grossberg. 1988. "Neural Dynamics of Category Learning and Recognition: Attention, Memory Consolidation and Amnesia," in *Brain Structure, Learning and Memory,* ed. J. Davis, R. Newburgh, I. Wegman. AAAS Symp. Series. Westview Press, Boulder, Colo.

Carpenter, G. A., and S. Grossberg. 1987. "A Massively Parallel Architecture for a Self-organizing Neural Pattern Recognition Machine," *Computer Vision, Graphics, and Image Proc.* 37: 54–115.

Duda, R. O., and P. E. Hart. 1973. *Pattern Classification and Scene Analysis,* New York: John Wiley and Sons.

Grossberg, S. 1977. *Classical and Instrumental Learning by Neural Networks. Progress in Theoretical Biology,* vol 3. New York: Academic Press, pp. 51–141.

Grossberg, S. 1982. *Studies of Mind and Brain: Neural Principles of Learning Perception, Development, Cognition, and Motor Control.* Boston: Reidell Press.

Hecht-Nielsen, R. 1987. "Counterpropagation Networks," *Appl. Opt.* 26(23): 4979–4984.

Hecht-Nielsen, R. 1988. "Applications of Counterpropagation Networks," *Neural Networks* 1: 131-139.

Hecht-Nielsen, R. 1990. *Neurocomputing.* Reading, Mass.: Addison-Wesley Publishing Co.

Kohonen, T. 1982. "A Simple Paradigm for the Self-Organized Formation of Structured Feature Maps," in *Competition and Cooperation in Neural*

Nets, Lecture Notes in Biomathematics, ed. S. Amari, M. Arbib. Berlin: Springer-Verlag.

Kohonen, T. 1984. *Self-Organization and Associative Memory.* Berlin: Springer-Verlag.

Kohonen, T. 1988. "The 'Neural' Phonetic Typewriter," *IEEE Computer* 27(3): 11–22.

Kohonen, T. 1990. "The Self-organizing Map," *Proc. IEEE* 78(9): 1464–1480.

Lippmann, R. P. 1987. "An Introduction to Computing with Neural Nets," *IEEE Magazine on Acoustics, Signal and Speech Processing* (April): 4–22.

Pao, Y. H. 1989. *Adaptive Pattern Recognition and Neural Networks.* Reading, Mass.: Addison-Wesley Publishing Co.

Simpson, P. I. 1990. *Artificial Neural Systems: Foundations, Paradigms, Applications, and Implementation.* New York: Pergamon Press.

Stork, D. G. 1989. "Self-organization, Pattern Recognition, and Adaptive Resonance Networks," *J. Neural Network Computing* (Summer): 26–42.

Tattershall, G. 1989. "Neural Map Applications," in *Neural Network Architectures,* ed. I. Alexander. Cambridge: The MIT Press.

Tou, J. T., and R. C. Gonzalez. 1974. *Pattern Recognition Principles.* Reading, Mass.: Addison-Wesley Publishing Co.

Wasserman, P. D. 1989. *Neural Computing Theory and Practice.* New York: Van Nostrand Reinhold.

8

APPLICATIONS OF NEURAL ALGORITHMS AND SYSTEMS

Nihil simul inventum est et per-fectum. (Nothing is invented and perfected at the same time.)

LATIN PROVERB

Our study thus far has focused on the theoretical framework and mathematical foundations of artificial neural systems. Having understood the computational principles of massively parallel interconnected simple "neural" processors, we may now put them to good use in the design of practical systems. Numerous clues and guidelines for applications of neural algorithms and systems were developed in preceding chapters. However, most such applications have been presented to illustrate the operating principles of neural networks rather than to reflect a practical focus. As we shall see in this chapter, neurocomputing architectures are successfully applicable to many real-life problems. Moreover, their application potential seems to be enormous but not yet fully realized.

Examples of diverse applications are tied together in this chapter. The published technical references on applications of neural networks number well over a thousand papers and perhaps several hundred more are printed every year. Instead of merely enumerating many successful project titles of that list in an encyclopaedic manner, the approach taken in this chapter is to study about a dozen applications in detail. The applications selected for coverage are believed to be representative of the field, and the depth of their coverage should prepare the readers to pursue their own application project development. However, since the area of neural networks is expanding very rapidly, new problems and solution approaches may emerge in the near future beyond those presented in this chapter.

First we discuss a single-layer fully coupled feedback network for solving classical optimization problems. The network used for this purpose is a gradient-type network and it can be designed so that it minimizes the linear cost function in the presence of linear constraints. Character recognition networks are discussed for both printed and written character evaluation. We shall see that although ordinary multilayer feedforward networks consisting of continuous perceptrons can be successfully used for this purpose, unconventional architectures and approaches result in even higher character recognition rates.

Selected approaches to building neurocontrollers are presented with explanations of how they make it possible to identify the plants, and how they can be used as controllers. Adaptive control issues as well as neurocontrol of the dynamic plant are examined and illustrated with application examples. Subsequently, techniques closely related to neurocontrol systems and applied to the control of robot kinematics are covered. Feedforward networks capable of performing kinematics transformations, trajectory control, and robot hand target point learning are examined.

Next, three connectionist expert systems are presented. The real-life examples of medical expert systems for diagnosis of skin diseases, low back pain, and heart diseases are examined. Their performance is reviewed and compared with the success rate of human experts. Finally, the applications for self-organizing semantic feature maps are covered. Their practical use can be envisaged for sentence processing and extraction of symbolic meaning and contextual information implicit in human language.

In this chapter an attempt is made to review a number of successful implementations of massively parallel networks, and to apply them to different tasks. We will try to determine the best architectures to accomplish certain functions, how the networks should be trained, whether or not they can be useful during the training phase, how well they perform in real-life training examples, and how they are able to generalize to unknown tasks from the already known ones. Most of these questions cannot be answered independently and some of them cannot be answered conclusively. By the end of the chapter, however, we will have an understanding of how to select and design networks to fulfill a number of particular goals.

8.1

LINEAR PROGRAMMING MODELING NETWORK

The interconnected networks of analog processors can be used for the solution of constrained optimization problems, including the linear programming problem. As studied in Chapter 5, properly designed single-layer feedback networks are capable of acquiring the properties of gradient-type systems. Such systems can be used to solve optimization problems since they minimize, in time, their energy function value. The crucial task in designing a system seeking the minimum of its energy function is the translation of the optimization problem into a suitable definition of the energy function. The gradient-type network of analog processors that can find the solution of the linear programming problem is discussed in this section.

The *linear programming problem* may be stated as follows: Find the unknowns $v_1, v_2, \ldots, v_n$, so as to minimize the cost function

$$c \overset{\Delta}{=} a_1 v_1 + a_2 v_2 + \cdots + a_n v_n \tag{8.1a}$$

where $a_1, a_2, \ldots, a_n$ are called price coefficients. The minimization is subject to the following conditions, which are linear constraints:

$$
\begin{aligned}
w_{11} v_1 + w_{12} v_2 + \cdots + w_{1n} v_n &\geq b_1 \\
w_{21} v_1 + w_{22} v_2 + \cdots + w_{2n} v_n &\geq b_2 \\
&\vdots \\
w_{m1} v_1 + w_{m2} v_2 + \cdots + w_{mn} v_n &\geq b_m
\end{aligned}
\tag{8.1b}
$$

where coefficients b_j, for $j = 1, 2, \ldots, m$, are called bounds or requirements.

The cost function (8.1a) may be equivalently expressed in matrix form using the price vector $\mathbf{a}$ and the variable vector $\mathbf{v}$

$$c = \mathbf{a}^t \mathbf{v} \tag{8.2a}$$

where

$$
\begin{aligned}
\mathbf{a} &\overset{\Delta}{=} \begin{bmatrix} a_1 & a_2 & \ldots & a_n \end{bmatrix}^t \\
\mathbf{v} &\overset{\Delta}{=} \begin{bmatrix} v_1 & v_2 & \ldots & v_n \end{bmatrix}^t
\end{aligned}
$$

The linear constraint condition (8.1b) now becomes

$$\mathbf{w}_j^t \mathbf{v} \geq b_j, \quad \text{for } j = 1, 2, \ldots, m \tag{8.2b}$$

where

$$\mathbf{w}_j \overset{\Delta}{=} \begin{bmatrix} w_{j1} & w_{j2} & \ldots & w_{jn} \end{bmatrix}^t$$

contains the n variable weight coefficients w_{ji} of each j'th linear constraint inequality (8.1b).

A gradient-type network based on the energy minimization concept can be used to compute the solution of problem (8.1) or (8.2). A variation of the mathematical analysis used in Chapter 5 leads to the network shown in Figure 8.1(a) for the case $n = 2$ and $m = 4$. The description below follows the approach and the network design example outlined in Tank and Hopfield (1986).

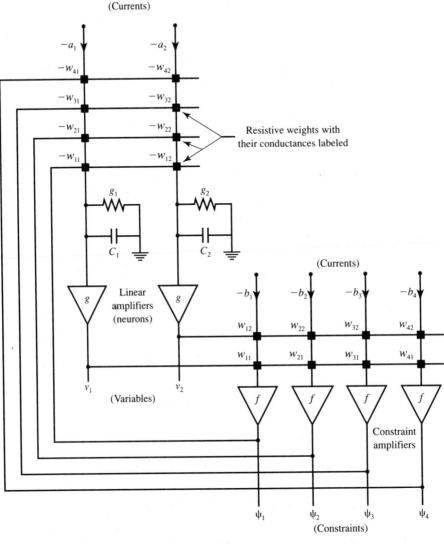

(a)

Figure 8.1a The architecture of a single-layer feedback network that solves a two-variable four-constraint linear programming problem: (a) network. [©*IEEE*; reprinted from Tank and Hopfield (1986) with permission.]

The network modeling the outlined minimization task consists of n neurons with output voltages v_i, for $i = 1, 2, \ldots, n$, which are variables in the linear programming problem. The input-output relationship of neurons is denoted as $v_i = g(u_i)$. Since the neurons are described here by a linear activation function, only n simple linear amplifiers of constant gain need to be used. The remaining

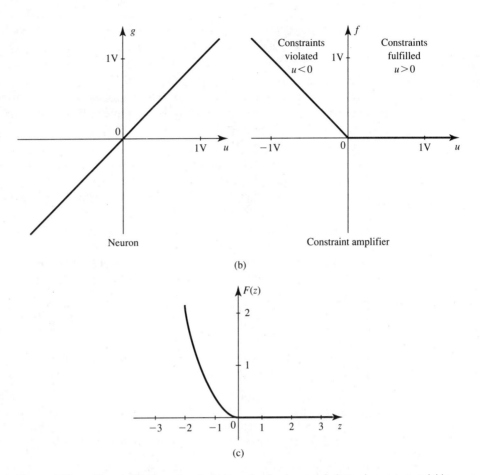

Figure 8.1b,c The architecture of a single-layer feedback network that solves a two-variable four-constraint linear programming problem *(continued):* (b) neuron and constraint amplifier characteristics, and (c) penalty function. [©*IEEE;* reprinted from Tank and Hopfield (1986) with permission.]

m amplifiers in the network are called constraint amplifiers and are characterized by the nonlinear relationship $\psi_j = f(u_j)$:

$$f(u_j) \triangleq \begin{cases} 0, & \text{for } u_j \geq 0 \\ -u_j, & \text{for } u_j < 0 \end{cases} \qquad (8.3a)$$

where

$$u_j = \mathbf{w}_j^t \mathbf{v} - b_j, \quad \text{for } j = 1, 2, \ldots, m \qquad (8.3b)$$

The voltage transfer characteristics of the neuron and of the constraint amplifier are shown in Figure 8.1(b). The nonlinear function definition (8.3a) provides for the output of the constraint amplifier to yield a large positive output value when the corresponding constraint inequality it represents is violated, i.e., when u_j is negative. Each of the constraint amplifiers receives constraint input current proportional to the bound value $-b_j$, and its additional input is expressed as the linear combination of neurons' outputs in the form $\sum_i w_{ji} v_i$.

The output voltage ψ_j of the j'th constraint amplifier produces the input currents to all neurons that are linear amplifiers. The input current of the i'th neuron is proportional to $-w_{ji}$, as well as to the price coefficient $-a_i$. As with the neurons of the Hopfield model network of Figure 5.4, the $g(u_i)$ amplifiers have input conductance and capacitance denoted as g_i and C_i, respectively. Although these components are not explicitly designed parts of the linear programming modeling network, they both represent the amplifiers' parasitic input impedance and are responsible for the appropriate time-domain behavior of the entire network. At the same time, we assume here that the response time of the $\psi(u_j)$ constraint amplifiers is negligibly small compared to that of the $g(u_i)$ amplifiers.

Under the assumptions stated, the KCL equation for the neuron input nodes of the network shown in Figure 8.1(a) can be expressed as it was in (5.11). It takes the form of the following state equation:

$$C_i \frac{du_i}{dt} = -a_i - u_i G_i - \sum_{j=1}^{m} w_{ji} \psi_j, \quad \text{for } i = 1, 2, \dots, n \qquad (8.4a)$$

where G_i denotes the sum of all conductances connected to the input of the i'th neuron and is equal to

$$G_i \stackrel{\Delta}{=} g_i - \sum_{j=1}^{m} w_{ji} \qquad (8.4b)$$

Using (8.3), the above formula can be expressed as follows:

$$C_i \frac{du_i}{dt} = -a_i - u_i G_i - \sum_{j=1}^{m} w_{ji} f(\mathbf{w}_j^t \mathbf{v} - b_j), \quad \text{for } i = 1, 2, \dots, n \qquad (8.5)$$

The discussed network for solving the linear programming task needs to minimize a meaningfully selected energy function. Assume now that the following Liapunov's function is an adequate choice for the energy function in this problem:

$$E(\mathbf{v}) \stackrel{\Delta}{=} \mathbf{a}^t \mathbf{v} + \sum_{j=1}^{m} F\left(\mathbf{w}_j^t \mathbf{v} - b_j\right) + \sum_{i=1}^{n} G_i \int_0^{v_i} g^{-1}(v) dv \qquad (8.6a)$$

where $F(z)$ is defined for dummy variable z as follows:

$$f(z) = \frac{dF(z)}{dz} \qquad (8.6b)$$

The components of the gradient vector of the assumed energy function (8.6a) can be expressed by finding its derivatives as follows

$$\frac{\partial E(\mathbf{v})}{\partial v_i} = a_i + u_i G_i + \sum_{j=1}^{m} w_{ji} f(\mathbf{w}_j^t \mathbf{v} - b_j) \qquad (8.7)$$

The time derivative of the energy function of (5.13) can now be expressed using (8.7):

$$\frac{dE}{dt} = \sum_{i=1}^{n} \frac{dv_i}{dt} \left(a_i + u_i G_i + \sum_{j=1}^{m} w_{ji} f(\mathbf{w}_j^t \mathbf{v} - b_j) \right) \tag{8.8}$$

Since the bracketed expression in (8.8) is the right side of the network state equation (8.4a), the time derivative of the energy function can be rewritten in the form similar to (5.17):

$$\frac{dE}{dt} = - \sum_{i=1}^{n} C_i \frac{dv_i}{dt} \cdot \frac{du_i}{dt} \tag{8.9a}$$

Using (5.18), the above expression can be rearranged as follows:

$$\frac{dE}{dt} = - \sum_{i=1}^{n} C_i g^{-1'}(v_i) \left(\frac{dv_i}{dt} \right)^2 \tag{8.9b}$$

Since $C_i > 0$, and $g^{-1}(v_i)$ is the monotone increasing function, the sum on the right side of (8.9) is nonnegative, and therefore we have $dE/dt \leq 0$, unless $dv_i/dt = 0$, in which case $dE/dt = 0$. Thus, the network shown in Figure 8.1 and described with the state equations (8.4) is a gradient-type network. During the transient period, the network seeks the minima of its energy function (8.6a) and the motion of the system stops there. It will seek the minima in space $v_1, v_2, \ldots, v_n$ in the direction which has the positive projection on the negative gradient vector, $-\nabla E(\mathbf{v})$, as explained in more detail in Section 5.3.

In fact, the cost term $\mathbf{a}'\mathbf{v}$ is only minimized during the transient state, while the second term of (8.6a) is needed to prevent the violation of the constraint relationship (8.2b) and to push the network equilibrium point toward the edge of the allowed region. This can be seen from Figure 8.1(c) which shows the nonzero penalty function $F(z)$ for inequality constraints that are not fulfilled. There is no penalty for constraints met when $z > 0$. However, a steep penalty applies if $F(z) = (1/2)z^2$ for $z < 0$. This results from integrating the function $f(u)$ introduced in (8.3a) and using the definition of $F(z)$ from (8.6b).

A small computational network has been developed using an electronic model as shown in Figure 8.1(a) (Tank and Hopfield, 1986) to solve a two-variable linear programming problem with four constraints. The constraint amplifiers with voltage transfer functions (8.3a) are operational amplifiers with diode circuitry to provide both clamping response ($\psi = 0$), and linear response ($\psi = -u$) circuits. The following constraint inequalities representing inequalities (8.1b) chosen arbitrarily for the experiment are

$$v_2 \leq 5$$
$$-v_1 \leq 5$$
$$\frac{5}{12}v_1 - v_2 \leq \frac{35}{12} \tag{8.10a}$$
$$\frac{5}{2}v_1 + v_2 \leq \frac{35}{2}$$

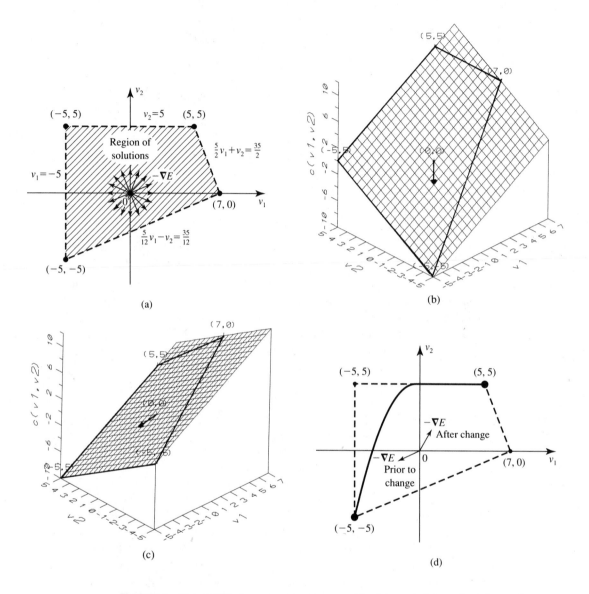

Figure 8.2 Two-variable linear programming example: (a) constraints and solution region, (b) cost plane $c = v_1 + v_2$, (c) cost plane $c = v_1 - v_2$, and (d) trajectory when gradient vectors are switched. [Parts (a) and (d) ©*IEEE*; adapted from Tank and Hopfield (1986) with permission.]

By comparing coefficients of inequalities (8.10a) with those of (8.1b), weight coefficients (conductances w_{ij}) and input biases (currents b_j) can be computed. Figure 8.2(a) shows constraint lines (8.10a) depicted with dashed lines on the plane v_1, v_2, which is the solution domain. The region of penalty-free solutions is within the shaded quadrangle and includes its edges and vertices. Indeed, the solution point minimizing the cost function (8.1a) is one of the four vertices of the quadrangle shown.

The choice of the solution point by the system modeling the problem is dependent on the orientation of the cost function. Let us look at the geometrical interpretation of the cost minimization issue. The cost function itself can be depicted as a plane in the three-dimensional space v_1, v_2, c, for $n = 2$. Moreover, the cost plane described by Equation (8.1a) always intersects the origin. The direction of the negative gradient vector of the linear two-variable cost function c can be represented as a vector from the origin pointing in one of the directions as shown in Figure 8.2(a). The negative gradient vector of the cost function c is given as

$$-\nabla c(\mathbf{v}) = \begin{bmatrix} -a_1 \\ -a_2 \end{bmatrix} \tag{8.10b}$$

As the cost function is changed, the cost plane tilts in a new direction, and the optimum solution of the linear programming problem may also change by displacement from one point to another. In such a case, the solution would dislocate from one vertex to another. Figures 8.2(b) and (c), show two sample cost planes defined by the cost function (8.1a) with price coefficients $a_1 = a_2 = 1$, and $a_1 = 1$, $a_2 = -1$, respectively. The corresponding vectors indicating the direction of the steepest descent of cost functions can be expressed as

$$-\nabla c = \begin{bmatrix} -1 \\ -1 \end{bmatrix} \tag{8.10c}$$

and

$$-\nabla c = \begin{bmatrix} -1 \\ 1 \end{bmatrix} \tag{8.10d}$$

The negative gradient vectors, shown for each of the planes in Figures 8.2(b) and (c) as coming out of the origin, indicate the directions of the transient solution of the problem for known constraints. As can be seen from Figure 8.2(a), the first vector would guarantee convergence of the network to the vertex $(-5, -5)$, the second would result in the solution at the vertex $(-5, 5)$.

For the series of experiments reported in Tank and Hopfield (1986), the output voltages v_1 and v_2 of the modeling network have consistently stabilized in one of the four vertices shown, dependent on the price coefficients chosen. The cost plane gradient vector was swept in a circle to check the convergence to the optimal solution in each case. Each time, the circuit stabilized at the minimum cost points corresponding to the correct constrained solution for a chosen gradient direction. In another set of experiments reported (Tank and Hopfield, 1986), the gradient vectors rapidly switched direction after the network had found the solution. This is illustrated in Figure 8.2(d). The stable solution of the problem found by the network moved accordingly from the vertex $(-5, -5)$ to the vertex $(5, 5)$ along the trajectory as shown. Since the solution area is always convex for linear programming problems (Simmons, 1972), the network is guaranteed to converge to the optimum solution.

8.2 CHARACTER RECOGNITION NETWORKS

As already discussed in Chapter 4, multilayer feedforward networks can be trained to solve a variety of data classification and recognition problems. Some of the examples of introductory classification applications were presented in Section 4.6. This section covers in more detail character recognition networks of both printed and handwritten characters. Initial emphasis is placed on the comparison of different learning techniques for feedforward architectures. We also demonstrate that handwritten character recognition tasks can be successfully performed by unusual and unconventional neural network designs. Specifically, successfully tested digit recognizers have employed hand-crafted multiple neural template windows, or transformations, and have involved specialized multilayer feature detectors with a limited number of degrees of freedom.

Multilayer Feedforward Network for Printed Character Classification

This section provides a comprehensive performance evaluation of the limitations and capabilities of multilayer feedforward networks for printed character recognition. Network learning parameters, architectures, and learning profiles are investigated (Zigoris 1989). Based on the comparison of different network architectures, the best size and training parameters will be devised for printed character classifiers (Zurada et al. 1991).

An introductory study of a multilayer continuous perceptron network for simple printed character recognition has been reported by Chandra and Sudhakar (1988). The performance of various classifiers was discussed and compared for recognition of digits "0" through "9" encoded as 20-tuple binary-valued input vectors representing black and white pixels. An error back-propagation network for classification of these data was evaluated. The network is of a 20–10–10 size denoting the number of input nodes, hidden-layer neurons, and output neurons, respectively. This convention for denoting network size using symbols I–J–K is consistent with Figure 4.7 an with the notation in earlier chapters. At least 1000 training cycles were used to develop the network, and reasonable classification results were achieved and reported by Chandra and Sudhakar (1988).

A similar study was done on pixel-image classification of amoebae nuclei images (Dayhoff and Dayhoff 1988). This application, which is similar in

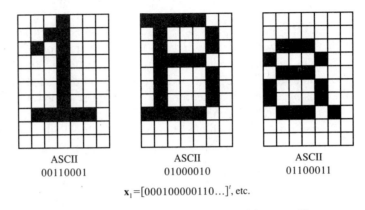

ASCII
00110001

ASCII
01000010

ASCII
01100011

$\mathbf{x}_1 = [000100000110\ldots]^t$, etc.

Figure 8.3 Bit maps for sample characters "1," "B," and "a," for recognition.

principle to printed character recognition, involved a gray-scale pixel matrix with geometric patterns that need to be recognized. The 7×9 pixel-grid signal was used and fed through 16 hidden-layer neurons to a 7×9 output grid. The study was based on four training images; 3000 cycles were required to train the network successfully.

Let us review the performance of multilayer feedforward architectures for classification of a full set of printed lowercase and uppercase letters, digits, and punctuation characters. In this application, standard dot-matrix printer characters need to be recognized robustly and correctly from a set of 95 characters. Each character is a 7-column $\times$ 10-row pixel matrix defined by Apple Computer (1986). The example bit maps for three characters from the set are shown in Figure 8.3. The training set consisting of 95 characters has also been used to test the performance of the trained network, and it has provided a relatively large number of input/output pattern pairs. Depending on the requirements for the classifying network, the output pattern has been chosen either as an 8-bit ASCII code of the character (distributed representation) or a single output bit that has been set to 1 for each character pattern to be recognized (local representation). The total of either 8 or 95 output neurons has been required, respectively, for the output layer trained in each of the output representations mentioned.

Continuous unipolar neurons are employed throughout this experiment for training and recall. The binary input vector representing the pixel pattern of each character has been fed directly into the network. No effort has been made to perform either preprocessing or feature extraction of any kind in this experiment. The outputs have been thresholded at 0.5 to obtain a binary output value in the test mode. The three basic network properties investigated for this application were the learning constant η, the activation function steepness coefficient λ, and the network architecture. The topologies of the network under study have been limited out of necessity since the number of different architectures potentially relevant for this classification task is enormous.

The number of input nodes I has been kept at a constant value of 70, equal to the number of pixels. Single and double hidden-layer networks with different layer sizes denoted as J have been evaluated for both 8 and 95 output neurons. The number of output neurons is denoted as K. Ideally, the network should be able to generate 8-bit ASCII encoded output. Such an 8-bit output architecture using eight output neurons is of particular importance because it combines two steps. Both recognition and encoding of the character pattern are performed by the network in a single processing step. In addition, this architecture yields more concise classification results compared to the local representation which requires 95 output nodes.

The simulation experiments described later in this section indicate that the number of neurons in each of the hidden layers can drastically affect both the accuracy and the speed of training. Some patterns require decision regions that cannot be realized by a low number of hidden layer neurons. Too many neurons in the hidden layer, however, can prevent effective training from occurring since the initial decision regions formed become too complex due to the excessive number of neurons for the application. The end result is often that the network weights get readily trapped in a local minimum during training and no further learning occurs.

The performance of the network has been measured in terms of its response errors with respect to correct classification results. Four different error measures have been monitored during the training and recall phases. They are E_{max}, E_{rms}, N_{err}, and E_d.

The maximum error denoted as E_{max} expresses the largest of the single neuron errors encountered during the full training cycle consisting of $P = 95$ steps, where P denotes the size of the training set. A value of 1 implies that at least 1 bit is totally incorrect. Since the character recognition application requires binary output, the network implements a postprocessing thresholding function to yield binary output decisions. The error E_{rms} is defined as in (4.35) and it serves as an ordinary root-mean-square normalized quadratic error measure, before thresholding. The absolute number of bit errors N_{err} at thresholded outputs during the single complete training cycle is also used as a local measure of comparison of learning quality and speed. The decision error E_d defined in (4.36) is used as a normalized error value computed over the total number of output bit errors N_{err} resulting at K thresholded outputs over the complete training cycle consisting of presentation of P patterns.

The simulated error back-propagation training runs were performed in two phases (Zurada et al. 1991). The first phase consisted of a large number of preliminary runs with various combinations of parameters and architectures. The runs were performed to determine an overall training effectiveness for various and often intentionally diversified learning conditions. This can be termed as a coarse search for suitable architectures. During the second phase of the runs, optimal parameters for network learning were explored. This second phase emphasized a fine heuristic search for optimum training conditions.

TABLE 8.1

Evaluation of 70–J–95 architecture, single hidden layer, $J = 35$ or 70 (printed character recognition network).

Run	Steepness Factor λ	Learning Constant η	Hidden Layer J	Training Length (cycles)	Max Error E_{max}	E_{rms}	Bit Errors N_{err}	Decision Error E_d
1	1	0.1	70	3600	0.9991	10^{-6}	1	0.0001
2		0.5	70	575	0.0209	10^{-6}	0	0
3	1	0.1	35	1900	0.1279	10^{-6}	0	0
				3975	0.0033	10^{-6}	0	0
4		0.5	35	1000	0.0627	10^{-6}	0	0
				3975	0.0004	0	0	0
5	1	0.1	35	3500	1	$2 \cdot 10^{-6}$	4	0.0004
6		0.5	35	3975		$2 \cdot 10^{-6}$	2	0.0004
7	2	0.1	70	3450	1	$4 \cdot 10^{-6}$	12	0.0013
				3975		$4 \cdot 10^{-6}$	12	0.0013
8		0.5	70	2400		$2 \cdot 10^{-6}$	5	0.0006
				3975		$2 \cdot 10^{-6}$	5	0.0006
9		0.1	35	3975		$8 \cdot 10^{-6}$	51	0.0057
10	5	0.1	70	2200	1	$9 \cdot 10^{-6}$	68	0.0075
				3975		$9 \cdot 10^{-6}$	68	0.0075
11		5	70	250		$1.9 \cdot 10^{-5}$	281	0.0311
				3975		$1.9 \cdot 10^{-5}$	280	0.0310

Table 8.1 shows results of the initial series of runs for a single hidden layer network of size 70–J–95 with $J = 35$ or 70. The training length for each run was different and involved up to several thousand cycles as listed in the fifth column of the table. The most important result of the preliminary training runs has been that for $\lambda = 5$ the network did not train properly (runs 9–11). The lowest number of single bit errors was 51 for 35 hidden units when $\eta = 0.1$. The number of errors got worse as the number of hidden units was increased. In practical simulation the error tends to oscillate. Since the activation function around zero has been very steep for this particular series of runs, this caused overcorrections and the weights did not settle at their proper value but instead

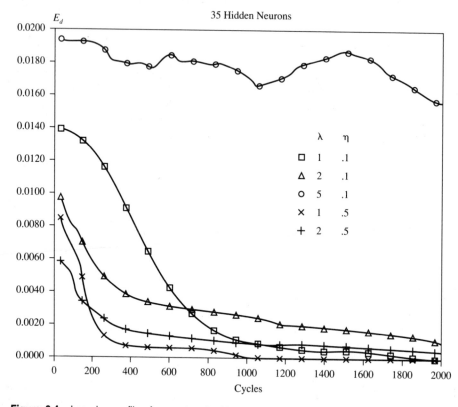

Figure 8.4 Learning profiles for a network with 35 hidden neurons; local representation.

swung from one extreme to another. Further increases of η tend to aggravate the problem by further overcorrections and have led to increased error values.

The problem of excessive errors is reduced with $\lambda = 2$, which ensures slower learning, but at least several bit errors have consistently occurred (runs 5–8). Finally, runs with $\lambda = 1$ seem to yield the best results (runs 1–4). Very small error values have been obtained for both 35 and 70 hidden units and for learning constants having a value of either 0.1 or 0.5. The training for 0 bit errors required fewer cycles with 70 hidden units (run 2); however, a 70–35–95 network with $\lambda = 1$ initially turned out to be the best for the task evaluated (runs 3 and 4). Simulations for 140 hidden units resulted in bit errors that were unacceptably high (637 and 1635), oscillatory, and involved prolonged training sessions.

Figure 8.4 illustrates the decision error of the recall phase versus the training length for the 70–35–95 network. It has been observed from a series of simulations that most training runs for the same network configuration and learning

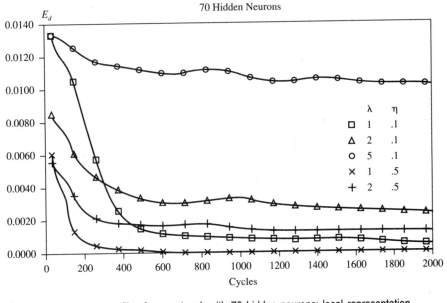

Figure 8.5   Learning profiles for a network with 70 hidden neurons; local representation.

parameters yield only a slightly different learning profile. This is due to the fact that weights are initialized at random values. Thus, the learning profiles shown in the figure can be considered typical, or average, for the selected network size and training parameters. The best learning profile and the least final error is achieved for $\lambda = 1$ and $\eta = 0.5$ (run 2). The decision error E_d typically reduces to zero after several hundred training cycles. The error curves on Figure 8.4 for $\lambda = 1$ and 2 also show reasonable training speed and accuracy.

In contrast, the decision error E_d for $\lambda = 5$, $\eta = 0.1$ does not converge to a reasonable value. Somewhat similar learning profiles have resulted for 70 hidden-unit networks. Training results for this network configuration are depicted in Figure 8.5. Figure 8.6 shows the results of a 140 hidden-neuron network training process. Notice that the error axis now starts at $E_d = 0.04$. The decision error does not undergo substantial reduction in spite of continued training. This configuration was therefore found to be unacceptable and was not pursued beyond the preliminary phase of training runs.

Table 8.2 shows the simulation results for double hidden-layer networks with the output layer of eight neurons. For this configuration the characters need to be encoded by the classifier in the ASCII format. Various architectures that have been tested employ the first hidden layer of size $J1 = 35$ and 70, and the second hidden layer of size $J2 = 8$ and 70. The results for double hidden layers are, in general, better than for a single hidden layer, and the final errors

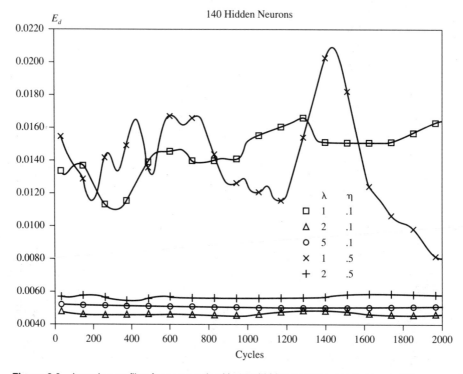

Figure 8.6 Learning profiles for a network with 140 hidden neurons; local representation.

are smaller. Three specific architectural hidden layer sizes $(J1, J2)$ that have been simulated are: $(70, 70)$, $(70, 8)$, and $(35, 8)$ (Zurada et al. 1991).

Simulations 1 through 6 correspond to $\lambda = 1$. Virtually all runs show reasonable results and a small number of bit errors. Runs 2 and 4 have the most bit errors, whereas all remaining runs converge to the single bit error. These particular runs have $\eta = 0.5$ in common. In addition to one bit error, runs 3, 5, and 6 also display the fastest convergence. Runs 7 through 12 are performed for $\lambda = 2$. These results are more varied and consist of some excellent results along with some extremely bad ones. The notably bad results are runs 10 and 12. Not only has training been excessively long, but run 10 resulted in an oscillatory bit error with a peak value of 103, and run 12 resulted in a large error of 150 incorrect decision bits. Runs 7 and 8 exhibited superb results since they both converged to zero bit errors. In addition, convergence of training to zero bit errors was extremely quick, 90 cycles for run 7, and only 40 cycles for run 8. Both these runs had $J1 = 70$ and $J2 = 70$ in common. Given this large number of hidden-layer units, the redundancy in feature recognition for this network is rather large. This seems to be the most likely reason for this particular network architecture to have produced no bit errors.

TABLE 8.2

Evaluation of 70–$J1$–$J2$–8 architecture, double
hidden layer (printed character recognition network).

Run	Steepness Factor λ	Learning Constant η	Hidden Layers $J1$	$J2$	Training Length (cycles)	Max Error E_{max}	E_{rms}	Bit Errors N_{err}	Decision Error E_d
1	1	0.1	70	70	2190	1	$58 \cdot 10^{-6}$	1	0.0013
2		0.5	70	70	310		$83 \cdot 10^{-6}$	3	0.0039
3	1	0.1	70	8	390	1	$98 \cdot 10^{-6}$	1	0.0013
4		0.5	70	8	980		$137 \cdot 10^{-6}$	8	0.0105
5	1	0.1	35	8	620	1	$80 \cdot 10^{-6}$	1	0.0013
6		0.5	35	8	870		$87 \cdot 10^{-6}$	1	0.0039
7		0.1	70	70	90	0.2034	$47 \cdot 10^{-6}$	0	0
	2				2520	0.0001	$3.6 \cdot 10^{-6}$	0	0
					4990	0.0001	$3.6 \cdot 10^{-6}$	0	0
8		0.5	70	70	40	0.9994	$58 \cdot 10^{-6}$	0	0
					210	0.0041	$11 \cdot 10^{-6}$	0	0
					830	0.0001	$3.6 \cdot 10^{-6}$	0	0
					3300	0.0000		0	0
9	2	0.1	70	8	2160	1	$51 \cdot 10^{-6}$	1	0.0013
10		0.5	70	8	4990	1	$435 \cdot 10^{-6}$	103	0.1355
11	2	0.1	35	8	110	1	$98 \cdot 10^{-6}$	1	0.0026
12		0.5	35	8	4990	1	$551 \cdot 10^{-6}$	150	0.1973

Table 8.3 summarizes the results of two runs with $J1 = J2 = 70$, $K = 8$, $\lambda = 2$, $\eta = 0.1$, and $\eta = 0.5$. Since this configuration with this choice of learning parameters has been so successful, additional simulations have been performed for this case to ensure consistency and to allow possibly for further optimization of the training. Both runs in Table 8.3 show excellent results, with run 1 converging to zero decision errors after 190 cycles, and run 2 converging to zero decision errors after only 60 cycles.

The discussion presented thus far indicates that the number of hidden layers and their sizes are of crucial importance for a particular application. Apparently a range of values exists for the number of hidden layers and their size that yields especially good results. Figure 8.7(a) shows the final decision error E_d for $\lambda = 1$

TABLE 8.3

Evaluation of 70–70–70–8 architecture (printed character recognition network).

Run	Steepness Factor λ	Learning Constant η	Hidden Layers J1	Hidden Layers J2	Training Length (cycles)	Max Error E_{max}	E_{rms}	Bit Errors N_{err}	Decision Error E_d
1	2	0.1	70	70	1	0.999	$798 \cdot 10^{-6}$	374	0.492
					10	0.999	$529 \cdot 10^{-6}$	160	0.210
					20	0.999	$428 \cdot 10^{-6}$	106	0.139
					30	0.998	$319 \cdot 10^{-6}$	50	0.066
					40	0.997	$214 \cdot 10^{-6}$	23	0.030
					50	0.997	$120 \cdot 10^{-6}$	4	0.005
					60	0.996	$98 \cdot 10^{-6}$	3	0.004
					70	0.996	$91 \cdot 10^{-6}$	3	0.004
					80	0.996	$76 \cdot 10^{-6}$	2	0.003
					90	0.993	$76 \cdot 10^{-6}$	2	0.003
					190	0.042	$29 \cdot 10^{-6}$	0	0
					200	0.020	$22 \cdot 10^{-6}$	0	0
					1500	0.0003	$3.6 \cdot 10^{-6}$	0	0
					2000	0.0002	$3.6 \cdot 10^{-6}$	0	0
2	2	0.5	70	70	1	0.997	$789 \cdot 10^{-6}$	329	0.433
					10	0.998	$660 \cdot 10^{-6}$	244	0.321
					20	0.999	$428 \cdot 10^{-6}$	105	0.138
					30	0.996	$192 \cdot 10^{-6}$	18	0.024
					40	0.910	$54 \cdot 10^{-6}$	1	0.001
					50	0.756	$51 \cdot 10^{-6}$	1	0.001
					60	0.005	$18 \cdot 10^{-6}$	0	0
					70	0.003	$14 \cdot 10^{-6}$	0	0
					420	0.002	$3.6 \cdot 10^{-6}$	0	0
					1990	0.000	$3.6 \cdot 10^{-6}$	0	0

and $\eta = 0.1$ versus the number of hidden units of the single hidden layer. The error has been computed after 500 training cycles for the number of hidden layer neurons covering the range from 5 to 150. The number of output units is kept equal to 8 thus ensuring an ASCII format for the output. The results indicate that low error values have been achieved within the range from 20 to 90 hidden units. The network with less than 20 hidden neurons has been incapable of learning all patterns, presumably, because the weight space has been too complicated. The error level has also become intolerable for more than 90 hidden units. The

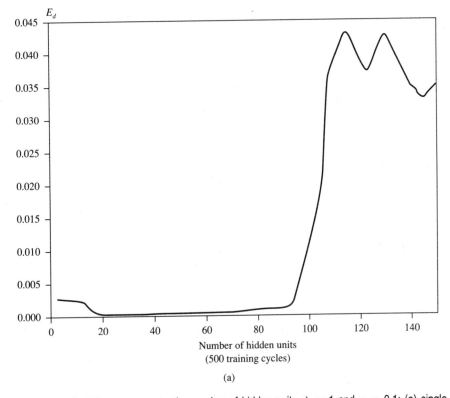

Figure 8.7a Decision error versus the number of hidden units, $\lambda = 1$ and $\eta = 0.1$: (a) single hidden-layer network.

system seems to be seriously overdetermined because of the large number of hidden units.

The training of a network with two hidden layers yielded superior results. Figure 8.7(b) shows the final decision error E_d versus the number of hidden units. In this training simulation, the number of hidden units is assumed to be variable but identical for both layers. The resulting optimum architecture is somewhat similar to that of the single hidden-layer network, ranging from 20 to 85 units. The primary difference was that the two hidden-layer network version tends to learn more reliably and quickly.

Figure 8.8 shows selected learning profiles for the training of single-layer networks. Several hidden-layer sizes covering the range from 20 to 80 units have been tested to find an optimum architecture. The number of training cycles needed to achieve a fixed decision error value seems to remain largely invariant with respect to the number of hidden-layer units. Although it is impossible to express analytically the error profiles as a function of training length, the simulations

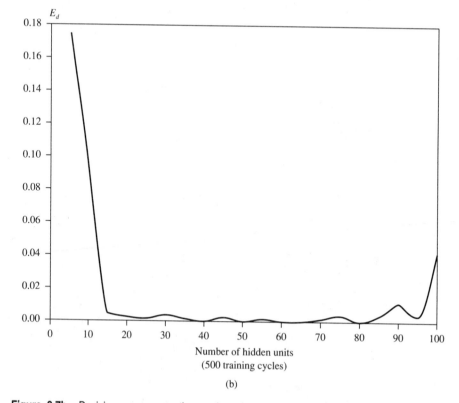

Figure 8.7b Decision error versus the number of hidden units, $\lambda = 1$ and $\eta = 0.1$ *(continued):* (b) double hidden-layer network of identical sizes $(J1 = J2)$.

seem to indicate that the decision error is approximately inversely proportional to the number of training cycles. With continued training, the error somewhat saturates at a low level. These conclusions seem to hold only for the case of feasible architectures, i.e., architectures that can learn the problem under study.

For this nontrivial application of multilayer feedforward networks for character classification, a number of reasonable solutions emerge. Let us summarize the results of the classification case study discussed in this section. The computationally most efficient value of activation steepness, λ , seems to be of unity value throughout each learning session. The learning constant of 0.5 works best with the number of hidden units ranging from 25 to 80. This size of hidden layer seems to be the most advantageous for both one and two hidden-layer systems. The best classification results are obtained with a two hidden-layer network employing about 70 hidden units per layer. Learning within this architecture has been quick and reliable; this size of layers presumably provides excellent redundancy. Remarkably, it has also been found that this size could be reduced

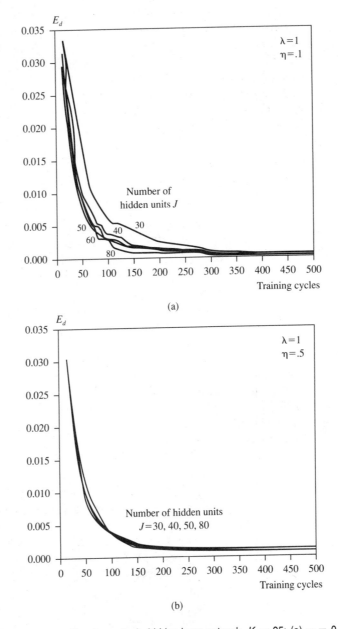

Figure 8.8 Learning profiles for a single hidden-layer network, $K = 95$: (a) $\eta = 0.1$ and (b) $\eta = 0.5$.

to approximately 25 without any major deterioration of classification. Training of networks with both too many or too few hidden units has resulted in slow learning with a somewhat excessive number of decision errors.

Finally, the configuration with 8 output neurons turns out to be generally superior compared to the local representation of classification involving 95 output neurons. Although both these architectures ensure a zero final decision error and thus both achieve perfect character classification, the configuration with 8 output neurons trains faster. It also results in a smaller network.

Handwritten Digit Recognition: Problem Statement

The ultimate success of neural networks depends on their effectiveness in solving a variety of real-life classification, recognition, or association problems that are more demanding and more difficult than any of the problems studied thus far. Let us look at recognition of objects that are drastically less structured than standard printed characters. In this group of problems, character recognition of handwritten digits represents an important example of a realistic, yet difficult, benchmark recognition task. This task has a clearly defined commercial importance and a level of difficulty that makes it challenging but still not so large and complex so as to be completely intractable. Recent technical reports have demonstrated that neural networks can perform handwritten digit recognition with state-of-the-art accuracy (Jackel et al. 1988; LeCun et al. 1989; Howard et al. 1990). In a number of respects, neural network solutions surpass even those obtained using other approaches. The basic neurocomputing techniques used for handwritten character classification are reviewed below.

Analysis shows that many difficult pattern recognition problems can be formulated as multidimensional curve fitting using the methods of approximation learning described in Section 2.4. In character recognition, however, the general rules for distinguishing between characters are neither known, nor have they been formulated. The best current process is to examine a large cross section of the character population with the goal of finding a function that adequately generalizes the exemplars from the training set. This would possibly allow for recognition of the test characters not contained in the original training set. Let us look at the neural network learning algorithms and approaches that first preprocess and then map handwritten digit character images to one of the ten categories. As we will see, neural network classifiers often yield comparable or better accuracy and, more importantly, require far less development time compared to conventional classifiers.

The example database used to train and test the network consists of 9298 isolated numerals digitized from handwritten zip codes that appear on U.S. mail envelopes (LeCun et al. 1989). Typical digit examples used for this project are

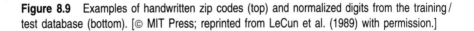

Figure 8.9 Examples of handwritten zip codes (top) and normalized digits from the training/test database (bottom). [© MIT Press; reprinted from LeCun et al. (1989) with permission.]

shown in Figure 8.9. The digits are written by many different people using a great variety of sizes, writing styles, instruments, and with a widely varying amount of care. It can be noted that many of the digits are poorly formed and are hard to classify, even for a human. Of the 7291 sample digits used for training, 2007 have been used for test purposes. The captured digits are first normalized to fill an area consisting of 40×60 black and white pixels. The resulting normalized patterns are presented to a neural network after being reduced to 16×16 pixel images. Further processing is performed by a mix of custom hardware and specialized software for image processing.

The general, common strategy for handwritten character processing is to extract features from the images and then perform the classification based on the resultant feature map (Graf, Jackel, and Hubbard 1988). As the first step of the recognition sequence, a digital computer equipped with frame-grab hardware captures a video image of a handwritten character. The computer thresholds the gray-level image into black and white pixels. This stage can be termed "image capturing." Next, the image is scaled both horizontally and vertically to fill a 16×16 pixel block. The 16×16 scaled character format appears to be of adequate resolution for the set of 10 digits, but would probably be too small to deal with letters or more complex characters.

Recognition Based on Handwritten Character Skeletonization

This section reports on one of the earlier attempts at building neural network-based handwritten character recognizers (Jackel et al. 1988; Graf, Jackel, and Hubbard 1988). The image capturing and scaling as described in the preceding paragraph is followed by the "skeletonization." This is a process that makes the lines one dimensional by removing meaningless linewidth variations. The rationale for line-thinning preprocessing is that a smaller number of features is sufficient to analyze the skeletonized images. Since the linewidth does not carry much information about the character itself, the skeletonization removes pixels of the image until only a backbone of the character remains, and the broad strokes are reduced to thin lines. Skeletonization is illustrated in Figure 8.10(a) where the gray area represents the original character, the digit 3, and the black area is its skeletonized image.

The skeletonization is implemented through scanning of the 5×5 pixel window template across the entire image. Twenty different 25-bit window templates are stored on the neural network chip. These templates are responsible for performing the skeletonization of the images. One of the templates is shown in Figure 8.10(b). During scanning each template tests for a particular condition that allows the deletion of the middle pixel in the window. If the match of the image pixels to any of the templates exceeds a preset threshold value, the center pixel of the character bit map is deleted.

In this manner, the entire 16×16 pixel image is scanned, and a decision is made for each pixel in the image whether that pixel just makes the line fat and can be deleted, or whether its presence is crucial to keep the connectivity of the character intact (Graf, Jackel, and Hubbard 1988). The 20 different templates for scanning images were crafted by network designers in a systematic but *ad hoc* manner. Examples of a single scanning pass through the image using four selected window templates are shown in Figure 8.11. The black pixels deleted

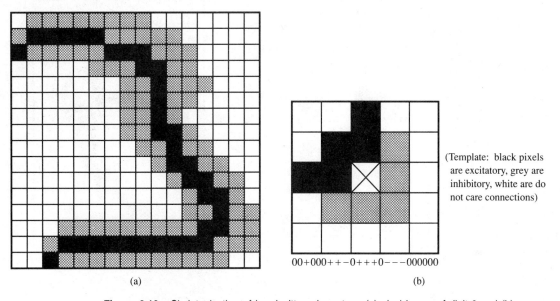

(Template: black pixels are excitatory, grey are inhibitory, white are do not care connections)

00+000++−0+++0−−−000000

(a)   (b)

Figure 8.10 Skeletonization of handwritten characters: (a) pixel image of digit 3 and (b) example of one of the window templates used for line thinning. [©*IEEE;* reprinted from Graf, Jackel, and Hubbard (1988) with permission]

in the images shown as a result of each template pass are marked in gray on the four images in each box.

The skeletonization process is followed by the feature extraction process for each character. In the feature extraction stage, the thinned image is presented to a number of 7×7 feature extracting pixel window templates. The neural network chip stores 20 different feature extracting window templates, again chosen *ad hoc,* but inspired by results from experimental neurobiology. Feature extraction processing by means of window templates is illustrated in Figure 8.12. The templates check for the presence of oriented lines, oriented line ends, and arcs in the image of a skeletonized character, for example, like the one displayed in Figure 8.12(a). Examples of the extracted features of line endstops and horizontal lines are shown in Figures 8.12(b), (c), and (d). Whenever a feature template match exceeds the preset threshold, a 1 is set in a blank feature map for that corresponding feature. In this way, a feature map is produced for every template. The maps of such features for each evaluated character skeleton are then subjected to an "OR" function after the scan is completed (Jackel et al. 1988).

The feature extraction process terminates by mapping the skeletonized input pattern of 16×16 size image into 20 different 16×16 feature images. To compress the data, each feature map is then coarse-blocked into a 3×3 array. As a final result of processing for feature extraction, 20 different 3×3 feature

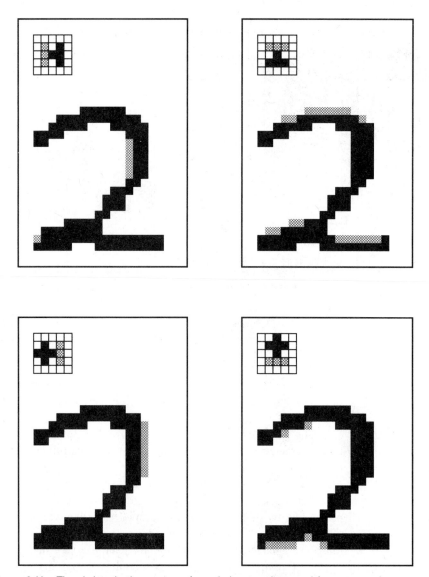

Figure 8.11 The skeletonization process, four window templates and four passes shown. (Templates: black pixels are excitatory, gray are inhibitory, white are do-not-care connections; digits: gray pixels are deleted by each template.) [©*IEEE;* adapted from Jackel et al. (1988) with permission.]

vectors, consisting jointly of 180 feature entries, are produced. These entries are then classified into one of the 10 categories signifying each of the 10 digits. Several conventional classification algorithms have been used to determine the class membership of the resulting vector. The overall results of this method

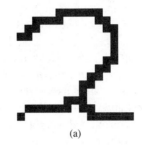

(a)

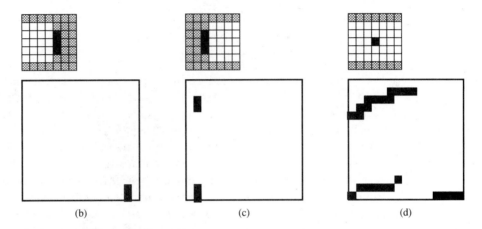

(b)   (c)   (d)

Figure 8.12 Examples of feature extraction: (a) skeletonized image for future extraction, (b) and (c) features of line endstops, and (d) features of horizontal lines. (Templates: black pixels are excitatory, gray are inhibitory, white are do-not-care connections.) [©*IEEE;* reprinted from Jackel et al. (1988) with permission.]

for handwritten character recognition have varied between 95% accuracy for hastily written digits and 99% accuracy for carefully written digits (Jackel et al. 1988). The tests were performed on digits taken again from the U.S. post office databases.

The approach to handwritten digit recognition described in this section is based on skeletonization and feature extraction using *ad hoc* experimentation and hand-chosen templates. This concept uses specially developed window templates and also a carefully organized scanning process. Through the scanning of suitable window templates across the character bit map, the original pattern of a character is decomposed into a single large-size feature vector. This is then followed by image compression. The sequence of processing is implemented by a neural network chip designed specifically for this purpose. The final classification of the feature vector obtained from each character is obtained using conventional computation.

The reader may have noticed that the approach presented in this section involves neither neural learning techniques nor the known recall algorithms described in the preceding chapters. Rather, the approach is based on analyzing the matching of the pattern with the number of movable window templates. The matching involves processing of the pattern segment through suitably chosen windows that represent weights for the pixels overlapping with the evaluated image. As we see, this approach, in which neural network learning has been replaced by using intuitively produced weight matrices associated with each window template, can be termed rather unconventional.

Recognition of Handwritten Characters Based on Error Back-propagation Training

Unlike the network described in the preceding section, the multilayer feed-forward neural network for handwritten character recognition can be directly fed with images obtained as slightly preprocessed original patterns containing low-level information. First, the 40×60 pixel binary input patterns are transformed to fit into a 16×16 pixel frame using a linear transformation. This frame contains the target image. The transformation preserves the aspect ratio of the character, but the resulting target image consisting of 256 entries is not binary. It has multiple gray levels because a variable number of pixels in the original input pattern can fall into a given pixel of the target image. The gray levels of each resulting target image are then scaled and translated to fall within the bipolar neuron's output value range, -1 to $+1$ (LeCun et al. 1989). This step is needed to utilize fully the mapping property of the activation function of the first layer of neurons.

The remainder of the recognition processing is performed by a rather elaborate multilayer feedforward network trained using the error back-propagation technique. The architecture of the network is shown in Figure 8.13. The network has three hidden layers, $J1$, $J2$, and $J3$, and an output layer consisting of 10 neurons. The hidden layers perform as trainable feature detectors.

The first hidden layer denoted as $J1$ consists of 12 groups of 64 units per group, each arranged in an 8×8 square. Each unit in $J1$ has connections only from the 5×5 contiguous square of pixels of the original input. The location of the 5×5 square shifts by two input pixels between neighbors in the hidden layer. The motivation for this is that high resolution may be needed to detect a feature while the exact position of it is of secondary importance. All 64 units within a group have the same 25 weight values so they all detect the same feature. Thus, a group in layer $J1$ serves as a detector of a specific feature across the entire input field. However, the units do not share their thresholds. The weight sharing and limitations to processing of 5×5 receptive input fields has resulted in a reduced number of connections equal to 19 968 or (12×64) by $(25 + 1)$, from

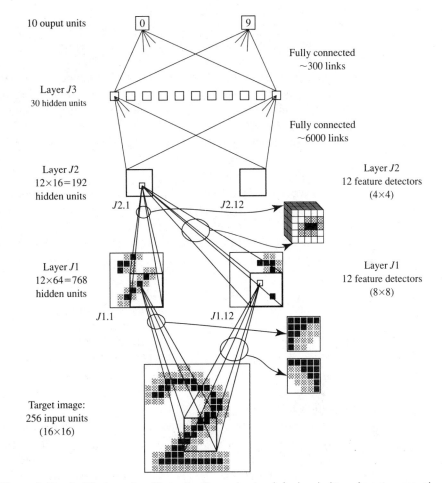

Figure 8.13 Architecture of multilayer feedforward network for handwritten character recognition. [© MIT Press; adapted from LeCun et al. (1989) and reprinted with permission.]

the ≅ 200 000 that would be needed for a fully connected first hidden layer. Due to the weight sharing, only 768 biases and 300 weights remain as free parameters of this layer during training.

The second hidden layer uses a similar set of trainable feature detectors consisting of 12 groups of 16 units, again taking input from 5×5 receptive fields. A 50% reduction of image size and weight sharing take place in this layer. The connection scheme is quite similar to the first input layer; however, one slight complication is due to the fact that $J1$ consists of multiple two-dimensional maps. Inputs to $J2$ are taken from 8 of the 12 groups in $J1$. This makes a total of 8×25 shared weights per single group in $J2$. Thus, every unit in $J2$ has 200 weights and a single bias. Since this $J2$ layer consists of 192 units, it employs

38 592 (192 × 201) connections. All these connections are controlled by only 2592 free trainable parameters. Twelve feature maps of this layer involve 200 distinct weights each, plus the total of 192 thresholds.

Layer $J3$ has 30 units and is fully connected to the outputs of all units in layer $J2$. The 10 output units are also fully connected to the outputs of layer $J3$. Thus, layer $J3$ contains 5790 distinct weights consisting of 30 × 192 units plus 30 thresholds. The output layer adds another 310 weights, of which 10 are thresholds of output neurons.

The discussed network has been trained using the error back-propagation algorithm. The training has involved only 23 full cycles. Thus, each character has been presented about 16 769 times to the network under the assumption that each digit occurs with the same probability in the training set of 7291 zip code digits. The weights were initialized with random values so that the total input to each neuron was within the operating range of its sigmoidal activation function. The target values for the output layer were chosen within the range of the sigmoid rather than at extreme ± 1 values, as is usually done for classifier training. This prevented the weights from growing indefinitely during the training. The weights were updated after the presentation of each single pattern.

Let us summarize the performance of the trained network of Figure 8.13 (LeCun et al. 1989). After completion of the training, only 10 digits from the entire training set had been misclassified (0.14%), thus yielding the decision error E_d as in (4.36) with a value 0.137×10^{-6}. However, 102 mistakes (5.0%) were reported on the test set and the decision error rose to $E_d = 0.0517$. The convergence to the correct response was found to be rather quick during the simulation of the test performance.

In a more realistic performance evaluation test, the rejection of marginal characters has been implemented that are very difficult to classify even for a human. In this approach, marginal characters are excluded from testing. The character rejection from the test set has been based on the criterion that the difference between the two most active output levels should exceed a certain minimum value to ensure reasonably reliable classification. To lower the error of 5% on the full test set to 1% using the rejection concept, the scribbled 12.1% of test patterns had to be removed because of their similarity to the classification of other digits.

Other networks with fewer feature mapping levels were also evaluated by LeCun et al. (1989) but they produced inferior results. For example, a fully connected network of 40 hidden units in a single layer was not able to generalize as well, compared to the architecture described. Misclassifications measured 1.6 and 8.1% on the training set and test set, respectively. In addition, 19.4% of the test set characters had to be removed to achieve the error of 1% when using the marginal character rejection concept.

It can be seen that the error back-propagation algorithm yielded the results that appear to be the state-of-the-art situation for handwritten digit recognition.

The trained network has many actual connections but only relatively few free parameters are selected during training. Also, distinct feature extraction constraints were imposed on the network. The training was implemented on commercial digital signal processing hardware that efficiently performed multiply/accumulate operations. The overall throughput rate of the complete, trained digit recognizer, including the image acquisition time, is reported to be 10 to 12 digit classifications per second.

8.3

NEURAL NETWORKS CONTROL APPLICATIONS

The use of neural networks in control applications—including process control, robotics, industrial manufacturing and aerospace applications, among others—has recently experienced rapid growth. The basic objective of control is to provide the appropriate input signal to a given physical process to yield its desired response. In control systems theory, the physical process to be controlled is often referred to as the plant. The plant input signals, called actuating signals, are typically needed to control motors, switches, or other actuating devices. If the actuating signal at the input to the plant shown in Figure 8.14 is generated by the neural network-based controller, the case can be termed *neural control,* or, briefly, *neurocontrol.* This section covers the basic concepts and examples of neural control techniques. Those neurocontrol aspects that deal specifically with robotics applications are discussed in the subsequent section.

Overview of Control Systems Concepts

This section presents an overview of the elementary concepts and terminology of control systems. The scope of presentation is limited only to issues that are later related in the context of neural controllers. Specifically, the concepts of transfer characteristics, transfer functions, and feedforward and feedback control are reviewed below. Readers familiar with such introductory material may proceed directly to the next section.

Solution of the control problem depends directly on the precision with which characteristics of the process are known. In a single-channel control problem

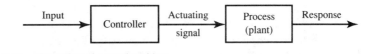

Figure 8.14   Illustration of control problem.

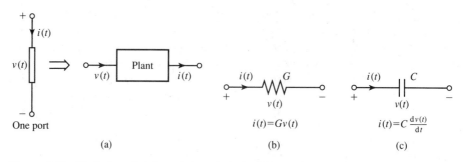

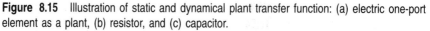

Figure 8.15   Illustration of static and dynamical plant transfer function: (a) electric one-port element as a plant, (b) resistor, and (c) capacitor.

when the plant input is a scalar variable, for example, the process, if known, can be described by a relationship between the plant actuating signal and the plant response. In general, this relationship is expressed as P, where P is the process *transfer function* in the form $P(s)$, and s is the complex variable. We consider only time-invariant plant characteristics in this section. In such cases, $P(s)$ includes the dynamic properties that relate the input and output signals of the plant. For plants that can be described in the time domain without a time variable, $P(s)$ is independent of s and reduces to the simple functional relationship between the actuating signal and the response. Such plants are called nondynamic, memoryless, or simply static. For static plants the transfer function $P(s)$ becomes P and is called the *transfer characteristics.*

Let us consider a simple example of static and dynamical plants. Assume that the current through a one-port electric element is the plant output, which needs to be controlled. The voltage across this one-port element is considered to be the plant's input, or actuating signal. The plant is shown in Figure 8.15(a). The figure also illustrates the equivalence between a specific electric one-port element and the commonly used general block diagram representation for the plant.

Since the plant transfer characteristics is defined as the ratio of its response to the excitation, we see that the description of a nondynamic plant yields a simple functional relationship. Now assume that the one-port plant is simply a resistor as shown in Figure 8.15(b). The plant transfer characteristic reduces to the following constant

$$P = \frac{i(t)}{v(t)} = G \tag{8.11a}$$

Thus, a static plant can be described by the transfer characteristics P. In the case of a static and linear process chosen here as an example (the resistor), the transfer characteristics is simply equal to the resistor's conductance, G.

Dynamical plants such as the capacitor shown in Figure 8.15(c) cannot be characterized by constants, not even by complex time-invariant functions because their responses, being solutions of differential or integrodifferential equations, are functions of time. The transfer function for such plants is defined as the ratio of the integral transforms of the output to the input signal. The Laplace transform, denoted here as $\mathcal{L}\{\cdot\}$ is the most commonly used transform to express the input and output signals of linear plants. Applying Laplace transform theory leads to the following transfer function for the capacitance plant of Figure 8.15(c):

$$P(s) = \frac{I(s)}{V(s)} = sC \qquad (8.11b)$$

where

$$I(s) \overset{\Delta}{=} \mathcal{L}\{i(t)\}$$

$$V(s) \overset{\Delta}{=} \mathcal{L}\{v(t)\}$$

denote transforms of current through the capacitor and voltage across it, respectively. Thus, the transfer function as in (8.11b) can be understood to be a ratio of the Laplace transform of current to the Laplace transform of voltage.

The reader may have noticed that the ratio of output response to the input signal yields the transfer characteristics of a static plant. Similarly, the ratios of the transforms of output to input yield the transfer function of a dynamical plant. We also should realize that the concept of a transfer characteristics is of no use for dynamical plants.

The significance of the transfer characteristics in system and control theory is based on the fact that response of a static system to an arbitrary excitation can be computed as a product of its transfer characteristics and of the excitation. Similarly, the transform of the response of a dynamical system can be expressed as a product of the transfer function and transform of the excitation.

For a plant that is completely known, any desired relationship between input and response can be realized by a simple *open-loop control configuration* as shown in Figure 8.16(a) (Mishkin and Braun 1961). The feedforward controller of Figure 8.16(a) consists of two parts connected in cascade. The second one cancels the process transfer function because its own transfer function has been chosen as the inverse of the known process transfer function. In addition, the front part of the controller introduces the desired overall transfer function of the controller and the plant equal to D. Thus, the controller's transfer function should be equal to D/P. This approach is known as *inverse control* since the most essential part of the controller should provide the inverse of the plant's transfer function. The transfer function of the inverse feedforward control system from Figure 8.16(a) computed between its input and output becomes

$$\frac{Y(s)}{X(s)} = D(s) \qquad (8.12a)$$

In this approach involving the cascade connection of the controller driving the plant and involving no feedback, the neural controller that acts as the plant inverse needs to be designed.

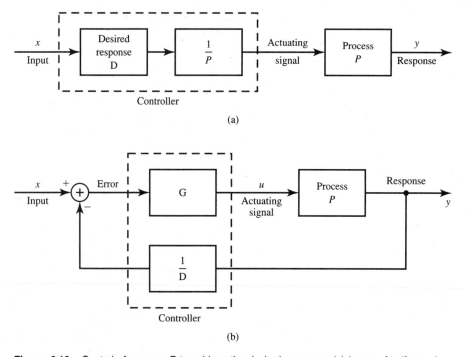

Figure 8.16 Control of process P to achieve the desired response: (a) inverse feedforward control and (b) feedback control.

Realize, however, that the inverse control method fails in any of the two important circumstances: (1) when the transfer function $P(s)$ or the transfer characteristics P varies during the course of normal operation of the plant, and (2) when $P(s)$ or P is not completely known in advance of design. We customarily turn to the feedback control systems to circumvent any or both of the two limitations mentioned. One of the most common feedback control arrangements is shown in Figure 8.16(b). That such a configuration is directly useful if $P(s)$ or P varies or is unknown is clear from simple analytical considerations. The feedback control system of Figure 8.16(b) is described with the transfer function between input and output

$$\frac{Y(s)}{X(s)} = \frac{G(s)P(s)}{1 + G(s)P(s)/D(s)} \tag{8.12b}$$

Note that the system designer can choose $G(s)$ and $D(s)$. If $G(s)/D(s)$ is made sufficiently large so that a quantity known as the loop-gain and denoted LG satisfies the condition

$$LG \triangleq \left| \frac{G(s)P(s)}{D(s)} \right|_{s=j\omega} \gg 1 \tag{8.13a}$$

for all frequencies ω of interest, then the transfer function (8.12b) reduces to the form approximately equal to (8.12a). Using the condition (8.13a), we easily obtain from (8.12b)

$$\frac{Y(s)}{X(s)} \cong D(s) \qquad (8.13b)$$

This result indicates that for high and fixed loop-gain values, the output now becomes independent of the plant transfer function $P(s)$, as desired. Therefore, the use of feedback provides a useful means for overcoming both the parameter variation of the plant and the ignorance of the designer as to the exact nature of the plant and its transfer function $P(s)$. These observations also apply to nondynamic plants. However, as mentioned earlier, for nondynamic plants, transfer functions $G(s)$, $P(s)$, and $D(s)$ in (8.12) and (8.13) become independent of complex variable s.

In this section we will approach the design of the controllers using the estimated information about the plant. We will assume that such information is gradually acquired during plant operation. Such control systems may be called *learning control systems*. Neural networks fit quite well into such a framework of control systems study. Plant identification techniques that make use of neural network techniques are reviewed first. Neural network applications for control of a nondynamic plant are then discussed. An example of a perceptron-based controller for a low-order dynamical plant will also be designed. The input signal to the perceptron controlling the dynamical plant, however, contains not only the present output of the plant but also its most recent output preceding the time the control decision was made. Finally, the discrete-time system control of the dynamical plant using the neurocontrol concept is studied. The concept involves adaptive control similar to the cerebellar model articulation controller (CMAC).

Process Identification

The introductory discussion above points out that plant identification can be distinctly helpful in achieving the desired output signal of the plant. In general, identification of the plant should result in usable terms such as coefficients of a plant differential equation or coefficients of its transfer function. The issue of identification is perhaps of even greater importance in the field of adaptive control systems. Since the plant in an adaptive control system varies in operation with time, the adaptive control must be adjusted to account for the plant variations. Neural networks used for identification purposes in this section typically have multilayer feedforward architectures and are trained using the error back-propagation technique.

The basic configuration for *forward plant identification* is shown in Figure 8.17(a). A nonlinear neural network receives the same input $\mathbf{x}$ as the plant, and

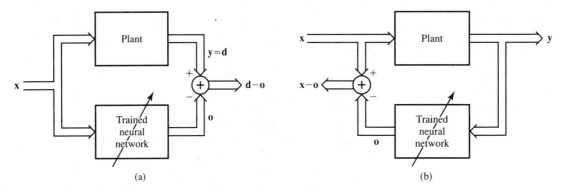

Figure 8.17a,b Neural network configuration for plant identification: (a) forward plant identification and (b) plant inverse identification.

the plant output provides the desired response **d** during training. The purpose of the identification is to find the neural network with response **o** that matches the response **y** of the plant for a given set of inputs **x**. During the identification, the norm of the error vector, $\|\mathbf{d} - \mathbf{o}\|$, is minimized through a number of weight adjustments. The minimization is achieved using learning techniques discussed in previous chapters. Figure 8.17(a) shows the case for which the network attempts to model the mapping of plant input to output, with both input and output measured at the same time. This is understandable since the trained neural network is feedforward and instantaneous; thus, we have $\mathbf{o}(t) = \mathbf{x}(t)$. However, more complex types of models for plant identification can also be employed. To account for plant dynamics, the input to the neural network may consist of various past inputs to the plant (Barto 1990). These can be produced by inserting the delay elements at the plant input.

In earlier discussions, we learned that the identification of the plant inverse may offer another viable alternative for designing the control system. In contrast to forward plant characteristics identification, now the plant output **y** is used as neural network input, as shown in Figure 8.17(b). The error vector for network training is computed as a $\mathbf{x} - \mathbf{o}$, where **x** is the plant input. The norm of the error vector to be minimized through learning is therefore $\|\mathbf{x} - \mathbf{o}\|$. The neural network trained this way will implement the *mapping of the plant inverse*. Once the network has been successfully trained to mimic the plant inverse, it can be used directly for inverse feedforward control as illustrated in Figure 8.16(a). The properly trained neural network acts as controller in this configuration, and the appropriate actuating signal for the plant is directly available at the network's output.

In both identification cases described, the neural network is trained to copy either the forward or inverse characteristics of the plant. Typically, multilayer feedforward networks are used for this purpose. A trained network as shown in

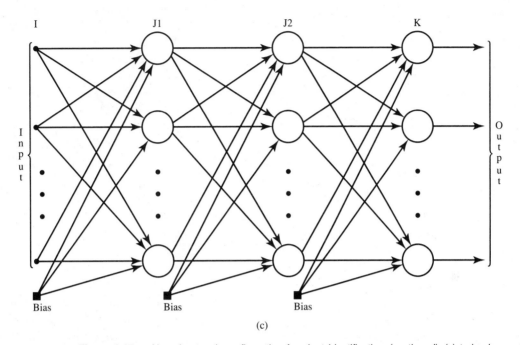

Figure 8.17c Neural network configuration for plant identification *(continued):* (c) trained neural network architecture.

Figure 8.17(c) can model the behavior of the actual plant in the forward or inverse mode of operation. Each of the identification modes has its advantages and disadvantages. Forward plant identification is always feasible; however, it does not immediately allow for construction of the plant controller. In contrast, plant inverse identification facilitates simple plant control; however, the identification itself is not always feasible.

A major problem with plant inverse identification arises when the plant inverse is not uniquely defined. This occurs for a plant when, as in Figure 8.18, *more* than one value of **x** exists that corresponds to one value of **y**. This particular condition coincides with the nonexistence of unique inverse mapping of **y** into **x**. Figure 8.18 illustrates this limitation of the plant inverse identification for the one-dimensional case. In the discussed case, the neural network modeling the plant inverse attempts to map a single input y^* to one of the two target responses x_1 or x_2. It may be that the eventual mapping learned would somewhat tend to average the two desired x values, but in no case can such identification of the plant inverse be considered adequate.

As an example of plant inverse identification, consider a static plant that converts polar (r, θ) to Cartesian (x, y) coordinates during its forward operation. The trained neural network should convert Cartesian to polar coordinates. A

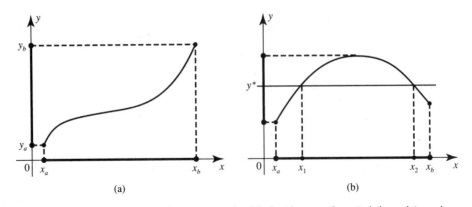

Figure 8.18 Plant inverse identification example: (a) plant inverse characteristics exists and (b) plant inverse characteristics does not exist.

two-layer feedforward architecture is chosen with two active inputs plus single bias input, 10 hidden-layer neurons, plus a single hidden biasing neuron, and two output neurons (Psaltis, Sideris, and Yamamura 1987, 1988). Hidden-layer neurons with unipolar activation function are selected with $\lambda = 1$. Two output neurons are chosen with the linear activation function $f(net) = net$ of unity slope so that they provide an unlimited range of output values. Initial weight values are chosen randomly at ± 0.5, and the learning constant used for training is 0.1.

The simulated learning experiment of plant inverse identification involves 10 points spread within the first quadrant such that $r \in [0, 10]$, and $\theta \in [0, \pi/2]$ (Psaltis, Sideris, and Yamamura 1987). The training set points are marked by circled g letters on Figure 8.19(a). The diagram shows the contour map of mapping error $\|\mathbf{x} - \mathbf{o}\|^2$, in Cartesian coordinates, before the training. Figure 8.19(b) shows the contour map of the error after 100 learning cycles. It can be seen that the conversion error has been reduced at and around the training points. Figure 8.19(c) indicates that the error after 1000 cycles has been totally suppressed at the training points. Continued training, however, gives rise to a problem shown in Figure 8.19(d). After 10 000 training cycles high-error pockets were observed outside the training areas. This phenomenon points out that the generalization ability of the network has actually decreased due to excessive training. Poor generalization also indicates that either the number of the training points is too low, or that the chosen architecture is not adequate for the problem requirements.

Let us note that the described training experiment is very similar to the one covered in Example 4.3. Indeed, the plant identification problem discussed here corresponds to a two-variable function approximation learning. The accurate values of the function to be approximated are outputs produced by the plant to be identified. These outputs are desired responses of the multilayer feedforward network, which undergoes the training.

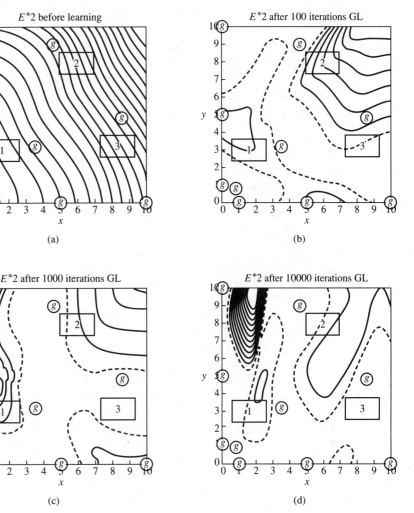

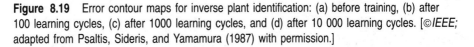

Dashed contours for $E^2 = 0$
Continuous contours for $E^2 = 10, 20, 30, \dots$

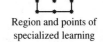

Region and points of
specialized learning

Figure 8.19 Error contour maps for inverse plant identification: (a) before training, (b) after 100 learning cycles, (c) after 1000 learning cycles, and (d) after 10 000 learning cycles. [©*IEEE;* adapted from Psaltis, Sideris, and Yamamura (1987) with permission.]

This description of identification procedures and example of plant identification overlook many details of real and complex identification problems. In particular, it does not completely cover the identification of the dynamical systems. It presents, however, the basic guidelines for plant modeling, which has many uses in signal processing and control. One usually assumes here that the model has a general mathematical form, and then its unknown parameters are estimated. Forward and inverse plant identification configurations seem to be somewhat natural applications for multilayer feedforward neural network models. The plant parameter estimation is implemented using the pairwise arranged examples of plant input/output values. The role of the teacher in plant identification is played by the system being modeled.

Basic Nondynamic Learning Control Architectures

Let us review a specific method of control in which multilayer neural networks are used as controllers of nondynamic plants (Psaltis, Sideris, and Yamamura 1987, 1988). The following discussion is closely related to the plant identification techniques discussed in the preceding section. The training of the neural network-based controller is also discussed in order to demonstrate the feasibility of the proposed architecture.

Figure 8.20 shows the feedforward controller implemented using a neural network. Neurocontroller *B* is an exact copy of neural network *A*, which undergoes training. Network *A* is connected in such a way that it gradually learns to perform as the unknown plant inverse. Thus, this configuration is implementing the inverse feedforward control similar to Figure 8.16(a). The input of the controller is **d**, which is the desired response of the plant. The plant's actual response is **y** due to its input **x** produced by the neurocontroller *B*. The error used for training the neural network is the difference between the output signals of networks *A* and *B*. Although the network *B* tracks *A* after each training step, **y** must exactly match **d** for this error to reduce to zero. We may note that this configuration becomes useless if the plant inverse is not uniquely defined, as illustrated by an example in Figure 8.18.

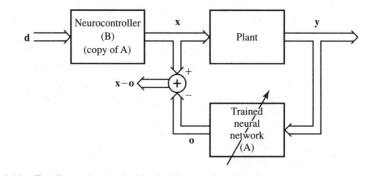

Figure 8.20   Feedforward control with plant inverse learning.

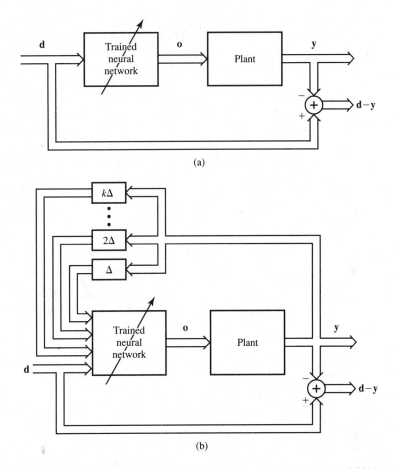

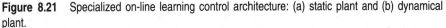

Figure 8.21 Specialized on-line learning control architecture: (a) static plant and (b) dynamical plant.

This control architecture is also called an *indirect learning architecture*. The distinct advantages of this configuration are obvious. The controller network can be trained on-line since it undergoes training while its copy performs the useful control function work. Thus, separate training sessions are no longer needed. Moreover, the inputs to the neurocontroller are the desired outputs of the plant. Thus, the controller's training can easily be performed in the region of interest of the output vector domain. Such training in the region of interest can be called specialized training. In addition, the neural network learns continually and is therefore adaptive.

A closely related control architecture for control and simultaneous specialized learning of the output domain of the static plant is shown in Figure 8.21(a). This control mode possesses all advantages of the control mode displayed in

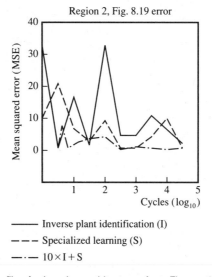

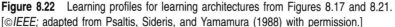

Figure 8.22   Learning profiles for learning architectures from Figures 8.17 and 8.21. [©*IEEE;* adapted from Psaltis, Sideris, and Yamamura (1988) with permission.]

Figure 8.20, but it uses only a single copy of the neural network instead of the two required by the control system of Figure 8.20.

The control objective of the specialized learning control architecture from Figure 8.21(a) is to obtain the desired output **d** of the plant under the condition that the plant input causing this output is unknown. For a dynamical plant, the trained neural network needs to be provided the sequence of recent output plant vectors in addition to present plant output. This would allow for reconstruction of the current state of the plant based on its most recent output history. Figure 8.21(b) shows a specialized learning control architecture of the dynamical plant of order k. In this case, the last k output vectors of the controlled plant are augmenting the present input of the trained neural network. It should be understood that the delay units Δ placed in the feedback loops denote the time elapsed between the samples of inputs used for training, and that the plant is controlled in real time. Under such conditions, k can be referred to as the order of the dynamical plant (Saerens and Soquet 1991).

Figure 8.19 illustrates three rectangular regions of specialized learning selected for the static neural network trained using the configuration shown in Figure 8.21(a). Ten points have been used within each rectangular learning specialization region as shown at the bottom of Figure 8.19. The learning profiles based on error $\|\mathbf{d} - \mathbf{y}\|$ are shown in Figure 8.22 (Psaltis, Sideris, and Yamamura 1988). The error analyzed and shown in the figure has been averaged for 10 points in region 2. The figure shows that errors for the plant inverse identification method (continuous line) and specialized learning (dashed line) are comparable.

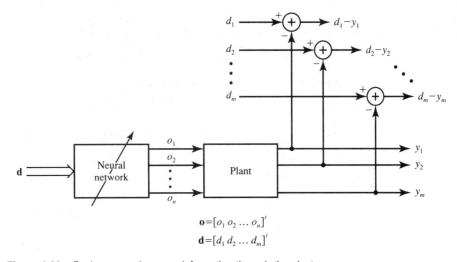

$$\mathbf{o} = [o_1 \, o_2 \, \dots \, o_n]^t$$
$$\mathbf{d} = [d_1 \, d_2 \, \dots \, d_m]^t$$

Figure 8.23 Back-propagating error information through the plant.

In addition, the learning experiment consisting of 10 cycles of plant inverse identification preceding the specialized learning has been carried out. The results have shown that this hybrid learning method may have a distinct advantage over each of the two learning methods applied separately. Combining the two learning approaches has resulted in the lowest error compared to other learning architectures. However, even with a series of extensive simulated experiments, it has not been possible to determine conditions under which the two learning methods have to be combined to achieve the best learning results.

The specialized on-line learning control architecture of Figure 8.21 suffers from one major weakness, which may result in slower training or other undesirable characteristics if the plant is known only approximately. We cannot apply the error back-propagation training for this configuration directly because only the error between the accessible plant output **y** and its desired output **d** is known to the user. The error **d** − **y** must be reduced to the input of the plant first.

The neural network to be trained using the error available at the plant output as shown in Figure 8.21 has been drawn in more detail in Figure 8.23. The customary error back-propagation rule (4.5a) for weight adjustment within the neural network can be rewritten in the form involving neural network outputs o_i as follows:

$$dw_{ij} = -\eta \frac{\partial E}{\partial o_i} \cdot \frac{\partial o_i}{\partial w_{ij}}, \quad \text{for } i = 1, 2, \dots, n, \quad j = 1, 2, \dots, m \quad (8.14)$$

where the plant output error E explicitly available from the teacher can be expressed as

$$E = \frac{1}{2} \sum_{i=1}^{m} (d_i - y_i)^2 \quad (8.15)$$

To compute the error E reflected at the plant's input we assume that the plant is described with the following algebraic equations:

$$y_i = y_i(\mathbf{o}), \quad \text{for } i = 1, 2, \ldots, m \tag{8.16}$$

The output error E propagates back to the input of the plant and $\partial E / \partial o_i$, $i = 1, 2, \ldots, n$, can be computed from (8.14), (8.15), and (8.16) as follows:

$$-\frac{\partial E}{\partial o_1} = (d_1 - y_1)\frac{\partial y_1}{\partial o_1} + (d_2 - y_2)\frac{\partial y_2}{\partial o_1} + \ldots + (d_n - y_n)\frac{\partial y_m}{\partial o_1}$$

$$-\frac{\partial E}{\partial o_2} = (d_1 - y_1)\frac{\partial y_1}{\partial o_2} + (d_2 - y_2)\frac{\partial y_2}{\partial o_2} + \ldots + (d_n - y_n)\frac{\partial y_m}{\partial o_2}$$

$$\vdots \tag{8.17}$$

$$-\frac{\partial E}{\partial o_n} = (d_1 - y_1)\frac{\partial y_1}{\partial o_n} + (d_2 - y_2)\frac{\partial y_2}{\partial o_n} + \ldots + (d_n - y_n)\frac{\partial y_m}{\partial o_n}$$

The expressions (8.17) can be rewritten in matrix form as below.

$$-\nabla_o E = \left(\frac{\partial \mathbf{y}}{\partial \mathbf{o}}\right)^t (\mathbf{d} - \mathbf{y}) \tag{8.18}$$

where

$$\nabla_o E \triangleq \begin{bmatrix} \dfrac{\partial E}{\partial o_1} \\[2mm] \dfrac{\partial E}{\partial o_2} \\[2mm] \vdots \\[2mm] \dfrac{\partial E}{\partial o_n} \end{bmatrix}$$

and

$$\left(\frac{\partial \mathbf{y}}{\partial \mathbf{o}}\right) \triangleq \left[\frac{\partial y_i}{\partial o_j}\right], \quad \text{for } i = 1, 2, \ldots, n, \quad j = 1, 2, \ldots, m$$

is the $m \times n$ Jacobian matrix of the plant. It can be seen from (8.18) that the plant output error $\mathbf{d} - \mathbf{y}$ propagates back through the plant according to the transpose of the plant's Jacobian matrix. This matrix describes the performance of the linearized plant (8.16) taken at the plant's operating point.

If the plant equations (8.16) are known, the Jacobian matrix can be easily produced in an analytical form at the plant's operating point. If the plant is not known, the array of partial derivatives $\partial y_i / \partial o_j$ can be determined by deviating the plant's input j by the amount Δo_j from its operating point and then measuring resulting changes $\Delta y_1, \Delta y_2, \ldots, \Delta y_m$. This approach is called the *perturbation method* and allows for measurement or simulation of approximate values of the

Jacobian matrix entries. The perturbation method yields approximate values only of $\partial y_i / \partial o_j$ since it involves finite differences Δy_i and Δo_j rather than infinitesimal differentials. However, the method is always applicable. Also, the evaluation of Jacobian matrix entries can be performed using the perturbation method either computationally or experimentally.

Inverted Pendulum Neurocontroller

In this section we will review the capability of a simple neural network to learn how to balance an inverted pendulum. The inverted pendulum (also called "broomstick balancing") problem is a classical control problem that has been extensively studied by many researchers and seems to be well understood. Also, the problem is representative of many typical dynamical plant control problems. Thus, designing the controller for this inherently unstable system will allow us to approach and solve a number of other, similar control tasks. The complexity of the task of inverted pendulum balancing is significant enough to make the problem interesting while still being simple enough to make it computationally tractable (Tolat and Widrow 1988).

A number of control techniques using neural networks to balance an inverted pendulum have been investigated (Barto, Sutton, and Anderson 1983; Anderson 1989). In the approach presented below we will use the simple and synergistic approach, which examines the merger of visual image acquisition, training, and neurocontrol (Tolat and Widrow 1988). Since the plant is inherently dynamical, the control must involve the plant's present and past state information.

The goal of the inverted pendulum task is to apply a sequence of right and left forces of fixed magnitude such that the pendulum is balanced, and the cart does not hit the edge of the track. The cart-pendulum physical system is shown in Figure 8.24(a). The cart and pendulum are constrained to move only within the vertical plane. Four time variables describe the state of the system: the horizontal position and velocity of the cart (x, v), the angle between the pendulum and vertical, and the angular velocity of the falling pendulum (θ, ω). The force required to stabilize the system is a function of four state variables x, v, θ, and ω as follows:

$$F(t) = ax(t) + b\dot{x}(t) + c\theta(t) + d\dot{\theta}(t), \tag{8.19}$$

$$\text{where } \dot{x}(t) = v(t), \quad \dot{\theta}(t) = \omega(t)$$

and a, b, c, and d are constant coefficients, which need to be found for each system since they are dependent on its physical characteristics.

Equation (8.19) approximates the motion of the system and assumes that it can be characterized by linear differential equations. Knowing the coefficients a,

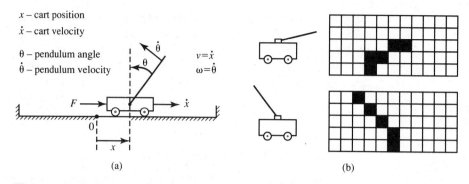

x – cart position
$\dot{x}$ – cart velocity

θ – pendulum angle
$\dot{\theta}$ – pendulum velocity

$v = \dot{x}$
$\omega = \dot{\theta}$

(a)

(b)

Figure 8.24 The inverted pendulum illustration: (a) physical system to be controlled and (b) two examples of computer-generated system images: left—real image; right—quantized image. [©*IEEE*; adapted from Tolat and Widrow (1988) with permission.]

b, c, and d and solving the system's modeling equation (8.19) would allow the user to compute the force that balances the plant. It is implied here, however, that neither Eq. (8.19) nor its coefficients are known both for the controller and for the observer. Let us consider that the only information available is about the order of equation and its general form. Since the equation is of first order, it can be expected that providing the present and most recent plant output value would enable us to train the controller adequately. As a result, the controller would need to generate the positive or negative force that would possibly stabilize the pendulum at its vertical position.

Since the balancing force can be assumed to be constant and of fixed magnitude for each push-pull action, and it differs only by direction, it may be postulated that the following force will stabilize the solution of the differential equation (8.19):

$$F(t) \cong \alpha \, \text{sgn} \left[ax(t) + b\dot{x}(t) + c\theta(t) + d\dot{\theta}(t) \right] \tag{8.20}$$

where α is a positive constant representing the force magnitude. Though the cart and pendulum velocities are involved in (8.20), they are more difficult to measure than linear distances and angles. To circumvent this difficulty, Equation (8.20) can be rewritten in the form of a difference equation:

$$F(t) \cong \alpha \, \text{sgn} \left[(a + b)x(t) - bx(t - 1) + (c + d)\theta(t) - d\theta(t - 1) \right] \tag{8.21}$$

This equation approximates the value of the balancing force $F(t)$ at the present time. It is assumed here that $x(t - 1)$ and $\theta(t - 1)$ are cart positions and pendulum angles at an earlier time preceding the evaluation of the plant and the computation of force.

The dynamics of the system remains largely unknown during the process of neurocontroller design. The knowledge of the system's dynamics is limited to the vague form of the difference equation (8.21) and it does not include its coefficients. In addition, the human observer who would measure cart positions and angles of pendulum at every instant is replaced by the input of the visual image of the cart and pendulum. Since it is essential to provide the controller with the present and most recent position and angle data, the present and most recent images arranged in pairs have been used to train the network (Tolat and Widrow 1988).

The neural network training was implemented by software simulation with the input of binary images providing the required state information $x(t)$, $x(t-1)$, $\theta(t)$, and $\theta(t-1)$. Examples of the quantized binary images are shown in Figure 8.24(b). The images were generated on a MacIntosh computer in the form of 5×11 pixel maps of the cart and pendulum. Images of finer granularity than 5×11 pixels were not used since they required extra computational effort and resulted in no improvement in controller performance. Pictures of smaller size, in contrast, did not provide an adequate resolution and input representation for the solution of this problem.

For the image resolution used and shown in Figure 8.24(b), there were 65 different images involving all possible combinations of 5 distinct cart positions with 13 different pendulum angles. Since the training objective was to produce $F(t)$ as in (8.21), both the present image and the most recent one representing the cart with pendulum at an earlier time, $t-1$, were used. The time elapsed between two consecutive state recordings, equal to the time between two successive force applications was 100 ms. This time and graphics resolution were found to be sufficient to balance the actual mechanical system investigated. With the two images completely combined, there were $65^2 = 4225$ training vectors in the training set. Each input vector used for training consisted of $2 \times 5 \times 11 = 110$ binary entries, not including the bias input.

Let us note how this method of controller design differs from more traditional control approaches. First, the plant's modeling equation (8.19) would have to be known to design a conventional controller. Specifically, the task would require finding initially unknown coefficients a, b, c, and d in (8.19) or (8.21). Analytical computation of force $F(t)$ would further require solution of the differential equation (8.19). Alternatively, the difference equation (8.21) obtained from (8.19) could be solved by the controller to approximate the value of $F(t)$ needed to provide the balance of plant.

The solution of (8.21) in the described experiment has been obtained without finding coefficients a, b, c, and d, and even without solving any equations, or measuring position and velocity of the cart, or even measuring the angle or angular velocity of the pendulum. Experiments have shown that a single discrete perceptron with 110 weights and one threshold weight can be trained to find the solution of (8.21). To train the perceptron, 4225 examples of image pairs were submitted along with the teacher's decision as to the desired $F(t)$ value for the specific set of observations $x(t)$, $x(t - 1)$, $\theta(t)$, and $\theta(t - 1)$. The teacher's input determines the sign of force ($F = 1$ or $F = -1$) needed to prevent the pendulum from falling. This input is based on the study of the present and most recent image. Note that both the present and most recent images on x and θ are presented as input patterns from the training set. Supervised training has replaced solving the system of 4225 linear equations with 111 unknowns. This has eliminated finding the best fit of unknowns in this overdetermined system of equations.

In the described control design experiment, the Widrow-Hoff training algorithm has been used to train the weights of the single perceptron controller consisting of 111 weights, one summing node, and one TLU. In addition, the network has proven capable of extracting necessary state information from crude visual images arranged in a time sequence without the need for measurements of motion coordinates or physical parameters of the system.

The learning profile for computation of the applied force in the experiment is shown in Figure 8.25(a). The error of force sign drops dramatically after several passes through the entire training set; then it flattens out. The reported error after 1000 training cycles was 3.4%. The example of final weight values coded into pixel map shade and intensity is shown in Figure 8.25(b). The sign of force F is found by combining the pixel images of the system with weights and creating an appropriate scalar product of the two 110-tuple vectors plus the threshold value.

In the next series of simulation experiments with inverted pendulum balancing, the training focused on analyzing the generalization capabilities of the trained controller. Only a fraction of the total of 4225 images was selected at random for training purposes. The training subsets were of different sizes and varied from 10 to 100%. Results were computed for four different training sets and then averaged. The final error after 300 training cycles is plotted in Figure 8.25(c) for six different training set sizes. The final error values indicate that the trained network is able to generalize fairly uniformly and well for training sets consisting of more than 40% of the patterns of the complete set.

The neurocontroller designed for keeping the pendulum from falling was able to perform successfully despite occasional failures. A single discrete perceptron was proven to be adequate for this task. More complicated control problems, however, will require larger neural networks with appropriate inputs (Fu 1986). The network used in this case has not made use of explicit decision, or control, rules. The only rules used were common sense teacher guidelines as to how to keep the pendulum vertical. The example remarkably demonstrates that a teacher-machine interaction can be gradually replaced by observing the environment and providing responses suitable for the observations. After training, the controller should be able to perform the control task autonomously by responding correctly to most situations, even those that were not specifically used for training.

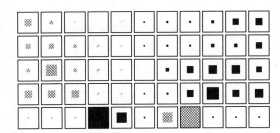

Weights, present image (t)

Weights, image at an earlier time ($t-0.1s$)

■ – positive weights
▨ – negative weights

(b)

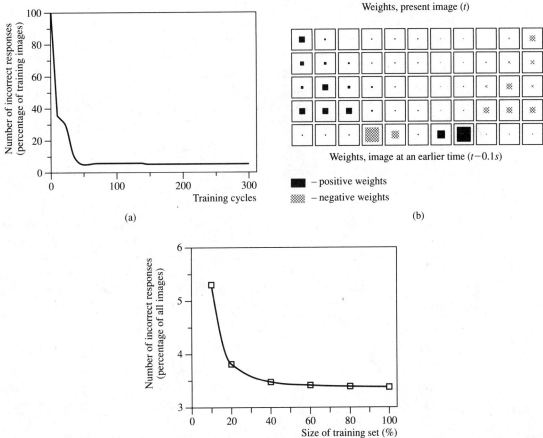

(a)

(c)

Figure 8.25 Training of the cart-pendulum controller: (a) learning profile example, (b) image of controller's final weights, 4225 images used, and (c) analysis of generalization capability of the trained controller. [©*IEEE;* adapted from Tolat and Widrow (1988) with permission.]

Cerebellar Model Articulation Controller

This section discusses the cerebellar model articulation controller (CMAC). Both the concept and the application case study for low-order CMAC control problems are reviewed here based on work by Kraft and Campagna (1990a, 1990b). The basic idea of the CMAC approach is to learn an approximation of the system characteristics and then to use it to generate the appropriate control signal. The approximation of the system characteristics is understood as gradual learning based on the observations of the plant input-output data in real time. The learning of a CMAC controller proceeds somewhat like the winner-take-all competitive learning discussed in Sections 2.5 and 7.2, however, without the competition enforcing the weight adjustment.

Let us consider the case of a first-order plant that needs to be controlled to yield a known, desired output signal. A sample discrete-time first-order plant is described with the difference equation

$$y(k + 1) = ay(k) + bx(k) \qquad (8.22a)$$

where $y(k)$ is the system output, $x(k)$ is the input, k is the time step number, and a and b are constant coefficients. Each point in plane $y(k)$, $y(k + 1)$ corresponds to a required value of control input $x(k)$. Interpreting the present and the next following output $y(k)$, and $y(k + 1)$, respectively, as two independent variables, input $x(k)$ can be represented as a so-called *characteristic surface* of the plant.

Two examples of characteristic surfaces are illustrated in Figure 8.26. For the linear plant as in (8.22a) with $a = b = 1$, the planar characteristic surface is shown in Figure 8.26(a). Nonlinear systems exhibit more diversified characteristic surface shapes that cannot be expressed through a linear form as in (8.22a). A sample nonplanar surface for the equation

$$y(k + 1) = y(k) + [x(k)]^{1/3} \qquad (8.22b)$$

is shown in Figure 8.26(b). Obviously, both for the linear or nonlinear plant that is completely known, the characteristic surface can be calculated and used to produce the present control input value $x(k)$. A simple look-up table or formulas such as (8.22) for $x(k)$ values at each coordinate pair $y(k)$, $y(k + 1)$ would provide, without computation, the appropriate value of the desired control signal. In a more realistic situation, however, when the system parameters are not known in advance or they vary in time, the characteristic surface can be learned gradually from the plant input-output data. This can be accomplished in an on-line control mode.

The block diagram of the complete learning and control system is shown in Figure 8.27. Let us assume a first-order discrete-time plant. For such a plant, the control signal $x(k)$ is determined by a pair of values $y(k)$ and $y(k + 1)$, which are the present and next plant outputs, respectively. The sequence of values $y(k)$, for

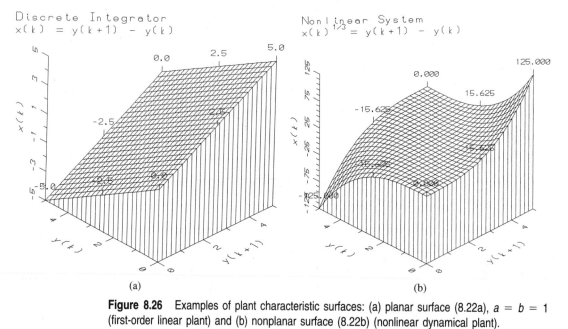

Figure 8.26 Examples of plant characteristic surfaces: (a) planar surface (8.22a), $a = b = 1$ (first-order linear plant) and (b) nonplanar surface (8.22b) (nonlinear dynamical plant).

$k = 1, 2, 3, \ldots$, is assumed to be known and is provided by the reference plant output generator.

The plant control signal $x(k)$ is initially produced by a conventional controller. The controller is used in a negative feedback configuration similar to the one shown in Figure 8.16(b). The reference plant output generator inputs the present output value of the plant to the summing node $S1$. This input is approximately equal to the actual output of the plant due to the fact that the closed-loop system between the reference plant output to the summing node $S1$ and the plant output has a transfer function of approximately unity value. For this condition to be valid, the closed-loop control system consisting of classical controller, plant, and node $S1$ must be both stable and it must use a high-gain classical controller. Note also that the neurocontroller provides little or no input to the summing node $S2$, at least at the initial training stage of the entire control system.

In the initial stage of operation, the plant derives almost all of its input from the classical controller. The neurocontroller, called here the CMAC memory, is not yet trained, and it initially outputs a zero value to $S2$. Therefore, initially, the classical controller output is the dominant component of the total actuating signal $x(k)$. In each control step, however, the control signal produced by the classical controller, $x(k)$, is used to build the value of the CMAC characteristic surface $x(k)$ having current coordinates $y(k)$, $y(k + 1)$. The characteristic surface adapts in each control step according to the following learning law, which is similar to

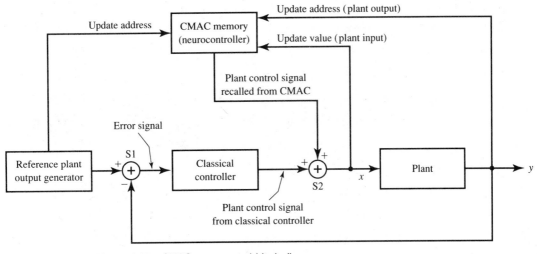

Figure 8.27　CMAC neurocontrol block diagram.

the learning rule (2.46):

$$w(k + 1) = w(k) + \alpha[x(k) - w(k)] \qquad (8.23)$$

In this weight adaptation formula, $\alpha > 0$ is a small positive learning constant, k denotes the learning (update) step number and also the number of the control step. As pointed out, the initial weight values are set to zero, which corresponds to setting the entire characteristic surface to zero at the beginning of training. The weights $w(k)$, which are built by the conventional controller, can be interpreted as iteratively updated control signal values $x(k)$, or memorized values of the characteristic surface that needs to be learned. The learning as in (8.23) should eventually end up at learned values w, which are averaged $x(k)$ values over a number of CMAC controller learning steps.

Despite the lack of competition between the neurons and the absence of the winner, the learning as in (8.23) follows the unsupervised winner-take-all learning rule. This is to provide matching between vectors $y(k)$, $y(k + 1)$ and vectors $x(k)$. The winning neuron during learning is always the one designated by the coordinates $y(k)$, $y(k + 1)$, of the learned characteristic surface. It is seen that CMAC characteristic surface learning represents an interesting case of supervised look-up memory training.

The described learning is of the local type, and more precisely can be called pointwise, since the only coordinates at which learning occurs are $y(k)$, $y(k + 1)$. No information is conveyed to nearby memory locations. The generalization of learning can be used, however, in order to update a neighborhood of the point to be learned. To accomplish the learning with neighborhood sensitivity, which can be also termed as learning with embedded generalization, the memory values

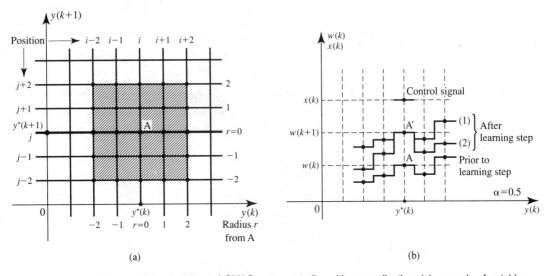

Figure 8.28 Learning of CMAC neurocontroller with generalization: (a) example of neighborhood learning radius of 2 and (b) learning at cross-section $y^*(k + 1)$ with generalization (two cases).

$w(k + 1)$ are assigned planar coordinates so that they become $w_{ij}(k + 1)$. It is now assumed that the memory has its values built over the discrete space with a certain neighborhood radius.

Figure 8.28(a) shows neighborhood sensitivity in the shaded region of generalized learning at point A with the neighborhood radius of 2. Learning at A in such cases and according to (8.23) is accompanied by the neighborhood learning at 24 adjacent memory locations falling within the shaded region. Learning at memory cross-section $y^*(k + 1)$ is displayed in Figure 8.28(b). The figure shows example memory adjustments at five neighborhood points. Curve (1) shows adjusted memory values with equal adjustments for each of the updated locations independent of their distance from A. Curve (2) exemplifies tapered learning with adjustments of $w_{ij}(k + 1)$ inversely proportional to the distance between the point A and the location i, j being adjusted within the neighborhood.

Figure 8.29 shows example learning of a characteristic surface without and with neighborhood generalization. Figure 8.29(a) depicts pointwise learning in several isolated locations of the controller's memory. Figure 8.29(b) depicts untapered neighborhood learning with uniform generalization built into the characteristic surface. It can be seen that the neighborhood weights are adjusted in this case by the same amount as for pointwise learning.

During the learning phase, the control signal coming from the classical controller of fixed high-gain is added in node $S2$ to the feedforward neurocontroller output. This output gradually increases from zero values as the weights are trained

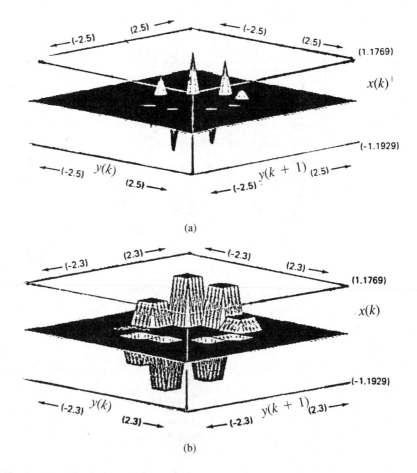

Figure 8.29 Learning of the characteristic surface: (a) pointwise learning mode (without generalization) and (b) neighborhood learning mode (with generalization). [©*MIT Press;* reprinted from Kraft and Campagna (1990b) with permission.]

to approximate the plant and as the characteristic surface is unfolding. As learning continues, the portion of the control signal derived from the neurocontroller increases. More precisely, the memorized weights of the CMAC controller are built up during control. As a result, the recalled control signal from the neural look-up memory gradually takes control of the plant. The conventional controller is excited by the error signal produced at the output of the summing node $S1$. Since this error signal gradually diminishes as the neurocontroller takes over the control function, the error signal input is reduced even further. As a result, the conventional controller is gradually eliminated from the control action.

For an accurately trained neurocontroller having the block diagram shown in Figure 8.27, the error signal of the classical controller reduces to zero, as does its output signal. An immediate consequence of the feedforward CMAC neuro-controller taking over the control function is the increased speed of the system's response. In the presence of noise, or variable plant parameters, however, the normally idle classical controller would assume partial control of the plant to compensate for partial uncertainties that may be present in the system but have not been learned from earlier experience.

The neurocontroller using the described concept has been designed to control a linear discrete integrator plant described by (8.22a) with $a = b = 1$ (Kraft and Campagna 1990b). The desired response $y(k)$ of the sample plant has been chosen to be the response of the unity-gain discrete integrator-filter with unity low-frequency gain and a pole at $z = 0.1$. The difference equation of the integrator-filter, which produces the desired sequence $y(k)$ at the output of the plant, is

$$y(k + 1) - 0.1y(k) - 0.9r(k) = 0 \qquad (8.24)$$

A unity magnitude, bipolar square wave of frequency 1 Hz has been chosen as the reference wave $r(t)$. Samples $r(k)$ of the continuous wave $r(t)$ have been assumed to be taken with frequency 9 Hz. Also, the plant was considered to be at rest initially. The reader can verify that this set of assumptions allows for computation of the entire sequence of plant output samples $y(k)$, for $k = 0, 1, 2, \ldots$, using Equation (8.24).

Three experiments for learning the characteristic surface with simultaneous control of the plant have been performed (Kraft and Campagna 1990a, 1990b). The first experiment was performed with noise-free input. The plant input and output measurements in the second experiment were contaminated with a significant amount of noise. The noise was white and uniformly distributed between -0.4 and 0.4. The third experiment involved no noise, but the plant to be learned was nonlinear. The plant had the linear characteristic surface augmented by the nonlinear term $-0.4[y(k)]^{1/3}$ to the form

$$y(k + 1) = y(k) - 0.4[y(k)]^{1/3} + x(k) \qquad (8.25)$$

Each of the three networks has been trained for 625 weights, or memory locations. The characteristic surface learned in the first experiment for $\alpha = 0.3$ and in the generalized learning mode is shown in Figure 8.30(a). The CMAC surfaces learned in the two remaining cases exhibit considerable similarities to the surface shown in the figure. The learning covers the domain $-1 < y(k) < 1$ and $-1 < y(k + 1) < 1$. The reader may notice that the plant output must be constrained to this region because of the choice of both the reference wave and the form of the difference equation (8.24). Specifically, the parts of the characteristic surface that are close to corners $(-1, 1)$, $(1, -1)$ in coordinates $y(k)$, $y(k + 1)$ indicate the largest and the smallest control signal values, respectively. Ideally, the learned surface should have been exactly as shown in Figure 8.26(a). However, the learning of the initially unknown surface remains notably localized.

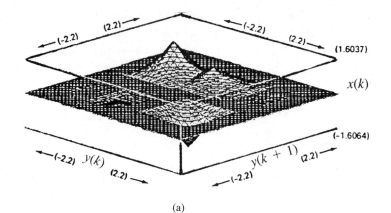

(a)

| Time | Reference | Plant Output | | Control |
| Instant | Wave | Present | Next | Signal |
k	$r(k)$	$y(k)$	$y(k + 1)$	$x(k)$
0	0	0	0	0
1	1	0	0.9	0.9
2	1	0.9	0.99	0.09
3	1	0.99	0.999	0.009
4	1	0.999	0.9999	0.0009
5	−1	0.9999	−0.8	−1.7999
6	−1	−0.8	−0.98	−0.1799
7	1	−0.98	−0.998	−0.018
8	1	−0.998	−0.9998	−0.0018
9	0	−0.9998	−0.1	0.8998
10	1	−0.1	0.8	0.9
11	1	0.8	0.98	0.18
12	1	0.98	0.998	0.018

$y(k + 1) = 0.1y(k) + 0.9r(k)$ (filter)
$x(k) = y(k + 1) - y(k)$ (plant)

(b)

Figure 8.30 CMAC learning: (a) characteristic surface learned and (b) control signals computed for the known plant. [Part (a), ©*MIT Press;* adapted from Kraft and Campagna (1990b) with permission.]

For the coordinates $y(k)$, $y(k + 1)$ that occur frequently, the learning resulted in local peaks; some other areas of the characteristic surface have not deflected from the initial value of $w_{ij} = 0$.

Figure 8.30(b) tabulates 12 initial steps of CMAC learning for the experiment described, with no input noise present. Plant outputs $y(k)$, $y(k + 1)$ have been computed from Eq. (8.24). The data tabulated in the plant input column $x(k)$ were obtained assuming a known plant rather than an unknown plant being identified using the signal provided by the conventional feedback controller. The controlled plant in this example is described by Eq. (8.22) with $a = b = 1$.

The measured signal tracking performance of the actual CMAC is plotted in Figure 8.31. The solid line represents the actual plant output, the dashed line indicates the desired output $y(k)$. It can be seen from the graphs that the trained controller's performance has proven to be at least satisfactory. For the no-noise case, 25 learning cycles involving a time frame of 25 full periods of the square wave $r(k)$ have been performed prior to the 30 output samples displayed in the figures. Learning with noise took longer, but the controller's final performance shown in Figure 8.31(b) was approximately the same as if it had learned without noise. Especially high performance was achieved for nonlinear plant learning. As shown in Figure 8.31(c), the tracking achieved was very good and output was very close to the required wave.

As can be seen, the controller under discussion is learning in a supervised mode. The controller's training involves characteristic surface buildup through weights gradually matching the plant inputs needed to produce the desired outputs. The neurons in this network are with the identity activation function and therefore they do not participate in the processing.

The CMAC, compared to conventional adaptive controllers performing the control task as described, has shown distinct desirable characteristics such as accuracy of learning and learning speed. In addition, it ranks favorably in terms of actual control speed. Upon learning, the control signal is instantaneously available, since it is derived directly from the look-up memory, which stores characteristic surface values. Moreover, the neurocontroller contains no restrictions regarding the plant and system linearity, and it seems to perform well in a noisy environment.

Concluding Remarks

The section on neural network control applications explores several central issues such as identification, control of static and dynamical plants, and example designs of selected low-order neurocontrollers. Control of example plants operating in both continuous- and discrete-time modes was considered. However, the exposition does not unveil a complete range of problems and ready-to-use solutions. Rather, basic concepts, problems, and solutions are outlined along with some promising directions for development of neurocontrol systems. The main reason for such a preliminary exposition is that the potential of artificial neural systems as neurocontrollers still has to be researched before it can be fully realized (Barto 1990). The study of the technical literature available seems

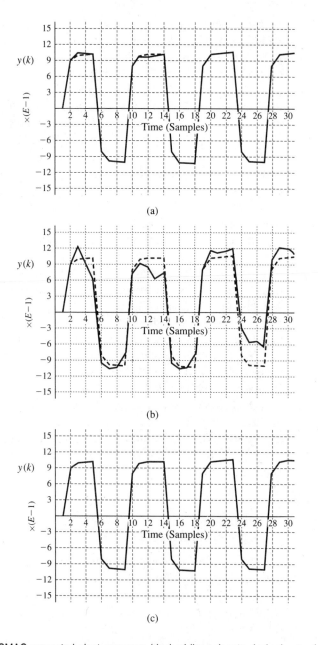

Figure 8.31 CMAC-generated plant response (dashed lines denote desired output): (a) plant as in (8.22a), $a = b = 1$, (b) same as part (a) but noise added, and (c) noise-free nonlinear plant as in (8.25). [©*MIT Press;* reprinted from Kraft and Campagna (1990b) with permission.]

to indicate that much has to be done before the systematic design of learning controllers can be undertaken.

At this stage of neurocontrol development, several areas of possible exploration are worth emphasizing. Neural networks can be used as models of dynamical systems with outputs dependent on input history. Suitable architectures and more systematic modeling approaches need to be devised for this purpose. Neural networks can also serve as controllers, and they seem to be especially promising for nonlinear dynamical systems control. Acquisition and storage of control information seems to be well suited to the applications of associative memory concepts. Such neurocontrollers would take full advantage of associative memory systems having high capacity, high speed, and the ability to interpolate and extrapolate control data in real time (Barto 1990). In addition, theoretical and experimental investigations of the stability of neurocontrollers needs to be undertaken. This would include both learning and control stability of such controllers.

To achieve this aim, novel architectures and training approaches, and an appropriate mixture of conventional and neural control need to be developed. The choices of the traditional identifier and controller structures are usually based on the well-established results of linear systems theory. However, existing design procedures for stable nonlinear dynamical systems are valid only for system-by-system cases. Such procedures are currently not available for designing large classes of such systems. The first comprehensive theoretical and experimental results in the identification and control of nonlinear dynamical systems using neural networks have been reported only recently (Narendra and Parthasarathy 1990, 1991).

One particularly interesting and promising concept is that of so-called dynamic back-propagation (Hecht-Nielsen 1990). Since most physical systems involve dynamics, their realistic modeling can involve a combination of linear dynamical systems and static multilayer neural networks. This combination can be considered as an extension of error back-propagation architectures for static systems. The study has shown that multilayer neural networks using dynamic error back-propagation can be very effective in performing identification and control tasks. The reader is encouraged to look to references for more advanced coverage of neurocontrol issues (Nguyen and Widrow 1990).

8.4 NETWORKS FOR ROBOT KINEMATICS

Although neural networks applicable to the solution of robotics control problems are, in fact, neurocontrollers, their function is specialized mainly to provide solutions to robot arm motion problems. In this section, neural network models

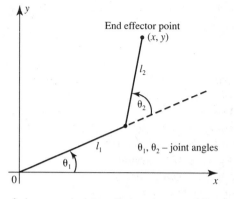

Figure 8.32   Geometry of planar manipulator with two degrees of freedom.

are considered for solving a number of robot kinematics problems. Robot kinematics involves the study of the geometry of manipulator arm motions. Since the performance of specific manipulator tasks is achieved through movement of the manipulator linkages, kinematics is of fundamental importance for robot design and control. Trajectory control and learning of the robot arms motions to achieve the desired final position are the main kinematics tasks covered below.

Overview of Robot Kinematics Problems

Our focus in this section is to provide the design fundamentals for neurocontrollers used in robotics systems. Trajectory control of robotic manipulators traditionally consists of following a preprogrammed sequence of end effector movements. Robot control usually requires control signals applied at the joints of the robot while the desired trajectory, or sequence of arm end positions, is specified for the end effector. Figure 8.32 shows the geometry of an idealized planar robot manipulator with two degrees of freedom. The robot arms operate in a plane. To make the arm move, the desired coordinates of the end effector point (x, y) are fed to the robot controller so that it generates the joint angles (θ_1, θ_2) for the motors that move the arms. To perform end effector position control of a robotic manipulator, two problems need to be solved (Craig 1986):

1. *Inverse kinematics problem:* Given the Cartesian coordinates of the end effector, specified either as a single point or as a set of points on a trajectory, joint angles or a set of joint angles need to be found.

2. *Target position control:* Given the final end effector position, a joint angles sequence suitable for achieving the final position needs to be found.

The kinematics considerations for the manipulator shown in Figure 8.32 are based on the *forward kinematic equation*. The forward kinematic equation involves mapping of joint angle coordinates (θ_1, θ_2) to the end effector position (x, y). The mapping expressions can be obtained by inspection of the figure as follows

$$x = l_1\cos\theta_1 + l_2\cos(\theta_1 + \theta_2)$$
$$y = l_2\sin\theta_1 + l_2\sin(\theta_1 + \theta_2)$$

(8.26)

where θ_1 and θ_2 are the joint angles of the first and second arm segments, respectively, and l_1, and l_2 are respective arm segment lengths. Relation (8.26) expresses the forward kinematic problem and implements unique mapping from the joint angle space to the Cartesian space.

The inverse kinematic problem is described by (Craig 1986):

$$\theta_2 = \cos^{-1}\left[\left(x^2 + y^2 - l_1^2 - l_2^2\right) \Big/ \left(2l_1l_2\right)\right]$$

$(8.27a)$

$$\theta_1 = \tan^{-1}(y/x) - \tan^{-1}\left[l_2\sin\theta_2 / (l_1 + l_2\cos\theta_2)\right]$$

$(8.27b)$

Since $\cos^{-1}$ is not a single-valued function in the range of angles of interest, two possible orientations typically result from (8.27) for the robot arm joint angles. The arm can be positioned with the elbow up or down, with the end effector still at the required (x, y) point. The inverse kinematic transformation (8.27) implementing mapping from Cartesian space to joint space is thus not unique.

As can be seen from Equation (8.27), control of robot arms requires the solution of the inverse kinematic equation system in real time. In the general case of an end effector with n degrees of freedom, the forward and inverse kinematic problems can be formulated, respectively, as

$$\mathbf{x} = \mathbf{h}(\boldsymbol{\theta})$$

(8.28)

$$\boldsymbol{\theta} = \mathbf{h}^{-1}(\mathbf{x})$$

(8.29)

where $\boldsymbol{\theta}$ and $\mathbf{x}$ are joint angles and end effector Cartesian coordinate vectors, respectively, which are defined as follows:

$$\boldsymbol{\theta} \overset{\Delta}{=} \begin{bmatrix} \theta_1 & \theta_2 & \dots & \theta_k \end{bmatrix}^t$$

$$\mathbf{x} \overset{\Delta}{=} \begin{bmatrix} x_1 & x_2 & \dots & x_n \end{bmatrix}^t$$

Even though the numerical solution of (8.29) can be found, this requires large, real-time computational resources. The neural network approach may be used here to solve both the problem of kinematic task formulation and the setting up of the equations. It also allows for circumvention of the computational complexity involved in their numerical solution.

Solution of the Forward and Inverse Kinematics Problems

The forward and inverse kinematics problems can be solved by multilayer feedforward networks as shown in the form of a block diagram in Figure 8.33. The network in Figure 8.33(a) needs to be trained to learn the set of end effector positions $\mathbf{x}$ from the given set of joint angle examples. The network in Figure 8.33(b) is trained to learn the set of joint angles $\boldsymbol{\theta}$ from the given set of end effector position examples. Each of the neural networks involved performs static mapping of two two-variable functions as discussed in earlier chapters.

The supervised learning diagram of both configurations from Figure 8.33 is shown in Figure 8.34. The reader may notice that this configuration falls into the general category of forward plant identification first introduced in Figure 8.17(a). The robot manipulator output $\mathbf{d}$ provides the teacher's signal, or the desired output value, which is compared with the network actual output $\mathbf{o}$. Based on the error value $\|\mathbf{d} - \mathbf{o}\|$, the neural network weights are tuned to achieve the required accuracy of mapping. Note that the teacher's signal $\mathbf{d}$ for the training set can be provided either by solving (8.28) or (8.29), or by taking the respective measurements of the Cartesian or joint coordinates of the actual manipulator. The learning of the manipulator proceeds off-line. Once the network has been trained and installed in the system, no more training is allowed since the neurocontroller is placed in front of the robot manipulator as discussed in the following paragraph. Therefore, the set of training data should be uniformly distributed over the robot's working area so that the network can make good generalizations for the intermediate points.

Obviously, once the network has been trained to perform the required kinematic transformation, it then needs to be employed in the inverse feedforward control mode. If the neural network has been trained to solve a forward kinematics problem, its natural application is to control the manipulator, which needs Cartesian coordinates $\mathbf{x}$ as input and produces joint angles $\boldsymbol{\theta}$ as outputs. This is shown in Figure 8.35(a). The input to the neural controller is the vector of desired joint angles, $\boldsymbol{\theta}_d$. After error-free training of the controller, we should have $\boldsymbol{\theta} = \boldsymbol{\theta}_d$ at the output of the robot manipulator. Using the trained network shown

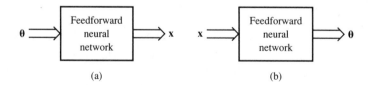

(a) (b)

Figure 8.33 Neural networks for robot kinematics transformation: (a) forward kinematics problem and (b) inverse kinematics problem.

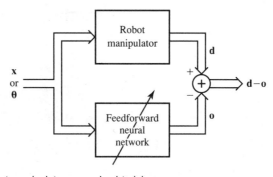

Figure 8.34 Robot manipulator supervised training.

in Figure 8.35(b) requires specification of the desired end effector coordinates $\mathbf{x}_d$. The network translates these coordinates to angles $\boldsymbol{\theta}$ and the robot manipulator should respond with $\mathbf{x} = \mathbf{x}_d$.

Let us review the forward kinematics trajectory learning for the two degrees of freedom (planar) manipulator. The concept of "trajectory" is understood here as the end effector workspace rather than as a sequence of points to be followed. In designing trajectory we are therefore dealing with specializing the robot end effector movement in a specific work area rather than training it to reach sequence of points ending at a target position. Target position learning is studied separately later in this chapter.

In this example the robot is required to learn Cartesian coordinates x, y for the circular trajectory of radius r. A network with two inputs (θ_1 and θ_2), four hidden nodes, and two output neurons yielding outputs x, y has been selected

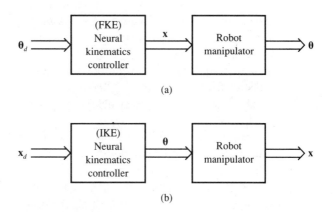

Figure 8.35 Controlling robot manipulator using neural controller: (a) joint angles input and (b) target coordinates (end effector) input.

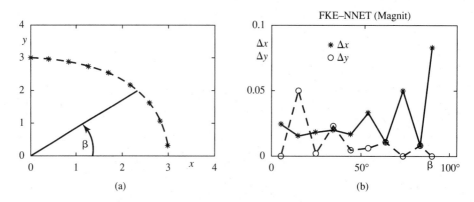

Figure 8.36 Forward kinematics solution for circular trajectory, $r = 3$: (a) response of the trained network and (b) mapping error for training data reused in the test mode. [©*IEEE*; adapted from Arteaga-Bravo (1990) with permission.]

to simulate the expression (8.26) (Arteaga-Bravo 1990). The constraint on the circular trajectory, which needs to be learned, is

$$x = r \cos \beta$$
$$y = r \sin \beta \tag{8.30}$$

where angle β is covering the first quadrant in this example. The training has been performed for $l_1 = 3$, $l_2 = 2$, and $r = 3$ at 10 points of the selected trajectory. The 2–4–2 network has been trained using the error back-propagation technique with learning constant $\eta = 0.9$, and $\alpha = 0.9$ for the momentum term. The training data of the trajectory with $r = 3$ contains angle β between 5 and 85°, spaced by 10°, and $\beta = 90°$.

The trained 2–4–2 network has subsequently been evaluated using the training data in the test mode. The results of training are shown in Figure 8.36(a). The figure illustrates an accurate mapping of angles into the desired end effector positions forming the trajectory $\sqrt{x^2 + y^2} = 3$. The differences between the accurate forward kinematics solutions and those computed by the neural network are illustrated in Figure 8.36(b). The maximum magnitude difference, or maximum absolute error, has been observed to be about 0.08 for the x coordinate at $\beta = 90°$.

A multilayer feedforward network with two hidden layers containing four neurons each has then been employed to perform the manipulator's inverse kinematic transformation for the same circular trajectory. The 2–4–4–2 network has been selected for training with parameters $\eta = 0.9$ and $\alpha = 0.3$. The results of the evaluation of the trained network for the training data θ_1 and θ_2 are illustrated in Figure 8.37(a). The figure illustrates a mapping of points from the trajectory (8.30) with $r = 3$ into joint angles θ_1 and θ_2. The differences between the accurate inverse kinematics solutions and those computed by the network at the training

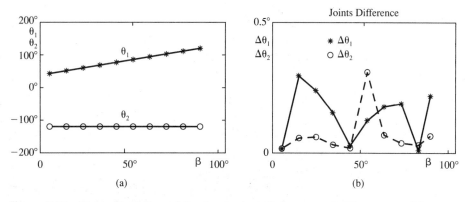

Figure 8.37 Inverse kinematics solution for circular trajectory, $r = 3$: (a) response of the trained network and (b) mapping error for training data in the test mode. [©*IEEE;* adapted from Arteaga-Bravo (1990) with permission.]

points are depicted in Figure 8.37(b). The largest absolute error of the joint angle has been approximately $0.33°$ for θ_2 at $\beta = 55°$.

Neurons with unipolar activation functions have been used in this experiment. Training input data for both cases have been mapped to the range $(0,1)$ in order to make more efficient use of the unipolar activation function and to obtain better results in training the networks.

Comparison of Architectures for the Forward Kinematics Problem

In this section, various feedforward neural networks are considered for solving the forward kinematics problem for robots with two degrees of freedom. Several network configurations have been designed and compared for modeling of the manipulator kinematics (Nguyen, Patel, and Khorasani 1990). A manipulator is treated in the description below as a black box for which the training samples are collected from geometrical measurements. The specific trajectory of the end effector is used to test the outcome of the training for selected neural architectures.

Each of the networks used for evaluation has two input nodes, θ_1 and θ_2, in addition to the bias node, and two output nodes, x and y. Since the unnormalized output values are Cartesian coordinates and exceed the range $(-1, 1)$ covered by the bipolar sigmoidal-type activation functions, output neurons are selected such that they have an identity activation function and perform scalar product computation only. Architectures studied have been: 2–10–10–2 for the network trained with the error back-propagation algorithm (BP), 2–10–10–2 for the network trained with the back-propagation algorithm but with output splitting (BPOS), 2–8–2 for the functional link network (FL). In addition, a counterpropagation

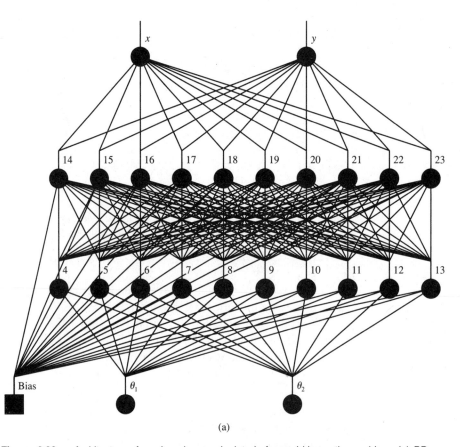

(a)

Figure 8.38a Architectures for a learning manipulator's forward kinematics problem: (a) BP [©*IEEE;* adapted from Nguyen, Patel, and Khorasani (1990) with permission.]

network (CP) has been used to provide trajectory mapping (Nguyen, Patel, and Khorasani 1990).

The networks have been trained using a set consisting of 64 input/output pairs obtained from measurements taken in the robot working area. Weights have been initialized at random values between -0.5 and 0.5, except for output layer weights, which have been initialized at zero. The joint angle values for training have been selected in the first quadrant in such a way that they uniformly cover the entire work area of interest defined by $0 < \theta_1 < 90°$ and $0 < \theta_2 < 90°$.

BP and BPOS error back-propagation architectures have been trained with $\eta = 0.1$ and $\eta = 0.4$ for the first and second hidden layers, respectively. The architecture of the BPOS network is the modified version of the common BP network. The nodes in both hidden layers of the BPOS network have been divided symmetrically into two groups. Both networks are shown in Figure 8.38. The FL network is composed of eight input nodes providing the following signals:

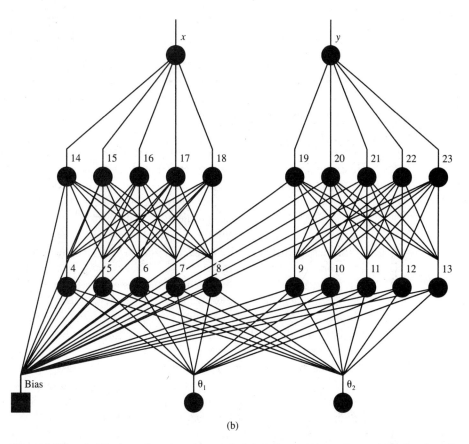

Figure 8.38b Architectures for a learning manipulator's forward kinematics problem *(continued):* (b) BPOS. [©*IEEE;* adapted from Nguyen, Patel, and Khorasani (1990) with permission.]

θ_1, θ_2, $\sin \theta_1$, $\sin \theta_2$, $\cos \theta_1$, $\cos \theta_2$, $\sin (\theta_1 + \theta_2)$, and $\cos (\theta_1 + \theta_2)$. A simple delta rule was used for learning of the single-layer feedforward FL network with a learning rate of $\eta = 0.4$.

The CP network design has followed the guidelines of Chapter 7 with the Kohonen layer used as a first CP network layer. This part of the network layer has been trained using the winner-take-all learning rule. The layer is followed by the Grossberg layer producing the desired network output. The input to the first layer of the CP network is provided by normalized input vectors. The CP network has performed here as a look-up table responding with the output, which is paired with the stored input that matches the output by being in the same training pair of vectors.

The following trajectory was used to train and test the discussed four architectures

$$\theta_1(t) = 3 \cdot 10^{-3}t$$
$$\theta_2(t) = 3 \cdot 10^{-3}t$$

(8.31)

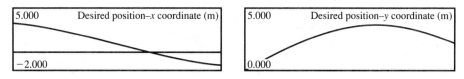

Figure 8.39 Trajectory for network testing. [©*IEEE;* adapted from Nguyen, Patel, and Khorasani (1990) with permission.]

where $0 < t < 500$ s. Figure 8.39 illustrates the trajectory used for network learning in Cartesian coordinates. The FKE equation (8.26) provides here the results for the Cartesian coordinates of the end effector.

The training of all four network architectures resulted in quick learning convergence to the desired trajectory. The basic BP network with two hidden layers gave a reasonably accurate solution. The error defined as distance (in centimeters) between the trajectory (8.31) and the one produced by the trained network is shown in Figure 8.40(a). The training of the BPOS network, which involved considerably fewer connections than the BP network, yielded comparable accuracy. This is shown in Figure 8.40(b). Although BPOS network training required 300 training cycles compared to 200 cycles for the same error of 10 percent for the BP network, its total training time has been shorter due to the smaller number of weights in the BPOS network.

The best solution of the trajectory learning task has been achieved with the FL network. The network required only 20 training cycles and the training resulted in the best approximation of the target trajectory (8.31) for all four cases studied. This can be seen from Figure 8.40(c).

In contrast with the multilayer feedforward networks and functional link network, the CP network implements a steplike approximation of the trajectory.

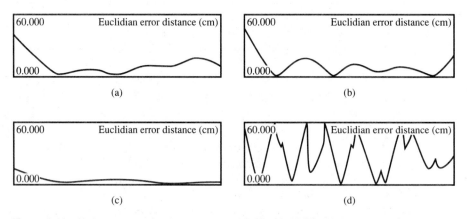

Figure 8.40 Trajectory error for the test mode: (a) BP, (b) BPOS, (c) FL, and (d) CP. [©*IEEE;* adapted from Nguyen, Patel, and Khorasani (1990) with permission.]

The training results in relatively fast approximation of the trajectory, but the end effector position error is rather large and uneven, as can be seen from Figure 8.40(d). Therefore, the CP network in this application can be recommended only if a short development time is required for low-precision trajectory tracking.

The discussion of neural network applications for solution of the forward and inverse kinematics problems and generation of the desired trajectories indicates that neural networks can efficiently learn manipulator kinematics. Modeling of the desired trajectories or kinematic transformations can be achieved with a considerable degree of accuracy using a number of network architectures. Training of a suitable neural network architecture can be performed based on geometrical measurements. Alternatively, training can be based on computed solutions of either forward or inverse kinematics problem for the robot working area of interest to the designer.

Target Position Learning

So far our discussion of applications of neural networks for robotics has only focused on memoryless mapping of manipulator kinematics. Neural networks, however, can also be employed to learn a *sequence of mappings*. This is understood as learning a sequence of space transformations. In this sense, the learning of a target position can be understood as dynamical control learning. Robotic arms can be treated as dynamical plant. In addition to learning the trajectory or working area, which is essentially static, or point-to-point transformation, robot arms can be controlled to follow a sequence of steps and to reach a desired target position. In this section the study of robot arm movement with two degrees of freedom and with a desired final end effector position is discussed based on the work of Sobajic, Lu, and Pao (1988). In particular, the presence of trajectory disturbances is evaluated in this study.

Our objective is to move the end effector of a two-link planar robot manipulator toward a target point until the positions of the two coincide. The specific task for the neural network designer is to generate the sequence of joint vector increments, thus providing the appropriate sequence of incremental control signals. In this discussion we assume that the target end effector position that needs to be learned is specified in polar coordinates $r_t \angle \theta_t$. An error back-propagation network with architecture 4–6–4–2 has been applied to perform the task (Sobajic, Lu, and Pao 1988). Network input signals are equal to the currently measured joint angles $\theta_1(t)$ and $\theta_2(t)$, and also to the fixed target coordinates r_t and θ_t. The network needs to map angles θ_1 and θ_2 into the two control actions $k_1 \Delta \theta_1$ and $k_2 \Delta \theta_2$, respectively. The control state equations have the following form:

$$\theta_1(t + 1) = \theta_1(t) + k_1(t)\Delta\theta_1$$
$$\theta_2(t + 1) = \theta_2(t) + k_2(t)\Delta\theta_2$$

$$(8.32)$$

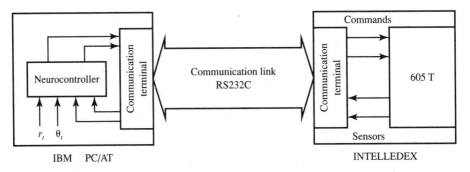

Figure 8.41 The communication scheme between the Intelledex 605T and the neurocontroller. [©*IEEE;* reprinted from Sobajic, Lu, and Pao (1988) with permission.]

The actual outputs of the neural network are $k_1(t)$ and $k_2(t)$. The values are limited to the range $(-1, 1)$ since bipolar activation functions are used. An Intelledex 605T-type robot and the neural network controller for that experiment have been configured in a closed-loop feedback system (Sobajic, Lu, and Pao 1988). As shown in Figure 8.41, the information exchange between the neurocontroller and the robot is carried by the RS232 serial port.

Two experiments have been performed. In the first experiment, the neural network controller has been trained to guide the arm end effector from any initial location to the specified single fixed target position. The training has been implemented based on the set of 26 input vectors covering the anticipated work area and involving a number of different initial points. Network training results are tabulated in Figure 8.42(a). Eight different initial point positions have been used for training as shown in the learning control experiment. The maximum relative target distance error reported in the experiment is 1.46 percent. All remaining relative target distance errors were below 1 percent.

The second experiment has been designed to move the robot arm from any initial location to one of a number of specified target positions. The training has been performed using the set of 64 training input vectors for each of the 14 specified target points being entrained. Results of the training have been tabulated in Figure 8.42(b) in 14 rows, with each row corresponding to one target point. All trials originated at $\theta_1 = \theta_2 = 0$. The maximum relative target distance error reported was 2.36 percent. The final weight values of the trained network of size 4–6–4–2 are listed in Figure 8.43.

In addition to testing the trained network under normal working circumstances as reported above, the controller was also investigated when affected by the presence of unforeseen disturbances. First, the network trajectory control was overridden first at time $t = t_1$, and then at time $t = t_2$. Thus, the robot arm was deflected twice to undesirable positions off the trajectory. In each case, the neural

Learning Experiment	Initial Position		Required Final Position		Implemented Final Position		Error
	θ_1	θ_2	r_t	θ_t	r_f	θ_f	
1	30.	30.	40.	−30.	39.96	−29.48	0.69%
2	30.	−90.	40.	−30.	39.66	−29.67	0.77%
3	−10.	30.	40.	−30.	39.91	−30.18	0.28%
4	−10.	−90.	40.	−30.	39.49	−30.86	1.46%
5	−50.	−30.	40.	−30.	40.24	−29.47	0.82%
6	−50.	90.	40.	−30.	39.92	−29.32	0.90%
7	−100.	−30.	40.	−30.	40.31	−30.36	0.75%
8	−100.	90.	40.	−30.	40.10	−30.39	0.54%

(a)

Learning Experiment	Initial Position		Required Final Position		Implemented Final Position		Error
	θ_1	θ_2	r_t	θ_t	r_f	θ_f	
1	0.	0.	40.	−45.	39.71	−44.99	0.54%
2	0.	0.	30.	−45.	30.00	−42.88	2.08%
3	0.	0.	20.	−45.	18.65	−46.63	2.73%
4	0.	0.	40.	−30.	39.71	−30.10	0.56%
5	0.	0.	30.	−30.	30.17	−27.70	2.28%
6	0.	0.	20.	−30.	18.81	−31.24	2.36%
7	0.	0.	40.	−15.	39.73	−15.28	0.62%
8	0.	0.	30.	−15.	30.26	−12.87	2.15%
9	0.	0.	20.	−15.	19.12	−15.82	1.72%
10	0.	0.	40.	0.	39.79	−0.62	0.90%
11	0.	0.	20.	0.	19.40	−0.43	1.16%
12	0.	0.	40.	15.	39.79	14.05	1.25%
13	0.	0.	30.	15.	30.57	16.63	1.93%
14	0.	0.	20.	15.	19.72	14.50	0.62%

(θ_1, θ_2)—initial position of the robot arm. (r_t, θ_t)—target position.
(r_f, θ_f)—final position of the robot arm. error—the relative error.

(b)

Figure 8.42 Result of the 4–6–4–2 network training: (a) fixed target position, different starting points, and (b) different target positions, different starting points. [©*IEEE;* reprinted from Sobajic, Lu, and Pao (1988) with permission.]

controller has shown remarkable response and it produced a new and correct trajectory, as illustrated in Figure 8.44(a). In another experiment, the target position was altered at $t = t_1$ while the robot arm was already following the desired trajectory. As a result of the sudden alteration of the target, the neural controller

Level 1						
			Weights			
		−0.028	8.578	−0.198	14.050	
		1.504	10.399	0.889	10.752	
		−1.535	16.108	0.417	14.590	
		−5.790	−5.707	3.421	−1.213	
		−1.192	−0.606	3.323	−3.638	
		18.238	2.350	−18.866	−0.189	
			Thresholds			
	−12.141	−12.409	−18.521	2.801	1.217	−5.061
Level 2						
			Weights			
	−0.472	−2.300	−3.269	−1.451	−3.404	−0.720
	5.670	5.270	8.206	−1.576	−2.693	−1.005
	1.330	0.618	−0.563	4.573	0.611	−9.513
	−0.595	−0.685	−0.402	−1.648	−1.439	−2.538
			Thresholds			
		0.921	−6.032	3.971	−0.422	
Level 3						
			Weights			
		−2.656	−0.059	−5.215	−2.623	
		4.642	−4.596	0.346	0.434	
			Thresholds			
			3.180	1.884		

Figure 8.43 Tabulated weights of the trained network for the different target points experiment. [©*IEEE;* reprinted from Sobajic, Lu, and Pao (1988) with permission.]

generated the revised set of command actions, and the new target position was reached. This is illustrated in Figure 8.44(b).

The described project with target position guidance control has made use of multilayer feedforward controllers trained using the error back-propagation techniques. The results achieved demonstrate their unusual efficiency and potential for use in robot kinematics control systems. The performance of neural controllers described in this section can be based entirely on actual geometrical conditions measured in the robot working space. Therefore, robot neurocontrollers can be developed without the need for complex mathematical transformations or even mathematical modeling of the problem. The discussed networks have been able to learn and generalize not only different static space-to-space mappings, but also the robot movement dynamics. The networks were also able to memorize the sequence of control signals needed to achieve one of the specified final positions.

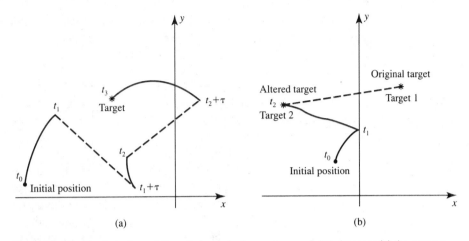

Figure 8.44 The trajectory of the robot arm in the presence of disturbances: (a) the arm position disturbance and (b) the target coordinates alteration. [©*IEEE;* reprinted from Sobajic, Lu, and Pao (1988) with permission.]

8.5

CONNECTIONIST EXPERT SYSTEMS FOR MEDICAL DIAGNOSIS

This section presents examples of connectionist expert systems for medical diagnosis. The introductory concepts of multilayer feedforward networks with error back-propagation training used for medical diagnosis have already been formulated in Section 4.6 and illustrated in Figure 4.24. This section discusses in more detail the specific capabilities and limitations of medical diagnosis connectionist expert systems. Example expert systems for diagnosis of skin, low back pain, and heart infarction diseases are presented.

Medical diagnosis is performed with multiple, often related, disease states that can occur with identical symptoms and clinical data. In addition, specific diseases are not always accompanied by the same symptoms and clinical and historical data. As a result of these difficulties, both physician accuracy and computer-aided diagnosis systems leave room for improvement. This is one of the reasons for our study. Let us review the basic issues of computer-aided diagnosis.

Computer-aided diagnosis systems have been successfully used in a number of areas of medicine. Among several approaches to automated diagnosis, rule-based systems and knowledge-based systems using the Bayesian approach seem to be the most widespread. Both approaches, however, seem to suffer from some problems in medical diagnosis applications. Rule-based systems typically require formulation of explicit diagnostic rules. Much of the human knowledge, and especially expert or medical expert knowledge, however, remain implicit. Implicit knowledge can be expressed neither as a mathematical function for numerical computation nor as an if-then rule for symbolic processing. Even expressing the implicit knowledge as a conditional probability density function encounters difficulties because of statistical interdependencies between the events.

Generally, implicit knowledge is difficult to quantize, formalize, or sometimes even express verbally. In addition to these difficulties, translation of implicit knowledge into explicit rules would thus lead to loss and distortion of information content. In other words, domains with implicit knowledge are difficult to express in terms of accurate specifications of decision rules. In addition, the knowledge engineer would have to understand thoroughly the domain and the expert reasoning in order to extract the rules for the system. Building an expert system for diagnosis using decision rules remains an expensive and time-consuming task.

The approach based on Bayes theorem involves comparisons of relative likelihoods of different diagnoses. The individual likelihoods of diseases are computed from individual patient information. Symptoms of diseases have to be assumed to be statistically independent in the Bayesian approach. This assumption underlying the Bayes theorem, however, does not apply widely in diagnostic practice. This is because several symptoms often arise due to the same organic cause. On the other hand, such symptoms have to be kept separated because they may provide vital decision information. Thus, a useful performance by practical diagnosis systems that are based on Bayes theorem is not always guaranteed.

The connectionist expert system can be trained to associate diagnoses with the symptom data. This presents an alternative approach that is essentially data driven. The connectionist approach lies in the middle ground between the rule-based and Bayesian approach. The experimental and heuristic approach prevailing in building connectionist expert systems focuses on repeated presentation of training examples of the various symptoms along with the diagnosed diseases. After training of a suitable network architecture is complete, test data and generalization by the network should lead to correct disease diagnosis.

Expert System for Skin Diseases Diagnosis

The expert system called DESKNET has been designed for instruction of medical students in the diagnosis of papulosquamous skin diseases. These are diseases that exhibit bumpiness or scaliness of the skin (Yoon et al. 1989). The system has been developed and used mostly for symptom gathering and for developing diagnosing skills rather than for replacing the doctor's diagnosis. The expert system uses multilayer feedforward network and employs the 96–20–10 architecture with a single hidden layer and continuous unipolar neurons.

Input for the system consists of the following skin disease symptoms and their parameters: location, distribution, shape, arrangement, pattern, number of lesions, presence of an active border, amount of scale, elevation of papuls, color, altered pigmentation, itching, pustules, lymphadenopathy, palmar thickening, results of microscopic examination, the presence of herald patch, and the result of the dermatology test called KOH. In addition to the current symptom-generated data from the above list, the duration of skin lesions in days and weeks are also represented at the input.

The system has a total of 96 inputs plus the fixed bias input, and 10 output neurons. Inputs of values 0 and 1 are fed to the network signifying the absence or presence of the symptoms and their respective durations. The output neurons used in the local representation mode are indicative of the following 10 diseases diagnosed: psoriasis, pityriasis rubra pilaris, lichen planus, pityriasis rosea, tinea versicolor, dermatophytosis, cutaneous T-cell lymphoma, secondary syphilis, chronic contact dermatitis, and seborrheic dermatitis.

The training data for the DESKNET system consisted of input specifications of 10 model diseases collected from 250 patients. If specific symptoms or their parameters were not known, the input was coded as 0.5. In this way the outputs of unipolar neurons used in this network were made independent of that input. The network was trained using the standard error back-propagation algorithm.

The performance of the developed network was tested for previously unused symptom and disease data collected from 99 patients. The correct diagnosis was achieved for 70% of the papulosquamous group skin diseases. The success rate was above 80% for the remaining diseases except for psoriasis. Psoriasis patients were diagnosed correctly only in 30% of the cases. According to the domain expert, however, psoriasis often resembles other diseases within the papulosquamous group, which makes it somewhat difficult to recognize even for specialists.

In case of a rule-based system whose knowledge base consists of a set of explicit rules, the decision path can be traced and explanation of the decision can be provided to the user. Connectionist expert systems reach conclusions through rather complex, nonlinear and simultaneous synergistic interaction of many units at a time. The accurate justification of an hypothesis, therefore, involves all nodes of the network. If the justification of a conclusion is expected from a discussed system, analyzing the effect of a single input, or selected group of inputs, would be very difficult and would yield inaccurate results.

However, some explanation capability exists within a trained connectionist expert system. Despite its limitations, this capability can offer certain interpretations to the user, and also reveals those input variables that are more important and are likely to contribute to decisions. For the local representation network, one of the output nodes is activated stronger than any of the remaining ones. Weights leading to this node with relatively large magnitudes are therefore contributing more to the decisions than the remaining weights, each considered separately. The positive and negative signs of relatively large weights can be looked at as indicative of positive and negative contributions, respectively. An additional consideration is that the hidden layer re-represents the input data and the outputs of hidden nodes are neither symptoms nor diagnostic decisions. In a network with a single hidden layer, internal data representation provided by the hidden layer rather than the original input data is used for generating the final decision. Internal representation can, however, offer further heuristic interpretations of the knowledge processing within the system.

In the case of the DESKNET expert system, which uses 20 hidden-layer nodes, the total of 20 hidden-layer factors attributed to the level of hidden node responses possess the discrimination capability for the set of 10 diseases. The factors are transmitted by large weights connected to the strongest activated output neuron of the output layer. With reference to Figure 4.7, such weights can be labeled $w_{k_1 j_1}, w_{k_1 j_2}, \ldots, w_{k_1 j_l}$, where k_1 is the output node number indicating the disease diagnosed, and there are l internal factors supporting it.

An example of the explanation potential of DESKNET is shown in Figure 8.45. The figure shows only the weights that are of relative importance for diagnosing a dermatophytosis disease. It can be seen that, although unnamed, internal factors numbered 13 and 14 are the two strongest in causing disease number 5. Thus, for this example case, we have $k_1 = 5$, $j_1 = 13$, $j_2 = 14$, and $l = 2$. Relatively large input weights now need to be found for each of the hidden nodes $j_1, j_2, \ldots, j_l$. Input nodes 1, 10, and 36 and 6, 10, 36, and 71 were identified as those that are affecting the internal factors of 13 and 14, respectively. Consequently, symptoms and their parameters numbered 1, 6, 10, 36, and 71 were found to be of dominant importance for the diagnosis of dermatophytosis.

Below we explain the methodology that has been used for identification of relatively large and contributive weights and symptoms in DESKNET. To determine internal decision factors, the largest and smallest weights of the output layer have been selected among all weights $w_{k_1,j}$, $j = 1, 2, \ldots, J$, for a given diagnosis k_1. The maximum difference between the largest and smallest weight constitutes the weight range. The range is then divided by 6 to estimate the standard deviation of weights. The doubled standard deviation is used as the cutoff point for discrimination of relatively large weights. For the data of Figure 8.45 with diagnosed disease 5, or $k_1 = 5$, weights with the largest magnitudes are $w_{5,13} = 2.86$, $w_{5,14} = 2.71$, $w_{5,2} = -2.68$, $w_{5,6} = -3.46$, $w_{5,10} = -2.38$, and $w_{5,17} = -3.31$. The range for this set of weights is

$$w_{5,13} - w_{5,6} = 6.32$$

This yields the standard deviation of approximately 1.05, and the cutoff points equal to $\pm 2(1.05) = \pm 2.1$ for selection of relatively large weights. Therefore, only two weights, $w_{5,13}$ and $w_{5,14}$, are found to support the decision of node $k_1 = 5$. The weights are shown in the figure and other weights are omitted. This analysis performed for the output layer needs to be repeated by using hidden nodes 13 and 14 as decision nodes. The full probability profile obtained for the diagnosis path of dermatophytosis is illustrated in the figure.

The discussion indicates the presence of the following symptoms and their parameters for this particular disease: lesions of weeks of duration, minimal

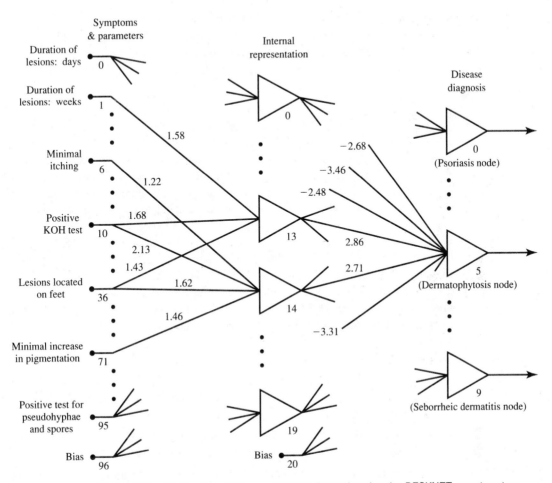

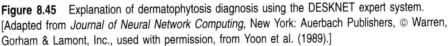

Figure 8.45 Explanation of dermatophytosis diagnosis using the DESKNET expert system. [Adapted from *Journal of Neural Network Computing*, New York: Auerbach Publishers, © Warren, Gorham & Lamont, Inc., used with permission, from Yoon et al. (1989).]

itching, positive KOH test, lesions on feet, minimal increase in pigmentation, and microscopic evaluation for pseudohyphae. The profile produced by this methodology rather closely matches the probability profile provided by the domain expert. Similar probability profiles can be obtained for the negative responses of the hidden nodes numbered 2, 6, 10, and 17 (not shown on Figure 8.45). These profiles indicate that absence of certain symptoms contribute to the positive diagnosis of a particular disease.

It should be noted that the discussed method of explanation extraction from the expert system is rather heuristic and somewhat inconclusive. Indeed, factors influencing the decision are usually distributed within the network in a complex, superimposed way. Thus, only fairly general and somewhat tentative conclusions can be drawn from the search for the largest and smallest weights connected to the neurons with the strongest responses within the layer.

Expert System for
Low Back Pain Diagnosis

The neural network-based expert system described in this section is used for low back pain disease diagnosis (Bounds et al. 1988). This expert system is somewhat better validated in practice and less experimental than DESKNET. After training, the system is able to provide correct diagnosis more often than any of the three groups of doctors or the fuzzy logic system when they are used for comparisons on the same data. This project offers an interesting and suggestive example of the useful performance of a neural network in an actual diagnosis application.

Back pain is one of the most common complaints encountered by doctors, and yet the diagnosis of the cause underlying the back pain is difficult. Common symptoms are often found in patients with serious spinal problems and in those with much less serious problems. In addition, nonorganic symptoms make the diagnosis of this disease more difficult.

For the purpose of patient treatment the back pain needs to be classified into four categories as follows (Bounds et al. 1988):

- Simple low back pain (SLBP)—simple backache
- Root pain (ROOTP)—nerve root compression due, for example, to disk prolapse
- Spinal pathology (SPATH)—due to tumor, inflammation, or infection
- Abnormal illness behavior (AIB)—back pain with significant psychological overlay.

Patients with AIB need to be separated from the population due to the difficulties of interpretation of clinical findings in patients of this group. Further comprehensive assessment is needed for such patients before a more detailed diagnosis is provided.

The set of patient data used referred to 200 patients with back pain. Lists of symptoms and medical history data were compiled for each patient for the purpose of producing the training and test sets. To ensure that the patients' problems were truly representative of one of the four classes, patients were followed up over a long period. Fifty examples of each class were used; 25 formed the training set and the remaining formed the test set for each class.

The input data were coded into 50 inputs in the unipolar values range [0, 1]. Many of the symptoms and medical history questions were responded to with "yes/no" answers and they were assigned binary 1/0 input values, respectively. The input was coded 0.5 where none of the answers was applicable. Answers to a few questions that were not binary were coded with the input values between 0 and 1. Unipolar continuous neurons arranged first in a single- and then in a double-hidden layer architecture were used for experiments. Both local and distributed representations were tested. Although local representation with a separate output neuron for each class worked reasonably well, better results were obtained for distributed coding as follows:

$$\mathbf{d} = \begin{cases} \begin{bmatrix} 0 & 0 \end{bmatrix}^t & \text{for SLBP} \\ \begin{bmatrix} 0 & 1 \end{bmatrix}^t & \text{for AIB} \\ \begin{bmatrix} 1 & 0 \end{bmatrix}^t & \text{for ROOTP} \\ \begin{bmatrix} 1 & 1 \end{bmatrix}^t & \text{for SPATH} \end{cases}$$

This coding improved the chances of a less serious cause (SLBP) being incorrectly attributed as the most serious cause (SPATH), and vice versa.

The training was implemented for the learning rate of 0.1 and with the momentum term of 0.9. Somewhere between 10 and 40 training runs were carried out, each starting from different initial random weights for each architectural configuration tested. A different number of hidden neurons were tried, ranging from 0 to 50 in a single hidden layer. Also, various sizes of double hidden layers were evaluated. Subsequent to training, feasible network architectures were selected. Final tests were made on the test set with a thresholding value of 0.5 for the output neurons so that they provided binary decisions. All units of the trained networks were fully connected.

The results were found to be somewhat insensitive for the number of single hidden layer units if it was selected between 0 and 50. The average success rate for test runs is depicted in Figure 8.46. Ten runs for each tested architecture are included in the average shown. Markedly, the large dimensionality of the input vector caused only a marginally worse decision rate for a single-layer network ($J = 0$) compared to a single hidden-layer network containing dozens of hidden neurons. Networks with double hidden layer have shown no practical advantage over the results illustrated in the figure for a single hidden layer. This conclusion, however, remains valid only for this particular problem, network input/output size, and the data used to train it.

To evaluate the performance of the developed expert system, the set of test data on symptoms and medical history of patients was given to both general practitioners and specialists. In addition, the set was used for testing a CAD system based on fuzzy logic (Bounds et al. 1988; Norris 1986). Comparison of performance has been made for the following diagnosis methods:

- BNS—Bristol neurosurgeons
- GOS—Glasgow orthopaedic surgeons

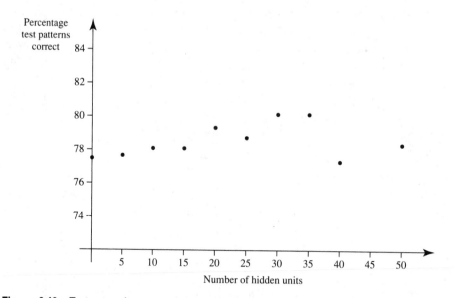

Figure 8.46 Test set performance of the back pain diagnosis expert system using a single hidden layer network with *J* hidden nodes. [©*IEEE;* adapted from Bounds et al. (1988) with permission.]

- ■ BGP—Bristol general practitioners
- ■ FLS—Fuzzy logic system (CAD)
- ■ MLP1—Best multilayer perceptron with architecture 50–30–2
- ■ MLP2—Mean of 10 MLP runs for 50–30–2 network
- ■ MLP3—Best multilayer perceptron with architecture 50–0–2
- ■ MLP4—Mean of 10 MLP runs for 50–0–2 network.

The results for each of the four diagnoses are summarized as bar charts in Figure 8.47. The results indicate that the overall performance of the multilayer perceptron network (black bars) exceeds that of three groups of doctors (blank bars). Also, the multilayer perceptron network reaches the level of performance of the fuzzy logic system (shaded bar). For the most serious disease, spinal pathology, the neural expert system outperforms the other methods as shown in Figure 8.47(d). It can be seen that any of the four selected architectures yields an equal or better diagnosis than each of the three teams of doctors and the fuzzy logic system. This outcome of the diagnosis is of special importance since undetected spinal pathology may have serious implications for a patient's health. On the other hand, the neural expert system performed much worse than any other method for diagnosis of simple low-back pain as illustrated in Figure 8.47(a).

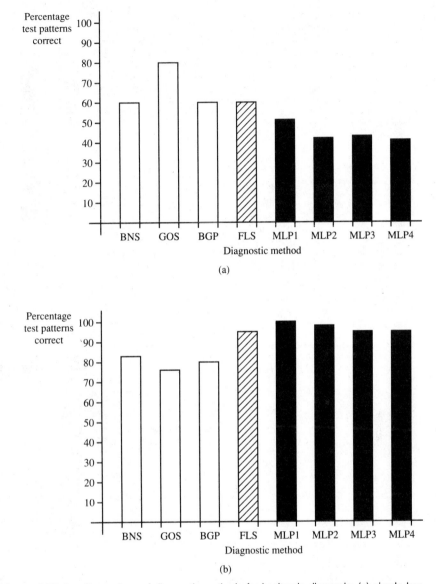

Figure 8.47a,b Comparison of diagnostic methods for back-pain diagnosis: (a) simple low back pain and (b) abnormal illness behavior. [©*IEEE;* reprinted from Bounds et al. (1988) with permission.]

In the opinion of the authors of the project, who are pattern recognition specialists and medical school faculty, the neural network could perform even better than reported provided a larger number of representative training examples were

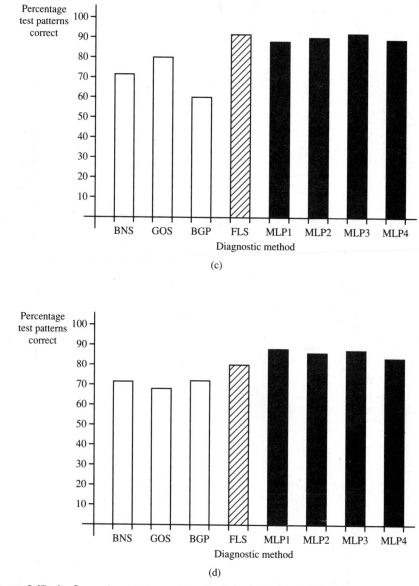

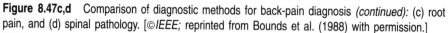

Figure 8.47c,d Comparison of diagnostic methods for back-pain diagnosis *(continued):* (c) root pain, and (d) spinal pathology. [©*IEEE;* reprinted from Bounds et al. (1988) with permission.]

used. Insufficient examples which do not span the entire spectrum of possible input patterns may have caused certain features of patterns not to be encoded in the network during the reported training experiment.

Expert System for Coronary
Occlusion Diagnosis

Acute myocardial infarction, also called coronary occlusion, is an example of another serious disease that has been difficult to diagnose accurately. A considerable number of methodologies have been developed in attempts to improve on the diagnosis accuracy of predicting acute myocardial infarction. The best of the diagnostic approaches using conventional computer-aided diagnostic systems has performed with a detection rate of 88 percent and a false alarm rate of 26 percent. These prediction rates are comparable to those by physicians, reported as equal to 88 and 29 percent for detection and false alarm rates, respectively (Baxt 1990).

A multilayer unipolar perceptron network trained using the error back-propagation technique was applied to the prediction of acute myocardial infarction in patients admitted to the emergency room with acute anterior chest pain. Because most patients in this population are not suffering from acute myocardial infarction, a subset of patients with a much greater probability of the disease was chosen for the study. Moreover, only patients later admitted to the coronary care unit were included in the evaluation. Understandably, only for these patients, the full present and retrospective data were available for analysis (Baxt 1990) and subsequent neural network training.

Consider that the present coronary care unit data confirm or rule out the presence of infarction. These data were presented as desired output and coded as 0 or 1 for an absent or present infarction, respectively. The retrospective data were clinical variables collected in the emergency department and submitted as input patterns to the network. The full list of predictive input variables for the diagnosis of coronary occlusion may include as many as 41 items. The tests performed on the neural network indicated, however, that only 20 of these variables were relevant for representing essential retrospective diagnostic data. The variables are tabulated in Figure 8.48(a). The inputs to the network were generated by a specially written program that coded most of these clinical variables into binary data 0 and 1 for the absence or presence of a finding.

The multilayer feedforward perceptron network that yielded the best results in the project has 20 input nodes, 1 output node, and two hidden layers consisting of 10 neurons each. The data involved a population of 356 patients randomly divided into two equal and permanent groups. In each of the groups there were 118 patients without acute myocardial infarction and 60 patients who sustained the disease. The network training was simulated starting at random initial weights with a learning rate of 0.05 and momentum term of 0.9.

The data on the first group of patients were first used to train the network, while the data on the second group were used to perform a test of the diagnostic expert system. It was found during tests that the output neuron indicating the

History	Past History	Examination	Electro-Cardiogram Findings
Age	Past AMI	Jugular venous distention	2 mm ST elevation
Sex	Angina		1 mm ST elevation
Location of pain	Diabetes	Rales	ST depression
Response to nitroglycerin	Hypertension		T wave inversion
Nausea and vomiting			Significant ischomic change
Diaphoresis			
Syncope			
Shortness of breath			
Palpitations			

(a)

Network Prediction	Absence of infarction		Infarction	
	cases of 236	%	cases of 120	%
Correct	226	95.7	111	92.5
Incorrect	10	4.3	9	7.5

(b)

Figure 8.48 Connectionist expert system for coronary occlusion diagnosis: (a) input variables and (b) test data performance summary. [Adapted from Baxt (1990)]

disease always exceeded 0.8, and the output indicating its absence was below 0.2. The network correctly diagnosed 55 of 60 test patients with infarction and 113 of 118 test patients without infarction. Secondly, the training and test sets were swapped and the training and test sessions repeated. The newly obtained network correctly diagnosed 56 of 60 test patients with infarction and 113 of 118 test patients without infarction on the new test data.

Figure 8.48(b) summarizes the network performance achieved in this project. The analysis of results reveals that the connectionist expert system has a disease detection ratio above 92 percent among sick patients. However, among healthy patients the system provides false alarms of disease in 4.3 percent of the cases. In spite of the errors, these results outperform the best previously reported diagnostic schemes, including trained physicians, which yield results of 88 and 26 percent, respectively.

Although the results presented above are very encouraging, further study needs to be made. Specifically, to draw conclusive comparisons, the experiments with different diagnosing techniques would have to use the same set of clinical and diagnostic data. Further, the study involved only patients admitted from the emergency department to the coronary care unit, which could have had consequences in terms of disease development. Despite the preliminary scope of the study, if the reported results hold up to further scrutiny, the connectionist expert system for infarction diagnosis could have a substantial impact on the reduction of health care costs.

Concluding Remarks

The three medical diagnosis expert systems presented in this section are able to store the model patient knowledge base. Moreover, the connectionist methodology to store knowledge can substantially ease the task of building an expert system. It is no longer necessary for a knowledge engineer to have a thorough understanding of implicit rules, links, and relations within the domain. Moreover, the amount of time for system development is substantially reduced compared to the systems that use either a tree structure of rule-based relationships or statistical calculations.

Although the performance achieved by the example expert systems discussed is impressive, the systems built and tested should be considered to be preliminary and tentative (Jones 1991). Although they compare rather advantageously and sometimes are even clearly superior to human experts, more detailed and exhaustive study is needed. Such a study would allow better assessment of all capabilities and limitations of connectionist methodology for expert systems applications. Also, a more comprehensive and versatile approach to the retrieval of the decision explanations of such expert systems is needed. It is almost certain that these and other relevant questions shall be explored by knowledge scientists in the near future.

8.6 SELF-ORGANIZING SEMANTIC MAPS

The semantic maps discussed in this section are implemented based on the self-organizing feature map concept described in Sections 7.4 and 7.5. This application example demonstrates that, in addition to processing quantitative data for feature extraction, the maps make it possible to display abstract data, such as words, arranged in topological neighborhoods. The maps extract semantic relationships that exist within the set of language data considered here as a collection of words. The relationships can be reflected by their relative distances on the map containing words positioned according to their meaning or context. This indicates that the trained network can possibly detect the logical similarity between words from the statistics of the contexts in which they are used. The context is understood here as an element of a set of attribute values that occur in conjunction with the words. In another approach, the context can be determined by the frequency of neighboring words without regard to the attribute values that are occurring. The discussion below is based on experiments and results described by Ritter and Kohonen (1989) and Kohonen (1990).

The self-organizing feature network consists of a number of laterally inter-acting adaptive neurons, usually arranged as a two-dimensional array. Although each array neuron is connected to each input node, only neighborhood neurons re-spond, after training, to specific inputs. The planar position of the excitation spec-ifies a mapping of the input pattern onto the two-dimensional topographic map. The map represents the distance relations within the original high-dimensional input space of input patterns compressed to the two-dimensional image space represented by a neural array. This remarkable property follows from the as-sumption of lateral interactions within the array and from the assumed weight adaptation law (7.28).

Let us restate that the resulting maps are nonlinear projections of the input space onto the feature array. The projection preserves the distance relationships between the patterns in the original multidimensional pattern space. Such implicit distances become explicit planar distances in low-dimensional image space called here the feature space. However, a mapping from a high-dimensional space to a low-dimensional one preserves only the most important neighborhood relation-ships within the input pattern. The less relevant properties are ignored. Moreover, the inputs that appear more frequently are mapped to larger and stronger domains at the expense of less frequent inputs. Data that are close, or similar, in the input space and appear frequently at the input are mapped into a cluster of images forming localized images on the map. Furthermore, the clusters of images are also arranged into topological neighborhoods that display the overall relationships within the entire input data set.

Extraction of features from geometrically or physically related input pattern data is usually a concrete task, as demonstrated in example of Figure 7.19. This and other self-organizing feature map examples of Chapter 7 have made use of the numerical values of data in the input space. Much more abstract data need to be processed, for example, in the case of cognitive and linguistic relations that may exist in the input space. Such processing reflects relationships that neural networks could extract for linguistic representations and relations. Self-organizing maps that display semantic relations between abstract language data are called *semantic maps* (Ritter and Kohonen 1989).

The most general concepts or abstractions needed to interpret the empirical world are called *categories*. They form an elementary lexicon embracing the whole domain of knowledge. They are commonly used for thinking and com-munication. The most common categories are (1) items (objects), (2) qualities (properties), (3) states (or state changes), and (4) relations (spatial, temporal, or other). The categories are formed on the basis of consciousness, and their typical counterparts in most languages are (1) nouns, (2) adjectives, (3) verbs, and (4) adverbs, prepositions, etc., but also order of words (syntax). Each category usually includes many subcategories such as persons, animals, and inanimate objects that are usually found within each category of items.

Difficulty results when trying to express the human language as neural network input data as opposed to nonsymbolic input data encoding. These data can be represented as continuous or discrete values arranged into a vectorial variable. The difficulty is due to the fact that for symbolic objects, such as words, no adequate metric has been developed. In addition, except for a few special words denoting sounds, the meaning of a word is usually disassociated from its encoding into letters or sounds. Moreover, no metric relations exist whatsoever between the words representing similar objects. To overcome the difficulties mentioned, we will therefore try to present the coded value for each symbol word expressed in appropriate context containing values of attributes.

One simple model for contextual representation of a symbol and its attribute enabling the topographical mapping on the semantic map is to concatenate the data vector as follows:

$$\mathbf{x} = \begin{bmatrix} \mathbf{x}_s \\ \mathbf{x}_a \end{bmatrix} \tag{8.33}$$

where the symbol and the attribute part of the data vector are expressed as column vectors $\begin{bmatrix} \mathbf{x}_s & \mathbf{0} \end{bmatrix}^t$ and $\begin{bmatrix} \mathbf{0} & \mathbf{x}_a \end{bmatrix}^t$, respectively.

We assume here that the symbol and attribute vectors are orthogonal. To reflect the metric relationship of the attribute sets, the norm, or the vector length, of the attribute vector is chosen as dominant over the norm of the symbol vector during the self-organizing process. Since both symbol and attribute part are included in each training input, however, topological neighborhoods are created by symbols and their attributes. The symbols can become encoded into a planar array so as to reflect their logic similarities. We would expect that the recall of only the symbol part with the attribute part of the data vector missing would provide us with the calibrated topological map of symbols. Such a map would show implicit logical similarities that potentially exist within the set of symbols in the form of geometrically explicit distances between symbols.

Assuming the local representation of the symbols, such that the i'th symbol in the set of P symbols is assigned a P-dimensional symbol vector $\mathbf{x}_{si}$ whose i'th component is equal to a fixed value of c, and all remaining components are zero. We thus have the symbol vectors of value

$$\begin{aligned} \mathbf{x}_{s1} &= \begin{bmatrix} c & 0 & \dots & 0 \end{bmatrix}^t \\ \mathbf{x}_{s2} &= \begin{bmatrix} 0 & c & \dots & 0 \end{bmatrix}^t \\ \mathbf{x}_{sP} &= \begin{bmatrix} 0 & 0 & \dots & c \end{bmatrix}^t \end{aligned} \tag{8.34}$$

The attributes are present or absent for each of the P symbols. The attribute

		dove	hen	duck	goose	owl	hawk	eagle	fox	dog	wolf	cat	tiger	lion	horse	zebra	cow
	small	1	1	1	1	1	1	0	0	0	0	1	0	0	0	0	0
is	medium	0	0	0	0	0	0	1	1	1	1	0	0	0	0	0	0
	big	0	0	0	0	0	0	0	0	0	0	0	1	1	1	1	1
	2 legs	1	1	1	1	1	1	1	0	0	0	0	0	0	0	0	0
	4 legs	0	0	0	0	0	0	0	1	1	1	1	1	1	1	1	1
has	hair	0	0	0	0	0	0	0	1	1	1	1	1	1	1	1	1
	hooves	0	0	0	0	0	0	0	0	0	0	0	0	0	1	1	1
	mane	0	0	0	0	0	0	0	0	0	1	0	0	1	1	1	0
	feathers	1	1	1	1	1	1	1	0	0	0	0	0	0	0	0	0
	hunt	0	0	0	0	1	1	1	1	0	1	1	1	1	0	0	0
likes	run	0	0	0	0	0	0	0	0	1	1	0	1	1	1	1	0
to	fly	1	0	0	1	1	1	1	0	0	0	0	0	0	0	0	0
	swim	0	0	1	1	0	0	0	0	0	0	0	0	0	0	0	0

Figure 8.49 Table of attributes for the set of $P = 16$ animal objects. [©*Springer-Verlag; reprinted from Ritter and Kohonen (1989) with permission.*]

column vector $\mathbf{x}_a$ contains the number of entries equal to the number of relevant attributes allocated to the set of symbols under consideration. The presence, or absence, of a particular attribute is indicated by a binary entry 1 or 0, respectively. Note also that the unnormalized similarity measure of two symbols is the scalar product of their respective attribute vectors.

Figure 8.49 illustrates a specific example input data case used for simulation by Ritter and Kohonen (1989). For $P = 16$ elements in the set of symbols being animals, the attribute vectors are specified by the attribute column vectors of the table shown. An example data vector for a cow is given as

$$\mathbf{x} = \begin{bmatrix} \mathbf{x}_{s16} & 0 & 0 & 1 & 0 & 1 & 1 & 1 & 0 & \dots & 0 \end{bmatrix}^t \qquad (8.35)$$

where $\mathbf{x}_{s16} = \begin{bmatrix} 0 & \dots & c \end{bmatrix}^t$ and $\mathbf{x}$ consists of $n = 29$ entries.

Let us note that the norm of the difference vector between each pair of symbol vectors is identical and equal to $\sqrt{2}c$. The numerical value of c is the norm of each symbol vector and it determines the relative weight of the symbol vector as compared to its attribute counterpart vector within the 29-entry data field. Input data vectors shown in the figure and used for training have been normalized to the unity length. To draw a comparison, this may correspond to the biological intensity normalization of the incoming stimuli.

Sixteen data vectors containing a symbol (object) part concatenated with its attribute part as displayed in Figure 8.49 have been used to produce a semantic map of the set of animals. The data vectors have been used to train a 10 × 10 planar array of neurons. The initial weights have been selected of random values so that no initial ordering was imposed. After about 2000 training input presentations, the neighborhood sensitivity has been ascertained. The neurons' responses became consistently stronger or weaker in certain regions. This has been learned due to either of the excitations $\mathbf{x} = \begin{bmatrix} \mathbf{x}_{si} & 0 \end{bmatrix}^t$, or $\mathbf{x} = \begin{bmatrix} 0 & \mathbf{x}_{ai} \end{bmatrix}^t$. The neurons with the strongest response due to the symbol vector excitation only (attribute part missing) are shown in Figure 8.50(a). They are labeled using the symbol that elicits the particular response. The neurons represented by dots indicate their nondominant responses on the map of symbols.

The spatial order of the responses has emerged on the semantic map as a result of the training. The order divides the symbols into three distinct groups of birds (left), hunters (right), and grass-eating animals (top). Within each group, certain similarities are also recognizable. "Dog" is located predominantly between "fox" and "wolf." It is somewhat less related to "cat" and "lion" and even less similar to hunting birds, however, it does not seem to be related at all to nonhunting birds such as a "duck" or "goose." This is also visible from Figure 8.50(b) showing the strongest response domains. Each neuron of this map is marked with the stimulus eliciting its strongest response.

The semantic maps of objects displaying logical distances between the animal symbols have been produced in this experiment using the static context of the relevant attribute vector. In language use, however, objects and their attributes often occur in temporal sequences. For a more comprehensive evaluation of the potential of self-organizing semantic maps, the concept of context needs to be broadened and to include the time domain. In the discussion to follow, the time variable present in semantic data will be represented as an order of word occurrence in their serial sequence.

Let us look at a mapping of a set of 30 test words listed as shown in Figure 8.51(a). The test set consists of nouns, verbs, and adverbs. The set is subdivided into 14 pairs or triples of related words. Let us attempt to build sensible sentence patterns on this set. Three-word sentences created from this semantic map-building lexicon and allowed in this experiment have to obey some rudimentary rules of grammar and semantic correctness.

Thirty-nine basic sentence patterns as shown in Figure 8.51(b) have been produced based on such rules. Test sentences are then created by plugging each member of the pair, or the triple, into the sentence patterns. In this mode, the basic sentence pattern 1–5–12, or "Bob runs fast" generates test sentences "Jim runs fast," "Mary runs fast," but also "Bob walks fast," etc. This way the total of 498 grammatically and semantically correct test sentences as in Figure 8.51(c) have been produced. The temporal context of a word in the experiment is made by the immediate predecessor and successor word. To build pairs for the first and the last word in the sentence, the randomly generated sentences were concatenated in the order in which they were produced.

Each word from the 30-word dictionary involved in the experiment can be defined by a vector with 30 entries with only one of them having a nonzero value. This would lead, however, to a rather sparse description of the input data.

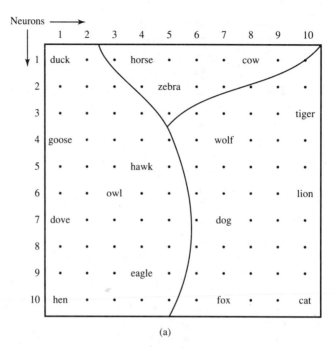

Figure 8.50 Semantic self-organizing symbol map obtained through training using attributes: (a) strongest responses due to the symbol part only excitation and (b) strongest response domains. [©*Springer-Verlag;* reprinted from Ritter and Kohonen (1989) with permission.]

Bob/Jim/Mary	1
horse/dog/cat	2
beer/water	3
meat/bread	4
runs/walks	5
works/speaks	6
visits/phones	7
buys/sells	8
likes/hates	9
drinks/eats	10
much/little	11
fast/slowly	12
often/seldom	13
well/poorly	14

(a)

Sentence patterns:

1–5–12	1–9–2	2–5–14
1–5–13	1–9–3	2–9–1
1–5–14	1–9–4	2–9–2
1–6–12	1–10–3	2–9–3
1–6–13	1–11–4	2–9–4
1–6–14	1–10–12	2–10–3
1–6–15	1–10–13	2–10–12
1–7–14	1–10–14	2–10–13
1–8–12	1–11–12	2–10–14
1–8–2	1–11–13	1–11–4
1–8–3	1–11–14	1–11–12
1–8–4	2–5–12	2–11–13
1–9–1	2–5–13	2–11–14

(b)

Mary likes meat
Jim speaks well
Mary likes Jim
Jim eats often
Mary buys meat
dog drinks fast
horse hates meat
Jim eats seldom
Bob buys meat
cat walks slowly
Jim eats bread
cat hates Jim
Bob sells beer
(etc.)

(c)

Figure 8.51 Words and sentences used for context production: (a) nouns, verbs, and adverbs, (b) sentence patterns, and (c) selected examples of sentences. [©*Springer-Verlag;* reprinted from Ritter and Kohonen (1989) with permission.]

For more economical encoding, a 7-tuple vector of unit length has been used (Ritter and Kohonen 1989). Such 7-tuple vectors have been generated at random for each word in the experiment, thus ensuring quasi-orthogonality of different word vectors. It follows then that the word in the context can be expressed using a single vector of 21 entries, where 14 entries represent the predecessor and successor context words. To perform training more efficiently, the average context of each word under consideration has been used instead of step-by-step learning with each sentence applied separately. Ten thousand sentences having all vectors have been used for averaging. The average word contexts were represented as 14 entries with word vectors scaled to unit length. They have been given a role similar to the attribute vector $\mathbf{x}_a$ described in the preceding simulation.

Each of the 7-tuple symbol-word vectors was scaled to the length $c = 0.2$ and combined with the 14-tuple average context vector. As a result, 21 scalar input data have been supplied as inputs to the array. A planar array of 10×15 neurons with 21 input nodes and weights randomly initialized prior to the training has been used for this semantic map design. Each of the 21 inputs has been connected to each of 150 neurons. After 2000 training presentations, the responses to symbol words alone have been tested. As can be seen from Figure 8.52(a), the training contexts have positioned the words in such an order that their mutual arrangements reflect existing semantic and grammatical relationships. A separate grouping for nouns, verbs, and adverbs has resulted, as marked by the partitioning curves. Each of the three domains clustering parts of speech has discernible subregions. For instance, names of persons or adverbs of opposite meaning tend to cluster together.

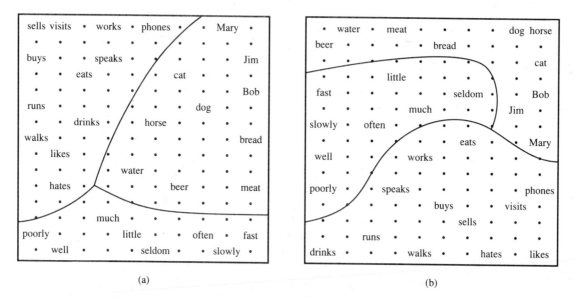

(a)   (b)

Figure 8.52 Semantic maps of words obtained by using their mutual context for training: (a) preceding-succeeding word context and (b) preceding word context. [©Springer-Verlag; reprinted from Ritter and Kohonen (1989) with permission.]

In a related semantic map generation experiment, the word context was limited to the immediately preceding word only. Even with that limited context, a map showing similar distance relationships has resulted as shown in Figure 8.52(b). It can be seen that even with the restricted context, a meaningful semantic map can be produced.

These feature extraction experiments have shown the extension of self-organizing neural arrays to processing of expressions that are of symbolic nature and display rather subtle and even evasive relationships. The simulations of semantic structures have resulted in semantic neighborhood maps that encode words into relative planar regions of localized responses. As seen, generated semantic maps allow the segregation and grouping of symbolic data based on an unsupervised learning approach. The topographic organization of concepts as discussed above may be offering us some clues as to why the information processing in the brain is spatially organized and distributed.

8.7 CONCLUDING REMARKS

The presentation focus of this chapter has been on neurocomputing engineering projects. Our concern has been analyzing and designing sample information processing systems that are nonprogrammable. We followed a fundamentally new and different information processing paradigm that is based on developing associations, mapping, or transformations between data in response to the environment. To achieve these objectives, we essentially pursued nonalgorithmic paths for solving specific engineering problems.

Well above a dozen representative engineering application problems have been explored in this chapter. Application examples have been selected so that they reinforce and illustrate basic theoretical concepts discussed in preceding chapters. Projects that seem exciting but are not easily traceable and reproducible have been excluded from coverage. Networks for constrained optimization, for printed and handwritten character recognition, for controlling static and dynamical plants and actuating robot arms, connectionist expert systems for medical diagnosis, and finally networks for processing semantic information have been studied. It is believed that the depth and diversity of the coverage in this chapter has prepared the reader at least for pursuing new application-specific projects, if not for independent research.

Due to the abundance and diversity of technical publications on artificial neural systems applications, many other interesting problem solutions could not be addressed in this book. A number of edited volumes on artificial neural systems (Denker 1986; Anderson and Rosenfeld 1988; Anderson 1988; Touretzky 1989, 1990; Omidvar 1992) and special issues of technical journals (*IEEE Computer,* March 1988; *IEEE Transactions on Circuits and Systems,* June 1990; *Proceedings of the IEEE,* September 1990 and October 1990) include discussion of different applications. In addition, the reader may refer to specific applications from the following partial list of projects:

- Trainable networks for solving matrix algebra problems (Wang and Mendel 1990)
- Reinforcement and temporal-difference learning controller for an inverted pendulum problem (Anderson 1989)
- Truck "backer-upper" neurocontroller and control of complex dynamical plant (Nguyen and Widrow 1990)
- Trajectory generation based on visual perception of mobile robots (Kawato et al. 1988)
- Sensor-based control of robots with vision (Miller 1989; Hashimoto et al. 1990)
- Networks for robot control (Liu, Iberall, and Bekey 1989; Wilhelmsen and Cotter 1990)
- Autonomous land vehicle neurocontroller/driver (Pomerleau 1989)
- Neural system NETTALK for continuous speech recognition (Sejnowski and Rosenberg 1987)
- General review of neural network performance for speech analysis (Lippman 1989)
- Temporal signals recognition networks (Gorman and Sejnowski 1988; Eberhart and Dobbins 1990)

- ■ Inspection of machined surfaces (Villalobos and Gruber 1990)
- ■ Connectionist expert system for bond rating (Dutta and Sekhar 1988).

Typical applications of neurocomputing indicate the ability of neural networks to handle multiple input and output variables, nonlinear relationships, past states, and implement fast network learning when suitable architectures are used. It is important to realize that these are not special, magical, or standalone techniques and applications. Rather, they can be looked at as outgrowth of long periods of research in function approximation, optimization, signal processing, pattern classification and decision theory, and stochastic approximation (Anderson 1989; Poggio and Girosi 1990; Tsypkin 1973). What makes neural network approaches different from conventional engineering is the methodology, specifically, the experimental methodology of learning and problem formulation that underlies neural network methods.

It seems somewhat easy to perceive the free-wheeling nature of many approaches we have taken during our discussion and the absence of theoretical guarantees, derivations, and proofs. Such approaches have often been present in earlier theoretical presentations and perhaps even more in the practical applications of artificial neural systems addressed in this chapter. However, we have made no restrictive assumptions or simplifications such as linearization, convergence, and stability. Interestingly, they have not been needed to accomplish a number of successful artificial neural system designs (Barto 1990).

As time passes, new neurocomputing engineering methods and applications will undoubtedly emerge. Despite spectacular successes, one should not be misled, however, about the still existing limitations of neural network technology. Currently neural networks can already be of great value in helping to solve real problems without exactly mimicking many functions performed by biological neural networks. Animals and humans can attain complex combinations of information processing, pattern recognition and feedback, and feedforward transmissions and of cognitive acts. While these very complex facets of neurocomputing may be considered as eventual aspirations for artificial neural systems, they should not be used as criterion for their present value.

PROBLEMS

Please note that problems highlighted with an asterisk (*) are typically computationally intensive and the use of programs is advisable to solve them.

$P8.1$ The cost function for a linear programming problem is $c = v_1 + 2v_2$. The constraints are known as

$$v_1 - v_2 \leq 2$$
$$2v_1 + 3v_2 \leq 12$$
$$v_1 \geq 0$$
$$v_2 \geq 0 .$$

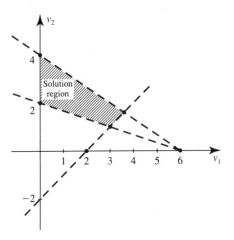

Figure P8.2 Linear programming problem of Problem P8.2.

(a) Find the solution of the problem by analyzing the conditions on the solution plane.

(b) Find the weights and currents of the gradient-type neural network similar to that shown in Figure 8.1 that would solve this task.

P8.2 For the linear programming problem with the cost function $c = 2v_1 + v_2$ and the constraints as shown in Figure P8.2, find

(a) the solution of the linear programming problem.

(b) the weights and currents of the gradient-type neural network similar to that shown in Figure 8.1 that would solve this task.

P8.3* The static plant shown in Figure P8.3 needs to convert Cartesian coordinates x, y, z, into cylindrical coordinates ρ, ϕ, z. The relations between input and output variables are also shown in the figure. Design a multilayer feedforward network that performs the forward identification and models the plant in the forward mode as shown in Figure 8.17(a). The training test points should be selected for the plant outputs in the range $0 < \rho < 1$, $0 < \phi < \pi/2$, and $0 < z < 1$. Select suitable architecture for the multilayer feedforward network and train the network.

P8.4* Repeat Problem P8.3 for the plant inverse identification by modeling the plant, which converts the Cartesian x, y, z coordinates into cylindrical coordinates ρ, ϕ, z in the same working region. [*Hint:* Use Figure 8.17(b) and model the inverse of the plant by training a multilayer feedforward network of suitable architecture. Study the mapping accuracy produced by the network by computing the differences between the network response and the accurate response value.]

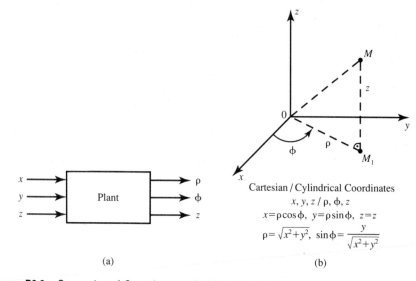

Cartesian / Cylindrical Coordinates

$x, y, z / \rho, \phi, z$

$x = \rho\cos\phi, \quad y = \rho\sin\phi, \quad z = z$

$\rho = \sqrt{x^2 + y^2}, \quad \sin\phi = \dfrac{y}{\sqrt{x^2 + y^2}}$

(a)   (b)

Figure P8.3 Conversion of Cartesian to cylindrical coordinates: (a) plant and (b) notation and relationships.

P8.5* The static plant shown in Figure P8.5 converts Cartesian coordinates x, y, z, into spherical coordinates r, ϕ, θ. The relations between the input and output variables are also shown in the figure. Design a multilayer feedforward network that performs the forward plant identification and models it in the forward mode as shown in Figure 8.17(a). The plant outputs, or training test points, should be selected in the range: $0 < r < 1$, $0 < \phi < \pi/2$, and $0 < \theta < \pi/2$.

P8.6* Repeat Problem P8.5 for plant inverse identification for the plant converting the Cartesian x, y, z coordinates into spherical ones, r, ϕ, θ, in the same working region. [*Hint:* Use Figure 8.17(b) and model the inverse of the plant by training a multilayer feedforward network of suitable architecture.]

P8.7 Network A needs to be trained to perform as plant inverse with its copy serving as neurocontroller B. The learning control system is shown in Figure P8.7(a). The expressions describing the plant are, in general, not known for this control arrangement. In this problem, however, it is assumed that the plant is known to be a Cartesian-to-cylindrical coordinates converter as illustrated in Figure P8.3. For the input **d** specified in Figure P8.7(b), the measurements of **x** and **o** have been obtained as indicated on the figure. Compute

(a) plant output vector **y**

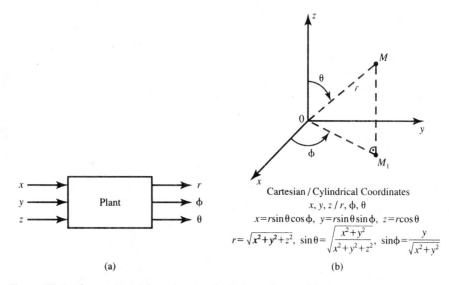

Figure P8.5 Conversion of Cartesian to spherical coordinates: (a) plant and (b) notation and relationships.

(b) control error $\|\mathbf{d} - \mathbf{y}\|$ at the plant output

(c) error $\|\mathbf{x} - \mathbf{o}\|$ which is used for training of network *A*.

Now assume that following the training, both networks *A* and *B* are ideally in tune with the plant inverse. Compute $\mathbf{x}$, $\mathbf{y}$, and $\|\mathbf{x}-\mathbf{o}\|$ for this condition if the neurocontroller input has changed to

$$\mathbf{d} = \begin{bmatrix} 0.275 \\ 0.725 \\ 0.300 \end{bmatrix}$$

P8.8 The plant shown in Figure P8.8 is controlled in a specialized on-line learning control architecture. In general, the plant equations $y_i = y_i(o_1, o_2)$, $i = 1, 2$, are not known; however, for the purpose of this exercise it is assumed that

$$y_1 = \frac{1}{2}o_1^2 + \sin o_2$$
$$y_2 = o_1 + o_1\sqrt{o_2}$$

(a) Compute the Jacobian matrix from the analytical description of the plant.

(b) Knowing that the operating point of the plant is $o_1{}^* = 0.472$ and $o_2{}^* = 0.125$, compute the four entries of the Jacobian matrix $\mathbf{J}$ at

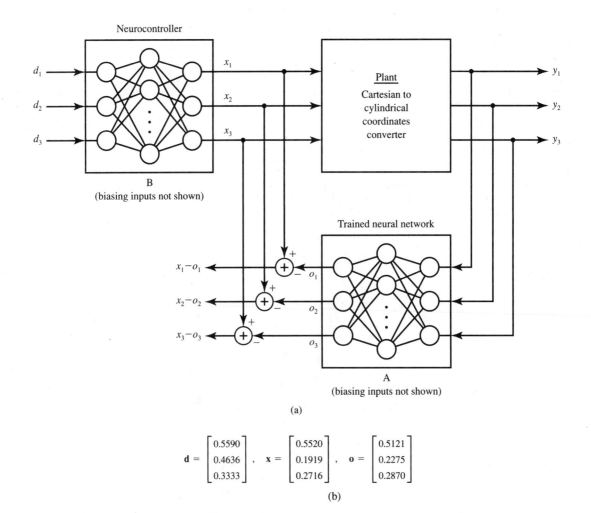

Figure P8.7 Feedforward control with plant inverse learning: (a) block diagram and (b) results of measurements before completion of training.

this point $\mathbf{o}^*$:

$$\mathbf{J}(\mathbf{o}^*) = \begin{bmatrix} \dfrac{\partial y_1}{\partial o_1} & \dfrac{\partial y_1}{\partial o_2} \\[2ex] \dfrac{\partial y_2}{\partial o_1} & \dfrac{\partial y_2}{\partial o_2} \end{bmatrix}.$$

P8.9 The plant of Problem P8.8 is working in the same learning control architecture as shown in Figure P8.8. Compute numerically the approximations

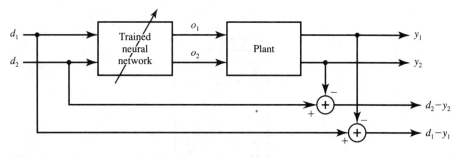

Figure P8.8 Specialized on-line learning control architecture.

for the Jacobian matrix entries at the quiescent operating point o* given as

$$\mathbf{o}^* = \begin{bmatrix} o_1{}^* \\ o_2{}^* \end{bmatrix} = \begin{bmatrix} 0.472 \\ 0.125 \end{bmatrix}$$

using the perturbation method. The disturbed values are to be assumed as deviated by +5 percent from the operating point, thus making the plant signal equal to 1.05 o*.

P8.10 The plant described with the following nonlinear equations

$$y_1 = o_1 o_2 + \frac{1}{\sqrt{o_2}}$$

$$y_2 = \sqrt{o_1} + o_1 \sin o_2$$

is used in the control arrangement shown in Figure P8.8. Its operating point is

$$\mathbf{o}^* = \begin{bmatrix} 0.721 \\ 0.293 \end{bmatrix}$$

and the desired response for this input is known to be

$$\mathbf{d} = \begin{bmatrix} 1.725 \\ 1.293 \end{bmatrix}$$

Compute numerically

(a) the plant output y*

(b) the output error $E = (1/2)\|\mathbf{d} - \mathbf{y}^*\|$

(c) the relative error values transferred to the plant input, i.e., $-\partial E/\partial o_1$ and $-\partial E/\partial o_2$, at this operating point.

P8.11 You need to use common-sense judgment and provide advice to balance the cart-pole system shown in Figures 8.24 and 8.25. Three sample pairs of quantized images are displayed in Figure P8.11. By analyzing each sequence of two images, determine what sign of the horizontal force needs

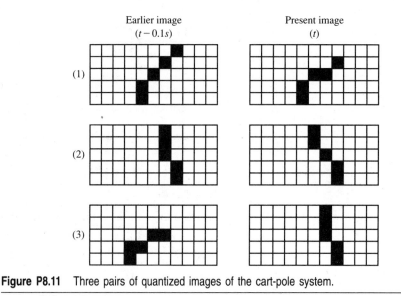

Figure P8.11 Three pairs of quantized images of the cart-pole system.

to be applied at present to improve the system's balance. Each of the three cases shown in rows (1), (2), and (3) of the figure should be treated separately. (Note: The force toward the right is positive; the force toward the left is negative.)

(a) Use your own judgment; assume that you are the teacher and you are trying to train the controller.

(b) Use the weights of the trained controller to obtain a crude approximation of the discrete perceptron activation value. Inspect Figure 8.25(b) for this purpose and draw conclusions as to the sign of the force needed for balancing.

P8.12 The discrete-time plant is described with the following difference equation:

$$x(k) = 2y(k + 1) - y(k) - 0.5$$

where $x(k)$ and $y(k)$ denote input and output, respectively, at time instant numbered k. The desired output wave of the plant is specified as

$$y(k) = \sin\left(\frac{k\pi}{6}\right) + 1$$

Assuming that a characteristic surface $x(k) = x\left[y(k), y(k + 1)\right]$ needs to be learned by the CMAC neurocontroller, identify the initial sequence of plant control signal values $x(0), x(1), \ldots, x(12)$, that would be located on the characteristic surface.

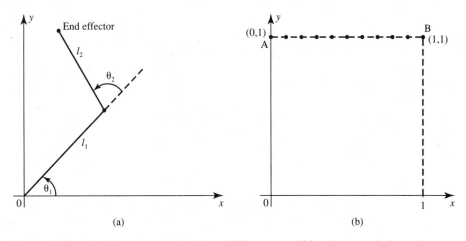

Figure P8.13 Two-link planar manipulators: (a) diagram and (b) trajectory to be learned.

P8.13 A multilayer feedforward network needs to be designed that solves the inverse kinematics problem as shown in Figure 8.33(b). The network's eventual use will be in the control arrangement from Figure 8.35(b).

The network should model the two-link planar manipulator as in Figure P8.13(a), with its end effector on a desired trajectory being a straight segment *AB* as shown in Figure P8.13(b).

(a) Draw the network architecture that would be expected to solve this problem.

(b) Prepare a training set of 11 pairs of input/output data. Note that the desired output data are θ_1, θ_2, in response to the end effector Cartesian coordinates x, y provided as inputs at each point. Assume $l_1 = l_2 = 1$ for this manipulator.

P8.14 Repeat Problem P8.13 for the elliptic end effector trajectory having the equation

$$\left(\frac{x}{2}\right)^2 + y^2 = 1$$

Select ten training points on the trajectory in the first quadrant. The points should be $\pi/18$ apart as indicated in Figure P8.14. Prepare complete training data for $l_1 = l_2 = 1$.

P8.15 A multilayer feedforward network needs to be trained to solve the forward kinematics problem. The desired trajectory of a two-link planar manipulator, in joint space, is given as

$$\theta_1(t) = \frac{\pi}{40}t$$

$$\theta_2(t) = \frac{\pi}{20}\left(1 - \frac{t}{20}\right)$$

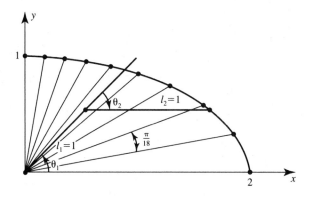

Figure P8.14 Trajectory to be learned by the two-link planar manipulator.

    (a) Produce 21 training pairs for trajectory points taken at $t = 0, 1, 2,$
    $\ldots, 20$; assume $l_1 = 2$ and $l_2 = 3$.

    (b) Devise a network architecture that would be expected to train properly
    for this problem.

P8.16* The multilayer feedforward network shown in Figure P8.16(a) needs to
be designed to solve the forward kinematics problem. The network working area is the circular trajectory with $r = 3$ shown in Figure 8.36(a).
Implement the training of the network using the training data from Figure
P8.16(b) [normalization of data may be needed to fit within the $(-1, 1)$
range].

P8.17* Repeat Problem P8.16 using a multilayer feedforward network of the architecture 2–4–4–2 as shown in Figure P8.17 to model the solution of the
inverse kinematics problem. Use the training data set of Figure P8.16(b).

P8.18 In this problem you are asked to design a simple "mini expert system"
called *free time advisor* (FTA) that would suit your personal needs. The
FTA is supposed to advise you which of the free time activities to choose
from given the circumstances preceding your decision making. The five
choices for the activities are

    (a) Socializing (date or visiting with friends, etc.)

    (b) Physical exercise (tennis, jogging, swimming, etc.)

    (c) Shopping or repairing things (taking care of necessities)

    (d) Cultural activities (seeing a good movie or reading a book, etc.)

    (e) Doing nothing (no suggestions needed here).

Factors determining your final choice of activity are virtually countless.
Limiting their number to a dozen or so (but no more than two dozen)
allows us to keep the expert system development work traceable. Prepare

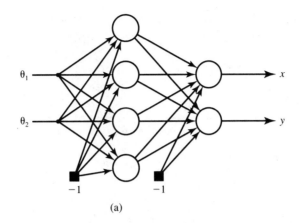

(a)

Point	Angle (deg)	End Eff. (Cartesian)		Joint Angles (rad)	
		x	y	θ_1	θ_2
1	5	2.9886	0.2615	0.7669	−1.9106
2	15	2.8978	0.7765	0.9414	−1.9106
3	25	2.7189	1.2679	1.1160	−1.9106
4	35	2.4575	1.7207	1.2905	−1.9106
5	65	2.1213	2.1213	1.4608	−1.9106
6	55	1.7207	2.4575	1.6396	−1.9106
7	65	1.2679	2.7189	1.8141	−1.9106
8	75	0.7765	2.8978	1.9886	−1.9106
9	85	0.2615	2.9886	2.1632	−1.9106
10	90	0	3.0000	2.2504	−1.9106

(b)

Figure P8.16 Figure for forward kinematics Problem P8.16: (a) network architecture and (b) training data.

your list of factors. These factors typically can be

(1) Money available

(2) Weather predicted

(3) Amount of time available

(4) A good book at hand

(5) Recent history of free time activities

(6) Empty refrigerator and pantry

(7) Car makes unusual noises and needs repair

(8) More sleep or rest needed.

For final lists of activities and factors that influence your decision, propose a set of test data consisting of the total of 10 to 20 pairs of input / output

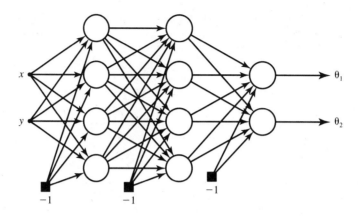

Figure P8.17 Network for inverse kinematics Problem P8.17.

vectors, with at least 2 pairs for each specific activity from the list. Code inputs as mixed variables (continuous and binary) as you see appropriate in the range $[-1, 1]$ and assign 0 to those inputs that do not matter.

P8.19* Develop a multilayer feedforward character classifier for five printed digits shown as 5×5 black-white pixel maps on Figure P8.19.

(a) Devise a suitable network architecture for a local representation classifier.

(b) Prepare the set of five input/output binary training vector pairs.

(c) Train the network for zero decision errors.

(d) Perform the recall of nondistorted digits by reusing the training input data.

(e) Perform the evaluation of the classifier by recalling digits distorted by the center pixel (pixel 13) of the 5×5 field being white rather than black.

(f) Evaluate the classifier by recalling digits distorted by reversal of input pixels 12, 13, and 14.

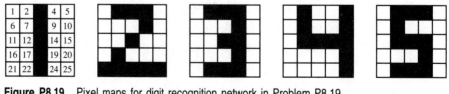

Figure P8.19 Pixel maps for digit recognition network in Problem P8.19.

REFERENCES

Anderson, C. W. 1989. "Learning to Control an Inverted Pendulum Using Neural Networks," *IEEE Control Systems Magazine,* (April): 31–37.

Anderson, D. Ed. 1988. *Neural Information Processing Systems.* New York: American Institute of Physics.

Anderson, J. A., and E. Rosenfield. Eds. 1988. *Neurocomputing: Foundations of Research.* Cambridge, Mass.: The MIT Press.

Apple Computer. 1986. *Imagewriter User's Manual, Part 1: Reference.* Cupertino, Calif.: Apple Computer.

Arteaga-Bravo, F. J. 1990. "Multi-Layer Back-Propagation Network for Learning the Forward and Inverse Kinematics Equations," in *Proc. Joint 1990 IEEE Int. Neural Network Conf.,* pp. II-319–321.

Barto, A. G., R. S. Sutton, C. W. Anderson. 1983 "Neuronlike Adaptive Elements That Can Solve Difficult Learning Control Problems," *IEEE Trans. Systems, Man, and Cybernetics* SMC-13(5): pp. 835–846.

Barto, A. G. 1990 "Connectionist Learning for Control: An Overview," in *Neural Networks for Control,* Eds. W. T. Miller, III, R. S. Sutton, P. J. Werbos. Cambridge, Mass.: The MIT Press.

Baxt, W. G. 1990. "Use of an Artificial Neural Network for Data Analysis in Clinical Decision-Making: The Diagnosis of Coronary Occlusion," *Neural Computation,* 2: 480–489.

Bounds, D. G., P. J. Lloyd, B. Mathew, and G. Wadell. 1988. "A Multilayer Perceptron Network for the Diagnosis of Low Back Pain," in *Proc. IEEE Int. Conf. on Neural Networks,* San Diego, California. pp. II-481–489.

Chandra, V., and R. Sudhakar. 1988. "Recent Developments in Artificial Neural Network Based Character Recognition: A Performance Study," *Proc. IEEE Southeastcon,* Knoxville, Tennessee. pp. 633-637.

Craig, J. J. 1986. *Introduction to Robotics Mechanics and Control.* Reading, Mass.: Addison Wesley Publishing Co.

Dayhoff, R. E. and J. E. Dayhoff. 1988. "Neural Networks for Medical Image Processing" in *Proc. IEEE Symp. on Computer Applications in Medical Care,* Washington, D.C. pp. 271–275.

Denker, J. S. Ed. 1986. *Neural Networks for Computing.* AIP Conference Proceedings. New York: American Institute of Physics.

Dutta, S., and S. Shekhar. 1988 "Bond Rating: A Non-conservative Application of Neural Networks," in *Proc. IEEE Int. Conf. on Neural Networks,* San Diego, California.

Eberhart, R. C. and R. W. Dobbins. 1990. *Neural Network PC Tools, A Practical Guide*. San Diego, Calif.: Academic Press.

Feldman, R. S. 1987 *Understanding Psychology*. New York: McGraw-Hill Book Co.

Fu, K. S. 1986. "Learning Control Systems—Review and Outlook," *IEEE Trans. Pattern Analysis and Machine Intelligence* 8(3): 327–342.

Gallant, S. I. 1988. "Connectionist Expert Systems," *Comm. ACM* 31(2): 152–169.

Gorman, R., and T. Sejnowski. 1988. "Learned Classification of Sonar Targets Using a Massively Parallel Network," *IEEE Trans. Acoustics, Speech, and Signal Proc.* 36: 1135–1140.

Graf, H. P., L. D. Jackel, and W. E. Hubbard. 1988. "VLSI Implementation of a Neural Network Model," *IEEE Computer* (March): 41–49.

Guez, A., J. L. Eilbert, and M. Kam. 1988. "Neural Network Architecture for Control," *IEEE Control Systems Magazine* (April): 22–25.

Hashimoto, H., T. Kubota, M. Kudon, and F. Harashima. 1990. "Visual Control of a Robotic Manipulator Using Neural Networks," in *Proc. 29th Conf. on Decision and Control,* Honolulu, Hawaii. pp. 3295–3302.

Hecht-Nielsen, R. 1990. *Neurocomputing*. Reading, Mass.: Addison-Wesley Publishing Co.

Hertz, J., A. Krogh, and R. G. Palmer. 1991 *Introduction to the Theory of Neural Computation*. Redwood City, Calif.: Addison-Wesley Publishing Co.

Howard, R. E., B. Boser, J. S. Denker, H. P. Graf, D. Henderson, W. Hubbard, L. D. Jackel, Y. LeCun, and H. S. Baird. 1990 "Optical Character Recognition: A Technology Driver for Neural Networks," *Proc. IEEE Int. Joint Neural Network Conf.* pp. 2433–2436.

Jackel, L. D., H. P. Graf, W. Hubbard, J. S. Denker, and D. Henderson. 1988. "An Application of Neural Net Chips: Handwritten Digit Recognition," in *Proc. IEEE Int. Conf. on Neural Networks,* San Diego, California. pp. II-107–115.

Jones, D. 1991. "Neural Networks for Medical Diagnosis," in *Handbook of Neural Computing Applications*. New York: Academic Press.

Josin, G., D. Charney, and D. White. 1988. "Robot Control Using Neural Networks," *Proc. IEEE Int. Conf. on Neural Networks*, San Diego, California. pp. II-615–631.

Kawato, M., Y. Uno, M. Isobe, and R. Suzuki. 1988. "Hierarchical Neural Network Model for Voluntary Movement with Applications to Robotics, *IEEE Control Systems Magazine* (April): 8–16.

Kohonen, T. 1990. "The Self-Organizing Map," *Proc. of the IEEE* 78(9): 1464–1480.

Kraft, L. G., and D. S. Campagna. 1990a. "A Comparison Between CMAC Neural Network Control and Two Traditional Adaptive Control Systems," *IEEE Control Systems Magazine* (April): 36–43.

Kraft, L. G., and D. S. Campagna. 1990b. "A Summary Comparison of CMAC Neural Network and Traditional Adaptive Control Systems," in *Neural Networks for Control*, ed. T. W. Miller III, R. S. Sutton, and P. J. Werbos. Cambridge, Mass.: The MIT Press.

LeCun, Y., B. Boser, J. S. Denker, D. Henderson, R. E. Howard, W. Hubbard, and L. D. Jackel. 1989. "Backpropagation Applied to Handwritten Zip Code Recognition," *Neural Computation* 1: 541–551.

Liu, H., T. Iberall, and G. A. Bekey. 1989. "Neural Network Architecture for Robot Hand Control," *IEEE Control Systems Magazine* (April): 38–43.

Lippman, R. P. 1989. "Review of Neural Networks for Speech Recognition," *Neural Computation* 1(1): 1–38.

Miller, W. T., III. 1989. "Real-Time Application of Neural Networks for Sensor-Based Control of Robots with Vision," *IEEE Trans. Systems, Man, and Cybernetics* 19(4): 825–831.

Mishkin, E., and L. Braun. Eds. 1961. *Adaptive Control Systems*. New York: McGraw-Hill Book Co.

Narendra, K. S., and K. Parthasarthy. 1990. "Identification and Control of Dynamical Systems using Neural Networks," *IEEE Trans. Neural Networks* 1(1): 4–21.

Narendra, K. S., and K. Parthasarathy. 1991. "Gradient Methods for the Optimization of Dynamical Systems Containing Neural Networks," *IEEE Trans. Neural Networks* 2(2): 252–262.

Nguyen, D. H., and B. Widrow. 1990. "Neural Networks for Self-learning Control Systems," *IEEE Control Systems Magazine* (April): 18–23.

Nguyen, L., R. V. Patel, and K. Khorasani. 1990. "Neural Network Architectures for the Forward Kinematics Problem in Robotics," in *Proc. Joint IEEE Int. Neural Networks Conf.*, San Diego, California. III-393–399.

Norris, D. E. 1986. "Machine Learning Using Fuzzy Logic with Applications in Medicine," Ph.D. diss., University of Bristol, United Kingdom.

Omidvar, O. M. Ed. 1992. *Progress in Neural Networks*. Norwood, N.J.: Ablex Publishing Co.

Poggio, T., and F. Girosi. 1990. "Networks for Approximation and Learning," *Proc. IEEE* 78(9): 1481–1497.

Pomerleau, D. A. 1989. "ALVINN: An Autonomous Land Vehicle in a Neural Network," in *Advances in Neural Information Processing Systems,* vol. 1, D. Touretzky. San Mateo, Calif.: Morgan Kaufmann Publishers.

Psaltis, D., A. Sideris, and A. Yamamura. 1987. "Neural Controllers," in *Proc. IEEE Int. Neural Networks Conf.,* San Diego, California. pp. IV-551–558.

Psaltis, D., A. Sideris, and A. Yamamura. 1988. "A Multi-layer Neural Network Controller," *IEEE Control Systems Magazine* (April): 17–21.

Ritter, H., and T. Kohonen. 1989. "Self-Organizing Semantic Maps," *Biolog. Cybern.* 61: 241–254.

Saerens, M., and A. Soquet. 1991. "Neural Controller Based on Back-Propagation Algorithm," *IEE Proc., Part F* 138(1): 55–62.

Sejnowski, T., and C. Rosenberg. 1987. "Parallel Networks that Learn to Pronounce English Text," *Complex Systems* 1: 145–168.

Simmons, D. M. 1972. *Linear Programming for Operations Research.* San Fransisco: Holden-Day.

Sobajic, D. J., J. J. Lu, and Y. H. Pao. 1988. "Intelligent Control for the Intelledex 605 T Robot Manipulator," in *Proc. 1988 IEEE Int. Neural Networks Conf.,* San Diego, California. pp. II-633–640.

Tank, D. W., and J. J. Hopfield. 1986. "Simple 'Neural' Optimization Networks: An A/D Converter, Signal Decision Circuit and a Linear Programming Circuit," *IEEE Trans. Circ. Syst.* CAS-33(5), 533–541.

Tolat, V. V., and B. Widrow. 1988. "An Adaptive 'Broom Balancer' with Visual Inputs," in *Proc. 1988 IEEE Int. Neural Networks Conf.,* San Diego, California. pp. II-641–647.

Touretzky, D. Ed. 1989. *Advances in Neural Information Processing Systems,* vol. 1. San Mateo, Calif.: Morgan-Kaufmann Publishers.

Touretzky, D. Ed. 1990 *Advances in Neural Information Processing Systems,* vol. 2. San Mateo, Calif.: Morgan-Kaufmann Publishers.

Tsypkin, Ya. Z. 1973. *Foundations of the Theory of Learning Systems.* New York: Academic Press.

Villalobos, L., and S. Gruber. 1990. "Interpolation Characteristics and Noise Sensitivity of Neural Network Based Inspection of Machined Surfaces," in *Proc. 1990 IEEE Int. Conf. on Robotics and Automation.*

Wang, L., and J. M. Mendel. 1990. "Structured Trainable Networks for Matrix Algebra," in *Proc. IEEE 1990 Joint Conf. on Neural Networks,* San Diego, California. pp. 125–132.

Widrow, B., and R. Winter. "Neural Nets for Adaptive Filtering and Adaptive Pattern Recognition," *IEEE Computer* (March): 25–39.

Widrow, B., and M. A. Lehr. 1990. "30 Years of Adaptive Neural Networks: Perceptron, Madaline, and Backpropagation," *Proc. IEEE* 78(9): 1415–1441.

Wilhelmsen, K., and N. Cotter. 1990. "Neural Network Based Controllers for a Single-Degree-of-Freedom Robotic Arm," in *Proc. 1990 Int. Joint Conf. on Neural Networks,* San Diego, California. pp. III-407–413.

Yoon, Y. O., R. W. Brobst, P. R. Bergstresser, and L. L. Peterson. 1989. "A Desktop Neural Network for Dermatology Diagnosis," *Journal of Neural Network Computing,* (Summer): 43–52.

Zigoris, D. M. 1989. "Performance Evaluation of the Back-Propagation Algorithm for Character Recognition," M. Eng. thesis, University of Louisville, Kentucky.

Zurada, J., D. M. Zigoris, P. B. Aronhime, and M. Desai. 1991. "Multi-Layer Feedforward Networks for Printed Character Classification," *Proc. 34th Midwest Symp. on Circuits and Systems,* Monterey, California, May 14-16.

NEURAL NETWORKS IMPLEMENTATION

*Physical models are as different
from the world as a geographical
map is from the surface of the earth.*

L. BRILLOUIN

A rtificial neural systems are currently realized in a number of ways. As we have seen, they can be implemented as computer simulations. This approach has been used for a number of examples in this text. Numerical simulations also support most of the computational end-of-chapter exercises involving training and recall. For the best results and real-life applications, however, artificial neural networks need to be implemented as analog, digital, or hybrid (analog/digital) hardware. Moreover, neural network processors rather than digital computer simulations seem to be the key ingredient to further expansion and commercialization of neural network technology. Fortunately, study of the technical reports and of products available indicates that electronic implementations of neural networks are feasible and promising. This provides us with the focus and justification for neural network hardware implementation study in this chapter.

While neural network hardware development is being pursued in a number of research centers, neurocomputing concepts and applications are usually tested through simulations of neural algorithms on digital computers. To this aim, a very wide spectrum of computers, called *programmable neurocomputers,* can be used.

A simple microcomputer running neural network training or recall software can therefore be termed a programmable neurocomputer. We should realize, however, that an especially efficient programmable neurocomputer can be built by tailoring its architecture to the flow of the neural algorithm. This would involve organizing the computations in parallel, scheduling appropriate data communication, and specializing in arithmetic or transfer operations that are performed frequently.

A number of companies have brought coprocessor accelerator boards on the market. They typically interface to personal computers or conventional workstations and are able to enhance the speed of numerical computations considerably. Coprocessor accelerator boards also make the simulations of neural algorithms faster and more accurate. A natural progression of these coprocessors has produced neural array processors with dedicated architecture and computation flow. A number of specialized parallel neurocomputers which are programmable have been developed.

However, any programmable sequential general-purpose neurocomputer is an order of magnitude slower than neural hardware, which could be directly produced using the same fabrication technology as the programmable neurocomputer. Our objective in this chapter is to review briefly programmable neurocomputers and provide extensive fundamentals on neural hardware. Such neural hardware is called a *neurocomputer.* Neurocomputers are dedicated computing devices working with embedded neural processing algorithms and employ parallel processing to increase the throughput. Programming is not required for their operation, but they often interface with a programmable training controller. The high-performance parallel computing unit must be matched with an efficient interface to avoid bottlenecks in training and recall network functions. We will focus in this chapter on silicon-based neural hardware which represents the largest category among special-purpose analog and digital neurocomputers.

9.1
ARTIFICIAL NEURAL SYSTEMS: OVERVIEW OF ACTUAL MODELS

Throughout the preceding chapters we have covered neural network concepts and applications, but only marginal attention has been paid to building actual working models of artificial neural systems. Our study thus far indicates, however, that the computation by neural networks whether implemented on a programmable or nonprogrammable neurocomputer is performed differently than computation by ordinary digital computers. In this section we attempt to address these differences. In addition, an overview of computational requirements for implementing connectionist models is the focus of this section.

The diversity of neural network concepts, algorithms, and abstractions, which dominated the coverage in previous chapters, also extends into the area of building their physical models. We will see that artificial neural networks can be built using analog, digital, or hybrid dedicated electronic or optical hardware. As mentioned before, neurocomputing algorithms can be tested and implemented on either dedicated or general-purpose conventional computers, called programmable neurocomputers. In addition, mixtures of computer simulations with digital or analog integrated circuit computations are often applied. These usually dedicated circuits can be built in a variety of technologies to assist with efficient implementations of specialized neurocomputing algorithms.

Let us look at an example of a neurocomputer that involves such mixed computations. One of the commercial neurocomputers involves simulation of error back-propagation training on a conventional programmable host computer. Subsequent transfer (downloading) and storage of weights, which result from the training, are performed by the digital circuitry. However, information stored in the network is recalled through analog computation within the designated electronic circuitry. In fact, the analog computation mode and parallel form of information processing and retrieval are responsible for the fast recall performed by the discussed network. In this neurocomputer we thus have numerical simulation of training, which is performed off-chip, digital transfer and data storage circuitry, and a dedicated analog neural network that performs recall only.

Let us focus on efficient hardware implementation of neural algorithms. Review of processing algorithms indicates that batch learning and incremental learning either from current errors or from past experience, as well as recall of stored information, are all executed as sequences of relatively simple arithmetic operations such as weighted product summation followed by a nonlinear mapping. The most commonly encountered operations are scalar and outer product vector multiplication and matrix-vector multiplication. These operations are performed as a series of multiply and/or multiply and add operations. Additions and subtractions of matrices and vectors, and ordinary multiplications often involving the generation of a nonlinear activation function, are less frequent, but are also indispensable for most learning and recall tasks.

Node Numbers and Complexity of Computing Systems

Let us attempt to position neural computation in the more general context of computation. One of the most important features of artificial neural systems is that they perform a large number of numerical operations in parallel. These operations involve simple arithmetic operations as well as nonlinear mappings and computation of derivatives. Almost all data stored in the network are involved in recall computation at any given time. The distributed neural processing is

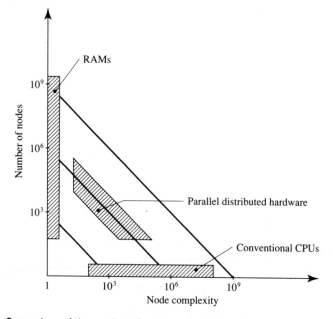

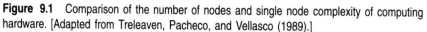

Figure 9.1 Comparison of the number of nodes and single node complexity of computing hardware. [Adapted from Treleaven, Pacheco, and Vellasco (1989).]

typically performed within the entire array composed of neurons and weights. This indicates that parallel distributed computing makes efficient use of the stored data (weights) and of the input data (inputs).

In contrast to the neural processor arrays performing parallel computations, conventional computers operate on a very limited number of data at a time. The arithmetic-logic unit within the processor of a conventional computer manipulates only two words just recently fetched from memory. Although the same processors can perform a variety of complex instructions very quickly, many megabytes of data are idle during any instruction cycle. The duty cycle of a processor is close to 100%, but that of the stored data is close to zero in conventional computation. This explains the computational bottleneck when conventional computers must deal with very large input/output data rates and perform tasks such as computer vision or speech recognition. This also explains why neural networks can handle massive amounts of input/output data more efficiently than conventional computers.

Figure 9.1 illustrates the comparison of conventional computers with the parallel distributed processing hardware. The parameters compared are the number of addressable computing nodes versus their complexity. We adopt for this comparison a rather broad concept of the computing node. Any addressable unit ranging from RAM cell to processor is understood in this discussion to be a computing node. The simplest processing node is the RAM cell, which typically consists of one and rarely more than three transistors. However, it has no processing power beyond its ability to retain the present binary content or to acquire a new one. In spite of their simplicity, millions of memory cells are needed for operation of a modern digital computer. We may place the central processing unit (CPU) of a computer at the other end of the spectrum of nodes. The CPU is the most complex processing node; however, only a limited number of CPUs are needed for a computer to operate.

Neural networks fall by nature of their parallel distributed processing into the middle ground between the two extreme examples of nodes of RAM cell and CPU. A medium number of processing nodes, each of low to medium complexity, perform local neurocomputing on local data. Ideally, each processing node, or neuron, should be rather simple and small to accommodate the placement of many of them on an integrated circuit chip. Since the neural processing node does not need to perform dozens of diversified logic and arithmetic operations, it can be hard-wired to perform just its basic computational function (Mackie et al. 1988). Its operation is rather straightforward and can often be tailored to a particular application or network paradigm.

Let us review the choice of an artificial neural system model, a choice that has to precede solution of a neurocomputing task. A specific neurocomputing task needs to be translated onto an artificial system model so that it can be implemented. Since the choice of an algorithm depends on the specific user's task to be accomplished, the user must first consider the selection of an optimal processing algorithm. The problem for which a suitable algorithm has been found is then transferred to the model to compute a solution.

This sequence of steps is illustrated in Figure 9.2 showing the problem-algorithm-model flowchart. Alternatively, the user's problem can be transferred directly to the artificial neural system model for execution. This may be the case for well-defined and known tasks for which the choice of the successful model has been made, and parameters of the algorithm have already been developed based on the previous experience of the user.

Neurocomputing Hardware Requirements

Artificial neural system models contain both invariant and variable parameters, which are called *characteristics* here and are essential for the system's operation (Reece and Treleaven 1988). Invariant characteristics are fixed in the neurocomputing model, while variable characteristics can be modified. Invariant characteristics usually include, among others, network topology, number of bits, or simply accuracy in expressing the weight value, number of bits describing the activation and output values of the neuron, and interconnection density. Variable characteristics of the model typically include its learning parameters, sequence

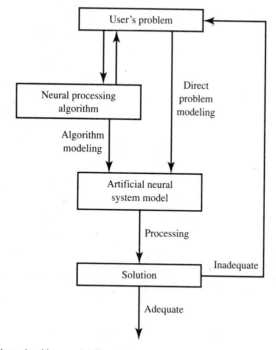

Figure 9.2　Problem-algorithm-model flowchart.

of learning and recall operations, as well as the presence or lack of synchronous neuron updates, etc.

Simulation of most neural network models in real-life applications can become computationally intensive to the degree that the processing bottleneck on conventional computers imposes constraints on practical explorations of large neural networks. In fact, limitations of computational power available has dwarfed the learning machines' research wave of a quarter century ago.

As mentioned before, there are two distinct approaches currently being taken for supporting artificial neural system modeling:

1. General-purpose computers, which are programmable and therefore able to simulate a variety of models

2. Special-purpose hardware, often dedicated to a specific neural processing model.

Let us first outline the requirements for neurocomputing hardware. This outline will allow us to specify the set of features that neuroemulators should have. Understandably, the features of any given artificial neural network depend primarily on its specific application. Let us look first at such properties as recall time, network size, and input layer size. Figure 9.3(a) tabulates five applications of layered feedforward networks. The applications listed differ widely from each

Application	Recall Time s	Network Size		Input Layer Size
		Neurons	Weights	
Radar Pulse Identification	$50 \cdot 10^{-6}$	384	32 k	128
Robot Arm Controller	0.01–1	312	3.6 k	5
Isolated Words Recognition (1024-word vocabulary)	.01	10 k	2.5 k	25
Low Level Vision 100 weights/neuron	.04	64 k	6400 k	64 k
Financial Risk Evaluation	1	5–10 k	4000 k	?

(a)

Figure 9.3a Neural network comparison for typical applications: (a) typical sizes and recall times. [Adapted from DARPA (1988).]

other in required processing speed and memory size. For example, for identification of radar pulse signals, processing time is the most severe constraint but memory size is not. On the other end, financial risk evaluation modeling requires a very large, but not necessarily very fast, network. The response time of financial risk evaluation can be in the range of a few seconds, while the radar pulse identification must be performed within 50 μs (Jutten, Guerin, and Herault 1990). Some other applications, such as vision, may require unusually large input/output bandwidth. The input/output bandwidth is understood here to be the number of bits per second that can be processed by the input/output unit. This brief comparison of computational requirements for various tasks indicates that a trade-off may be necessary between a network's processing time, memory size, and the input/output bandwidth. When considering particular applications, these three features should be balanced and geared toward the specific problem requirements.

Let us now consider the memory and network size of an artificial neural system. The size of a neural network is determined by the overall number of neurons and the total number of inputs, but mainly by the number of its weights. Thus, neural network size is about directly proportional to the number of weights. For example, there are $(n-1)^2$ weights in fully coupled single-layer networks with n neurons. Since the number of weights drastically exceeds the number of neurons, the size of the network is determined primarily by the number of weights.

Assume that a neural network model is simulated on a digital computer. Each weight is typically characterized by a single value, and only the current

Application	Memory Size Words	Word Length Bits	I/O Bandwidth W/s or b/s	CPS Measure (Recall)	MFLOPS Measure (Recall)
Radar Pulse Identification	< 32 k	1/neuron 32/synapse	2.5 Mb/s	640 M	1.3 G
Robot Arm Controller	4.5 k	32	< 600 W/s	< 350 k	< 700 k
Isolated Words Recognition (1024-word vocabulary)	300 k	32	2.5 kW/s	24 M	48 M
Low Level Vision 100 weights/neuron	6.4 M	1/neuron 8/synapse	1.6 Mb/s	156 M	312 M
Financial Risk Evaluation	4.1 M	?	< 7 kW/s	4 M	8 M

(b)

Figure 9.3b Neural network comparison for typical applications *(continued):* (b) hardware requirements. [Adapted from DARPA (1988).]

weight value needs to be stored during learning. This also applies to error back-propagation training of multilayer feedforward networks. However, if either cumulative weight adjustment training, or training with a momentum term, is implemented, the most recent weight value must be memorized in addition to its present value. Furthermore, activation values, output values, and the error term value must be stored for each neuron of the layer that undergoes training.

At the data format level, the machine representation must be more accurate for weights than for any of the remaining data. In particular, weight updates resulting during incremental supervised or unsupervised learning are relatively small to provide training stability and convergence. A *floating-point* format for representing weights by number is therefore necessary. Floating-point representation for weights typically requires a mantissa with 24 or 32 bits (Bessiere et al. 1991).

The external environment in which the neural network is used usually imposes the speed of data transfer. A high sampling rate, for example, would be necessary to process large video images. In addition to communication speed requirements, a neural network can be characterized by its computational bandwidth. The computational bandwidth for conventional computers is typically expressed in units such as MFLOPS (million of floating-point operations per second), or MIPS (million of instructions per second). For simulation of artificial neural systems the "CPS" (connections per second) unit has recently emerged as an efficiency measure (Bessiere et al. 1991).

The CPS unit has become the popular catch phrase for neurocomputing products. Its generality is severely limited, however. It describes only the processing speed for the recall mode of a multilayer feedforward network. CPS units neither reflect the speed of learning of any architecture nor the processing speed within recurrent networks. Also, the number of CPS units does not include auxiliary system operations, which support inputs and outputs.

Let us compare the units of CPS and FLOPS for feedforward networks simulated on a conventional computer. The recall pass through a single neuron with n connections requires approximately n multiplication-accumulation operations, one for each weight. Assuming that multiplication-accumulation is equivalent to approximately two floating-point operations of the CPU, we can establish that there is $1 : 2$ ratio between CPS measure and FLOPS measure.

Figure 9.3(b) outlines the hardware requirements for the five artificial neural systems discussed earlier in Figure 9.3(a). The table lists the required CPS and FLOPS measures expected for each of the five applications. It can be seen from the table that each of the networks not only requires a different size of the memory measured in terms of memory words, but memory word lengths also differ. In addition, I/O bandwidth requirements differ widely among networks for different applications.

As an example, the application of radar pulse identification requires 2.5 Mb/s I/O bandwidth, which corresponds to the transfer of a 128-tuple binary vector every 50 μs. The network performing this task is of rather moderate size starting at 32 000 weights and having 256 binary neurons arranged in two layers plus one layer of input nodes. If a binary input vector must be processed every 50 μs, then 32 000 connections must be implemented 20,000 times per second. We would thus have the required CPS measure of approximately 640 MCPS. This corresponds to a computational power of about 1.3 MFLOPS of the computer simulating efficiently the recall stream of radar pulses that needs to be recognized.

Let us attempt to outline the general computational requirement estimates for two important cases of neural processing. Our concern will be digital computer simulation of learning in feedforward networks of multilayer perceptrons, and simulation of recall in discrete-time, fully coupled recurrent networks. Figure 9.4 lists the average number of multiplication-accumulation operations per weight. Single-layer and multilayer feedforward network learning, and single-layer and recurrent network recall are included in this comparison. The number of operations listed in the figure are understood to be estimates and are specified as range of values. This allows accounting for supporting operations other than multiplication and addition. Also, the precise average number of operations would depend on the complexity of the activation function computation. The function can be defined for computation as a permanent look-up table, generated by polynomial expansion or calculated directly. Each of the methods requires a different computational expense.

Processing Mode	Single-layer Network	Multilayer Network	Recurrent Network (Discrete-time)
Learning	4 − 10	7 − 12	Batch
Recall	2 − 3	2 − 3	$(2 - 3) \times R$
Total	6 − 13	9 − 15	

R—number of recurrent updates of all neurons until stability.

Figure 9.4 Average estimated number of multiplication-accumulation operations per weight for three selected architectures. [Adapted from Jutten, Guerin, and Herault (1990).]

It can be seen that the learning of a multilayer feedforward architecture is the most computationally intensive neural processing form. Let us use the data of Figures 9.3 and 9.4 to estimate the required computational power of a conventional computer performing efficient learning of isolated word recognition using a 1024-word vocabulary. Assume that the training needs to take 4000 full presentation cycles. Thus, about 4 M input vectors are submitted to the network during learning, or 4 M incremental learning steps are needed. Since the network contains 2500 weights, assuming 12 operations per single weight adjustment would yield the total of 120 G required operations. It then takes about 42 min of computing time for a 48-MFLOPS computer to complete the training, or only 1 min for a 2000-MFLOPS computer to accomplish the same task.

The calculation shows that the powerful computer can produce the multilayer feedforward network in question within a reasonable training time, provided the training converges to an acceptable solution. Improvements of training efficiency can be achieved in a number of forms. Some of them are:

- Dedicated hardware architectures of conventional programmable computers
- Parallel distributed architectures of densely interconnected computing neural nodes containing conventional multiply or multiply-add processors
- Reduction of the volume of the training data through the use of the generalization properties of networks
- Designing neurocomputing integrated circuits using digital, analog, or digital/analog arrays performing simultaneous local computations within the entire array.

As stated before, the availability of neurocomputing integrated circuits offers the most advantageous alternative for multifaceted utilization of neural networks.

Not only would the processing time drastically decrease for integrated neurocomputing circuits, but also the size, power supply requirements, and the retraining possibility of networks would render miniature neurocomputers very attractive.

Digital and Analog Electronic Neurocomputing Circuits

To review special-purpose neurocomputing hardware, the exposition of artificial neural systems must descend to the level of the neuron. The basic processing unit defined as the processing node (neuron) and weights (synaptic connections) was shown earlier in Figure 2.4. The processing unit needs to memorize data stored as connection weights, to generate a neuron's activation value, and to compute the unit's output signal. These features would make it possible for the unit to perform recall functions. In addition, the ability to store the learning rule and to adapt weights according to the rule would be the most desirable property of the processing node. The processed signals and functions of the node can be either analog, digital, or of a combined type (Goser et al. 1989).

Let us review some basic issues of building a neural processing node. To calculate the activation value using the conventional digital computer simulation method, the weight values stored in a local memory cell are first multiplied by the input values and then the products are added. More efficiently, the activation value can be compounded through serial calculation as follows

$$net_i \leftarrow 0 \tag{9.1}$$

$$net_i \leftarrow net_i + w_{ij}x_j, \quad \text{for } j = 1 \text{ TO } n \text{ STEP } 1$$

This commonly used multiply-accumulate sequence (9.1) requires synchronous operation of related digital hardware. High-precision calculations and considerable noise immunity are inherent in this computing method. While high-precision computation of a neuron's response as in (9.1) is often indispensable for the learning mode, the recall function usually does not require the same degree of accuracy. Furthermore, it is difficult to avoid the view that the computation algorithm (9.1) cannot be substantiated by any biological analogies. Let us now therefore look at analog computation performed by a neural processing node. Analog computation is not only more plausible in biological neural networks, but constitutes the fundamental form of processing for nonprogrammable neural hardware.

In the case of an analog processing node, knowledge is encapsulated in analog weights w_{ij}. Learning of the network proceeds via relatively slow changes of weights w_{ij} and only in the training mode. Recall proceeds as simultaneous analog computing within the entire array encompassing all nodes. In a simple version, weights can be determined by resistance values, and the analog computation of

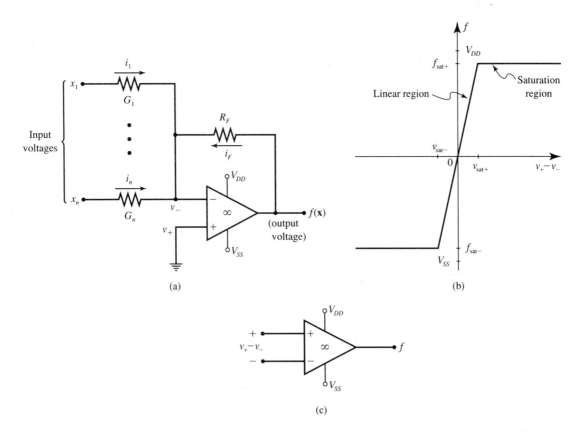

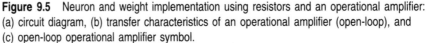

Figure 9.5 Neuron and weight implementation using resistors and an operational amplifier: (a) circuit diagram, (b) transfer characteristics of an operational amplifier (open-loop), and (c) open-loop operational amplifier symbol.

the scalar product and subsequent nonlinear mapping can be performed by a summing amplifier with saturation.

A conventional operational amplifier can implement these node functions as follows

$$f(\mathbf{x}) = f\left(\sum_{j=1}^{n} w_j x_j\right) \tag{9.2}$$

A sample analog implementation of the processing node performing Equation (9.2) is shown in Figure 9.5(a). The neuron, or cell body, is formed from an infinity-gain operational amplifier with strong negative feedback. Weight value w_j is proportional to the conductance G_j. As derived below, the feedback resistance R_F provides here a proportionality factor common for all weights. Let us analyze the computing node circuit and evaluate its weights in terms of circuit components.

Figure 9.5(b) illustrates the voltage transfer characteristics $f(v_+ - v_-)$ of the open-loop high-gain operational amplifier. Figure 9.5(c) shows the circuit symbol of the open-loop operational amplifier for which the characteristics shown are valid. In the linear region, the open-loop operational amplifier performs as a constant-gain amplifier of high gain. The open-loop gain value of the operational amplifier in the linear region corresponds to the slope of the steep part of the characteristics displayed in Figure 9.5(b). The output voltage f of the operational amplifier, however, can neither exceed the f_{sat+} value, nor can it drop below the f_{sat-} value. This is due to the saturation of transistors within the device. Typically, saturation voltages f_{sat-} and f_{sat+} are of equal magnitude and of opposite signs. The values of f_{sat+} and f_{sat-} are about 1 V below the operational amplifier supply voltage V_{DD}, and 1 V above V_{SS}, respectively.

As a consequence, an operational amplifier operates within a very narrow range of input voltages. This range is (v_{sat-}, v_{sat+}). However, the differential input voltage $v_+ - v_-$ remains in this range only if the operational amplifier is in its linear region of operation. Note that only the operational amplifier with a closed negative feedback loop remains in the linear region. The negative feedback loop is closed when the resistance R_F connects the output with an inverting input of the operational amplifier. The neuron's circuit from Figure 9.5(a) can be considered as having the discussed properties.

It can be seen that any rise in output voltage f causes an increase of current i_F, which in turn elevates the potential v_-. Such an increase is caused as the result of an additional voltage drop across the device input resistance R_i. This resistance can be measured between the noninverting and inverting input terminals and is typically of large value. The increase of voltage across R_i, however, results in a decrease in the output voltage since an increase in v_- brings about a decrease in the voltage f. The final outcome of this process is that the negative feedback around the operational amplifier enforces its stabilization in the linear region. More precisely, the existing negative feedback attempts to stabilize its differential input voltage $v_+ - v_-$ near 0 V.

Inspection of Figure 9.5(a) indicates that the negative feedback enforces the condition $v_+ - v_- \cong 0$ V. Since the noninverting input of the operational amplifier is grounded and thus $v_+ = 0$ V, potential v_- remains very close to 0 V. This phenomenon is called *virtual ground* and it makes the analysis of operational amplifier circuits rather simple. The advantage of the virtual ground node is that while being separated from the ground by a very large resistance R_i, the node behaves as grounded. The property holds for the operational amplifier inverting input node of Figure 9.5(a). This remains true as long as the negative feedback prevails.

The KCL equation for the inverting input node of the circuit from Figure 9.5(a) can be obtained as

$$i_1 + i_2 + \ldots + i_n = -i_F \qquad (9.3a)$$

which is equivalent to

$$(x_1 - v_-)G_1 + (x_2 - v_-)G_2 + \cdots + (x_n - v_-)G_n = (v_- - f)\frac{1}{R_F}$$

Using the virtual ground property we obtain

$$x_1G_1 + x_2G_2 + \ldots + x_nG_n = -\frac{f}{R_F} \tag{9.3b}$$

The output voltage of the neuron can now be obtained from (9.3b) for the linear range of operation as

$$f(\mathbf{x}) = \sum_{j=1}^{n} x_j(-R_FG_j) \tag{9.4a}$$

where

$$\sum_{j=1}^{n} x_j(-R_FG_j) \triangleq net \tag{9.4b}$$

Comparison of the coefficients in expressions (9.2) and (9.4) leads to the conclusion that the weights implemented by the circuit of Figure 9.5(a) are

$$w_j = -R_FG_j \tag{9.5a}$$

Furthermore, considering the definition of activation *net* as in (9.4b), the neuron implements here a unity-gain activation function in the linear region. In fact, the amplifier produces a linear combination of input voltages with weights (9.5a). The amplifier saturates whenever $f(\mathbf{x})$ reaches and attempts to exceed $f_{\text{sat}+}$. It also saturates when $f(\mathbf{x})$ attempts to drop below $f_{\text{sat}-}$. This allows for expression of the activation function in the following form:

$$f(net) = \begin{cases} f_{\text{sat}-}, & \text{for } net < f_{\text{sat}-} \\ net, & \text{for } f_{\text{sat}-} < net < f_{\text{sat}+} \\ f_{\text{sat}+}, & \text{for } net > f_{\text{sat}+} \end{cases} \tag{9.5b}$$

The activation value *net* is not measurable or physically present anywhere in the discussed neural computing node circuitry. It is helpful, however, to define and use this variable as a hypothetical input voltage of a unity-gain saturating amplifier.

Note that the discussed processing node configuration is somewhat preliminary. The unit basically implements the identity activation function. Also, positive weights cannot be achieved in this circuit without some additional modifications. However, it is possible to produce a nonzero bias level in this configuration. This can be easily accomplished by connecting the noninverting input terminal of the operational amplifier to the bias voltage T. As a consequence, the virtual ground potential of the inverting operational amplifier input is shifted to the value of T. Alternatively, the fixed bias can be produced by fixing at a constant value one of the input voltages $x_1, x_2, \ldots, x_p$ in the circuit of Figure 9.5(a).

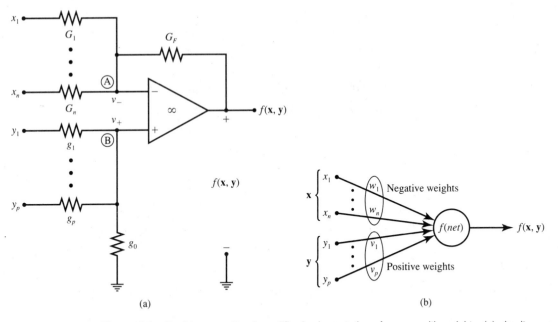

Figure 9.6 Resistor-operational amplifier implementation of neuron with weights: (a) circuit diagram and (b) computing node symbol.

Figure 9.6(a) shows the resistor-operational amplifier implementation of an electronic neuron with the output voltage being weighted input voltages. Both negative and positive signs of weighting coefficients can be produced in this circuit. Negative weights are formed in the same way as in the configuration of Figure 9.5(a). In addition, positive weights are produced by a voltage divider circuitry connected to the noninverting input of the operational amplifier. We assume here that negative weights w_i are associated with inputs x_i, for $i = 1, 2, \ldots, n$, and positive weights v_i are associated with inputs y_i, for $i = 1, 2, \ldots, p$.

Let us perform the analysis of this network by using the superposition principle. Our objective is to express the neuron's weight values and its range of linear operation in terms of circuit component values. We assume momentarily that the neuron made of an operational amplifier operates in the linear region. According to the superposition technique, $f(\mathbf{x}, \mathbf{y})$ can be computed as the sum of individual $n + p$ responses, which are the results of each separate excitation. The resulting neuron's weights that need to be computed are shown in symbolic form in Figure 9.6(b). Markedly, results obtained in (9.4a) and (9.5a) are already available for negative weights. These weights are responsible for computing the contribution of inputs $x_1, x_2, \ldots, x_n$ to the total neuron's response.

Let us note that the response due to the individual input y_k when all remaining inputs are short-circuited to ground can be computed using the following expansion of the output voltage $f(y_k)$

$$f(y_k) = \left(\frac{f(y_k)}{v_+}\right) \cdot \left(\frac{v_+}{y_k}\right) y_k \tag{9.6}$$

The first ratio of (9.6) can be computed by setting $v_+ \cong v_-$ due to the virtual ground property, and by writing the KCL equation for the node labeled A:

$$(f(y_k) - v_+) G_F - v_+ \sum_{j=1}^{n} G_j = 0 \tag{9.7a}$$

We thus obtain

$$\frac{f(y_k)}{v_+} = 1 + R_F \sum_{j=1}^{n} G_j \tag{9.7b}$$

The second ratio of (9.6) can be easily computed from the voltage division at node B as follows:

$$\frac{v_+}{y_k} = \frac{g_k}{\sum_{j=0}^{p} g_j}, \quad \text{for } k = 1, 2, \ldots, p \tag{9.8}$$

Combining expression (9.7b) and (9.8) yields the neuron's response $f(y_k)$ due to y_k from (9.6) as

$$f(y_k) = y_k \left(1 + R_F \sum_{j=1}^{n} G_j\right) \frac{g_k}{\sum_{j=0}^{p} g_j} \tag{9.9}$$

Summarizing the results of the analysis for this elementary neural processing node, the final negative and positive weight values expressed in terms of circuit components result, respectively, as

$$w_i = -R_F G_i, \quad \text{for } i = 1, 2, \ldots, n$$

$$v_k = \left(1 + R_F \sum_{j=1}^{n} G_j\right) \frac{g_k}{\sum_{j=0}^{p} g_j}, \quad \text{for } k = 1, 2, \ldots, p \tag{9.10}$$

The total output voltage of the analyzed neuron is expressed as

$$f(\mathbf{x}, \mathbf{y}) = \begin{cases} f_{\text{sat}-}, & \text{for } net < f_{\text{sat}-} \\ net, & \text{for } f_{\text{sat}-} < net < f_{\text{sat}+} \\ f_{\text{sat}+}, & \text{for } net > f_{\text{sat}+} \end{cases} \tag{9.11}$$

where

$$net = \mathbf{w}^t \mathbf{x} + \mathbf{v}^t \mathbf{y}$$

Noticeably, the assumption of linear operation remains valid only when the condition $f_{\text{sat}-} < net < f_{\text{sat}+}$ holds. For a *net* value outside this range, the performed analysis of the neuron of Figure 9.6 remains invalid and the neuron's output latches at one of its saturation voltage levels $f_{\text{sat}-}$ or $f_{\text{sat}+}$.

EXAMPLE 9.1

This example illustrates the typical design steps of an electronic neural network for cluster detection. Assume that a three-neuron network has been trained in the winner-take-all mode as described in Section 7.2. The network needs to be able to identify one of the three input vector clusters. Network weight vectors that need to be implemented are

$$\mathbf{w}_A = \begin{bmatrix} -2.897 \\ 0.776 \end{bmatrix}, \quad \mathbf{w}_B = \begin{bmatrix} 2.121 \\ 2.121 \end{bmatrix}, \quad \mathbf{w}_C = \begin{bmatrix} -1.026 \\ -2.819 \end{bmatrix} \quad (9.12)$$

A network with three operational amplifiers, each using four resistors, as shown in Figure 9.7, can be employed to fulfill the design specifications (9.12). Detectors of clusters 2 and 3 require two positive and two negative weights, respectively, while cluster 1 needs weights of both signs. Let us observe that each of the three computing neurons has only two associated weights and four or five resistors. Since we have some freedom of choice here, all but two weight-determining resistor values will thus need to be assumed. Design assumptions for further considerations are $R_F = r_0 = 1 \text{ k}\Omega$.

Cluster 1 Neuron: Using Equations (9.10) for $n = p = 1$, we obtain from (9.12)

$$\begin{cases} -R_F G_1 = -2.897 \\ (1 + R_F G_1) \dfrac{g_1}{g_0 + g_1} = 0.776 \end{cases} \quad (9.13a)$$

Letting $R_F = r_0 = 1/g_0 = 1 \text{ k}\Omega$ simplifies the expressions (9.13a) to the form

$$\begin{cases} G_1 \cdot 10^3 = 2.897 \\ 3.897 \dfrac{g_1}{10^{-3} + g_1} = 0.776 \end{cases} \quad (9.13b)$$

The reader can verify that $R_1 = 1/G_1 = 345.2 \ \Omega$, and $r_1 = 1/g_1 = 4022 \ \Omega$ are the solutions of (9.13b). This completes the design of the neuron that detects cluster 1.

Cluster 2 Neuron: Using Equations (9.10) for $p = 2$, we obtain from (9.12)

$$\begin{cases} (1 + R_F G_1) \dfrac{g_1}{g_0 + g_1 + g_2} = 2.121 \\ (1 + R_F G_1) \dfrac{g_2}{g_0 + g_1 + g_2} = 2.121 \end{cases} \quad (9.14)$$

Note that a dummy G_1 conductance between the inverting node of the operational amplifier and ground is used here to provide the fixed gain f/v_+ of the circuit. This gain is now $1 + R_F G_1$. Since the ratios on the left side

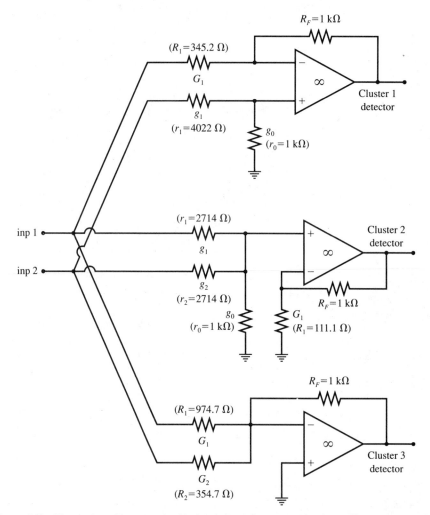

Figure 9.7 Cluster detecting network with the three resistor-operational amplifiers neurons of Example 9.1.

---

of (9.14) are smaller than unity, $1 + R_F G_1$ should be chosen in the order of tens so that the positive weights can be in the required range. Since $R_F = 1$ kΩ, then for $1 + R_F G_1 = 10$ we obtain $R_1 = 1/G_1 = 111.1$ Ω, and (9.14) simplifies as follows

$$\begin{cases} \dfrac{g_1}{g_0 + g_1 + g_2} = 0.2121 \\ \dfrac{g_2}{g_0 + g_1 + g_2} = 0.2121 \end{cases} \qquad (9.15)$$

Since we assume $r_0 = 1/g_0 = 1$ kΩ, the solutions of (9.15) are obtained as follows:

$$r_1 = r_2 = \frac{1}{g_1} = \frac{1}{g_2} = 2.714 \text{ k}\Omega$$

This completes the design of a neuron that detects cluster 2.

Cluster 3 Neuron: Using the first of two equations (9.10) for case $n = 2$ we have

$$\begin{cases} R_F G_1 = 1.026 \\ R_F G_2 = 2.819 \end{cases} \tag{9.16}$$

Again using $R_F = 1$ kΩ, the remaining resistances of the network can be computed from (9.16) as $R_1 = 1/G_1 = 974.6$ Ω, and $R_2 = 1/G_2 = 354.7$ Ω. This completes the design of the entire cluster detecting network. ■

The techniques described in this subsection apply equally both to neuron circuits with zero and nonzero bias levels. Assume that a fixed bias of nonzero value is needed for a neuron. This can be achieved by augmenting the input vector $\mathbf{x}$ by a single fixed component x_{n+1}. This component is used to produce the bias signal and can be called the reference voltage. Stage 1 of the circuit from Figure 9.8(a) depicts an example neuron with the weights of values $-w_i$, for $i = 1, 2, \ldots, n$, and the nonzero bias produced by the input x_{n+1}. Applying relationships (9.10) and (9.11) allows for computation of the output voltage of the first stage as

$$f_{o1}(x_1, \ldots, x_{n+1}) = \sum_{i=1}^{n} (-w_i)x_i - x_{n+1} \tag{9.17}$$

As for previous configurations, the stage from Figure 9.8(a) also works with the linear transfer characteristics of unity slope, provided $f_{\text{sat}-} < f_{o1} < f_{\text{sat}+}$. Otherwise, the stage saturates at $f_{\text{sat}-}$ or $f_{\text{sat}+}$ for the output voltages that attempt to exceed the linear range of an operational amplifier.

In cases for which a high-gain neuron is needed, the unity-gain neurons, examples of which are shown in Figures 9.5, 9.6, and 9.7, should be connected in cascade with a high-gain amplifier. Stage 2 of the circuit from Figure 9.8(a) provides the gain of value $-K$, but it also reverses the polarity of all weights. The overall transfer characteristics, or activation function of this two-stage neuron, is given by the following formula:

$$f_{o2}(\mathbf{x}) = K \left(\sum_{i=1}^{n} w_i x_i + x_{n+1} \right) \tag{9.18}$$

Again, whenever the value $f_{o2}(\mathbf{x})$ computed from (9.18) falls outside the range $(f_{\text{sat}-}, f_{\text{sat}+})$, the neuron's output saturates at either $f_{\text{sat}-}$, or $f_{\text{sat}+}$. The resulting transfer characteristics of the two-stage neuron is shown in Figure 9.8b. It can

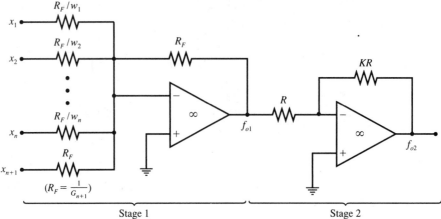

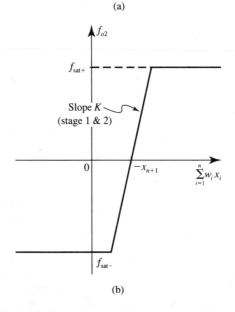

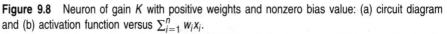

Figure 9.8 Neuron of gain K with positive weights and nonzero bias value: (a) circuit diagram and (b) activation function versus $\sum_{i=1}^{n} w_i x_i$.

be seen that the neuron's bias, or threshold, value is T and has now an opposite sign with respect to the reference voltage x_{n+1}, since we have $T = -x_{n+1}$.

In this subsection we introduced the simple electronic model of a processing neural node. It is a node that sums a number of weighted input voltages and produces an output voltage that is a nonlinear function of that sum. The nonlinear function of a processing node plays the same role as an activation function of a neuron. The activation functions implemented thus far with resistors and operational amplifiers have been piecewise linear with controlled slope near the origin, and having symmetrical saturation for large activation levels.

The resistor-operational amplifier circuits introduced in this section rather lucidly illustrate the basic design concepts of the neural network computing nodes. Nevertheless, they are of limited practical significance due to several important reasons. Some of them are limitations of the shape of the produced transfer characteristics, excessive power consumption, and large area occupied by discrete resistors and operational amplifiers. In addition, the main problem with the electronic neural networks just discussed is that weight values are encapsulated in the values of resistances of fixed, discrete resistors. Such resistors are not easily adjustable or controllable. As a consequence, they can be used neither for learning, nor can they be reused for recall when another task needs to be solved.

As will be shown in the subsequent sections, the discussed circuits from Figures 9.5 through 9.8 play an important role in more advanced neural network implementations. More sophisticated, integrated circuit neural networks are often based on the simple principles just illustrated with resistive networks and operational amplifiers. In fact, conversion of input voltages into weighted currents highlighted in (9.2) is one of the most frequent intermediate operations encountered in electronic neural network implementations. Another commonly used technique is the summation of currents into a proportional voltage response with nonlinear saturation. More specialized design techniques for electronic neural processing nodes are discussed below in more detail.

9.2
INTEGRATED CIRCUIT SYNAPTIC CONNECTIONS

Artificial neural networks usually contain a very large number of synaptic connections and much fewer processing neurons. As mentioned before, conventional resistors can be used to produce synaptic connections in the form of weights. Nonlinear voltage amplifiers can be used to accomplish weighted summation of input voltages into the activation value, and also produce nonlinear mapping of an activation into the output voltage.

The central problem of implementation of artificial neural networks is to make weights that are continuously adjustable, preferably in response to an analog control signal. In addition, weights should not require many transistors for their implementation and for control of their values. Ideally, weights should also be capable of learning under a specified learning rule. We should realize from previous study that the requirement of adjustable weights is easier to implement than this one of learning weights. Indeed, a learning weight must not only be adjustable but it also must respond to a learning signal according to the training rule it implements.

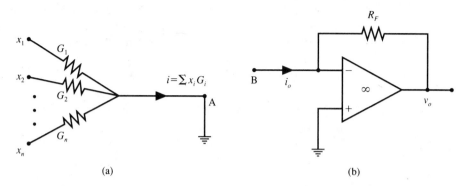

Figure 9.9 Functional blocks of the basic circuit of a neuron with fixed weights: (a) resistive synaptic connections and (b) current-to-voltage converter.

Adjustable weights are weights that can be modified off-line as a result of the learning process. *Learning weights* are understood as weights that modify by themselves on-line during learning. The learning signal in such cases is provided to the weight circuitry that allows the weight modification. The learning weight modification can be an outcome of either the current continuous or step-like learning. Usually, weight modification depends on the neuron's output signal, but it may also involve other quantities.

Neurobiology solves an on-line learning problem by using chemical modifications of ionic conductances, and by constructing a synapse that is a complex signal transmitting device with history-dependent properties. Making artificial neural network connections at least partially as clever as the natural connections could have great impact on the effectiveness of analog implementations of neural networks (Hopfield 1990). Let us focus, however, on studying microelectronic techniques that are presently available rather than on imitating neurobiological processes that are too involved to be duplicated in present-day integrated circuits.

As discussed in the previous section, inputs to the electronic model of a neural network are assumed to be voltages x_i, for $i = 1, 2, \ldots, n$. To produce a weighted sum of inputs, the input voltages are first converted into branch currents $x_i G_i$ as shown in Figure 9.9(a). The values G_i are branch conductances of resistors connected between the i'th input and ground. The branch currents must then be summed and the sum converted back to voltage using, for example, a current-to-voltage converter depicted in Figure 9.9(b). The converter output voltage v_o is equal

$$v_o = -i_o R_F \tag{9.19}$$

To implement a neural processing node following the description above, two functional blocks from Figure 9.9(a) and (b) must be connected in cascade. Node

A needs to be connected to virtual ground node B instead of to the actual ground node as in Figure 9.9(a). This connection enforces $i = i_o$, and the output voltage value becomes as expressed by (9.3) and (9.4). The two connected networks yield a basic neural processing node identical to the one introduced earlier in Figure 9.5(a).

In this section we will study analysis and design of adjustable microelectronic synaptic connections. Our focus is on voltage-controlled resistors that implement such connections. We will see in the following discussion that both analog and digital control can be used to produce variations of weight values. The performance of learning synapses that are trained according to the Hebbian rule will also be studied.

Voltage-controlled Weights

The resistive synaptic connection circuit with electrically tunable weights can be developed using the basic electronic neuron concept of Figure 9.9. Assume that there is a voltage-controlled switch available with performance as depicted in Figure 9.10. Figure 9.10(a) shows a symbol of the switch, and the typical characteristics of a switch are displayed in Figure 9.10(b). The switch can operate between an ON state (short-circuit), $V_{AB} = 0$, and an OFF state (open-circuit), $I_{AB} = 0$. If neither of the two states applies, the switch assumes the resistance between terminals A and B, equal to R_{AB}. The value of R_{AB} can be made dependent on the controlling voltage V_C. It can be seen from Figure 9.10(b) that R_{AB} decreases with the increase of the control voltage V_C.

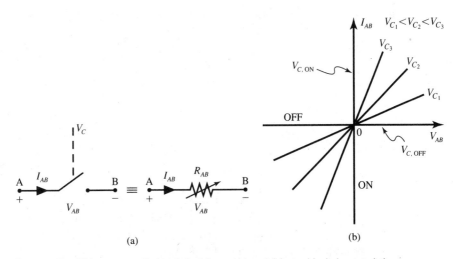

(a)   (b)

Figure 9.10 Voltage-controlled switch: (a) symbol and (b) graphical characteristics.

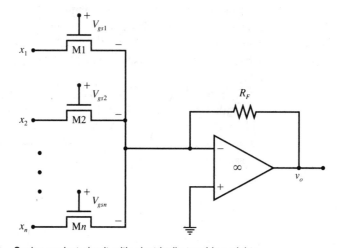

Figure 9.11 Scalar product circuit with electrically tunable weights.

The voltage-controlled switch can be implemented using a single field-effect or MOS transistor operating in the resistive (ohmic, also called linear) region. Figure 9.11 shows a neuron with n synaptic connections, each of them consisting of a single enhancement mode NMOS transistor performing as a voltage-controlled switch. With reference to Figures 9.10 and 9.11, terminals A or B of the switch can be either the drain or source of the transistor since the device is electrically symmetric. Node B is the source for positive input voltage, otherwise node A becomes the source, so that the channel current always flows toward the source terminal. For this discussion, we assume that the source is at the virtual ground potential and input voltages are positive. The input voltage is thus applied at the drain terminal of an enhancement mode NMOS transistor. The channel resistance R_{ds}, or the resistance between the drain and source of the i'th transistor, is controlled by the gate to source voltage V_{gs}.

Let us express the transistor channel resistance R_{ds} as a function of controlling voltage V_{gs}. The drain to source current, I_{ds}, for the transistor depicted in Figure 9.12(a) is given by the following expression (see Appendix)

$$I_{ds} = k' \frac{W}{L} \left[(V_{gs} - V_{th})V_{ds} - \frac{V_{ds}^2}{2} \right] \tag{9.20}$$

for $V_{ds} < V_{gs} - V_{th}$ (resistive region), where k' is the process transconductance (typically of value 20 $\mu A/V^2$), W and L are channel width and length, respectively, and V_{th} is the transistor threshold voltage (typically between 1 and 2.5 V for enhancement mode NMOS devices).

Figure 9.12(b) shows the output characteristics of an NMOS device operating in the resistive region. The characteristics depict $I_{ds}(V_{ds})$ with the gate to

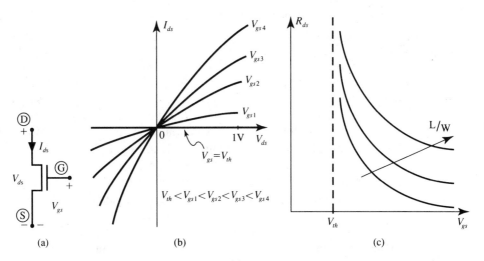

Figure 9.12 Enhancement mode NMOS transistor as a voltage-controlled switch for weight tuning: (a) device symbol, (b) output characteristics in the resistive region, and (c) channel resistance versus controlling voltage.

source voltage V_{gs} as a parameter for each curve. Comparing the switch characteristics of Figure 9.10(b) with the transistor characteristics of Figure 9.12(b), the reader may notice that $V_{C,OFF} = V_{th}$. Voltage $V_{C,ON}$ is not defined for the NMOS transistor configured as a switch, since R_{ds} is always of nonzero value. Noticeably, the first quadrant characteristics of the switch also extend into the third quadrant, which makes it possible to apply not only positive but also negative input voltages to the synaptic connection. If $V_{ds} \ll V_{gs} - V_{th}$, then the quadratic-type relation (9.20) becomes approximately linear in V_{ds} and we have

$$I_{ds} \cong k'\frac{W}{L}(V_{gs} - V_{th})V_{ds} \tag{9.21a}$$

This linear approximation of (9.20) as in (9.21a) can be considered accurate for practical purposes for $V_{ds} < 0.5(V_{gs} - V_{th})$. For this condition to be fulfilled, the voltage-controlled resistance value R_{ds} equal to the ratio of V_{ds} to I_{ds} becomes from (9.21a)

$$R_{ds} \cong \frac{L}{k'W(V_{gs} - V_{th})} \tag{9.21b}$$

It can be seen that R_{ds} is controllable in a very wide range and V_{gs} can be used as the control voltage. As illustrated in Figure 9.12(c), the switch remains open for $V_{gs} \le V_{th}$, and then with V_{gs} increasing above V_{th}, the R_{ds} value drops quickly. An additional advantage of this simple configuration is that the value of R_{ds} can be scaled by the choice of the channel length to width ratio, L/W. Obviously, for large L/W values, the channel resistance is limited to large values. This becomes the case for so-called "long channel" or "long transistors."

When applying this controlled switch as a tunable resistance, keep in mind that, ideally, the linear resistances of values as in (9.21b) are only obtainable at the origin $I_{ds} = V_{ds} = 0$. Otherwise, slight nonlinearity due to the quadratic term in (9.20) is always present, and the weights can only be approximately considered as linear voltage-controlled resistances. This should not be a serious problem, however, since no great precision of weight values is usually required for a neural network operating in the recall mode. Also, only positive resistances can be produced by the discussed switch and thus only weights of one sign can be implemented by the circuit configuration of Figure 9.11.

One possible way of producing both positive and negative weights is to · use an additional network of positive synaptic weights in the form of a voltage divider at the noninverting input of an operational amplifier. This concept was illustrated earlier in Figure 9.6 for discrete resistor circuitry. Another possible solution is to use complementary output operational amplifiers, which would provide both positive and negative weight values by producing output voltages of both signs.

At this point we have gained insight into the analysis and design of neurons' weights, which can be adapted electrically by means of a control voltage. In addition to this very desirable feature of tunability, however, voltage-controlled weight values should be stored to ensure proper synapse operation over a period of time. This issue will be covered following the example below which focuses on analysis of a neuron circuit with electrically controlled weights.

EXAMPLE 9.2 ■■■■■■■■■■■■■■■■

Let us analyze the neuron circuit illustrated in Figure 9.11 with three weights. Following are the data on transistors, control voltages, and the circuit elements used to design this circuit.

Transistors: $k' = 20\,\mu\text{A}/\text{V}^2$ (for all transistors)

                          $V_{th} = 1$ V (for all transistors)

$$\left(\frac{L}{W}\right)_1 = 1, \; \left(\frac{L}{W}\right)_2 = \frac{1}{3}, \; \left(\frac{L}{W}\right)_3 = \frac{1}{3}$$

Control Voltages: $V_{gs1} = 5$ V , $V_{gs2} = 3$ V, $V_{gs3} = 3.75$ V

Circuit: $R_F = 100$ kΩ

Our objective is to find the neuron's output voltage v_o as a function of $\mathbf{x}$ where $\mathbf{x} = \begin{bmatrix} x_1 & x_2 & x_3 \end{bmatrix}^t$.

Let us initially assume that the drain-source resistances of NMOS transistors are exactly linear because $V_{dsi} \ll V_{gsi} - V_{th}$, for $i = 1, 2, 3$. This would require that a small range of input voltages be maintained. With this assumption, the transistors are in resistive regions and their channel resistances R_{dsi}, for $i = 1, 2, 3$, can be determined from (9.21b) as follows

$$R_{dsi} = \frac{(L/W)_i}{20 \cdot 10^{-6}(V_{gsi} - 1)}, \quad \text{for } i = 1, 2, 3 \qquad (9.22a)$$

Performing calculations as in (9.22a) for the specified network parameters yields the following channel resistance values

$$R_{ds1} = 12.5 \text{ k}\Omega$$
$$R_{ds2} \cong 8.33 \text{ k}\Omega$$
$$R_{ds3} \cong 6.06 \text{ k}\Omega$$

Considering that the feedback resistance R_F is 100 kΩ and that in the linear range of operation we have

$$v_o = -R_F \left(\frac{x_1}{R_{ds1}} + \frac{x_2}{R_{ds2}} + \frac{x_3}{R_{ds3}} \right) \qquad (9.22b)$$

then the resulting weight values are as follows:

$$w_1 = -8, \quad w_2 = -12, \quad w_3 = -16.5$$

Let us now verify the accuracy of the computed weights and determine a reasonable operating voltage range for the circuit. Limiting the range of input voltages so that $V_{dsi} \leq 0.5(V_{gsi} - V_{th})$, the maximum values of input voltages for linear approximation of R_{ds} as in (9.21b) become equal:

$$V_{dsi} = \frac{1}{2}(V_{gsi} - 1) \qquad (9.22c)$$

Given the specified control voltages, V_{gsi}, the values of maximum input voltage, V_{dsi}, are 2, 1, and 1.375 V for each transistor, respectively. It is interesting to compute the actual values of implemented weights considering the condition that the input voltage has reached the maximum level beyond which the channel resistance cannot be considered linear.

For such a case, R_{ds} cannot be computed from a closed-form expression (9.21b) since its value also depends on the drain current. Using expression (9.20) we thus have for the transistor $M1$

$$I_{ds1} = 20 \cdot 10^{-6}(1) \left(4 \cdot 2 - \frac{2^2}{2} \right) \text{ A}$$

which yields

$$I_{ds1} = 120 \, \mu\text{A}$$

For the maximum input voltage level of value $V_{ds1} = 2$ V, the resulting actual channel resistance is R'_{ds1}

$$R'_{ds1} \cong 16.6 \text{ k}\Omega$$

It can be seen that the discrepancy between the newly computed accurate value of the channel resistance R'_{ds1} and the original approximate value of $R_{ds1} = 12.5$ kΩ is 33.3%. This indicates that for the working region of input voltages $V_{ds1} < 2$ V, the actual channel resistance is between 12.5 and 16.6 kΩ, with the resistance error ranging between 0 and 33.3%. In fact, the precise value of the resistance depends on the input voltage value.

The reader can easily verify that similar analysis results in the following actual resistance values in the bordercase of input voltages:

$$R'_{ds2} \cong 11.1 \text{ k}\Omega \quad \text{for } V_{ds2} = 1 \text{ V}$$
$$R'_{ds3} \cong 8.08 \text{ k}\Omega \quad \text{for } V_{ds3} = 1.375 \text{ V}$$

The actual weight values implemented by the circuit for the maximum level of inputs are now resulting in fairly different values than originally specified for this neuron which are valid for very small input voltages. The output voltage would be now of the value

$$v_o = -R_F \left(\frac{x_1}{16.6 \text{ k}\Omega} + \frac{x_2}{11.1 \text{ k}\Omega} + \frac{x_3}{8.08 \text{ k}\Omega} \right)$$

and the weights implemented by this network are $w'_1 = -6$, $w'_2 = -9$, and $w'_3 = -12.37$. This example demonstrates that in order to preserve the linearity of transistor operation and to produce constant values of weights, the input voltages should be kept well below the upper limit of channel resistance linearity, which has been set at $x_{i\max} = 0.5(V_{gsi} - V_{th})$, for $i = 1, 2, 3.$ ▬

Analog Storage of Adjustable Weights

Storage of adjustable analog weights is one of the most important problems faced in analog implementation of artificial neural systems. The storage form can be analog; it would thus have the properties of an analog memory cell. Storage cells should also be as small as possible since one memory cell would be required per every weight (Vittoz et al. 1991) and the overall size of a neural network is determined primarily by its number of weights.

A commonly used storage technique is based on storing charge across a capacitive circuit element. Note that voltage-controlled weights outlined in the previous section use the gate of an NMOS transistor as the weight control terminal. Since no current is needed to drive the transistors' gates, the simple, natural method to store the weight value is to store it as a voltage across the gate capacitance (Tsividis and Anastassiou, 1987). The gate capacitance can be either intrinsic or intentionally added to the circuit to enhance its storage capability.

Figure 9.13(a) illustrates the concept of storing a weight as a voltage across a capacitor C at the gate of transistor $M1$. The weight control voltage v_c that needs to be stored is sampled by means of a sample-and-hold circuit. Transistor $M2$ shown in Figure 9.13(b) functions as a sample-and-hold gate and provides

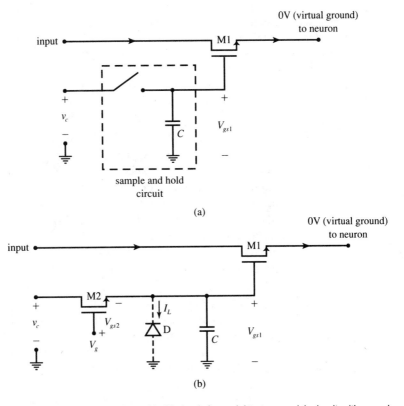

Figure 9.13 Elementary sample-and-hold circuit for weight storage: (a) circuit with sample-and-hold switch and (b) all transistor implementation.

the ON/OFF operation of the switch. The voltage V_{gs1} directly controls the channel resistance of transistor $M1$.

For an ideal operation of switch $M2$, V_{gs1} exactly tracks the weight control voltage v_c when the switch is at least partially ON. This corresponds to $M2$ being conductive and $V_{gs1} \cong v_c$. To ensure the voltage tracking, the switch control voltage V_g must be well above the level of the weight control voltage v_c. This is due to the fact that the voltage actually controlling the gate of the switch, V_{gs2}, has to be in excess of V_{th2}. This condition ensures that the switch $M2$ remains conductive between the drain and source. By inspection of Figure 9.13(b) we obtain

$$V_g = V_{gs1} + V_{gs2} \tag{9.23a}$$

For both $M1$ and $M2$ conducting, the following conditions must be met, respectively:

$$V_{gs1} > V_{th1}$$
$$V_{gs2} > V_{th2} \tag{9.23b}$$

Assuming that threshold voltages of both transistors are identical and equal to V_{th}, we obtain from (9.23a)

$$V_g > 2V_{th} \tag{9.23c}$$

This conclusion supports an intuitively obvious statement that both transistors must operate with their gate-to-source voltages above V_{th}. In such a case, $M2$ conducts the current (sampling mode) and adjusts the amount of charge that is to be stored in the capacitance C. The voltage across the capacitance, V_{gs1}, in turn controls the weight value. To ensure the analog storage of the weight value (hold mode), the open-circuit switch condition $V_{gs2} < V_{th2}$ must subsequently be enforced to trap the charge at the capacitor.

In the absence of a positive pulse V_g at the gate of the switch, the capacitor C holds the charge, which has been stored during the most recent conductive (sampling) period of $M2$. When the switch is OFF and the drain and source of $M2$ are disconnected, only a small leakage current I_L flows through a reverse-biased diffusion-to-bulk junction of $M2$ (these regions are not shown in Figure 9.13(b)). As a result, the storage capacitor will slowly discharge. For today's conventional MOS technologies, the retention, or storage, time is of the order of several milliseconds. To store the weight control voltage for longer periods, the charge stored at the capacitance C needs to be refreshed once every few milliseconds. This leakage and refresh phenomena here are analogous to the phenomena encountered in the dynamical memory RAM cell, which also needs to be refreshed periodically.

For a number of weight values to be electrically tuned, one control voltage generator providing voltages v_c can be time-shared by many neurons. As each switch closes in turn so that sampling can take place, v_c assumes an appropriate value for charging the corresponding capacitor. Note that the capacitors of the various neurons and weights can be accessed using well-known addressing schemes from semiconductor memories. The basic difference is that the data stored now are in the form of analog control voltage rather than in the binary form (Tsividis and Anastassiou, 1987).

Once the appropriate control voltages have been stored on the gate capacitors, the network is ready to perform recall. Upon completion of recall, the storage capacitors can be accessed again, either to refresh the existing weight values or to impose new weight values that may result as an outcome of the incremental learning step.

The natural decay of a capacitor's charge that represents the learned weight value is one of the inherent limitations of the analog storage of weights. Essentially, this is the implementation problem shared by all analog nonvolatile memories. Advanced circuit techniques exist that extend the storage time of analog microelectronic memory through either additional special circuitry or special refresh signals. The reader is referred to the technical references for more details on special refresh circuitry (Vittoz et al. 1991). Other, alternative techniques for analog memory for weight storage make use of electrically programmable non-volatile memory cells. Electrically programmable memory cells will be examined in Section 9.4.

Digitally Programmable Weights

As stressed earlier in this chapter, one of the most desirable features of neuron's weights is their tunability. In addition to the tunability of weights with the use of an analog voltage control signal, weights implemented as integrated circuits can be controlled digitally. This technique for weight tuning allows for increased flexibility compared to the analog tuning mode due to the fact that weights can be both programmed and stored digitally. Weight control data, arranged in digital control words, are easily stored in digital registers. Understandably, the accuracy of the weight setting in this mode depends mainly on the length of the control word. This accuracy limitation is common for any digital-to-analog conversion task and is known as the *finite resolution and conversion error.* Moreover, the accuracy of the subsequent analog signal processing is also of importance. The key consideration here is that once the weight values have been set digitally, all subsequent network computation during the recall mode is performed with analog signals. This involves multiplication, addition, and nonlinear mapping by the neuron.

In addition to flexibility and accuracy, the digital tunability of weights provides a convenient interface between the training and recall mode of operation of the neural hardware. Since learning often requires considerable accuracy, it is usually performed off-line and with the use of high-precision digital computation. Weight values computed as a final result of simulated off-line training are subsequently programmed on the neural network chip using the digital-to-analog interface. In addition, digital weight storage in RAM cells or registers of a digital computer is easily available.

A block diagram of a circuit producing a single digitally programmable weight and employing a multiplying digital-to-analog converter (MDAC) is shown in Figure 9.14. MDAC circuits are used in many electronic circuits that require the use of digitally tunable resistances and a flexible digital-to-analog interface (Zurada 1981). The converter circuit shown in the figure performs the decomposition of an input voltage x_i into binary weighted currents i_1, i_2, ..., i_n, which are proportional to x_i. The binary weighted currents are then summed and converted back into the output voltage in the current-to-voltage converter identical to the one depicted in Figure 9.9(b).

Assume that register bits of value 0 or 1 represent the entries of the binary control word $b_N b_{N-1} ... b_1$, where the most-significant bit (MSB) is that corresponding to b_N, while the least-significant bit (LSB) corresponds to b_1. Although a digital word can be presented in a variety of codes, the one assumed

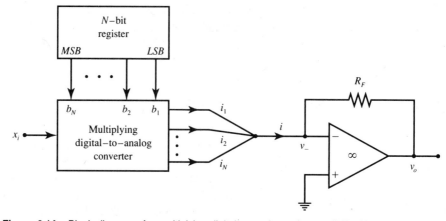

Figure 9.14 Block diagram of a multiplying digital-to-analog converter (MDAC).

here for expressing the weight value is simply its pure binary representation. Figure 9.15(a) shows the circuit diagram of a *weighted-resistor MDAC* (Sedra and Smith 1991). Successive resistances in the network are inversely proportional to the numerical significance of an appropriate bit. It can be seen that b_i of value 0 directs the weighted current to ground by positioning the respective switch S_i in its left-hand position. Switches for which $b_i = 1$ direct the binary weighted currents to the summing node B. Let us note that the currents can be considered as binary weighted since node B serves as a virtual ground. The expression for current at the input of the summing current-to-voltage converter becomes

$$I = \frac{x_i}{R}b_N + \frac{x_i}{2R}b_{N-1} + \ldots + \frac{x_i}{2^{N-1}R}b_1 \qquad (9.24a)$$

This expression simplifies to

$$I = \frac{2}{R}x_i\left(\frac{b_N}{2} + \frac{b_{N-1}}{4} + \ldots + \frac{b_1}{2^N}\right) \qquad (9.24b)$$

Let us define the digital control word D as

$$D \triangleq \frac{b_1}{2^N} + \frac{b_2}{2^{N-1}} + \ldots + \frac{b_N}{2}$$

and rewrite (9.24) in a more concise form:

$$I = \frac{2}{R}x_iD \qquad (9.25)$$

Note that D can take values $0, 1/2^N, 1/2^{N-1}, \ldots, 1 - 1/2^N$. These values uniformly cover the range $[0, 1 - 1/2^N]$ with the resolution 2^{-N}. The resolution, for instance, is about 0.1% for a 10-bit converter, but it is only 6.25% for a four-bit converter. Depending on the scaling required, different R_F values can be used in the feedback loop of the current-to-voltage converter. Assuming $R_F = (1/2)R$,

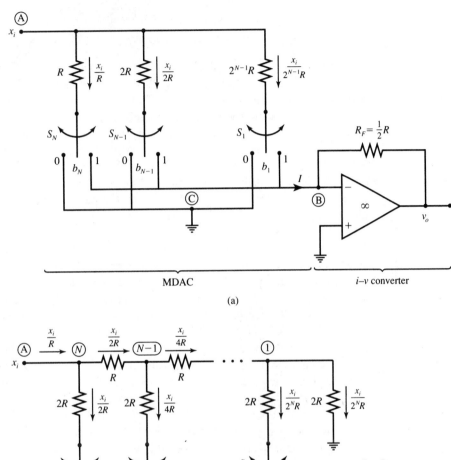

(a)

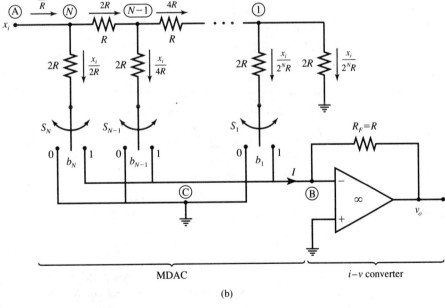

(b)

Figure 9.15 Circuit diagram of a digitally programmable weight: (a) using a weighted-resistor MDAC and (b) using a ladder-resistor MDAC.

we obtain from (9.25) and (9.19)

$$v_o = -Dv_i \tag{9.26}$$

The neuron's output voltage (9.26) is the product of the digital control word D representing the weight value and of the analog input voltage. That is why this particular configuration can be referred to as a *programmable attenuator*. However, by using appropriate scaling and selecting a suitable R_F value, the range of weight values can be adjusted and increased above the unity value according to specific design requirements. The value of R_F must be chosen in excess of $R/2$ if the weights of magnitudes larger than unity are required. Similar to the circuits described earlier in this chapter, however, a large R_F causes saturation of v_o at low levels of currents I. In such cases, the neuron's response will approach the bipolar binary activation function and make it resemble the hard-limiting response of the threshold logic unit.

Figure 9.15(b) shows an alternative converter circuit called a *ladder-resistor MDAC* (Sedra and Smith 1991). The network operates on the same principle of producing binary weighted currents. Instead of binary weighted resistances, however, now a ladder network of $R - 2R$ resistors is used as a current splitting structure. We observe from the figure that at any of the ladder nodes, the resistance is $2R$ looking to the right from each node numbered $1, 2, \ldots, N$. This is due to the fact that the horizontal resistance R of the ladder adds with a parallel combination of two resistances of value $2R$, each being connected to ground. Thus, such a series connection of R, with $2R$ parallel to $2R$, yields the resistance $2R$. This particular property applies at each of the nodes $2, 3, \ldots, N$.

As a result, the current entering each node from the left splits into two equal parts, one flowing down toward the switch, the other half toward the adjacent node to the right. Current is halved this way in every upper node of the ladder network yielding the total number of splits equal to N. However, only the currents for which switches are in the right-hand positions contribute to the current I entering the node B of the current-to-voltage converter. The output current of the MDAC thus has the value

$$I = \frac{x_i}{R} \left(\frac{b_N}{2} + \frac{b_{N-1}}{4} + \ldots + \frac{b_1}{2^N} \right) \tag{9.27a}$$

or

$$I = \frac{x_i}{R} D \tag{9.27b}$$

A formula identical to (9.26) for the output voltage in terms of input x_i can be obtained if we let the feedback resistance R_F of the operational amplifier be of value R.

Clearly, each MDAC configured as discussed and shown in Figure 9.15 can implement a single digitally controlled weight. The total of $n + p$ MDACs needs to be connected to a current-to-voltage converter arrangement to implement the set of n negative and p positive digitally controlled weights. Assume that the

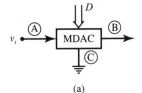

(a)

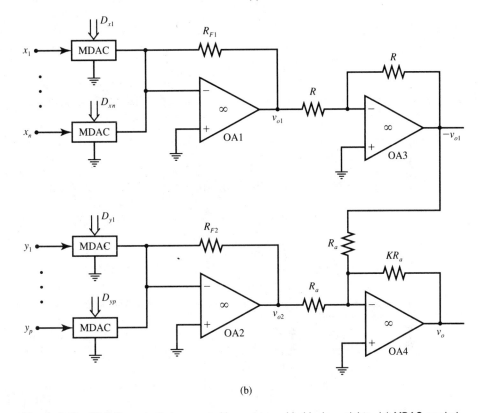

(b)

Figure 9.16 Digitally controlled neuron with programmable bipolar weights: (a) MDAC symbol and (b) circuit diagram for n negative and p positive weights of a single neuron.

MDAC is represented in the form of a block diagram with the signal input voltage at node A, converter output at node B, and the ground terminal at node C as shown in Figure 9.16(a). An example neuron's circuit diagram can take the form of Figure 9.16(b). The neuron shown in the figure implements n negative and p positive weights. Operational amplifiers $OA1$ and $OA2$ produce output voltages as a function of both inputs and digital control words. We thus have for the output voltages

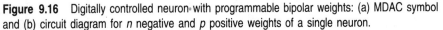

$$v_{o1} = -(x_1 D_{x1} + x_2 D_{x2} + \ldots + x_n D_{xn}) \qquad (9.28a)$$

and

$$v_{o2} = -(y_1 D_{y1} + y_2 D_{y2} + \ldots + y_p D_{yp})$$

or, briefly

$$v_{o1} = -\sum_{i=1}^{n} x_i D_{xi}$$

$$v_{o2} = -\sum_{i=1}^{p} y_i D_{yi}$$

(9.28b)

Operational amplifier $OA3$ serves as a unity-gain inverter. Linear combination of the two inputs $-v_{o1}$ and v_{o2} is subsequently computed by the inverting amplifier of gain $-K$ based on the operational amplifier $OA4$. We thus have for the output voltage

$$v_o = K(v_{o1} - v_{o2})$$

(9.29a)

The substitution of (9.28) into (9.29a) yields the neuron's output voltage determined by n negative and p positive weights as follows:

$$v_o = -\sum_{i=1}^{n} K D_{xi} x_i + \sum_{i=1}^{p} K D_{yi} y_i$$

(9.29b)

Again, this neuron implements a linear activation function of identity value with weights $-KD_{xi}$, for $i = 1, 2, \ldots, n$, and KD_{yi}, for $i = 1, 2, \ldots, p$. If, however, the output voltage v_o computed from (9.29) falls outside the linear output range (f_{sat-}, f_{sat+}) of an operational amplifier, then the neuron's output saturates at one of the levels f_{sat-} or f_{sat+}.

Both weighted-resistor and ladder-resistor MDACs can be implemented in integrated circuit technologies. Weighted-resistor MDACs require only as many individual resistors as bits in contrast to the ladder-resistor MDAC, which requires twice as many resistors. However, the spread of resistance values, or the ratio of the largest to the smallest resistance for weighted-resistor MDACs, is 2^N. Fabrication of integrated circuit resistors with extreme yet precise resistance values encounters technological difficulties. This limits the use of this type of MDAC to usually up to 5 or 6 bits. The ladder-type converter avoids this difficulty of extreme resistance values and is more suitable for high-accuracy resistance fabrication.

Let us look at an example of a neural network implementation that directly utilizes the described concepts. A neural network integrated circuit chip has been designed and fabricated using standard 3 μm CMOS technology MDAC's (Raffel et al. 1989). The converters are 4-bit with the fifth bit controlling the sign of the implemented weight. Converters are addressed using a 10-bit address bus, thus allowing for handling of 1024 programmable weights. In addition, there are 32 analog signal inputs to the chip. Up to 16 neurons can be configured using the chip circuitry when external amplifiers serving as current-to-voltage converters and neurons are added. The chip outputs 16 excitatory and 16 inhibitory currents to off-chip current-to-voltage converters. The outputs of the two converters are then fed into a differential amplifier-neuron providing analog levels compatible with the input levels on the chip. This particular feature enables building layered networks. The chip thus has a total of 79 analog and digital inputs and outputs, plus power supply lines. It is packaged in an 84-pin package. It occupies an active silicon area of 28 mm^2 and uses 28 500 transistors.

Let us look at some of the particularly interesting features of the chip. Figure 9.17(a) shows the circuit diagram of a pair of MDACs. The top converter produces an excitation current I_E, or positive weights; the other produces an inhibition current I_I, or negative weights. The E/I control bit determines which of the two converters is active. Weight voltages are encoded in 4-bit register $B1$ through $B4$. Weighted resistors are built of NMOS transistors biased in the resistive mode and controlled at their gates by the binary voltage levels. This should ensure the resistors' linearity for the limited range of input voltages as expressed by formula (9.21). Here, instead of adjusting the R_{ds} of individual weighted resistances through design of a suitable ratio W/L of individual transistors, all transistors have been made of identical sizes. The resulting weighted resistance value is determined by the configuration of transistors controlled by each bit. It can be seen that $B1$ controls two transistors in series; thus their total resistance is $2R_{ds}$. In contrast, $B4$ controls four transistors connected in parallel so their total resistance is $0.25R_{ds}$. In series with the weight-producing transistors are switch transistors controlled by the E/I bit. This bit determines whether the excitation MDAC (top) or the inhibition MDAC (bottom) contributes the current to the output currents I_E and I_I, respectively.

Figure 9.17(b) depicts the family of measured output current characteristics of a single MDAC as a function of input voltage v_{in}. The values of the digital control word D serve as parameters for each curve shown. The lowest nonzero $I(v_{in})$ characteristics is produced for $D = 1/16$; the top one is for $D = 15/16$. To maintain the linearity of the weighted resistances of the MDAC, the converter input voltage v_{in} was kept below 1 V. The output current nonlinearity was found to be within 5% for this input range.

The described chip has been successfully tested in several applications (Raffel 1989). In the first experiment, a Hamming network has been designed using the approach outlined in Section 7.1. The network has been implemented for 16-dimensional input vectors representing six different classes ($n = 16, p = 6$). Each of the six neurons in the Hamming network must be provided with bias input; therefore, fixed input voltages must be applied in addition to the weighted input voltages. The Hamming network requires weights with a single-bit resolution only since its binary weights are of values ± 1. Six distinct prototype vectors labeled A through F, one of each class, have been stored in the weights of the tested network.

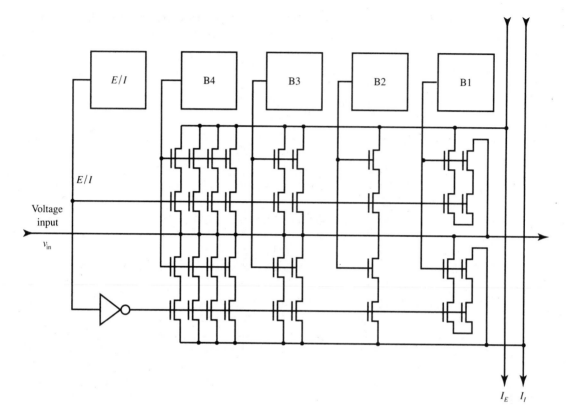

(a)

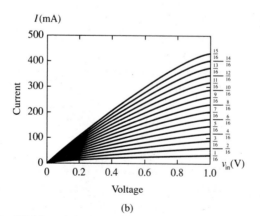

Voltage

(b)

Figure 9.17 MDACs pair for implementing positive or negative weights with 6.25% resolution: (a) circuit diagram and (b) output current of one of the MDACs. [©*Lincoln Laboratory Journal*, reprinted from Raffel et al. (1989) with permission.]

Figure 9.18(a) tabulates the results of the recall experiment performed by the network. Applied input vectors numbered 1 through 6 have been identical to the stored prototypes A through F. Each of the six output nodes labeled A through F is associated by the neural network with a stored vector bearing the same label. As expected, the corresponding output neuron's response A through F is the strongest for this set of inputs. This is highlighted on the diagonal of the matrix shown containing the highest responses circled and having measured values of 1130 or 1125 mV. The boxed numbers in the table of responses correspond to $HD = 8$, or a difference of 8 bits between an input and a stored prototype. For input vectors 7, 8, and 9 applied to the network, the detected prototypes at the smallest Hamming distance value are A, C, and A or B, respectively.

To test the chip operating with its full 4-bit resolution of weights, the network was configured as a 22-component vector correlator-classifier (first layer), followed by the MAXNET network (second layer and output node). The network diagram is depicted in Figure 9.18(b). Twenty two analog input voltages drive seven neurons, each of them representing one class, equivalent to a single cluster. This layer consists of 154 MDACs, one for each weight, connected to seven summing current-to-voltage converters. The second layer is configured as seven amplifiers, which amplify the difference of the input and feedback voltages. Inputs to this layer of neurons are from the first layer neurons, and from the single summing output node called here the feedback node. This node provides the output sum which is fed back to the inverting inputs of the differential amplifiers that constitute the second layer. The second layer of seven neurons and the output summing node operate jointly as MAXNET.

The discussed network configuration has been tested for classification of speech samples. The speech samples were the seven spoken numbers from "one" to "seven." The inputs to the network represent two concatenated 11-tuple vectors, each containing the spectral components from two 10-ms frames of the spoken numbers' samples. The network has been tested for 182 trials of different spoken digits. Seven misclassifications by the network were identified during the test.

Another implementation of programmable weights using MDACs is reported by Moopenn et al. (1990). A chip with 1024 weights utilizes 7-bit data latches to store the control words for the 7-bit weighted-resistance MDACs. The programmable weights implemented on the chip are of 6-bit resolution; the seventh bit is used for producing the weight polarity. To ensure the linearity of weights made of the drain-source resistances of NMOS transistors, long channel transistors are used in this design. Also, the high gate voltage of the switching transistor ensures operation within the linear range of drain-source characteristics of individual transistors serving as programmable resistances. The performance of the chip configured as a Hopfield network was successfully tested for generating the solution of the eight-city traveling salesman problem described in Section 5.6. The intercity distances were encoded in the programmable weight values.

Applied vector	Nearest stored vector	Output in millivolts					
		A	B	C	D	E	F
1	A	(1,130)	695	556	556	775	300
2	B	710	(1,125)	554	700	636	559
3	C	556	560	(1,125)	555	637	560
4	D	556	695	558	(1,125)	493	845
5	E	780	631	629	485	(1,130)	353
6	F	303	556	557	840	358	(1,130)
7	A	1,065	628	480	627	705	352
8	C	428	556	705	557	640	560
9	A & B	705	695	557	415	493	300

(a)

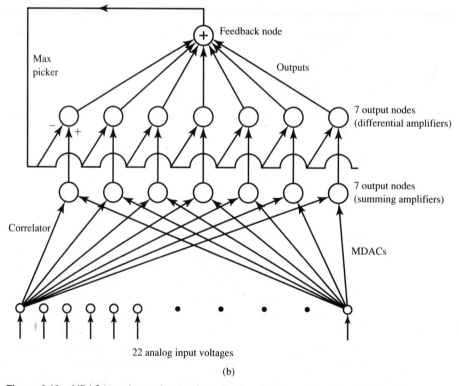

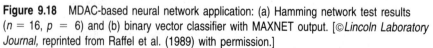

(b)

Figure 9.18 MDAC-based neural network application: (a) Hamming network test results ($n = 16$, $p = 6$) and (b) binary vector classifier with MAXNET output. [©*Lincoln Laboratory Journal,* reprinted from Raffel et al. (1989) with permission.]

Learning Weight Implementation

In our discussion so far, microelectronic analog weight, which transmits the signals between neurons, is typically represented by a channel conductance of an MOS transistor. The transistor's gate voltage is stored across the gate capacitance and performs the weight control function. Learning algorithms, however, have been considered so far to be running off-line. In this section we take a more challenging approach. Learning examined in this section is regarded as a continuous-time on-chip process, occurring while the network is responding to the present inputs. The learning signal is not switched on and off; thus, learning and recall are concurrent. However, the learning proceeds with its own dynamics, which is usually slower than the dynamics of the neural network recall.

Figure 9.19(a) shows an integrated circuit weight implementation that makes use of this concept. Weight value w_{ij} is determined by the weight control voltage v_c, which is supplied by the learning algorithm. One of the most interesting learning modes is Hebbian learning for which the learning signal is simply available at the neuron's output. This section covers the design of weights that learn according to the Hebbian rule discussed earlier in Section 2.5. The weight adjustments according to this unsupervised learning rule are $\Delta w_{ij} = c o_i x_j$ as expressed in (2.32).

The learning weight performs the computation of weight adjustment locally at the synapse. The key component for weight adjustment is the product of analog input and output voltages, $o_i x_j$. This particular computation can be implemented by components called *analog multipliers*. A number of multiplier configurations is available for integrated circuit implementation (Geiger, Allen, and Strader 1990; Allen and Holberg 1987). As we will see below, the analog product computation can be implemented by a simple two-transistor circuit.

Figure 9.19(b) shows the learning synapse using the simple circuit of an analog multiplier consisting of a pair of identical transistors $M3$, and $M4$ (Card, Schneider, and Moore 1991). Transistor $M1$ performs functions identical to transistor $M1$ on Figure 9.13. The synapse qualitatively approximates the multiplicative Hebbian correlation of input and output voltage levels, x_j and o_i. The learning current i_L is approximately proportional to the product $o_i x_j$ when voltage $v_c \cong 0$. This approximation for current is valid conditionally for an existing correlation between the variables x_j and o_j. It is supported by the following discussion as well as by the measurements illustrated below. Assume that current i_L starts flowing at $t = t_0$ into capacitor C due to the existing correlation between x_j and o_i. The weight control voltage v_c increases since

$$v_c(t) = \frac{1}{C} \int_{t_0}^{t} i_L(t) dt \tag{9.30a}$$

When continuous learning occurs and constant current $i_L(t) = I_L$ is assumed,

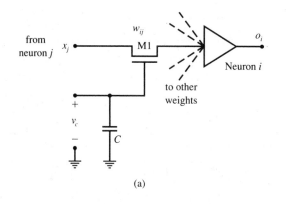

(a)

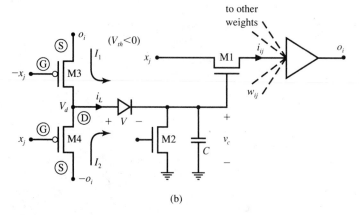

(b)

Figure 9.19 Electrically tunable weight w_{ij}: (a) without learning and (b) with learning embedded into the weight structure. [Part (b) adapted from Card, Schneider, and Moore (1991); © IEE, with permission.]

voltage $v_c(t)$ increases linearly in time since

$$v_c(t) = \frac{1}{C}\left[v_c(t_o) + tI_L\right] \tag{9.30b}$$

Let us examine in more detail how the learning of the weight value is accomplished in this circuit. Assume that the levels of neuron outputs exceed the magnitude of the threshold voltage of the enhancement mode PMOS devices used, thus $|x_j| > V_{th}$ and $|o_i| > |V_{th}|$. Three distinct learning conditions can be identified in this circuit as follows:

1. Both x_j and o_i are positive and therefore correlated. For $x_j > 0$ and $o_i > 0$, assume that $M3$ is conducting and $M4$ is cut-off. For $M3$, $M4$ we have, respectively

$$V_{gs3} = -x_j - o_i < V_{th}$$
$$V_{gs4} = x_j + o_i > V_{th}$$

Both inequalities are fulfilled unconditionally; our assumption has thus been correct; therefore, $M3$ is indeed conductive and $M4$ remains cut-off. Current I_1 flows through $M3$, provided that the diode is forward biased. This, in turn, is only guaranteed as long as the voltage v_c remains small enough, or o_i large enough, to keep the diode conductive.

Under certain conditions, $M3$ is found to be saturated and thus I_1 remains constant in time and independent of v_c, which increases linearly in such circumstances. Since the condition for saturation of a PMOS device, $V_{ds} < V_{gs} - V_{th}$, is equivalent to $V_d < V_g - V_{th}$, we obtain the following condition for saturation of $M3$:

$$V_d < -x_j - V_{th}$$

or

$$v_c + V < -x_j - V_{th}$$

The above formula indicates that $M3$ indeed remains saturated below a certain level of v_c. Otherwise, the condition is not fulfilled and $M3$ is operating in the resistive range.

2. Both x_j and o_i are negative and therefore correlated. For $x_j < 0$ and $o_i < 0$, assume that $M3$ is cut-off and $M4$ saturated. For $M3$, $M4$ we have, respectively

$$V_{gs3} = -x_j - o_i > V_{th}$$
$$V_{gs4} = x_j + o_i < V_{th}$$

Again, this proves that the assumption about the operating regions of $M3$ and $M4$ is correct; thus, $M3$ is indeed cut-off and $M4$ is conductive. Current I_2 flows through $M4$ provided again that the diode is forward biased. Similarly as in case 1 the voltage v_c can be shown to increase as a result of this process due to the existing correlation of x_j and o_i. Again, as in the previous case, I_2 remains constant in time for $M4$ saturated. The reader can verify that $M4$ is saturated when

$$v_c + V < x_j - V_{th}$$

Otherwise, $M4$ operates in the resistive range if this condition is not met.

3. For $x_j < 0$ and $o_i > 0$ with an additional assumption of $|x_j| \cong |o_i|$, we obtain $V_{gs3} = V_{gs4} \cong 0$. Both transistors are thus cut-off. As required, no learning takes place in this case and $I_L = 0$, since x_j and o_i are obviously anticorrelated.

Let us summarize the learning progress in this circuit. As the capacitor charges due to the computed correlation of o_i and x_j, the weight w_{ij} increases. The voltage at the node D is equal to v_c plus the forward-biased diode voltage drop V. It can be noticed that for a certain level of $v_c + V$, the voltage v_c ceases to increase and i_L stops flowing even though the product $o_i x_j$ is positive. Thus, the learning signal represented by i_L becomes affected by the acquired weight value $w_{ij}(t)$ and the weight learning process slows down, or even vanishes. It can therefore be seen that this circuit implements the Hebbian learning with saturation, because high weight values slow down further learning. Transistor $M2$ is used to control the leakage current, which now produces the intentionally embedded weight forgetting property of this circuit. The decay of weights because of leakage current through $M2$ occurs much slower than the learning so that the weight can memorize a large number of inputs / output pairs. The diode allows for decoupling of the learning and forgetting process so that their rates may be independently adjusted. The forgetting rate is usually several orders of magnitude slower than the learning rate.

The dimension of each synapse from Figure 9.19(b) implemented in 1.2-μm CMOS technology is 115×10.9 μm. The smallest length of the CMOS transistor channel in this technology is 1.2 μm. A synapse chip with an area of 1 cm^2 could contain approximately 75 000 individual learning weights. SPICE simulations have been performed for the weight model discussed (Card, Schneider, and Moore 1991). Figure 9.20(a) depicts the current i_{ij} through the weight as a function of the weight input voltage x_j with v_c being the parameter. Figure 9.20(b) shows the learning current i_L versus o_i, with x_j being a parameter for each of the four characteristics shown. The figure corresponds to the case $v_c = 0$ and therefore represents the maximum learning rate. It can be seen that the pair $M3$ and $M4$ performs well as an analog voltage multiplier, except for values o_i and x_j near the origin. The graphs reveal that small correlations existing between o_i and x_j are ignored by this multiplier.

Figure 9.20(c) illustrates the weight control voltage curves, v_c, versus current i_L. The figure displays four different positive correlation learning cases between o_i and x_j: (5 V, 5 V), (5 V, 3 V), (3 V, 5 V), (3 V, 3 V). Note that the fastest learning is observed for (5 V, 5 V); however, faster learning occurs for case (5 V, 3 V) than for case (3 V, 5 V). The figure clearly illustrates the learning with saturation by this weight circuit. It can also be seen, that the weight decay starts at $t = 30$ ns when the learning ceases and a slow weight value decay begins due to the discharge of C through $M2$.

9.3

ACTIVE BUILDING BLOCKS
OF NEURAL NETWORKS

Although the number of weights usually outnumbers the number of computing nodes, and the majority of the artificial neural network circuitry is composed of connections, an important part of the processing is performed outside synapses. Specifically, functions such as summing, subtracting, computing scalar products,

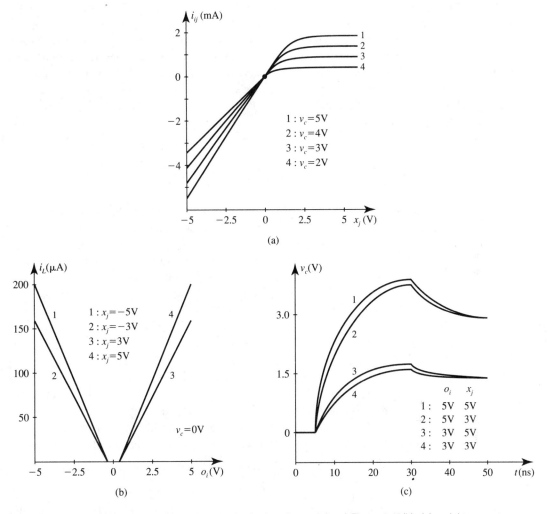

Figure 9.20 Simulation results for learning weight of Figure 9.19(b): (a) weight current versus input voltage, (b) learning current versus output voltage, and (c) learning rate and saturation phenomena ($t < 30$ns); followed by forgetting through weight decay ($t \geq 30$ns). [Adapted from Card, Schneider, and Moore (1991); © IEE, with permission.]

or nonlinear mapping are for the most part performed independently of synaptic weighting. A number of electronic functional circuits such as current mirrors, inverters, differential amplifiers, transconductance amplifiers, analog multipliers, and scalar product circuits can perform these operations. Integrated circuits able to implement these functions and designed using CMOS technology are covered in this section. To avoid duplication and maintain our focus of study on neural networks, the coverage of these building blocks is less comprehensive in this text than in more advanced microelectronic texts. Primary attention is devoted in this chapter to the circuits' applications in artificial neural systems rather than in their typical switching or amplifying configurations. For a more comprehensive study of building block circuit analysis and design, the reader may refer to a number of specialized microelectronic circuits texts available (Geiger, Allen, and Strader 1990; Allen and Holberg 1987; Millman and Grabel 1987; Sedra and Smith 1991).

Current Mirrors

A *current mirror* is one of the most essential building blocks of many analog integrated circuits, with artificial neural systems being no exception. A current mirror takes its input current and creates one or more copies of it at one or more of its outputs. The term *current amplifier* is also used for a current mirror since an input current change results in an output current change.

Figure 9.21(a) shows an example of a simple current mirror consisting of two matching NMOS transistors, $M1$ and $M2$. The current mirror produces output current I_{out} proportional to the input current I_{in} so that $I_{out} = \alpha I_{in}$, where α is the proportionality constant dependent on the transistor sizes and the fabrication process constants. For practical purposes, the relationship $I_{out} = \alpha I_{in}$ should be maintained in large range of input current variations. Note that since $V_{gs1} = V_{ds1}$, then the condition $V_{ds1} > V_{gs1} - V_{th1}$ is always fulfilled and, therefore, $M1$ is permanently saturated. Assuming that an additional condition is met, $V_{ds2} = v_{out} > V_{gs2} - V_{th2}$, both devices can be considered to be saturated. We thus obtain the mirror output/input current ratio (see Appendix):

$$\frac{I_{out}}{I_{in}} = \frac{k'(W_2/L_2)(V_{gs2} - V_{th2})^2(1 + \lambda V_{ds2})}{k'(W_1/L_1)(V_{gs1} - V_{th1})^2(1 + \lambda V_{ds1})} \tag{9.31a}$$

where λ stands for the channel length modulation effect. In our previous discussion of MOS transistor modeling, λ has been assumed to have a zero value without making a significant error. For the current mirror study, however, the simplifying assumption $\lambda = 0$ may lead to essential inaccuracies of the analysis. Since $V_{gs2} = V_{gs1}$ and $V_{th1} = V_{th2}$ for matching transistors, we obtain from (9.31a)

$$\frac{I_{out}}{I_{in}} = \frac{W_2/L_2}{W_1/L_1}\left(\frac{1 + \lambda V_{ds2}}{1 + \lambda V_{ds1}}\right). \tag{9.31b}$$

Ideally, I_{out}/I_{in} should only be a function of the aspect ratios (W/L) of both transistors. For identically sized transistors, and $V_{ds1} = V_{ds2}$, input and output current are then exactly equal. In such an ideal case, the current gain value α is equal to unity. In the case of $V_{ds2} \neq V_{ds1}$, however, the channel length modulation

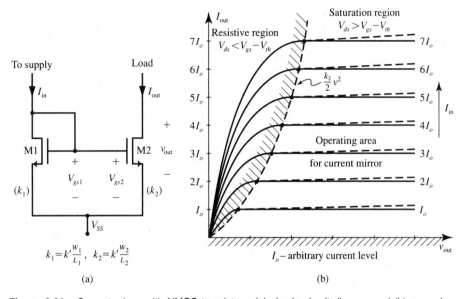

Figure 9.21 Current mirror with NMOS transistors: (a) simple circuit diagram and (b) example $I_{out} = f(I_{in})$ characteristics for unity-gain case [$(W_1 / L_1) = (W_2 / L_2)$].

factor λ causes the output current to be slightly different than the input current. For $\lambda = 10^{-2}V^{-1}$ (typically), I_{out} displays then a slight deviation from I_{in} that can be computed from (9.31b) for given values of drain-to-source voltages for both $M1$ and $M2$.

Figure 9.21(b) depicts the unity-gain current mirror characteristics. The current mirror operating area should be maintained in the saturation region of transistor $M2$. Therefore, v_{out} must satisfy the condition $v_{out} > V_{gs2} - V_{th2}$, which easily translates into the following inequality

$$v_{out} > \sqrt{\frac{2I_{out}}{k_2}} \tag{9.32}$$

where $k_2 = k'W_2/L_2$.

The output characteristics of the current mirror are shown in the figure as horizontal lines for the idealized case when $\lambda = 0$, thus indicating that the device reproduces the input current at its output in a wide range of output voltages v_{out}. A current mirror therefore behaves as both current source and current replicator. For more realistic MOS transistor modeling with $\lambda \neq 0$, the output current characteristics in the saturation region have nonzero slopes. This is shown in Figure 9.21(b) with dashed lines. It can be seen that the output current produced by the current mirror also depends to some extent on its output voltage. As a result, the device can therefore be considered a nonideal current source.

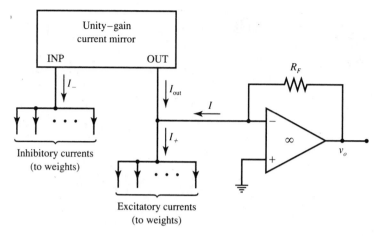

Figure 9.22 Current mirror use for computing the difference between the excitatory and inhibitory currents.

Current mirrors are ideally suited for detecting the differences of two currents. Specifically, they can be applied in artificial neural networks to compute the difference between an excitatory and an inhibitory current. This function can be performed by the unity-gain current mirror loaded with a current-to-voltage converter as shown in Figure 9.22. Noting that the current I to be converted is equal to the following current difference

$$I = I_+ - I_{out} \tag{9.33a}$$

and using the current mirror property of $I_- = I_{out}$ we obtain

$$I = I_+ - I_- \tag{9.33b}$$

Thus, the converter output voltage is of value

$$v_o = (I_+ - I_-)R_F \tag{9.34}$$

This result is valid provided the operational amplifier remains in the linear region and does not saturate. Otherwise, output voltage v_o takes either the positive or negative saturation value, f_{sat+} or f_{sat-}, respectively.

Three main reasons make the actual current mirror perform as a nonideal device: the channel length modulation effect, threshold voltage differences between transistors used, and imperfect geometrical matching of the fabricated transistors. Figure 9.23 shows three circuit diagrams of improved current mirrors. They are cascode (a), Wilson (b), and modified Wilson (c) types (Millman and Grabel 1987; Geiger, Allen, and Strader 1990; Sedra and Smith 1991). All of the current mirrors shown have distinctly more constant current I_{out} versus v_{out}, and reduced channel length modulation effect compared to the original simple two-transistor circuit from Figure 9.21(a).

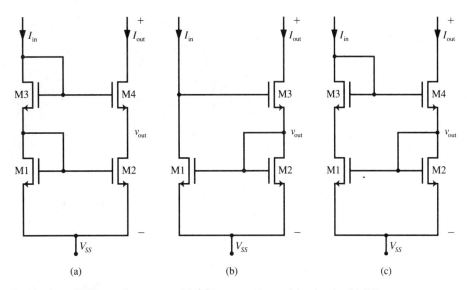

Figure 9.23 Basic configurations of MOS current mirrors: (a) cascode, (b) Wilson, and (c) modified Wilson

Inverter-based Neuron

Most neuron elements presented in this chapter have consisted of a suitably coupled operational amplifier circuit that simultaneously performed current summation, current-to-voltage conversion, and nonlinear mapping. We have noticed, however, that the activation functions of neurons designed so far with operational amplifiers are of limited form only. As discussed, they are (1) linear, (2) of finite gain, with the gain value determined by the slope of the linear part of the characteristics near the origin, and (3) beyond the linear region the characteristics saturated at f_{sat+} and f_{sat-} levels. In summary, all activation functions produced thus far have been either linear or piece-wise linear.

In numerous applications, however, the neurons' characteristics are required to have a sigmoidal shape of the activation function. "Sigmoidal" is used here in the sense of any smooth S-shaped curve, and it does not refer to any specific function. Such characteristics can be obtained as voltage transfer characteristics of a simple complementary circuit known in electronics as a "push-pull amplifier." This circuit behaves as a voltage inverter and is often used in logic circuits.

The CMOS inverter circuit is shown in Figure 9.24 and consists of complementary NMOS and PMOS transistors with drains tied together that also act as the output terminal. Gates are also connected to form the input, and sources are tied to two opposite supply voltages V_{DD} and $V_{SS} = -V_{DD}$, where $V_{DD} > 0$. The circuit performs as an inverting voltage amplifier with considerable voltage

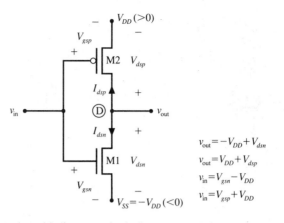

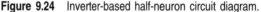

Figure 9.24   Inverter-based half-neuron circuit diagram.

gain near the origin. To derive the activation function for this circuit, we assume that there is full electrical symmetry between the NMOS and PMOS devices, or $k_n = k_p$. Symmetry also requires that both transistors' threshold voltages be of the same magnitude, which means $V_{thn} = -V_{thp}$.

To obtain the voltage transfer characteristics $v_{out}(v_{in})$ for this circuit let us use the equation

$$I_{dsn} + I_{dsp} = 0 \tag{9.35}$$

valid for the case of open-circuit inverter output. It can be seen that each of the transistors can be in one of the three regions: cut-off, resistive, or in saturation (see Appendix). Although the number of combinations of regions for two transistors in the pair is nine, only five pairs of stable states can exist in the entire range of input and output voltages (Zurada, Yoo, and Bell 1989).

To construct the output characteristics, we start with large negative input voltages v_{in} such that $v_{in} + V_{DD} < V_{thn}$. Since by inspection of the figure we have for the NMOS transistor

$$V_{gsn} = v_{in} + V_{DD} \tag{9.36a}$$

thus $M1$ remains as the cut-off. However, at the same time transistor $M2$ is fully on since its gate-to-source voltage is below V_{thp}. Indeed, we have for $M2$,

$$V_{gsp} = v_{in} - V_{DD} < V_{thp} \tag{9.36b}$$

However, since no current can flow through any of the two transistors connected in series due to the cut-off of $M1$, transistor $M2$ behaves as a short circuit between the drain and source. Also, the following condition holds for the resistive region of $M2$:

$$V_{dsp} > V_{gsp} + V_{thp} \tag{9.37}$$

We thus have for this region

$$v_{\text{out}} = V_{DD}, \quad \text{for } v_{in} < -V_{DD} + V_{thn}$$

Figure 9.25(a) shows the voltage transfer characteristics of this circuit. The discussed part of the characteristics is marked AB. In this operating range of the neuron transistor, $M1$ is the cut-off and $M2$ is in the resistive region.

When the input voltage reaches the level slightly above $-V_{DD} + V_{thn}$, the NMOS device enters the saturation region, the PMOS device remains in the resistive region and the channel currents start flowing with the following values:

$$I_{dsn} = \frac{k}{2}(V_{gsn} - V_{thn})^2 \tag{9.38a}$$

$$I_{dsp} = -k\left[(V_{gsp} - V_{thp})V_{dsp} - \frac{V_{dsp}^2}{2}\right] \tag{9.38b}$$

Let us now notice that (9.38a) and (9.38b) remain valid for the following conditions, respectively:

$$V_{dsn} > V_{gsn} - V_{thn} \ (M1 \ \text{saturated}) \tag{9.39a}$$

and

$$V_{dsp} > V_{gsp} - V_{thp} \ (M2 \ \text{resistive}) \tag{9.39b}$$

Using identities labeled on Figure 9.24 and expressing v_{in}, and v_{out} in terms of the transistors' terminal voltages and supply voltages allows for the expression of all voltages between transistor terminals as follows

$$V_{dsn} = v_{\text{out}} + V_{DD} \tag{9.40a}$$

$$V_{dsp} = v_{\text{out}} - V_{DD} \tag{9.40b}$$

$$V_{gsn} = v_{\text{in}} + V_{DD} \tag{9.40c}$$

$$V_{gsp} = v_{\text{in}} - V_{DD} \tag{9.40d}$$

Conditions (9.39) for the transistors' operating regions can now be rewritten to the form

$$v_{\text{out}} > v_{\text{in}} - V_{thn} \ (M1 \ \text{saturated}) \tag{9.41a}$$

$$v_{\text{out}} > v_{\text{in}} - V_{thp} \ (M2 \ \text{resistive}) \tag{9.41b}$$

The line $v_{\text{out}} = v_{\text{in}} - V_{thn}$ obtained from (9.41a) separates the resistive and saturation regions of $M2$ as shown in Figure 9.25(a). A straight line $v_{\text{out}} = v_{\text{in}} - V_{thp}$ obtained from (9.41b) is also shown in the figure. The line passes through point C and separates the saturation and resistive regions of $M1$.

Our objective in this step is to find v_{out} versus v_{in} for $M1$ saturated and $M2$ resistive, or beyond point B of the characteristics. This part of the input/output curve is responsible for the sigmoidal part of the neuron's activation function. Using relationships (9.40) again allows for rearranging expressions for currents

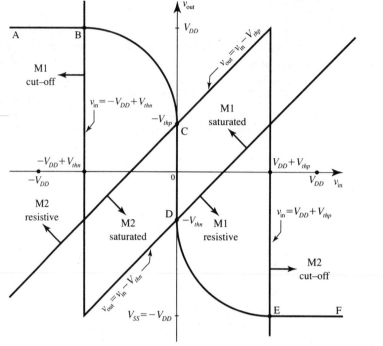

(a)

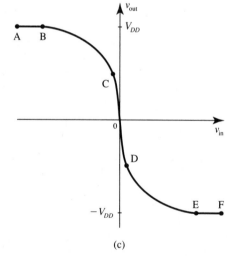

Region	M1	M2
AB	Cut-off	Resistive
BC	Saturated	Resistive
CD	Saturated	Saturated
DE	Resistive	Saturated
EF	Resistive	Cut-off

(b)

(c)

Figure 9.25 Voltage transfer characteristics of an inverter-based neuron (device and power supply symmetry assumed): (a) v_{out} versus v_{in} ($\lambda = 0$) (ideal transistors case), (b) regions of transistors operation, and (c) v_{out} versus v_{in}, ($\lambda \neq 0$) (nonideal transistors case).

as in (9.38) to the form

$$I_{dsn} = \frac{k}{2}(v_{\text{in}} + V_{DD} - V_{thn})^2 \tag{9.42a}$$

$$I_{dsp} = -k\left(v_{\text{in}} - V_{thp} - \frac{v_{\text{out}} + V_{DD}}{2}\right)(v_{\text{out}} - V_{DD}) \tag{9.42b}$$

It now follows from (9.35) that (9.42) can be rewritten as:

$$\frac{1}{2}(v_{\text{in}} + V_{DD} - V_{thn})^2 = \left(v_{\text{in}} - V_{thp} - \frac{v_{\text{out}} + V_{DD}}{2}\right)(v_{\text{out}} - V_{DD}) \tag{9.43}$$

This relationship is somewhat unwieldy for hand calculation but does provide the desired relationship between v_{in} and v_{out} in the concerned region of operation of the neuron. The relationship is graphed as part BC of the characteristics in Figure 9.25(a). When v_{in} reaches 0 V, the characteristics at point C crosses the region borderline and transistor $M2$ enters the saturation region. This results in two transistors being saturated simultaneously. The output voltage remains undefined in this CD part of the characteristics and $-V_{thn} < v_{\text{out}} < -V_{thp}$ for $v_{\text{in}} = 0$.

A summary of the operating regions for both transistors covering the complete characteristics is illustrated in Figure 9.25(b). The remaining part DEF of the characteristics can be obtained from a similar analysis using data in the two bottom rows of Figure 9.25(b). The discussion above makes use of the assumption that the channel length modulation effect is negligible in both transistors, or $\lambda = 0$. For a more realistic assumption $\lambda \neq 0$ We obtain the inverter characteristics as shown in Figure 9.25(c). The main difference here is that in contrast to the ideal case, this curve is of finite slope in the region CD when both $M1$ and $M2$ are saturated.

It is obvious that connecting two inverting half-neurons from Figure 9.24 in cascade yields a complete neuron element. The resulting input/output characteristics of the cascade connection is of the noninverting type and has a sigmoidal shape. This neuron configuration is especially well suited for building associative memory circuits or continuous-time gradient-type networks. Figure 9.26 depicts an example of a circuit diagram of an n-bit single-layer recurrent autoassociative memory using a cascade connection of two push-pull inverters as neurons. Due to the availability of both v_i and inverted output $\bar{v}_i$, positive as well as negative weights can be implemented in this circuit. The weight matrix of the memory network shown contains weights made of single-transistor resistances and controlled by the gate voltages. The transistors of this circuit need to operate in their linear region to maintain constant weight values as has been discussed in Section 9.2.

Differential Voltage Amplifiers

Throughout this chapter we have most often used integrated circuit operational amplifiers as versatile building blocks of microelectronic neural systems.

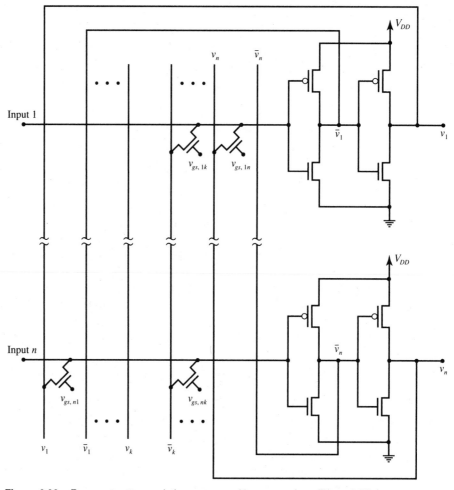

Figure 9.26   Recurrent autoassociative memory with neurons from Figure 9.25.

An operational amplifier is essentially a differential voltage amplifier of very high gain with voltage output. As we have seen, the negative feedback loop of the operational amplifier has to be closed to achieve its stable operation. However, differential voltage amplifiers exist that can operate without the negative feedback loop and their voltage gain is typically a hundred or more times lower than that of operational amplifiers. Such differential voltage amplifiers are very often used as input stages of operational amplifiers. This section is concerned with the properties of such *differential voltage amplifiers*. It also covers the basic concept of the transconductance amplifier. These two simple and closely related circuits have characteristics that make them desirable building blocks of microelectronic neural networks.

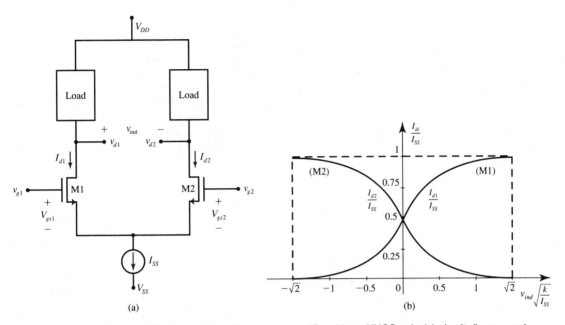

Figure 9.27 Basic differential voltage amplifier with an NMOS pair: (a) circuit diagram and (b) normalized transconductance characteristics for normalized differential input voltage.

Figure 9.27(a) shows the schematic of an NMOS differential voltage amplifier called briefly the differential pair. The circuit consists of a pair of matching NMOS transistors $M1$ and $M2$, two possibly symmetric loads, and a reference current source I_{ss}. Let us examine the pair's transfer characteristics, noting that the circuit should primarily serve as an amplifier of the differential voltage signal v_{ind} defined as follows:

$$v_{ind} \triangleq V_{gs1} - V_{gs2} \qquad (9.44a)$$

which is equal to

$$v_{ind} = v_{g1} - v_{g2} \qquad (9.44b)$$

Assume that transistors $M1$ and $M2$ are always in saturation, which is a reasonable assumption as we will see later from subsequent discussion and from the lines separating operating regions on Figure 9.28(a). For the saturation condition, we have the drain-to-source current of both transistors:

$$I_{di} = \frac{k_i}{2}(V_{gsi} - V_{thi})^2, \quad \text{for } i = 1, 2 \qquad (9.45a)$$

which leads to the following expression for V_{gs1} and V_{gs2}:

$$V_{gsi} = \sqrt{\frac{2I_{di}}{k_i}} + V_{thi}, \quad \text{for } i = 1, 2 \qquad (9.45b)$$

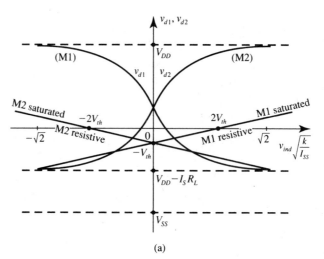

(a)

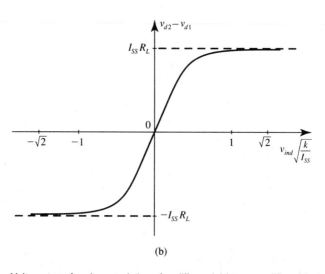

(b)

Figure 9.28 Voltage transfer characteristics of a differential input amplifier: (a) single-ended output configuration and (b) double-ended output (differential output) configuration.

This allows us to express v_{ind} from (9.44a) as a function of currents I_{d1} and I_{d2}:

$$v_{ind} = \sqrt{\frac{2I_{d1}}{k}} - \sqrt{\frac{2I_{d2}}{k}} \tag{9.46}$$

provided $V_{th1} = V_{th2}$, and $k_1 = k_2 = k$ for matching transistors. Observing that the reference current source establishes the sum of both channel currents I_{ds1} and I_{ds2} as equal to I_{ss}

$$I_{ss} = I_{d1} + I_{d2} \tag{9.47}$$

and forming a quadratic solution of (9.46) and (9.47) for I_{d1} and I_{d2} leads to

$$I_{d1} = \frac{I_{ss}}{2} + \frac{I_{ss}}{2}\left(\frac{kv_{ind}^2}{I_{ss}} - \frac{k^2 v_{ind}^4}{4I_{ss}^2}\right)^{1/2} \tag{9.48a}$$

$$I_{d2} = \frac{I_{ss}}{2} - \frac{I_{ss}}{2}\left(\frac{kv_{ind}^2}{I_{ss}} - \frac{k^2 v_{ind}^4}{4I_{ss}^2}\right)^{1/2} \tag{9.48b}$$

Due to the assumed saturation condition, expressions (9.48) are valid for the following limited range of differential input voltages:

$$-\sqrt{\frac{2I_{ss}}{k}} < v_{ind} < \sqrt{\frac{2I_{ss}}{k}} \tag{9.49}$$

The transfer characteristics I_{d1} versus v_{ind} and I_{d2} versus v_{ind} can now be sketched using (9.48) in the region of v_{ind} specified by (9.49). Figure 9.27(b) shows a plot of the normalized drain currents through transistors $M1$ and $M2$.

Assume that the loads of the driving transistors $M1$ and $M2$ from Figure 9.27(a) are resistors of an arbitrary value R_L. It can be seen that the output voltages v_{d1} and v_{d2} can be expressed as

$$\begin{aligned} v_{d1} &= V_{DD} - I_{d1}R_L \\ v_{d2} &= V_{DD} - I_{d2}R_L \end{aligned} \tag{9.50}$$

Equations (9.50) are plotted in Figure 9.28(a). The graphs depict the voltage transfer characteristics of a single-ended output differential-input amplifier with outputs being either v_{d1} or v_{d2}. The saturation regions for both transistors are also graphed on the figure. The equations of lines separating the transistors' operating regions are

$$\begin{aligned} v_{d1} &= \frac{v_{ind}}{2} - V_{th} \\ v_{d2} &= -\frac{v_{ind}}{2} - V_{th} \end{aligned} \tag{9.51}$$

and this indicates that the initial assumption about the two transistors being saturated is fulfilled in a rather large range of the differential input voltages. Let us also notice that the amplifier output can also be configured in the differential mode so that $v_{out} = v_{d2} - v_{d1}$. Such a connection ensures that the range of the output voltage covered by this configuration is between $-I_{ss}R_L$ and $I_{ss}R_L$. This can be seen from the double-ended differential-input characteristics shown in Figure 9.28(b).

Although the double-ended, or differential output, amplifier provides a desirable shape for the transfer characteristics and its gain is twofold compared to the single-ended stage, none of its two output terminals are grounded. To circumvent this rather impractical load configuration, a current mirror can be used to form the load. The advantage of such a configuration is that the differential output signal in the form of drain currents in the circuit of Figure 9.27(a) is converted to a single-ended output with the load grounded at one terminal.

The circuit configuration implementing this concept is shown in Figure 9.29(a). In this circuit, the output voltage or current is taken from the connected drains of transistors $M2$ and $M4$. The most essential feature of this arrangement is that by definition of the current mirror as in (9.33) we have in this circuit

$$I_{\text{out}} = I_{d1} - I_{d2} \tag{9.52}$$

This circuit providing the output variable of current I_{out} is also called the *transconductance amplifier*. It behaves like current source controlled by the differential input voltage v_{ind}.

Expressing currents I_{d1}, I_{d2} as in (9.48) allows for rewriting (9.52) as follows:

$$I_{\text{out}} = I_{ss} \left(\frac{kv_{ind}^2}{I_{ss}} - \frac{k^2 v_{ind}^4}{4I_{ss}^2} \right)^{1/2} \tag{9.53}$$

The transconductance of this circuit, g_m, is defined as

$$g_m = \frac{d(I_{\text{out}})}{d(v_{ind})} \bigg|_{v_{ind}=0} \tag{9.54}$$

Computation of g_m from (9.54) using (9.53) indicates that the transconductance g_m of the amplifier is identical to the transconductance of a single transistor $M1$ or $M2$ of the pair (Geiger, Allen, and Strader 1990) and is equal to

$$g_m = \sqrt{kI_{ss}} \tag{9.55}$$

If the load of the transconductance amplifier is resistive, then the circuit performs like an ordinary differential voltage amplifier with the voltage gain of value

$$\frac{d(v_{\text{out}})}{d(v_{ind})} = g_m R_L \tag{9.56}$$

The symbol of the transconductance amplifier is shown in Figure 9.29(b). It can be seen in this figure that the amplifier load is resistive. The differential voltage gain expression of (9.56) is only valid near the origin $v_{ind} = v_{\text{out}} = 0$. Similar to the transfer characteristics from Figures 9.27(b) and 9.28(b), the characteristics of the transconductance amplifier with resistive load also becomes strongly nonlinear for larger differential inputs v_{ind} and eventually it saturates. Typical curve v_{out} versus v_{ind} is shown in Figure 9.29(c). Since the currents of the differential amplifier in saturation are limited to $\pm I_{ss}$, the output voltage of the loaded transconductance amplifier is limited to between $-I_{ss}R_L$ and $I_{ss}R_L$.

The transconductance amplifier has several distinct characteristics different from the conventional high open-loop gain differential operational amplifier.

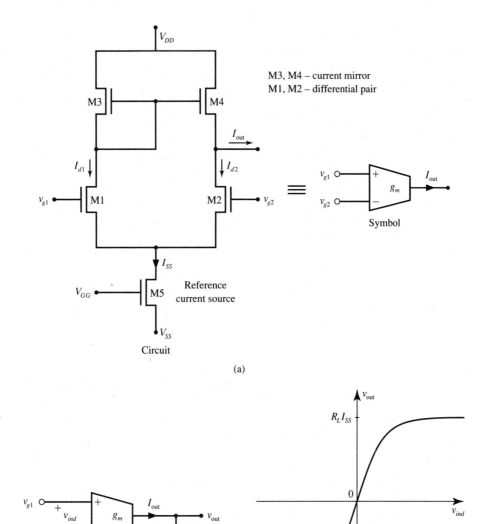

Figure 9.29 Transconductance (voltage-to-current) amplifier: (a) circuit diagram, (b) symbol of the transconductance amplifier loaded by a resistance R_L, and (c) voltage transfer characteristics for the circuit of part (b).

They are:

1. The voltage gain level of an operational amplifier is controlled by the ratios of resistance in the feedback loop to the resistances between the signal input and the operational amplifier input. In the transconductance amplifier, the gain is proportional to g_m, which is controlled by the internal supply current I_{ss}, as can be seen from expressions (9.55) and (9.56).

2. The voltage gain of the operational amplifier does not depend on the load resistance R_L as is the case for the transconductance amplifier [see Equation (9.56)]. This difference is due to the fact that the operational amplifier performs as a voltage source, and it has output stages with low output resistance. The transconductance amplifier performs as a current source producing current of certain value; its output voltage is thus proportional to the load resistance value.

3. The input/output voltage or current transfer characteristics of the transconductance amplifier characteristics have a sigmoidal shape. The transconductance amplifier computes an activation function with a smooth transition from the linear behavior to the behavior that is saturated. The counterpart characteristics of the operational amplifier are, rather, linear next to the origin and then displaying flat saturation far from the origin.

The simplicity of the design and the sigmoidal shape of the produced transfer characteristics make the transconductance amplifier a versatile building block of neural networks as will be shown later. One additional desirable feature of the transconductance amplifier is its high input resistance.

Scalar Product and Averaging Circuits with Transconductance Amplifiers

Transconductance amplifiers can be used to process voltage input signals and are able to produce current or voltage outputs. The circuit can be configured in a number of ways depending on its intended function. Figure 9.30(a) shows the voltage follower circuit using the transconductance amplifier with a negative feedback loop closed. Its output current i_o is proportional to the difference between the output voltage and the input voltage and is expressed by the following formula:

$$i_o = g_m(v_{in} - v_o) \tag{9.57}$$

Substituting $i_o = v_o/R$, the expression for the voltage gain of the voltage follower circuit becomes

$$\frac{v_o}{v_{in}} = \frac{g_m R}{1 + g_m R} \tag{9.58a}$$

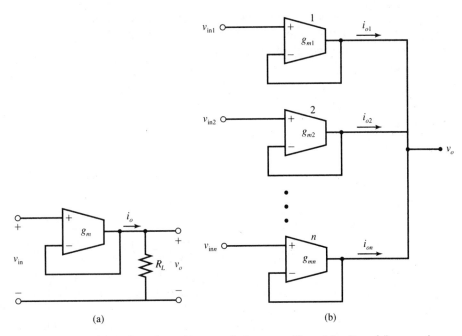

Figure 9.30 Useful configurations of transconductance amplifiers: (a) voltage follower and (b) follower-aggregation circuit.

If the follower is connected to a high-resistance load and $g_m R \gg 1$, the output voltage approximately follows the input voltage since we have

$$\frac{v_o}{v_{in}} \cong 1 \qquad (9.58b)$$

The most attractive property of the voltage follower as an electronic circuit building block is that the output voltage follows the input. However, no current is taken at its input, thus the circuitry that provides the signal v_{in} to the follower's input is not loaded due to the follower's very large input resistance value. Also, the follower's output voltage depends only on the input voltage and remains invariant under variable load conditions.

Several voltage followers can be connected to compute a scalar product or the average value of several input voltages (Mead 1989). The circuit diagram for such a computational function of interconnected transconductance amplifiers is depicted in Figure 9.30(b). The configuration is called the *follower-aggregation circuit*. Each amplifier i has a transconductance g_{mi}. Each voltage follower supplies an output current proportional to the difference between the input voltage and the output voltage. The contribution of each input v_{ini} is weighted by the transconductance of the associated amplifier.

For the output node of voltage v_o we can express the total current as a sum of contributions $g_{mi}(v_{\text{in}i} - v_o)$, for $i = 1, 2, \ldots, n$. Since no current leaves the output node we have

$$\sum_{i=1}^{n} g_{mi}(v_{\text{in}i} - v_o) = 0 \tag{9.59}$$

Rearranging the terms of (9.59) and computing v_o yields

$$v_o = \frac{\sum_{i=1}^{n} g_{mi} v_{\text{in}i}}{\sum_{i=1}^{n} g_{mi}} \tag{9.60}$$

Equation (9.60) shows that the output voltage v_o is the weighted average of inputs $v_{\text{in}i}$, and that each input voltage is weighted by its transconductance. Thus, the follower-aggregation circuit shown in the figure computes the weighted sum of n input voltages, with transconductances g_{mi} serving as the weighting coefficients. This function can also be interpreted as computing the average value of an ensemble of inputs. In another interpretation, the output voltage v_o as in (9.60) can be understood to be a scalar product of weights and inputs, with the expression $\left(\sum_{i=1}^{n} g_{mi}\right)^{-1}$ serving as the proportionality constant.

Formula (9.60) is only valid for the range of input voltages $v_{\text{in}i}$ that ensures the linear operation of each transconductance amplifier. If one of the input voltages $v_{\text{in}i}$ is of excessive positive or negative value, the corresponding transconductance amplifier saturates and does not contribute beyond its bias current. This feature limits the effect of a possible faulty or out of bounds value in the averaging of a large number of signals. Thus, the voltage v_o will not follow a few off-scale inputs. The discussed implementation of the averaging circuit using voltage followers has great robustness against bad data points (Mead 1989).

Current Comparator

A current comparator circuit offers another useful alternative solution to the task of summation of inhibitory and excitatory currents, which are produced in synaptic connections at the neuron's input. The comparator sums the inhibitory and excitatory currents flowing through the weights and performs the nonlinear mapping of their difference into the output voltage. The comparator's output voltage may be required to have sigmoidal characteristics as a function of a differential current $I_+ - I_-$. Figure 9.31 shows a typical circuit diagram for a CMOS current comparator. It uses two p-channel current mirrors consisting of transistors $M1$, $M2$ and $M3$, $M4$, one n-channel current mirror consisting of transistors $M5$, $M6$, and one CMOS inverter as a thresholding element (Bibyk and Ismail 1990). The inverter, composed of $M7$ and $M8$, should preferably be electrically symmetric.

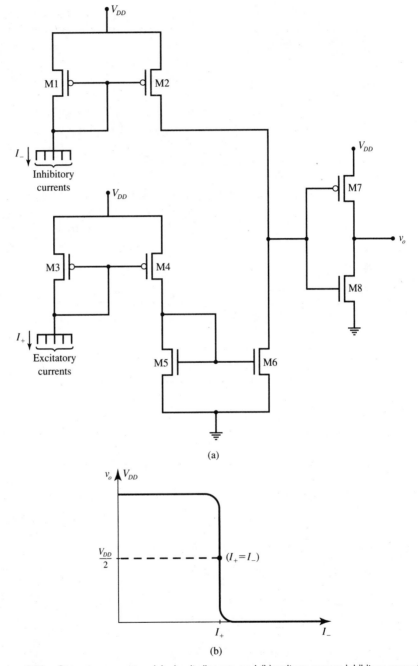

Figure 9.31 Current comparator: (a) circuit diagram and (b) voltage versus inhibitory current characteristics.

The sum of all excitatory currents, I_+, is mirrored through the n-channel current mirror, and it flows through $M6$. At the same time the sum of all inhibitory currents flows out from transistor $M2$. If $I_+ = I_-$, then $M2$ and $M6$ will source and sink, respectively, the same amount of current. The output voltage in such a case is equal to $V_{DD}/2$. Any imbalance of currents such that $I_+ < I_-$ causes the output voltage v_o to decrease from its quiescent, center value of $V_{DD}/2$. This is shown in Figure 9.31(b). When $I_+ > I_-$, a reverse situation occurs and the output voltage increases. For proper operation of this circuit, the sizing of transistors must be such that the current mirror transistor in each of the three mirrors must remain in saturation during the entire operating range of total excitatory and inhibitory currents. Each of the currents consists of n synaptic component currents produced by the input component signal weight. In addition, the current mirror design has to provide for accurate balance such that $v_o = V_{DD}/2$ at $I_- = I_+$. This is ensured when $M2$, $M6$ and $M7$, $M8$ are electrically identical transistor pairs.

Template Matching Network

As discussed in previous chapters, template matching represents one of the frequently used forms of neural processing. Template matching can be of particular importance for handling images in bit-map form, and is especially suitable for preprocessing of the binary data. Template matching networks are typically required to decode binary n-tuple vectors and output the logic level that is unique and different from any outputs that are produced for n-tuple inputs that do not match the specified template. From this standpoint, an output of the template matching network can be expressed as a combinational Boolean function. Perhaps the most suitable Boolean function for this task is called an equivalency function. It is defined as a complement of an XOR function. A number of techniques exist to design Boolean functions of interest. Although the operation of matching using these well-known techniques can be easily implemented using conventional digital logic gates, we will focus in this section on a design that is analog in nature and possibly involves only a single transistor per bit to be matched (Chung 1991). This ensures the minimum size of the matching network, with only a single transistor per weight, and it provides for analog operation and binary decision output.

An example bit-map template to be matched is shown in Figure 9.32(a). The template shown is represented by the vector $\mathbf{x} = \begin{bmatrix} 1 & 0 & \times & 1 \end{bmatrix}^t$, where $\times$ stands for a "do not care" condition. The simple CMOS network of Figure 9.32(b) consists of up to four transistors $M0$–MB, one per bit, plus a bias transistor MB, and it can realize the template bit-map matching function of interest. The transistors are sized in such a way that only the matching bit input pattern results in $v_{\text{in}} > V_{DD}/2$. This requires symmetrical transfer characteristics for the

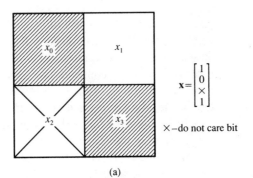

$$\mathbf{x} = \begin{bmatrix} 1 \\ 0 \\ \times \\ 1 \end{bmatrix}$$

$\times$ – do not care bit

(a)

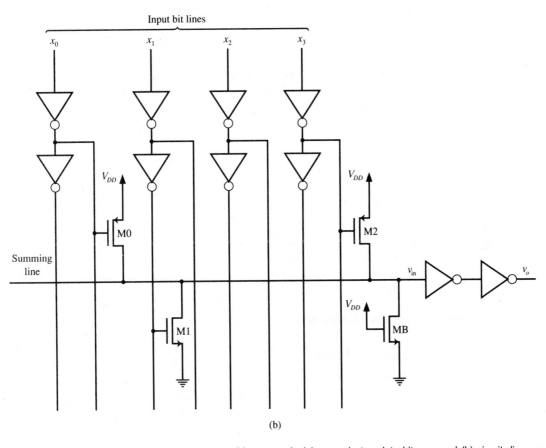

(b)

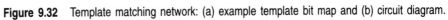

Figure 9.32 Template matching network: (a) example template bit map and (b) circuit diagram.

two output inverters, which produce the voltage v_o as a function of v_{in} such that $v_o = V_{DD}/2$ when $v_i = V_{DD}/2$.

When the input matches the value of 1 stored in the template, this turns on the single PMOS bit transistor. This occurs since the gate voltage of the PMOS device is pulled down to zero; see transistors $M0$ and $M2$ as examples. The channel resistance of value R then connects the power supply to the summing line, as would be the case when $x_0 = x_3 = 1$ for the example network. For a matching bit of zero value, the corresponding bit transistor of the NMOS type remains open. This will be the case for $M1$ responding to $x_1 = 0$.

Assume now that the bias transistor MB, which is always conductive, also has a channel resistance value of R. Note that when $M0$ and $M2$ are turned on in parallel, they represent the total resistance of $0.5R$ from the summing line to the V_{DD} node. Since the total resistance connected between the summing line and the ground is of value R, this yields a value of ⅔ for the voltage division ratio at the summing line. As a result, $v_{in} = (2/3)V_{DD}$, and the output voltage is high, thus indicating that a matching input vector is present at the input bit lines. The reader can easily verify that for a mismatch of one or more bits, the summing line voltage drops below the value $V_{DD}/2$ and the output voltage v_o can be interpreted as assuming a logic low value.

To design the more general bit template matching network exemplified in Figure 9.32, all transistors must be electrically identical. This requires their device transconductances to be identical so as to yield the resistances of value R when the devices are conductive. In addition, the bias transistor MB needs to be sized properly so that the matching input vector yields the value of v_{in} above $0.5V_{DD}$. More detailed inspection of the network leads to the observation that the bias transistor resistance should be chosen equal to $R/(n-1)$, where R is the resistance of each of the bit transistors and n is the number of bits equal to 1 in the template to be matched (see Problem 9.20).

9.4

ANALOG MULTIPLIERS AND SCALAR PRODUCT CIRCUITS

Electrically tunable synapses make it possible to multiply the input signal x_i times the associated adjustable weight value. In a case for which the weight value w_i is a function of the control voltage, the scalar product of input and weight vector can be expressed in the following form:

$$net = \sum_{i=1}^{n} w_i(v_{ci})x_i \tag{9.61a}$$

where the i'th weight value is dependent on the controlling voltage v_{ci}, for $i = 1, 2, \ldots, n$. This approach to computing the product of weight and the input signal based on (9.61a) has been used in most discussions of the analog implementations of neural circuitry with tunable weights presented thus far in this chapter.

Alternatively, the scalar product of an electrically tunable weight vector and of the n-tuple input signal vector can be obtained as a sum of outputs $v_i x_i$ of analog voltage multipliers as follows:

$$net = c \sum_{i=1}^{n} v_i x_i \tag{9.61b}$$

where v_i is the voltage directly proportional to the weight value w_i, and c is the proportionality constant common for all n weights under consideration. In contrast to the approach taken in (9.61a), now the weight value can be represented directly using the variable voltage v_i.

Essentially, the approach based on (9.61b) tends to be slightly more costly to use. Expression (9.61a) allows for implementation of the product of an input variable and of a weight value dependent on a weight control voltage considered to be a parameter. In (9.61b), weights are treated as direct voltage variables rather than as constants controlled by electrical variables. Thus, the products of input signals and weights are obtained through simple analog multiplication.

Below we look at several implementation techniques of analog multipliers. We will also cover scalar product circuits that make use of analog multipliers. Such circuits often prove useful for building artificial neural systems.

Depletion MOSFET Circuit

A simple integrated circuit analog multiplier can be built from all MOS components (Khachab and Ismail 1989a). The circuit requires an operational amplifier and fully matched depletion mode NMOS transistors working in pairs. The multiplier can operate with both positive and negative input voltages. The basic multiplier circuit diagram is shown in Figure 9.33(a). The input voltage is x, and the gate voltage v of transistor $M2$ is used to express the weight value.

Since both transistors need to remain in the resistive region in this circuit arrangement, their drain currents for $V_{gs} < V_{ds} - V_{dep}$ are expressed as

$$I_{ds} = k \left[(V_{gs} - V_{dep}) V_{ds} - \frac{V_{ds}^2}{2} \right] \tag{9.62}$$

where V_{dep} is the depletion voltage of each transistor, typically having a value between -2 and -4 V. Since for $M1$ we have $V_{ds} = V_{gs} = x$, expression (9.62) can be rewritten for this device:

$$I_{ds1} = k \left[(x - V_{dep})x - \frac{x^2}{2} \right] \tag{9.63a}$$

Note that for the transistor $M2$ we have $V_{ds} = x$ and $V_{gs} = x + v$; thus, expression

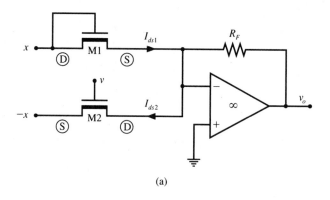

(a)

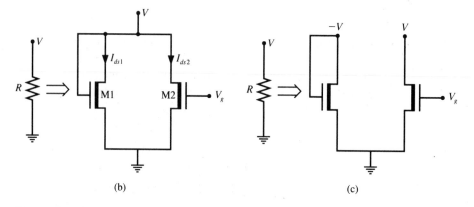

(b)   (c)

Figure 9.33 Analog multiplier with two depletion mode MOS transistors and an operational amplifier: (a) circuit diagram, (b) integrated circuit implementation of resistance, and (c) another version of part (b).

(9.62) for the drain current becomes

$$I_{ds2} = k\left[(x + v - V_{dep})x - \frac{x^2}{2}\right] \tag{9.63b}$$

Figure 9.33(a) shows that the difference between currents I_{ds1} and I_{ds2} is converted to the output voltage v_o by the closed-loop operational amplifier configured as a current-to-voltage converter. We thus have

$$v_o = -(I_{ds1} - I_{ds2})R_F \tag{9.64a}$$

Plugging expressions (9.63) into (9.64a) results in the following output voltage for the analyzed analog multiplier when it is working in the linear region of the operational amplifier:

$$v_o = R_F kvx \tag{9.64b}$$

The nonlinear (quadratic) terms of I_{ds1} and I_{ds2} have canceled due to the subtraction of both currents. Expression (9.64b) therefore remains valid provided both depletion mode transistors operate in the resistive region. Thus, the following condition must be fulfilled:

$$|v + x| \le \left| V_{\text{dep}} \right|$$

Formula (9.64b) implies that the circuit of Figure 9.33(a) is able to perform four-quadrant multiplication. The multiplication constant of the obtained multiplier is proportional to the transconductance value k of the transistors used, and to the user-selected feedback resistance R_F. Thus, the multiplication constant can be suitably adjusted by the choice of R_F.

An all-MOS realization of this multiplier can be accomplished by replacing the feedback resistor with two depletion mode transistors operating again in the resistive region. Two possible replacement circuit diagrams for resistors are shown in Figures 9.33(b) and 9.33(c). Drain currents for transistors $M1$, and $M2$ can be obtained for the matching transistor pair $M1$, $M2$ of Figure 9.33(b), respectively, as

$$I_{ds1} = kV \left(\frac{V}{2} - V_{\text{dep}} \right) \tag{9.65a}$$

$$I_{ds2} = k \left[(V_g - V_{\text{dep}})V - \frac{V^2}{2} \right] \tag{9.65b}$$

Expression (9.65b) is in a standard form (see Appendix) with the condition $V_{ds} = V$. Expression (9.65a) is obtained from the same standard form with additional simplification such that $V_{ds} = V = V_{gs}$. Since the value of the equivalent resistance implemented by the two transistors connected in parallel can be expressed as follows

$$R = \frac{V}{I_{ds1} + I_{ds2}} \tag{9.66a}$$

substituting I_{ds1} and I_{ds2} from (9.65) into (9.66a) results in the following formula:

$$R = \frac{1}{k(V_g - 2V_{\text{dep}})} \tag{9.66b}$$

It can be seen that V_g is the control voltage used to tune the value of the equivalent feedback resistor. The resistance value also depends on the depletion voltage V_{dep} of the transistors used. Figure 9.34(a) shows the voltage/current characteristics of the all-MOS resistor of Figure 9.33(b). The curves shown were obtained from the circuit simulation using the SPICE2G.1 program for $V_g = 2$ V, $k = 20$ $\mu A/V^2$, and for four values of V_{dep} as tabulated in Figure 9.34(b) (Rao 1988).

As stated before, the discussed circuit configuration functions properly only for the resistive mode of operation of both $M1$ and $M2$ and thus the following

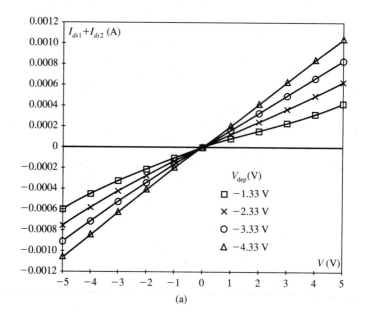

(a)

V_{dep}(V)	R at V = 0 V (simulated) (kΩ)	R (from (9.66b)) (kΩ)
−1.33	10.7	10.729
−2.33	7.5	7.507
−3.33	5.8	5.774
−4.33	4.5	4.609

(b)

Figure 9.34 Characteristics of the all-depletion mode MOS resistor of Figure 9.33(b) (V_g = 2 V) for V_{dep} as a parameter: (a) voltage versus current characteristics and (b) equivalent resistance values.

condition must apply:

$$V + V_g \leq \left| V_{dep} \right| \tag{9.67a}$$

In this particular circuit application, the general condition (9.67a) takes the form

$$v_o + V_g \leq \left| V_{dep} \right| \tag{9.67b}$$

In contrast to the configuration discussed, the resistance produced by the configuration illustrated in Figure 9.33(c) does not depend on the value of the depletion voltage V_{dep} of the transistors used. Calculations similar to those performed for the resistor of Figure 9.33(b) yield the following equivalent resistance value

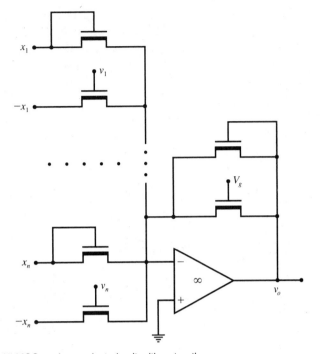

Figure 9.35 All-MOS scalar product circuit with saturation.

for this circuit:

$$R = \frac{1}{kV_g} \tag{9.68}$$

However, to achieve cancellation of both nonlinear terms in the current expressions (9.65) and of V_{dep}, the input voltages to the multiplier of opposite polarities must be produced and used as inputs for this configuration.

The discussed analog multiplier cell from Figure 9.33(a) can be replicated n times to implement the full scalar products as expressed in (9.61b). Weight coefficients can be either positive or negative—depending on the polarity of voltage v used to control the sign and weight value. Figure 9.35 shows the circuit diagram of the scalar product circuit. It computes the following expression, which is a linear combination of the terms of Equation (9.64b):

$$v_o = R_F(k_1 v_1 x_1 + k_2 v_2 x_2 + \ldots + k_n v_n x_n) \tag{9.69}$$

where k_i is the transconductance coefficient of transistors in the i'th input pair, for $i = 1, 2, \ldots, n$.

Expression (9.69) becomes similar to (9.61b) for all transistors of identical electrical parameters when $k_1 = k_2 = \ldots = k_n$. The saturation level, as well as the steepness of the activation function, are set by the voltage V_g, which controls the feedback resistance R_F according to either (9.66b) or (9.68), depending on the resistor configuration used. Both voltage values x_i and $-x_i$ are required to drive the inputs of a single synapse of this scalar product circuit. These double-polarity inputs are intrinsically available when neurons are comprised of cascaded inverting amplifiers, or push-pull inverters, as described earlier in this chapter (Bibyk and Ismail 1989).

Enhancement Mode MOS Circuit

The basic concept of analog multipliers using all-MOS integrated circuitry presented in the last section can be extended to circuits with enhancement mode field-effect devices or other types of active devices. Again, the common-mode nonlinear terms of a transistor's nonlinear current characteristics can be eliminated, and the difference current signal can develop the product of two input voltages at the output of the analog multiplier. The circuit diagram of the analog multiplier cell is depicted in Figure 9.36 (Khachab and Ismail 1989b). The circuit comprises a single operational amplifier and four electrically identical, matched MOS input transistors that could be enhancement or depletion, and both either n- or p-type.

Using the model of the transistors in the resistive region and with reference to the notation of Figure 9.36, the current differences at the inputs of the operational amplifier can be expressed as follows (Khachab and Ismail 1989b):

$$I_1 - I_2 = k' \left(\frac{W}{L}\right)_i (x_1 - x_2)(y_1 - y_2) \tag{9.70a}$$

$$I_1' - I_2' = k' \left(\frac{W}{L}\right)_f v_o(z_1 - z_2) \tag{9.70b}$$

where $(W/L)_i$ and $(W/L)_f$ are width/length ratios of the transistors' channels in the input and feedback paths, respectively. Applying the KCL at each input node of the operational amplifier we obtain

$$I_1 - I_2 = I_2' - I_1' \tag{9.71}$$

Hence, the output voltage v_o becomes from (9.70)

$$v_o = \frac{(W/L)_i}{(W/L)_f} \frac{(x_1 - x_2)(y_1 - y_2)}{z_1 - z_2} \tag{9.72}$$

To ensure the operation of all transistors in the resistive region, the following conditions must apply at the input and output, respectively, of the multiplier

$$x_1, x_2 \le \min(y_1 - V_{th}, y_2 - V_{th})$$
$$v_o \le \min(z_1 - V_{th}, z_2 - V_{th}) \tag{9.73}$$

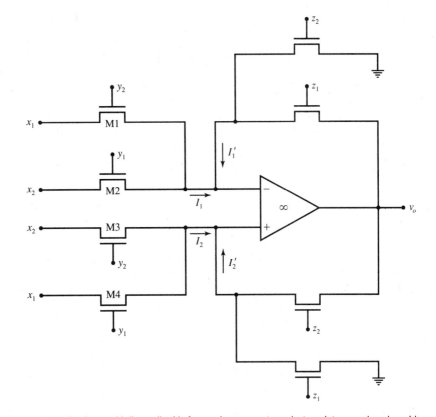

Figure 9.36 Analog multiplier cell with four enhancement mode transistors and a closed-loop operational amplifier.

where V_{th} is the threshold voltage of the matched MOS devices. As can be seen from (9.72), the circuit achieves the product computation of difference input voltages $x_1 - x_2$ and $y_1 - y_2$. In addition, the necessary biasing levels must be provided at the feedback transistors' gates dependent on the type of transistors used. Enhancement mode n-type transistors require positive gate voltages exceeding V_{th} if they are to operate properly. Depletion transistors, however, can accept positive, zero, or negative bias voltages at their gates.

Let us require the four-quadrant multiplication to be performed by the multiplier cell with weight control voltage v, and for the input voltage x applied at gate and input terminals, respectively. Letting

$$x_1 = -x_2 = x$$
$$y_1 = Q_o + v, \quad y_2 = Q_o - v \qquad (9.74)$$
$$z_1 = V_{g1}, \quad z_2 = V_{g2}$$

we obtain expression (9.72) for the multiplier's output voltage, which reduces to the desired form containing a product of analog voltages x and v:

$$v_o = \frac{4(W/L)_i}{(W/L)_f(V_{g1} - V_{g2})}xv \tag{9.75}$$

Note that a scalar product of two n-tuple vectors can be achieved by a straight-forward extension of the simple two-input multiplier just described. In such a case, a total of n four-transistor circuits (as in Figure 9.36) is needed to combine into products all n inputs and n weight control voltages applied at gates. Weights are set equal to the gate control voltages v_i, for $i = 1, 2, \ldots, n$, and inputs are x_i, for $i = 1, 2, \ldots, n$.

Analog Multiplier with Weight Storage

An alternative analog multiplier circuit useful for neural network applications can be designed using a matched pair of enhancement type NMOS and PMOS transistors connected in a differential mode (Kub et al. 1990). An example of a circuit that uses two PMOS devices is shown in Figure 9.37. The weight values are represented by the analog voltage v at the output of the switch $M3$, which serves as an access transistor. The short-term weight storage capacitor C is connected to the gate of transistor $M1$. The capacitor is charged to the weight control voltage v for normal weight operation during recall. Capacitor C can be either an intrinsic gate capacitance of transistor $M1$ or a specially formed capacitor structure.

For transistors $M1$ and $M2$, both in resistive regions, the drain-to-source currents can be expressed as

$$I_{ds1} = k\left[(v - V_{th})x - \frac{x^2}{2}\right] \tag{9.76a}$$

$$I_{ds2} = k\left[(v_R - V_{th})x - \frac{x^2}{2}\right] \tag{9.76b}$$

where v_R is the weight reference voltage applied at the gate of transistor $M2$ and assumed here to be constant. It is also assumed that $V_{ds} > V_{gs} - V_{th}$ since both $M1$ and $M2$ must remain in the resistive region to ensure an appropriate operation of this multiplier. The difference current can be obtained using (9.76) as

$$I_{ds1} - I_{ds2} = k(v - v_R)x \tag{9.77}$$

Inspection of Figure 9.37 reveals that the output voltages v_{o1} and v_{o2} are equal, respectively,

$$\begin{aligned} v_{o1} &= I_{ds1}R_F \\ v_{o2} &= I_{ds2}R_F \end{aligned} \tag{9.78}$$

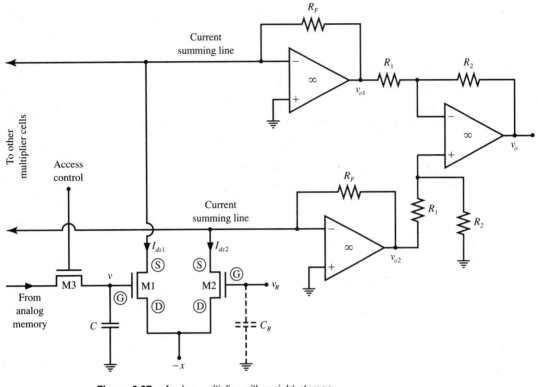

Figure 9.37 Analog multiplier with weight storage.

provided that both current-to-voltage converters work in the linear part of their operational amplifier characteristics. The output operational amplifier is connected as a difference amplifier so as to yield the amplified difference voltage of value

$$v_o = (v_{o2} - v_{o1})\frac{R_2}{R_1} \qquad (9.79a)$$

In the linear range of operation of the output operational amplifier its output voltage can be expressed from (9.77-9.78) as given:

$$v_o = k\frac{R_2}{R_1}R_F(v_R - v)x \qquad (9.79b)$$

Note from (9.79b) that the resistances R_1, R_2, and R_F can be used to control the steepness of the activation function in the linear region. As explained in the previous section, these values also set the range of the analog product value and its linear or nonlinear mapping to the output v_o. Obviously, if n multipliers are connected to each of the current summing lines, we obtain the total of I_{ds} currents of each line as n-tuple sums. In such cases, the output voltage v_o expressed for a single weight by expression (9.79) yields the scalar product as follows:

$$v_o = k\frac{R_2}{R_1}R_F \sum_{i=1}^{n}(v_{Ri} - v_i)x_i \tag{9.80}$$

where v_{Ri} is the reference voltage of the i'th weight.

A 11×11 matrix-vector multiplier based on the discussed concept has been implemented in CMOS p-well technology (Kub et al. 1990). Measurements of analog capacitive storage characteristics have shown that the weight decay rate due to the lack of weight refresh has been 30 mV/s at room temperature. The intrinsic gate capacitances with an estimated value of 90 fF have been used as capacitive storage elements. The weight values have been permanently stored in electrically erasable programmable read-only memory (EEPROM) or RAM in digital form. The analog weight voltage values have been provided at the inputs to the access transistors as output signals of digital-to-analog converters.

Substantial reduction of the weight control voltage decay rate has been achieved in the circuit of Figure 9.37 by adding a second capacitance C_R at the gate of transistor $M2$. Since the leakage currents of the gate capacitances of $M1$ and $M2$ are similar, they tend to cancel each other when the multiplier output currents are subtracted. In the measured integrated circuit with both C and C_R used, the decay rate has dropped to 0.6 mV/s. This configuration, however, has required the addition of another access transistor $M4$ to store the weight reference voltage v_R (transistor $M4$ not shown in the figure). The multiplier cell from Figure 9.36 with three transistors fabricated using the 3-μm p-well CMOS technology was of 56 μm^2. The entire chip consisted of 11×11 matrix-vector multiplier circuitry. It has been configured to compute 11 scalar products simultaneously, each with 11-tuple vectors.

Floating-Gate Transistor Multipliers

Floating-gate transistors offer rather simple and efficient circuit implementation techniques for artificial neural systems. In particular, the technique is suitable for designing large networks fabricated with modern VLSI technologies (Bibyk and Ismail 1990). The most attractive feature of floating-gate MOS transistors used as analog multipliers for neural networks is that both the weight storage and analog multiplication of weights and inputs are implemented concurrently and by the same circuitry. The floating-gate transistors provide an adjustable, non-volatile analog memory, and, simultaneously, they behave as analog processors when appropriately connected.

The cross-section of a floating-gate MOS transistor is shown in Figure 9.38(a). The device is similar to the MOS transistor, but in addition to the regular gate shown as a top layer, it has one more layer of polysilicon to store a trapped charge. Once the charge is trapped in this layer called the floating gate,

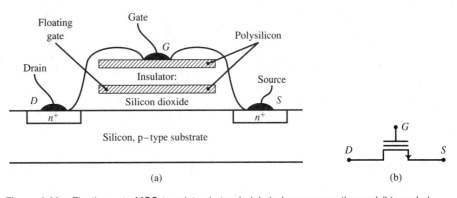

Figure 9.38 Floating-gate MOS transistor (n-type): (a) device cross-section and (b) symbol.

it produces a shift in the threshold voltage of the transistor. Figure 9.38(b) shows the symbol of the device. Note that the floating gate is not connected to any other part of the circuitry.

Let us briefly examine the operation of the floating-gate transistor. Before the device is programmed, it behaves as a regular n-channel enhancement mode MOSFET. In this case its threshold voltage is rather low. To program the floating-gate transistor, a large pulse voltage of about 20 V is applied between the gate and source terminals. Simultaneously, a large 25 V pulse of voltage is applied between the drain and source terminals. Due to the physical phenomena described in more detail elsewhere in the literature (Sedra and Smith 1991), the floating gate acquires charge. In this state, called the programmed state, the device threshold voltage is substantially higher than in the nonprogrammed state. Moreover, the value of the programmed threshold voltage can be controlled through the duration and level of voltage pulses applied. Once programmed, the device is able to retain the threshold value for years.

To return the floating-gate MOS transistor to the non-programmed state, the erasure process needs to take place. The erasure corresponds to the removal of the charge from the floating gate. It is accomplished by illuminating the floating gate with ultraviolet light of a suitable wavelength.

Let us now focus on the application of floating-gate devices for analog multipliers with simultaneous weight storage. The multiplier consists of a single-transistor current sink and two threshold-programmable transistors with gates tied together and connected as a differential pair as shown in Figure 9.39(a). Because transistors $M1$ and $M2$ are a perfectly matched pair, and thus nonprogrammed, I_{d1} and I_{d2} remain exactly the same. Through device programming, the threshold voltages are made unequal. The resulting difference of drain currents I_{d1} and I_{d2} becomes proportional to the difference of the programmed threshold voltages.

Assume that the current differences are sensed at the input of the neuron that produces the scalar product function and its sigmoidal mapping as discussed

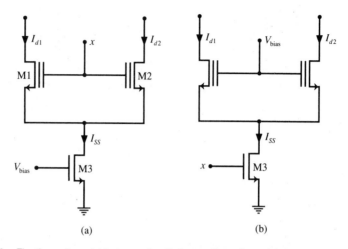

Figure 9.39 Floating-gate weight storage / multiplier configurations: (a) circuit diagram and (b) modified circuit.

earlier in this chapter. When input x is low, the circuit makes no current contribution to the neuron since $M1$ and $M2$ are cut-off and $I_{d1} = I_{d2} \cong 0$. For x larger and positive, the difference current I_{diff} becomes proportional to the threshold voltage difference of the two transistors.

An analysis of this circuit (Borgstrom, Ismail, and Bibyk 1990) shows that the differential current can be expressed:

$$I_{diff} \overset{\Delta}{=} I_{d1} - I_{d2} \tag{9.81a}$$

$$I_{diff} = V_{thd} \sqrt{\frac{kI_{ss}}{2}} \tag{9.81b}$$

where the threshold voltage difference is $V_{thd} = V_{th2} - V_{th1}$, and k is the device transconductance common for both $M1$ and $M2$. It is seen from (9.81b) that the current I_{diff} is proportional to V_{thd}, and also to the input voltage x in a narrow range of values. Although the latter relationship is not explicit in (9.81b), note that x establishes the level of the total current I_{ss}. To improve the performance of the circuit, simple modification of swapping x and V_{bias} as shown in Figure 9.39(b) can be undertaken. The current I_{diff} for this modified circuit is of approximate value

$$I_{diff} \cong xV_{thd} \sqrt{\frac{1}{2} k_{inp} k} \tag{9.82}$$

where k_{inp} is the device transconductance of the input transistor $M3$. Thus, the differential current I_{diff} in (9.82) is proportional to the product of both the input voltage x and of V_{thd}. The value of V_{thd}, however, is made through programming proportional to the weight value. Figure 9.40 shows the differential current

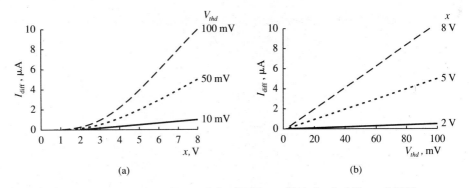

Figure 9.40 Differential current characteristics for the modified circuit of Figure 9.39(b): (a) versus the input voltage and (b) versus the difference of threshold voltages. [© IEE; adapted from Borgstrom, Ismail, and Bibyk (1990) with permission.]

responses of the modified multiplier circuit from Figure 9.39(b). The graphs have been obtained through circuit simulations. They illustrate excellent linearity of I_{diff} with respect to V_{thd}, and good linearity with respect to x, in particular for large values of inputs. This can be seen from comparison of curves from Figures 9.40(a) and (b).

Floating-gate multipliers from Figure 9.39(a) can be used with a current comparator, example of which are shown in Figure 9.31(a). The inputs to the synapses, x, are single-ended voltages. The effective "weight" represented by the synapse is proportional to the difference of the two currents I_{d1} and I_{d2}, which is, in turn, proportional to the preprogrammed difference in the threshold voltages V_{th2} and V_{th1}. A single neuron with floating-gate programmable synapses can be obtained by connecting inputs I_{d1} of a number of synapses from Figure 9.39 to the input I_+ of the current comparator of Figure 9.31(a), and by connecting inputs I_{d2} of the synapses to the input I_- of the current comparator.

An experimental prototype of the neural network described above has been designed, fabricated, and tested (Borgstrom, Ismail, and Bibyk 1990). The chip was implemented with a 2-μm CMOS double-poly p-well process. Poly 1 layer has been used to make the floating gate, and the poly 2 layer as the top gate. The transistors' aspect ratio used in the multiplier has been 20 μm/20 μm, and large W and L values have been selected to minimize mismatch due to the geometrical inaccuracies. The designed neural network uses the described current-mode technique and is especially attractive for modern VLSI technology. It offers programmable weights, excitatory and inhibitory current summation, the sigmoidal nonlinearity function of the current comparator, and the output in the form of voltage. The current-mode processing and current-mode building blocks used by the network are of special importance for microelectronic technologies where voltage signal handling is often limited for analog applications.

9.5

ASSOCIATIVE MEMORY IMPLEMENTATIONS

This section briefly describes how to integrate electronic circuit components into an associative memory circuit. Since only modest precision is required for the nonlinear processors (neurons) and coupling elements (weights), associative memories are particularly convenient and attractive for microelectronic implementation. In a typical memory circuit, input and output data are in binary form. However, as explained in Chapter 6, analog computation is performed by the network throughout the recall phase. This feature makes it easy to integrate an associative memory circuit as a specialized module within large digital systems. Although feedforward networks can also be termed, at least in a certain respect, as associative memories, we have reserved the term "memories" for networks that are typically trained in the batch mode, and are dynamical systems with feedback, which is activated during the recall phase. Only such dynamical memory systems are discussed here.

Figure 9.41 shows a general schematic representation of a single-layer associative memory. The programming of the connection matrix is performed by a weight control network, which is responsible for storing appropriate weights at suitable locations within the connection matrix. The connection matrix contains

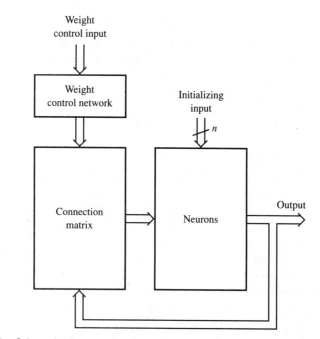

Figure 9.41 Schematic diagram of a single-layer autoassociative memory network.

binary or, more accurately, ternary weights of values 0, $+1$, and -1; sometimes weights need to be set with higher resolutions. The weight control network can be designed either as a microprocessor-based controller or as a dedicated memory control network. This type of weight control network usually involves either a digital memory of RAM type, or registers, as well as address decoders, transmission gates, and buffers.

One of the first associative memory circuits involves implementation of binary weights of values 0, $+1$, and -1 (Graf and Vegvar 1987). The weight circuitry has been designed as shown in Figure 9.42. The figure depicts a single weight configuration and an associated weight control circuitry. The circuit from Figure 9.42(a) uses two RAM cells to program the single weight value. If DataOut1 = 0 and DataOut2 = 1, both transistors $M2$ and $M4$ are cut-off, thus allowing no current to or from the input line of the i'th neuron. This programs a missing connection, or $w_{ij} = 0$.

Assume now that $v_j = V_{DD}$. An excitatory current flowing toward the i'th neuron can be produced by programming DataOut1 = DataOut2 = 0. The excitatory current i_{exc}, which is sourced to the line, can be denoted as shown on the diagram of Figure 9.42(b). Tied transistors $M3$ and $M4$ can be represented as their respective channel resistances R_{ds3} and R_{ds4}. This set of control signals from RAM cells implements $w_{ij} = 1$.

When the memory outputs DataOut1 = DataOut2 = 1, while v_j remains positive, the direction of current reverses as shown in Figure 9.42(c). In this way $w_{ij} = -1$ is produced due to the sinking of current away from the current input line of the i'th neuron. This circuit arrangement imitates the apparent negative conductance $g_{ij} = w_{ij}$ of unity value between the output of the j'th neuron and the input of the i'th neuron. This negative conductance effect is due to the counterflow of sinking current i_{inh} with respect to the sourced current i_{exc}.

The circuitry of Figure 9.42 implements fixed and ternary weight values. It is obvious that by selecting weighted resistances of MOSFET devices, the amount of current sourced, i_{exc}, or current sinked, i_{inh}, could be controlled with better resolution. Several circuit techniques to achieve a higher resolution of resistances along with the principle of analog or digital tunability of weights that could be used for associative memory circuits were discussed earlier in this chapter.

An example auto-associative memory chip was fabricated with 2.5 μm CMOS technology (Graf and Vegvar 1987). The chip contained about 75 000 transistors in an area 6.7 mm $\times$ 6.7 mm. Figure 9.43 shows the schematic of memory interface with the data input/output. There are 54 neuron-amplifier pairs used in the memory, each neuron-amplifier being a simple inverter. Data input and output are made through transmission gates $T1$ and $T2$, respectively. Data are fed through a buffer containing one storage cell, each connected to the output neuron. The content of the buffer can be utilized to program synaptic connections using the approach shown in Figure 9.42.

To initialize the memory output, the READ/WRITE transistor needs to conduct in order to pass the signal to the neuron from the buffer. The memory

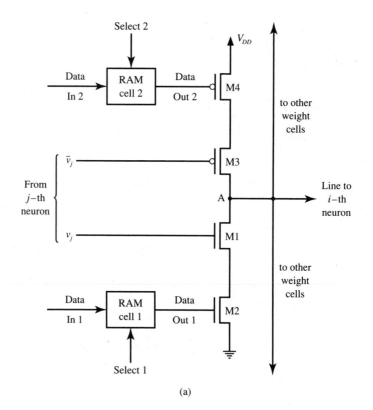

(a)

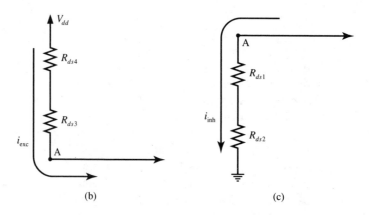

(b) (c)

Figure 9.42 Implementation of binary weights: (a) w_{ij} weight cell diagram, (b) current sourcing for $w_{ij} = 1$, and (c) current sinking for $w_{ij} = -1$.

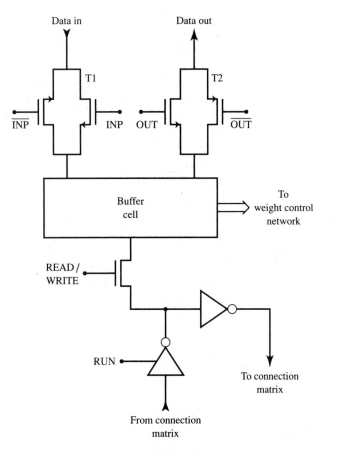

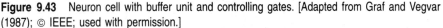

Figure 9.43 Neuron cell with buffer unit and controlling gates. [Adapted from Graf and Vegvar (1987); © IEEE; used with permission.]

feedback loop remains open during the initialization. Following initialization, the RUN control signal is turned to initiate recall, and the network evolves to an equilibrium state. After the circuit has reached a stable state, the READ/WRITE transistor passes the output voltage data to the buffer. These data can be read out as the components of the memory recalled binary vector.

The fabricated network consists of $54^2 = 2916$ binary weights designed according to the concept of Figure 9.42(a) (Graf and Vegvar 1987). Tests on the chip have been run with up to 10 vectors programmed as stable states. Auto-associative recall has been performed reliably, and only the states programmed into the circuit and no spurious states have been retrieved during experiments. A large spread of convergence times has been observed dependent on the overlap of the input and memory vector. The measured recall times have been between 20 and 600 ns. In more general cases, the convergence time scale would depend on the product of weight resistances times the intrinsic input capacitances of the neurons used. The power dissipation measured for the single convergence of the memory has been typically of the order of 200 mW, reaching 500 mW in the worst case.

The drawback of single input line current summation used in this memory design is that excitatory and inhibitory currents may not be the same due to the mismatching between the sourcing and sinking circuitry. Since the mismatches are subsequently summed, this can produce a substantial error in the total input current value (Verleysen and Jespers 1991). To compensate for potential lack of symmetry due to the mixture of n- and p-type MOSFETs in weight circuitry as in Figure 9.42, a two-line system can be used instead. Such arrangements were already discussed in more detail in Section 9.3 for neural network architectures other than associative memories.

In this technique, excitatory and inhibitory currents are summed on separate lines and weight currents are contributed to each of the lines by the same type transistors. Figure 9.44(a) illustrates a two-line current summation. Each synapse is a differential pair controlled by two RAM cells as shown in more detail in Figure 9.44(b) (Verleysen and Jespers 1991). If DataOut1 = 1, current is sunk through M0, provided either $M1$ or $M2$ is conductive. Transistor $M1$ conducts and contributes to the excitatory current when Out is high. At the same time $M2$ remains cut-off. The contribution to the inhibitory current is generated when Out is low, thus $M2$ is conducting and $M1$ is cut-off. The current mirror circuit needs to be used as described in previous sections in order to compare the excitatory and inhibitory currents and to produce the output voltage as a function of their difference.

As suggested earlier, associative memories can also utilize the channel resistances of MOSFET devices as tunable weights to achieve weight setting with higher resolution. The concept of using properly biased field-effect transistors to implement weights was discussed in more detail in Section 9.2. Let us now look at an example of a hardware implementation of a versatile and expandable connection matrix chip reported by Moopenn et al. (1988).

A single synaptic chip with 1024 weights has been implemented that contains an array of 32×32 "long channel" NMOS transistors as illustrated in Figure 9.45. Since neurons are kept off-chip, the circuit remains purely "synaptic" and is thus easily cascadable with identical chips. Such a multichip architecture allows for expansion of the chip up to the size of 512×512 weights, if chips are arranged in an array. In addition, the chips can be connected in parallel, thus allowing for higher than binary weight resolution. In this type of connection mode, the conductances are added since individual weights are connected in parallel. To ensure low-power dissipation within the connection matrix, weight resistances are selected from large values, thus taking small current levels. For this reason, large L/W (long channel) transistors are used on the chip ($L = 244$ μm, $W = 12$ μm). This ensures typical channel resistance R_{ds} values greater than 200 kΩ in the

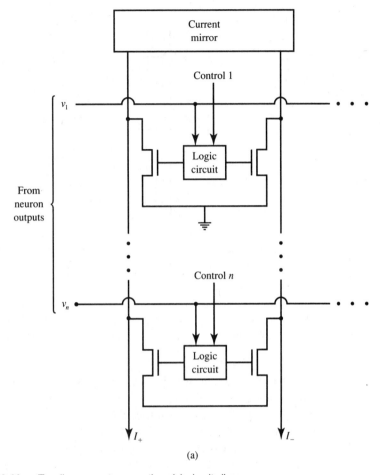

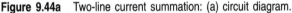

(a)

Figure 9.44a Two-line current summation: (a) circuit diagram.

entire operating range [see formula (9.21)]. Also, a large ratio L/W enhances the linearity of the controlled weights, for a given range of operating voltages, thus it results in increased weight accuracy. This also increases the precision of implemented weights, which becomes of particular importance when connection matrices need to be connected in parallel in order to achieve better resolution.

Figure 9.45(a) depicts the block diagram of the fabricated synaptic chip and also shows an expanded single weight cell. Transistor $M2$, controlled by the gate with voltage Q, acts as an ON/OFF switch. The Q output is provided by the latch, which is externally addressed via the row and column address decoders. Transistor $M1$ operates as a long channel resistance R_{ds} controlled by the gate voltage V_G. Since V_G takes only one nonzero value in this circuit arrangement,

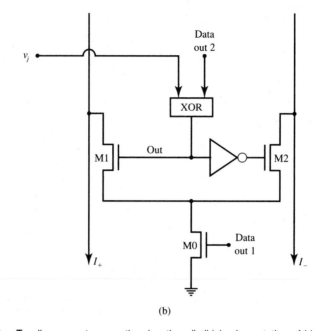

(b)

Figure 9.44b Two-line current summation *(continued):* (b) implementation of binary weight.

only binary unipolar weights can be produced in this circuit. With a weight control voltage V_G of 5 V, for example, values for R_{ds} of about 200 kΩ can be obtained over an input operating range. The weights' linearity of 5% has been measured for the input voltage in the range up to 1.5 V.

Figure 9.45(b) shows the microphotograph of the 32 × 32 connection chip. The synaptic chip has been fabricated using 3 μm bulk CMOS process. A microcomputer interface needs to be used in this project to program the weight values, to initialize the memory, and to provide read-out of the recalled vector. The chip has been used as a basic building block for a number of associative memory experiments. An average convergence time within the connection chip has been observed of 10 μs, with some recalls taking up to 50 μs. The discussed associative memory network has demonstrated an excellent stability and associative recall performance.

Another approach to building a reconfigurable memory connection matrix is shown schematically in Figure 9.46. The weight value can be adjusted by turning the binary weighted resistances on or off. The resistances are controlled by 1-bit RAM memory switches (Lee and Sheu 1991). The figure exemplifies weights that can be arranged externally for up to 3-bit resolution. Resistances can be realized either as channel resistances of MOS transistors or as current sinks/sources connected to current mirrors.

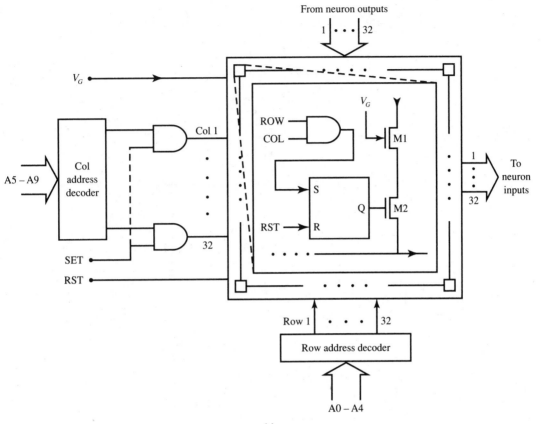

(a)

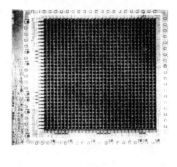

(b)

Figure 9.45 Synaptic chip with long channel MOSFETs and binary weights: (a) chip architecture and single weight implementation and (b) microphotograph of a CMOS 3-μm chip with 1024 weight cells. [© American Institute of Physics; adapted from Moopenn (1988) with permission.]

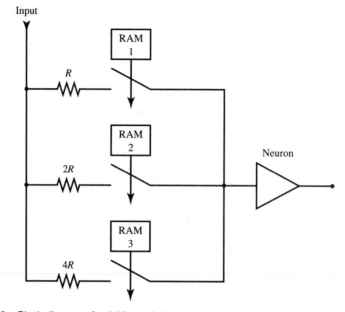

Figure 9.46　Block diagram of a 3-bit resolution associative memory weight cell.

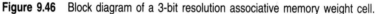

9.6

ELECTRONIC NEURAL PROCESSORS

In this chapter we have formulated the basic requirements and outlined the operational parameters of artificial neural hardware processors. We also discussed numerous issues related to the design of special-purpose artificial neural systems. Much of the material presented to this point has been oriented toward the implementation of the basic building blocks of neural hardware. Synaptic connections, neuron elements, elementary current-mode processors, and scalar product circuits have been among the main building blocks covered. Our emphasis on the analog neural processing has been due to the fact that it offers size and speed advantages compared to conventional numerical simulations. Analog neural processing is also much more efficient than purely digital hardware computation since convergence times for parallel analog hardware are significantly smaller. We have also seen that some electronic implementations can be made as combinations of analog and digital processors. While recall and often also learning are carried out as analog processes, digital programmability and digital control and interface offer increased accuracy and flexibility.

This section discusses sample electronic neural network implementations. Rather than continue to focus on the principles and basic building blocks, here we outline the main features of ready-to-use neural processors. Some of them appear experimental, some are available commercially—nevertheless, all of the discussed systems are reported to be complete and functional as described in the technical literature. Included in this section are Intel's ETANN chip (Intel 1991), the analog programmable neural processor (Fisher, Fujimoto, and Smithson 1991), a general-purpose neural computer (Mueller et al., 1989, 1989b), and an optically controlled neural network (Frye et al. 1989).

The Electrically Trainable Analog Neural Network (ETANN) 80170 integrated circuit chip is a commercial product suitable for real-time neurocomputing applications. Its applications include recognition of printed or handwritten characters, diagnosis of fault patterns, signal recognition, image processing and convolution, speech recognition, nonlinear process control, robotic motion control and tactile pattern recognition. The chip operates in the recall phase with a speed of $2 \cdot 10^9$ CPS, which is well beyond the capabilities of both the neural network software and hardware accelerator boards.

The ETANN 80170 chip is trainable in two modes. Given a specific mapping task to be performed, synaptic weights can be trained for a selected neural network model. This task can be done off-chip either by the user's software or by the learning simulation software provided with the chip. Downloading the weights on the chip terminates this learning performed "off-the-chip" on a programmable host neurocomputer. Also, off-chip learning maximizes the flexibility of training approaches and of architectures potentially chosen for the network.

Alternatively, the chip can be subject to "chip-in-the-loop" learning. In this mode of training, the network itself performs the recall function and is trained on-line, while software is used for recomputing the weights during training. This mode of learning enables more realistic network development because the chip characteristics and imperfections are included and accounted for in each weight adaptation step. Because the chip uses EEPROM technology, the weights can be changed many times. The programmable weights are trainable with up to six bits of resolution.

The ETANN chip comes in a 208-pin package. It consists of 64 programmable neurons and a total of 10 240 programmable weights. The block diagram of the chip is shown in Figure 9.47(a). Each neuron is capable of computing the output for 128 input weights with variable inputs and 32 fixed-bias weights. Figure 9.47(b) illustrates programmable synapse operation. The weight value is programmed and stored as threshold voltages of a pair of floating-gate MOS transistors as described in detail in Section 9.4. The circuit shown in the figure performs the analog multiplication of the differential voltage Δv_{in} times the weight value, which, in turn, is proportional to the threshold voltage difference. The output from the synapse is in the form of the current difference ΔI_{out}.

Families of the synaptic connections' current characteristics shown in Figure 9.48 illustrate the performance of programmable weights. Figure 9.48(a) shows the differential output current as a function of the weight input voltage with

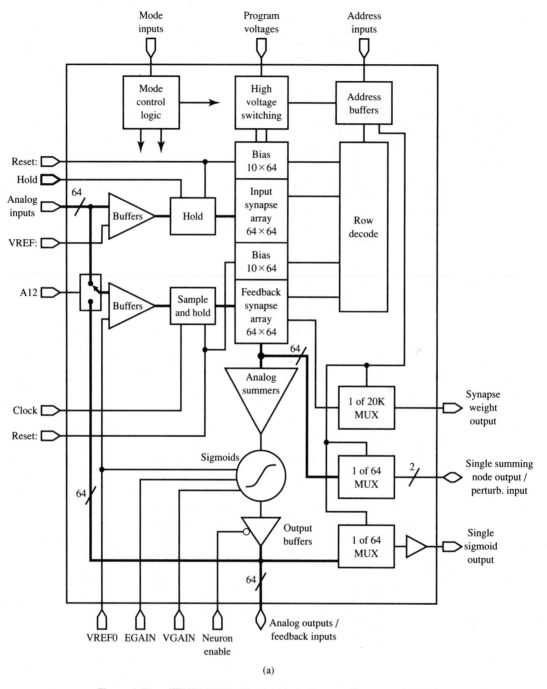

Figure 9.47a ETANN 80170 chip: (a) block diagram. (Courtesy of Intel Corporation)

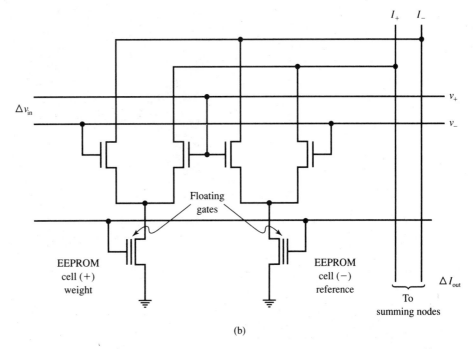

Δv_{in}

Floating gates

EEPROM cell (+) weight

EEPROM cell (−) reference

I_+ I_-

v_+

v_-

ΔI_{out}

To summing nodes

(b)

Figure 9.47b ETANN 80170 chip *(continued):* (b) synaptic connection implementation. (Courtesy of Intel Corporation)

the threshold voltage difference V_{thd}, called here $V_{t-\mathrm{Diff}}$ as a parameter for each curve shown. The six different values of weights displayed in the figure have been obtained with the threshold voltage value of one of the transistors fixed as a reference, V_{ref1}. The graphs show that the weights can be set with fine accuracy and a considerable linearity of weights is achieved. Figure 9.48(b) shows the differential input current versus the difference of the threshold voltages V_{thd} with the input voltage as a parameter for the family of curves. Noticeably, the inputs and outputs of the weight cell are both differential. Weight changes are accomplished by applying high-voltage pulses to the ETANN chip and causing the floating gate to store the weight value as described earlier in Section 9.4.

Currents generated by products of up to 160 weights times the inputs are summed and converted to an output voltage. This is accomplished by the neuron characterized by an activation function as shown in Figure 9.49. The sigmoidal function takes a voltage-controlled shape. The neuron's output voltage corresponds to a "squashed" scalar product of input and weight vectors, and it depends on the value of the control voltage VGAIN.

The ETANN chip can be programmed and trained using a development system that plugs into a personal computer, which serves as a host. The development system contains converters, conditioners, multiplexers, and logic controllers,

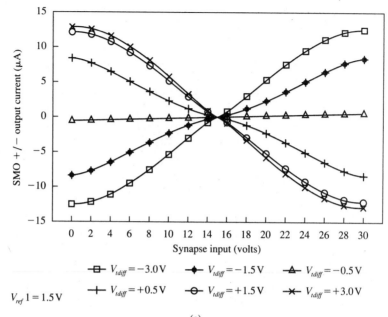

$V_{ref}1 = 1.5\,V$

(a)

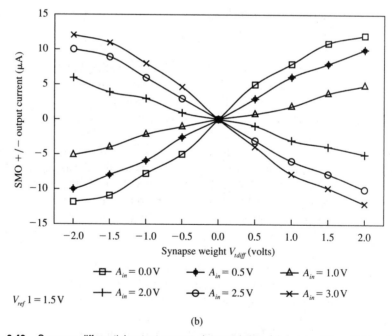

$V_{ref}1 = 1.5\,V$

(b)

Figure 9.48 Synapse differential output current characteristics: (a) versus differential input voltage, V_{thd} as a parameter and (b) versus V_{thd}, differential input voltage as a parameter. (Courtesy of Intel Corporation)

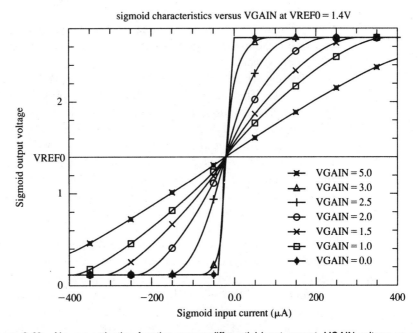

Figure 9.49 Neuron activation function versus differential input current, VGAIN voltage as a parameter. (Courtesy of Intel Corporation)

which are needed to program the neural network chip. System software is available to either verify the downloaded weights or read weights out of a chip that has been previously trained in an on-line mode. The ETANN chip can be wire-wrapped into a variety of architectures. Either cascaded or parallel architectures can be developed that employ up to 1024 neurons and up to 81 920 weights in the interconnected network.

The analog neural network processor described by Fisher, Fujimoto, and Smithson (1991) and discussed below represents a somewhat different category of neural hardware. In contrast to the ETANN concept, the processor can be reprogrammed on the fly as if it were read/write memory. The processor's analog throughput does not need to be halted during the weight adaptation or reprogramming. Thus, while ETANN is best suited for ultrafast execution of problems that require rather infrequent retraining, the analog neural network processor can be modified while working. In addition, the ETANN chip uses current-mode signal processing rather than the voltage-mode processing employed in an analog neural network processor.

The processor can be connected so it functions as either a feedforward or feedback network. The 256 neurons are made of operational amplifiers. The processor weights are arranged in an array of custom programmable resistor chips assembled at the board level. The 2048 programmable resistors are physically located on 16 boards. The overall architecture of the processor is shown in Figure 9.50(a). Input to the network can be simply analog, or from 12-bit digital sources converting the digital signal to analog form in the block of 256 digital-to-analog (D/A) converters.

The experimentally tested D/A conversion rate for the processor built has been 5 kHz. The processor input data can be provided externally or from the computer. The analog output data can be monitored after a conversion of up to 256 outputs by a set of 256 A/D converters. The interconnection boards used by the processor adjust it to the problem class and are architecture specific, while the rest of the processor is general-purpose. While the system requires more space than an integrated neural network chip, the use of the boards and wire-wrap interconnect boards makes it possible to reconfigure the network easily.

The heart of the analog network of the processor is made up of the digitally programmable analog resistors. A single programmable weight diagram is shown in Figure 9.50(b). The resistors are made on a gate array chip. This weight implementation concept is similar to that described in Section 9.2 for MDACs with binary weighted resistances. This processor, however, uses integrated circuit resistors rather than MOSFETs. Each weight consists of a buffer connected to five polysilicon resistors through analog bipolar switches. The resistors range from 8 to 128 kΩ and can be set up with an 8- kΩ step, thus providing 4-bit resolution. This resolution has been found adequate for the neural control applications studied by Fisher, Fujimoto, and Smithson (1991). The buffered design allows for the connection of many resistors to the neuron's input without placing excessive current load on the summing and amplifying neuron. Also, since the weight program data are stored in digital form within computer memory, or registers, no refresh signals are required to store their values.

The programmable neural network processor has been successfully tested for control of adaptive mirrors' actuators. The purpose of adaptive mirrors is to undo the distortions of images of solar or celestial objects. Such images are distorted when the light forming the image passes through the atmosphere. The light reflected from adaptive mirrors can produce corrected images. However, the mirror adaptation cycle must not take longer than 10 ms to keep up with atmospheric changes. The neural processor described has been able to control the mirrors significantly faster than any of the conventional digital control methods attempted.

Another example of an electronic neural network is described by Mueller et al. (1989a, 1989b). The network is designed and implemented in the form of a general-purpose analog neural computer. It consists of three types of interconnected modules. They are dedicated VLSI chips: neurons, modifiable synapses, and routing switches. The neurocomputer runs entirely in the analog mode but the architecture, weights, neuron parameters, and time constants are all set digitally from a host computer.

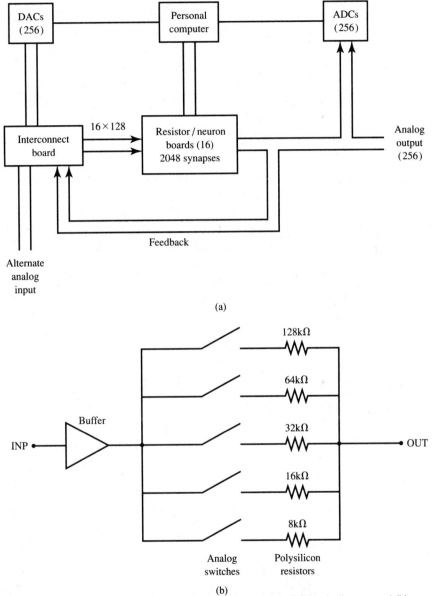

(a)

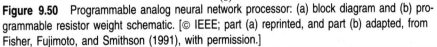

(b)

Figure 9.50 Programmable analog neural network processor: (a) block diagram and (b) programmable resistor weight schematic. [© IEEE; part (a) reprinted, and part (b) adapted, from Fisher, Fujimoto, and Smithson (1991), with permission.]

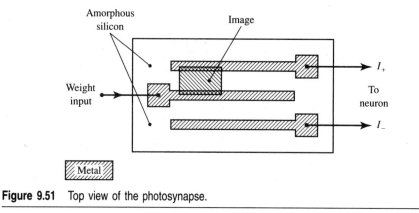

Figure 9.51 Top view of the photosynapse.

An interesting feature of this neurocomputer is that the analog outputs of the neurons are read through analog multiplexers. Subsequently, these data are digitized and stored in digital memory. During training, the weights and threshold values of the neurons are computed by the host computer and set on the neuron and synaptic chips. The multiplexing operation does not interfere with the actual analog computation.

The synaptic weights are implemented by current mirrors that scale the currents with 5-bit resolution. Since the neurons' outputs are voltages, voltage-to-current converters have been used to provide appropriate current inputs to the current mirrors. The converters are followed by the current dividers consisting of current mirrors in series. To retain the weight value, synaptic cells are provided with local 6-bit weight control memory. Five bits determine the weight magnitude and the sixth bit is used to determine the sign of the weight. The memory consists of shift registers that read the data during the programming phase.

The neuron circuit consists of a rectified summing amplifier, comparator, and an output driver. Inputs to the neurons are currents; outputs are analog voltages. Digital control can be used to adjust the following neuron parameters: bias (threshold), minimum output, and the choice of a linear or sigmoidal transfer function. The sigmoidal transfer function is obtained by adding one or more non-linear devices in parallel with the feedback resistor of the summing operational amplifier. The neuron chip fabricated consisted of 16 neurons implemented in 2-μm CMOS technology. The reader is encouraged to refer to the literature for more detail on this versatile circuit (Mueller et al. 1989a, 1989b).

An interesting example of a neural network with optically controlled hardware has been described by Frye et al. (1989). Synaptic weights can be built using amorphous silicon photoconductors. Such weights, which can be called "photosynapses," react to the amount of light energy projected onto them. A schematic illustration of a photosynapse (top view) is shown in Figure 9.51. The photosynapse is composed of three narrow strips of metal deposited on a layer

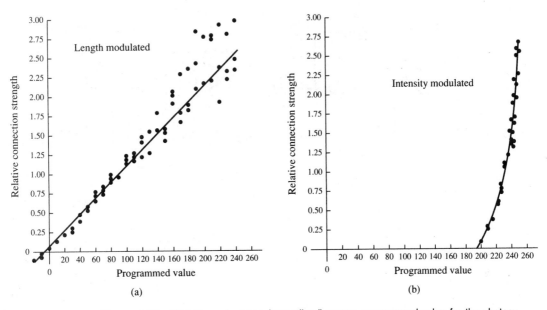

Figure 9.52 Weight conductance (normalized) versus programmed value for the photosynapse: (a) image length modulation and (b) image intensity modulation, full bar length. [© IEEE; reprinted from Frye et al. (1989); with permission.]

of glow-discharge amorphous silicon. The region between input and either the negative or positive output line forms a photoconductor whose electrical conductance can be controlled by an image projected on the synapse. The weight conductance is a function of the length of the bar of light projected and also of its intensity. In addition, the length of the bar is proportional to the length of the image.

The image projected on the matrix of synaptic connections has been generated by a high-intensity CRT. The length of the image bar spanned 240 pixels. The weight conductance has been coded accordingly into the integer values between 0 and 240. Alternatively, the intensity of light alone has been used to control the conductance encoded as an integer ranging from 0 to 255. This intensity has been projected on the photosynapse when using a full-length bar of 240 pixels.

Measured values for the normalized weight conductance are shown in Figure 9.52. It can be seen that the conductance modulated by the length of the bar at full intensity displays a linear relationship. The behavior of weight as a function of bar intensity, however, shows a very different functional dependence. Because of the nature of the CRT light and of the properties of the photoconducting material employed to make the photosynapse, the intensity-modulated conductance is a strongly nonlinear function of the programmed value, showing only a small value of conductance for programmed intensity values below 200 (Frye et al. 1989).

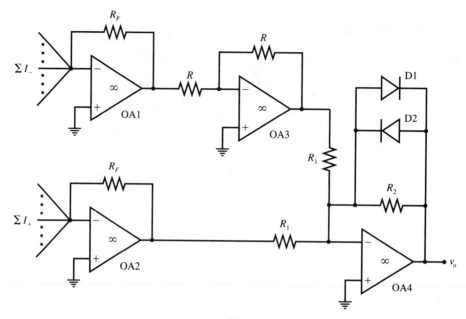

(a)

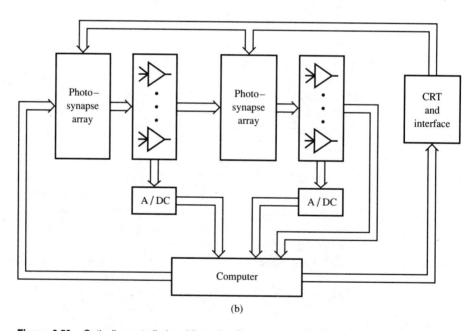

(b)

Figure 9.53 Optically controlled multilayer feedforward network: (a) neuron circuit diagram and (b) block diagram of the system. [Adapted from Frye et al. (1989); © IEEE; with permission.]

As shown in Figure 9.51, the weight current can be either excitatory when $I_+ > 0$, or inhibitory when $I_- > 0$. A simple neuron circuit performing an aggregation of currents $\sum I_+$ and $\sum I_-$ is shown in Figure 9.53(a). The first stage consists of current-to-voltage converters, or transconductance amplifiers built with operational amplifiers $OA1$ and $OA2$. A unity-gain inverter built with $OA3$ provides the sign change for the voltage but without scaling of its magnitude. An inverting summer mode with $OA4$ provides for the summation of the voltages of both channels. The two diodes in the feedback loop are provided to give the neuron sigmoidally-shaped response characteristics rather than piecewise linear-shaped characteristics.

The described network with photosynaptic connections has been used in a multilayer feedforward architecture trained in the error back-propagation mode. The block diagram of the overall error back-propagation training system is illustrated in Figure 9.53(b). The external computer is used to generate the training data and to evaluate the error produced by the actual system with the current setting of weights. Then, the new images are produced and sent to the photosynapses that correspond to the newly adjusted weight values. The output of the neural system and of the hidden neurons is monitored in each training step so that the new set of weights can be recomputed and translated into light images. The described network has been successfully trained to locate the target point of a ballistic trajectory. The system has proven very useful despite some disadvantages displayed by the actual hardware.

9.7 CONCLUDING REMARKS

Throughout this book we have seen that a wide variety of problems can be solved by using the neural network computing framework. However, each of the classes of problems that needs to be solved usually requires a different architecture and training approach as well as different data stored in the network in the form of weights. The exposition in this chapter has focused on building working models of neural networks which we called neural processors. Among the numerous approaches to implementation of artificial neural systems we have stressed microelectronic hardware realizations. We have emphasized analog circuits to implement neural systems because they provide high synapse density and high computational speed (Satyanarayana, Tsividis, and Graf 1990). Once the algorithms are developed and the networks trained, such realizations provide an efficient way of solving a variety of technical problems. In most cases, neural analog processors offer improvement over both software simulations and digital circuits emulating analog operation.

Most real-life applications of artificial neural networks appear to typically require at least several hundred neurons. An essential aspect of neural hardware implementation is the mechanism used to represent and manipulate the weights. Although more difficult to accomplish than weight adjustment, learning also appears to be an essential ingredient for most neural network applications. A number of designs to accomplish these features within the neural network hardware rather than on the host computer have been presented in this chapter.

While some approaches use off-line learning to train an artificial neural system, which is both possible and practical, the inherent ability to learn on the chip as more information becomes available to the system is invaluable. However, the development of an artificial neural system chip with on-chip learning seems to be a nontrivial task. Even for limited learning capability, the network design becomes quite complex (Collins and Penz 1990). Development of standard digital application-specific integrated circuit hardware requires high expenditures to design, fabricate, and test the digital circuit chip. Development of neural network hardware seems to be even more costly. This is one of the reasons why the neural network chips currently available often involve technology demonstrations as opposed to the easily usable, perhaps even hand-held circuits for practical applications. The task of making a universal and usable neural network chip still remains a challenging one.

Let us consider what could be called an "ideal" neural network. Such a network should possess the following characteristics:

- Work for any neural processing algorithm
- Contain at least 1000 neurons, which can be interconnected globally
- Have programmable analog weights
- Be able to learn on-chip
- Consist of small-area neurons and interconnections
- Operate at low-power levels
- Be stable, reproducible, and extendable so that larger systems can be built through interconnecting neural network building blocks
- Be affordable.

Let us compare the above requirements with the present capabilities of integrated circuit technology. One of the most complex semiconductor chips currently available (early 1992) is the 1-Mbit DRAM. One can say that a 1-Mbit DRAM is roughly equivalent to a 1000-neuron network, which involves about one million weights. The DRAM network, however, stores binary information in contrast to the expected analog weight storage of the neural hardware. Therefore, just from the standpoint of granularity of data storage, it is much easier to fabricate a 1-Mbit DRAM chip than a 1000 neuron network chip. Additional expectations such as weight tunability, learning capability and required nonlinear processing by the neuron bring even more complexity to the neural hardware picture (Collins and Penz 1989).

Neural network chips available at present, including those discussed in this chapter, meet somewhat relaxed criteria compared to the above list of desirable features and are of reduced complexity and size. The chips made thus far contain on the order of 100 processing nodes. We can state that the currently available neural hardware, including VLSI chips, still lags somewhat behind the neural networks' theoretical computational capabilities. Therefore, most large-scale neural computation is still done on serial computers, special-purpose accelerator boards, or by theoretical analysis.

Out of necessity, the exposition of neural network implementation in this chapter has been limited to a number of approaches and design techniques. Also, microelectronic VLSI technology has been emphasized for the most part. Other designs and approaches are available and are described in more specialized technical reports. The reader may refer to the literature for further study of the subject.

Below is a partial list of topics and related literature:

- Neurocomputing architectures (Bessiere et al. 1991; Goser et al. 1989; Jutten, Guerin, and Herault 1990; Morton 1991; Ouali, Saucier, and Thrile 1991; Ramacher 1991; Vidal 1988)

- Architecture of neural VLSI chips (Wasaki, Itario, and Nakamura 1990; Schwartz and Samalam 1990; Foo, Anderson, and Takefuji; 1990; Kaul et al. 1990; Mack et al. 1988; Mann 1990; Lambe, Moopenn, and Thakoor 1988)

- Silicon implementation of neural networks (Maher et al. 1989; Murray 1991; Paulos and Hollis 1988; Reed and Geiger 1990; Rossetto et al. 1989; Salam and Choi 1990; Verleysen and Jespers 1989; Wang and Salam 1990)

- Optoelectronic implementations of neural networks (Farhat 1989; Lu et al. 1989; Psaltis et al. 1989; Szu 1991; Wagner and Psaltis 1987).

In addition, a pioneering monograph on neurobiologically inspired neural networks is available (Mead 1989). The book is mainly devoted to microelectronic hardware emulation of a number of the powerful organizing principles found in biological neural systems. Integrated circuit design techniques are employed in the book to implement certain features of biological networks. Examples include imitation of human senses such as hearing, vision, and other perceptions. Most of the circuits developed by Mead (1989) operate in the subthreshold range of transistors. MOS transistors in the subthreshold range have beneficial properties such as extremely low power consumption and the transistor's current versus voltage characteristics is described with exponential relationships rather than quadratic with additional saturation.

As stated before, efficient neural processing hardware is crucially important for the success of neural network technology if we are going to take full advantage of its learning and processing capabilities. There is strong and growing activity in this area. Analog semiconductor technology, charge-coupled devices, and optical implementation are all among the explored technologies. Although semiconductor technology is presently the most widespread, the capabilities of the other technologies have not yet been fully evaluated for efficient implementation of neural network hardware.

PROBLEMS

Please note that problems highlighted with an asterisk (*) are typically computationally intensive and the use of programs is advisable to solve them.

P9.1 Analyze the neuron circuit from Figure P9.1 and compute its weight values. Compute the neuron's response $f(\mathbf{x})$ for the following inputs knowing that $f_{\text{sat}+} = -f_{\text{sat}-} = 13$ V:

(a) $\mathbf{x} = \begin{bmatrix} -1 & 3 & 0.5 \end{bmatrix}^t$

(b) $\mathbf{x} = \begin{bmatrix} 0 & 0.5 & 1.5 \end{bmatrix}^t$

(c) $\mathbf{x} = \begin{bmatrix} -1 & -2 & -0.5 \end{bmatrix}^t$

(The input vector components are specified in Volts.)

P9.2 Design the neuron circuit as in Figure 9.5 with weights of values -3, -4, and -6. Use the feedback resistance value of 1200 Ω. By writing appropriate inequalities, determine in which segments of the input space, x, the neuron saturates and assumes the values $f_{\text{sat}+}$ or $f_{\text{sat}-}$. Assume $f_{\text{sat}+} = -f_{\text{sat}-} = 13$ V.

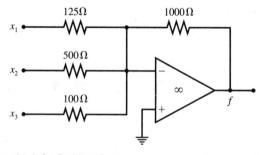

Figure P9.1   Neuron circuit for Problem P9.1.

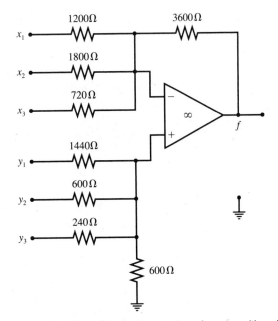

Figure P9.3 Resistor-operational amplifier implementation of neuron with weights for Problem P9.3.

P9.3   The neuron circuit shown in Figure P9.3 implements the following mapping:

$$f(\mathbf{x}, \mathbf{y}) = \begin{bmatrix} w_1 & w_2 & w_3 \end{bmatrix} \begin{bmatrix} x_1 \\ x_2 \\ x_3 \end{bmatrix} + \begin{bmatrix} v_1 & v_2 & v_3 \end{bmatrix} \begin{bmatrix} y_1 \\ y_2 \\ y_3 \end{bmatrix}$$

(a) Find weights w_1, w_2, w_3 and v_1, v_2, v_3.

(b) Assume that input to this single neuron network is now the vector with entries being voltages

$$\mathbf{a} = \begin{bmatrix} x_1 & x_2 & x_3 & y_1 & y_2 & y_3 \end{bmatrix}^t$$

such that (1) $\|\mathbf{a}\| = 1$ and (2) the input exactly matches the total weight vector defined as

$$\mathbf{w}_{tot} \overset{\Delta}{=} \begin{bmatrix} w_1 & w_2 & w_3 & v_1 & v_2 & v_3 \end{bmatrix}^t$$

so that $\mathbf{w}_{tot}^t \mathbf{a} = \|\mathbf{w}_{tot}\|$. Find the neuron's output voltage $f(\mathbf{a}, \mathbf{w}_{tot})$ due to $\mathbf{a}$.

P9.4   The operational amplifier-resistor neuron circuit from Figure P9.4(a) needs to be analyzed. Compute f_{o2} as a function of w_1, w_2, and w_3, and of the bias T as indicated on the neuron symbol of Figure 9.4(b). Assume for computation purposes that the two neurons are equivalent.

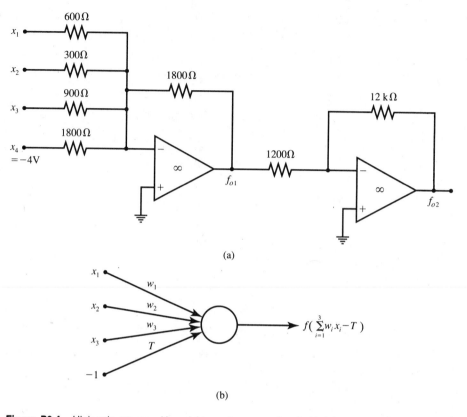

(a)

(b)

Figure P9.4 High-gain neuron with weights and nonzero threshold: (a) circuit diagram and (b) symbol.

(a) Draw the neuron's transfer characteristics as a function of $z=\sum_{i=1}^{3} w_i x_i$.

(b) Determine the range of activation z that allows for the linear operation of the neuron. Assume $|f_{sat-}| = |f_{sat+}| = 14$ V.

(c) Assume that the neuron needs to classify patterns of two classes and find its responses due to the eight individual input values, which are vertices of a three-dimensional $[-1, 1]$ cube.

P9.5   The perceptron shown in Figure P9.5 needs to classify input patterns into two classes. The centers of gravity for each class are known as follows:

$$\mathbf{x}_1 = \begin{bmatrix} 5 \\ 4 \\ 7 \end{bmatrix} : \text{class 1}$$

$$\mathbf{x}_2 = \begin{bmatrix} -1 \\ 0 \\ 4 \end{bmatrix} : \text{class 2}$$

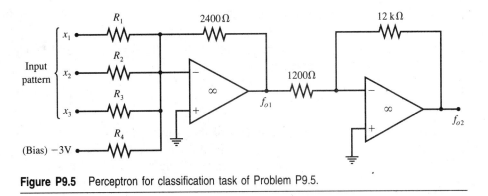

Figure P9.5 Perceptron for classification task of Problem P9.5.

Design the minimum-distance dichotomizer that would best classify patterns from the two classes. Follow the design steps below:

(a) Compute the weights and threshold value of the bipolar binary perceptron.

(b) Find R_1, R_2, R_3, and R_4 for the high-gain perceptron from Figure 9.5 that approximates the bipolar binary perceptron.

(c) Identify the region of linear response of the designed perceptron. This region contains inputs that are falling between the two distinct classes and produce response in the range between $f_{\text{sat}-}$ and $f_{\text{sat}+}$. Assume for computations that $|f_{\text{sat}-}| = |f_{\text{sat}+}| = 14$ V.

P9.6   The enhancement-mode NMOS transistor shown in Figure P9.6 is configured to function as a voltage-controlled synaptic weight. Voltage $V_G = V_{gs}$ is the weight control voltage. It sets the drain-to-source, or channel, resistance R_{ds} that determines the weight current, I_{ds}. Knowing that $k' = 20$ μA/V^2, $W/L = 10$, and $V_{th} = 1.5$ V, evaluate the value of R_{ds} as follows:

(a) Compute and sketch R_{ds} as a function of V_{gs} for 1.5 V $< V_{gs} < 5$ V. Assume that the channel resistance is linear because of linearization

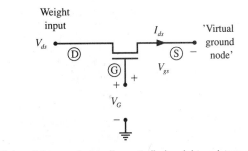

Figure P9.6   NMOS transistor as electrically controlled weight resistance.

of $I_{ds}(V_{ds})$ due to the limited input levels, which fulfill condition $V_{ds} < 0.5(V_{gs} - V_{th})$.

(b) Compute and sketch $R_{ds} = V_{ds}/I_{ds}$ using the following unabbreviated formula for I_{ds}:

$$I_{ds} = k' \frac{W}{L} \left[(V_{gs} - V_{th})V_{ds} - \frac{V_{ds}^2}{2} \right]$$

Solve this part of the problem for the condition $V_{ds} = 0.5(V_{gs} - V_{th})$. Again, V_{gs} should be maintained in the range from 1.5 V to 5 V. Notice the increase of the computed resistance value compared to case (a) due to the quadratic term now present in the expression for I_{ds}.

P9.7 The scalar product circuit with electrically tunable weights as illustrated in Figure 9.11 uses $R_F = 10$ kΩ and NMOS transistors with $k' = 20$ μA/V^2, $W/L = 10$, and $V_{th} = 2$ V. The circuit needs to implement the function

$$v_o = -2.5x_1 - 6x_2 - 4x_3$$

Complete the design of the circuit by computing

(a) the gate control voltages V_{gs1}, V_{gs2}, and V_{gs3} producing the specified scalar product

(b) the range of input voltages x_1, x_2, and x_3 ensuring the linearity of the channel resistance. Use the linearity condition $V_{dsi} = V_i < 0.5(V_{gsi} - 2)$, for $i = 1, 2, 3$.

P9.8 (a) Two 3-bit MDACs are connected in a circuit as shown in Figure P9.8(a). Calculate the output voltage v_{o1} assuming that x_1 and x_2 are input voltages.

(b) Calculate the output voltage v_{o2} for the input voltages y_1 and y_2 by analyzing the circuit shown in Figure P9.8(b).

(c) A difference voltage amplifier is used to combine excitatory voltage v_{o1} [from part (a)] with inhibitory voltage v_{o2} [from part (b)] as shown in Figure P9.8(c). Find

$$v_{o3}(\mathbf{w}) = \begin{bmatrix} w_1 & w_2 & w_3 & w_4 \end{bmatrix} \begin{bmatrix} x_1 & x_2 & y_1 & y_2 \end{bmatrix}^t$$

for this neuron circuit when all operational amplifiers operate in their linear regions.

P9.9 A linear activation function neuron needs to be designed using three weighted-resistor MDACs as shown in Figure 9.15(a). MDACs are controlled by 4-bit words. The neuron's output voltage needs to be

$$v_o = -8v_{i1} - 4.5v_{i2} - 2.5v_{i3}$$

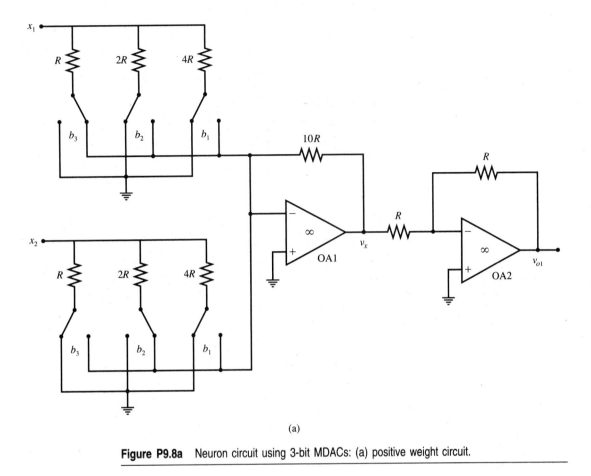

(a)

Figure P9.8a Neuron circuit using 3-bit MDACs: (a) positive weight circuit.

provided the operational amplifier operates in the linear region. Select $R_F = 4.5R$, where R is the resistance determining the MSB switch current, or S_4 current. Calculate the control word settings D_1, D_2, and D_3 that best approximate the required output. Upon completion of the design, find:

(a) the percent errors in approximation of the specified weight coefficients -8, -4.5, and -2.5 through control words D_1, D_2, and D_3, respectively

(b) the output voltage for $v_{i1} = v_{i2} = v_{i3} = 100$ mV with control word settings as in part (a)

(c) the percent error of the output voltage computed in part (b) as compared with the accurate output voltage required.

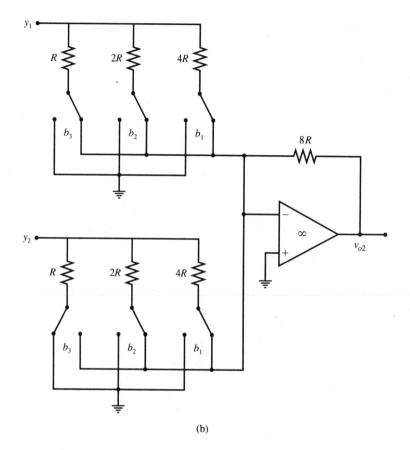

(b)

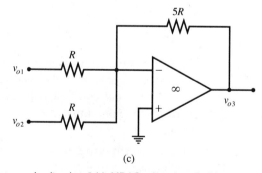

(c)

Figure P9.8b,c Neuron circuit using 3-bit MDACs *(continued):* (b) negative weight circuit, and (c) neuron circuit.

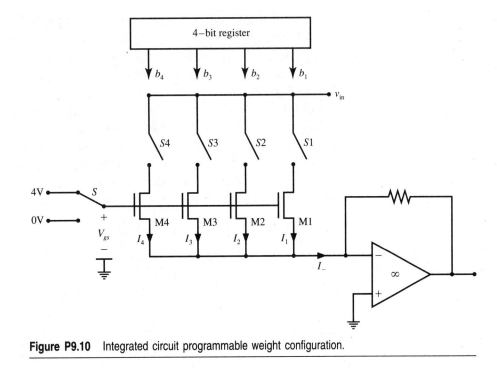

Figure P9.10 Integrated circuit programmable weight configuration.

P9.10 The circuit configuration shown in Figure P9.10 is used to produce a single digitally programmable weight. Weighted currents in vertical branches of the MDAC are obtained by proper sizing of enhancement mode NMOS transistors $M4$ through $M1$. Each of the transistors is assumed conductive and behaves as an integrated circuit linear resistance between the drain and source, R_{ds}, for $V_{gs} = 4$ V provided $0 < v_{in} < 1$ V. The threshold voltage of transistors used is $V_{th} = 1$ V, the process transconductance is $k' = 20 \ \mu A/V^2$.

Transistor current in the resistive region is approximated by the expression

$$I_{ds} \cong k' \frac{W}{L}(V_{gs} - V_{th})V_{ds} \quad \text{for } V_{ds} < V_{gs} - V_{th}$$

The following design conditions need to be assumed:

(1) $v_{in,max} = 1$ V

(2) $I_{-max} = 1.875 \ \mu A$ when b_1, b_2, b_3, b_4 are of unity value and S_1, S_2, S_3, and S_4 are short-circuited

(3) $V_{gs} = 4$ V

Complete the design by computing required value W/L of transistors $M1$ through $M4$ used to produce the weight.

P9.11 Consider the current mirror as in Figure 9.21 with $V_{ss} = 0$ V, $I_{in} = 10$ μA and assume transistors $M1$ and $M2$ to be identical, with $V_{th} = 1$ V, $k' = 20$ μA/V^2, $L = 10$ μm, and $W = 40$ μm. Find $V_{gs1} = V_{gs2}$ and the lowest allowable output voltage v_{out} at the present current level $I = 10$ μA for proper operation of the current mirror.

P9.12 The basic differential amplifier as shown in Figure 9.27(a) with differential input and single-ended output and resistive loads R_L has voltage transfer characteristics as shown in Figure 9.28(a). For this case, compute the voltage gains A_{v1}, and A_{v2} defined as

$$A_{v1} = \left(\frac{\partial v_{d1}}{\partial v_{ind}} \right) \Bigg|_{v_{ind}=0}$$

$$A_{v2} = \left(\frac{\partial v_{d2}}{\partial v_{ind}} \right) \Bigg|_{v_{ind}=0}$$

Express computed gains in terms of k, and I_{ss}.

P9.13 Design a template matching network using the concept of one transistor per single bit matching element as illustrated in Figure 9.32(b). The input vector representing the template bit map to be matched is $\mathbf{x} = \begin{bmatrix} 1 & 0 & \times & 1 & 0 & 0 \end{bmatrix}^t$, where $\times$ denotes a "do not care" bit.

P9.14 The double-ended operational amplifier shown in Figure P9.14 that performs as a neuron element implements simultaneously summation and current-to-voltage conversion. It uses two matching depletion mode transistors with device transconductance and depletion voltage values k and V_{dep}, respectively. Show that both networks of Figure P9.14 are identical if (9.68) holds, or

$$R_F = \frac{1}{kV_g}$$

P9.15 A simple way to reduce the nonlinearity of a weight consisting of an MOS transistor is to use a properly biased transmission gate as shown in Figure P9.15. Show that if both transmission gate transistors remain in the resistive region (NMOS: $V_{ds} < V_{gs} - V_{thn}$, PMOS: $V_{ds} > V_{gs} - V_{thp}$), the resistance of the produced weight is equal

$$R \triangleq \frac{V_1 - V_2}{I} = \frac{1}{2k(V_g - V_{thn})}$$

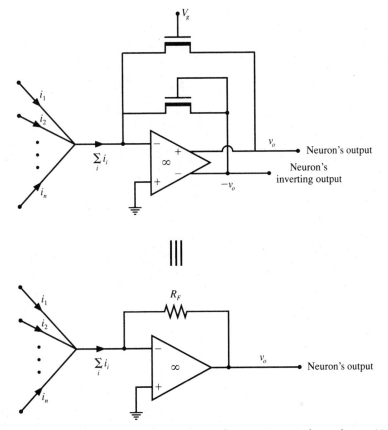

Figure P9.14 Integrated circuit feedback resistance for current summation and current-to-voltage conversion for Problem P9.14.

Assume:

$$I_{dsn} = k_n \left[(V_{gs} - V_{thn})V_{ds} - \frac{V_{ds}^2}{2} \right] \quad \text{for NMOS device}$$

$$I_{dsp} = k_p \left[(V_{gs} - V_{thp})V_{ds} - \frac{V_{ds}^2}{2} \right] \quad \text{for PMOS device}$$

$$k = k_n = k_p, \quad V_{th} = V_{thn} = -V_{thp}$$

(*Hint:* Assume initially $V_1 > V_2$ for derivation purposes. Since the weight circuitry is electrically symmetrical, the weight resistances remain identical when $V_1 < V_2$ is subsequently assumed.)

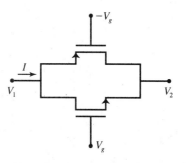

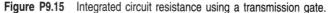

Figure P9.15 Integrated circuit resistance using a transmission gate.

P9.16 The output stage of a neuron with the sigmoidal transfer characteristics can be designed with two diodes connected in parallel to the
operational amplifier feedback resistor. The diodes cause the approximate saturation voltages of the neuron, which are substantially lower
than the saturation voltages produced without the diodes in place.
The resulting current-to-voltage converter that needs to be analyzed
in this problem is shown in Figure P9.16(a). Assume that $D1$ and
$D2$ are identical and described by the model approximated as shown
in the box of Figure P9.16(b). Provide the answer to the problem
in the form of the graphical characteristics of v_o versus I for the
current-to-voltage converter.

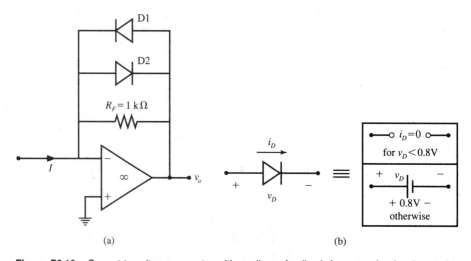

Figure P9.16 Current-to-voltage converter with nonlinear feedback for saturation level control.

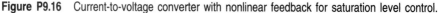

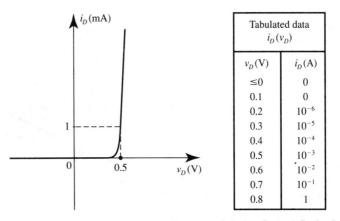

Tabulated data $i_D(v_D)$	
v_D (V)	i_D (A)
≤ 0	0
0.1	0
0.2	10^{-6}
0.3	10^{-5}
0.4	10^{-4}
0.5	10^{-3}
0.6	10^{-2}
0.7	10^{-1}
0.8	1

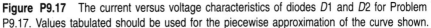

Figure P9.17 The current versus voltage characteristics of diodes *D*1 and *D*2 for Problem P9.17. Values tabulated should be used for the piecewise approximation of the curve shown.

P9.17 Repeat Problem P9.16 after replacing diodes *D*1 and *D*2 with the diode model characteristics sketched in Figure P9.17. The piecewise linear characteristics of the diodes as provided in the table can be used for obtaining the graphical solution.

[*Hint:* The parallel connection of R_F, *D*1, and *D*2 may be treated as a single nonlinear resistor carrying current i_{tot}. Current versus voltage characteristics $i_{tot}(v_o)$ of this composite nonlinear resistor can be obtained graphically by adding the currents through R_F, *D*1, and *D*2. The current-to-voltage conversion curve $v_o(I)$ can then be found since $i_{tot} = -I$].

P9.18 An analog voltage multiplier has the following transfer characteristics:

$$v_o = cv_i V_{thd}, \quad \text{where } V_{thd} > 0$$

where v_i, and v_o are input and output voltages, respectively, V_{thd} is the difference in threshold voltages of the MOSFET devices used, and $c > 0$ is a constant. Measurements of the multiplier output voltage versus its input voltage have been taken and are illustrated in Figure P9.18. Based on the characteristics shown:

(a) Compute the multiplication constant c of this multiplier.

(b) Draw the characteristics v_o versus V_{thd} with the input voltage as a parameter taking values $v_i = 0$; 0.25; 0.5; 0.75; 1.0 (V).

P9.19 Analyze the neuron circuit shown in Figure 9.53(a) and obtain its transfer characteristics v_o versus the difference of total excitatory and

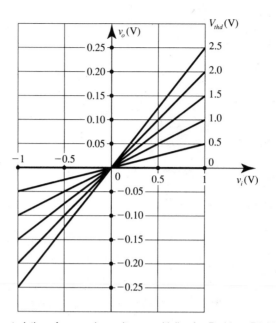

Figure P9.18 Characteristics of an analog voltage multiplier for Problem P9.18.

inhibitory currents as follows:

$$v_o = f(\Sigma I_+ - \Sigma I_-)$$

Assume that the circuit components have the values $R_F = 10$ kΩ, $R_1 = 1$ kΩ, and $R_2 = 5$ kΩ. Assume also that all operational amplifiers operate in their linear regions. Solve the problem for two separate cases as follows:

(a) Diodes $D1$ and $D2$ are disconnected.

(b) Diodes $D1$ and $D2$ are connected as shown and modeled by the equivalent circuit as depicted in Figure P9.16(b)

P9.20 This problem requires the analysis of the template matching network shown in Figure 9.32(b), for which n denotes the number of bits equal to 1 in the original template vector to be matched. Assume that the bit transistor resistances are R, and that the bias transistor resistance is chosen to have the value $R/(n-1)$. Show that the following properties of the network apply for this choice of component values:

(a) $v_{in} = V_{DD}n/(2n - 1) > V_{DD}/2$ for a perfect match

(b) $v_{in} = V_{DD}/2$ for the mismatch of a single input bit originally "0"

(c) $v_{in} = V_{DD}/2$ for the mismatch of a single input bit originally "1"

REFERENCES

Allen, P. E., and D. R. Holberg. 1987. *CMOS Analog Circuit Design.* New York: Holt, Rinehart and Winston.

Alspector, J., B. Gupta, and R. B. Allen. 1989. "Performance of a Stochastic Learning Microship," in *Advances in Neural Information Processing Systems.* San Mateo, Calif.: Morgan Kaufmann Publishers.

Bessiere, P., A. Chams, A. Guerin, J. Herault, C. Jutten, and J. C. Lawson. 1991. "From Hardware to Software and Designing a Neurostation," in *VLSI Design of Neural Networks,* ed. U. Ramacher, U. Rueckert. Boston: Kluwer Academic Publishers.

Bibyk, S., and M. Ismail. 1989. "Issues in Analog VLSI and MOS Techniques for Neural Computing," in *Analog Implementation of Neural Systems,* ed. C. Mead, M. Ismail. Boston: Kluwer Academic Publishers.

Bibyk, S., and M. Ismail. 1990. "Neural Network Building Blocks for Analog MOS VLSI," in *Analogue IC Design: The Current Mode Approach,* ed. C. Toumazou, F. J. Lidgey, D. G. Haigh. London: Peter Peregrinus, Ltd.

Borgstrom, T. H., M. Ismail, and S. B. Bibyk. 1990. "Programmable Current-Mode Neural Network for Implementation in Analogue MOS VLSI," *IEE Proc. Part G* 137(2): 175–184.

Card, H. C., C. R. Schneider, and W. R. Moore. 1991. "Hebbian Plasticity in MOS Synapses," *IEE Proc. Part F* 138(1): 13–16.

Chung, H. W. 1991. "CMOS VLSI Implementation of Neural Networks," in *Proc. '91 Neural Networks and Fuzzy Systems Application Workshop,* Seoul, South Korea, June 7-8, 1991. pp. 209–225.

Collins, D. R., and P. A. Penz. 1989. "Considerations for Neural Network Hardware Implementations," in *Proc. 1989 IEEE Int. Symp. on Circuits and Systems,* Portland, Oregon, May 9–12, 1989. pp. 834–837.

Collins, D. R., P. A. Penz, and J. B. Barton, "Neural Network Architectures and Implementations," in *Proc. 1990 IEEE Int. Symp. on Circuits and Systems,* New Orleans, Louisiana, May 1–3, 1990. pp. 2437–2440.

DARPA. 1988. *Neural Network Study.* Fairfax, Virginia: AFCEA Int. Press.

Farhat, N. H. 1989. "Optoelectronic Neural Networks and Learning Machines," *IEEE Circuits and Devices Magazine* (September): 32–41.

Fisher, W. A., R. J. Fujimoto, and R. C. Smithson. 1991. "A Programmable Analog Neural Network Processor," *IEEE Trans. Neural Networks* 2(2): 222–229.

Foo, S. Y., L.R. Anderson, and Y. Takefuji. 1990. "Analog Components for the VLSI of Neural Networks," *IEEE Circuits and Devices Magazine* (July): 18–26.

Frye, R. C., R. A. Rietman, C. C. Wong, B. L. Chin. 1989. "An Investigation of Adaptive Learning Implemented in an Optically Controlled Neural Network," in *Proc. Joint IEEE Int. Conf. on Neural Networks,* San Diego, California. pp. 457–463.

Geiger, R. L., P. E. Allen, and N. R. Strader. 1990. *VLSI Design Techniques for Analog and Digital Circuits.* New York: McGraw Hill Book Co.

Goser, K., U. Hilleringmann, U. Rueckert, and K. Schumacher. 1989. "VLSI Technologies for Artificial Neural Networks," *IEEE Micro* (December): 28–43.

Graf, H. P., and P. D. Vegvar. 1987. "CMOS Associative Memory Chip Based on Neural Networks," in *Proc. 1987 IEEE Int. Solid State Conf.,* February 27, 1987. pp. 304–305, 347.

Hopfield, J. J. 1990. "The Effectiveness of Analogue 'Neural Network' Hardware," *Network* 1: 27–40.

Howard, R. E., L. D. Jackel, and H. P. Graf. 1988. "Electronic Neural Networks," *AT&T Technical J.* (May): 58–64.

Intel Corporation. 1991. *Electrically Trainable Analog Neural Network ETANN Intel 80170NX.*

Jutten, C., A. Guerin, and J. Herault. 1990. "Simulation Machine and Integrated Implementation of Neural Networks: A Review of Methods, Problems, and Realizations," in *Neural Networks, Proc. of EURASIP Workshop,* Sesimbra, Portugal, February 15–17, 1990, ed. L. B. Almeida, C. J. Wellekens.

Kaul, R., S. Bibyk, M. Ismail, and M. Andro. 1990. "Adaptive Filtering Using Neural Network Integrated Circuits," in *Proc. 1990 IEEE Symp. on Circuits and Systems,* New Orleans, Louisiana, May 1–3, 1990. pp. 2520–2523.

Khachab, N. I., and M. Ismail. 1989a. "A New Continuous-Time MOS Implementation of Feedback Neural Networks," in *Proc. 32nd Midwest Symp. on Circuits and Systems,* Urbana, Illinois, August 1989. pp. 221-224.

Khachab, N. I., and M. Ismail. 1989b. "MOS Multiplier/Divider Cell for Analogue VLSI," *Electron. Lett.* 25(23): 1550–1552.

Kub, F. J., K. K. Moon, I. A. Mack, and F. M. Long. 1990. "Programmable Analog Vector-Matrix Multiplier," *IEEE J. of Solid-State Circuits* 25(1): 207–214.

Lambe, J., A. Moopenn, and A. P. Thakoor. 1988. "Electronic Neural Networks," *IEEE Eng. Medicine and Biology Magazine* (December): 56–57.

Lee, B. W., and B. J. Sheu. 1991. *Hardware Annealing in Analog VLSI Neurocomputing.* Boston: Kluwer Academic Publishers.

Lu, T., S. Wu, X. Xu, and F. T. S. Yu. 1989. "Two-Dimensional Programmable Optical Neural Network," *Appl. Opt.* 28(22): 4908–4913.

Mackie, S, H. P. Graf, D. B. Schwartz, and J. S. Denker. 1988. "Microelectronic Implementations of Connectionist Neural Networks," in *Neural Information Processing Systems,* ed. D. Z. Anderson. New York: American Institute of Physics.

Maher, M. A. C., S. P. Deweerth, M. A. Mahowald, and C. A. Mead. 1989. "Implementing Neural Architectures Using Analog VLSI Circuits," *IEEE Trans. Circuits and Systems* 36(5): 643–652.

Mann, J. 1990. "The Effects of Circuit Integration on a Feature Map Vector Quantizer," in *Advances in Neural Information Processing Systems,* ed. D. Touretzky, vol. 2. San Mateo, Calif.: Morgan Kaufmann Publishers.

Mead, C. 1989. *Analog VLSI and Neural Systems.* Reading, Mass.: Addison-Wesley Publishing Co.

Millman, J., and A. Grabel. 1987. *Microelectronics,* 2nd Ed. New York: McGraw Hill Book Co.

Moopenn, A., H. Langenbacher, A. P. Thakoor, and S. K. Khanna. 1988. "Programmable Synaptic Chip for Electronic Neural Networks," in *Advances in Neural Information Processing Systems,* ed. D. Touretzky, vol. 2. San Mateo, Calif.: Morgan Kaufmann Publishers.

Morton, S. G. 1991. "Electronic Hardware Implementation," in *Handbook of Neural Computing and Applications.* New York: Academic Press.

Mueller, P., J. V. D. Spiegel, D. Blackman, T. Chiu, T. Clare, C. Donham, T. P. Hsieh, M. Loinaz. 1989a. "Design and Fabrication of VLSI Components for a General Purpose Analog Neural Computer," in *Analog Implementation of Neural Systems,* ed. C. Mead, M. Ismail. Boston: Kluwer Academic Publishers.

Mueller, P., J. V. D. Spiegel, D. Blackman, T. Chiu, T. Clare, C. Donham, T. P. Hsieh, M. Loinaz. 1989b. "A Programmable Analog Neural Computer and Simulator," in *Advances in Neural Information Processing Systems,* ed. D. Touretzky, vol. 1. San Mateo, Calif.: Morgan Kaufmann Publishers.

Murray, A. F. 1991. "Silicon Implementation of Neural Networks," *IEE Proc. Part F* 138(1): 3–12.

Ouali, J., G. Saucier, and J. Thrile. 1991. "Fast Design of Dedicated Neuro-Chips," in VLSI Design of Neural Networks, ed. U. Ramacher, U. Rueckert. Boston: Kluwer Academic Publishers.

Paulos, J. J., and P. W. Hollis. 1988. "Neural Networks Using Analog Multipliers," in *Proc. 1988 IEEE Int. Symp. on Circuits and Systems,* Helsinki, Finland. pp. 494–502.

Psaltis, D., D. Brady, S. G. Gu, and K. Hsu. 1989. "Optical Implementation of Neural Computers," in *Optical Processing and Computing.* New York: Academic Press.

Rao, S. 1988. "Design and Analysis of MOSFET Resistors in VLSI," MSEE thesis, University of Louisville, Kentucky.

Raffel, J. I., J. R. Mann, R. Berger, A. M. Soares, and S. Gilbert. 1989. "A Generic Architecture for Wafer-Scale Neuromorphic Systems," *Lincoln Lab. J.* 2(1): 63–75.

Ramacher, U. 1991. "Guidelines to VLSI Design of Neural Nets," in *VLSI Design of Neural Networks,* ed. U. Ramacher, U. Rueckert. Boston: Kluwer Academic Publishers.

Recce, M., and P. C. Treleaven. 1988. "Parallel Architectures for Neural Computers," in *Neural Computers,* ed. R. Eckmiller, Ch. v. d. Malsburg. Berlin: Springer Verlag.

Reed, R. D., and R. L. Geiger. 1989. "A Multiple-Input OTA Circuit for Neural Networks," *IEEE Trans. Circuits and Systems* 36(5): 767–770.

Rossetto, O., C. Jutten, J. Herault, and I. Kreutzer. 1989. "Analog VLSI Synaptic Matrices as Building Blocks for Neural Networks," *IEEE Micro* (December): 56–63.

Salam, F. M. A., and M. R. Choi. 1990. "An All-MOS Analog Feedforward Neural Circuit with Learning," in *Proc. 1990 IEEE Int. Symp. on Circuits and Systems,* New Orleans, Louisiana, May 1–3, 1990. pp. 2508–2511.

Satyanarayana, S., Y. Tsividis, and H. P. Graf. 1990. "A Reconfigurable Analog VLSI Neural Network Chip," in *Advances in Neural Information Processing Systems,* ed. D. Touretzky, vol. 2. San Mateo, Calif.: Morgan Kaufmann Publishers.

Schwartz, D. B., and V. K. Samalam. 1990. "Learning, Function Approximation and Analog VLSI," in *Proc. 1990 IEEE Int. Symp. on Circuits and Systems,* New Orleans, Louisiana, May 1–3, 1990. pp. 2441–2444.

Sedra, A. S., and K. C. Smith. 1991. *Microelectronic Circuits.* Orlando, Fla.: Saunders College Publ.

Szu, H. H. 1991. "Optical Neuro-Computing," in *Handbook of Neural Computing and Applications.* New York: Academic Press.

Treleaven, P., M. Pacheco, and M. Vellasco. 1989. "VLSI Architectures for Neural Networks," *IEEE Micro* (December): 8–27.

Tsividis, Y. P., and D. Anastassiou. 1987. "Switched-Capacitor Neural Networks," *Electron. Lett.* 23(18): 958–959.

Tsividis, Y., and S. Satyanarayana. 1987. "Analogue Circuits for Variable-Synapse Electronic Neural Networks," *Electron. Lett.* 23(24): 1313–1314.

Verleysen, M., and P. G. A. Jespers. 1989. "An Analog Implementation of Hopfield's Neural Network," *IEEE Micro* (December): 46–55.

Verleysen, M., B. Sirletti, A. Vandemeulerbroeke, and P. G. A. Jespers. 1989. "A High-Storage Capacity Content-Addressable Memory and Its Learning Algorithm," *IEEE Trans. Circuits and Systems* 36(5): 762–766.

Verleysen, M., and P. Jespers. 1991. "Precision of Computations in Analog Neural Networks," in *VLSI Design of Neural Networks,* ed. U. Ramacher, U. Rueckert. Boston: Kluwer Academic Publishers.

Vidal, J. J. 1988. "Implementing Neural Nets with Programmable Logic," *IEEE Trans. Acoustics, Speech, and Signal Proc.* 36(7): 1180–1190.

Vittoz, E., H. Ougney, M. A. Maher, O. Nys, E. Dijkstra, and M. Chevroulet. 1991. "Analog Storage of Adjustable Synaptic Weights," in *VLSI Design of Neural Networks,* ed. U. Ramacher, U. Rueckert. Boston: Kluwer Academic Publishers.

Wagner, K., and D. Psaltis. 1987. "Multilayer Optical Learning Networks," *Appl. Opt.* 26(23): 5061–5075.

Wang, Y., and F. M. A. Salam. 1990. "Design of Neural Network Systems from Custom Analog VLSI Chips," in *Proc. 1990 IEEE Int. Symp. on Circuits and Systems,* New Orleans, Louisiana, May 1–3, 1990. pp. 1098–1101.

Wasaki, H., Y. Hario, and S. Nakamura. 1990. "A Localized Learning Rule for Analog VLSI Implementation of Neural Networks," in *Proc. 33rd Midwest Symp. Circuits and Systems,* Calgary, Alberta, Canada, August 12–14, 1990.

Zurada, J. M. 1981. "Application of Multiplying Digital-to-Analogue Convertor to Digital Control of Active Filter Characteristics," *IEE Proc. Part G* 128(2): 91–92.

Zurada, J. M. 1981. "Programmable State Variable Active Biquads," *J. Audio Eng. Soc.* 29(11): 786–793.

Zurada, J. M., Y. S. Yoo, and S. V. Bell. 1989. "Dynamic Noise Margins of MOS Logic Gates," in *Proc. 1989 IEEE Int. Symp. on Circuits and Systems,* Portland, Oregon, May 9–11, 1989.

APPENDIX

This appendix gives a brief introduction to basic mathematical concepts used throughout this text. It also contains the listing of the main procedures of the ANS program. Reading this appendix should give the student a good understanding of most of the definitions, interpretations, and operations. Reviewing the listing of the source code would provide the reader with an understanding of the programming of neural network computing algorithms in the Pascal language.

A1

VECTORS AND MATRICES

Definition of Vectors

Consider n real numbers (scalars) x_1, x_2, ..., x_n. These numbers can be arranged so as to define a new object $\mathbf{x}$, called a *column vector:*

$$\mathbf{x} \triangleq \begin{bmatrix} x_1 \\ x_2 \\ \vdots \\ x_n \end{bmatrix} \tag{A1.1}$$

A1

A lowercase boldface letter will always denote a column vector in this text, for example, $\mathbf{x}$, $\mathbf{y}$, $\mathbf{w}$. The numbers x_1, x_2, $\ldots$, x_n are the *components* of the vector. The vector itself can be called an n-component, n-tuple, or n-dimensional vector.

We can associate with the $\mathbf{x}$ vector its *transpose vector,* denoted by $\mathbf{x}^t$ and defined as follows:

$$\mathbf{x}^t \overset{\Delta}{=} \begin{bmatrix} x_1 & x_2 & \ldots & x_n \end{bmatrix} \tag{A1.2}$$

where superscript t denotes the transposition. Note that $\mathbf{x}^t$ is a row vector.

Operations on Vectors

Consider the column vectors

$$\mathbf{x} = \begin{bmatrix} x_1 \\ x_2 \\ \vdots \\ x_n \end{bmatrix}, \ \mathbf{y} = \begin{bmatrix} y_1 \\ y_2 \\ \vdots \\ y_n \end{bmatrix}, \ \mathbf{z} \overset{\Delta}{=} \begin{bmatrix} x_1 + y_1 \\ x_2 + y_2 \\ \vdots \\ x_n + y_n \end{bmatrix} \tag{A1.3}$$

We define the *sum of the column vectors* $\mathbf{x}$ and $\mathbf{y}$, $\mathbf{x} + \mathbf{y}$, to be the column vector $\mathbf{z}$ as in (A1.3). Note that adding two n-component vectors requires adding their respective components.

The *product of a column vector* $\mathbf{x}$ *by a scalar* c is defined as a vector whose components are products cx_i such that

$$c\mathbf{x} \overset{\Delta}{=} c \begin{bmatrix} x_1 \\ x_2 \\ \vdots \\ x_n \end{bmatrix} = \begin{bmatrix} cx_1 \\ cx_2 \\ \vdots \\ cx_n \end{bmatrix} \tag{A1.4}$$

Linear Dependence of Vectors

Consider a set of n-dimensional vectors $\mathbf{x}_1$, $\mathbf{x}_2$, $\ldots$, $\mathbf{x}_m$ used to construct a vector $\mathbf{x}$ such that

$$\mathbf{x} = c_1 \mathbf{x}_1 + c_2 \mathbf{x}_2 + \ldots + c_m \mathbf{x}_m = \sum_{i=1}^{m} c_i \mathbf{x}_i \tag{A1.5}$$

where c_1, c_2, $\ldots$, c_m are scalars. The vector $\mathbf{x}$ is a *linear combination* of vectors $\mathbf{x}_i$, for $i = 1, 2, \ldots, m$. A set of vectors $\mathbf{x}_1$, $\mathbf{x}_2$, $\ldots$, $\mathbf{x}_m$ is said to be *linearly dependent* if numbers c_1, c_2, $\ldots$, c_m, exist and are not all zero, such that

$$c_1 \mathbf{x}_1 + c_2 \mathbf{x}_2 + \ldots + c_m \mathbf{x}_m = \mathbf{0} \tag{A1.6}$$

If vectors $\mathbf{x}_1$, $\mathbf{x}_2$, $\ldots$, $\mathbf{x}_m$ are not linearly dependent, we say that they are *linearly independent*.

EXAMPLE A1.1 ■■■■■■■■■■■■■

Consider three vectors

$$\mathbf{x}_1 = \begin{bmatrix} 1 \\ -1 \\ 0 \end{bmatrix}, \ \mathbf{x}_2 = \begin{bmatrix} 0 \\ -2 \\ 1 \end{bmatrix}, \ \mathbf{x}_3 = \begin{bmatrix} 2 \\ 4 \\ -3 \end{bmatrix}$$

Since $2\mathbf{x}_1 + (-3)\mathbf{x}_2 + (-1)\mathbf{x}_3 = \mathbf{0}$, the vectors are linearly dependent.
Consider three vectors

$$\mathbf{x}_1 = \begin{bmatrix} 1 \\ 0 \\ 0 \end{bmatrix}, \ \mathbf{x}_2 = \begin{bmatrix} 0 \\ 1 \\ 0 \end{bmatrix}, \ \mathbf{x}_3 = \begin{bmatrix} 0 \\ 0 \\ 1 \end{bmatrix}$$

No constants, c_i, $i = 1, 2, 3$, which are not all zero, can be found such that $c_1\mathbf{x}_1 + c_2\mathbf{x}_2 + c_3\mathbf{x}_3 = \mathbf{0}$. Therefore, vectors $\mathbf{x}_1, \mathbf{x}_2$, and $\mathbf{x}_3$ are considered to be linearly independent. ■

Definition of Matrices

A rectangular array $\mathbf{A}$ as in (A1.7) of $n \cdot m$ numbers a_{ij}, where $i = 1, 2, \ldots, n$, and $j = 1, 2, \ldots, m$, arranged in n rows and m columns is called an $n \times m$ *matrix*

$$\mathbf{A} \triangleq \begin{bmatrix} a_{11} & a_{12} & \cdots & a_{1m} \\ a_{21} & a_{22} & \cdots & a_{2m} \\ \vdots & \vdots & \cdots & \vdots \\ a_{n1} & a_{n2} & \cdots & a_{nm} \end{bmatrix} \tag{A1.7}$$

We denote matrices by uppercase boldface letters, for example, $\mathbf{A}, \mathbf{W}, \mathbf{V}$.

We can associate with the $\mathbf{A}$ matrix its *transpose matrix,* denoted by $\mathbf{A}^t$ and defined as follows:

$$\mathbf{A}^t \triangleq \begin{bmatrix} a_{11} & a_{21} & \cdots & a_{n1} \\ a_{12} & a_{22} & \cdots & a_{n2} \\ \vdots & \vdots & \cdots & \vdots \\ a_{1m} & a_{2m} & \cdots & a_{nm} \end{bmatrix} \tag{A1.8}$$

Note that $\mathbf{A}^t$ is formed from the matrix $\mathbf{A}$ by interchanging its rows with columns. Therefore, the first column of $\mathbf{A}$ becomes the first row of $\mathbf{A}^t$, the second column of $\mathbf{A}$ becomes the second row of $\mathbf{A}^t$, and so on. Thus, $\mathbf{A}^t$ is an $m \times n$ matrix.

Operations on Matrices

Consider two $n \times m$ matrices, $\mathbf{A}$ and $\mathbf{B}$, with their respective elements a_{ij} and b_{ij}, for $i = 1, 2, \ldots, n$, and $j = 1, 2, \ldots, m$. The *sum of matrices* $\mathbf{A}$ and $\mathbf{B}$ is the $n \times m$ matrix whose elements are the sums of the corresponding elements:

$$
\mathbf{A} + \mathbf{B} = \begin{bmatrix} a_{11} & a_{12} & \cdots & a_{1m} \\ a_{21} & a_{22} & \cdots & a_{2m} \\ \vdots & \vdots & \cdots & \vdots \\ a_{n1} & a_{n2} & \cdots & a_{nm} \end{bmatrix} + \begin{bmatrix} b_{11} & b_{12} & \cdots & b_{1m} \\ b_{21} & b_{22} & \cdots & b_{2m} \\ \vdots & \vdots & \cdots & \vdots \\ b_{n1} & b_{n2} & \cdots & b_{nm} \end{bmatrix}
$$

$$
= \begin{bmatrix} a_{11} + b_{11} & a_{12} + b_{12} & \cdots & a_{1m} + b_{1m} \\ a_{21} + b_{21} & a_{22} + b_{22} & \cdots & a_{2m} + b_{2m} \\ \vdots & \vdots & \cdots & \vdots \\ a_{n1} + b_{n1} & a_{n2} + b_{n2} & \cdots & a_{nm} + b_{nm} \end{bmatrix} \tag{A1.9}
$$

The *product of an $n \times m$ matrix $\mathbf{A}$ by a scalar c* is defined as an $n \times m$ matrix whose elements are products ca_{ij} such that

$$
c\mathbf{A} \overset{\Delta}{=} c \begin{bmatrix} a_{11} & a_{12} & \cdots & a_{1m} \\ a_{21} & a_{22} & \cdots & a_{2m} \\ \vdots & \vdots & \cdots & \vdots \\ a_{n1} & a_{n2} & \cdots & a_{nm} \end{bmatrix} = \begin{bmatrix} ca_{11} & ca_{12} & \cdots & ca_{1m} \\ ca_{21} & ca_{22} & \cdots & ca_{2m} \\ \vdots & \vdots & \cdots & \vdots \\ ca_{n1} & ca_{n2} & \cdots & ca_{nm} \end{bmatrix} \tag{A1.10}
$$

The *product $\mathbf{AB}$* of an $n \times m$ matrix $\mathbf{A}$ and of an $m \times q$ matrix $\mathbf{B}$ is the $n \times q$ matrix $\mathbf{C}$ such that

$$
c_{ik} = \sum_{j=1}^{m} a_{ij} b_{jk} \tag{A1.11}
$$

for $i = 1, 2, \ldots, n$, and $k = 1, 2, \ldots, q$. In matrix notation, the product is written

$$
\mathbf{C} = \mathbf{AB} \tag{A1.12}
$$

Formula (A1.11) indicates that the element c_{ik} at the intersection of the i'th row and k'th column of the product matrix is computed by multiplying the i'th row of $\mathbf{A}$ by the k'th column of $\mathbf{B}$. Note that for the product $\mathbf{AB}$ to make sense, the number of columns of $\mathbf{A}$ must be equal to the number of rows of $\mathbf{B}$ [both are m in expression (A1.11)]. The reader should notice that matrix multiplication is not commutative.

EXAMPLE A1.2

Let us illustrate the use of (A1.11) by multiplying two matrices as shown below:

$$\mathbf{A} = \begin{bmatrix} a_{11} & a_{12} \\ a_{21} & a_{22} \\ a_{31} & a_{32} \end{bmatrix}, \; \mathbf{B} = \begin{bmatrix} b_{11} & b_{12} \\ b_{21} & b_{22} \end{bmatrix}$$

Matrix $\mathbf{A}$ is 3×2, matrix $\mathbf{B}$ is 2×2, thus the product matrix is 3×2:

$$\mathbf{AB} = \begin{bmatrix} a_{11} & a_{12} \\ a_{21} & a_{22} \\ a_{31} & a_{32} \end{bmatrix} \begin{bmatrix} b_{11} & b_{12} \\ b_{21} & b_{22} \end{bmatrix} = \begin{bmatrix} a_{11}b_{11} + a_{12}b_{21} & a_{11}b_{12} + a_{12}b_{22} \\ a_{21}b_{11} + a_{22}b_{21} & a_{21}b_{12} + a_{22}b_{22} \\ a_{31}b_{11} + a_{32}b_{21} & a_{31}b_{12} + a_{32}b_{22} \end{bmatrix}$$

Note that, for example, element c_{12} of $\mathbf{C}$ computed from (A1.11) is

$$c_{12} = \sum_{j=1}^{2} a_{1j}b_{j2} = a_{11}b_{12} + a_{12}b_{22}$$

and the element c_{21} computed from (A1.11) is

$$c_{21} = \sum_{j=1}^{2} a_{2j}b_{j1} = a_{21}b_{11} + a_{22}b_{21}$$

■

Multiplication of Matrices and Vectors

An m-tuple vector $\mathbf{x}$ defined in (A1.1) can be interpreted as a matrix with m rows and one column. Let us consider the problem of *postmultiplying an $n \times m$ $\mathbf{A}$ matrix with a vector $\mathbf{x}$*, which is equivalent to an $m \times 1$ matrix. If we let

$$\mathbf{y} \stackrel{\Delta}{=} \mathbf{Ax} \tag{A1.13a}$$

or, in an expanded form

$$\begin{bmatrix} y_1 \\ y_2 \\ \vdots \\ y_n \end{bmatrix} = \begin{bmatrix} a_{11} & a_{12} & \cdots & a_{1m} \\ a_{21} & a_{22} & \cdots & a_{2m} \\ \vdots & \vdots & \cdots & \vdots \\ a_{n1} & a_{n2} & \cdots & a_{nm} \end{bmatrix} \begin{bmatrix} x_1 \\ x_2 \\ \vdots \\ x_m \end{bmatrix} \tag{A1.13b}$$

then we can compute components y_i of the vector $\mathbf{y}$ using (A1.11) as follows:

$$y_i = \sum_{j=1}^{m} a_{ij}x_j, \quad \text{for } i = 1, 2, \ldots, n \tag{A1.14}$$

Note that the vector $\mathbf{y}$ resulting as a product is n-dimensional.

EXAMPLE A1.3 ■■■■■■■■■■■■

Let us illustrate the multiplication of a 3×2 matrix $\mathbf{A}$ by a two-component vector $\mathbf{x}$. In the general case, we have

$$\mathbf{y} = \mathbf{A}\mathbf{x} = \begin{bmatrix} a_{11} & a_{12} \\ a_{21} & a_{22} \\ a_{31} & a_{32} \end{bmatrix} \begin{bmatrix} x_1 \\ x_2 \end{bmatrix} = \begin{bmatrix} a_{11}x_1 + a_{12}x_2 \\ a_{21}x_1 + a_{22}x_2 \\ a_{31}x_1 + a_{32}x_2 \end{bmatrix}$$

■

Symmetric Matrices and Their Properties

Let us suppose that $\mathbf{A}$ is an $n \times n$ matrix. Such a matrix is called a *square matrix* since it has the same number of rows and columns. Let us note that a square matrix can be *symmetric*. This property applies when

$$\mathbf{A}^t = \mathbf{A} \tag{A1.15}$$

A square matrix $\mathbf{A}$ whose elements not on the main diagonal are zero is called a *diagonal* matrix. The general form of a diagonal matrix is

$$\mathbf{A} = \begin{bmatrix} a_{11} & 0 & \cdots & 0 \\ 0 & a_{22} & \cdots & 0 \\ \vdots & \vdots & \cdots & \vdots \\ 0 & 0 & \cdots & a_{nn} \end{bmatrix} \tag{A1.16}$$

The *unity* or *identity* matrix denoted as $\mathbf{I}$ is a special case of the diagonal matrix in (A1.16) such that $a_{ii} = 1$, for $i = 1, 2, \ldots, n$. We thus have

$$\mathbf{I} = \begin{bmatrix} 1 & 0 & \cdots & 0 \\ 0 & 1 & \cdots & 0 \\ \vdots & \vdots & \cdots & \vdots \\ 0 & 0 & \cdots & 1 \end{bmatrix} \tag{A1.17}$$

The *determinant* of a square matrix is a scalar and is denoted by

$$\det \mathbf{A} = \begin{vmatrix} a_{11} & a_{12} & \cdots & a_{1n} \\ a_{21} & a_{22} & \cdots & a_{2n} \\ \vdots & \vdots & \cdots & \vdots \\ a_{n1} & a_{n2} & \cdots & a_{nn} \end{vmatrix} \tag{A1.18}$$

(It is assumed that the reader is familiar with the computation of determinants.)

Norms, Products, and Orthogonality of Vectors

The *Euclidean norm,* or *length,* of an *n*-tuple vector $\mathbf{x}$ is denoted as $\|\mathbf{x}\|$ and defined

$$\|\mathbf{x}\| \overset{\Delta}{=} (\mathbf{x}^t\mathbf{x})^{1/2} \tag{A1.19}$$

Note that the Euclidean norm as in (A1.19) can be computed by using the concept of matrix multiplication. Indeed, for an *n*-component vector $\mathbf{x}$ we have from (A1.19)

$$\|\mathbf{x}\| = \left(\begin{bmatrix} x_1 & x_2 & \dots & x_n \end{bmatrix} \begin{bmatrix} x_1 \\ x_2 \\ \vdots \\ x_n \end{bmatrix} \right)^{1/2} = \sqrt{\sum_{i=1}^{n} x_i^2} \tag{A1.20}$$

This result is in agreement with the principles of matrix multiplication rules (A1.11) and (A1.12) for multiplication of a $1 \times n$ matrix by an $n \times 1$ matrix.

The *scalar (inner, dot) product* of two *n*-component vectors $\mathbf{x}$ and $\mathbf{y}$ is the scalar (number) defined as

$$\mathbf{x}^t\mathbf{y} = x_1y_1 + x_2y_2 + \dots + x_ny_n = \sum_{i=1}^{n} x_iy_i \tag{A1.21}$$

Note that both vectors $\mathbf{x}$ and $\mathbf{y}$ are column vectors and that their scalar product is computed as a sum of *n* products of corresponding components.

An important property as below holds for the scalar product that links the Euclidean norms of vectors $\mathbf{x}$ and $\mathbf{y}$ and the angle ψ between them:

$$\mathbf{x}^t\mathbf{y} = \|\mathbf{x}\| \cdot \|\mathbf{y}\| \cos \psi \tag{A1.22}$$

This property is illustrated in Figure A1 for the two-dimensional case of vectors $\mathbf{x}$ and $\mathbf{y}$, where

$$\mathbf{x} = \begin{bmatrix} x_1 \\ x_2 \end{bmatrix}, \mathbf{y} = \begin{bmatrix} y_1 \\ y_2 \end{bmatrix} \tag{A1.23}$$

The reader should note that the scalar product operation on two vectors is commutative. We thus have $\mathbf{x}^t\mathbf{y} = \mathbf{y}^t\mathbf{x}$. In the text the scalar product of input and weight vectors is often denoted by *net*, which is the argument of the activation function.

Vectors $\mathbf{x}$ and $\mathbf{y}$ are said to be *orthogonal* if and only if their scalar product is zero. There is a simple connection between linear independence and orthogonality. If the nonzero vectors $\mathbf{x}_1$, $\mathbf{x}_2$, ..., $\mathbf{x}_n$ are mutually orthogonal (every vector is orthogonal to each other), then they are linearly independent. The three

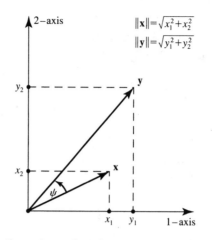

$$\|\mathbf{x}\| = \sqrt{x_1^2 + x_2^2}$$
$$\|\mathbf{y}\| = \sqrt{y_1^2 + y_2^2}$$

Figure A1   Illustration for the scalar product of two vectors, **x** and **y**.

vectors of Example A1.1

$$\mathbf{x}_1 = \begin{bmatrix} 1 \\ 0 \\ 0 \end{bmatrix}, \ \mathbf{x}_2 = \begin{bmatrix} 0 \\ 1 \\ 0 \end{bmatrix}, \ \mathbf{x}_3 = \begin{bmatrix} 0 \\ 0 \\ 1 \end{bmatrix}$$

are examples of three mutually orthogonal vectors. They also are linearly independent.

EXAMPLE A1.4

Let us find the scalar product of two vectors **x** and **y**, their lengths, and the angle between them. The vectors are

$$\mathbf{x} = \begin{bmatrix} 2 \\ 1 \\ 2 \end{bmatrix}, \ \mathbf{y} = \begin{bmatrix} 1 \\ -1 \\ 4 \end{bmatrix}$$

The definition (A1.21) yields the following scalar product value

$$\mathbf{x}^t \mathbf{y} = 2 \cdot 1 + 1 \cdot (-1) + 2 \cdot 4 = 9$$

The angle between the vectors can be found from expression (A1.22) as follows

$$\cos \psi = \frac{\mathbf{x}^t \mathbf{y}}{\|\mathbf{x}\| \cdot \|\mathbf{y}\|} \tag{A1.24}$$

Since the lengths of the vectors $\mathbf{x}$ and $\mathbf{y}$ computed from (A1.20) result as

$$\|\mathbf{x}\| = \sqrt{2^2 + 1 + 2^2} = 3$$
$$\|\mathbf{y}\| = \sqrt{1 + 1 + 4^2} = \sqrt{18}$$

we obtain from (A1.24)

$$\cos \psi = \frac{9}{3\sqrt{18}} = \frac{1}{\sqrt{2}}$$

We thus conclude that $\psi = 45°$.
■

The *outer (vector, cross) product* of two n-component vectors $\mathbf{x}$ and $\mathbf{y}$ is defined as

$$\mathbf{x} \times \mathbf{y} \stackrel{\Delta}{=} \mathbf{x}\mathbf{y}^t \qquad \text{(A1.25)}$$

Note that the outer product is an $n \times n$ matrix as shown below:

$$\mathbf{x} \times \mathbf{y} = \begin{bmatrix} x_1 \\ x_2 \\ \vdots \\ x_n \end{bmatrix} \begin{bmatrix} y_1 & y_2 & \cdots & y_n \end{bmatrix} = \begin{bmatrix} x_1y_1 & x_1y_2 & \cdots & x_1y_n \\ x_2y_1 & x_2y_2 & \cdots & x_2y_n \\ \vdots & \vdots & \cdots & \vdots \\ x_ny_1 & x_ny_2 & \cdots & x_ny_n \end{bmatrix} \qquad \text{(A1.26)}$$

Note that the outer product of two identical n-tuple vectors results in symmetrical $n \times n$ matrix.

Linear Systems, Inverse and Pseudoinverse Matrices

Consider a linear system of n equations with m unknowns $x_1, x_2, \ldots, x_m$. The general form of the equation system is as in (A1.13)

$$\mathbf{y} = \mathbf{A}\mathbf{x} \qquad \text{(A1.27)}$$

In a case where $m = n$ and $\det \mathbf{A} \neq 0$, the exact solution of (A1.27) is

$$\mathbf{x} = \mathbf{A}^{-1}\mathbf{y} \qquad \text{(A1.28)}$$

where $\mathbf{A}^{-1}$ is the inverse matrix. In a case where $m < n$, equation (A1.27) does not have an accurate solution for $\mathbf{x}$. We may therefore be interested in obtaining the approximate solution, $\bar{\mathbf{x}}$, such that it minimizes the error $\|\mathbf{A}\mathbf{x} - \mathbf{y}\|$. This solution is

$$\bar{\mathbf{x}} = \mathbf{A}^+\mathbf{y} \qquad \text{(A1.29)}$$

In the case when $m > n$, equation (A1.27) has an infinite number of solutions. Again, we may be interested in the solution, $\bar{\mathbf{x}}$, which has the smallest norm, i.e., $\|\bar{\mathbf{x}}\| \leq \|\mathbf{x}\|$ for each $\mathbf{x}$ such that $\mathbf{A}\mathbf{x} = \mathbf{y}$. This solution is

$$\bar{\mathbf{x}} = \mathbf{A}^+\mathbf{y} \qquad \text{(A1.30)}$$

In both cases (A1.29) and (A1.30) matrix $\mathbf{A}^+$ is called the *pseudoinverse* of matrix $\mathbf{A}$.

When $m < n$ we have the pseudoinverse matrix of value

$$\mathbf{A}^+ = (\mathbf{A}'\mathbf{A})^{-1}\mathbf{A}' \tag{A1.31}$$

When $m > n$ we have the pseudoinverse matrix of value

$$\mathbf{A}^+ = \mathbf{A}'(\mathbf{A}\mathbf{A}')^{-1} \tag{A1.32}$$

A2

QUADRATIC FORMS AND DEFINITE MATRICES

Definition of Quadratic Forms

Quadratic form $E(\mathbf{x})$ of a vectorial variable, $\mathbf{x}$, is of fundamental importance for studying multi-input/multi-output physical systems. The *quadratic form* is a scalar-valued function of $\mathbf{x}$ defined through a symmetric $n \times n$ matrix $\mathbf{A}$ as defined in expression (A1.7). The quadratic form is equal

$$E(\mathbf{x}) = \mathbf{x}'\mathbf{A}\mathbf{x} \tag{A2.1}$$

which is equivalent to

$$E(\mathbf{x}) = \begin{bmatrix} x_1 & x_2 & \dots & x_n \end{bmatrix} \begin{bmatrix} a_{11} & a_{12} & \cdots & a_{1n} \\ a_{21} & a_{22} & \cdots & a_{2n} \\ \vdots & \vdots & \cdots & \vdots \\ a_{n1} & a_{n2} & \cdots & a_{nn} \end{bmatrix} \begin{bmatrix} x_1 \\ x_2 \\ \vdots \\ x_n \end{bmatrix} \tag{A2.2}$$

Assuming the symmetric matrix $\mathbf{A}$ and performing the multiplication from left to right of matrices $1 \times n$ by $n \times n$ by $n \times 1$ yields the scalar function 1×1, which is the polynomial in the form

$$\begin{aligned} E(x_1, x_2, \dots x_n) = a_{11}x_1^2 &+ 2a_{12}x_1x_2 + 2a_{13}x_1x_3 + \dots + 2a_{1n}x_1x_n \\ &+ a_{22}x_2^2 + 2a_{23}x_2x_3 + \dots + 2a_{2n}x_2x_n + \cdots + a_{nn}x_n^2 \end{aligned} \tag{A2.3}$$

Note that the assumption about the symmetry of matrix $\mathbf{A}$ causes all terms without the squared variables x_i, for $i = 1, 2, \dots, n$, to be doubled in (A2.3) since $a_{ij} = a_{ji}$. If the matrix $\mathbf{A}$ were not symmetric, we would have terms $(a_{ij} + a_{ji})x_ix_j$ for all terms of (A2.3) without the squared variable. In short, the quadratic form of (A2.2) or (A2.3) can be rewritten as

$$E(\mathbf{x}) = \sum_{i=1}^{n} \sum_{j=1}^{n} a_{ij} x_i x_j \tag{A2.4}$$

EXAMPLE A2.1 ■■■■■■■■■■

Let us compute the quadratic form $E(\mathbf{x})$ defined as in (A2.1), where

$$\mathbf{x} = \begin{bmatrix} x_1 \\ x_2 \end{bmatrix}, \quad \mathbf{A} = \begin{bmatrix} 1 & 2 \\ 2 & 3 \end{bmatrix}$$

Using either of the formulas (A2.2), (A2.3), or (A2.4) yields the quadratic form as

$$E(\mathbf{x}) = x_1^2 + 4x_1x_2 + 3x_2^2 \qquad ■$$

Properties of Quadratic Forms

Let us define the most important properties of quadratic forms related to their value in terms of the vectorial variable, $\mathbf{x}$. If for all nonzero $\mathbf{x}$ $(\mathbf{x} \neq \mathbf{0})$ $E(\mathbf{x}) = \mathbf{x}^t\mathbf{Ax}$ is

(a) non-negative, then $E(\mathbf{x})$ is called a *positive semidefinite form* and $\mathbf{A}$ is called a positive semidefinite matrix.

(b) positive, then $E(\mathbf{x})$ is called a *positive definite form* and $\mathbf{A}$ is called a positive definite matrix.

(c) non-positive, then $E(\mathbf{x})$ is called a *negative semidefinite form* and $\mathbf{A}$ is called a negative semidefinite matrix.

(d) negative, then $E(\mathbf{x})$ is called a *negative definite form* and $\mathbf{A}$ is called a negative definite matrix.

Below we outline the procedure for the testing of quadratic forms for conditions (a) through (d). We begin with case (b).

The form $E(\mathbf{x})$ is said to be positive definite if and only if, for the symmetric matrix $\mathbf{A}$

$$\mathbf{A} = \begin{bmatrix} a_{11} & a_{12} & \cdots & a_{1n} \\ a_{12} & a_{22} & \cdots & a_{2n} \\ \vdots & \vdots & \cdots & \vdots \\ a_{1n} & a_{2n} & \cdots & a_{nn} \end{bmatrix} \qquad (A2.5)$$

its principal determinants $\det A_{11}$, $\det A_{22}$, ..., $\det A_{nn}$, defined as below fulfill the conditions

$$\det A_{11} \stackrel{\Delta}{=} |a_{11}| > 0$$

$$\det A_{22} \stackrel{\Delta}{=} \begin{vmatrix} a_{11} & a_{12} \\ a_{12} & a_{22} \end{vmatrix} > 0$$

$$\vdots \qquad (A2.6)$$

$$\det A_{nn} \stackrel{\Delta}{=} \det \mathbf{A} > 0$$

The test conditions are tabulated below for all relevant cases. Similar to (A2.6), the test involves evaluation of the signs of the principal determinants of matrix **A**.

Case	Class	Test
(a)	Positive semidefinite	$\det A_{11} \geq 0$, $\det A_{22} \geq 0$, ..., $\det A_{nn} \geq 0$
(b)	Positive definite	$\det A_{11} > 0$, $\det A_{22} > 0$, ..., $\det A_{nn} > 0$
(c)	Negative semidefinite	$\det A_{11} \leq 0$, $\det A_{22} \geq 0$ ... etc.
		(note alternating signs)
(d)	Negative definite	$\det A_{11} < 0$, $\det A_{22} > 0$, ..., etc.
		(note alternating signs)
(e)	Indefinite	none of the above.

(A2.7)

Note that the quadratic form $E(\mathbf{x})$ is said to be *indefinite* if it is positive for some **x** and negative for other **x**. This points out that the sign of an indefinite quadratic form depends on **x**.

EXAMPLE A2.2 ■

Let us look at an example of a quadratic form with a symmetric 2×2 matrix **A** such that its diagonal elements are zero:

$$\mathbf{x}'\mathbf{A}\mathbf{x} = \begin{bmatrix} x_1 & x_2 \end{bmatrix} \begin{bmatrix} 0 & a \\ a & 0 \end{bmatrix} \begin{bmatrix} x_1 \\ x_2 \end{bmatrix}$$

Since we have

$$\det A_{11} = 0, \ \det A_{22} = -a^2 < 0$$

we can conclude that the evaluated quadratic form is indefinite. Indeed, multiplication of matrices or using expansion of the evaluated form as in (A2.3) yields the quadratic form

$$E(\mathbf{x}) = \begin{bmatrix} ax_2 & ax_1 \end{bmatrix} \begin{bmatrix} x_1 \\ x_2 \end{bmatrix} = 2ax_1x_2$$

The sign of the resulting function $E(\mathbf{x})$ depends on **x**. If x_1 and x_2 are of identical signs, $E(\mathbf{x})$ remains positive, otherwise it is negative. Therefore, vectors **x** from the first and third quadrant render the discussed form positive, otherwise it is negative. ■

A3

TIME-VARYING AND GRADIENT VECTORS, JACOBIAN AND HESSIAN MATRICES

Time-Varying Vectors

A *time-varying vector* $\mathbf{x}(t)$ is defined as a column vector (A1.1), but its components are themselves functions of time, i.e.,

$$\mathbf{x}(t) = \begin{bmatrix} x_1(t) \\ x_2(t) \\ \vdots \\ x_n(t) \end{bmatrix} \tag{A3.1}$$

The time derivative of the vector $\mathbf{x}(t)$ is defined as

$$\frac{d\mathbf{x}(t)}{dt} = \begin{bmatrix} \dfrac{dx_1(t)}{dt} \\ \dfrac{dx_2(t)}{dt} \\ \vdots \\ \dfrac{dx_n(t)}{dt} \end{bmatrix} \tag{A3.2a}$$

or in a shorthand notation as

$$\dot{\mathbf{x}}(t) = \begin{bmatrix} \dot{x}_1(t) \\ \dot{x}_2(t) \\ \vdots \\ \dot{x}_n(t) \end{bmatrix} \tag{A3.2b}$$

Gradient Vectors

Consider a scalar function $E(\mathbf{x})$ of a vectorial variable $\mathbf{x}$, which is defined as an n-component column vector as in (A1.1). The *gradient vector* of $E(\mathbf{x})$ with respect to the column vector $\mathbf{x}$ is denoted as $\nabla_x E(\mathbf{x})$ and is equal

$$\nabla_x E(\mathbf{x}) \overset{\Delta}{=} \begin{bmatrix} \dfrac{\partial E}{\partial x_1} \\ \dfrac{\partial E}{\partial x_2} \\ \vdots \\ \dfrac{\partial E}{\partial x_n} \end{bmatrix} \tag{A3.3}$$

Note that the gradient is also an n-tuple column vector.

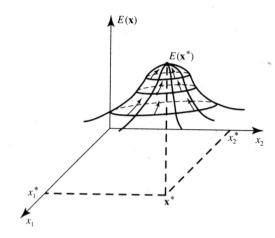

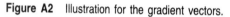

Figure A2 Illustration for the gradient vectors.

Notice that the immediate consequences of the definition of the gradient vector as in (A3.3) are

$$\nabla_x(\mathbf{x}^t\mathbf{y}) = \mathbf{y} \qquad\qquad \text{(A3.4a)}$$

$$\nabla_x(\mathbf{x}^t\mathbf{A}\mathbf{y}) = \mathbf{A}\mathbf{y} \qquad\qquad \text{(A3.4b)}$$

$$\nabla_x(\mathbf{x}^t\mathbf{A}\mathbf{x}) = \mathbf{A}\mathbf{x} + \mathbf{A}^t\mathbf{x} \qquad\qquad \text{(A3.4c)}$$

When dealing with quadratic forms and when $\mathbf{A}$ is a symmetric matrix, we have $\mathbf{A} = \mathbf{A}^t$ and (A3.4c) simplifies to

$$\nabla_x(\mathbf{x}^t\mathbf{A}\mathbf{x}) = 2\mathbf{A}\mathbf{x} \qquad\qquad \text{(A3.5)}$$

The geometrical interpretation of a gradient is often useful. Figure A2 shows a function $E(\mathbf{x})$ with $\mathbf{x}$ restricted to two components, x_1 and x_2. Vector $\nabla_x E(\mathbf{x})$ at a given point $\mathbf{x}_0$ specifies the direction of the maximum increase of $E(\mathbf{x})$. Note that at the maximum point, $\mathbf{x}^*$, we have

$$\nabla_x E(\mathbf{x}^*) = \mathbf{0} \qquad\qquad \text{(A3.6)}$$

The property of the zero gradient also holds at a minimum point.

Gradient of Time-Varying Vectors

Assume that $\mathbf{x}$ is a time-varying n-component vector and that a scalar function $E[\mathbf{x}(t)]$ (not necessarily a quadratic form) is defined for such a vectorial variable. The time derivative $dE[\mathbf{x}(t)]/dt$ for the evaluated scalar function can be computed by the chain rule as follows

$$\frac{dE[\mathbf{x}(t)]}{dt} = \frac{\partial E}{\partial x_1} \cdot \frac{dx_1(t)}{dt} + \frac{\partial E}{\partial x_2} \cdot \frac{dx_2(t)}{dt} + \ldots + \frac{\partial E}{\partial x_n} \cdot \frac{dx_n(t)}{dt} \qquad \text{(A3.7a)}$$

or, briefly

$$\frac{dE[\mathbf{x}(t)]}{dt} = \sum_{i=1}^{n} \frac{\partial E}{\partial x_i} \dot{x}_i(t) \qquad \text{(A3.7b)}$$

We may notice from (A3.3) that the derivative (A3.7) can be expressed succinctly using the gradient vector as follows:

$$\frac{dE[\mathbf{x}(t)]}{dt} = [\nabla_x E(\mathbf{x})]^t \dot{\mathbf{x}}(t) \qquad \text{(A3.8)}$$

Here we have used the notation of (A3.2b) for brevity.

EXAMPLE A3.1 ■■■■■■■■■■

Consider that the following quadratic form with the matrix **A** as in Example A2.1 is to be evaluated for changes in time:

$$E[\mathbf{x}(t)] = \begin{bmatrix} e^{2t} & t \end{bmatrix} \begin{bmatrix} 1 & 2 \\ 2 & 3 \end{bmatrix} \begin{bmatrix} e^{2t} \\ t \end{bmatrix}$$

Notice that in our example we have

$$\mathbf{x}(t) = \begin{bmatrix} x_1(t) \\ x_2(t) \end{bmatrix} = \begin{bmatrix} e^{2t} \\ t \end{bmatrix}$$

Using expression (A3.8) allows the result to be rewritten as a scalar product of the gradient vector

$$\nabla_x E(\mathbf{x}) = \begin{bmatrix} \dfrac{d}{dx_1}(x_1^2 + 4x_1 x_2 + 3x_2^2) \\[2mm] \dfrac{d}{dx_2}(x_1^2 + 4x_1 x_2 + 3x_2^2) \end{bmatrix} = \begin{bmatrix} 2x_1 + 4x_2 \\ 4x_1 + 6x_2 \end{bmatrix}$$

times the vector $\dot{\mathbf{x}}(t)$ of value

$$\dot{\mathbf{x}}(t) = \begin{bmatrix} 2e^{2t} \\ 1 \end{bmatrix}$$

Combining the two results we obtain

$$\frac{dE[\mathbf{x}(t)]}{dt} = \begin{bmatrix} 2e^{2t} + 4t & 4e^{2t} + 6t \end{bmatrix} \begin{bmatrix} 2e^{2t} \\ 1 \end{bmatrix}$$

$$= 2[2e^{4t} + (4t + 2)e^{2t} + 3t] \qquad ■$$

Jacobian Matrix

Let us consider m functions $E_i(\mathbf{x})$, for $i = 1, 2, \ldots, m$, of the vectorial variable $\mathbf{x}$ defined as

$$E_1(\mathbf{x}) = E_1(x_1, x_2, \ldots x_n)$$
$$E_2(\mathbf{x}) = E_2(x_1, x_2, \ldots x_n)$$
$$\vdots$$
$$E_m(\mathbf{x}) = E_m(x_1, x_2, \ldots, x_n)$$

(A3.9)

The matrix $d\mathbf{E}/d\mathbf{x}$ called the *Jacobian matrix* and denoted $\mathbf{J}(\mathbf{x})$ can be defined for (A3.9) as:

$$\mathbf{J}(\mathbf{x}) = \begin{bmatrix} \dfrac{\partial E_1}{\partial x_1} & \dfrac{\partial E_1}{\partial x_2} & \cdots & \dfrac{\partial E_1}{\partial x_n} \\ \dfrac{\partial E_2}{\partial x_1} & \dfrac{\partial E_2}{\partial x_2} & \cdots & \dfrac{\partial E_2}{\partial x_n} \\ \vdots & \vdots & \cdots & \vdots \\ \dfrac{\partial E_m}{\partial x_1} & \dfrac{\partial E_m}{\partial x_2} & \cdots & \dfrac{\partial E_m}{\partial x_n} \end{bmatrix}$$

(A3.10)

EXAMPLE A3.2 ■■■■■■■■■

Let us compute the Jacobian matrix at $\mathbf{x} = \begin{bmatrix} 2 & 1 \end{bmatrix}^t$ for the following functions of $E_1(\mathbf{x})$ and $E_2(\mathbf{x})$:

$$E_1(\mathbf{x}) = x_1^2 - x_1 x_2$$
$$E_2(\mathbf{x}) = x_1 x_2 + x_2^2$$

The Jacobian matrix expressed from (A3.10) is

$$\mathbf{J}(\mathbf{x}) = \begin{bmatrix} 2x_1 - x_2 & -x_1 \\ x_2 & x_1 + 2x_2 \end{bmatrix} = \begin{bmatrix} 3 & -2 \\ 1 & 4 \end{bmatrix}$$

■

Hessian Matrix

For a scalar-valued function $E(\mathbf{x})$, a matrix of second derivatives called the *Hessian matrix* is defined as follows:

$$\nabla_x^2 E(\mathbf{x}) = \nabla_x \left[\nabla_x E(\mathbf{x}) \right]$$

(A3.11)

$$\nabla_x^2 E(\mathbf{x}) \triangleq \begin{bmatrix} \dfrac{\partial^2 E}{\partial x_1^2} & \dfrac{\partial^2 E}{\partial x_1 \partial x_2} & \cdots & \dfrac{\partial^2 E}{\partial x_1 \partial x_n} \\[2mm] \dfrac{\partial^2 E}{\partial x_2 \partial x_1} & \dfrac{\partial^2 E}{\partial x_2^2} & \cdots & \dfrac{\partial^2 E}{\partial x_2 \partial x_n} \\[2mm] \vdots & \vdots & \cdots & \vdots \\[2mm] \dfrac{\partial^2 E}{\partial x_n \partial x_1} & \dfrac{\partial^2 E}{\partial x_n \partial x_2} & \cdots & \dfrac{\partial^2 E}{\partial x_n^2} \end{bmatrix} \tag{A3.12}$$

Note that the Hessian matrix is of size $n \times n$ and is symmetric. The matrix is often denoted by $\mathbf{H}$.

EXAMPLE A3.3 ■■■■

Let us compute the Hessian matrix and determine whether it is positive definite for the function

$$E(\mathbf{x}) = (x_2 - x_1)^2 + (1 - x_1)^2$$

Computing first the gradient vector yields

$$\nabla_x E(\mathbf{x}) = 2 \begin{bmatrix} 2x_1 - x_2 - 1 \\ x_2 - x_1 \end{bmatrix}$$

and the Hessian matrix of size 2×2 becomes

$$\nabla_x^2 E(\mathbf{x}) = 2 \begin{bmatrix} 2 & -1 \\ -1 & 1 \end{bmatrix}$$

Since the principal determinants of the matrix are 4 and 2, the Hessian matrix is positive definite. Note that the Hessian matrix is constant in this example and independent of $\mathbf{x}$. ■

A4 ■■■■■■■■■

SOLUTION OF OPTIMIZATION PROBLEMS

Unconstrained Optimization Problem

An optimization problem is usually defined in terms of the *minimization of a scalar function* of a number of variables. If the variables are not constrained by inequalities or equality relationships, the optimization is said to be *unconstrained*. The function to be minimized is an *objective function,* sometimes also called a cost function or criterion function. In neural network studies, the objective functions take the forms that follow:

1. *For feedforward networks:* The scalar error function $E(\mathbf{w})$ in the weight space is the objective function.
2. *For recurrent networks:* The scalar energy function $E(\mathbf{v})$ in the network output space is the objective function.

For a scalar valued objective function $E(x)$ of a single variable x, the well-known conditions for a minimum at $x = x^*$ are

$$\frac{dE(x^*)}{dx} = 0$$
$$\frac{d^2E(x^*)}{dx^2} > 0 \tag{A4.1}$$

For a scalar valued function $E(\mathbf{x})$ of a vectorial variable $\mathbf{x}$ we generalize conditions (A4.1) as given below:

$$\nabla_x E(\mathbf{x}^*) = \mathbf{0} \tag{A4.2a}$$

$$\nabla_x^2 E(\mathbf{x}^*) \text{ is positive definite} \tag{A4.2b}$$

Condition (A4.2a) requires the gradient vector at a minimum of $E(\mathbf{x})$ to be a null vector. Condition (A4.2b) requires the Hessian matrix at a minimum of $E(\mathbf{x})$ to be positive definite. The evaluation of conditions (A4.2) is possible only for continuous functions involved in expressions for $E(\mathbf{x})$, and in matrices $\nabla_x E(\mathbf{x})$ and $\nabla_x^2 E(\mathbf{x})$ for all values of $\mathbf{x}$.

To derive conditions (A4.2), let us inspect a two-variable function $E(\mathbf{x})$ expanded in a Taylor series at $\mathbf{x} = \mathbf{x}^*$ and retain the linear and quadratic term of the expansion:

$$E(\mathbf{x}) \cong E(\mathbf{x}^*) + (x_1 - x_1^*)\frac{\partial E(\mathbf{x}^*)}{\partial x_1} + (x_2 - x_2^*)\frac{\partial E(\mathbf{x}^*)}{\partial x_2}$$
$$+ \frac{1}{2}(x_1 - x_1^*)^2\frac{\partial^2 E(\mathbf{x}^*)}{\partial x_1^2} + \frac{1}{2}(x_2 - x_2^*)^2\frac{\partial^2 E(\mathbf{x}^*)}{\partial x_2^2} \tag{A4.3a}$$
$$+ (x_1 - x_1^*)(x_2 - x_2^*)\frac{\partial^2 E(\mathbf{x}^*)}{\partial x_1 \partial x_2}$$

Equation (A4.3a) rewritten in the matrix form becomes for $\Delta x_1 \overset{\Delta}{=} x_1 - x_1^*$ and $\Delta x_2 \overset{\Delta}{=} x_2 - x_2^*$:

$$E(\mathbf{x}) \cong E(\mathbf{x}^*) + \begin{bmatrix} \dfrac{\partial E(\mathbf{x}^*)}{\partial x_1} & \dfrac{\partial E(\mathbf{x}^*)}{\partial x_2} \end{bmatrix} \begin{bmatrix} \Delta x_1 \\ \Delta x_2 \end{bmatrix}$$
$$+ \frac{1}{2}\begin{bmatrix} \Delta x_1 \\ \Delta x_2 \end{bmatrix}^t \begin{bmatrix} \dfrac{\partial^2 E(\mathbf{x}^*)}{\partial x_1^2} & \dfrac{\partial^2 E(\mathbf{x}^*)}{\partial x_1 \partial x_2} \\ \dfrac{\partial^2 E(\mathbf{x}^*)}{\partial x_2 \partial x_1} & \dfrac{\partial^2 E(\mathbf{x}^*)}{\partial x_2^2} \end{bmatrix} \begin{bmatrix} \Delta x_1 \\ \Delta x_2 \end{bmatrix} \tag{A4.3b}$$

Using the gradient vector (A3.3), Hessian matrix (A3.12), and the notation

$$\Delta \mathbf{x} \triangleq \begin{bmatrix} \Delta x_1 \\ \Delta x_2 \end{bmatrix}$$

we obtain the following matrix form of (A4.3b):

$$E(\mathbf{x}) \cong E(\mathbf{x}^*) + \left[\boldsymbol{\nabla}_x E(\mathbf{x}^*) \right]^t \Delta \mathbf{x} + \frac{1}{2} \Delta \mathbf{x}^t \left[\boldsymbol{\nabla}_x^2 E(\mathbf{x}^*) \right] \Delta \mathbf{x} \qquad \text{(A4.3c)}$$

If $\mathbf{x}^*$ is to be a minimum of $E(\mathbf{x})$ as in (A4.3c), any infinitely small change $\Delta \mathbf{x}$ at $\mathbf{x}^*$ should result in $E(\mathbf{x}^* + \Delta \mathbf{x}) > E(\mathbf{x}^*)$. This requires the following:

1. The gradient vector at $\mathbf{x}^*$ vanishes and makes the linear term in (A4.3c) of zero value, and

2. The Hessian matrix at $\mathbf{x}^*$ is positive definite, which makes the last term in the quadratic form (A4.3c) positive independently of $\Delta \mathbf{x}$.

Analytical Solution of a Selected Optimization Problem

Suppose that

$$E(\mathbf{x}) = \frac{1}{2} \mathbf{x}^t \mathbf{A} \mathbf{x} + \mathbf{b}^t \mathbf{x} \qquad \text{(A4.4)}$$

where $\mathbf{x}$ is an n-dimensional column vector; $\mathbf{A}$ is an $n \times n$ symmetric, positive definite matrix; and $\mathbf{b}$ is an n-dimensional constant vector.

The scalar multivariable function $E(\mathbf{x})$ as defined in (A4.4) is one of the few functions for which an analytical solution for the unconstrained minimum exists. Computing the gradient vector and the Hessian matrix of $E(\mathbf{x})$ yields:

$$\boldsymbol{\nabla}_x E(\mathbf{x}) = \mathbf{A}\mathbf{x} + \mathbf{b} \qquad \text{(A4.5a)}$$

$$\boldsymbol{\nabla}_x^2 E(\mathbf{x}) = \mathbf{A} \qquad \text{(A4.5b)}$$

Setting condition (A4.2a) for the minimum at $\mathbf{x}^*$, we obtain the equation for $\mathbf{x}^*$:

$$\mathbf{A}\mathbf{x}^* + \mathbf{b} = \mathbf{0} \qquad \text{(A4.6a)}$$

which has the solution

$$\mathbf{x}^* = -\mathbf{A}^{-1}\mathbf{b} \qquad \text{(A4.6b)}$$

Note that the Hessian matrix as in (A4.5b) has been assumed to be constant and positive definite; therefore, the solution found at $\mathbf{x}^*$ in (A4.6b) is a minimum.

EXAMPLE A4.1 ■■■■■■■■■■■■■■

Let us evaluate the location of the minimum of the following function having the form of Equation (A4.4):

$$E(\mathbf{x}) = \frac{1}{2} \begin{bmatrix} x_1 & x_2 \end{bmatrix} \begin{bmatrix} 2 & 2 \\ 2 & 8 \end{bmatrix} \begin{bmatrix} x_1 \\ x_2 \end{bmatrix} + \begin{bmatrix} 1 & 0 \end{bmatrix} \begin{bmatrix} x_1 \\ x_2 \end{bmatrix}$$

This quadratic form, supplemented by the linear term, is equivalent to the expanded polynominal of two variables:

$$E(\mathbf{x}) = x_1^2 + 2x_1x_2 + 4x_2^2 + x_1$$

Equation (A4.5a) takes the form:

$$\begin{bmatrix} 2 & 2 \\ 2 & 8 \end{bmatrix} \begin{bmatrix} x_1 \\ x_2 \end{bmatrix} + \begin{bmatrix} 1 \\ 0 \end{bmatrix} = \mathbf{0}$$

Solving it yields vector $\mathbf{x} = \mathbf{x}^*$ such that

$$\begin{bmatrix} x_1^* \\ x_2^* \end{bmatrix} = -\frac{1}{6} \begin{bmatrix} 4 & -1 \\ -1 & 1 \end{bmatrix} \begin{bmatrix} 1 \\ 0 \end{bmatrix} = \begin{bmatrix} -\dfrac{2}{3} \\ \dfrac{1}{6} \end{bmatrix}$$

Checking the principal determinants of the Hessian matrix, $\mathbf{A}$, we obtain

$$\det A_{11} = 2 > 0$$
$$\det A_{22} = 2 \cdot 8 - 4 = 12 > 0$$

Therefore, because the Hessian matrix is positive definite, the point $\mathbf{x}^*$ is the minimum of $E(\mathbf{x})$.

Note that selecting an arbitrary $\Delta\mathbf{x}$ value yields a vanishing linear term and the quadratic term of the series expansion (A4.3c) is equal:

$$\begin{bmatrix} \Delta x_1 & \Delta x_2 \end{bmatrix} \begin{bmatrix} 1 & 1 \\ 1 & 4 \end{bmatrix} \begin{bmatrix} \Delta x_1 \\ \Delta x_2 \end{bmatrix} = (\Delta x_1)^2 + 2\Delta x_1 \Delta x_2 + 4(\Delta x_2)^2$$

This result is equivalent to the expression

$$(\Delta x_1 + \Delta x_2)^2 + 3(\Delta x_2)^2 > 0$$

which is always positive if Δx_1 and Δx_2 are not both equal to zero. ■

Geometrical Interpretation

Note that the gradient vector nullification at $\mathbf{x} = \mathbf{x}^*$ as in (A4.2a) is necessary for the existence of the minimum at $\mathbf{x}^*$. The same property of gradient vector nullification, however, is also shared by maxima and saddle points. This is illustrated for a function $E(x_1, x_2)$ of two variables in Figure A3. The figure shows the shapes of $E(x_1, x_2)$ for the case of a minimum (a), and of a saddle (b).

Assume that the functions represented by the surfaces shown are quadratic forms with the linear term in the form as in (A4.4). Matrix $\mathbf{A}$ must be positive definite for the function shown in Figure A3(a). The figure illustrates conditions described in Example A4.1 with the minimum at $\mathbf{x} = \mathbf{x}^* = \begin{bmatrix} -2/3 & 1/6 \end{bmatrix}'$. Figure A3(b) displays contour maps showing constant value lines for the function from Figure A3(a).

A quadratic form is, however, indefinite for the function depicted in Figure A3(c) because it can take either sign depending on $\Delta\mathbf{x}$. The function itself is shaped like a saddle. The function increases in one direction $\Delta\mathbf{x}$, but decreases in the other and the form is said to be *indefinite* at the saddle point. Also, matrix $\mathbf{A}$ is indefinite at the saddle.

The reader may verify that if $\mathbf{A}$ is chosen in Example A4.1 as

$$\mathbf{A} = \begin{bmatrix} 2 & 2 \\ 2 & -8 \end{bmatrix}$$

matrix $\mathbf{A}$ becomes indefinite based on the test from Section A2.2 since

$$\det A_{11} = 2 > 0$$
$$\det A_{22} = -20 < 0$$

The saddle point is the solution of the equation

$$\begin{bmatrix} 2 & 2 \\ 2 & -8 \end{bmatrix} \begin{bmatrix} x_1 \\ x_2 \end{bmatrix} + \begin{bmatrix} 1 \\ 0 \end{bmatrix} = 0$$

which is

$$\mathbf{x}^* = \begin{bmatrix} -0.4 \\ -0.1 \end{bmatrix}$$

This case of a two-variable function is depicted in Figure A3(c). Figure A3(d) displays contour maps for the function from Figure A3(c) that possesses a saddle.

A5

STABILITY OF NONLINEAR DYNAMICAL SYSTEMS

Preliminary Considerations

Late in the nineteenth century, the Russian mathematician A. M. Lyapunov developed an approach to stability analysis of dynamical systems. The unique feature of the approach is that only the form of the differential or difference

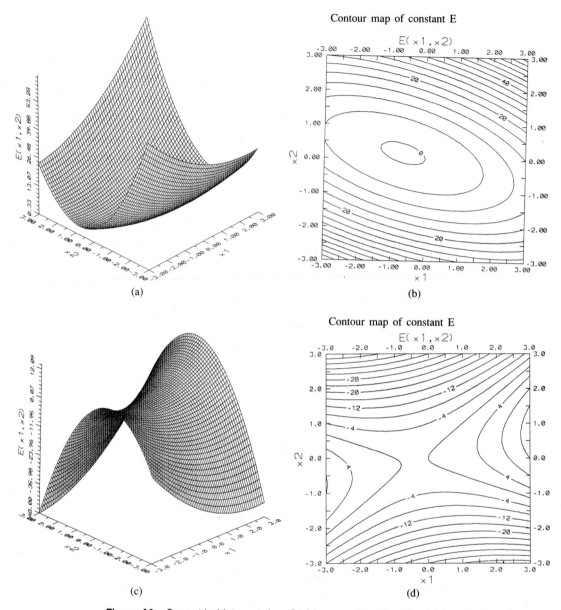

Figure A3 Geometrical interpretation of minimum and saddle point: (a) function from Example A4.1 with minimum, (b) contour map for (a), (c) function with saddle point, and (d) contour map for (c).

equations needs to be known, not their solutions. The method, called *Lyapunov's method,* is based on the generalized energy concept. The method requires evaluation of a so-called Lyapunov function. Consider first an analogy between Lyapunov's function and the energy function of a physical system.

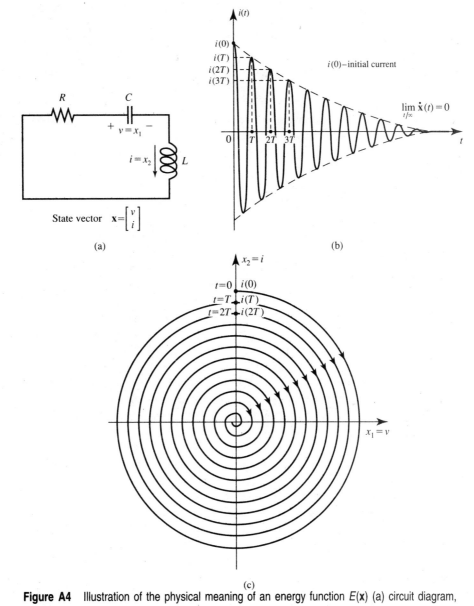

Figure A4 Illustration of the physical meaning of an energy function $E(\mathbf{x})$ (a) circuit diagram, (b) current waveform, and (c) state vector trajectory.

Figure A4(a) shows an autonomous (i.e., unforced) second-order electric system consisting of a series RLC connection. In this case, capacitor voltage v and inductor current i can be defined as state variables, and $\mathbf{x}$ is the state vector

$$\mathbf{x} = \begin{bmatrix} x_1 \\ x_2 \end{bmatrix} \overset{\Delta}{=} \begin{bmatrix} v \\ i \end{bmatrix} \tag{A5.1}$$

The total physical energy stored in the system is known to be

$$E(\mathbf{x}) = \frac{1}{2}Cv^2 + \frac{1}{2}Li^2 = \frac{1}{2}[v \quad i]\begin{bmatrix} C & 0 \\ 0 & L \end{bmatrix}\begin{bmatrix} v \\ i \end{bmatrix} \tag{A5.2}$$

Thus the energy function is a quadratic function of state variables and

$$E(\mathbf{x}) > 0 \tag{A5.3}$$

unless $\mathbf{x} = \mathbf{0}$. We can, therefore, say that the energy function is positive definite. When the energy function rate of change in time is evaluated we notice that

$$\mathbf{x}(t) = \begin{bmatrix} v(t) \\ i(t) \end{bmatrix} \tag{A5.4a}$$

and from (A3.7a) we obtain

$$\frac{dE(\mathbf{x})}{dt} = \frac{\partial E(\mathbf{x})}{\partial x_1}\dot{x}_1 + \frac{\partial E(\mathbf{x})}{\partial x_2}\dot{x}_2 \tag{A5.4b}$$

which is equivalent to

$$\frac{dE(\mathbf{x})}{dt} = [\nabla_x E(\mathbf{x})]^t\,\dot{\mathbf{x}} \tag{A5.4c}$$

Using (A5.2) the derivative of the energy function versus time becomes

$$\frac{dE(\mathbf{x})}{dt} = [Cv \quad Li]\begin{bmatrix} \dot{v} \\ \dot{i} \end{bmatrix} = Cv\,\dot{v} + Li\,\dot{i} \tag{A5.5}$$

Knowing the form of the differential equations describing system $\dot{x}_1 = f_1(\mathbf{x})$, $\dot{x}_2 = f_2(\mathbf{x})$ is usually sufficient for evaluation of the expressions for $E(\mathbf{x})$ and $dE(\mathbf{x})/dt$. For our sample circuit from Figure A4(a) the equation describing the system is

$$L\frac{di(t)}{dt} + \frac{1}{C}\int_{-\infty}^{t} i(t)\,dt + Ri(t) = 0 \tag{A5.6a}$$

This integrodifferential equation can be rewritten as a system of two first-order equations using the state vector as defined in (A5.1):

$$\begin{aligned} \frac{dv(t)}{dt} &= \frac{i(t)}{C} \\ \frac{di(t)}{dt} &= -\frac{v(t)}{L} - \frac{Ri(t)}{L} \end{aligned} \tag{A5.6b}$$

which is equivalent to

$$\begin{bmatrix} \dot{v} \\ \dot{i} \end{bmatrix} = \begin{bmatrix} 0 & \dfrac{1}{C} \\ -\dfrac{1}{L} & -\dfrac{R}{L} \end{bmatrix}\begin{bmatrix} v \\ i \end{bmatrix} \tag{A5.6c}$$

Now we can evaluate the sign of the rate of change of $E[\mathbf{x}(t)]$ versus time using (A5.5):

$$\frac{dE(\mathbf{x})}{dt} = i(t)v(t) - i(t)v(t) - Ri^2(t) \tag{A5.7a}$$

which reduces to

$$\frac{dE(\mathbf{x})}{dt} = -Ri^2(t) < 0 \tag{A5.7b}$$

The discussed energy function always decreases in time unless $i = 0$. The result (A5.7b) can be easily interpreted physically. The circuit of Figure A4(a) represents a lossy resonant circuit. Once the circuit is energized with $v(0) \neq 0$ or $i(0) \neq 0$, it starts producing damped oscillations as illustrated.in Figure A4(b). The damping phenomena are a result of the nonzero resistance value in the circuit, which makes the system actually dissipative.

The evaluated solution for $v(t)$ and $i(t)$ can also be represented as a trajectory $v(i)$, with the time variable eliminated. The damped oscillations from Figure A4(b) take the form of a state trajectory as in Figure A4(c), which is drawn to the origin after a sufficiently long time has elapsed. Again, neither the time-domain solution nor knowledge of the trajectories is required to prove that the system is stable. Evaluation of the energy function alone allows the stability of the system to be proven or disproven.

Lyapunov's Theorem

Consider the autonomous (i.e., unforced) system described with a system of n first-order linear or nonlinear differential equations:

$$
\begin{aligned}
\dot{x}_1 &= f_1(\mathbf{x}) \\
\dot{x}_2 &= f_2(\mathbf{x}) \\
&\;\;\vdots \\
\dot{x}_n &= f_n(\mathbf{x})
\end{aligned}
\tag{A5.8a}
$$

which is equivalent to

$$\dot{\mathbf{x}} = \mathbf{f}(\mathbf{x}) \tag{A5.8b}$$

We assume that the equations have been written so that $\mathbf{x} = 0$ is an equilibrium point that satisfies equations $\mathbf{f}(0) = \mathbf{0}$. We formulate a condition for the equilibrium $\mathbf{x} = \mathbf{0}$ to be asymptotically stable which means that the state vector goes to zero as time goes to infinity. The argument goes like this: *If a positive definite function $E(\mathbf{x})$ can be found such that*

1. *E is continuous with respect to all components x_i, for $i = 1, 2, \ldots, n$, and*
2. *$dE[\mathbf{x}(t)]/dt < 0$, which indicates the energy function decreasing in time, then the origin is asymptotically stable.*

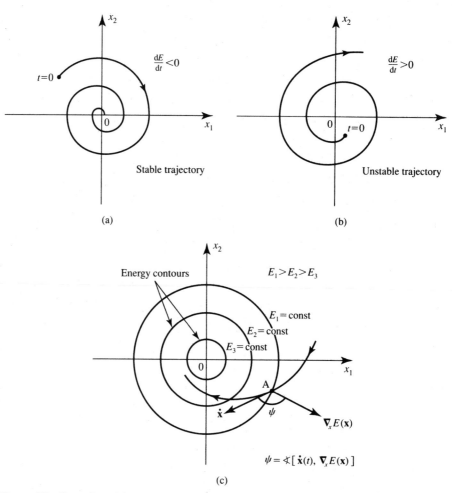

Figure A5 Illustration of the Lyapunov theorem: (a) stable trajectory, (b) unstable trajectory, and (c) respective positions of velocity and gradient vectors.

Function $E(\mathbf{x})$ satisfying the above requirements is called a *Lyapunov function*. The function is not unique; rather, many different Lyapunov functions can be found for a given system. If at least one function is known that meets conditions 1 and 2 given above, the system is asymptotically stable. This means that its attractor is a point rather than a bounded trajectory. Figure A5(a) illustrates asymptotical stability, which we simply call *stability* in our neural network studies. This trajectory is of the same type as that shown in Figure A4(c) representing the decaying oscillations from Figure A4(b). Figure A5(b) shows an unstable trajectory of a system with an increasing energy function such that $dE[\mathbf{x}(t)]/dt > 0$. This case would correspond to the negative resistance value in (A5.7b) and to the energy function increasing in time.

Note that modifying condition 2 so as not to have strictly negative but non-positive derivatives of the energy function would allow for so-called *limit cycles,* which correspond to limited but nondamped and steady oscillations. Indeed, for the example circuit from Figure A4(a) with $R = 0$ we obtain from (A5.7b):

$$\frac{dE(\mathbf{x})}{dt} = 0 \qquad (A5.9)$$

In this case the energy function remains constant in time. This corresponds to the lossless LC resonant circuit, which produces nondecaying sinusoidal oscillations. Since the circuit does not dissipate its energy in the resistance, the oscillations are of constant amplitude. This case corresponds to a circular trajectory on the plane x_1, x_2 rather than decreasing (stable) or increasing (unstable) spiral trajectories on the state plane.

Figure A5(c) provides an interesting observation relating the energy function $E(\mathbf{x})$ and the trajectories of the stable system. Let us note that based on (A3.8) condition 2 is equivalent to

$$\frac{dE[\mathbf{x}(t)]}{dt} = [\nabla_x E(\mathbf{x})]^t \, \dot{\mathbf{x}}\,(t) \qquad (A5.10)$$

which is the scalar product of the energy function gradient vector and of the velocity of the state vector $\dot{\mathbf{x}}\,(t)$. The velocity vector is obviously tangent to the trajectory. The gradient vector is normal to the energy contour line. These conditions are illustrated in Figure A5(c). Since stability condition 2 requires the scalar product (A5.10) to be negative, the angle between the two vectors

$$\psi \overset{\Delta}{=} \sphericalangle[\dot{\mathbf{x}}\,(t), \nabla_x E(\mathbf{x})] \qquad (A5.11)$$

must be bounded as follows

$$-180° < \psi < -90° \qquad (A5.12)$$

This, in turn, means that the state velocity vector $\dot{\mathbf{x}}\,(t)$ must have a negative projection on the gradient vector, $\nabla_x E(\mathbf{x})$. This also indicates that the state velocity vector $\dot{\mathbf{x}}\,(t)$ has a positive projection on the negative gradient vector, $-\nabla_x E(\mathbf{x})$.

As a final note, the energy function having physical energy meaning often fits as a Lyapunov function. In many cases, however, in which a system model is described with differential equations, it may not be clear what "energy" of the system means. Therefore, the conditions that $E(\mathbf{x})$ must satisfy to be a Lyapunov function are based on mathematical rather than physical considerations. For our neural network studies of fully coupled single-layer networks, the Lyapunov function is often called the *computational energy function* and has no physical energy relation. Note also that the inability to find a satisfactory Lyapunov function does not mean that the evaluated system is unstable.

No unique and best method exists to identify a Lyapunov function for a given system. A form $E(\mathbf{x})$ can be assumed either as a pure guess or obtained by physical insight and energy-like considerations. Following the choice of the hypothetical energy function which is positive definite, $dE(\mathbf{x})/dt$ needs to be tested involving the equations $\mathbf{f}(\mathbf{x}) = \dot{\mathbf{x}}$ in the process.

EXAMPLE A5.1 ■■■■■■■■■■

Let us check the stability of the closed feedback loop control system shown in Figure A6. The system is described by the equation

$$U(s) - Q(s)\frac{K}{s(s + \alpha)} = Q(s)$$

where α and K are positive constants. To evaluate the stability of the closed-loop system we use the equation for an autonomous system and assume $U(s) = 0$. This corresponds to the relationship

$$s^2Q(s) + \alpha sQ(s) + KQ(s) = 0$$

In the time domain, the autonomous system is described with the equation

$$\ddot{q} + \alpha \dot{q} + Kq = 0$$

The following definitions of state variables can be introduced in order to identify the system of first-order differential equations:

$$x_1 \overset{\Delta}{=} q$$

$$x_2 \overset{\Delta}{=} \dot{q}$$

Since $x_2 = \dot{x}_1$, we have $\dot{x}_2 = \ddot{q}$, and Equation (A5.8) can be written as follows:

$$\dot{x}_1 = 0x_1 + 1x_2$$

$$\dot{x}_2 = -Kx_1 - \alpha x_2$$

We thus have the $\dot{\mathbf{x}} = \mathbf{f}(\mathbf{x})$ relationship as given below:

$$\dot{\mathbf{x}} = \begin{bmatrix} 0 & 1 \\ -K & -\alpha \end{bmatrix} \mathbf{x}, \text{ where } \mathbf{x} \overset{\Delta}{=} \begin{bmatrix} x_1 \\ x_2 \end{bmatrix}$$

Let our first guess for the energy function $E(\mathbf{x})$ be

$$E(\mathbf{x}) = x_1^2 + x_2^2$$

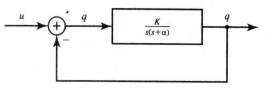

Figure A6 Illustration for Lyapunov function evaluation in Example A5.1.

Since the function is positive definite and fulfills condition 1, checking condition 2 yields:

$$\frac{dE[\mathbf{x}(t)]}{dt} = \begin{bmatrix} \frac{\partial E(\mathbf{x})}{\partial x_1} & \frac{\partial E(\mathbf{x})}{\partial x_2} \end{bmatrix} \begin{bmatrix} \frac{dx_1}{dt} \\ \frac{dx_2}{dt} \end{bmatrix} = 2x_1\dot{x}_1 + 2x_2\dot{x}_2$$

Using the equations describing the system, the rate of change of the energy function in time becomes

$$\frac{dE[\mathbf{x}(t)]}{dt} = 2x_1x_2 + 2x_2(-Kx_1 - \alpha x_2) = 2x_1x_2(1 - K) - 2\alpha x_2^2$$

To check whether or not this result is always positive independent of $\mathbf{x}$ we can make it equivalent to the following quadratic form:

$$2x_1x_2(1 - K) - 2\alpha x_2^2 = \begin{bmatrix} x_1 & x_2 \end{bmatrix} \begin{bmatrix} 0 & 1 - K \\ 1 - K & -2\alpha \end{bmatrix} \begin{bmatrix} x_1 \\ x_2 \end{bmatrix}$$

Since $\det A_{11} = 0$, the derivative of the energy function is not negative and the system cannot be asserted to be stable. In fact, it cannot be called an unstable system either. However, another choice of the Lyapunov function can be attempted. Assuming

$$E(\mathbf{x}) = Kx_1^2 + (x_2 + \alpha x_1)^2$$

we have selected a positive definite function satisfying condition 1. Checking condition 2 yields:

$$\frac{dE[\mathbf{x}(t)]}{dt} = [2x_1K + 2(x_2 + \alpha x_1)\alpha]x_2 + 2(x_2 + \alpha x_1)(-Kx_1 - \alpha x_2) = -2\alpha Kx_1^2$$

This concludes the proof that the chosen energy function has a negative definite derivative versus time and therefore the system is stable. ■

A6

ANALYTIC GEOMETRY IN EUCLIDEAN SPACE IN CARTESIAN COORDINATES

The point $P_0(x_0, y_0)$ in the two-dimensional Euclidean space in Cartesian coordinates can be represented as a two-component column vector $\mathbf{x}_0$ defined as

$$\mathbf{x}_0 = \begin{bmatrix} x_0 \\ y_0 \end{bmatrix}$$

Equation Forms of a Straight Line on a Plane

For this section, refer to Figure A7.

1. The *gradient form:*

$$y = kx + q \qquad (A6.1)$$

2. The *intercept form:*

$$\frac{x}{p} + \frac{y}{q} = 1, \ p \neq 0, \ q \neq 0 \qquad (A6.2)$$

where p and q are intercept coordinates with the x and y axes, respectively.

3. The *general form*

$$ax + by + c = 0, \quad a^2 + b^2 > 0 \qquad (A6.3)$$

where constants a and b are coordinates of a vector $\mathbf{n}$:

$$\mathbf{n} = \begin{bmatrix} a \\ b \end{bmatrix}$$

which is normal to the line. The vector is called a *normal vector* and has the property that it points to the side of a line for which $ax + by + c > 0$, which is called the *positive half-plane*. This property is proven below.

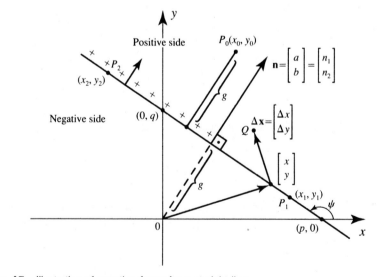

Indeed, for a point $\begin{bmatrix} x & y \end{bmatrix}^t$ on the line we have from (A6.3)

$$\mathbf{n}^t \begin{bmatrix} x \\ y \end{bmatrix} + c = 0 \tag{A6.4}$$

Assume that a vector $\Delta\mathbf{x}$ has been added to $\mathbf{x}$ so that point $Q(x + \Delta x, y + \Delta y)$ is on the upper side of the line of Figure A7. Computing from (A6.4) yields

$$\mathbf{n}^t \begin{bmatrix} x + \Delta x \\ y + \Delta y \end{bmatrix} + c = \left(\mathbf{n}^t \begin{bmatrix} x \\ y \end{bmatrix} + c \right) + \mathbf{n}^t \begin{bmatrix} \Delta x \\ \Delta y \end{bmatrix}$$
$$= \mathbf{n}^t \begin{bmatrix} \Delta x \\ \Delta y \end{bmatrix} \tag{A6.5}$$

Since the vectors $\mathbf{n}$ and $\Delta\mathbf{x} = \begin{bmatrix} \Delta x & \Delta y \end{bmatrix}^t$ are both nonzero and the angle between them is between $-90°$ and $90°$, their scalar product (A6.5) is always positive. This proves that $\mathbf{n}$ always points to the positive half-plane. Note that the positive half-plane is denoted by $+$ signs, or by a small arrow pointing toward the positive side of the line.

Note that this equation form can be used with the unit normal vector $\mathbf{r}$ rather than the normal vector.

4. The *two-point form:*

$$\frac{y - y_1}{x - x_1} = \frac{y_2 - y_1}{x_2 - x_1}, \text{ or} \tag{A6.6a}$$

$$\begin{vmatrix} x & y & 1 \\ x_1 & y_1 & 1 \\ x_2 & y_2 & 1 \end{vmatrix} = 0 \tag{A6.6b}$$

The line passes through points $P_1(x_1, y_1)$ and $P_2(x_2, y_2)$

5. The *normal vector-point form:*

$$\mathbf{n}^t(\mathbf{x} - \mathbf{x}_1) = 0, \text{ or} \tag{A6.7a}$$

$$n_1(x - x_1) + n_2(y - y_1) = 0 \tag{A6.7b}$$

The line is perpendicular to its normal vector $\mathbf{n} = \begin{bmatrix} n_1 & n_2 \end{bmatrix}^t$ and passes through point $P_1(x_1, y_1)$. This form of the equation remains valid also for the unit normal $\mathbf{r}$ used rather than the normal vector. Indeed, dividing both sides of (A6.7a) by $(n_1^2 + n_2^2)^{1/2}$ we obtain:

$$\frac{\mathbf{n}^t}{\|\mathbf{n}\|}(\mathbf{x} - \mathbf{x}_1) = 0 \tag{A6.8}$$

Using the definition of the unit normal vector

$$\mathbf{r} \triangleq \frac{\mathbf{n}}{\|\mathbf{n}\|}$$

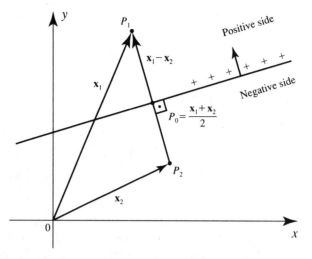

Figure A8   Illustration of a line bisecting the segment between $\mathbf{x}_1$ and $\mathbf{x}_2$.

we obtain an alternative normal vector-point form equation:

$$\mathbf{r}^t(\mathbf{x} - \mathbf{x}_1) = 0 \qquad\qquad (A6.9)$$

6. The *form for bisecting a segment between* $\mathbf{x}_1$ *and* $\mathbf{x}_2$:

$$(\mathbf{x}_1 - \mathbf{x}_2)^t\mathbf{x} + \frac{1}{2}\left(\|\mathbf{x}_2\|^2 - \|\mathbf{x}_1\|^2\right) = 0 \qquad\qquad (A6.10)$$

This line passes through the center of gravity of two points—point $P_1(x_1, y_1)$ represented by the vector $\mathbf{x}_1$, and point $P_2(x_2, y_2)$ represented by the vector $\mathbf{x}_2$—and is perpendicular to the line's normal vector $\mathbf{x}_1 - \mathbf{x}_2$. The coordinates of the center of gravity point P_0 are $0.5(\mathbf{x}_1 + \mathbf{x}_2)$. This line is illustrated in Figure A8.

The derivation below of Equation (A6.10) is based on the Equation (A6.7a). Indeed, the line of interest is normal to the vector $\mathbf{x}_1 - \mathbf{x}_2$ and passes through the center point P_0. We thus have from (A6.7a)

$$(\mathbf{x}_1 - \mathbf{x}_2)^t(\mathbf{x} - \mathbf{x}_0) = 0 \qquad\qquad (A6.11a)$$

which is equivalent to

$$(\mathbf{x}_1 - \mathbf{x}_2)^t\mathbf{x} - \frac{1}{2}(\mathbf{x}_1 - \mathbf{x}_2)^t(\mathbf{x}_1 + \mathbf{x}_2) = 0 \qquad\qquad (A6.11b)$$

Performing multiplication and reducing similar terms we obtain

$$(\mathbf{x}_1 - \mathbf{x}_2)^t\mathbf{x} + \frac{1}{2}(\mathbf{x}_2^t\mathbf{x}_2 - \mathbf{x}_1^t\mathbf{x}_1) = 0 \qquad\qquad (A6.11c)$$

Using the identity $\mathbf{x}^t\mathbf{x} = \|\mathbf{x}\|^2$ we notice that (A6.11c) becomes identical to (A6.10).

Useful Relationships

For this section, refer to Figure A7. The *distance g from the line ax + by + c = 0 to the point* $P_0(x_0, y_0)$ is

$$g = \left| \frac{ax_0 + by_0 + c}{\sqrt{a^2 + b^2}} \right| \tag{A6.12}$$

For special cases when the point P_0 is the origin, the distance from the origin to the line equals

$$g = \left| \frac{c}{\sqrt{a^2 + b^2}} \right| \tag{A6.13}$$

Note that the distance is always a non-negative quantity by definition.

EXAMPLE A6.1 ■■■■■■■■■■■■■■■■

This example reviews the main forms of equations of a straight line and illustrates useful relationships. Let us begin by finding the gradient form of an equation for the line shown in Figure A9. Since

$$k = \tan \psi = \frac{3}{2}, \quad q = -3$$

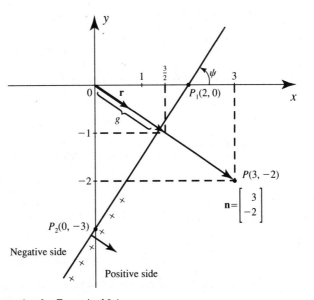

Figure A9 Illustration for Example A6.1.

then Equation (A6.1) has the form

$$y = \frac{3}{2}x - 3$$

Since $p = 2$ and $q = -3$, the intercept form of equation is

$$\frac{x}{2} - \frac{y}{3} = 1$$

The general form of the equation can be obtained by rearranging either of the two forms above to the following form:

$$3x - 2y - 6 = 0$$

The resulting normal vector perpendicular to the line and pointing to the positive side of the line is $\begin{bmatrix} 3 & -2 \end{bmatrix}^t$

The unit normal vector $\mathbf{r}$ is

$$\mathbf{r} = \frac{\begin{bmatrix} 3 \\ -2 \end{bmatrix}}{\sqrt{3^2 + 2^2}} = \frac{1}{\sqrt{13}} \begin{bmatrix} 3 \\ -2 \end{bmatrix}$$

Note that the length of the normal vector remains irrelevant for this form of line equation. Indeed, $\begin{bmatrix} 3/2 & -1 \end{bmatrix}^t$ is another normal vector to the line. The line's general equation for this normal vector is obtained by dividing the original line equation in the general form by 2 as given below:

$$\frac{3}{2}x - y - 3 = 0$$

The distance from the line to the origin is

$$g = \left| \frac{6}{\sqrt{3^2 + 2^2}} \right| = \frac{6}{\sqrt{13}}$$

The two-point form equation (A6.6) for the line passing through points $(2, 0)$ and $(0, -3)$ is

$$\frac{y}{x - 2} = \frac{-3}{-2}$$

Knowing the line normal vector and a single point P on the line, the equation as in (A6.7) can be obtained:

$$\begin{bmatrix} 3 \\ -2 \end{bmatrix}^t \left(\begin{bmatrix} x \\ y \end{bmatrix} - \begin{bmatrix} 2 \\ 0 \end{bmatrix} \right) = 0$$

or

$$3x - 2y - 6 = 0$$

This concludes the review of the example forms of straight line equations.■

Equation Forms of a Plane in Three-dimensional Space

1. The *intercept form*:

$$\frac{x}{p} + \frac{y}{q} + \frac{z}{s} = 1, \; p \neq 0, \; q \neq 0, \; s \neq 0 \qquad \text{(A6.14)}$$

where p, q and s, are plane intercept coordinates with the x, y and z axes, respectively.

2. The *general form*:

$$ax + by + cz + d = 0, \; a^2 + b^2 + c^2 > 0 \qquad \text{(A6.15)}$$

The constants a, b and c determine the normal vector $\mathbf{n}$

$$\mathbf{n} = \begin{bmatrix} a \\ b \\ c \end{bmatrix}$$

which points to the *positive side* of the plane, usually denoted by an arrow. Equation (A6.15) can be rewritten in vectorial notation:

$$\mathbf{n}^t \begin{bmatrix} x \\ y \\ z \end{bmatrix} + d = 0 \qquad \text{(A6.16)}$$

3. The *three-point form*:

$$\begin{vmatrix} x & y & z & 1 \\ x_1 & y_1 & z_1 & 1 \\ x_2 & y_2 & z_2 & 1 \\ x_3 & y_3 & z_3 & 1 \end{vmatrix} = 0 \qquad \text{(A6.17)}$$

The plane passes through three non-linear points $P_1(x_1, y_1, z_1)$, $P_2(x_2, y_2, z_2)$, and $P_3(x_3, y_3, z_3)$.

4. The *normal vector-point form*:

$$a(x - x_1) + b(y - y_1) + c(z - z_1) = 0 \qquad \text{(A6.18a)}$$

or

$$\mathbf{n}^t(\mathbf{x} - \mathbf{x}_1) = 0 \qquad \text{(A6.18b)}$$

where

$$\mathbf{x} = \begin{bmatrix} x \\ y \\ z \end{bmatrix}, \; \text{and} \; \mathbf{x}_1 = \begin{bmatrix} x_1 \\ y_1 \\ z_1 \end{bmatrix}$$

The plane is perpendicular to the normal vector $\mathbf{n}$ and passes through point

$P_1(x_1, y_1, z_1)$. This form or equation also remains valid for the unit normal vector $\mathbf{n}$ used rather than normal vector.

5. The *form for bisecting a segment between* $\mathbf{x}_1$ *and* $\mathbf{x}_2$:

$$(\mathbf{x}_1 - \mathbf{x}_2)^t \mathbf{x} + \frac{1}{2}\left(\|\mathbf{x}_2\|^2 - \|\mathbf{x}_1\|^2\right) = 0 \qquad (A6.19)$$

This plane passes through the center point between two points—$P_1(x_1, y_1, z_1)$ represented by the vector $\mathbf{x}_1$, and $P_2(x_2, y_2, z_2)$ represented by the vector $\mathbf{x}_2$—and is perpendicular to the plane's normal vector $\mathbf{x}_1 - \mathbf{x}_2$. The coordinates of the center point P_0 are $0.5(\mathbf{x}_1 + \mathbf{x}_2)$.

Useful Relationships in Three-dimensional Euclidean Space

1. Distance of point $P_0(x_0, y_0, z_0)$ from the plane $ax + by + cz + d = 0$

$$g = \left|\frac{ax_0 + by_0 + cz_0 + d}{\sqrt{a^2 + b^2 + c^2}}\right| \qquad (A6.20)$$

When the point P_0 is the origin, the distance (A6.20) reduces to

$$g = \left|\frac{d}{\sqrt{a^2 + b^2 + c^2}}\right| \qquad (A6.21)$$

2. The distance between two points $P_1(x_1, y_1, z_1)$ and $P_2(x_2, y_2, z_2)$ is equal to the length of vector $\mathbf{x}_1 - \mathbf{x}_2$:

$$\|\mathbf{x}_1 - \mathbf{x}_2\| = \sqrt{(x_1 - x_2)^2 + (y_1 - y_2)^2 + (z_1 - z_2)^2} \qquad (A6.22)$$

where

$$\mathbf{x}_1 \triangleq \begin{bmatrix} x_1 \\ y_1 \\ z_1 \end{bmatrix}, \ \mathbf{x}_2 \triangleq \begin{bmatrix} x_2 \\ y_2 \\ z_2 \end{bmatrix}$$

3. The *mid-point of the line segment* connecting points P_1 and P_2 as in (A6.22) corresponds to a vector $\mathbf{x}_m$ such that

$$\mathbf{x}_m = \frac{\mathbf{x}_1 + \mathbf{x}_2}{2} \qquad (A6.23)$$

4. The center of gravity of a system with K masses m_k distributed at points $\mathbf{x}_k$ is at $\mathbf{x}_c$ such that

$$\mathbf{x}_c = \frac{\displaystyle\sum_{k=1}^{K} m_k \mathbf{x}_k}{\displaystyle\sum_{k=1}^{K} m_k} \qquad (A6.24)$$

Note that the center $P(x, y, z)$ of mass of a triangle is given by

$$\mathbf{x}_c = \frac{\mathbf{x}_1 + \mathbf{x}_2 + \mathbf{x}_3}{3}, \text{ i.e.,}$$

$$x = \frac{x_1 + x_2 + x_3}{3}, \quad y = \frac{y_1 + y_2 + y_3}{3}, \quad z = \frac{z_1 + z_2 + z_3}{3}$$

EXAMPLE A6.2

This example reviews some forms of equations for a plane and illustrates useful relationships. Let us find the equations of a plane perpendicular to the vector $\begin{bmatrix} 2 & 3 & 6 \end{bmatrix}^t$ and passing through point $(0, 7, 0)$. The normal vector-point equation (A6.18) for the plane can be obtained:

$$2x + 3(y - 7) + 6z = 0, \text{ or}$$
$$2x + 3y + 6z - 21 = 0$$

To sketch the plane, it is convenient to rearrange the plane equation to the intercept form (A6.14) as follows:

$$\frac{x}{21/2} + \frac{y}{7} + \frac{z}{7/2} = 1$$

The plane is shown in Figure A10. The unit normal vector for the plane is

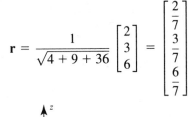

$$\mathbf{r} = \frac{1}{\sqrt{4 + 9 + 36}} \begin{bmatrix} 2 \\ 3 \\ 6 \end{bmatrix} = \begin{bmatrix} \frac{2}{7} \\ \frac{3}{7} \\ \frac{6}{7} \end{bmatrix}$$

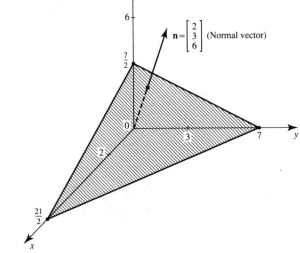

Figure A10 Plane for Example A6.2.

Note that the distance between the origin and the plane is

$$g = \left| \frac{21}{\sqrt{2^2 + 3^2 + 6^2}} \right| = 3$$

Since the normal vector points to the upper part of the plane, the upper part is the positive half-space; the lower part, including the origin, is the negative half-space.

■

A7

SELECTED NEURAL
NETWORK RELATED
CONCEPTS

Exclusive OR (XOR) Operation

The *Exclusive OR*, denoted with operator $\oplus$, is a binary operation on logic arguments x_1 and x_2. It assigns the value 1 to the two arguments if and only if they have complementary values; that is, $x_1 \oplus x_2 = 1$ if either x_1 or x_2 is 1, but not when both x_1 and x_2 are 0, or when both x_1 and $x_2 = 1$. The truth table for Boolean variables 0, 1 is

x_1	x_2	$x_1 \oplus x_2$
0	0	0
0	1	1
1	0	1
1	1	0

Let us note that the operation is associative since

$$(x_1 \oplus x_2) \oplus x_3 = x_1 \oplus (x_2 \oplus x_3) = x_1 \oplus x_2 \oplus x_3$$

This allows the extension of the XOR operation for n logic arguments as

$$\text{XOR}(x_1, x_2, \ldots, x_n) = x_1 \oplus x_2 \oplus \ldots \oplus x_n$$

The multivariable XOR function is called the *parity function* since it assigns the value 1 to n arguments if and only if the number of the arguments of value 1 is odd.

Hamming Distance

The *Hamming distance* (HD) between two binary codes α and β of the same length is defined as the number of places in which α_i and β_j differ. The Hamming distance is denoted as $HD(\alpha, \beta)$. For example, when

$$\alpha = 1 \quad -1 \quad 1 \quad 1 \quad 1 \quad 1$$
$$\beta = 1 \quad 1 \quad -1 \quad -1 \quad 1 \quad 1$$

then $HD(\alpha, \beta) = 3$.

The Hamming distance between 2-, 3-, 4-bit codes can be advantageously illustrated using two-, three-, or four-dimensional cubes. This is shown in Figure A11. Binary codes can be seen as vertices of the cube and the distances between the two codes can be interpreted as the lowest number of edges that must be traversed between the two relevant codes. Accordingly, the $HD(00, 11) = 2$ for a 2-bit code. Figure A11(c) shows a 3-dimensional cube within a cube so that together they compose a 4-dimensional cube (hypercube) with 16 vertices. Another version of a 4-dimensional cube (hypercube) is shown in Figure A11(d).

Assume that the two binary sequences are represented as n-tuple vectors $\boldsymbol{\alpha}$, $\boldsymbol{\beta}$ with bipolar binary components. The scalar product of vectors $\boldsymbol{\alpha}$, $\boldsymbol{\beta}$ is equal to the number of positions in which the components of $\boldsymbol{\alpha}$, $\boldsymbol{\beta}$ agree minus the number of positions in which they differ, the latter being the Hamming distance. We thus can write

$$\boldsymbol{\alpha}'\boldsymbol{\beta} = [n - HD(\boldsymbol{\alpha}, \boldsymbol{\beta})] - HD(\boldsymbol{\alpha}, \boldsymbol{\beta}) \qquad (A7.1)$$

which is equivalent to

$$\boldsymbol{\alpha}'\boldsymbol{\beta} = n - 2HD(\boldsymbol{\alpha}, \boldsymbol{\beta}) \qquad (A7.2)$$

Note that the formulas above are valid for components of $\boldsymbol{\alpha}$ and $\boldsymbol{\beta}$ of the value ± 1.

A8

MOSFET MODELING FOR NEURAL NETWORK APPLICATIONS

The Metal-Oxide Semiconductor Field-Effect Transistor (MOSFET) can be seen as the gate (metal or conductor) over the insulator (oxide), which is in turn over the subsrate (semiconductor) (see Figure A12(a)). When the externally applied gate-source voltage is greater then the threshold voltage of the n-type

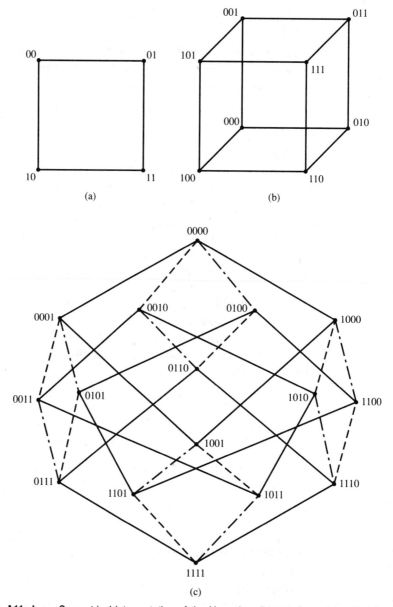

Figure A11a,b,c Geometrical interpretation of the Hamming distance for codes with (a) two bits (b) three bits (c) four bits.

device, the MOS transistor is said to be operative in the *resistive region* prior to the pinching of the channel between drain and source. In this region the drain-to-source current I_{ds} is positive and it increases with increasing drain-to-source

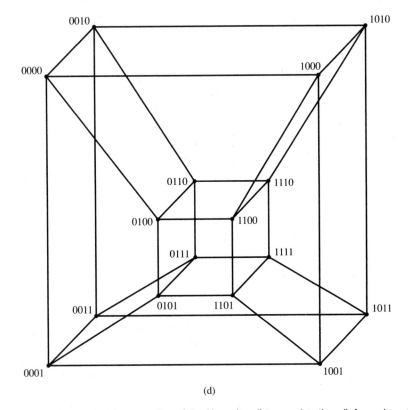

Figure A11d Geometrical interpretation of the Hamming distance, *(continued)*, for codes with (d) four bits.

voltage. This can be seen from Figure A12(b) and(c) showing the device symbol and output current / voltage characteristics.

When the channel is pinched off, the value of the drain-to-source current remains approximately constant as a function of drain-to-source voltage. The transistor is said to operate in the *saturation region*. If the gate-to-source voltage is less then the threshold voltage, no drain-to-source current flows through the channel and the device is in the *cutoff region*. The gate current I_g remains at zero all three regions of operation.

A summary of a MOFSET model that is adequate for most neural network implementations using these devices appears in Table A1. Note that the channel length modulation parameter λ of non-zero value causes that the I_{ds} current in the saturation region increases slightly and in approximately linear manner with V_{ds}. The channel length modulation effect is depicted with dashed lines on characteristics of Figure A12(c).

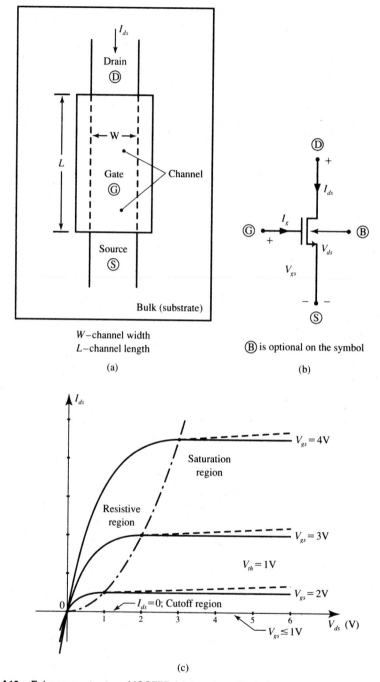

Figure A12 Enhancement *n*-type MOSFET (a) top view, (b) device symbol and reference quantities, and (c) output characteristics for the threshold voltage $V_{th} = 1$ V.

TABLE A.1

Summary of MOSFET devices characteristics.

Device	Current ($I_g = 0$)	Condition (Region)
NMOS $\quad I_{ds} =$	$\begin{cases} 0 \\[1em] k'\dfrac{W}{L}\left(V_{gs} - V_{th} - \dfrac{V_{ds}}{2}\right) \\[1em] k'\dfrac{W}{2L}(V_{gs} - V_{th})^2(1 + \lambda V_{ds}) \end{cases}$	$V_{gs} < V_{th}$ (cutoff) $V_{gs} > V_{th},\ 0 < V_{ds} < V_{gs} - V_{th}$ (resistive) $V_{gs} > V_{th},\ V_{ds} > V_{gs} - V_{th}$ (saturation)
PMOS $\quad I_{ds} =$	$\begin{cases} 0 \\[1em] -k'\dfrac{W}{L}\left(V_{gs} - V_{th} - \dfrac{V_{ds}}{2}\right) \\[1em] -k'\dfrac{W}{2L}(V_{gs} - V_{th})^2(1 - \lambda V_{ds}) \end{cases}$	$V_{gs} > V_{th}$ (cutoff) $V_{gs} < V_{th},\ 0 > V_{ds} > V_{gs} - V_{th}$ (resistive) $V_{gs} < V_{th},\ V_{ds} < V_{gs} - V_{th}$ (saturation)

W—channel width
L—channel length
k'—process transconductance
λ—channel length modulation parameter ($\lambda > 0$)
V_{th}—threshold voltage

For n-channel transistors the devices are termed *enhancement* if $V_{th} > 0$ and *depletion* if $V_{th} < 0$. For p-channel transistors the devices are *enhancement* mode MOFSETs if $V_{th} < 0$ and *depletion* type if $V_{th} > 0$.

A9

ARTIFICIAL NEURAL SYSTEMS (ANS) PROGRAM LISTING

The program ANS,[a] written in Borland Turbopascal, version 6.0, implements basic neural network training and recall algorithms covered in the text. The listing below contains the source code of procedures of the ANS program and is limited to the neural algorithms coding only.

The full program contains, in addition to the control program, menu and help screens and a number of data files for examples selected from the text and

---

[a] The program is contributed by W. F. Hahnert, C. D. Perttunen, and J. M. Zurada.

for selected end-of-chapter problems. The program is menu-driven and runs on IBM-PC and compatible microcomputers under MS-DOS, version 3.1, or higher. To obtain a diskette with the full version of the program write to:

West Publishing Company
College Department
610 Opperman Drive
P.O. Box 64526
St. Paul, MN 55164-0526

```
1   (**********************************************************************)
2   (*** SINGLE BIPOLAR PERCEPTRON DICHOTOMIZER **************************)
3
4   procedure dichot_output(finished : boolean);
5   var i : integer;
6   begin
7      check_key;
8      gotoxy(1,4);
9      textbackground(7); textcolor(0);
10     writeln('Training Cycle ',iter,': Weight Vector');
11     writeln;                       (Note: this routine ignores linect ..)
12     textbackground(0); textcolor(7); (     since only one neuron.)
13     for i := 1 to leninvecs+1 do write(weightvecs[1][i]:7:3,' ');
14     writeln;
15     write_outputend(finished);
16  end;
17
18  procedure dichotomizer;
19  var sum    : real;
20      i, j   : integer;
21  begin
22     load_patterns(1);
23     for i := 1 to numinvecs do        (uses augmented input as a +1)
24        inputvecs[i][leninvecs+1] := 1.0;
25     repeat
26        for i:=1 to leninvecs+1 do weightvecs[1][i] := 2.0*random-1.0;
27        write('Enter learning constant: ');
28        readln(alpha);
29        linect := linect + 1;
30        alpha := -abs(alpha);          (force alpha neg for later use)
31        iter := 0;
32        clear_work_area;
33        print_fkey_footings;
34        dichot_output(false);
35        if not abort then
36        repeat
37           iter := iter + 1;
38           finished := true;           (assume a successful training cycle)
39           for i := 1 to numinvecs do  (for each input vector ...)
40              begin
41                 sum := 0.0;                       (... calc scalar product)
42                 for j:= 1 to leninvecs+1 do
43                    sum := sum + weightvecs[1][j]*inputvecs[i][j];
44                 if sgn(sum) <> outputvecs[i][1] then (... if not correct sign)
45                    begin                          (... cycle is not success)
46                       finished := false;
47                       for j:=1 to leninvecs+1 do   (... adjust weights +/-)
48                          weightvecs[1][j] := weightvecs[1][j] +
49                                    alpha*sgn(sum)*inputvecs[i][j];
50                    end;
51              end;
52           dichot_output(finished);
53        until finished or abort or quittrain;
54        if not abort then
55           while not abort and not quittest do    (allow testing of new patts)
56           begin
57              writeln;
58              write('Enter a test vector of dimension ',leninvecs,': ');
59              for i := 1 to leninvecs do read(testvec[i]);
60              readln;
61              testvec[leninvecs+1] := 1.0;
62              sum := 0.0;
63              for i:= 1 to leninvecs+1 do
64                 sum := sum + weightvecs[1][i]*testvec[i];
65              if sgn(sum) < 0.0 then writeln('Classified as pattern 1')
66                              else writeln('Classified as pattern 2');
67              hitakey;
68           end;
69     until quitruns;
70  end;
71
72
```

```
73  {**********************************************************************}
74  {*** DISCRETE, BIPOLAR DISCRETE PERCEPTRON LAYER *********************}
75
76  procedure dpl_output(finished : boolean);
77  var i,j,lines : integer;
78  begin
79     check_key;
80     gotoxy(1,4);
81     textbackground(7); textcolor(0);
82     write('Training Cycle ',iter,': Weight Matrix');
83     textbackground(0); textcolor(7);
84     writeln('  (rows,cols) = (inputs,neurons)');
85     writeln;
86     linect := 6;
87     lines := (numclasses div 11) + 1;
88     for i := 1 to leninvecs+1 do
89        begin
90        if screen_full(lines) then clear_work_area;
91        for j := 1 to numclasses do write(weightvecs[i][j]:7:3,' ');
92        writeln;
93        linect := linect + lines;
94        end;
95     write_outputend(finished);
96  end;
97
98  procedure dpl;
99  var
100     i,j,k     : integer;
101     net,fnet  : vector;
102  begin
103     load_patterns(1);
104     repeat
105        write('Enter learning constant: ');
106        readln(alpha);
107        linect := linect + 1;
108        alpha := -abs(alpha);              {force alpha negative for later}
109        for i := 1 to leninvecs+1 do
110           for j := 1 to numclasses do
111              weightvecs[i][j] := 2.0*random-1.0;
112        for i := 1 to numinvecs do         {augment with a + 1}
113           inputvecs[i][leninvecs+1] := 1.0;
114        clear_work_area;
115        print_fkey_footings;
116        iter := 0;
117        dpl_output(false);
118        if not abort then
119           repeat
120              iter := iter + 1;
121              finished := true;            {assume no weight changes required}
122              for i := 1 to numinvecs do   {for all training vectors do}
123                 begin
124                 for j := 1 to numclasses do  {calc scalar prod and perceptron ..}
125                    begin                       {.. outputs}
126                    net[j] := 0.0;
127                    for k := 1 to leninvecs + 1 do
128                       net[j] := net[j] + weightvecs[k][j]*inputvecs[i][k];
129                    fnet[j] := sgn(net[j]);
130                    end;
131                 for j := 1 to numclasses do  {if any output not as desired ...}
132                    if fnet[j] <> outputvecs[i][j] then
133                       begin
134                       finished := false;    {... not trained, update weights}
135                       for k := 1 to leninvecs + 1 do
136                          weightvecs[k][j] := weightvecs[k][j] +
137                                              fnet[j]*alpha*inputvecs[i][k]
138                       end;
139                 end;
140              dpl_output(finished);
141           until abort or finished or quittrain;
142           if not abort then
143              while not abort and not quittest do
144                 begin
145                 writeln;
146                 write('Enter a test vector of dimension ',leninvecs,': ');
147                 for i := 1 to leninvecs do read(testvec[i]);
148                 readln;
149                 testvec[leninvecs+1] := 1.0;
150                 for i:= 1 to numclasses do
151                    begin
152                    net[i] := 0;
153                    for j := 1 to leninvecs + 1 do
154                       net[i] := net[i] + weightvecs[j][i]*testvec[j];
155                    fnet[i] := sgn(net[i]);
156                    end;
157                 k := 0;
158                 for i := 1 to numclasses do
159                    if fnet[i] > 0.0 then
160                       begin
161                       k := k + 1;
162                       j := i;
163                       end;
```

```
164              if k = 1 then writeln('Classified as pattern ',j)
165                       else writeln('Not Classified');
166           hitakey;
167           end;
168     until quitruns;
169  end;
170
171  {*********************************************************************}
172  {*** CTS, BIPOLAR SINGLE LAYER DELTA LEARNING NETWORK ***************}
173
174  procedure delta_output(finished : boolean);
175  var i,j,lines : integer;
176  begin
177     check_key;
178     gotoxy(1,4);
179     textbackground(7); textcolor(0);
180     write('Training Cycle ',iter,': Weight Matrix');
181     textbackground(0); textcolor(7);
182     writeln('   (rows,cols) = (inputs,neurons)');
183     writeln;
184     linect := 6;
185     lines := (numclasses div 11) + 1;
186     for i := 1 to leninvecs+1 do
187        begin
188        if screen_full(lines) then clear_work_area;
189        for j := 1 to numclasses do write(weightvecs[i][j]:7:3,' ');
190        writeln;
191        linect := linect + lines;
192        end;
193     writeln;
194     if iter <> 0 then writeln('Error = ',error:8:4);
195     write_outputend(finished);
196  end;
197
198  procedure delta;
199  var i, j, k : integer;
200      sigma   : real;
201      net     : vector;
202      ok      : vector;
203  begin
204     load_patterns(1);
205     repeat
206        write('Enter the learning constant: ');
207        readln(alpha);
208        write('Enter termination error: ');
209        readln(term_error);
210        for i := 1 to leninvecs + 1 do
211           for j := 1 to numclasses do
212              weightvecs[i][j] := 2.0*random - 1.0;   {init on [-1,1]}
213        for i := 1 to numinvecs do                    {augment input +1}
214           inputvecs[i][leninvecs+1] := 1.0;
215        iter := 0;
216        clear_work_area;
217        print_fkey_footings;
218        delta_output(false);
219        if not abort then
220        repeat
221           iter := iter + 1;
222           error := 0.0;
223           for i := 1 to numinvecs do          {each iter one training cycle}
224              begin
225              for k := 1 to numclasses do
226                 begin
227                 net[k] := 0.0;;              {calc scalar prod and output}
228                 for j := 1 to leninvecs+1 do
229                    net[k] := net[k] + weightvecs[j][k] * inputvecs[i][j];
230                 ok[k] := fnet(net[k]);
231                 error := error + sqr(ok[k] - outputvecs[i][k])/2.0;
232                 sigma := alpha*(outputvecs[i][k]-ok[k])*(1-sqr(ok[k]))/2;
233                 for j := 1 to leninvecs+1 do  {always adjust weights}
234                    weightvecs[j][k] := weightvecs[j][k]+sigma*inputvecs[i][j];
235                 end;
236              end;
237           finished := error <= term_error;
238           delta_output(finished);
239        until abort or finished or quittrain;
240        if not abort then                    {submit vecs for classification}
241        while not abort and not quittest do
242           begin
243           writeln;
244           write('Enter a test vector of dimension ',leninvecs,': ');
245           for i := 1 to leninvecs do read(testvec[i]);
246           readln;
247           testvec[leninvecs+1] := 1.0;
248           for i:= 1 to numclasses do
249              begin
250              net[i] := 0.0;;
251              for j := 1 to leninvecs+1 do
252                 net[i] := net[i] + weightvecs[j][i] * testvec[j];
253              end;
```

```
254                 k := 0;
255                 for i := 1 to numclasses do
256                     if fnet(net[i]) > 0.5 then
257                         begin
258                         k := k + 1;
259                         j := i;
260                         end;
261                 if k = 1 then writeln('Classified as pattern ',j)
262                          else writeln('Not Classified');
263                 hitakey;
264                 end;
265         until quitruns;
266     end;
267
268     (**********************************************************************)
269     (*** CTS, BIPOLAR BACKPROPAGATION TRAINING **************************)
270
271     procedure backprop_headings;
272     begin
273         check_key;
274         gotoxy(1,4);
275         textbackground(7); textcolor(0);
276         write('Training Cycle ',iter,': Outputs');
277         textbackground(0); textcolor(7);
278         writeln('   (rows,cols) = (input vectors,neurons)');
279         writeln;
280         linect := 6;
281     end;
282
283     procedure backprop_outline(vecnum : integer;
284                                vec    : vector;
285                                finished : boolean);
286     var i,j,lines : integer;
287     begin
288         lines := (numclasses div 11) + 1;
289         if screen_full(lines) then
290             begin
291             clear_work_area;
292             backprop_headings;
293             end
294         else if vecnum = 1 then backprop_headings;
295         for j := 1 to numclasses do write(vec[j]:7:3,' ');
296         writeln;
297         linect := linect + lines;
298         if vecnum = numinvecs then
299             begin
300             if screen_full(2) then backprop_headings;
301             writeln;
302             writeln('Error = ',error:8:4);
303             linect := linect + 2;
304             write_outputend(finished);
305             end;
306     end;
307
308     procedure backprop_outweights( w: wmatrix;
309                                    rows,cols,layer : integer);
310     var i,j,lines : integer;
311     begin
312         clear_work_area;
313         textbackground(7); textcolor(0);
314         if layer = 1 then write('Final hidden layer weights')
315                      else write('Final output layer weights');
316         textbackground(0); textcolor(7);
317         if layer = 1 then writeln('  (row, column) = (hidden,input)')
318                      else writeln('  (row, column) = (output,hidden)');
319         writeln;
320         linect := linect + 2;
321         lines := (cols div 11) + 1;
322         for i := 1 to rows do
323             begin
324             if screen_full(lines) then clear_work_area;
325             for j := 1 to cols do write(w[i][j]:7:3,' ');
326             writeln;
327             linect := linect + lines;
328             end;
329         hitakey;
330     end;
331
332     procedure backprop;
333     var sum     : real;
334         o1, o2,
335         delta_j,
336         delta_k : vector;
337         i,j,k : integer;
338         numhiddennodes : integer;
339     begin
340         load_patterns(1);
341         repeat
342             write('Enter # of hidden nodes: ');
343             readln(numhiddennodes);
```

```
344        write('Enter learning constant: ');
345        readln(alpha);
346        write('Enter termination error: ');
347        readln(term_error);
348        iter := 0;
349        for i := 1 to numinvecs do
350          inputvecs[i][leninvecs+1] := 1.0;
351        for i := 1 to max_vec_len do
352          for j:= 1 to max_vec_len do
353            begin
354              weightvecs[i][j] := 2.0 * random - 1.0;
355              weight2vecs[i][j] := 2.0 * random - 1.0;
356            end;
357        clear_work_area;
358        backprop_headings;
359        print_fkey_footings;
360        repeat
361          iter := iter + 1;
362          error := 0.0;
363          for i := 1 to numinvecs do
364            begin
365              for j := 1 to numhiddennodes do
366                begin
367                  sum := 0;
368                  for k := 1 to leninvecs+1 do
369                    sum := sum + weightvecs[j][k]*inputvecs[i][k];
370                  o1[j] := fnet(sum);
371                end;
372              o1[numhiddennodes+1] := 1.0;
373              for j := 1 to numclasses do
374                begin
375                  sum := 0;
376                  for k := 1 to numhiddennodes+1 do
377                    sum := sum + weight2vecs[j][k]*o1[k];
378                  o2[j] := fnet(sum);
379                  error := error + sqr(o2[j]-outputvecs[i][j])/2;
380                end;
381              for j:= 1 to numclasses do
382                delta_k[j] := (outputvecs[i][j]-o2[j])*(1-sqr(o2[j]))/2;
383              for j := 1 to numhiddennodes+1 do
384                begin
385                  sum := 0;
386                  for k := 1 to numclasses do
387                    sum := sum + delta_k[k] * weight2vecs[k][j];
388                  delta_j[j] := (1 - sqr(o1[j]))*sum/2;
389                end;
390              for j := 1 to numclasses do
391                for k := 1 to numhiddennodes+1 do
392                  weight2vecs[j][k] := weight2vecs[j][k]+
393                                       alpha*delta_k[j]*o1[k];
394              for j := 1 to numhiddennodes+1 do
395                for k := 1 to leninvecs+1 do
396                  weightvecs[j][k] := weightvecs[j][k]+
397                                      alpha*delta_j[j]*inputvecs[i][k];
398              finished := error <= term_error;
399              backprop_outline(i,o2,finished);
400            end;
401        until abort or finished or quittrain;
402        if not abort then
403          begin
404            output_mode := screenoutput;    {force to view each screenful}
405            backprop_outweights(weightvecs,numhiddennodes,leninvecs+1,1);
406            backprop_outweights(weight2vecs,numclasses,numhiddennodes+1,2);
407          end;
408        if not abort then
409          while not abort and not quittest do
410            begin
411              writeln;
412              writeln('Enter a test vector of dimension ',
413                      leninvecs,': ');
414              for i := 1 to leninvecs do read(testvec[i]);
415              readln;
416              testvec[leninvecs+1] := 1.0;
417              for j := 1 to numhiddennodes do
418                begin
419                  sum := 0;
420                  for k := 1 to leninvecs+1 do
421                    sum := sum + weightvecs[j][k]*testvec[k];
422                  o1[j] := fnet(sum);
423                end;
424              o1[numhiddennodes+1] := 1.0;
425              for j := 1 to numclasses do
426                begin
427                  sum := 0;
428                  for k := 1 to numhiddennodes+1 do
429                    sum := sum + weight2vecs[j][k]*o1[k];
430                  o2[j] := fnet(sum);
431                end;
432              k := 0;
433              for i := 1 to numclasses do
```

```
434                    begin
435                    if o2[i] > 0.5 then
436                       begin
437                       k := k + 1;
438                       j := i;
439                       end;
440                    end;
441                 if k = 1 then writeln('Classified as pattern ',j)
442                          else writeln('Not Classified');
443              hitakey;
444              end;
445       until quitruns;
446    end;
447    (**********************************************************************}
448    (*** DISCRETE BIPOLAR HOPFIELD ASSOCIATIVE MEMORIES ******************}
449
450    procedure hopfield_output(finished : boolean);
451    var i,j,lines : integer;
452    begin
453       check_key;
454       gotoxy(1,4);
455       textbackground(7); textcolor(0);
456       writeln('Training vector ',iter,': Weight Matrix T');
457       textbackground(0); textcolor(7);
458       writeln;
459       linect := 6;
460       lines := (leninvecs div 21) + 1;
461       for i := 1 to leninvecs do
462          begin
463          if screen_full(lines) then clear_work_area;
464          for j := 1 to leninvecs do
465             write(trunc(weightvecs[i][j]):3,' ');
466          writeln;
467          linect := linect + lines;
468          end;
469       write_outputend(finished);
470    end;
471
472    procedure hopfield;
473    var i, j, k, numrelax : integer;
474        sum              : real;
475    begin
476       load_patterns(1);
477       hitakey;
478       clear_work_area;
479       print_fkey_footings;
480       for i := 1 to leninvecs do
481          for j := 1 to leninvecs do
482             weightvecs[i][j] := 0;      {init weights zero}
483       iter := 0;                        {simple training algorithm}
484       repeat
485          iter := iter + 1;
486          for j := 1 to leninvecs do
487             for k := 1 to leninvecs do
488                if (j<>k) then weightvecs[j][k] := weightvecs[j][k] +
489                               (inputvecs[iter][j]*inputvecs[iter][k]);
490          finished := iter = numinvecs;
491          hopfield_output(finished);
492       until abort or finished or quittrain;
493       if not abort then.               {submit vectors to classify}
494          while not abort and not quittest do
495             begin
496             writeln;
497             writeln('Enter a discrete, bipolar test vector of dimension '
498                      leninvecs,': ');
499             for i := 1 to leninvecs do read(testvec[i]);
500             readln;
501             for i := 1 to leninvecs do outputvecs[1][i] := 0;
502             i := 0;
503             repeat
504                i := i + 1;
505                for j := 1 to leninvecs do
506                   begin
507                   sum := 0.0;
508                   for k := 1 to leninvecs do
509                      sum := sum + weightvecs[j][k]*testvec[k];
510                   testvec[j] := sgn(sum);
511                   end;
512                finished := true;
513                for j := 1 to leninvecs do
514                   begin
515                   if testvec[j] <> outputvecs[1][j] then finished := false;
516                   outputvecs[1][j] := testvec[j];
517                   end;
518             until finished or (i > 100);
519             writeln;
520             writeln('Output Vector:');
521             for i := 1 to leninvecs do write(trunc(outputvecs[1][i]),' ');
522             writeln;
523             hitakey;
524             end;
525    end;
```

```
526
527
528  (*******************************************************************)
529  (*** DISCRETE BIPOLAR BIDIRECTIONAL ASSOCIATIVE MEMORY ***************)
530
531  procedure bam_output(finished : boolean);
532  var i,j,lines : integer;
533  begin
534     check_key;
535     gotoxy(1,4);
536     textbackground(7); textcolor(0);
537     write('Training vector ',iter,',: Weight Matrix W');
538     textbackground(0); textcolor(7);
539     writeln('  (rows,cols) = (inputs,neurons)');
540     writeln;
541     linect := 6;
542     lines := (numclasses div 11) + 1;
543     for i := 1 to leninvecs do
544        begin
545        if screen_full(lines) then clear_work_area;
546        for j := 1 to numclasses do
547           write(trunc(weightvecs[i][j]):3,' ');
548        writeln;
549        linect := linect + lines;
550        end;
551     write_outputend(finished);
552  end;
553
554
555  procedure bam;
556  var i,j,k              : integer;
557      a                  : vector;
558  begin
559     load_patterns(1);
560     hitakey;
561     clear_work_area;
562     print_fkey_footings;
563     for i := 1 to leninvecs do
564        for j := 1 to numclasses do
565           weightvecs[i][j] := 0;
566     iter := 0;
567     repeat
568        iter := iter + 1;
569        for j := 1 to leninvecs do
570           for k := 1 to numclasses do
571              weightvecs[j][k] := weightvecs[j][k]+
572                              inputvecs[iter][j]*outputvecs[iter][k];
573        finished := iter = numinvecs;
574        bam_output(finished);
575     until abort or finished;
576     if not abort then
577        while not abort and not quittest do
578           begin
579           writeln;
580           writeln('Enter a discrete, bipolar test vector of dimension ',
581                    leninvecs,': ');
582           for i := 1 to leninvecs do read(testvec[i]);
583           readln;
584           for i := 1 to leninvecs do a[i] := testvec[i];
585           repeat
586              for i := 1 to numclasses do
587                 begin
588                 outputvecs[1][i] := 0;
589                 for j := 1 to leninvecs do
590                    outputvecs[1][i] := outputvecs[1][i]+a[j]*weightvecs[j][i];
591                 outputvecs[1][i] := sgn(outputvecs[1][i]);
592                 end;
593              finished := true;
594              for i := 1 to leninvecs do
595                 begin
596                 outputvecs[2][i] := 0;
597                 for j := 1 to numclasses do
598                    outputvecs[2][i] := outputvecs[2][i]+
599                                    outputvecs[1][j]*weightvecs[i][j];
600                 outputvecs[2][i] := sgn(outputvecs[2][i]);
601                 if outputvecs[2][i] <> testvec[i] then finished := false;
602                 testvec[i] := outputvecs[2][i];
603                 end;
604           until finished;
605           writeln;
606           writeln('Output Vector:');
607           for i := 1 to numclasses do write(trunc(outputvecs[1][i]),' ');
608           writeln;
609           hitakey;
610           end;
611  end;
612
```

```
613  {*************************************************************************}
614  {*** HAMMING/MAXNET TRAINING ****************************************}
615
616  procedure hamming_outweights;      {output weights used for training}
617  var i, j : integer;
618  begin
619     check_key;
620     clear_work_area;
621     textbackground(7); textcolor(0);
622     writeln('Maxnet Weights');
623     textbackground(0); textcolor(7);
624     writeln;
625     for i := 1 to numinvecs do
626        begin
627        for j := 1 to numinvecs do write(weightvecs[i][j]:7:3,' ');
628        writeln;
629        end;
630     linect := linect + numinvecs + 1;
631     hitakey;
632  end;
633
634  procedure hamming_output(vec  : vector;
635                           patt : integer;
636                           finished : boolean);
637  var i : integer;
638  begin
639     check_key;
640     gotoxy(1,4);
641     textbackground(7); textcolor(0);
642     write('Classification Step ',iter,': Outputs');
643     textbackground(0); textcolor(7);
644     writeln('   (rows) = (input vecs)');
645     writeln;
646     linect := 6;
647     for i := 1 to numinvecs do writeln(vec[i]:7:3);
648     if output_mode = screenoutput then hitakey;
649  end;
650
651  procedure hamming;
652  var net,                  {current similarity value for each class}
653      oldfnet,              {previous neuron outputs for comparison}
654      fnet      : vector;   {current class (neuron) output for each}
655      i,j,                  {misc counters}
656      patt,                 {current cluster matched with}
657      numnonzero : integer; {number nonzero outputs in current iteration}
658      temp      : real;     {misc value}
659  begin
660     load_patterns(2);
661     repeat
662        write('Enter the learning constant (less than ',
663                (1/numinvecs):6:3,'): ');
664        readln(alpha);
665        write('Enter a discrete, bipolar test vector of dimension ',
666                leninvecs,': ');
667        for i := 1 to leninvecs do read(testvec[i]);
668        readln;
669        linect := linect + 2;
670        for i := 1 to numinvecs do        {create weight matrix}
671           for j := 1 to numinvecs do
672              if i = j then weightvecs[i][j] := 1
673                       else weightvecs[i][j] := -alpha;
674        hamming_outweights;             {output weight matrix}
675        if not abort then
676           begin
677           for i := 1 to numinvecs do   {scalar prod of each input vec}
678              begin
679              temp := 0;
680              for j := 1 to leninvecs do
681                 temp := temp + inputvecs[i][j]*testvec[j];
682              net[i] := (temp + leninvecs)/2;
683              fnet[i] := net[i]/leninvecs;
684              end;
685           iter := 0;
686           clear_work_area;
687           hamming_output(fnet,0,false);
688           end;
689        if not abort then
690           repeat                        {until all but one output = 0}
691              numnonzero := 0;           {assume all outputs > 0}
692              iter := iter + 1;
693              for i := 1 to numinvecs do oldfnet[i] := fnet[i];  {save outputs}
694              for i := 1 to numinvecs do
695                 begin
696                 net[i] := 0;            {calc new scalar prod outputs}
697                 for j := 1 to numinvecs do
698                    net[i] := net[i] + weightvecs[i][j]*oldfnet[j];
699                 fnet[i] := rmax(net[i],0.0);
```

```
700              if abs(fnet[i]) > 0.001 then    {see how many > 0 and save}
701                begin
702                  numnonzero := numnonzero + 1;
703                  patt := i;
704                end;
705              end;
706          finished := numnonzero <= 1;
707          hamming_output(fnet,patt,finished);    {display new outputs}
708        until finished or abort or quittrain;
709        if not abort then
710          begin
711          writeln;
712          writeln('Training Complete');
713          if numnonzero = 1 then writeln('Classified as pattern ',patt)
714                             else writeln('Not classified.');
715          end;
716    until quitruns;
717  end;
718
719
720  {*************************************************************************}
721  {*** WINNER TAKE ALL TRAINING **********************************************}
722
723  procedure wta_output(finished : boolean);
724  var i,j,k,lines : integer;
725  begin
726    check_key;
727    gotoxy(1,4);
728    textbackground(7); textcolor(0);
729    write('Training Step ',iter,': Weight Matrix');
730    textbackground(0); textcolor(7);
731    writeln('   (rows,cols) = (neurons,inputs)');
732    writeln('Alpha = ',alpha:0:4);
733    writeln;
734    linect := 7;
735    lines := (leninvecs div 11)+1;              {lines for one neuron weights}
736    for i := 1 to numclasses do
737      begin
738      if screen_full(lines) then clear_work_area;
739      for j := 1 to leninvecs do write(weightvecs[i][j]:7:3,' ');
740      writeln;
741      linect := linect + lines;
742      end;
743    write_outputend(finished);
744  end;
745
746  procedure normalize_vector(var vec : vector;
747                                 len : integer);
748  var i    : integer;
749      temp : real;
750  begin
751    temp := 0;
752    for i := 1 to len do temp := temp + sqr(vec[i]);
753    temp := sqrt(temp);
754    if temp <> 0 then
755      for i := 1 to len do vec[i] := vec[i]/temp;
756  end;
757
758  procedure winnertakeall;
759  var i,j,k,               {misc counters}
760      successes,           {number of consecutive succesful training iters}
761      minneur   : integer; {vector with max scalar product in curr iter}
762      temp      : real;    {misc value}
763      success   : boolean; {is current iter a success}
764      dist      : vector;
765  begin
766    load_patterns(2);
767    repeat
768      write('Enter number of classes: ');
769      readln(numclasses);
770      write('Enter similarity error limit: ');
771      readln(term_error);
772      for i := 1 to numinvecs do normalize_vector(inputvecs[i],leninvecs);
773      for j := 1 to numclasses do    {weights random on [-1,1], then normalized}
774        for k := 1 to leninvecs do
775          weightvecs[j][k] := 2.0*random -1.0;
776      for j := 1 to numclasses do normalize_vector(weightvecs[j],leninvecs);
777      iter := 0;
778      successes := 0;
779      i := 0;
780      clear_work_area;
781      print_fkey_footings;
782      alpha := 0.7;
783      wta_output(false);
784      if not abort then
785        repeat                               {til abort or complete cycle of success}
786          iter := iter + 1;
787          alpha := 0.7*exp(-iter/1000);
788          if i = numinvecs then i := 1
789                            else i := i + 1;
```

```
790            for j := 1 to numclasses do
791              begin
792              dist[j] := 0.0;
793              for k := 1 to leninvecs do
794                dist[j] := dist[j] +sqr(inputvecs[i][k]-weightvecs[j][k]);
795              end;
796            minneur := 1;
797            for j := 2 to numclasses do
798              if dist[j] < dist[minneur] then minneur := j;
799            for k := 1 to leninvecs do   {save old weights for success calc and ..}
800              begin                      {.. update new weights for the winner}
801              weight2vecs[1][k] := weightvecs[minneur][k];
802              weightvecs[minneur][k] := weightvecs[minneur][k] +
803                        alpha*(inputvecs[i][k] - weightvecs[minneur][k]);
804              end;
805            normalize_vector(weightvecs[minneur],leninvecs);
806            success := true;            {... assume successful adjustment}
807            successes := successes + 1;
808            for k := 1 to leninvecs do   {.. exceed error constant}
809              if abs(weight2vecs[1][k]-weightvecs[minneur][k]) > term_error then
810                success := false;
811            if not success then successes := 0;  {if no succ reset count to 0}
812            finished := successes = numinvecs;
813            wta_output(finished);          {display adjusted weights}
814          until abort or finished or quittrain;
815          if not abort then
816            while not abort and not quittest do
817              begin
818              writeln;
819              write('Enter a test vector of dimension ',leninvecs,': ');
820              for i := 1 to leninvecs do read(testvec[i]);
821              readln;
822              normalize_vector(testvec, leninvecs);
823              for j := 1 to numclasses do
824                begin
825                dist[j] := 0.0;
826                for k := 1 to leninvecs do
827                  dist[j] := dist[j] +sqr(testvec[k]-weightvecs[j][k]);
828                end;
829              minneur := 1;
830              for j := 2 to numclasses do
831                if dist[j] < dist[minneur] then minneur := j;
832              writeln('Classified as pattern ',minneur);
833              hitakey;
834              end;
835      until quitruns;
836    end;
837
838  {****************************************************************************}
839  {*** KOHONEN FEATURE MAPPING *********************************************}
840
841  procedure fmap_output(nrad: integer; {output weights}
842                        adj : real;
843                        finished : boolean);
844  var i,j,k,lines : integer;
845  begin
846    check_key;
847    gotoxy(1,4);
848    textbackground(7); textcolor(0);
849    write('Training Step ',iter,': Weights');
850    textbackground(0); textcolor(7);
851    writeln('  (rows,cols) = (inputs,neurons)');
852    writeln('Neighborhood = ',Nrad,', Alpha = ',alpha:7:3,
853            ', Total Ajdustment = ',adj:10:3);
854    writeln;
855    linect := 7;
856    lines := (leninvecs div 11) + 1;   {lines for one neuron weights}
857    for i := 1 to leninvecs do          {for all neurons}
858      begin
859      if screen_full(lines) then clear_work_area;
860      for j := 1 to numclasses do write(weightvecs[j][i]:7:3,' ');
861      writeln;
862      linect := linect + lines;
863      end;
864    write_outputend(finished);
865  end;
866
867  procedure featuremap;          {feature map training}
868  var
869    i,j,k,m,indx,          {misc counters and array indices}
870    minneur,              {neuron with minimum dist inputs to weights}
871    Nrad,                 {curr radius of neighborhood for wvec adjust}
872    alphadectime,         {time at which alpha starts to decline}
873    Ndecint,              {interval at which Nrad continues to decline}
874    successes,            {# of consecutive successes current cycle}
875    rows, cols  : integer; {dimensions of feature mapping grid}
876    dist        : vector;  {distance weights to inputs at curr iter}
877    adjust,               {adj to indiv neur weights during current iter}
878    totadjust   : real;    {tot adj to all neur weights during curr iter}
879    success     : boolean; {is curr input a success}
```

```
880  begin
881    load_patterns(2);
882    repeat
883      write('Enter # rows in rectangular feature space (1 for 1-D): ');
884      readln(rows);
885      write('Enter # cols in rectangular feature space: ');
886      readln(cols);
887      write('Enter total adjustment limit: ');
888      readln(term_error);
889      write('Enter iterations before begin reducing alpha: ');
890      readln(alphadectime);
891      write('Enter iterations between neighborhood reductions: ');
892      readln(Ndecint);
893      numclasses := rows*cols;
894      for i := 1 to numclasses do          {initial weights random on (0,1)}
895        for j := 1 to leninvecs do
896          weightvecs[i][j] := random;
897      alpha := 0.95;
898      Nrad := trunc(sqrt(sqr(rows-1)+sqr(cols-1)));  {init cover all neurs}
899      successes := 0;
900      iter := 0;
901      i := 0;
902      clear_work_area;
903      print_fkey_footings;
904      fmap_output(nrad,0.0,false);
905      if not abort then
906      repeat
907        iter := iter + 1;
908        if iter >= alphadectime then      {reduce alpha if necessary}
909          alpha := 0.95*exp((alphadectime-iter)/(200*numclasses));
910        if (Nrad > 0) and (iter mod ndecint = 0) then   {adjust Nrad if necc}
911          Nrad := Nrad - 1;
912        if i = numinvecs then i := 1
913                           else i := i + 1;
914        for j := 1 to numclasses do      {calc dist neuron weights to inputs}
915          begin
916          dist[j] := 0;
917          for k := 1 to leninvecs do
918            dist[j] := dist[j] + sqr(inputvecs[i][k]-weightvecs[j][k]);
919          end;
920        minneur := 1;                     {assume first is smallest}
921        for j := 2 to numclasses do       {find actual smallest - the winner}
922          if dist[j] < dist[minneur] then minneur := j;
923        totadjust := 0.0;
924        for j := 1 to rows do             {if neuron is w/in Nrad of winner..}
925          for k := 1 to cols do           {.. adjust its weights}
926            if sqrt(sqr(j-((minneur-1) div cols + 1)) + sqr(k-
927                    ((minneur-1) mod cols + 1))) <= Nrad then
928              for m := 1 to leninvecs do
929                begin
930                indx := (j-1)*cols+k;
931                adjust := alpha*(inputvecs[i][m]-weightvecs[indx][m]);
932                totadjust := totadjust + adjust;
933                weightvecs[indx][m] := weightvecs[indx][m]+adjust;
934                end;
935        success := true;                  {assume successful (minimal) adjustment}
936        successes := successes + 1;
937        for k := 1 to leninvecs do        {.. exceed error constant}
938          if abs(totadjust) >= term_error then
939            success := false;
940        if not success then successes := 0;  {if no succ reset count to 0}
941        finished := successes = numinvecs;
942        fmap_output(nrad,totadjust,finished);
943      until abort or finished or quittrain;
944      if not abort then
945      while not abort and not quittest do
946        begin
947        writeln;
948        writeln('Enter a test vector of dimension ',leninvecs,': ');
949        for i := 1 to leninvecs do read(testvec[i]);
950        readln;
951        for i:= 1 to numclasses do
952          begin
953          dist[i] := 0.0;;
954          for j := 1 to leninvecs do
955            dist[i] := dist[i] + sqr(testvec[j]-weightvecs[i][j]);
956          end;
957        minneur := 1;
958        for i := 2 to numclasses do
959          if dist[i] < dist[minneur] then minneur := i;
960        writeln('Classified as pattern ',minneur);
961        hitakey;
962        end;
963    until quitruns;
964  end;
965
966  {*******************************************************************}
967  {*** ART1 TRAINING *************************************************}
968
969  procedure art1_headings(patt : integer;
970                          thresh : real);   {display output headings}
```

```
971    begin
972       check_key;
973       clear_work_area;
974       textbackground(7); textcolor(0);
975       write('Input Pattern ',patt,' of ',numinvecs);
976       textbackground(0); textcolor(7);
977       writeln('  Threshold = ',thresh:7:3);
978       writeln;
979       linect := linect + 2;
980    end;
981
982    procedure art1_outweights( patt,neur : integer;
983                                        thresh : real);
984    var  i,j,k, lines : integer;
985    begin
986       check_key;
987       lines := (leninvecs div 11) + 1;
988       if screen_full(lines+1) then art1_headings(patt,thresh);
989       writeln('Weight Vector W, Neuron ',neur,':');
990       for i := 1 to leninvecs do write(weightvecs[neur][i]:7:3,' ');
991       writeln;
992       linect := linect + lines + 1;
993       if screen_full(lines+1) then art1_headings(patt,thresh);
994       writeln('Weight Vector V, Neuron ',neur,':');
995       for i := 1 to leninvecs do write(weight2vecs[neur][i]:7:3,' ');
996       writeln;
997       linect := linect + lines + 1;
998       hitakey;
999    end;
1,000
1,001  procedure art1;
1,002  var
1,003     fnet          : vector; {current scalar prod inputs to each neuron}
1,004     disabled      : array[1..max_vec_len] of boolean;
1,005                              {neur discarded as choice for current pattern?}
1,006     i,j,k,               {misc counters}
1,007     maxneuron,           {curr neuron considered with max output}
1,008     maxusedneuron,       {curr last neuron assigned to a class}
1,009     numdisabled   :integer; {num neurs discarded in classing curr pattern}
1,010     temp,
1,011     thresh,              {user supplied threshold value}
1,012     maxval,              {output value of maxneuron}
1,013     simtest,             {scalar product of revweights and curr pattern}
1,014     mag           : real;   {number of 1's in current pattern}
1,015     finished      : boolean;{finished training}
1,016  begin
1,017     load_patterns(2);
1,018     repeat
1,019        write('Enter vigilance threshold on (0,1): ');
1,020        readln(thresh);
1,021        maxusedneuron := 0;              {so far no classifications made}
1,022        for i := 1 to max_neurons do    {init wvecs as in text}
1,023           for j := 1 to leninvecs do
1,024              begin
1,025                 weightvecs[i][j] := 1/(leninvecs+1);
1,026                 weight2vecs[i][j] := 1;
1,027              end;
1,028        i := 1;                          {first invec auto class one}
1,029        art1_headings(i,thresh);
1,030        print_fkey_footings;
1,031        writeln('Automatically mapped to pattern one');
1,032        linect := linect + 1;
1,033        simtest := 0;                    {calc rev scalar prod neur one}
1,034        for j := 1 to leninvecs do
1,035           simtest := simtest + weight2vecs[i][j]*inputvecs[i][j];
1,036        for j := 1 to leninvecs do       {adjust weights as neccesary}
1,037           begin
1,038              if inputvecs[i][j] = 1 then
1,039                 weightvecs[i][j] := (weight2vecs[i][j]*inputvecs[i][j])/
1,040                                       (0.5+simtest);
1,041              weight2vecs[i][j] := inputvecs[i][j]*weight2vecs[i][j];
1,042           end;
1,043        art1_outweights(1,i,thresh);     {display new weights}
1,044        maxusedneuron := 1;
1,045        while (i < numinvecs) and (not abort) do   {for all input patterns}
1,046           begin
1,047              i := i + 1;
1,048              art1_headings(i,thresh);
1,049              for j := 1 to maxusedneuron do   {calc each active neuron output}
1,050                 begin
1,051                    fnet[j] := 0;
1,052                    for k := 1 to leninvecs do
1,053                       fnet[j] := fnet[j] + weightvecs[j][k]*inputvecs[i][k];
1,054                 end;
1,055              for j:= 1 to maxusedneuron do disabled[j] := false;{all are eligible}
1,056              numdisabled := 0;
1,057              repeat                       {until classified or new class activated}
1,058                 finished := true;
1,059                 maxneuron := 0;
1,060                 repeat                    {find first eligible neuron for input patt}
1,061                    maxneuron := maxneuron + 1
```

```
1,062          until not disabled[maxneuron];
1,063          k := maxneuron;        {assume this is the maximum output}
1,064          for j := k+1 to maxusedneuron do  {find true max of all eligible}
1,065              if (fnet[j] > fnet[maxneuron]) and not disabled[j] then
1,066                  maxneuron := j;
1,067          simtest := 0;
1,068          mag := 0;
1,069          for j := 1 to leninvecs do   {calc rev scal prod and invec mag ..}
1,070              begin                    {... for similarity test}
1,071              simtest := simtest + weight2vecs[maxneuron][j]*inputvecs[i][j];
1,072              mag := mag + inputvecs[i][j];
1,073              end;
1,074          write('Testing against pattern '+chr($30+maxneuron)+
1,075                  ', Sim = ',(simtest/mag):7:3,' --> ');
1,076          if simtest/mag > thresh then {if exceed threshold, use that neur}
1,077              begin
1,078              writeln('Passed');
1,079              linect := linect + 1;
1,080              for j := 1 to leninvecs do {update weights}
1,081                  begin
1,082                  if inputvecs[i][j] = 1 then
1,083                      weightvecs[maxneuron][j]:=(weight2vecs[maxneuron][j]*
1,084                          inputvecs[i][j])/(0.5+simtest);
1,085                  weight2vecs[maxneuron][j] := inputvecs[i][j]*
1,086                          weight2vecs[maxneuron][j];
1,087                  end;
1,088              art1_outweights(i,maxneuron,thresh);
1,089              end
1,090          else    {failed threshold test, try remaining eligibles or ...}
1,091              begin {... create new class}
1,092              writeln('Failed');
1,093              linect := linect + 1;
1,094              disabled[maxneuron] := true;
1,095              numdisabled := numdisabled + 1;
1,096              if maxusedneuron >= max_neurons then  {exceed pgm constraints}
1,097                  begin
1,098                  writeln('# of needed classes exceeds program maximum');
1,099                  linect := linect + 1;
1,100                  end
1,101              else
1,102                  if numdisabled < maxusedneuron then finished := false
1,103                  else                            {form a new class}
1,104                      begin
1,105                      maxusedneuron := maxusedneuron + 1;
1,106                      maxneuron := maxusedneuron;
1,107                      writeln('Adding as new pattern '+chr($30+maxneuron));
1,108                      linect := linect + 1;
1,109                      temp := 0;
1,110                      for j := 1 to leninvecs do
1,111                          temp := temp+weight2vecs[maxneuron][j]*inputvecs[i][j];
1,112                      for j := 1 to leninvecs do
1,113                          begin
1,114                          if inputvecs[i][j] = 1 then  {adjust new neur weights}
1,115                              weightvecs[maxneuron][j] :=
1,116                                  (weight2vecs[maxneuron][j]*inputvecs[i][j])/
1,117                                  (0.5+temp);
1,118                          weight2vecs[maxneuron][j] := inputvecs[i][j]*
1,119                                  weight2vecs[maxneuron][j];
1,120                          end;
1,121                      art1_outweights(i,maxneuron,thresh);
1,122                      end;
1,123              end;
1,124          until finished or abort;
1,125          end;
1,126      if not abort then writeln('Classification Complete');
1,127  until quitruns;
1,128  end;
1,129
```

REFERENCES

Athans, M., M. L. Dertouzos, R. N. Spann and S. J. Mason. 1974. *Systems and Computation: Multivariable Methods,* New York: McGraw-Hill Book Co.

Brogan, W. L. 1991. *Modern Control Theory,* 3rd Ed. Englewood Cliffs, N. J.: Prentice Hall.

Calahan, D. A. 1972. *Computer-Aided Network Design,* Revised Ed. New York: McGraw-Hill Book Co.

Franklin, G. F., J. D. Powell and A. Emami-Naeimi. 1986. *Feedback Control of Dynamic Systems.* Reading, Mass.: Addison-Wesley Publishing Co.

Kaplan, W. 1981. *Advanced Mathematics for Engineers.* Reading, Mass.: Addison-Wesley Publishing Co.

Kohavi, Z. 1978. *Switching and Finite Automata Theory.* New York: McGraw-Hill Book Co.

Rektorys, K. 1969. *Survey of Applicable Mathematics.* Cambridge, Mass.: The MIT Press.

Strang, G. 1976. *Linear Algebra and its Applications.* New York: Academic Press.

Vlach, J., and K. Singhal. 1983. *Computer Methods for Circuit Analysis and Design.* New York: Van Nostrand Reinhold.

de Larminat, P., and Y. Thomas. 1977. *Automatique des Systemes Lineares.* 2. Identification, Paris: Flammarion Sciences.

Geiger, R. L., P. E. Allen, and N. R. Strader. 1990. *VLSI Design Techniques for Analog and Digital Circuits.* New York: McGraw-Hill Book Co.

Index

I1